The
Windows 95
Bible

by

Fred Davis

PEACHPIT PRESS

The Windows 95 Bible
Fred Davis

Peachpit Press
2344 Sixth Street
Berkeley, CA 94710
(510) 548-4393
(510) 548-5991 (fax)
(800) 283-9444

Find us on the World Wide Web at: http://www.peachpit.com

Peachpit Press is a division of Addison Wesley Longman
Copyright © 1996 by Fred Davis

Editor: Roslyn Bullas
Copyeditor: Kathleen Christensen
Cover design: The Visual Group
Interior design: Olav Martin Kvern
Icon design: Lynda Banks
Production: Rick Gordon and Myrna Vladic, Emerald Valley Graphics (rcgordon@linex.com)

This book was created with QuarkXPress® 3.31, Nisus Writer® 4.1.3, Adobe Photoshop® 3.0.5, Adobe Illustrator® 5.5, and Microsoft Word® 6.0.1 on a Power Macintosh 7100/66. The fonts used were Minion, Minion Expert, Dom Casual, Tekton, Prestige Elite, and ITC Zapf Dingbats from Adobe.

ISBN 0-201-88388-0

9 8 7 6 5 4 3 2

Printed and bound in the United States of America

 Printed on recycled paper

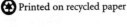

Contents

· ·

Acknowledgments xv

PART 1   **Mastering the Windows 95 Environment** 1

CHAPTER 1   **Introducing Windows 95** 3

     The Launch Party 4
     What This Book Is About 5
     What's New in Windows 95 5
     Why Bother to Read This Book 6
     The Windows Family Tree 8
     Comparing Windows 95 with Windows 3.1 10
     What's in the Box 13
     Microsoft Plus 14
     What's Ahead for Windows 16

CHAPTER 2   **The Windows 95 Interface** 17

     Windows, Menus, Icons, and Dialog Boxes 18
         Windows 22
         Menus 33
         Icons 37
         Dialog Boxes 41
     Summary 43

CHAPTER 3   **Navigating Windows 95** 45

The Windows 95 Taskbar 46

    The Start Button 47

    The Task List 52

    The Notify Area 53

    Control Panels 53

    Shutting Down the Windows 95 System 56

An Object-Oriented View of Your Computer 57

My Computer 58

    Folder Views: Your Window on Objects 59

    Hello, Toolbar 63

    Grappling with Device Objects 66

    How to Find Anything 68

The Windows 95 Explorer 72

    Exploring Other Resources 74

    Manipulating Objects 76

    What's in an Object 81

    Shortcuts 84

Fancy Fingerwork 88

Summary 91

CHAPTER 4   **Ready, Set, Run!** 93

What Runs with Windows 95 94

    DOS Applications 95

    Win16 Applications 95

    Win32 Applications 96

Jump Start 96

    Hit Start 96

    Use a Folder View 98

    Launching Applications from an MS-DOS Command Prompt . . 100

    The Run Dialog Box 101

    The Documents Submenu 103

Programs A-Go-Go 104

    File Operations 104

    Multitasking with Windows 95 108

    The Windows 95 Clipboard 111

    Hot Links with DDE 113

Viewing the Clipboard's Contents 114

Object Linking and Embedding 115

Quitting Applications 119

Summary 120

CHAPTER 5   **Playing with Your New Toys** 121

A Lightweight Software Sampler 122

How to Get There 123

WordPad 124

Paint 132

Notepad 139

Character Map 140

Phone Dialer 141

Calculator 142

The Briefcase 144

Windows 95 Games 148

On-Line Help 153

Summary 159

CHAPTER 6   **Personalizing Windows 95** 161

Designing Your Desktop 162

Background 163

Color Schemes 165

Screensavers 167

Customizing the Taskbar 170

Messing with the Start Menu 174

Multiple Users 179

How to Set It Up 180

Working with User Profiles 181

Date and Time 182

Regional Settings 183

Accessibility Options 185

Keyboard 185

Sound 187

Display 187

Mouse 188

General 189

Summary 189

CHAPTER 7   **Of Displays, Mice, and Keyboards** 191

Display Systems 192

Display Standards 193

Expanding the Desktop 196

Graphics Accelerators 201

Monochrome VGA 204

Display Drivers 205

Display Ergonomics 211

What the Future Brings 213

Mice and Other Pointing Devices 214

Pointing Device Ergonomics 214

Mice, Trackballs, Graphics Tablets, and Pens 215

Resolution of the Mouse 217

Pointing Device Product Overview 218

Keyboard and Pointer Combinations 223

The Mouse Control Panel 224

Keyboards 230

Keyboard Ergonomics 230

Keyboard Device Drivers 232

The Keyboard Control Panel 232

The Dvorak Keyboard Layout 236

ANSI Characters 238

Summary 241

PART 2   **Inside Windows 95** 243

CHAPTER 8   **Fonts** 245

Typography 247

A Triad of Fonts 248

Font Compatibility 248

Screen Fonts, Printer Fonts, and Substitutes 249

TrueType Fonts 250

Printing TrueType Fonts 258

PostScript Fonts 261

TrueType versus PostScript 262

System Fonts 264

Fonts and DOS Applications 267

Installing Fonts 268

The Fonts Folder 269

Removing Fonts 274

Character Map 274

Summary 276

CHAPTER 9 **Printing** 277

The Printers Folder 278

Bidirectional Communication 279

Enhanced Metafile Spooling 280

Extended Capabilities Port Support 280

Image Color Matching 280

Installing a Printer 281

Choosing a Printer Port 282

Installing a Printer Twice 285

Removing a Printer 286

Printing from Windows Applications 286

Appearance 286

Printing from DOS Applications 287

Managing Print Queues 288

Changing Print Speed 290

Printer Drivers 291

Options 292

Printer Support 294

Bundled Drivers 296

Network Printers: Point and Print 308

Sharing a Printer 308

Printing 309

When It's Ready 309

Netware Print Servers 310

Print It Later 310

What to Buy 310

Get a Windows Driver 311

Go Laser 311

Go Color 312

Summary 313

CHAPTER 10   **Networking and Communications** 315

Built-in Network Support 316

     One on One 317

     Setting Up a Network 318

     Adding Network Components 319

     From the Cockpit 321

     Clients, Protocols, Adapters, and Services 322

     Browsing the Network 325

     Connecting to Network Resources 326

     Mapping Network Drives 328

     Printing across a Network 329

     Searching for Network Resources 331

     Network Security 332

     Sharing a Resource 334

     The Properties Dialog Box 337

     Managing Network Printing and Other Resources 339

     Net Watcher 339

Data Communications 340

     COM Ports and Windows 95 341

     Modem Installation 342

     Configuring the Modem 343

     Installing a Network Fax Modem 345

     Reach Out with HyperTerminal 347

     Dial-Up Networking 351

     Direct Cable Connection 354

Surfing the Internet 355

     Installing TCP/IP for Internet Access 356

     Cruising the Internet 359

Summary 361

CHAPTER 11   **Microsoft Exchange** 363

What It Is 364

Installing and Running Exchange 365

     Working with Profiles 366

     Sending and Receiving Mail Periodically 372

     Sending and Receiving Mail on Demand 373

Creating Mail 373
Addressing a Message 375
Sending a Message to a Distribution List 376
Entering Recipients' Names by Hand 378
Sending Blind Courtesy Copies 378
Customizing Exchange's Toolbars 378
Composing a Message 379
Posting a Message 383
Setting a Message's Priority 385
Sensitivity Options 386
Receipt Options 387
Retaining Copies of Posted Messages 388
Reading and Replying to Mail 388
Notification Options 388
Replying to Mail 389
Forwarding Messages 391
Editing Messages 391
Saving Attachments 391
Printing Messages 392
Moving or Copying Messages to Other Folders 392
Deleting Messages 392
Managing Addresses and Address Books 392
Displaying Address Books 393
Finding an Addressee 394
Maintaining a Personal Address Book 394
Managing Folders 398
Managing Exchange Windows 399
Managing Mail Among Folders 400
Sorting Messages 400
Dial-Up Networking with a Local Area Network Mail System . . 404
Microsoft Fax 408
New Features 409
Setting Up Microsoft Fax 410
Configuring Microsoft Fax 411
Adding Fax Recipients to Your Personal Address Book 413
Sending a Fax 414

The Compose New Fax Wizard 415
Options for Sending Faxes 418
Receiving Faxes 421
Reading and Replying to Incoming Faxes 423
The Fax Viewer 424
Providing Security for Your Faxes 425
Cover Page Editor 430
Using a Fax-on-Demand Service 435
Using a Shared Fax Modem 436
Summary 437

PART 3   **Advanced Windows 95 Techniques** 439

CHAPTER 12   **Multimedia** 441
The Mechanics of Multimedia 443
Graphics 444
Still Images 444
Video 446
Animation 450
Sound 451
Digital Audio 451
CD-ROMs 453
Other CD-ROM Formats 454
The MPC Standard 455
Multimedia Applets 457
CD Player 458
Media Player 459
Sound Recorder 461
MIDI 466
Summary 471

CHAPTER 13   **Optimizing Windows 95 Resources** 473
The Compatibility Myth 474
The Central Processing Unit 475
Standard versus Enhanced Mode 477
The Best Processor for Your Needs 477
Processor Cache 479
Upgrading Your Processor 480

The Math Coprocessor Chip 481

The System Bus 482

Plug and Play 487

Memory 487

RAM 488

What's a Hexadecimal Memory Address 493

Conventional Memory 494

Upper Memory Area 496

Expanded Memory 498

Extended Memory 502

Hard-Disk Storage 504

Getting More 505

Virtual Memory 509

File System Settings 512

Caching 513

DriveSpace 514

Heap Space in Windows 95 521

Summary 522

CHAPTER 14 **Integrating Applications with DDE and OLE** 523

The Clipboard 524

Dynamic Data Exchange 528

What DDE Can Do 528

How DDE Works 529

Object Linking and Embedding 531

Uses for OLE 531

OLE Terminology 532

How OLE Works 533

OLE Clients and OLE Servers 534

The Client Side of OLE 535

The Object Packager 546

The Registry 550

Summary 553

CHAPTER 15 **Windows 95 and DOS** 555

The Big Picture 557

Boot Action 558

Egad! CONFIG.SYS and AUTOEXEC.BAT Still Live 559

The Windows 95 Command Prompt 561
   The Toolbar 562
   Starting Programs from a Command Prompt 565
   Configuring DOS Program Properties 565
Advanced DOS Configuration Topics 576
   What Is MS-DOS Mode 577
Windows 95 and DOS Memory Managers 580
Summary 581

CHAPTER 16   **Inside the Windows 95 Installation Process** 583
The Starting Players 584
Starting the Setup Process 586
   How Long Does It Take 588
   Choosing the Directory for Windows 95 589
   Creating a Dual-Boot System 590
   Choosing the Type of Installation 592
   The Hardware Detection Phase 594
   The File Copy Phase 598
   The Final Configuration Phase 600
Adding New Hardware 601
Custom-Design Your Own Installation 601
   The [Setup] Section 602
   The [System] Section 605
   The [NameAndOrg] Section 607
   The [InstallLocationsMRU] Section 607
   The [OptionalComponents] Section 608
   The [Network] Section 609
   Security Parameters 615
   The Network Cards Section 616
   The [NWLink] Section 618
   The [NWRedir] Section 619
   The [NWServer] Section 620
   The [VServer] Section 621
   The [Printers] Section 621
   The [Strings] Section 622
   The [Install] Section 623

Choosing a Work Group 623
   The [Options] Section 624
   The [Workgroups] Section 624
Installing Custom DOS Programs 625
   The [PIF95] Section 625
   The [Strings] Section of APPS.INF 626
   The Application Sections 626
Customizing Setup Scripts 627
Creating Your Own Setup Script with NETSETUP.EXE 629
Using BATCH.EXE to Make a Script 630
About the .INF Generator 631
Summary 632

Index 633

Acknowledgments

. . . .

I'd like to thank the following cast of characters for helping me create this book: Sylvia Paull, for her devotion to editing the beast through numerous drafts and revisions; Ted Nace, Roslyn Bullas, Kaethin Prizer, and Kate Reber at Peachpit Press for steadfastly guiding this book through production; Jim Larkin and Chris DeVoney, for their significant writing contributions; Rick Gordon, for his skillful layout and production work; Kathleen Christensen, for her meticulous job of copyediting; Lenny Bailes and Karl Schmidtman, who helped provide technical feedback; Serge Vladimiroff, for patiently taking hundreds of screenshots; and Steve Rath for providing an excellent index.

Many other people, most notably my father, Don Davis, a former IBM-lifer and proficient Windows-user, prodded and encouraged me along the way, and I'd like to thank every one of them as well. Thanks, too, to my mother, Doris Vladimiroff, who instilled me with a love of language and encouraged me to develop the writing skills that helped carry me through this work.

For anyone I forgot to thank, thank you one and all for helping—I couldn't have done it without you.

1

Mastering the Windows 95 Environment

Introducing Windows 95

Windows 95. You have to be a hermit not to have heard about it. Its release was backed by a quarter-billion dollar marketing blitzkrieg, but Windows 95 didn't remain just the focus of Microsoft's promotions. The product became the epicenter of a media quake, with shock waves spreading to newspaper headlines, television news, radio talk shows, and the most critical communications medium of all—office gossip. Microsoft cleverly picked August—a slow month at the office—to roll out Windows 95, and during that time it seemed as if everyone was talking about the new operating system. Never has the introduction of a computer product received as much attention.

The Launch Party

Massive media exposure and manipulative marketing maneuvers transformed the release of Windows 95 from a mundane operating system upgrade into a cultural event of the first magnitude. My head spun as I attended the Windows 95 launch event at Microsoft's Redmond, Washington, campus on August 24, 1995. Carnival tents and a Ferris wheel were set up to welcome the Windows elite, and security seemed assured with scores of Seattle police surrounding the perimeters. The gala event was hosted by Jay Leno of "Tonight Show" fame. Not coincidentally, Microsoft and NBC announced a deal related to the Microsoft Network that same day. Leno flaunted the tie-in with a joke about Bill Gates, chairman of Microsoft, saying, "NBC . . . it means Now Bill Compatible." Most of Leno's jokes played on the fact that Gates—who shared the stage with the comedian—is a nerd. Leno rode off toward the horizon in a midget car shaped like a Microsoft Mouse.

Then Gates took center stage and invited the two Brads who helped build Windows 95—Brad Silverberg and Brad Chase—to join him onstage. As a giant Windows 95 Start button rose above them, the lights dimmed, and Gates popped a $12 million token into a virtual jukebox. (Microsoft paid that amount to gain rights to "Start Me Up" by the Rolling Stones, the first time the rock group had permitted commercial use of one of their songs.) The speakers blared, and Gates jumped and gyrated to the music in an attempt to disprove Leno's portrayal of him.

Then the stage split open. The backdrop was pulled up like a curtain to reveal oudoor bleachers packed with the Windows 95 product development team, all dressed in rainbow-colored crew shirts bearing the Windows 95 logo. Like that of their suddenly rhythmic chairman, the wholesome faces of Microsoft were charged with excitement as they swayed to the music. We attendees were then ushered through the opening in the stage into the sunshine outside, with the music blaring and the dancing Bill guiding us through like Moses leading the Israelites through the Red Sea into the promised land.

All the hoopla left little time to think about Windows 95 itself. Even at the press conference, no one seemed to care about the operating system; most of the questions centered around problems the Justice Department was having with the Microsoft Network, which was finally permitted to be part of the

Windows 95 package. But Windows 95 isn't about marketing or about Jay Leno or the Rolling Stones or even the Microsoft Network. It's about a new version of Windows, the most popular and prominent operating system in all of computerdom. And the changes that Microsoft has made to this important piece of software dramatically change the way you work with your computer. That's what this book is about.

What This Book Is About

According to the hype surrounding the launch of Windows 95, some 500 books have been written on the topic. I'm glad you chose this one. Hundreds of those books were available simultaneously with the launch; because it takes several months to produce a book, that means those books were not based on the final product. I've tried to describe the real world of Windows 95, and that's why I waited to finish the book until Windows 95 was also finished. I've used the final product and installed it on several different machines. And I like to tell it like it is, so you can count on me to give you the straight scoop and sound advice, based on hard experience with the real product.

When you strip away all the hyperbole, you have an operating system that's evolutionary, not revolutionary. Most people will still be doing pretty much the same things with Windows 95 that they were doing with Windows 3.1. Yes, it will be a little easier and a little prettier, but it won't change your life, and it won't turn your PC into a Mac. A PC is a PC is a PC—despite the much-touted Plug and Play feature—so you might have to confront the technical complexities of your hardware setup sometime in the near future. Don't get me wrong. I think Windows 95 is a big improvement over Windows 3.1. It's just important to keep everything in perspective.

What's New in Windows 95

Windows 95 raises computing on a PC to a higher threshold in three important areas: features, performance, and ease of use. To start with, Windows 95 introduces a substantially new graphical user interface, or GUI (Figure 1.1). Windows 95 also improves the performance of your operating system in areas such as graphics, multitasking, memory management, and hardware device drivers. And Windows 95 adds new features such as built-in networking and "auto-play" technology for CD-ROMs; the latter enables a music CD to begin playing all by itself and a software CD-ROM to start up all by itself when you pop the disc into the drive. All the improvements to Windows also enrich the entire environment for building application programs.

• • • • • • • • • • • • • •
FIGURE 1.1
Windows 95
GUI

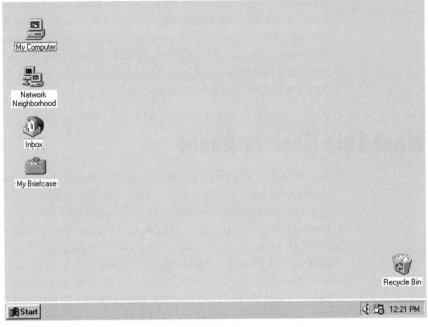

Windows 95 introduces a brand-new graphical user
interface, which shares more with the Macintosh
than with previous versions of Windows.

One of the most important things about Windows 95 isn't new; it's the
ability to use almost all the existing software applications written for Windows 3.1 and DOS. The tens of thousands of applications created for those
older operating systems run the gamut from spreadsheets and word processors to shareware utilities and music software. Microsoft actually put reins on
the advancement of Windows to retain compatibility with existing Windows
3.1 and DOS applications.

Why Bother to Read This Book?

The megabucks Microsoft set aside to blitz the media with Windows 95 has
paid off handsomely. I'm assuming that you, too, have been swept up in the
wave of Windows 95 enthusiasm. But even if you're someone without the
faith, someone who's had Windows 95 foisted on you by your boss, why just
tolerate it when you can actually put it to work for you? Either way, without

a detailed understanding of the software and hardware resources that the environment offers, and without a command of the utilities that enable you to control and customize it, you aren't able to take full advantage of Windows. And as with any software product, it's the extras—the tips, the tricks, the little insights—that give you the incomparable pleasure that comes with truly understanding and mastering your environment.

If you stop your efforts after installing the Windows 95 environment along with an application or two, you're bound to miss out on some important advances in personal computing, advances that can help increase your productivity and creativity and even enhance your enjoyment of computing. With Windows 95 you can make your personal computer more personal. You can customize your screen by selecting or designing icons, changing the colors of menus and buttons, and splashing the desktop with any pattern, from fleur-de-lis to flying toasters. Windows brings individuality to the forefront, so every system can reflect the personality and preferences of its user (Figure 1.2).

FIGURE 1.2

*Personalized
Desktop*

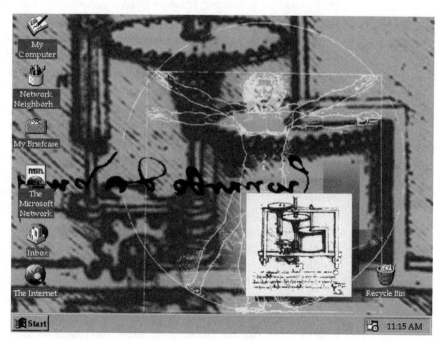

*A host of products enable you to customize your
Windows 95 desktop. This screen shows the
Leonardo da Vinci desktop look provided by the
Microsoft Plus! package.*

Underlying the capabilities and flexibility of Windows 95 is a vast array of features and options. This book is designed to help you learn the inner secrets of Windows 95 so you can optimize your system and your software. Those secrets will help you harness all the power that Windows 95 offers. Imagine that you've driven home the car of the future. This book shows you all the new controls and how best to use them to rev up your engine.

The Windows Family Tree

Windows 95 is a graphical user interface with a long evolutionary history. Windows belongs to a larger family of interfaces that are all derived from the same source: Xerox's Palo Alto Research Center (Xerox PARC). During the 1960s and 1970s, PARC was home to seminal work by computer scientists such as Doug Englebart (inventor of the mouse), Alan Kay (now an Apple Fellow), and John Warnock (chairman of Adobe Systems). Products emanating from ideas developed at Xerox PARC revolutionized the computer industry. They include Xerox's own Star Workstation (a commercial failure), Apple Computer's failed Lisa and its highly successful Macintosh (which catalyzed an industry-wide move to GUIs), and the UNIX interfaces, including Open-Look from Sun Microsystems, Open Software Foundation's Motif, NeXT's NextStep, and IBM's OS/2 Presentation Manager and Workplace Shell.

Of course, Windows 95 is also a member of its own species: Windows. As such, Windows 95 represents the latest step in the evolution of Windows. Inaugurating a long-standing policy of preannouncing software, Microsoft first announced Windows 1.0 in 1983 but didn't ship it for two years, until 1985. Thus Windows was released a year after Apple launched the Macintosh, which came with the first successful operating system based on a graphical user interface. By the late 1980s, Windows reached a new evolutionary plateau that included versions 2.0, 2.1, and 2.2 and Windows 386. In 1990 the first commercially successful version of Windows—3.0—appeared, ultimately selling about 7 million copies.

Windows 3.0 introduced many of the features and concepts that remain today in Windows 95. Windows 3.1 represented a relatively minor step forward in the technical evolution of Windows; its GUI was almost identical to that of Windows 3.0. However, it was a huge success in the marketplace, its installed base soaring to include over 50 million users by the time Windows 95 was launched in August 1995. Although Windows 95 is often seen as a new product, it's almost as long-lived as the Macintosh operating system.

The Windows interface is based loosely on a software design specification called the SAA CUA, for System Application Architecture Common User Access, developed several years ago by IBM. When IBM first outlined SAA CUA, the intent was to make all user interfaces look similar, especially OS/2 Presentation Manager and Windows. Indeed, Windows 2.x (that is, all the versions of Windows 2) and Presentation Manager 1.x shared a similar appearance. However, in 1991 IBM and Microsoft severed their long-standing joint development efforts, the very efforts that had lead to the creation of DOS and the PC standard. The result was the end of the look-alike quality of OS/2 and Windows, with Microsoft taking its portion of the OS/2 code and renaming it Windows NT.

Because Microsoft designed much of the original OS/2 operating system, Windows and OS/2 have many similarities. Microsoft could take the portion of the OS/2 code it owned and rework it so that it became even more similar to Windows. With both hindsight and foresight, Microsoft decided to have NT support both native Windows NT applications (32-bit applications specifically designed for Windows NT) and existing 16-bit Windows 3.1 applications. Windows 95 is a step closer to the full 32-bit world of Windows NT; the two operating systems use many of the same internal programming codes, called application programming interfaces (APIs). This means that Windows NT can also run applications designed for Windows 95, and because Windows 95 programs are based on the 32-bit API, they run faster on Windows NT than do Windows 3.1 programs.

Windows NT offers several advantages over Windows 95. It's a full, 32-bit operating system, whereas Windows 95 is a hybrid 16-bit/32-bit system, which impairs its overall performance and limits its capabilities. Furthermore, Windows 95 can run only on a single Intel processor, whereas Windows NT can run on more than one processor and on non-Intel processors. The ability to run on more than one processor means that you can build a powerful desktop and server system by using two or more processors simultaneously. Because Windows NT was designed to be "portable," it is relatively easy for Microsoft to port the code from the Intel processor to other types of CPUs. So far Microsoft has ported Windows NT to the PowerPC chip, the MIPS 4000-series chip, and the DEC Alpha chip. The PowerPC, MIPS, and Alpha chips are all state-of-the-art RISC processors, which are capable of providing performance levels greater than the current Intel offerings. The combination of multiprocessing and the ability to run on different types of processors makes Windows NT suitable for a broad range of powerful applications, such as engineering workstations, servers, and even supercomputers.

Comparing Windows 95 with Windows 3.1

Windows 95 is more than a face-lift of Windows 3.1; Microsoft put a whole new face on the operating system. Windows 3.1 is actually two-faced; to work with it you have to interact with both the Program Manager and the File Manager. To use a program, you have to run Program Manager, whose colorful icons are just aliases—that is, you cannot manipulate them to control the program files they represent. Instead the icons act as buttons that give you access to the actual files. Thus, if you delete an icon, you don't delete the file it represents. To work with your actual files in Windows 3.1—say, to clean up a directory or copy a file to a floppy disk—you have to fire up the File Manager, a file-browsing utility so weak that power users often resort to using the DOS command line instead.

Windows 95 scraps the Windows 3.1 interface altogether and presents a look that is more reminiscent of the Macintosh or even of IBM's OS/2. The design of almost every interface component has changed, from dialog boxes to menus to icons. Not only have the look and feel changed, but so has the way you operate your computer. Gone are the Program Manager and File Manager Siamese twins. Instead Windows 95 gives birth to interface triplets: My Computer, the Taskbar, and the Windows Explorer. Unlike the twins, the triplets are independent: each one gives you a unique and stand-alone way to manipulate the look and functions of your computer.

My Computer, as its name suggests, presents the warmest, fuzziest way to view your system (Figure 1.3). My Computer bears an uncanny resemblance to the Macintosh interface, which should be no surprise to Macintosh aficionados, who know that the Macintosh offers the most intuitive of any computer interface. Macintosh users will feel right at home with My Computer. It is organized into a system of file folders that represent directories. Inside those folders are icons, which represent programs, data, and other files. There's even a trash can, although on the advice of Microsoft's legal department, it's called the Recycle Bin. Like the Macintosh, My Computer enables you to double-click on a drive's icon to view the contents of that drive and double-click on a folder to open up that folder. Even if you are not a Macintosh user, if you have not used Windows before, My Computer is the easiest place to start.

• • • • • • • • • • • • • • •
FIGURE 1.3

My Computer

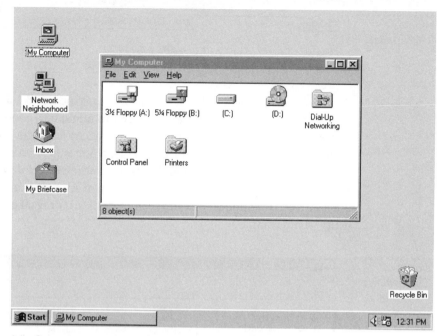

*My Computer, with its file folders and icons,
is the portion of the Windows 95 interface
that most resembles the Macintosh.*

Speaking of starting, a great big button labeled Start sits at the bottom left-hand corner of your screen. It's the lead item of the **Taskbar**, as well as the Windows tie-in to that rocking Rolling Stones song, "Start Me Up" (Figure 1.4). An animated message pops up when you install Windows, pointing to the Start button and inviting you to click on it to start. Despite all this attention, the Start button isn't really for beginners (as I said earlier, My Computer is the real starting place). The Start button provides a handy way for Windows power users to get things going. When you push on that puppy, you access a cascading array of menus that can resemble a maze, depending on how many files and folders you've created. Like a trained rat, though, your mouse hand can quickly learn its way through the maze, and the Start button could become your favorite starting place.

FIGURE 1.4

The Taskbar

The Taskbar is your handy dandy control center for running Windows 95 applications.

The **Explorer** could be described as the Windows 3.1 File Manager on steroids (Figure 1.5). If you're a 3.1 user, this might be a good place for you to start, because it will look somewhat familiar. At least you'll spot icons. The alias icons in the Windows 3.1 File Manager were tiny and not very informative. The Windows 95 Explorer dishes up a more powerful system of managing files, letting you choose from a variety of icon sizes and displaying the actual icons for applications and many data files. It only takes a glance to identify what's what.

FIGURE 1.5

The Explorer

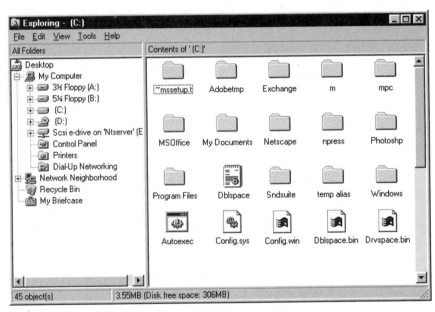

The Explorer is a more sophisticated version of the Windows 3.1 File Manager.

The differences between Windows 95 and Windows 3.1 are more than skin deep. In addition to gaining cute icons and a more advanced interface, Windows has undergone major surgery. The guts of the operating system have been reconstructed, resulting in more features and better performance. But there's a catch: to benefit from its greater strength, you have to feed Windows 95's enormous appetite.

Given the way it consumes system resources, Windows 95 truly is a generation ahead. Microsoft claims on the box that Windows 95 runs on a 386 processor, but I consider that more fiction than fact. Running Windows 95 even stresses out a 486 processor unless it has lots (32 bits) of RAM. Most serious users will find a fast 486 or a Pentium the realistic minimum. Windows 3.1 runs so-so with 4 megabytes of RAM; it really starts cooking when the RAM is pumped up to 8 megabytes. Windows 95 runs so-so on 8 megabytes and starts to simmer with 16. If you use graphics, Computer Aided Design (CAD), or animation programs, you may not find the sizzle until you've fed the beast a whopping 32 megabytes.

What's in the Box

Windows 95 is a retail software product, sold either on its own or bundled with a computer system. Windows 95 comes in the following four versions:

➤ A floppy-disk version called the "full version," which means you don't need to have an earlier version of Windows already running on your system to install Windows 95. This version includes a boot disk and 13 installation disks, for a total of 14 floppy disks.

➤ A floppy-disk upgrade version that requires you to have installed Windows 3.0 or 3.1 on your computer already. This version ships on 13 disks.

➤ A CD-ROM full version that does not require you to have an earlier version of Windows already installed. The CD-ROM version neatly eliminates the hassle of feeding a fistful of floppy disks into the computer during setup.

➤ A CD-ROM upgrade version that requires you to have installed Windows 3.0 or 3.1.

The version is identified on the box when the product is sold at retail. The term "full version" is confusing but merely means it's the version for people who have never installed earlier incarnations of Windows; in other words it's not an upgrade version. The CD-ROM versions (either full or upgrade) are actually more complete than either of the floppy-disk versions. Microsoft uses the extra space available on the CD-ROM to add information, such as the Windows 95 Resource Kit (an excellent technical reference) and even some visual treats, such as full-motion video clips.

The prices of the full and upgrade versions differ significantly. The upgrade version carries a street price of $80 to $90, whether you purchase it on CD-ROM or floppy disk. The full version can cost $200 or more because you aren't given the price break for already being a Windows owner. Obviously, the CD-ROM upgrade version is the best value, because you get the extra goodies at the low price. Don't overzealously wipe out your old Windows installation in anticipation of Windows 95, because the upgrade version checks for existing Windows components before it installs Windows 95.

Most computer manufacturers will preinstall Windows 95 on the hard disk of a system as part of a so-called bundle. The same doesn't hold for dealers, however; if they include bundled software, it may not have been pre-installed. Because of its popularity and value, Windows 95 is frequently bundled with other products, such as mice, multimedia upgrade kits, and software programs. Whether you buy straight from the computer maker or from a dealer, your copy of Windows 95 should contain a set of installation disks or a CD-ROM and a slim user guide, *Introducing Microsoft Windows 95*.

Many computer makers place their labels on Windows when they bundle it with their systems. In those cases the manuals and software are usually identical to what Microsoft has produced, despite the change on the cover. However, sometimes the software has been modified. This can affect how your system operates, particularly if the setup program has been altered.

For the remainder of this book, I refer to the installation software, whether on floppy disks or on CD-ROM, as the Windows installation disks. Keep those disks handy even after you've installed Windows. As I point out later in the book, you may need them from time to time.

Microsoft Plus!

When Microsoft's product developers met to plan Windows 95, they filled a white board with all sorts of great ideas. However, many of the ideas were erased when it became apparent that they were not feasible. And even the final list of features didn't make it into the Windows 95 retail box. Had all those grand features been incorporated into Windows 95, it would not run on a 386 system. Because the Microsoft marketing department viewed the millions of 386 computer users—many of whom are using Windows 3.1—as a potentially profitable market, they convinced the techies to yank out a few things and make a lean, mean Windows 95 that would still run on a 386.

That's what the programmers did. The leftover features that would require a 486 or larger processor were pulled out of Windows 95 and packaged into Microsoft Plus! for Windows 95, which retails for $49.95. But as I have mentioned, even though the Windows 95 box claims the program runs on a 386, I am skeptical about whether Microsoft really met that goal. (The bottom line: If you've got a 386, consider sticking with Windows 3.1.)

Microsoft Plus! for Windows 95 contains a mixed assortment of goodies, including the following:

➤➤ **System Agent**. A software scheduling utility.

➤➤ **DriveSpace 3**. An advanced data-compression utility.

➤➤ **3D Pinball**. Yet another reason for your boss to yell at you.

➤➤ **Desktop Themes**. A collection of wallpaper, icons, and other designs that can spiff up your Windows 95 desktop.

➤➤ **Visual Enhancements**. Utilities that don't work on anything less than a 486, including a program that smooths fonts and another that enables you to drag a full window (not just its outline).

The Microsoft Plus! package also contains a collection of Internet-related utilities called the Internet Jumpstart Kit. The kit contains three programs:

➤➤ **The Internet Setup Wizard**. An automated script that helps you set up Windows 95 to connect to the Internet through any Internet service provider (including, of course, Microsoft Network).

➤➤ **Internet Extensions**. Software extensions to Windows 95 that, through the magic of OLE, provide better integration between Windows 95 and the Internet.

➤➤ **The Internet Explorer**. Microsoft's World Wide Web browser, based on NCSA Mosaic.

Most of those components meld seamlessly into your Windows environment, providing desktop delights such as designer backgrounds and more sophisticated sounds. The Internet components can be downloaded from microsoft.com free of charge, so don't purchase Microsoft Plus! if they are all you want. Also, I recommend Netscape Navigator as a better World Wide Web browser than Microsoft's Internet Explorer, at least at the time of this writing.

What's Ahead for Windows

The name Windows 95 implies that there might be a Windows 96. Microsoft officials are still debating whether another version will be out in 1996, but given the sluggish pace of operating system development, I predict that Microsoft will probably sit out a year. Ultimately, however, Microsoft does plan to achieve an annual upgrade cycle, which I'm sure makes their spreadsheets light up with dollar signs.

By the time Windows 97 or 98 becomes a reality, you may decide it's time to take an altogether different route—Windows NT. In fact, if you're a power user, you may find that Windows 95 is just a small stepping-stone on your way to Windows NT, which is undergoing more rapid upgrades than Windows 95. Windows NT already sports an interface that is almost identical to Windows 95's. And as I mentioned earlier, Windows NT is a true 32-bit, multitasking operating system that can take your computing platform to a higher level.

Insider's Tip

The folks on the Windows 95 product development team are pretty darn proud of themselves. To show off and give themselves a virtual pat on the back, they embedded an elaborate Easter egg inside Windows 95. Easter eggs are secret software routines that are usually activated by a series of keyboard entries or menu selections. To demonstrate that Windows 95 is more sophisticated than older versions of Windows, the Microsoft team concocted a sophisticated way to activate its Easter egg. Here's how to do it:

➤ Move the mouse to a blank space on your desktop and click on the right mouse button.

➤ Select New Folder and name the new folder "and now, the moment you've all been waiting for." (Don't type in the quotation marks or the period.)

➤ Point to the folder, click the right mouse button on it, select Rename, and this time name it "we proudly present for your viewing pleasure." (Again, don't type in the quotation marks or the period.)

➤ After renaming the folder, click the right mouse button on it again and rename it one more time, to "The Microsoft Windows 95 Product Team!" (Don't type in the quotation marks; do type in the exclamation point.)

➤ Open the folder, making sure your speakers are turned on, and you'll see (and hear) the lengthy multimedia Easter egg crediting the entire Windows 95 team.

The Windows 95 Interface

Welcome to virtual reality! It's time to sit down at your virtual desk. In an attempt to make running a computer program as intuitive as working with paper and pencil, Windows 95 has adopted the desktop look. It's far from an original concept; a desktop is the predominant metaphor adopted by many **graphical user interfaces**, or **GUIs**. In fact, Microsoft has clearly borrowed some concepts from competitors' products—most notably the Macintosh—in crafting the Windows 95 interface.

The Windows 95 GUI was designed to mirror everything on your desk—including, in some cases, the clutter. What you see is what you've got: the full-screen background is your desktop, and windows and icons represent items you work with every day, such as papers (documents), filing drawers (volumes), file folders (folders), and tools (applications). Icons in Windows 95 can also depict devices such as printers and fax machines. Windows 95 adheres to the look and feel of a desktop more than any earlier incarnation of this middle-aged operating system.

An obvious advantage of the desktop metaphor is easy orientation. If you get lost, just hone in on the desktop, where you can view your tools, rearrange documents, and solve thorny problems in a familiar setting. Luckily, Windows 95 lets you arrange the desktop almost any way you like, so you can organize the Windows environment to suit your personal preferences, no matter how idiosyncratic. In fact, sometimes we think Windows 95 was designed to satisfy the needs of those with weird tastes. To make the most of your design options, become familiar with the main components of your desktop, as described below.

Windows, Menus, Icons, and Dialog Boxes

The Windows 95 interface is constructed of four main types of building blocks: windows, menus, icons, and dialog boxes. Both Windows 95 and the software programs that run on it use those four elements to communicate with you and to help you operate your computer.

As its name suggests, the **window** is the most basic building block of the Windows 95 environment. A window visually defines a work space on the computer display and can be manipulated in various ways; you can move, shrink, expand, and (usually) change the dimensions of a window. You can rearrange windows on the screen just as you would rearrange papers on an actual desktop. In fact, the computer screen—upon which the windows are displayed—is called the desktop.

Most computer programs and applications use **menus** to present commands. The people at Microsoft basically force all application developers to present commands in the same way, so you find the File and Edit menus in the same places in most Windows programs. Not only that, those menus often contain the same or similar commands from program to program. Even the keyboard shortcuts that activate commands on the menu are fairly consistent. For example, the exit command—Alt,F,X—is the same in almost every Windows program. Windows 95 takes menus to the extreme, allowing you to use the Start button to access your entire system from one menu.

Icons are pictures that represent elements of your computer system. Sometimes intuitive, sometimes obtuse (depending on the artist's talent), icons can represent programs, documents, files, directories (called folders), and special controls. Ideally, the meaning of an icon is obvious. For example, the icons for printers, disks, and documents are literal representations of those items (Figure 2.1).

FIGURE 2.1
Icons

[C:]   3½ Floppy (A:)   HP LaserJet 4 Plus   Bootlog   Examples   Bubbles

Icons visually suggest what they represent—at least usually.

Dialog boxes are like New York taxicab drivers: they talk back. In that sense, they are the most interactive element of the Windows 95 graphical user interface. Basically, Windows 95 dialog boxes relay or request information in one of three ways. One variety simply presents a message, such as "The operation was completed successfully." Another common kind of dialog box asks you to make a yes-or-no choice—for example, "Save Changes Before Quitting?" The most complex (and often annoying) kind of dialog box presents an almost bewildering array of options, which in turn may include dialog boxes that bring up dialog boxes that bring up even more dialog boxes, like the Russian doll within a doll.

Upgrade Alert

New in Windows 95 are tabbed dialog boxes. By using index tabs, each of these dialog boxes can present you with a bewildering array of options (Figure 2.2).

•••••••••••••
FIGURE 2.2

*Tabbed Dialog
Box*

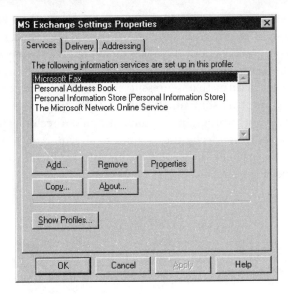

*Click on a tab to view a
page of options in these
new multilayered dialog
boxes.*

Windows 95 is designed so that windows, menus, icons, and dialog boxes can be manipulated best with some sort of pointing device, most commonly a **mouse.** As you move the mouse around on the top of your desk, a small pointer, usually shaped like an arrow, appears on the screen. The pointer sometimes changes its shape to let you know it can be used for a special task (Figure 2.3).

•••••••••••••
FIGURE 2.3

Cursors

*Cursors are used to show your location on
the desktop and to perform special tasks.*

You can use a mouse to activate objects on your computer screen. First you point to an item on screen and then you click or double-click on it. Clicking is simple: just give the left mouse button a quick push (tip for lefties: yes, you can change that to the right button, as described in Chapter 7). Double-clicking means just that: two quick clicks of the mouse in rapid succession. To adjust the period of time between the two clicks, use the Mouse Control Panel. Once you've pointed and clicked, you can drag an item around the screen. Dragging involves a series of actions: point to something on the screen, press and hold down the left mouse button, and "drag" whatever you have thus grabbed to its new location. Finally, release the mouse button to drop the repositioned object into place.

Upgrade Alert

Windows 95 introduces a new use for the **right mouse button**, which was treated like a useless appendage by previous versions of Windows. The right mouse button now enables you to perform actions on objects throughout the interface. For example, to rename a file—in this case the file is the object—select it with the left button, then click on it with the right button, which brings up a pop-up menu (Figure 2.4). The pop-up menu in this example features standard commands used to manipulate files, including the Rename command.

FIGURE 2.4

A Pop-up Menu

Point to an on-screen object and click with the right mouse button to reveal a pop-up menu pertinent to that object.

Insider's Tip

You can manipulate windows, menus, icons, and dialog boxes from the keyboard. In fact, Microsoft has made sure you can operate everything in Windows 95 without a pointing device. Experienced DOS users and proficient typists may find it faster to issue many Windows commands from the keyboard rather than take their hands off the keyboard to use the mouse. That's why this book includes the keyboard equivalents for all the commands I mention.

The rest of this chapter gives you a closer look at windows, icons, menus, and dialog boxes. If you're an experienced Windows user, you can skip to the next chapter—you probably know these tricks by now. If you're new to Windows, it wouldn't hurt to read on. Consider this your orientation to computer life.

Windows

Although Windows 95 has received a major interface lift, it is still haunted by remnants of its older versions. That's because many Windows applications—mostly from companies other than Microsoft—still use part of an old scheme for displaying windows that was originally developed by IBM. The scheme is confusing, and a lot of programs, including Windows 95, now use the newer, simpler interface. However, the old system—called **MDI,** for **Multiple Document Interface**—is still not out the door, so I'm going to explain how it works. By the way, IBM developed MDI with the best of intentions—to create a standard look for programs and applications. MDI also provides a way for applications to display many documents within one window.

With the MDI system, a document window is displayed only inside the main window of the application or program that created the document. In other words, if you create a document in WordPerfect, you can open that document's window only inside the main WordPerfect window. Windows 95 displays a document in its own window, independent of the application that created the document.

Another characteristic of the MDI system is hierarchical windows. An application window defines the screen; document windows—called **child windows**—are found within the application window. Some people call child windows **secondary windows**—I presume they don't like the anthropomorphic connotations—but I stick to the term *child window* or *child document window.* A child document window can contain various elements, from text to video images to groups of icons or even graphical control panels.

Upgrade Alert

With the release of Windows 95, Microsoft has begun to discourage the use of the MDI in favor of what it feels is a more intuitive interface, one that places both documents and applications in their own separate windows. The old MDI system was developed when a document was created by only a single application. For example, word processors created word-processing documents, and paint programs created graphics documents. Nowadays, technologies such as OLE allow a single document to contain data from several applications. This brings document windows up to the full status of application windows. The Macintosh works along these lines, displaying documents and applications in separate windows. In this way (as well as in several others) Windows 95 more closely resembles the Macintosh than earlier Windows versions did.

Insider's Tip

Most of the Windows 95 interface is designed without the use of the old MDI. Someday all Windows applications will also abandon the MDI. For the time being, however, you'll probably see a mixture of both the old and the new schemes.

Figure 2.5 shows a Windows 95 desktop. The main components of the interface are identified.

• • • • • • • • • • • • • •
FIGURE 2.5
The Windows 95 Desktop with Several Applications Open

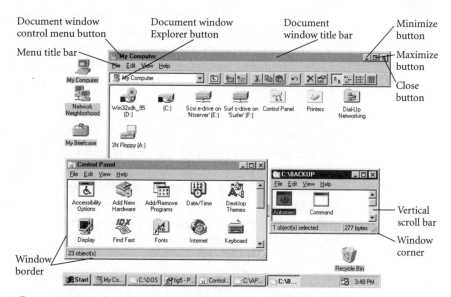

The anatomy of a Windows application: a menu bar, a document window Control menu button, a document window Explorer button, a window border, a window corner, a vertical scroll bar, a Maximize button, a Minimize button, and a Close window button.

Moving and Resizing Windows. You can move any application window and the new Windows 95 **independent document windows** around on the desktop and position them any way you like, even with portions moved off the screen. The older, child document windows, however, can be moved around only within the parent application window to which they belong. Windows 95 helps mitigate this limitation by enabling you to move any type of window with a mouse: grab the window's title bar by pointing at it and pressing down on the mouse button, drag the window to a new location (its outline will move as you drag it), and release the mouse button when the window is positioned at the desired location. To abort the move at any time, press the Esc key before releasing the mouse button.

Upgrade Alert

For the most part, the new independent document windows look and behave much the same as application windows.

To reposition just one edge of a window, move the cursor to whichever of the four sides you want to move; the pointer changes into a two-headed arrow when it's on target. Then simply drag the window border with the mouse. You can also grab a window corner to lengthen or shorten two adjacent sides at the same time. To abort a resizing, press the Esc key before releasing the mouse button. The minimum size for any window is about two inches wide by one inch tall, but this varies depending on the resolution and size of the display.

Windows can also be moved or resized with the cursor control, or arrow, keys. To select an application window, press Alt+Tab to cycle through application windows until you reach the one you want. When you have selected a window, issue the appropriate command (Resize or Move) from the window's Control menu, as described later in this chapter. The pointer changes shape into a four-headed arrow. If you have selected Move, pressing any arrow key causes an outline of the window to move accordingly. When the window has reached its new position, press Enter. If you have selected Resize, use an arrow key to select a window border. For example, press the up arrow to select the top window border. To grab a window corner, press two of the arrow keys together; for example, pressing down arrow+right arrow selects the lower right-hand corner of the window. Then you can use the arrow keys to resize the window; press Enter when you're done. To abort the moving or resizing process, press Esc.

Scroll Bars. Scroll bars enable you to move contents of a window into view when the window is too small to display all its contents at once. Application windows, document windows, and even sections of dialog boxes can have scroll bars. Scroll bars usually appear only when they might be needed, so if you alter the contents of a window so that everything can be viewed on one screen, the scroll bar usually disappears. The reverse happens when you add items to a window so that it can no longer display all its contents at once.

The vertical scroll bar appears along the right-hand side of a window, and the horizontal scroll bar is located at the bottom of the window. The position of a button in the scroll bar provides a visual indication of your location in the window.

You can scroll the contents of a window in several ways:

»+ Grab the scroll button in the middle of the bar and drag it with the mouse. To move to the top of the window's contents, drag the scroll button to the top of the vertical bar. To get to the bottom of the window, drag the scroll button down the bar.

»+ Click on the arrow buttons on either end of the scroll bar to move the contents up or down in small increments.

»+ Hold the mouse button down while pointing at one of the arrow buttons on the scroll bar to scroll the contents continuously.

»+ Click on the scroll bar itself, in between the scroll button and the appropriate arrow button, to move the window's contents one windowfull at a time.

With some applications, you can scroll using the keyboard. Table 2.1 lists the commonly supported conventions for keyboard scrolling.

TABLE 2.1
Common Conventions for Keyboard Scrolling

Keystroke	Scrolls
Up arrow	Up one line.
Down arrow	Down one line.
Page Up	Up one screen.
Page Down	Down one screen.
Ctrl+Page Up	One screen to the left.
Ctrl+Page Down	One screen to the right.
Home	To the beginning of the line.
End	To the end of the line.
Ctrl+Home	To the beginning of the document.
Ctrl+End	To the end of the document.

Folder Windows. In earlier versions of Windows, an application window almost always contained a running program, and document windows were displayed within the application window. As mentioned earlier, Windows 95 now allows documents to occupy their own independent windows that behave like application windows. To add more confusion, Windows 95 has introduced a new type of window called a **folder window.** The folder window has the status of an application window; it's definitely a daddy or a mommy window, not a child window. That's because a folder window performs a powerful function: it enables you to view and organize the contents of your computer. When they are minimized, folder windows are represented by small file folder icons (Figure 2.6).

FIGURE 2.6

A Folder Window That Contains File Folder Icons

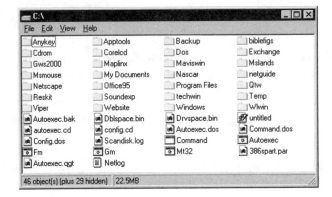

In Windows 95, folders represent the directories on your storage devices, and the icons inside the folders represent the files.

Folder icons and folder windows represent the directories on storage devices such as floppy-disk drives, hard-disk drives, CD-ROM drives, and network servers. When you double-click on a folder icon, it opens to display the contents of the directory it represents. (No, Virginia, this is not a novel concept. Macintosh users will experience déjà vu because this is the way the Mac has always worked.)

Title Bars and Control Menus. You can find the name of a window and other information about it (including the generating application) in the **title bar** at the top of every standard window. If you open more than one window, the title bar of the active window—the window you most recently selected— appears in a different color or intensity from the title bars of the dormant windows.

At the right end of a window's title bar, you'll see three small buttons: the **Minimize button,** the **Maximize button,** and the **Close button** (Figure 2.7). Pressing the Minimize button shrinks the window down into a button on the Taskbar; pressing the button is like selecting the Minimize command from the Control menu (discussed later in this chapter). The Maximize button enlarges the window to fill the entire screen or, if the window is already maximized, restores the window to its original size. The Maximize button is equivalent to the Maximize and Restore commands on the Control menu. The last button on the title bar is the Close button, which closes the window and, if it's an application window, quits the application.

• • • • • • • • • • • • • •

FIGURE 2.7

Main Components of the Title Bar

This screen shows the Control menu, the window's name, the Minimize button, the Maximize button, and the Close button.

The left end of the window's title bar contains the **Control menu**, also called the System menu. In Windows 95, this menu is represented by a small icon, which varies depending on the type of window:

➤ Application windows are represented by miniature versions of their application icons.

➤ Independent document windows are designated by small versions of their file icons.

➤ Folder windows display an icon of an open folder.

The Control menu icons clue you in about the window you are viewing. To access a Control menu, click once on its small icon, or press Alt,spacebar. If the window contains a DOS session, press Alt+spacebar. The Control menu contains commands that enable you to move, resize, and close windows, and it's particularly well suited for keyboard users; mouse handlers can accomplish most of these tasks in other ways. For example, you can shrink an application window down into an icon either by clicking the window's Minimize button or by typing Alt,spacebar,N. To expand the window to fill the entire screen, press the Maximize button or type Alt,spacebar,X. The Control menus of most application windows include the commands shown in Table 2.2.

To close an application window, double-click on its Control menu button, choose Close from the Control menu (Alt+F4), select Exit from the File menu (Alt,F,X), or click on the window's Close button (located in the upper right-hand corner, the one with the *X*).

• • • • • • • • • • • • • •
TABLE 2.2
*Common
Control Menu
Commands for
Windows*

Menu Command	Keystroke	Description
Restore	Alt,spacebar,R	Restores window to previous size.
Move	Alt,spacebar,M	Enables you to move window using arrow keys.
Size	Alt,spacebar,S	Enables you to resize window using arrow keys.
Minimize	Alt,spacebar,N	Reduces window to icon on Taskbar.
Maximize	Alt,spacebar,X	Enlarges window to full screen.
Close	Alt+F4	Closes window; quits if it's an application.

Application windows that contain DOS sessions can also include the menu selections shown in Table 2.3

• • • • • • • • • • • • • •
TABLE 2.3
*Common
Control Menu
Commands for
Windows That
Contain DOS
Applications*

Menu Command	Keystroke	Description
Edit	Alt+spacebar,E	Displays a cascading menu with Mark, Copy, Paste, and Scroll.
Settings	Alt+spacebar,T	Displays dialog box that enables you to toggle the toolbar.

Insider's Tip

If you're running a full-screen DOS session, you can still press Alt+spacebar to bring up the Control menu.

Child Document Windows. What's in a child document window depends on the nature of a program or an application. For example, in a child document window for Microsoft's Word for Windows, you find word-processing documents, whereas Adobe Photoshop uses child document windows to display image files.

Child document windows share the menu bar of their so-called parent application window. If you select a command from a menu, it usually affects the contents of the active document window. To activate a document window, click on it anywhere, or press Ctrl+Tab repeatedly until the window is selected. When more than one document window is open, the active one displays a different-colored title bar and appears in front of any overlapping document windows.

The Control menu buttons in parent applications and child document windows have some similarities and some differences. The icon in the center of a button is smaller in a document window and changes to reflect the window's contents. To get to a document window's Control menu, click on its button or type Alt,minus. Control menus sometimes contain special commands for particular applications, but almost all Control menus for document windows contain the commands shown in Table 2.4.

. . . .

TABLE 2.4
*Common
Child Window
Control Menu
Commands*

Menu Command	Keystroke	Description
Restore	Alt,minus,R	Restores document window to its previous size.
Move	Alt,minus,M	Enables you to move document window with arrow keys.
Size	Alt,minus,S	Enables you to resize document window with arrow keys.
Minimize	Alt,minus,N	Reduces document window to an icon within the application window.
Maximize	Alt,minus,X	Enlarges document window to the full size of the application window.
Close	Ctrl+F4	Closes document window.
Next	Ctrl,F6 or Ctrl+Tab	Switches to next document, regardless of whether it is a window or a minimized document icon.

The button for a child document window's Control menu is positioned at the left end of the document window title bar. If you press the window's Maximize button or double-click on the window's title bar—or if you issue the Maximize command from the keyboard by typing Alt,minus,X—the document window expands to fill the entire application window, and a number of changes occur (Figures 2.8 and 2.9).

FIGURE 2.8

*Before
Maximize*

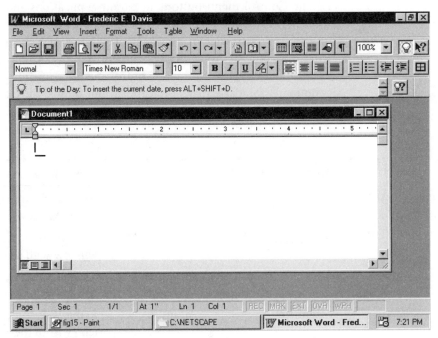

*Word before you press the Maximize button
on one of its document windows.*

When a document window is maximized, it loses its own title bar; as a result, the document window title is usually incorporated into the application window title bar. Other changes occur when you maximize: the document window's Control menu appears at the left end of the menu bar, and the Restore button is at the right end of the menu bar. The Restore button contains two tiny squares on top of each other. If you click on the Restore button, the document window shrinks back to its previous size.

FIGURE 2.9

*After
Maximize*

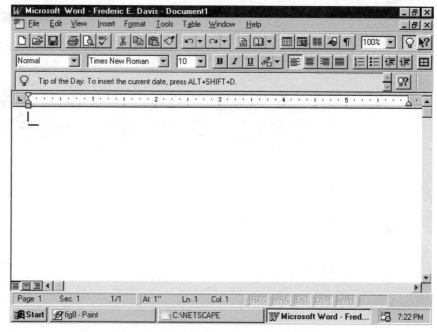

*Same Word application window as in Figure 2.8
after you have pressed the Maximize button.*

Oops! A big problem with the old MDI is that child windows sometimes get cropped by parent application windows (Figure 2.10). Consequently, their scroll bars and other controls are sometimes out of reach. To view the portions of a child document window that are out of sight, you can use the scroll bars, or you can move and resize the document window itself. But there's an easier solution. Many Windows applications provide commands that automatically arrange the document windows inside the application window. Microsoft Word, for example, offers **Tile** commands (found on the Windows menu). The Tile command arranges all the document windows so they fit inside the application window without overlapping (Figure 2.11).

• • • • • • • • • • • • • •
FIGURE 2.10
*Cropped
Document
Windows*

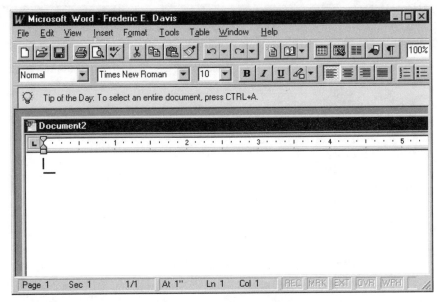

In Windows 95, application windows, such as the one
shown here for Microsoft Word, sometimes crop
document windows, making their controls inaccessible.

• • • • • • • • • • • • • •
FIGURE 2.11
Tiled Windows

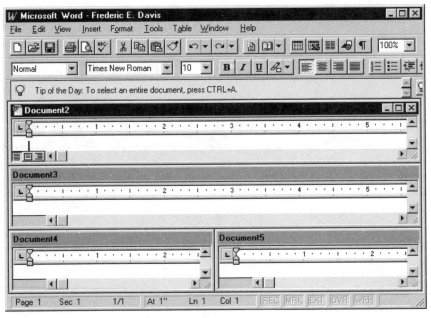

The Tile command partitions the application window
equally among all the open document windows.

Even if you have only one window open, the Tile command can prove handy. For example, if the scroll bars of a document window are inaccessible because that window is cropped by an application window, issuing the Tile command resizes the document window so that it fits entirely within the open application window, revealing all the controls.

To close a document window within an application window, double-click on its Control menu button, choose Close from the Control menu (Ctrl+F4), select Close from the File menu (Alt,F,C), or click the Close Window button. At this point a dialog box may appear to ask if you want to save any changes before closing the window—just in case you have made changes since you last saved.

Menus

Menus offer the primary commands for operating Windows and its applications. This à la carte system enables you to issue a command simply by selecting a choice from a menu. Menus are also informative because they present the commands and options for an application in an organized fashion that makes it easy for you to browse. Menus offer an incomparable advantage over a command-based environment like DOS, in which you have to recall the exact spelling or syntax of a command to issue it. In addition to commands, menus can contain lists of open files or windows, font styles, and the names of cascading menus, which in turn reveal further choices.

To make this movable feast possible, Windows uses two types of menus: **control menus** and **application menus.** Control menus are generic and change little from application to application. Application menus, however, are the command centers of Windows programs and contain the basic commands specific to each application. Because Microsoft has rigorously encouraged developers to standardize the layout of the command structure, you'll find that you can use some of the same commands—such as Alt,F,X to exit an application—for almost any Windows application. Application menus are found on the menu bars of virtually all application windows, and although they vary widely from program to program, the first two menus are usually a File menu followed by an Edit menu (Figure 2.12).

FIGURE 2.12

*Application
Window with
File Menu
Pulled Down*

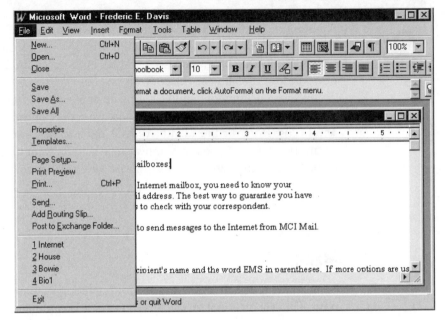

*Menus contain the main commands for an application,
and almost every program includes a File menu.*

The menu bar shows the names of menus from which you can select commands. Menus can be pulled up or down, depending on their length and the available space on the display (Figure 2.13).

Selecting a menu with a mouse is easy; you can either pop it up or pull it down. To pop it up, point to the name on the menu bar and click once. Point to an item on the menu and click once again to select it. Alternatively, you can use the pull-down method familiar to Macintosh users: point to the menu, hold the mouse button down, drag the mouse to an item (which is then highlighted), and release the button to select the item. Pulling a menu up works the same way: just point and drag up instead of down.

Insider's Tip

The mouse is not always the fastest way to work in Windows 95. You can use the Alt key in combination with other keys to select frequently issued commands without having to take your fingers off the keyboard. To access a menu, press the Alt key (or F10), followed by the underlined letter in the menu's name. Then select an item by typing the underlined letter in that item's name. For example, to quit a program, use the standard Alt,F,X command: Alt accesses the menu bar, F selects the File menu, and X chooses the Exit command on

FIGURE 2.13
Application Window with Menu Pulled Up

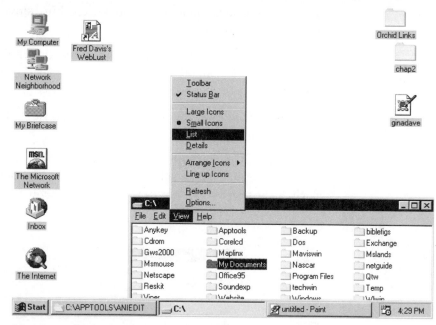

Menus are bidirectional: you can pull them up or down depending on where you have the most space.

the menu. In those rare cases when the menu names do not include an underlined letter, you can press Alt to select the menu bar and then use the right or left arrow key to highlight the name of the menu you wish to select. Similarly, once the menu is open, you can use the up and down arrow keys to highlight a menu item and then press the Enter key to select the item. To deselect a menu and return to the application, click anywhere outside the menu or press Alt (or F10). To close the menu but remain on the menu bar ready to select a different menu, press Esc.

Sometimes a command is placed directly on the Start menu. In this case, you can press Ctrl+Esc to reveal the Start menu and then type the underlined letter in a menu option to select it.

Menus also follow certain other conventions:

➻ Items appear dim on a menu to indicate that a command or an option is not available at the time. Often you need to take another step, such as selecting text for formatting, before the command can be applied.

➤+ Menu items are often followed by keyboard combinations—these are keyboard shortcuts for the option.

➤+ A menu item preceded by a check mark means this choice is already in effect. To turn the item off and remove the check mark, reselect the command. To toggle the item on and off, just keep selecting it.

➤+ Any menu item followed by an ellipsis (...) means you'll elicit a dialog box by selecting that item.

➤+ Any menu item ending with a small triangle means it's a cascading menu. If you choose this item, a submenu appears offering additional choices, which can be selected in the same way as regular menu items (Figure 2.14).

FIGURE 2.14

Cascading
Menu

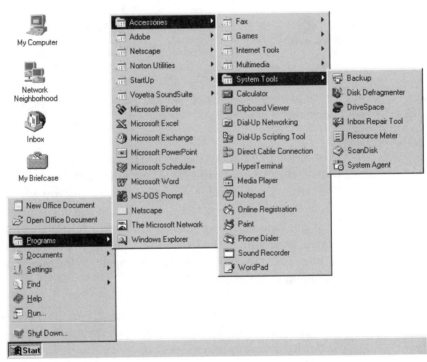

A cascading menu item, marked by a small triangle after the item's name, reveals a menu within a menu when selected. A good example is the Windows 95 Start Button menu.

Icons

Icons defy any one definition because they can represent a hodgepodge of materials and functions, including applications, documents, disk files, directories, and special controls. Every Windows program contains at least one if not several unique icons, and developers seem to strive for individuality in their icon designs. Although icons should give you some visual clue as to what they represent, sometimes creativity gets out of hand.

Icons often represent programs and data files. Sometimes icons act like buttons. Clicking or double-clicking on an icon usually activates it. For example, to open a folder on the Windows 95 desktop, double-click on its folder icon.

Microsoft has created five primary types of Windows 95 icons:

➤ Application icons.

➤ Child document icons.

➤ Volume icons.

➤ Folder icons.

➤ File icons.

You'll also encounter many other types of icons in specific applications.

Application Icons. One of the most common types of icon, the **application icon,** represents a program that is stored somewhere on one of your computer's mass storage devices (a hard disk, a floppy disk, or even a network server). Double-clicking on an application icon causes Windows 95 to load the program's code into memory so that Windows can execute—in other words, run—the program (Figure 2.15).

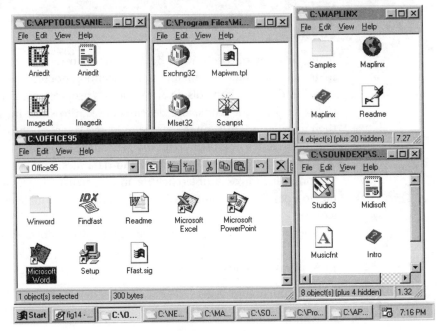

FIGURE 2.15

*Application
Icons*

This Windows 95 desktop shows a number of open
folders, each containing application icons.

**Upgrade
Alert**

The ability to move application icons almost anywhere in the interface—
including the desktop—is new to Windows 95. In Windows 3.1, for example,
application icons were found almost exclusively in the Program Manager
application. Also, when an application window was minimized, its application icon appeared at the bottom of the screen. With Windows 95, on the
other hand, minimized applications are found on the Taskbar.

Child Document Icons. A **document icon** can represent one of two things.
In Windows 95, document icons usually represent actual document files, such
as a text file or a graphics file. But in the case of an application that follows
the old MDI, a document icon is simply a child document window that you
have minimized. This kind of icon is found only inside a parent application's
window (Figure 2.16).

Although **child document icons** (and their corresponding document windows) often do represent traditional documents such as word-processing and
paint files, they can designate anything the individual program designers wish
—within reason, that is. Microsoft encourages Windows developers to adhere
to certain guidelines.

FIGURE 2.16
*Child
Document
Icons in Word*

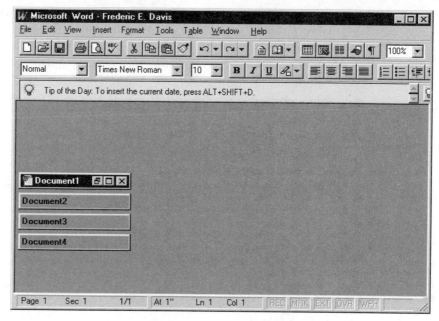

Child document windows and their icons in Word
appear only inside Word's application window.

You can minimize an active child document window into a document icon by clicking on the Minimize button or by typing Alt,minus,N. The child window implodes into an elongated icon bar that often takes its place along the bottom of its parent application window. You can move document icons freely within the parent window by dragging them with a mouse (or by typing Alt,minus,M and using the arrow keys), but you can't move them outside the boundary of the parent application's window onto the desktop. (OK, try it and see what happens!)

Here are two ways to explode the icon back into a document window:

≫→ Double-click on the icon, or click once on the icon to pop up the Control menu, then choose Restore from the menu. From the keyboard, use Ctrl+Tab to cycle through the document icons; when the one you want is selected, issue the Restore command by typing Alt,minus,R.

➺ To maximize the document icon so that the resultant document window fills the entire application window, click once on the icon to pop up the Control menu, and choose Maximize from the menu. Or double-click on the icon to restore it to a window, then press its Maximize button if needed. From the keyboard, select the document icon (use Ctrl+Tab to cycle through the document icons), then type Alt,minus,X to issue the Maximize command.

Volume, Folder, and File Icons. Icons, icons, icons. You also need to know about three other major types of icons: **volume, folder, and file icons.** All of these are used to represent the contents of your system (Figure 2.17).

FIGURE 2.17
A Volume, a Folder, and a File Icon

[C:]   My Documents   Bio1

These icons can be used to depict what's in your system.

Volume icons represent the storage volumes that Windows recognizes as being connected to your system. Commonly, you find volume icons for a floppy disk, a hard disk (or a hard-disk volume partition), a RAM disk, a CD-ROM drive, and a network volume. Volume icons appear in the My Computer folder and usually depict the type of storage device they represent, whether a floppy disk or a piece of hardware. Volume icons are always followed by a letter that represents the drive letter used by DOS (such as A:).

Folder icons normally represent directories and subdirectories; you'll recognize them on screen as yellow file folders. Keep in mind that every folder is tied to the storage volume that contains the directory the folder represents. As you can see in Figure 2.20, an open file folder icon represents an open file folder; likewise, a closed file folder icon stands for a closed file. Such literalmindedness!

Upgrade Alert

Windows 95 introduces another type of document icon called a file icon. This icon appears within file folder windows. File icons let you know which application created the document file represented by the icon. For example, Windows 95 gives every document created by Word a file icon that is similar to Word's own application icon. This makes it easy to identify a document file created by Word; it also lets you know that opening that icon will cause Word to load so you can edit the file's contents.

In addition to document file icons, you'll also run across a variety of other file icons, such as application icons, font icons, and system component icons (Figure 2.18). Something almost always happens when you double-click on one of these icons. If it's a volume, a window opens to reveal the contents of that storage device. If it's a folder, a window displays the contents of the directory or subdirectory represented by that folder icon. If it's an application program, the program runs. Or if it's a document icon, the program that created the document will run, with the document already loaded into it.

· · · · · · · · · · · · · ·

FIGURE 2.18

Folder with File Icons

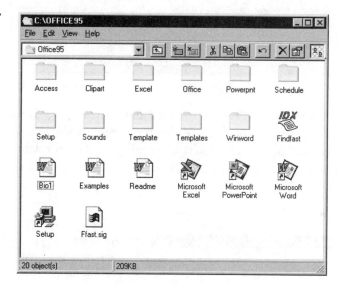

A folder can contain a variety of file icons, representing anything from a document to an application.

· ·

Dialog Boxes

Dialog boxes make you work. That's because Windows 95 uses dialog boxes to request information that it needs to complete an action, or to present you with an important message. An ellipsis (…) following a menu item indicates that a dialog box will pop up when you select that item.

Often a dialog box presents you with a selection of options related to a command or a procedure that you initiated by choosing a menu item. The options are pretty standard fare: you usually get to press some buttons, check a box or two, or select options from a list. Then there's a checkpoint: you're asked to press an OK button to carry out the task, or you can bail with a Cancel button (Figure 2.19).

FIGURE 2.19

Dialog Box

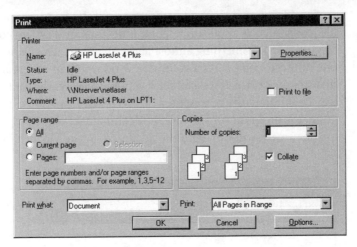

A dialog box
provides
options
for you
to press,
check, or
select.

Some dialog boxes—also called **alert boxes**—display warnings and cautionary information. These dialog boxes either warn you about the dire consequences of an action you're attempting to take or explain why you can't do what you're trying to do. To make an alert box go away, click on the Yes button (Figure 2.20).

FIGURE 2.20

Alert Box

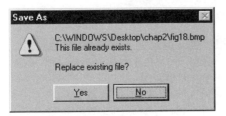

An alert box presents a warning
or a message explaining why your
action either is dangerous or
can't be completed.

If a dialog box contains a title bar, you can move the box to a different spot on the screen either by grabbing the title bar with the mouse and dragging the dialog box to its new location or by using the dialog box's Control menu: type Alt,spacebar,M and move the box with the arrow keys. You can move among the pages of a **tabbed dialog box** by clicking on each page's tab, which includes a title for the page (Figure 2.21).

•••••••••••••
FIGURE 2.21

*A Tabbed
Dialog Box*

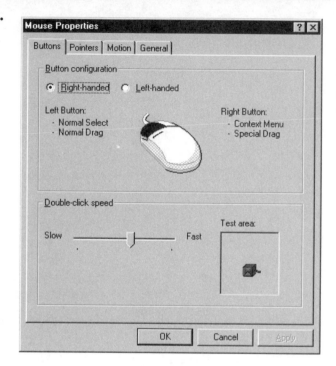

*Tabbed dialog
boxes let you flip
through more
than one page of
options within a
single dialog box.*

Summary

This chapter introduced you to the building blocks of the Windows 95 graphical user interface. Most of those elements—windows, icons, and dialog boxes—are all too familiar to users of previous versions of Windows (not to mention Macintosh crossovers). Windows 95 spruces up those features and adds a few more as well—sort of like a face-lift plus a hair implantation. You get the picture. All in all, though, the changes make it easier not only to look at the screen but to figure out how to use what's there.

If you haven't at least glanced at the Upgrade Alerts I've scattered throughout this chapter, you're missing out on some hints I've dropped about how to take advantage of the new interface developments. These changes are important: not only do they affect Windows 95 itself, they also affect all the applications, utilities, and other items that you encounter in your Windows wanderings.

Buckle your flight belt! In the next chapter, I'll show you how to take the controls to navigate the Windows environment.

Navigating Windows 95

Windows 95 introduces three new tools for navigating and operating Windows and Windows applications: the **Taskbar**, **My Computer**, and the **Explorer**. These three tools replace the Program Manager and the File Manager found in previous versions of Windows. I say good riddance. Not only were those artifacts limited, they were also codependent: you needed to use them both to operate your system. In response to a severe round of criticism, Microsoft has introduced not one but three tools, each of which is functional enough on its own to enable you to run your computer. The only drawback to this embarrassment of riches is determining which tool to use. Reading this chapter will help you make an informed decision, but in most cases there's no one right choice. Ultimately, your decision will be based mostly on personal preference.

Of the three new interface tools, the Taskbar offers the most concentrated functionality. Its push-button control center places an almost staggering arrray of commands and options at your fingertips. You can usually find the Taskbar resting at the bottom of your screen, ready to spring into action whenever you need it.

My Computer uses icons to depict the elements that make up your computer and its software—including documents, applications, the printer, and Windows 95 itself—in what is called an **object-oriented** view. You can look at My Computer to scan and access the entire contents of your computer. Because Macintosh users (and Apple Corporation lawyers) might find noticeable similarities between My Computer and the Macintosh Finder, My Computer offers those people the easiest way to approach Windows 95.

The Explorer offers the most literal representation of what's on your system. This souped-up file browser presents a hierarchical view of your computer system based on your storage devices, folders, and files. The Explorer is like the old Windows 3.1 File Manager on steroids; for Windows 3.1 users, this tool will provide a familiar environment in which to get a handle on Windows 95.

The Windows 95 Taskbar

The Taskbar is like one of those leather tool cases electricians strap onto their hips in an attempt to carry the entire shop around with them. Like a virtual wraparound belt, the Taskbar provides a compact way to get at myriad tools and services. The Taskbar is normally found along the bottom of the screen and serves as the resting place for minimized windows. You'll notice that the Taskbar is often visible while you are running applications, which makes it handy to switch quickly from one window to another. The Taskbar also includes the powerful Start button, which provides a grab bag of shortcuts for getting to almost anywhere in your system (Figure 3.1).

FIGURE 3.1

The Basic Taskbar

| Start | C:\NETSCA... | fig21 - Paint | My Compu... | C:\ | Microsoft W... | 7:55 PM |

You'll find the helpful Taskbar along the bottom of your Windows screen.

Because you can use the Taskbar both for accessing minimized windows and for tapping the potent Start button, the Taskbar is the Windows navigational tool you'll probably find yourself using the most, especially once you become familiar with Windows 95.

Insider's Tip

When you first install Windows 95, the Taskbar appears as a horizontal band across the bottom of the screen. In line with the have-it-your-way attitude behind the design of Windows 95, you can move the Taskbar if you like. Click on any blank space left on the Taskbar, hold down the mouse button, and drag the Taskbar to any edge of the screen: top, bottom, or either side. When the Taskbar borders the top or the bottom of the screen, it maintains its horizontal orientation, but if you drag it to one side or the other, the Taskbar becomes vertical. A vertical Taskbar provides more room for stacking icons but also usually truncates names (Figure 3.2). Once you are familiar with what your icons represent, however, this can be a good way to stuff more into your Taskbar.

. . . .
FIGURE 3.2
Vertical
Taskbar

You can turn the Taskbar on end
to stuff more icons into it.

. . . .

The Start Button

The Taskbar starts off with—what else—the **Start button.** The Start button is the single most important button you can press in all of Windows 95. Every major Windows 95 function—from starting an application program to configuring your system's hardware—can be accessed from this button. When you first boot Windows 95, the Taskbar immediately points to the Start button with the message "Click here to start" (Figure 3.3).

When you first click on the Start button, an intimidating array of menu choices pops up. When you click on one of them, you'll probably see a whole new crop of choices. It's like trying to stamp out ants—kill a few, and their reinforcements keep on coming. Actually, this endless potential for issuing commands from a single button is what makes the Start menu so powerful. Once you've mastered its subtleties (by reading this chapter word by word), you will be completely in command of Windows 95 at the push of a button (Figure 3.4).

FIGURE 3.3
FIGURE 3.3

*The Initial
Taskbar
Prompt*

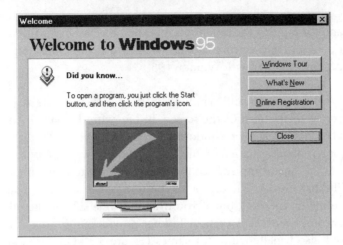

This start-up
prompt gets
you to take the
next step with
a message
that says:
*"Click here
to start."*

FIGURE 3.4

*The Start
Menu*

*Master this menu, and you'll
be in charge of Windows 95.*

Many of the commands and options that you can access from the Start button provide shortcuts to operations I cover in greater detail further along in this chapter. I'll start at the beginning, with an overview of the Start button's basic submenus and their functions.

Insider's Tip

It can be a real drag holding the mouse button down while you drag your pointer through a complex array of cascading submenus. Guess what? It's not necessary. With Windows 95, you simply click on the Start button once and then let your mouse pointer hover for a moment over each menu item to bring up its submenu; the same technique works for the submenu. Once you've pointed your way through the menu maze to the item you want, click once more to select it.

Programs. The first Start menu selection you notice is the **Programs submenu.** Here you see additional submenus, each representing a program or a group of programs that has been installed on your system. By default, you find submenus for items such as the Windows 95 Accessories (more on these in Chapter 5), Multimedia (covered in Chapter 12), and the Startup folder (which lists programs that should be started automatically by Windows 95 when you boot it up) (Figure 3.5).

• • • • • • • • • • • • • •

FIGURE 3.5

The Programs Submenu

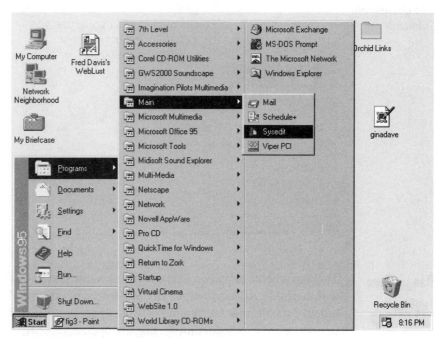

This submenu depicts additional submenus, each representing programs or groups of programs installed on your system.

The Programs menu also contains icons for running specific applications or utilities. On a new installation of Windows 95, you find icons for the MS-DOS prompt (see Chapter 4), the Microsoft Network on-line service, and usually, at the bottom of the menu, an icon for the powerful Explorer utility, which we cover later in this chapter.

To start one of those programs, highlight its menu entry and click. This quick-click action is a new feature of Windows 95 and is designed to make the environment easier for novices. You don't have to worry about folders or volumes or even double-clicking—just highlight an entry in the Start menu, click once, and you're on your way.

Documents. The Documents submenu lists the most recently used data files. You don't have to locate a particular folder to recall items you handled recently. Think of the Documents submenu as a bookmark for your system. By listing your most recently used documents, Windows 95 makes it easy for you to start working where you last left off (Figure 3.6).

FIGURE 3.6
The Documents Submenu

This feature acts like a bookmark by listing the documents you most recently handled.

Danger Zone

The Documents submenu lists only documents that you open directly from within a folder. If, for example, you first start a program and then load a document data file, that file's name will not appear on the Documents submenu. In other words, only documents that are opened directly, by double-clicking on their icons in a folder, are added to this list.

Settings. The **Settings submenu** provides quick access to three of the main configuration options for the Windows 95 environment. The first, **Control Panels,** enables you to alter the appearance and behavior of Windows 95. The second option, **Printers**, lets you install new printers, change the configuration of existing printers, and view currently spooled print jobs. Finally, a **Taskbar option** lets you alter the behavior of the Taskbar (Figure 3.7). All of these options are discussed later in this chapter.

• • • • • • • • • • • • • •
FIGURE 3.7
*The Settings
Submenu*

This submenu enables you to
change the configuration of
Windows 95, your printers,
and the Taskbar itself.

Find. The **Find submenu** brings up three flavors of the Windows 95 Find
utility, which tracks down missing objects. The first flavor, **On the Microsoft
Network,** enables you to search for a resource on Microsoft's own on-line
service. The second, **Find Files or Folders,** enables you to search disk and network volumes for a particular set of files or folders by name, date, or contents.
Finally, **Find Computer** enables you to search for a particular network
resource, such as a file server (Figure 3.8). We'll be taking a closer look at the
Find utility later on in this chapter.

• • • • • • • • • • • • • •
FIGURE 3.8
*The Find
Submenu*

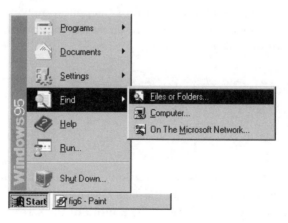

The new Find submenu
makes searching for a
disk, network, volume,
file, folder, or network
resource a snap.

Help and Run. Two additional Start menu items—**Help** and **Run**—provide functions that I discuss in detail later in the book. The Help item brings up the Windows 95 context-sensitive help system, which includes an on-line reference to all the major functions and features of the environment. There is help on Help in Chapter 5. The Run item brings up a dialog box that enables you to run a program by typing its name—useful when you can't find the program in the Start menu's submenus (Figure 3.9). I cover the Run command in Chapter 4.

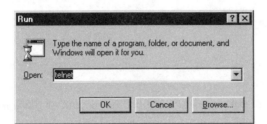

*This dialog box allows you
to run a program by
typing in its name.*

The Task List

Besides providing a handy spot for the Start button, the Windows 95 Taskbar also functions as a **task list**—that is, Windows 95 uses the Taskbar to keep track of all open application windows. The list is displayed as a series of horizontal boxes, each containing the title of an application window, a miniature version of its application icon, and in some cases the name of a related open document or data file (Figure 3.10).

FIGURE 3.10
*Application
Icons on the
Taskbar*

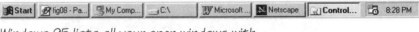

*Windows 95 lists all your open windows with
these icons on the Taskbar.*

**Upgrade
Alert**

If you've worked with previous versions of Windows, you'll see that the Windows 95 Taskbar combines the Task Manager program and the application icons that used to appear at the bottom of the screen in the Program Manager. When a program's application window is minimized, it no longer produces an icon on the Windows desktop (which was the case with Windows

3.0 and 3.1); now the window is minimized on the Taskbar. Instead of bringing up the Windows Task List to switch between running programs, you now use the Taskbar's version of a task list, which is similar to the push-button channel controls on a radio. Click on the Taskbar entry for a particular program, and its application window is immediately brought to the "top" of the desktop.

The Notify Area

The final piece of the Windows 95 Taskbar is the **notify area.** This small region at the right end of the Taskbar provides useful information about system events. It also serves as a standard location for hardware controls, such as the volume control for a sound card installed in a Windows 95 system (Figure 3.11).

FIGURE 3.11
*The Notify
Area*

 The notify area hosts a variety of controls and alerts.

　　By default the notify area displays only a small digital clock. But the area can be used for a variety of tasks: for example, it can alert you to incoming e-mail messages, indicate battery power level on a notebook or a portable computer, and provide a modem-line monitor for the **Windows 95 Remote Access Services**. (See Chapter 10 to find out more about all the cool networking and communications features that have been built into Windows 95.)

Control Panels

Like a film director in the editing room, you can use Control Panels to manipulate what goes into your Windows 95 environment, from sounds to sights and keyboard options to time settings. This is your chance to play the all-powerful computerist—with the Control Panels, you can configure and customize Windows 95 to your nerdliest delight.

　　You can get more Control Panels if you install certain options in Windows such as Exchange or if you have certain hardware options such as a joystick or PCMIA card. You can also get other Control Panels from third-party software vendors and hardware manufacturers, but Windows 95 already comes with an array of default Control Panels, which cover your basic needs. Here's a brief description of what you'll find:

Accessibility
Options

Accessibility Options. Enables you to configure Windows 95 to be more easily manipulated by individuals with physical disabilities.

Add New
Hardware

Add New Hardware. Brings up the Windows 95 hardware auto-detection and installation wizard. This Control Panel enables you to install new hardware and device drivers.

Add/Remove
Programs

Add/Remove Programs. Enables you to install new software programs, remove existing programs, and selectively install and remove optional portions of Windows 95.

Date/Time

Date/Time. Enables you to set the system's date and time and adjust the settings for location and time zone.

Display

Display. Enables you to control all aspects of your Windows 95 display configuration, including video drivers, resolution, background patterns, color schemes, and screensavers.

Fonts

Fonts. Displays currently installed typefaces and provides the controls for installing or removing typefaces.

Keyboard

Keyboard. Enables you to fine-tune your keyboard's operation.

Mail and Fax

Microsoft Exchange Profiles. Enables you to set options for the Microsoft Exchange program.

Microsoft Mail
Postoffice

Microsoft Mail Post Office. Enables you to use your computer as an e-mail post office.

Modems

Modems. Provides controls for the installation and configuration of modems attached to your system.

Mouse

Mouse. Enables you to fine-tune your mouse's operation, including tracking speed and right- or left-handedness.

Multimedia

Multimedia. Provides a control center for multimedia devices.

Network

Network. Enables you to configure your network hardware and software.

Passwords

Passwords. Enables you to set security parameters for your system.

Printers

Printers. Similar to the Printers item in the Settings submenu of the Start button, enables you to install, configure, and manage printers.

Regional
Settings

Regional Settings. Enables you to control the display of formats for currency, date, time, and other items.

Sounds

Sounds. Enables you to attach sounds to specific system events.

System

System. Provides you with access to advanced system features, including the Windows 95 hardware configuration tree.

All of those options are described in more detail as we progress through *The Windows 95 Bible.* Once you're familiar with them, you will be able to exercise a great deal of control over your computing environment.

Upgrade Alert

Users of previous Windows versions will notice several differences in the Control Panels feature. Windows 3.0 and 3.1 treated all control panels as sub-sections of a single program, called the Control Panel. In Windows 95, the Control Panels (notice the plural) exist as independent programs and can be executed directly. Another difference is that the Control Panels offer a broader range and more depth in controlling configuration parameters than was possible in previous Windows versions. Finally, many functions of the old 3.1 version of Windows Setup have been replaced by function-specific Control Panels, such as Display. Not only is this design cleaner, you can find things more easily.

- -

Shutting Down the Windows 95 System

Danger Zone

After you've finished your work, it is important to shut down the environment properly before you hit the power switch and call it a day. With previous versions of Windows, this meant closing the Program Manager, which terminated the Windows environment and left you at a DOS prompt. Because Windows 95 is more tightly integrated with DOS, you encounter a few new wrinkles in the shutdown procedure.

The **Shutdown option** itself is located at the bottom of the Start menu. Selecting this option brings up the Shutdown dialog box (Figure 3.12).

FIGURE 3.12

The Shutdown Dialog Box

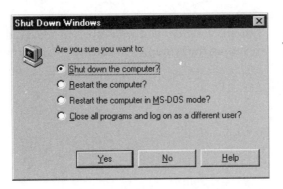

You need to shut down your system gracefully with this dialog box to keep Windows 95 running smoothly.

The Shutdown dialog box provides you with four choices:

➤ Shut down the computer?

➤ Restart the computer?

➤ Restart the computer in MS-DOS mode?

➤ Close all programs and log on as a different user?

Selecting the first option causes all of your running programs to close. (Don't worry—if you haven't saved your data, the editing program prompts you to do so.) The program then clears the Windows 95 desktop and displays a message that the computer is ready to be turned off.

Selecting the second option produces the same results as the first, except that instead of telling you to turn off the computer, the program reboots the computer automatically. If Windows 95 is the default operating system, you return to Windows 95 (this process is commonly referred to as a "warm boot").

Selecting "Restart the computer in MS-DOS mode" forces Windows 95 into a special MS-DOS compatibility mode. This is desirable when you run a tricky DOS program, such as a game, that has proven to be incompatible with DOS application support in Windows 95. You'll learn more about MS-DOS mode in Chapter 4.

Finally, the "log on as a different user" option works in conjunction with the Windows 95 user account feature. Unlike previous versions of Windows, Windows 95 can be set up to maintain multiple, independent configurations of the desktop for different users—a feature I'll show you how to use in Chapter 6.

An Object-Oriented View of Your Computer

Now that you're familiar with the basic features of Windows 95, it's time to explore objects, one of the most powerful concepts of the operating system. The Windows 95 interface is what is commonly referred to as an **object-oriented interface.** Computer scientists and other purists contend that Windows 95 doesn't really qualify as a true object-oriented system because it is not designed that way from a programming perspective. That's true for programmers. But for users of Windows 95, the system definitely looks like an object-oriented interface—at least there are graphical objects on screen designed to represent the hardware and software components of your system.

Windows 95 is designed to act as a natural extension of your physical work space, with objects that represent familiar tools hiding the complexities of the underlying hardware and software. Fundamental to the new look and feel of Windows 95 is the **desktop**. As part of the object-oriented design, the desktop itself is an object, much like your real desk is an object in your office, as are paper, pencils, and card files. You work in the Windows 95 environment by opening objects and displaying them on the desktop. For example, to edit a word-processing document, you first open the folder in which it is stored, then open the document file. Windows 95 then loads the appropriate tool and displays the document on the desktop for editing. The entire operation is like opening a file cabinet, removing a folder, and opening the folder on your desk. Computers are finally simulating reality.

In another design shift, Windows 95 helps you move your focus away from applications, such as word processors and spreadsheets, and toward the **documents** you are handling. With this heightened emphasis both on documents (rather than applications) and on objects, the document object is one of the most important concepts in Windows 95. Document objects are represented by a much wider variety of icons than in previous versions of Windows. Windows 95 enables you to start applications and even to load documents into already running applications by double-clicking on document icons.

To master this major shift away from applications and toward documents, Windows 95 has boosted its use of **OLE,** a powerful software standard that enables applications and documents to share information. With OLE embedded in Windows 95, you can create a single document that contains data generated by several applications. For example, a single document file can contain text created by a word processor, graphics designed with a paint program, and a table generated by a spreadsheet. And by means of a powerful new interface mechanism known as **Scraps,** you can actually keep snippets of data from individual files, then drag and drop them at will throughout the Windows 95 interface. We'll teach you lots more about OLE in Chapter 14.

. . . .

My Computer

What's the use of an object-oriented interface without a bevy of objects? That's the point behind the Windows 95 interface—you interact with it by manipulating numerous objects that appear on the screen. Windows 95 organizes these objects by grouping them into larger objects, so some objects represent just a single item—like a document—whereas other objects, such as file folders, contain many other objects. The metaphor is that of a desktop—the primary object in Windows 95—containing the rest of your objects, whether they are on your system or connected to your computer through a network.

In the upper left-hand corner of the Windows 95 desktop is My Computer, an object that contains all the other objects on your system (as opposed to, say, objects you access via a local area network, which would be found inside the Network Neighborhood icon). If you want an eagle's-eye view of what's on your computer system, double-click on My Computer (Figure 3.13).

FIGURE 3.13
My Computer

Check out what's on your computer with the My Computer icon.

When you select My Computer, a window pops up containing a variety of icons. These include volume icons, which represent the mass storage devices attached to your computer, and several special-settings folder icons, which contain Control Panels and other items related to the configuration of your system. Typical volume icons include floppy-disk drives, hard-disk drives, attached CD-ROM drives, and in some cases network drives that have been mapped to your computer.

Insider's Tip

My Computer presents information in a way similar to how the Macintosh does. So if you're coming to Windows 95 from a Mac, this is probably the best way to get started.

Folder Views: Your Window on Objects

Normally, if you double-click on any of the icons in My Computer, Windows 95 opens a new window displaying the object's contents. For example, if you double-click on a volume object, you see a window displaying all the folders and files stored in that particular volume. This type of window is commonly called a **folder view,** and it's a key visual tool in the Windows 95 interface.

Folders are software containers in which collections of icons are stored, and folder views are windows that display the same collections of icons. Several types of icons open up to display folder views, including volume icons and folder icons. My Computer itself opens into a folder view, as do all the volume and folder objects within My Computer—including, for example, the settings folders for the Windows 95 Control Panels (Figure 3.14).

FIGURE 3.14

Viewing the Contents of a Folder

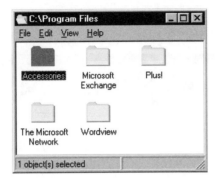

Double-click on a volume icon to obtain a folder view, which displays the folders and files stored on that volume.

Folder views make it easy to view and work with hard disks and other storage devices. That's because data on a **mass storage device**—be it floppy disk, hard disk, or network drive—is organized by a folder view into a hierarchical, branching pattern so that you can let your eyes do the searching. The trunk, or root directory, of the drive may have any number of subdirectories branching from it. These subdirectories, in turn, may contain additional subdirectories of their own, forming a pattern reminiscent of a tree with many branches.

The Windows 95 folder view was designed to reflect neatly the hierarchy of your storage volumes. For example, when you first open a volume icon, you are presented with a folder view of the volume's root directory. Included in that view are any file icons located in the root directory, as well as folder icons representing additional directories that branch from the root. Double-clicking one of those folders opens a new window displaying a folder view of its contents. This view may include additional nested folders, files, or a combination of both (Figure 3.15).

FIGURE 3.15

Easy Navigation

Navigating volumes is easy thanks to the Windows 95 folder mechanism.

The folder view concept of Windows 95 makes navigating your disks and other storage volumes a snap. Simply double-click, and you've changed directories. Every folder and file in the Windows 95 interface is part of the treelike, hierarchical file system.

Custom-Designed Folder Views. Windows 95 enables you to customize your folder views to create a desktop that suits your needs, tastes, and whims. If you like, for example, you can adjust the way icons are displayed, prod the system into displaying more information, or change your method of navigating through directories. You can even access a special toolbar to use in a folder view window.

Changing the View Style. Want to change the size and style of the icons inside your folder view windows? As you've noticed, Windows 95 displays the folder view contents using large, made-for-the-myopic icons. These are easy to read but take up more real estate than you might want to give them. Also, these mega-icons don't provide more information about what they represent than smaller icons could (Figure 3.16).

· · · · · · · · · · · · · ·
FIGURE 3.16
*The Default
Folder View*

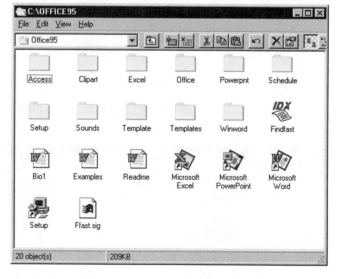

This view displays large, easily visible icons but takes up too much space for the dribble of information it leaves behind.

I suggest that intermediate users—those of you ready to handle having more objects squeezed into the folder view—switch to the Details view. Select Details from the View menu, and check out the view. It's like going from the *Weekly Reader* to the *New York Times:* expect to see considerably more information about each object's size, its type, and the last time it was modified (Figure 3.17).

••••••••••••
FIGURE 3.17

The Details View

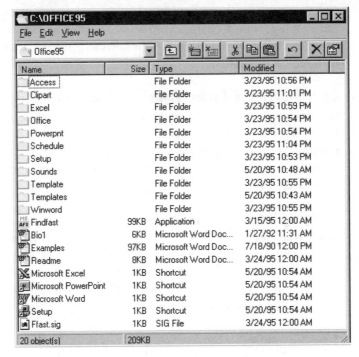

The Details view provides information about the type of object, its size, and the date it was last modified.

Want another view option? Try one of these:

➻ **List.** Sorts the icons from left to right (Figure 3.18).

➻ **Small Icons.** Sorts the icons from top to bottom (Figure 3.19).

••••••••••••
FIGURE 3.18

List View

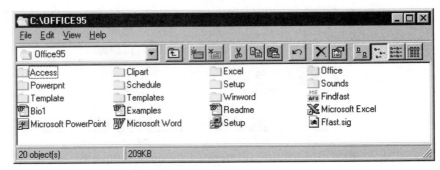

The List view sorts icons in a folder view from left to right.

FIGURE 3.19
Small Icons View

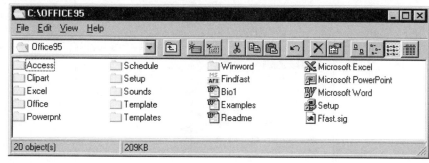

The Small Icons view arranges icons
alphabetically from top to bottom.

Hello, Toolbar

Because the **toolbar** offers shortcuts for a variety of handy commands, you often want it in a folder view window. Normally, though, the toolbar is hidden. By default, folder view windows don't display the toolbar for two sensible reasons: to reduce clutter and to clear up as much viewing space as possible. But if you're willing to sacrifice a little space, you can turn on the toolbar and gain push-button access to frequently used functions. For example, you can click on one button to connect to a network drive or click on another to change your style of view to Small Icons, List, or Details. To display the toolbar in a folder view window, select Toolbar from the View menu (Figure 3.20).

FIGURE 3.20
Toolbar in the Folder View

Turn on the toolbar to take shortcuts for
some commonly used commands.

If you feel particularly nimble (intermediate to advanced computerists), you can take advantage of the first item on the toolbar. This is a drop-down list box that provides a treelike overview of your entire Windows 95 system, including My Computer and all open folder windows. This system tree makes it easy to jump from directory to directory with a minimum of clicking (Figure 3.21).

FIGURE 3.21
The Toolbar's Drop-Down List Box

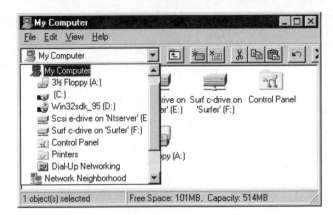

The toolbar's drop-down list box makes jumping from point to point as easy as knowing where you want to go.

The system tree drop-down list box appears on all toolbars in folder windows. But that's about the only consistent feature of folder view window toolbars. As you might imagine, different toolbars contain different buttons, depending on the nature of the folder view window. For example, the toolbar in a folder view window of My Computer contains buttons for connecting to and disconnecting from a network, whereas you won't find those buttons in the folder view of the Control Panel window. Other toolbars contain unique, special-purpose buttons; for example, the toolbar in a folder view of a Fonts folder window contains a Similarity button, which enables you to determine how similar one font is to another (you'll find out more about that later in the book).

Here's a roundup of the most common buttons you'll find on toolbars in folder view windows:

 Up One Level. Moves up one step in the directory tree to the previous or parent folder.

 Map Network Drive. Enables you to connect to a drive or storage volume across a network.

 Disconnect Net Drive. Enables you to disconnect from a drive or storage volume.

 Cut. Cuts whatever is selected in the window and places it in the Clipboard.

Copy. Copies whatever is selected in the window and places the copy in the Clipboard.

Paste. Pastes the contents of the Clipboard into the window at the location of the cursor or insertion point.

Undo. Undoes your most recent action.

Properties. Displays the Properties dialog box for whatever object is selected in the window.

Large Icons. Switches to the default, Large Icons view.

Small Icons. Switches to the Small Icons view.

List. Changes the window to the List view.

Details. Displays the full Details view.

A Change of View. As if all those folder view options weren't enough, you can also change the very nature of the way you browse through folders and windows. By default, Windows 95 creates a new window for each new folder view. So each time you click on a folder view icon within a folder view window, a new folder view opens to display the contents of the icon you just selected. If you're cruising through many folders, the screen can quickly become overrun with hordes of open windows. Windows 95 comes to the rescue with a feature that enables you to display a single window that depicts only the contents of the currently opened folder.

To access the feature, select Options from the View menu; this brings up a tabbed dialog box. The first tab, labeled Folder, enables you to select the viewing modus operandi (Figure 3.22). You can choose one of two views:

➣ Browse folders using a separate window for each folder (Alt+S).

➣ Browse folders by using a single window that changes as you open each folder (Alt+N).

....
FIGURE 3.22
*Changing the
Viewing
Behavior*

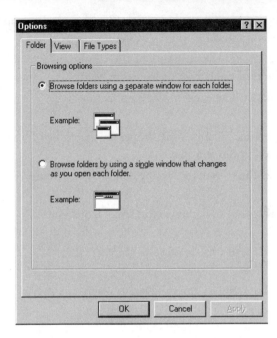

*To change the
viewing behavior,
select Options.*

Danger Zone

Although the single-window viewing approach spares you from window clutter, you might forget your place in the overall tree structure. That's why it's a good idea to turn on the toolbar when you use this viewing method. With the toolbar in place, you can use the Up One Level button and the drop-down list box to locate your position in the directory tree and to jump quickly from directory to directory.

Grappling with Device Objects

Objects, objects everywhere could be the leitmotif for Microsoft's Windows 95 interface-design team. **Device objects** are yet another type of object in the grand scheme of Windows 95; they represent peripheral hardware devices that are attached to your system. For example, a printer connected to your computer's parallel port is a device object. It's represented by an object icon, which you can manipulate as you would other objects in Windows 95.

Device objects have properties intrinsic to the nature of the devices they represent. For example, printers maintain a print queue that contains the pending print jobs requested by applications you are running. To view the print queue, you can double-click on the icon that represents the printer, which brings up a window displaying the contents of the print queue (Figure 3.23).

FIGURE 3.23

Right on Cue

HP LaserJet 4 Plus

Printer   Document   View   Help

Document Name	Status	Owner	Progress	Started At
Remote Downlevel Document	Printing	FRED	0 bytes of 0 ...	3:42:55 PM 7/17/95

To view the print queue for a printer, double-click on the printer's icon.

The window that's displayed when you open a device object icon bears a fair resemblance to a folder view. However, if you look closely, you'll see some differences related to the kind and particular brand of device you're viewing. For example, in addition to displaying the print queue, a printer object window typically contains the menu options you need to control your printer. As shown in Figure 3.24, the Properties command on the Printer menu brings up a dialog box that contains a large number of controls specific to your printer, including options for paper handling, graphics, font management, and devices. The controls enable you to tell Windows 95 how much memory you have installed in your printer so Windows can optimize printing speed.

FIGURE 3.24

Examining the Device Options Properties for a Device Object

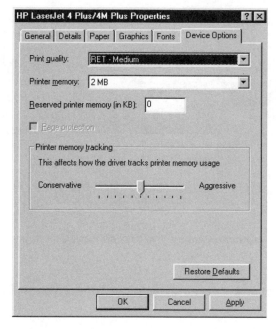

The Device Options page of the Properties dialog box lets you tell Windows 95 how much memory is installed in your printer.

. . . .

How to Find Anything

Microsoft definitely went gung ho—maybe even overboard—in providing a cornucopia of techniques to accomplish the same task. I've already surveyed several ways to navigate through folders and directories, and believe it or not, there's more to come. All this flexibility can drive you crazy, which is why I encourage you to keep reading this book.

Although folders can help you organize data, they can also make finding a particular file or other object a daunting task, especially on a fully loaded system. With this unhappy scenario in mind, Microsoft made sure to include a powerful search utility with Windows 95. The result is the **Find utility**—a feature that can streamline your computer life considerably. That's because the Find utility makes it easy to put your finger on files, folders, and even other computers across a network without having to double-click your way through mountains of nested folders.

To summon the Find utility, go to the Taskbar's Start menu and select Find. From the short submenu that pops up, select whatever type of object you're seeking (Figure 3.25).

. . . .
FIGURE 3.25
*The Find
Submenu*

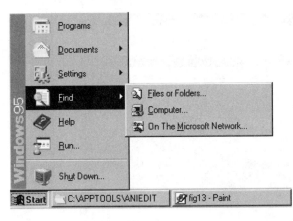

It's not as simple as merely picking the Find command from the Taskbar's Start menu. You also need to choose the kind of object you want to find from the pop-up submenu.

The Find submenu enables you to send out a search party for three types of objects:

➤ Files, programs, or device drivers located on the Microsoft Network on-line service.

➤ Specific files or folders on a local or networked drive.

➤ Other computers on your network, so you can tap into their resources, including storage volumes, printers, and other peripherals.

Surprise, Surprise! It's Microsoft Network. Leave it to Microsoft to give itself a pitch right off the bat. The first option in the Find submenu, On the Microsoft Network, lets you search for a specific piece of software or other resource on Microsoft's on-line service. If you've already signed up for the Microsoft Network on-line service, Windows 95 automatically connects you to the service when you select this Find option. Once it successfully connects to Microsoft Network, this Find option uses the search facilities of the on-line service to locate specific resources, such as an elusive printer driver or an on-line database.

Finding Files or Folders. You'll use the Files and Folders option more often than any of the others, so if you're skimming, it's time to slow down and pay special attention. Select Files and Folders from the Find submenu to bring up a tabbed dialog box containing three pages: Name & Location, Date Modified, and Advanced. The first page enables you to search for an object based on its name and its location in your system. Use this page if you know the object's name; enter the name into the Named box and click the **Find Now button** (Figure 3.26).

• • • • • • • • • • • • • •
FIGURE 3.26
The Find Now Button

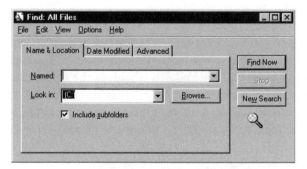

Type the name of an object into the Named box and click the Find Now button to start the search.

By default, the Find utility searches for a file or a folder on the hard disk you used to boot Windows 95, but you can expand the search to include all your volumes. To do so, select the My Computer option in the Look In drop-down list box. This tells the Find utility to search every volume in the My Computer folder, which should contain every volume currently attached to your system. Once the Find utility's detective work is done, it displays its results in a folder view window that gets tacked onto the bottom of the Find dialog box (Figure 3.27). You can then manipulate the contents of this folder view as you would with any other folder.

FIGURE 3.27
The Results Window from a File-Name-Based Search

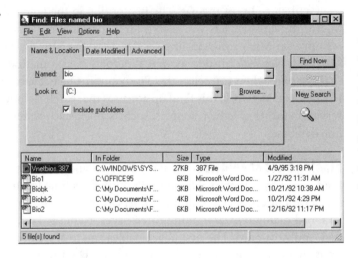

The Find utility displays the results of its search in a folder view window grafted onto the bottom of the Find dialog box.

The search results window is really a fully functional folder view. For example, you can open a data file by double-clicking on its icon, and you can drag and drop objects from the search results window into other folder views or onto the Windows 95 desktop.

Knowing an object's name makes finding the object easier, but it's not the only way to track down what you're searching for. For example, you can also find an object based on its date stamp. Windows 95 stamps each file with a date and a time that are updated whenever the file's contents are modified. For example, if you know that a particular file was changed within the past 24 hours, you can use the **Date Modified page** of the Find dialog box to round up all the files that have changed during this time period (Figure 3.28).

FIGURE 3.28
Using the Date Modified Page

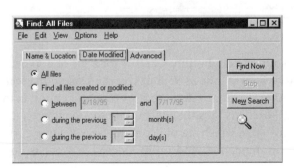

Use the Date Modified page of the Find dialog box to track down objects based on the time they were last used.

You can also use the Date Modified page to search for file objects that fall within a range of dates. Or you can look for objects that were changed within a specific number of days or months.

If you want to search through your system with a fine-tooth comb, tab over to the **Advanced page** in the Find dialog box. The Advanced page enables you to search for a file object based on several criteria:

>→ **Containing text.** Enables you to search for files that contain a specific word or fragment of text. This is a great feature because it enables you to find files just by remembering words, names, or other bits of text. But watch out—this option takes by far the most time to complete its search.

>→ **Of type.** Enables you to find all the objects of a specific type, such as all the animated cursors.

>→ **Size is.** Enables you to find an object of a specific file size.

You can combine options to narrow your search. For example, to look for all the Word documents containing the phrase "Dear Bill," you would first specify Word in the Of Type drop-down list box, then enter the words "Dear Bill" in the Containing Text box and click on the Find Now button (Figure 3.29).

• • • • • • • • • • • • • •
FIGURE 3.29
*The Advanced
Page of the
Find Utility*

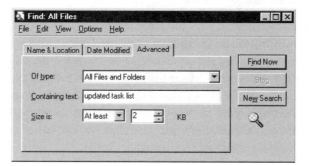

*Use the Advanced
page of the Find
dialog box to track
down an object
based on the text it
contains, its file size,
or its file type.*

Once you've completed searching for a particular object, you can begin a new query by clicking the New Search button. This resets all the search criteria so you can start afresh.

Finding Objects on Other Computers.
If you are overly curious, work for the CIA, or are a network administrator, you may need to look for an object that's located on another computer connected to yours over a network. That's when you need to select Computer from the Find submenu.

When you choose Computer, you bring up a relatively simple dialog box with only a single field: Named. If you know the name of the computer or other network resource, enter it into the Named field and click on the Find Now button. The Find utility searches your network for a computer or a resource with that name. The results are displayed in the same tacked-on folder view window you see in the Find Files or Folders dialog box. You can open and view the contents of any of the found resources—such as shared network volumes or printers—by double-clicking on their icons (Figure 3.30).

FIGURE 3.30

Network Computer Search

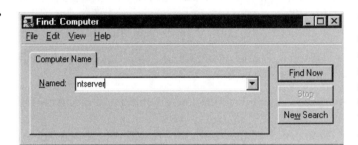

To find a computer over the network, select Computer from the Find submenu.

The Windows 95 Explorer

So far in this chapter, I've described how the Taskbar can provide you with quick, push-button access to frequently used documents, programs, and utilities. And for Macintosh crossovers, I've reviewed the My Computer icon, which deftly presents a Macintosh-like system for working with Windows. I've saved the trickiest—or shall I say, the most sophisticated—tool for last. That's the Explorer, a file-browsing utility that presents all the elements of your system in a treelike hierarchy so that you can easily see the structure of the directories on any storage device.

Upgrade Alert

In true Darwinian fashion, the Explorer has evolved from its 3.1 presence as the File Manager. It incorporates some of the old features, such as a split-window view with the tree on the left side and the contents window on the right. But as you'll soon see, the Explorer is much more powerful than the old File Manager.

The Explorer enables you to browse effortlessly through every folder in your system by combining a treelike map of your system's resources with a custom folder view window. Both Explorer elements—the tree and the folder view—share a single window on the Windows 95 desktop; a split screen separates the tree from the folder view (Figure 3.31).

•••••••••••••••
FIGURE 3.31
*The Windows
95 Explorer*

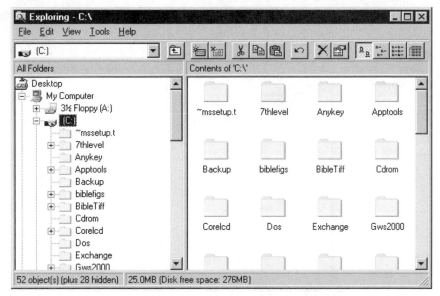

*The Windows 95 Explorer displays a treelike view of your
computer's contents and updates the accompanying folder
view automatically to reflect what you select in the tree.*

To view a resource, click on its icon in the tree on the left side of the
Explorer window. You can look at the icon's contents in the folder view on the
right side of the window. As you move through the tree on the left side, the
folder view on the right is updated automatically. This enables you to jump
from resource to resource without digging through a bunch of folders (as you
have to do with My Computer).

The Explorer is fashioned like an upside-down tree; its root is at the top,
with everything else branching off below. At the base of the Explorer's object
tree is the Windows 95 desktop—your starting point for the entire Windows
95 interface. Branching from this root are all the folders and other resources
you can access in Windows 95, such as the My Computer folder, complete
with volumes, Control Panels, and all the other items it normally contains
(Figure 3.32).

Each branch of the Explorer's object tree can be expanded or collapsed
to broaden or narrow the scope of what you see. By default, only top-level
resources, like the Desktop and My Computer icons, are shown in the tree. To
expand a branch—and thus delve deeper into the system's hierarchy—click
on the small plus sign next to the branch's name. To collapse a branch, click on
its minus sign. A branch without a sign signifies a top-level branch that contains no additional folders nested within it.

FIGURE 3.32

*Viewing the
My Computer
Folder's Object
Tree Branch*

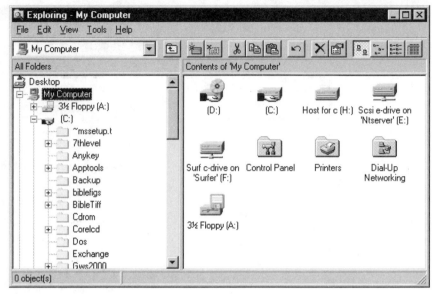

*Click on the My Computer branch of the Explorer's
object tree to open My Computer.*

Exploring Other Resources

The Explorer's object tree can contain everything, from directory folders and files inside those folders to Resource icons representing objects like Control Panels or the desktop. Because the Explorer's folder view window can display the contents of just about any resource you encounter, you can take advantage of the Explorer to explore and peer into everything in your system, from the Fonts folder to the desktop itself (Figure 3.33).

In addition, the Explorer's folder view window is fully functional, so you can manipulate each object within the contents window as if you were working with a normal folder view window. For example, if you're viewing the contents of the Control Panels folder, you can double-click on any Control Panel to bring it up.

Even network resources—if you're connected—can be viewed with the Explorer. Select Network Neighborhood and expand it into an open branch. You'll see a list of computers in your network work group or domain. To view the contents of their shared resources, select computers in the object tree and expand branches as necessary (Figure 3.34).

FIGURE 3.33

Examining the Windows 95 Desktop from the Explorer

The Explorer provides an easy way to
survey your system's contents.

FIGURE 3.34

Viewing Network Resources with Explorer

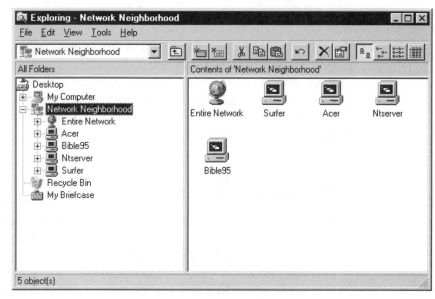

If you are connected to a network, you can
view that network's resources with Explorer.

Changing Explorer Views. As with a normal folder view window, the way the Explorer displays items in the contents window can be customized. For example, you can tell it to use either large or small icons or to display contents in list form. The Explorer also features the same multipurpose toolbar that is found in traditional folder view windows. Notice the similarity between the Explorer's object tree and the tree displayed in the drop-down list box of the toolbar (Figure 3.35).

FIGURE 3.35
*Comparing
Explorer and
Folder View
Object Trees*

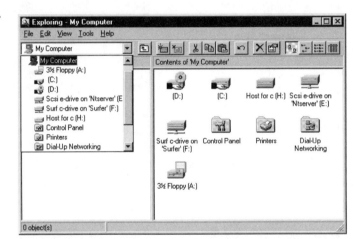

*All trees are
not alike, but
the Explorer
tree bears a
marked
resemblance
to folder view
object trees.*

All of the configuration options described previously are available from the Explorer's View menu. In fact, aside from the separate object tree, nearly every other major Explorer function is identical to that of the normal folder view. This design feature reflects a planned consistency among the three interface tools—the Explorer, My Computer, and the Taskbar—so you can manipulate the interface in similar ways.

Manipulating Objects

Now that I've surveyed the variety of ways in which Windows 95 lets you view objects in your system, the next step is to begin working with the objects themselves. As I mentioned earlier, Windows 95 treats each software and hardware resource in your computer as an individual object. For example, a file stored on your hard disk is a file object, and the directory in which it is stored is a folder object. Folder objects are containers that hold collections of other objects. The Windows 95 desktop is itself an object, and peripheral hardware devices are represented by device objects.

Most objects perform unique functions; that's why every object bears a unique name. Objects are visually identified by icons that specify the type of object—whether Word object or document object. If you want to find out more about an object, check out its Properties sheet, which lists specific characteristics of the object, such as its name, its size, its location on the system, and the dates it was created and last modified.

First Drag, Then Drop. The best way to manipulate objects is to **drag and drop** them with the mouse. Because objects represent items such as files and programs and devices connected to your computer, dragging and dropping let you move, start, close, and otherwise mess around with things on, in, and connected to your computer. For example, you can drag the on-screen icon of a file and drop it into the Recycle Bin to delete the file. This mirrors the act of crumpling a piece of paper and tossing it into the trash.

Not only is the drag-and-drop concept meant to make it easier to learn the system, it's also a handy way to get things done. Often the quickest way to perform a task is to drag an icon and drop it somewhere else. Dragging and dropping are just what they sound like: you "grab" an object with the mouse— place the mouse pointer over an icon and hold down the left mouse button —then drag the object to its destination and drop the object by releasing the mouse button (Figure 3.36).

••••••••••••••
FIGURE 3.36
Drag and Drop

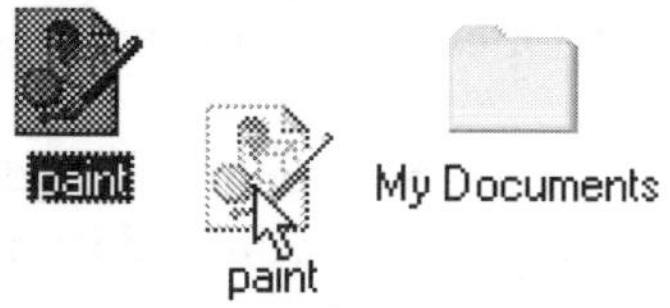

    My Documents

The quickest way to move an object is by dragging it from where it is and dropping it at its destination.

Danger Zone

Although the drag-and-drop process is fairly straightforward, the same action can cause entirely different results, depending on what you drag and where you drop it. For example, if you drag a file icon from one folder to another on the same drive, your action moves the file. But if you drag that same icon to a folder on another volume, your action copies the file instead of moving it. But there's a wrinkle: if you drag an application icon somewhere, your action creates a shortcut instead of moving or copying the application. You can perform this same sort of drag-and-drop operation on folders, too. But watch out—when you drag and drop a folder, the entire contents, including any nested folders and their contents, are affected.

Normally Windows 95 moves an object in response to your performing a drag-and-drop operation. Sometimes you may want to copy an object instead—that is, make a duplicate and place it in a different folder. To tell Windows 95 to copy an object instead of moving it, hold down the Ctrl key during the entire drag-and-drop operation, provided the items are on the same disk. A new copy of the object appears in the destination folder, and the original remains in place (Figure 3.37).

• • • • • • • • • • • • •
FIGURE 3.37
Copying an Object

To copy an object, hold down the Ctrl key and drag the object to its destination.

Those two drag-and-drop procedures—move and copy—can be used in virtually every part of the Windows 95 interface, with a few exceptions. Some objects, such as the volume objects in My Computer, should never be moved, and Windows 95 does its best to restrict this kind of drag-and-drop operation.

Digging Deeper into Drag and Drop. The simplest use for drag and drop is moving and copying files between folders. By creating folders for different topics and placing related files in each folder, you're practicing good house-keeping and creating an oganizational structure for your system. Because Windows places few restrictions on how you organize things, you can drag and drop to your heart's content. Of course, there may be some unexpected results, so keep reading.

When you drag and drop an object across volumes, Windows 95 copies the object instead of moving it. For example, dragging a document icon from its folder on a hard disk and dropping it onto a floppy-disk drive makes a copy (Figure 3.38).

• • • • • • • • • • • • •
FIGURE 3.38
A Drag-and-Drop Operation across Volumes

[C:]

When you drag an object from one storage volume to another, Windows 95 copies the object into the destination volume.

You can, however, override this behavior and force Windows 95 to move instead of copy the file. First select the file with the left mouse button, then hold down the Shift key while you perform the drag-and-drop operation. This places the file in the destination volume and deletes the original from the source volume.

Drag and drop is particularly handy when you move objects onto icons that represent device objects. For example, if you drop a file object onto one of the printer objects in the Printers folder, Windows 95 interprets this action as a request to print the document. Windows loads the application that created the file and instructs that application to print the document. Finally, Windows closes the application, and the document prints in the background using the Windows print spooler. Similarly, you can drag the same file and drop it onto a fax object to send the document out as a fax.

Microsoft has gone out of its way to make drag and drop pervasive throughout the interface. For example, you can even drag icons and drop them into some dialog boxes, as you'll find out later in this book.

The Recycle Bin. These are politically correct times, even for operating systems. In Windows 95, you don't delete objects—you recycle them. Actually, the concept's not new, just the terminology: what's known as a trash can on the Macintosh is called a **Recycle Bin** in Windows 95. That's considered enough of a difference to keep the Apple lawyers at bay. The Recycle Bin is technically a folder object, but it has a special purpose: if you want to delete an object, just drag it to the Recycle Bin and drop it onto the Bin's icon (Figure 3.39).

•••••••••••••
FIGURE 3.39
*The Recycle
Bin*

untitled   untitled

Recycle Bin

*Drag and drop an object into the
Recycle Bin if you want to trash it.*

If you're bent on a course of mass destruction and deletion, you can drag a folder full of stuff to the Recycle Bin. But be advised: if you drag a folder to the Recycle Bin, you are also dragging any nested folders that reside within the first folder. Also, Windows 95 doesn't let you put certain things in the Recycle Bin, including device objects and configuration folders. Basically, icons for objects that represent either hardware or important system software components can't be thrown out—at least not without a lot of extra effort.

Well, *The Windows 95 Bible* can't tell you where people go when they die, but this book can tell you where objects go when you've marked them for death by dropping them into the Recycle Bin. They don't go far at first; the icons have simply been moved from their old locations into the Recycle Bin's folder, and the objects represented by the icons are still intact. If you change your mind about deleting them, you can double-click on the Recycle Bin's icon to open its folder, then drag the objects back to their original locations, preventing their ultimate demise (Figure 3.40).

••••••••••••••
FIGURE 3.40
*Recovery
Action*

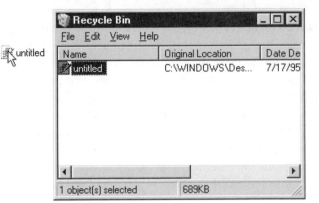

To recover an
object from
the Recycle
Bin, drag it out
before the next
recycling.

Be forewarned, however, that icons don't stay in the Recycle Bin forever; if you don't do anything, the objects they represent are ultimately deleted. The Recycle Bin dedicates a percentage of each volume's storage space to recently deleted objects. As the number of items in the Recycle Bin grows, older objects are purged to make space for newer objects. This means that the more recently you threw out an icon, the more likely you are to be able to retrieve it from the Recycle Bin. You should notice which Recycle Bin files have been deleted at the DOS command prompt or have been deleted by DOS applications— so be careful, because those get zapped as soon as you delete them.

You can control the Recycle Bin's behavior by calling up its object menu. To do so, point to the Recycle Bin and click the *right* mouse button, instead of the more commonly used left button. Almost every object in Windows 95 has a similar pop-up menu offering a list of commands and options specific to that object.

To set the options for the Recycle Bin, select Properties from the pop-up menu. The resulting dialog box features a page containing the overall configuration options and includes pages that enable you to set recycling options individually for each storage volume connected to the system (Figure 3.41).

If it's time to take out the trash, you can check a box that forces the Recycle Bin to purge files immediately. If you're a person who has trouble making up your mind, a slider control enables you to specify how much space is set aside for recoverable files on your hard disk, setting a limit on your indecisiveness. Finally, either you can set these options globally, so they control the recycling on all your storage devices, or you can choose a different recycling schedule for each storage volume.

FIGURE 3.41
*Configuring
the Recycle Bin*

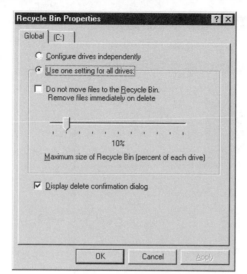

*Select Properties
from the Recycle
Bin's pop-up menu
to adjust the
behavior of your
Recycle Bin.*

What's in an Object?

Each object has unique properties related to its function. For example, each file object has a unique file name that corresponds to a specific disk file located in one of a system's volumes. Similarly, each folder object contains a corresponding subdirectory name. Device objects each control the connection and configuration of a particular device.

Windows 95 provides a **Properties dialog box** for each object in a system. Each Properties dialog box contains information about its object—rather like a driver's license or a police record contains information about a person. These dialog boxes also display Control Panels that enable you to select options related to the object. For some objects, such as file objects, the Properties dialog box is relatively simple, providing basic information like the object's file name and size in only a single page. Device objects, at the other extreme, often have extensive Properties dialog boxes that feature multiple pages covering a number of configuration parameters (Figure 3.42).

FIGURE 3.42
*Properties
Dialog Boxes*

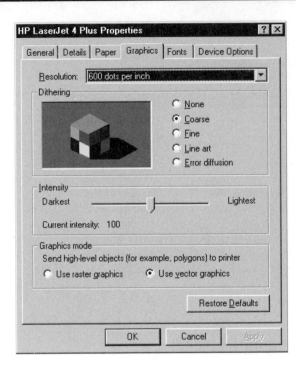

*A Properties dialog
box can be simple or
complex, depending
on the nature of the
object.*

FIGURE 3.43
*A Device
Object's
Pop-Up Menu*

*An object's pop-up menu
often gives you access to
the object's most
frequently used options.*

To view an object's Properties dialog box, point at the object with the mouse and click on the object with the right mouse button; this brings up a pop-up menu. Then select Properties, which is usually at the bottom of the menu.

Quite a few objects provide items in their pop-up menus that give you quick access to frequently used options. A printer object, for example, may place controls on its pop-up menu that enable you to pause the printer or purge its queue. It's handy to be able to control some of an object's properties without having to open a Properties dialog box (Figure 3.43).

Once you've explored enough pop-up menus, you're bound to notice that each one contains commands that replicate drag-and-drop operations, including copy, move, delete, and in some cases print. Once again Microsoft has provided more than one way to accomplish the same task. If you prefer menus to drag and drop, remember that clicking on an object with the right mouse button brings up the object's pop-up menu.

Object Face-Lifts. Once you've gotten the hang of viewing an object's properties, you'll probably want to do some reconstruction. The most direct way to change the way an object looks or performs is to bring up the object's Properties dialog box. Device objects, in particular, can be modified. These often feature multipage dialog boxes chock-full of **configuration parameters** (Figure 3.44).

FIGURE 3.44
*Changing the
Properties of a
Device Object*

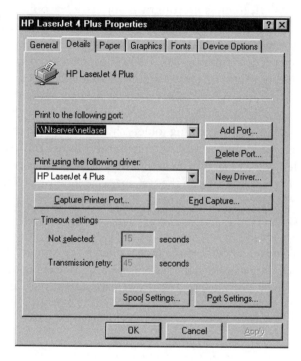

*Use the Properties
dialog box to change
an object's
configuration options.*

But what about a simple operation like renaming an object? Windows 95 offers three ways to do this. The first, and simplest, method is to select the object's icon with the mouse pointer, then reselect the object with the mouse pointer positioned directly over the title. The title field changes into an edit field, and you can alter the text at will (Figure 3.45).

FIGURE 3.45
*Editing the
Title Text of an
Object*

*To edit the text of an object, keep
the mouse pointer hovering above
the title for a moment, then make
your changes.*

You can also edit an object's title by selecting Rename from the object's pop-up menu. If the object is located in a folder, you can perform the Rename function a third way, by highlighting the object in the folder view window and selecting Rename from the folder window's File menu.

Don't Touch That Object!

Danger Zone

Although it's OK to mess up your own objects, a few objects in Windows 95 should be off-limits unless you know exactly what you're doing. Most of these critical system objects reside in the Windows 95 folder on your boot disk (probably called something like c:\WINDOWS or c:\WIN95). Some of the objects lurking within this main Windows 95 folder are very sensitive.

For example, the System folder contains the core of the Windows 95 operating system, including the 32-bit code that makes up the interface. The System folder and surrounding folders should not be renamed, or Windows will not be able to find critical systems and will most likely crash. Nor should you delete any file objects from within these folders unless you are absolutely certain what role they play in the system. Accidentally deleting the wrong file can leave Windows 95 unbootable, forcing you to reinstall the operating system from scratch.

Insider's Tip

For your convenience, I have documented every single Windows 95 file object, including its role in the system, as part of the appendices of this book. When in doubt, don't delete. And if you just can't resist, check the back of the book first.

· ·

Shortcuts

Shortcuts work the way the little programs called macros do—they let you circumvent normal routes to get to frequently used programs. Windows 95 includes Shortcut icons that work like buttons. Clicking on a Shortcut icon is like clicking on the icon that the Shortcut icon represents (Figure 3.46).

FIGURE 3.46
Shortcuts

Shortcut to
Scsi e-drive on
'Ntserver' (E)

Shortcut to HP
LaserJet 4
Plus

Shortcut to
Bio2

Shortcuts enable you to reference any object in your system quickly.

For example, to provide quick access to the superimportant Freecell game, you can create a shortcut to it on the Windows 95 desktop. When you double-click on the Freecell shortcut icon, Windows 95 uses a special pointer inside the shortcut to track the original program down. Windows then opens the original just as if you had opened it directly from within its folder.

Insider's Tip

You can create a shortcut to any object in the system. Especially handy are shortcuts to frequently used storage volumes. By placing those shortcuts on the Windows 95 desktop, you don't have to use an interface browser like My Computer. Instead, you can open the volumes directly via their desktop shortcuts. The same can be done for file, folder, or device objects, and these shortcuts can be placed anywhere on your desktop or in a folder.

Creating a New Shortcut. Hey, this is Windows, so of course several techniques exist for creating shortcuts. The first and easiest method is to select an object with the mouse, pop up the object's menu with the right mouse button, and select Create Shortcut. This creates a new shortcut to the object in the same folder as the original. You can then move the shortcut anywhere you like, and it remembers where its original resides (Figure 3.47).

Another way to create a shortcut is to select the original object and drag it to a new location with the right (not the left) mouse button. Using the right mouse button during a drag operation causes Windows 95 to prompt you with a small menu when you attempt to drop the item at its new location. Menu choices include Copy Here, Move Here, and Create Shortcut Here. Selecting the latter tells Windows 95 to create a new shortcut to the object at the target location (Figure 3.48).

••••••••••••••
FIGURE 3.47
*Shortcut
Number One*

You can create a shortcut using an object's pop-up menu.

••••••••••••••
FIGURE 3.48
*Shortcut
Number Two*

untitled

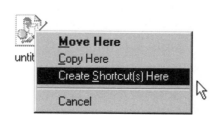

This shortcut was made with a right mouse button drag-and-drop operation.

Managing Shortcuts. Once a shortcut is created, you can move it virtually anywhere within the confines of your Windows 95 system. Should you ever need to locate the original object, you can use the shortcut's Properties dialog box to track down the original. Point to the shortcut with the mouse and click on the right mouse button to bring up the shortcut's pop-up menu, then select Properties (Figure 3.49). Next, click on the Shortcut tab to bring the second page of the dialog box to the front. Notice that the dialog box keeps track of the complete path to the object's file. This is why you can move shortcuts around your system at will: Windows 95 can always extract the location of the original from the shortcut's properties. To bring up the folder view containing the original object, click the Find Target button. Up pops a folder view of the object in its folder (Figure 3.50).

FIGURE 3.49
*Tracing the
Origins of a
Shortcut*

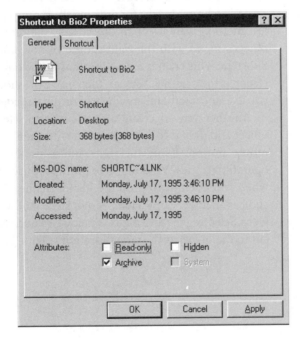

*View the shortcut's
Properties dialog box
to track down the
original object.*

FIGURE 3.50
Another Search Method

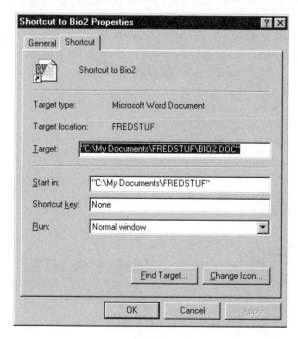

To locate the original object, use the Find Target button.

Repairing Broken Shortcuts.

Danger Zone

Taking shortcuts—like leaping over crevasses—can sometimes be dangerous. Certain changes to an original object may break the link between it and its shortcut. For example, if you create a shortcut to a document and then either rename the document or move it to another folder, the shortcut might not be able to locate the original.

Windows 95 does make an attempt to reestablish broken shortcut links, but it is limited to searching on the volume that held the original when the shortcut was created. If the original object is moved to a different volume, the shortcut becomes completely severed (Figure 3.51).

FIGURE 3.51
Shortcut Saver

Windows 95 automatically attempts to reestablish broken shortcut links.

When it comes to repairing a broken shortcut, Windows 95 provides you with several options. The first and probably easiest option is simply to recreate the shortcut. Locate the original and then use one of the techniques I mentioned earlier to create a new shortcut. If you're not sure where the original was moved, use the Windows 95 Find utility to track it down.

Alternatively, you can bring up the shortcut's Properties dialog box and enter the new file and directory information directly onto the Shortcut page. The shortcut is reestablished when you exit the dialog box.

Finally, while Windows 95 is searching for the original as part of its attempt to reestablish the link, you can click on the Browse button in the Missing Shortcut dialog box to bring up a simple file-browsing window. You can then click your way to the original's folder and reestablish the link manually (Figure 3.52).

FIGURE 3.52
*Missing
Shortcut
Dialog Box*

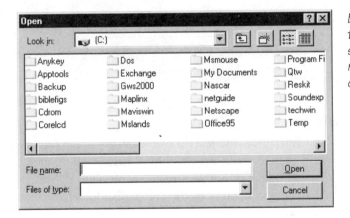

*Browse
through your
system for a
missing
original.*

Fancy Fingerwork

Now that I've covered the basics of operating Windows 95, let's take a moment to relax and forget about all those fancy GUI (graphical user interface) advances like Taskbars and Explorers. It's time to regress. It's time to do what they did in the good old days of DOS: acquire some mind-blowing skills that will amaze your hacker friends, impress your boss, and limber up your fingers. I'm going to provide you with some keyboard shortcuts and other insider tricks that will enable you to fly through Windows 95. If you take the extra time to memorize a few keyboard commands, you can save yourself from clicking through menus and dialog boxes and instead get right to the point.

Keystroke	Command
F1	Start the Windows help system.
F2	Rename an object.
F3	Start the Find utility.
F4	In the Explorer, display the drop-down list box that contains a system tree; in an Open or Save dialog box, display the Look In list.
F5	Refresh the view or contents of a window (use if a disk's or folder's contents have changed since the window was opened).
F6	Move the focus between the tree portion of the Explorer window and the contents portion.
F10	Switch to menu mode.
Shift+F10	Display pop-up menu for selected object.
Ctrl+A	Select all.
Ctrl+C	Copy an object.
Ctrl+V	Paste an object.
Ctrl+X	Cut an object.
Ctrl+Z	Undo last action.
Ctrl+G	Choose the Go To command in the Explorer.
Del	Mark a selected object for deleting by placing it in the Recycle Bin.
Shift+Del	Delete the selected object instantly without first placing it in the Recycle Bin.
Ctrl+Tab	Move forward through pages in dialog boxes.
Ctrl+Shift+Tab	Move backward through pages in dialog boxes.
Alt+Enter	Display the Properties dialog box of an object.
Backspace	Go to the parent folder.
* on numeric keypad	Expand the entire Explorer tree under the current selection.
+ on numeric keypad	Expand only the currently selected branch of the Explorer tree.
– on numeric keypad	Collapse the currently selected branch of the Explorer tree.

Keystroke	Command
Right arrow	Expand a selected branch of the Explorer tree; if it's already expanded, step down to the first child folder.
Left arrow	Collapse a selected branch of the Explorer tree; if it's already collapsed, step up to parent folder.
Ctrl+arrow key	Scroll the Explorer tree without changing the current selection.
Ctrl+Esc	Move the focus to the Taskbar and display Start menu.
Esc or Ctrl+Esc	Move the focus to the Taskbar (use Tab and then Shift+F10 to access pop-up menus for objects; use Tab and arrow keys to switch among tasks; use Tab to go to the desktop).
Alt+Tab	Switch to the next running application.
Alt+M	Minimize all open windows and move the focus to the desktop.
Alt+S	When no windows are open and no items are selected on the desktop, display the Start menu (use arrow keys to select menu commands).
Win*+R	Bring up the Run dialog box.
Win*+M	Minimize all open windows.
Shift+Win*+M	Undo the Minimize All command.
Win*+F1	Help.
Win*+E	Start the Explorer utility.
Win*+F	Use the Find utility to locate files or folders.
Ctrl+Win*+F	Use the Find utility to locate a computer resource.
Win*+Tab	Cycle through the buttons on the Taskbar.
Win*+Break	Display System Properties dialog box.
Ctrl+drag	Copy a file into another folder on the same storage volume (instead of moving it).
Ctrl+Shift+drag	Create a shortcut.
Alt+double-click	Display the Properties dialog box of an object.
Ctrl+right-click	Show any alternate choices on an object's pop-up menu.

Keystroke	Command
Shift+double-click	Explore the selected object; if there is no Explore command for the selected object, issue the default action for the object (typically, Open).
Shift+click the Close button	Close a folder and all its parent folders.
Shift+insert a CD	Bypass the Auto-Run function for audio CDs and CD-ROMs.

*Note: The Win key—which contains a small Windows icon—is available only on Microsoft Natural and compatible keyboards.

. . . .

Summary

If you didn't read this chapter, you are missing out on vital features new to Windows 95. In fact, you should go back right now and read about the three new interface tools—the Taskbar, My Computer, and the Explorer—and learn how they can help you move around, look at the stuff in your computer, and manipulate just about anything you want. It's important to be able to find things like folders and documents; if you don't know how, you can waste a lifetime (or more) looking for lost files. For keyboard crazies, I offer some great shortcuts for getting to do what you want to without using all the new graphical user interface tools it took Microsoft programmers years to develop.

4

Ready, Set, Run!

It's not quite the universal operating system, but Windows 95 is getting close to that point. Or at least closer. With Windows 95, you can run applications created for three other platforms: DOS, Win16, and Win32. This new capability extends your range considerably. You can take advantage of programs written for a text-based operating system—MS-DOS—

and programs written for Windows 3.1. You can also run 32-bit applications developed for the most advanced Windows territory—Windows NT, used on high-end workstations and servers.

What Runs with Windows 95?

Windows supersedes DOS but is actually built on top of it. Of the world's 140 million PC users, almost half still use DOS as their primary operating system. Even if you use Windows as your main platform, you may find it handy to run DOS applications from time to time. For this reason, Microsoft made sure that Windows 95 retains full compatibility with DOS. That's the good news. The bad news is that to maintain this compatibility, Microsoft had to make certain compromises in Windows 95. That's why you cannot use long file names—ones over eight letters long—in Windows 95, although originally Microsoft intended to incorporate this capability into its operating system. When the company discovered a longer file name would create incompatibilities with DOS and older Windows programs, this feature was dropped. Compatibility was given priority over other design considerations.

Win16 applications are the most prevalent kind of Windows programs on the market today. In fact, almost all Windows applications are Win16 programs. Win16 applications are **16-bit applications** designed for Windows 3.1, which is basically a 16-bit operating system (as is DOS). Newer operating systems, such as Windows NT, the Macintosh, and UNIX, are **32-bit operating systems,** which are the best suited to take advantage of today's 32-bit microprocessors. Windows 95 is a hybrid operating system; part of it is designed for 16-bit systems, part of it for 32-bit systems. This means Windows 95 still contains several core components from its 16-bit heritage but can also run newer 32-bit programs. The reason for maintaining the 16-bit components is so your new operating system can still run DOS and Win16 programs. Again, compatibility rules.

Win32 programs are the latest and the greatest. They can take advantage of large amounts of RAM and can handle sophisticated tasks involving, for example, multimedia and graphics. Win32 programs are harder to find than Win16 applications because they are newer and also slightly harder to create. But if you're running a performance-hungry type of application, a Win32 program will probably work better than its Win16 counterpart. Vendors don't always inform you on the package whether a program is Win16 or Win32, so you may have to ask. It may be worth the effort, though. Win32 programs run even better under Windows NT, so any investment you make in these more advanced applications can be carried with you should you upgrade to NT.

DOS Applications

Windows 95 provides extensive support for DOS applications—most importantly, for DOS games. You can run these applications either full screen or in a window on the Windows 95 desktop. Running a DOS application full screen is just like running it in native DOS; the program occupies the entire display, while the Windows 95 desktop "hides" in the background. **Full-screen mode** provides the best DOS compatibility and is required for certain finicky DOS programs. But if you want to use other applications at the same time— including other DOS windowed programs—you can run a DOS program in a window. This mode lets you make full use of the Windows 95 Clipboard for transferring data.

A tremendously useful capability of Windows 95 is that it allows you to use multiple DOS applications simultaneously. For example, you can run a lengthy DOS telecommunications downloading session in the background while playing a DOS game in the foreground. In fact, instead of running only one application at a time as does MS-DOS, Windows 95 lets you open dozens of applications at the same time. The applications can run either full screen or windowed on the desktop, and you can switch among them at will.

Upgrade Alert

Windows 95 has new features that make working with DOS applications easier. A new toolbar providing quick access to frequently used functions is available for windowed DOS applications. And to improve the way you view text in a windowed DOS application, Windows 95 can automatically adapt the screen font based on the size of the window itself.

Win16 Applications

Win16 applications are the most common type of Windows program. Designed for Windows 95's predecessor, Windows 3.1, 16-bit Windows titles number in the thousands and cover the spectrum of application categories.

Windows 95 supports virtually all Windows 3.1–compatible Win16 applications. Win16 applications gain some of the Windows 95 look and feel when they run under the new environment. However, in many ways a Windows 3.1 program is still a Windows 3.1 program. For example, the more common dialog boxes don't look any different than they did under Windows 3.1, and many applications still use the old MDI interface system, which places documents in child windows within application windows.

Win32 Applications

Win32 applications are designed specifically for Windows 95 or Windows NT. Also referred to as **native** applications, Win32 programs take full advantage of the advanced features found in Windows 95. Those include new interface features, such as the revised dialog boxes for opening and saving files.

Win32 applications can take control of the Windows 95 desktop directly. For example, an electronic mail application can use a custom icon in the Taskbar's notify area to alert you when a new message has arrived. There's no doubt about it: if you want to get the most out of your computer, upgrade to a Win32 version of an application—if it's available. These programs tend to incorporate the latest code from the vendor, and they work smoothly under Windows 95, thanks to their 32-bit design.

Jump Start

No matter what type of application you run—Win16, Win32, or DOS—Windows 95 offers many ways to start a program. There's the nouvelle, **object-oriented** way we discussed in the preceding chapters: you double-click on an object, and Windows 95 figures out what to do. If you've clicked on an application, Windows 95 runs it. If the object represents a data file, Windows 95 loads the appropriate application together with the file, ready for you to edit. Of course, since it's Window 95, there's more than one way to start a program. You can start applications using any of Windows 95's three main interface tools: the Taskbar, My Computer, or the Explorer. Each provides its own way to get at the objects on your system. Perhaps the most convenient is the Taskbar, with its primal Start button—an excellent place to begin our tour.

Hit Start

Nested within the many branches of the Start menu are entries for virtually every application you have installed on your PC. To launch an application, find the appropriate Start menu item and click (Figures 4.1 and 4.2).

There are entries for the bundled Windows 95 mini-applications, as well as for system maintenance tools such as the Backup program. In addition, Windows applications create custom Start menu entries as part of the installation process.

FIGURE 4.1
The Start Menu

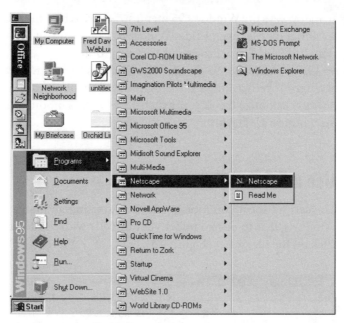

The Start menu is often the quickest way to launch an application. Application programs add their own entries to the Start menu when they are installed.

FIGURE 4.2
An Application's Start Menu Entry

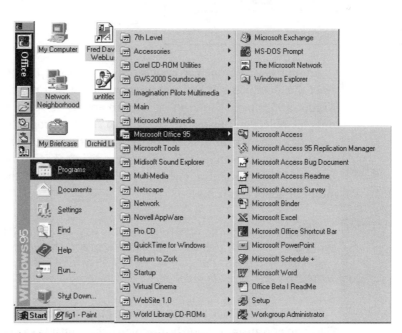

Application programs add their own Start menu entries as part of the installation process.

Upgrade Alert

In many ways the Windows 95 menu structure is reminiscent of the Windows 3.1 Program Manager. Under Windows 3.1, when you install a new application, it creates a new Program Manager group.

When Windows 95 is first installed, application program entries are arranged together under the Programs submenu. In Chapter 6, you'll learn how to customize this menu structure, as well as modify other aspects of the Start button's behavior.

Use a Folder View

The second most common method of starting an application program in Windows 95 is to open a folder view directly with its file object. Just double-click on the file object (Figure 4.3).

FIGURE 4.3
Launching from a File Object

The simplest way to launch an application from a folder view is to double-click on the application's file object.

Another way to launch an application is to bring up its pop-up menu and select the Open item. When you open an object that represents a program, Windows 95 runs it. You can also start an application by creating a shortcut to its file object and using the shortcut to run the program. **Mini-tip:** Keep shortcut icons on your desktop for the applications you use most frequently, so you can get to them quickly. This method gives you flexibility because you can move the shortcut anywhere you like, whether to the desktop or to another folder (Figure 4.4).

FIGURE 4.4
Launching from a Shortcut

You can create a shortcut to an application program and use the shortcut to start the application. The shortcut can be moved anywhere in the system to provide quick access to the application.

Finally, you can take advantage of the object-oriented nature of Windows 95 to bring up an application by double-clicking on an associated data file. For example, if you double-click on a Paintbrush document, Windows 95 launches the Paintbrush program with the document preloaded and ready for editing.

Insider's Tip

Windows 95 enables you to create a new document file without having to load the corresponding program first. Use the Windows 95 pop-up menu system to create new data files for most Windows applications, just as if you were grabbing a fresh, blank sheet from a stationery pad or a book of forms. First click the right mouse button while the cursor is hovering inside a folder view (which can be the Windows 95 desktop) and open the New submenu. You see a list of data file types, as well as more common entries such as folders. Select Word Document, for example, and Windows 95 creates a new Word document in the current folder view. You can rename the document, and Windows 95 loads it into Word. The newly created document is then ready for your input when you double-click on its icon (Figure 4.5).

• • • • • • • • • • • • •
FIGURE 4.5
*Creating a
Data File*

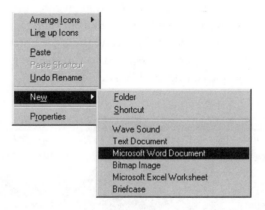

Windows 95 enables you to create a data file directly, without first loading the application program. Bring up the pop-up menu in a folder view and select the appropriate file type from the New submenu.

Insider's Tip

If an application you launch is an MDI program—that is, if it opens document windows within its own application window—you can drag and drop to open data files for editing. Drag a data file from its folder view and drop it onto the title bar of the target program's application window (Figure 4.6). If the program is maximized, click on its Restore button—or select Restore from the System menu—and resize the window so that you can see both the folder view of your data files and the application's title bar.

• • • • • • • • • • • • •
FIGURE 4.6
*Dragging and
Dropping to
Open a File*

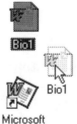

Dragging a data file and dropping it onto a running program's title bar is the same as using the program's File menu to open the data file. Note that only MDI programs support this kind of drag-and-drop operation.

Launching Applications from an MS-DOS Command Prompt

As part of its support for DOS applications, Windows 95 provides a Start menu item—the MS-DOS prompt—that brings up a DOS command prompt, indicating that DOS is running. DOS can run either full screen or in a window on the Windows 95 desktop.

Virtually all DOS commands are supported during an MS-DOS command prompt session. You can also launch both DOS and Windows application programs directly from a command prompt (Figure 4.7). To do so, you use the DOS Change Directory command (CD), then enter the name of the program's file. To start Word for DOS from the root directory of the drive, for example, you would first type CD Word and press the Enter key to enter that directory, then type Word and press Enter to run the program. Similarly, to run the DOS game Tetris, you would change to its directory and type tetris.

FIGURE 4.7

*Starting an
Application
from a
Command
Prompt*

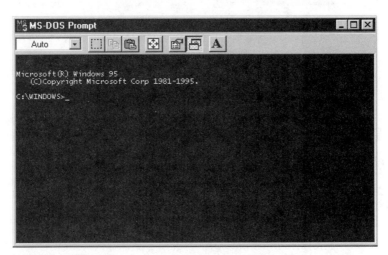

Windows 95 enables you to launch both DOS
and Windows applications from an MS-DOS
command prompt.

A launched DOS program takes over the command prompt and maintains control of a session until it has finished executing. It then returns you to the command prompt. In contrast, when you launch a Windows program, Windows 95 only loads the program into a window before returning you to the command prompt.

Upgrade Alert

Two convenient ways to start a program have been introduced in Windows 95: typing the program's name at the MS-DOS command prompt and using the START command in conjunction with the MS-DOS command prompt. By using START, you can specify how Windows 95 displays an application once it is loaded. For example, if you want to load a program now but don't plan to use it until later, you can load it in a minimized state, so that only its Taskbar is visible on the screen.

Here are some possible variations on the START command:

➺ START WINWORD   Starts Word and returns control to the command prompt.

➺ START DOOM   Starts Doom in its own window.

➺ START /M PBRUSH   Starts the Paintbrush program minimized.

➺ START /MAX NOTEPAD   Starts the Notepad program maximized.

➺ START /R SOL   Starts the Solitaire game restored (windowed).

Insider's Tip

By default, after Windows 95 launches a Windows application from the command prompt, the prompt returns to the desktop. However, you can tell Windows 95 to suspend the command prompt until the launched application has quit by adding /W to the end of a START command line.

• •

The Run Dialog Box

The final way to launch an application directly is to select Run from the Start menu. This brings up a Run Application dialog box, into which you can enter the complete pathname of any application you'd like to launch (Figure 4.8).

• • • • • • • • • • • • •
FIGURE 4.8
The Run Application Dialog Box

Selecting Run from the Start menu brings up the Run Application dialog box, which enables you to select a program by providing its complete pathname.

For example, to launch Word from the Run Application dialog box, you type the path to the Word program files into the Open field. Typically the pathname is something like C:\WINWORD\WINWORD.EXE. Then you click on the OK button, and Windows 95 launches the program.

Windows 95 maintains a list of programs that have been launched recently from the Run Application dialog box. This means you can repeat a Run operation without reentering the entire pathname. Simply expand the drop-down list box—part of the Open field—and click on the matching entry (Figure 4.9).

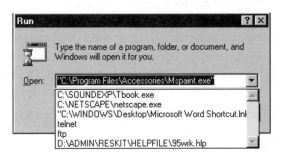

The Run Application
dialog box maintains a
list of recently launched
applications, making it
easy to repeat a launch
operation.

To locate an application, use the Browse dialog box, which you can bring up by clicking on the Browse button in the Run Application dialog box (Figure 4.10). The Browse dialog box provides you with a wealth of information. For starters, it includes a folder view of your desktop; you can navigate this view as you would any other. You can also perform maintenance tasks, such as creating a new folder, by using the right mouse button to bring up the view's pop-up menu. Finally, a drop-down list box labeled Look In enables you to switch among volumes, including network drives. If you know what kind of file you're trying to find, you can select its type from the Of Type dialog box (which is set to All Files and Folders by default).

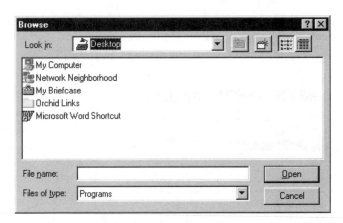

The Browse
dialog box
makes it easy
to hunt down
an application
program.

When you are already working (or playing) on your computer, you can access the Browse dialog box by double-clicking on folder icons. For example,

to find Word—located in this example in the Winword folder on the C:
volume—first open the My Computer folder, then the volume storing the
Word program. Finally, burrow through the folder structure until you find
the folder containing the Word program files.

Selecting the Winword icon causes Word to fill in its file name automatically. Clicking on the Open button returns you to the Run Application dialog
box, with the complete pathname now stored in the Open field. Click once
more, this time on the OK button, and Word is launched (Figure 4.11).

• • • • • • • • • • • • • •
FIGURE 4.11
*Selecting an
Application
Program with
the Browse
Dialog Box*

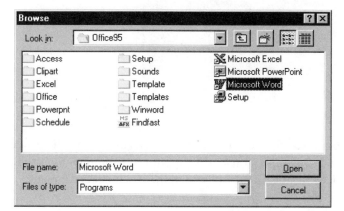

*Once you
navigate your
way to the
appropriate
folder, select
the program,
then click on
OK to return
to the Run
Application
dialog box.*

The Documents Submenu

The approach to launching a program that I just described incorporates the
formerly revolutionary notion of object orientation into interface design.
Basically, Windows 95 enables you to launch a program through an associated data file. Because the data—rather than the application that was used to
create it—is the focus, you have a more direct approach to your work. In
other words, Windows is beginning to work more like you do, focusing more
on content and less on technique.

Another way Windows 95 attempts to make computer life more closely
resemble your work life (at least if you don't suffer from short-term memory
loss) is by remembering which data files you used most recently. Windows
95 maintains a list of those files for quick access in the Documents submenu
of the Windows 95 Start menu (Figure 4.12). The Documents submenu
reminds you what you were working on last; at the top of the menu is the most
recently used data file. You can click on it to bring up the appropriate editing
tool (such as Word or Excel), then load the file.

FIGURE 4.12
*The
Documents
Submenu*

By maintaining a list of the most recently used data files in the Documents submenu, Windows 95 makes it easy to resume working where you last left off.

Insider's Tip

Only data files that are opened directly are listed in the Documents submenu. If, for example, you load an application and then use its File menu to open a data file, the file is not listed in the Documents submenu.

Programs A-Go-Go

Once you start a program with Windows 95, myriad opportunities are available to you. Of course you can open, save, and close data files. You can also multitask to your brain's full extent, use OLE, and copy and paste with the Windows 95 Clipboard. How much you can do depends on the range of your application. Some operations—like opening, saving, and closing data files— are universal. Others, like OLE, are not always built into software programs.

Insider's Tip

When shopping for Windows applications, look for programs that support OLE. Because OLE is a powerful mechanism for sharing data among application programs, products that exploit this technology provide more flexibility and are more intuitive to use.

File Operations

Most applications use the procedures developed by Microsoft for opening, saving, and closing files. Read on for more details.

Open. To load a data file into a running Windows application, select Open from the File menu. The application presents you with a dialog box showing a folder view of available data files and folders (Figure 4.13).

• • • • • • • • • • • • • •
FIGURE 4.13
*The Open
Dialog Box*

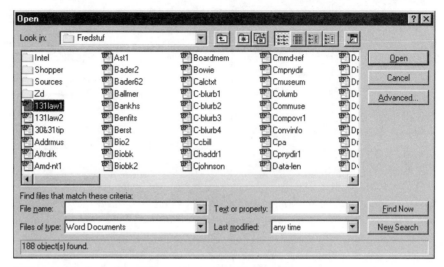

| Open | | | | | ? ✕ |

Look in: Fredstuf

Intel	Ast1	Boardmem	Cmmd-ref	Dε	Open
Shopper	Bader2	Bowie	Cmpnydir	Di	Cancel
Sources	Bader62	Calctxt	Cmuseum	Dr	Advanced...
Zd	Ballmer	C-blurb1	Columb	Dr	
131law1	Bankhs	C-blurb2	Commuse	Dι	
131law2	Benfits	C-blurb3	Compovr1	Dι	
30&31tip	Berst	C-blurb4	Convinfo	Dp	
Addrmus	Bio2	Ccbill	Cpa	Dr	
Aftrdrk	Biobk	Chaddr1	Cpnydir1	Dr	
Amd-nt1	Biobk2	Cjohnson	Data-len	Dι	

Find files that match these criteria:

| File name: | | Text or property: | | Find Now |
| Files of type: | Word Documents | Last modified: | any time | New Search |

188 object(s) found.

*When you select Open from an application's File menu,
you are presented with a dialog box showing a folder
view of your PC's contents.*

If this dialog box looks familiar, that's because it's the same one used by the Browse function of the Run Application dialog box. In fact, aside from its title (which changes from application to application), this dialog box is universal to all Windows 95 applications. It introduces a number of powerful new features.

First, the folder view itself is fully functional. You can copy, rename, delete, and create new files and folders just as you would in a view that is opened from a volume icon. Click the right mouse button to open the view's pop-up menu, then select the desired action (Figure 4.14).

The Open dialog box also provides a limited version of the folder view toolbar. It includes a Parent Folder button for navigating "upward" in the folder hierarchy, as well as buttons for selecting List or Details view (no Large Icons view is provided). A Create Folder button creates a new folder within the currently selected folder view.

To make navigating across volumes easier, a Look In drop-down list box provides access to all your PC's attached volumes, including network drives. Click on the list box and select the desired volume; the folder view is updated automatically to reflect the new volume's contents.

FIGURE 4.14

*A Fully
Functional
Folder View*

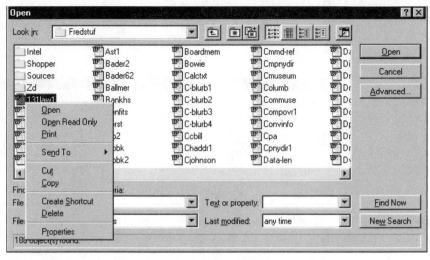

The folder view provided by the Open dialog box is fully functional.
You can perform file-related chores by accessing the view's pop-up
menu with a click on your right mouse button.

Finally, a File of Type drop-down list box filters the information in the
folder view to display only data file objects that meet certain criteria (for
example, Word documents). By default, this list box displays the file type of
the application that presented the dialog box. For example, in Microsoft Word
the list box is set to display Word files. However, you can override the default
type and either broaden or narrow the search based on options presented in
the box.

To open a data file, first apply the navigational tools of the Open dialog
box to locate the appropriate folder, then select the desired data file and click
on the Open button. The application loads the data file, and you're on your
way (Figure 4.15).

FIGURE 4.15

*A Fully
Configured
Open Dialog
Box*

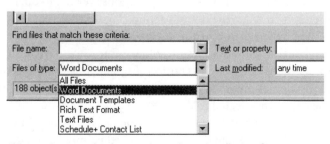

By combining the navigational tools of the Open
dialog box, you can quickly locate a file in a sea of
folders and volumes.

Save. Saving a file is similar to opening one. In fact, when you select Save As from the File menu of an application, you see the same dialog box as when you select Open, except that a Save button replaces the Open button. Otherwise the two dialog boxes are identical, and you can perform the same navigational and maintenance chores in either by bringing up the pop-up menu for the folder view (Figure 4.16).

. . . .
FIGURE 4.16
The Save As
Dialog Box

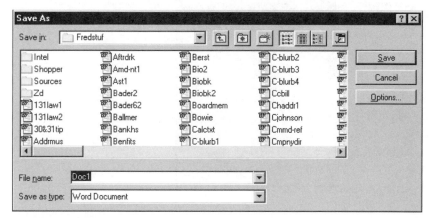

The Save As dialog box is almost
identical to the Open dialog box.

To save a new data file in a Windows 95 application, select either Save or Save As from the File menu. If this is the first time the data has been saved, the Save As dialog box appears regardless of which of the two menu items you chose. Type a name into the File Name field and click on the Save button. Windows 95 supports file names of up to 255 characters; it warns you if you exceed this limit or if you enter unacceptable punctuation.

If you are saving a file that has already been stored to disk, Windows 95 does not prompt you with the Save As dialog box unless you specifically choose it. If you select Save, Windows 95 assumes that you wish to save the data to the existing file, updating its contents.

The same thing happens with a so-called empty data file. You create an empty file by choosing the New menu option in a folder view, then double-clicking either on the data file itself or on the Open menu item within the application. Selecting Save does not bring up the Save As dialog box because, even though the new data file object is empty, it already exists as a file object on a volume.

Normally you want to save a file under the name you first assigned it. Sometimes, however, you want to change the name of a file. For example, to keep several revisions of the same document, you need to save them under different file names. Fortunately, virtually all File menus in Windows applications provide the Save As option. Selecting Save As brings up the Save As dialog box so that you can enter a new file name (Figure 4.17).

FIGURE 4.17
*Selecting the
Save As Menu
Item*

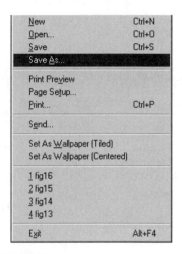

*Virtually all Windows applications provide
a Save As menu item in addition to the
Save and Open items.*

Close. If you use an application based on the older, MDI interface, you will discover a third universal File menu option: Close. Close tells the application to remove the currently selected data file from memory and close its disk file. Close is useful when you work with multiple documents simultaneously. As you finish with a document, you can close it to free up memory and unclutter the application window. Microsoft suggests that Windows 95 applications not use MDI but instead place documents in independent windows, eliminating the need for a Close command on the File menu.

Insider's Tip

Although all Windows 95 applications use common dialog boxes for opening and saving data files, older applications, especially those written for Windows 3.1, can't access the new dialog boxes. Those applications use an older dialog box familiar to users of Windows 3.1. Most of the old-style dialog boxes include a Help button; click on it or press the F1 key for further instructions.

• •

Multitasking with Windows 95

One of the most powerful features of Windows 95 is its support for **multitasking.** Multitasking is the ability to do more than one thing at a time. In the case of Windows 95, this means that you can run more than one program at once and that you can switch among those programs at will.

Multitasking enables your computer to mirror more fully the richness of your work. Instead of focusing on a single task at a time—as you are limited to doing with DOS—you can open multiple applications concurrently, each providing a specific tool or function. The net result is a more natural working environment. Unless you are the head of a large corporation—in which case your desk may be dramatically bare—your real desk probably serves as the resting ground for multiple ongoing jobs. On one side is that stack of unfinished reports. At the top is a copy of a memo you were reading. On one corner is a letter to your congressperson, while sitting center stage is the latest stock report from Wall Street.

Similarly, multitasking enables you to keep lots of things open at once on your virtual desktop. A database program might contain those unfinished reports, and Word might contain that letter to your congressperson. The memo could be an e-mail message, and the stock report could be a spreadsheet file in Excel. You get the picture (Figure 4.18).

FIGURE 4.18

The Windows 95 Desktop with Multiple Applications Open

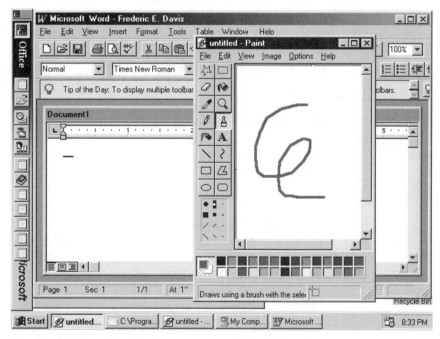

Windows 95 enables you to run multiple applications
simultaneously, simulating the sometimes desirable
chaos of a real desk.

Opening Multiple Applications. In practice, each time you launch a program from the Start menu or open a data file in a folder view, you are multitasking. Windows 95 folder views are considered application programs, so just by navigating the Windows 95 interface, you tap into its multitasking capabilities.

However, opening multiple applications is only the tip of the multitasking iceberg. Windows 95 also allows applications to operate simultaneously, letting you continue to work in one application while a complex, time-consuming operation (like a print job) takes place in another.

This multitasking sleight of hand is accomplished by dividing up the amount of processing time available on your PC. By giving each application a slice of the computer's processing capacity, and by switching quickly between applications behind the scenes, Windows 95 creates the illusion that more than one thing is happening at once. In reality, Windows is simply switching between tasks every few milliseconds.

The net result is that you can do more because you no longer have to wait for an application to finish a complex procedure before continuing. Now, instead of going for coffee while that 100-page report is printing, you can switch to another running application—or open a new data file for editing—while the print job continues to churn away in the background (Figure 4.19).

• • • • • • • • • • • • • •
FIGURE 4.19
Word
Printing in the
Background

With multitasking, you can do more with your PC because time-consuming tasks like print jobs no longer tie up the entire system.

The Windows 95 interface remains responsive even when multiple applications are performing heavy processing in the background. You can continue to navigate folders, open other applications from the Start menu, and perform virtually any other task in the foreground while your computer chugs away on other jobs in the background.

Switching Applications. Windows 95 makes it easy to exploit its multitasking capabilities by providing a running list of open applications on the Taskbar. This task list includes full-blown programs, like Word, as well as the folder views you use to navigate the Windows 95 interface (Figure 4.20).

• • • • • • • • • • • • • •
FIGURE 4.20
The Windows
95 Taskbar
Task List

Windows 95 maintains a running list of all open applications on the Taskbar.

To switch to a different application, click on its entry on the task list. The application appears at the top of the desktop. Do the same for applications that have been minimized. Although you can't see their application windows, you can always locate them by looking at the task list. A simple click on a program on the task list restores that application's window and places it at the top of the desktop pile (Figure 4.21).

FIGURE 4.21
*Switching
between
Applications
with the
Task List*

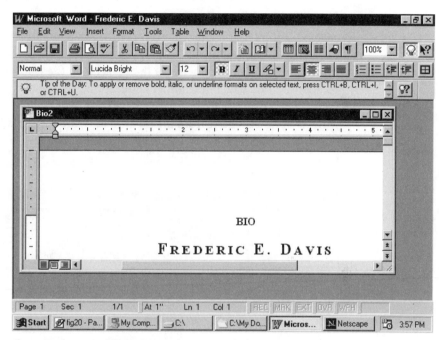

*To switch to a different application, click on it on the
task list. The application is moved to the top of the
desktop and is ready for use.*

The Windows 95 Clipboard

Under Windows 95, no application is an island. That's because Windows 95 provides bridges that enable applications to communicate with one another in powerful ways. The most well known of those bridges is the ubiquitous Windows 95 Clipboard.

Based on a concept borrowed from the Macintosh (again, let's give credit where credit is due), the Windows 95 Clipboard is sort of a universal scratch pad. When data is placed on the Clipboard by one application, it becomes available to any other application. Text, graphics, and even more complex amalgamations can all be copied to the Clipboard. If you want to copy worksheet data from Excel, for example, into a document you are writing in Word, you use the Clipboard as the go-between. Word and Excel use different data formats, so the Clipboard acts as a neutral depository and translator that can be filled with and communicate virtually any kind of data regardless of its source.

Cut, Copy, and Paste. To place data on the Windows 95 Clipboard, you use an application's Edit menu. For example, to copy a range of cells from an Excel worksheet to the Clipboard, you highlight the cells in Excel and select Copy from the Edit menu. The cells are then placed on the Clipboard.

To insert that data into another application, you use that application's Edit menu. For example, to insert the data into Word, you switch to Word's window and select Paste from the Edit menu. The data is pasted into the current Word document, where it can be formatted and integrated with the document text for printing (Figure 4.22).

FIGURE 4.22

Copying and Pasting from Excel to Word

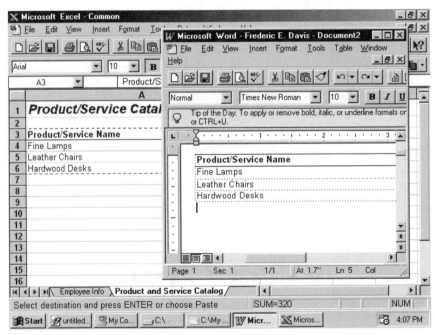

To copy data from Excel to Word, highlight the data in Excel, select Copy from the Edit menu to place it on the Clipboard, then select Paste from Word's Edit menu to insert the data into the current Word document.

Suddenly Windows 95 becomes more than a cluttered desk—it's a United Nations that works. Not only can you run multiple applications concurrently, but you can also share data among them virtually at will.

A third option, cutting data, actually removes data from a program into the Clipboard. Thus if you cut a range of cells from an Excel worksheet, the data ceases to exist in the worksheet and is present only in the Clipboard. Cutting is less popular than copying because it destroys the data in the original, leaving the data only in the Clipboard and in any applications into which it is pasted.

Hot Links with DDE

Although cutting, copying, and pasting are powerful mechanisms for sharing data, they can become tedious, especially with data that is frequently updated. For example, if you generate a monthly report in Word that includes worksheet data pasted from multiple Excel data files, updating that information manually can become a real chore.

Fortunately, Windows 95 provides a mechanism for automating Clipboard exchanges. By means of **Dynamic Data Exchange (DDE),** you can instruct Windows 95 to update data automatically, copying and pasting it into a document whenever it is changed in the original file. When you update the original, DDE searches out and updates each pasted link.

To use DDE, first copy the data from the source file to the Clipboard. In the scenario just mentioned, this would mean highlighting cells in the Excel worksheet and selecting Copy from the Edit menu. Next you would switch to Word and select Paste Link from the Edit menu.

Selecting Paste Link (as opposed to Paste) tells Windows 95 to establish a DDE link between the two data files. Instead of merely pasting the data, Windows establishes a dynamic link between the cells in the Excel worksheet and their pasted equivalents in the Word document. Now each time the data in the Excel file is updated, all of the references to it in the Word document are also updated. This takes place automatically the next time you open the Word document (Figure 4.23).

Insider's Tip

Keep in mind a few caveats when you work with DDE. First, the source of the data must be an actual disk file. That means the data you copy to the Clipboard must be part of a file that has been saved to disk; using data from a new, unsaved document or worksheet is not allowed. Also, DDE links are sensitive to the location of the source file. If you move a file, you will likely break any links made to its data. If you accidentally break a link, try moving the file back to its original location.

FIGURE 4.23
*Using DDE to
Establish a
Dynamic Link*

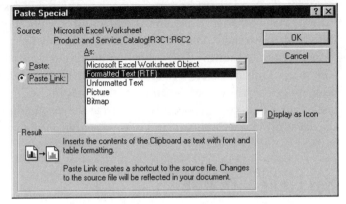

DDE enables you to establish a dynamic link
between data files in different applications.
Changes made to the original are automatically
reflected in the linked version.

Viewing the Clipboard's Contents

If you work for the CIA or if you're just nosy, you might want to be able to
view the Clipboard's contents—especially when you're preparing to paste
data into a sensitive document. Even if you just work for the lumber company,
you might not want to paste your company's private profit statements inadvertently into the staff newspaper.

Fortunately, Windows 95 provides a convenient mechanism for viewing
the contents of the Clipboard. The Clipboard Viewer is a Windows 95 accessory program that enables you to view the contents of the Clipboard, as well
as save those contents to a disk file that can later be reloaded into the Clipboard manually (Figure 4.24).

FIGURE 4.24
*The Windows
95 Clipboard
Viewer*

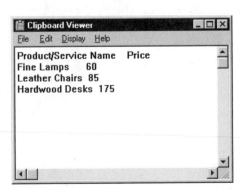

*The Clipboard Viewer
enables you to view the
contents of the Clipboard,
as well as save the
contents to a disk file.*

The Clipboard Viewer can display Clipboard data in a variety of ways—for example, as raw or OEM text (a special font for displaying oddball characters). The Clipboard Viewer selects the most appropriate way to view the data at hand. However, the View menu provides additional viewing formats, and you can override the Clipboard Viewer's default settings at any time.

Saving Clipboard Data. To save Clipboard data, select Save As from the Clipboard Viewer's File menu. The Viewer uses its own data file format, so you have to reload the data into the Clipboard Viewer before inserting it into a data file in an application (Figure 4.25).

FIGURE 4.25

Saving Clipboard Data

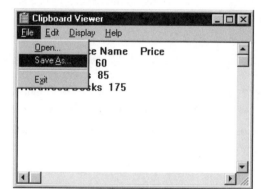

To save Clipboard data, select Save As from the Clipboard Viewer's File menu.

Object Linking and Embedding

Although the Windows 95 Clipboard and DDE are able to link your data regardless of which application created it, these mechanisms do have their limitations. For starters, data that is placed on the Clipboard is generic; once pasted into another application, it loses its original characteristics. This means that when you paste Excel data from the Clipboard into a Word document, the data ceases to be Excel data and is converted into raw text. And although DDE may be able to update this pasted raw text automatically, the data itself cannot be manipulated with worksheet commands; it is text and nothing more.

Fortunately, Windows 95 provides an even more sophisticated mechanism for sharing data among applications. Called **Object Linking and Embedding (OLE),** this mechanism builds upon the foundation of the Windows 95 Clipboard and DDE, expanding their capabilities in powerful ways.

In-Place Editing. OLE enables an application to edit data that has been pasted into another application. Called in-place editing, the feature enables you to edit data that has been transferred into a host, or "container," document. Data pasted with OLE is called an *embedded object;* you use a variant of the Paste command, Paste Special, to paste OLE data.

When you double-click on an OLE embedded object, Windows 95 interprets this as a request to edit the object in place and searches the system for an appropriate "server" application to handle the editing chores. Once found, the server application essentially takes over the application window of the "client" application—the one in which the embedded object and its container document reside—providing all the necessary tools and menu options to edit the data (Figure 4.26).

FIGURE 4.26

In-Place Editing with Word and Excel

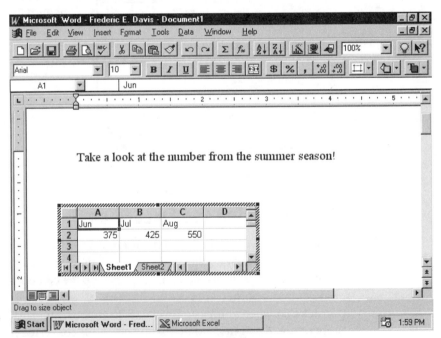

When you double-click on an OLE embedded object, Windows 95 searches for an appropriate server application to provide the necessary editing functions. Once found, this application takes over the application window of the client application, providing tools and menu items to edit the embedded object in place.

To see in-place editing in action, open an OLE-aware application such as Excel. Next, copy a range of cells to the Clipboard using the Copy command on the Edit menu. Now launch another OLE-aware application—for example, Word. When you select Paste Special from the Edit menu, a dialog box appears with a list of possible data types. Select the entry for an Excel worksheet object, click on the OK button, and the data is pasted into Word as an embedded object.

If you subsequently double-click on the embedded Excel data, the Excel program takes over the Word application window, and you gain access to all of Excel's menus and toolbars. It's as if you were editing the data in Excel itself, except that you can also see the data of the container document in which the Excel object resides.

The advantage of in-place editing is obvious. You can see exactly how changes made to the data affect the overall container document, and this in turn makes it easy to format the information precisely.

Drag-and-Drop Embedding.

In-place editing makes it easy to change information that has been embedded as an OLE object. Drag-and-drop embedding makes it easy to share that data among OLE-capable applications by automating the Copy/Paste Special operation. Instead of a three-step process —highlighting data, copying it to the Clipboard, and selecting the Paste Special command—you highlight and then drag data from application window to application window (Figure 4.27).

FIGURE 4.27

Using Drag and Drop to Embed an Object

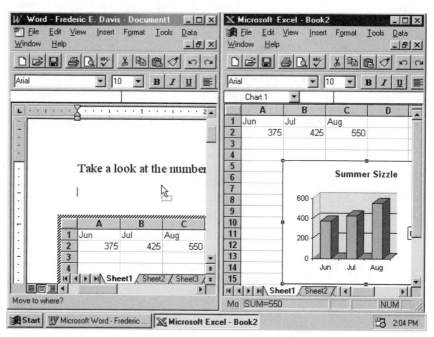

By using drag-and-drop embedding, you can bypass all those Edit menu commands and drag an object to its destination container document.

To illustrate drag-and-drop embedding, I use the Excel/Word example again. First you highlight a range of cells in Excel, then you drag them from the Excel application window and drop them when the cursor is over the Word application window. The cells are embedded into the current Word document as an OLE object, and you can now edit them using in-place editing.

Scraps. One of the most revolutionary features of the Windows 95 interface is its level of support for OLE. Although previous versions of Windows supported OLE operations such as drag-and-drop embedding and in-place editing, Microsoft has expanded OLE support in Windows 95 by making folder views OLE aware. Since each folder view is a potential OLE container, you can drag and drop or copy and paste snippets of data into folder views just as if you were embedding the data into another program.

These miscellaneous pieces of data—called **Scraps** in Windows 95—feature their own icon, which can be manipulated just like any other desktop object. You can drag Scraps from folder to folder, delete them using the Recycle Bin, and even rename them with more descriptive titles (Figure 4.28).

● ● ● ● ● ● ● ● ● ● ● ● ●
FIGURE 4.28
Scraps in
Windows 95

Scraps are data objects that represent snippets of application data. You can drag and drop or copy and paste these objects among applications at will.

You can use Scraps in a number of productive ways. To begin with, you can store interesting data items as Scraps without having to create an entire data file (Scraps take up less disk space than most data files). These data items can be grouped together in their own folder for quick access (Figure 4.29).

● ● ● ● ● ● ● ● ● ● ● ● ●
FIGURE 4.29
A Folder Full
of Scraps

Scraps can be grouped together to provide quick access to frequently used data items.

You can also use the Scraps mechanism as a scratch pad for data. Simply drag the data from an OLE application onto the desktop for later use in another application. The advantage of using Scraps instead of the Clipboard is that you don't lose the data in the Scrap if you should accidentally copy something else onto the Clipboard, overwriting its contents.

Scraps also make it easy to copy multiple individual data items for later use. Whereas the Clipboard holds only one item at a time, you can create dozens of Scraps and later drag them back into applications as desired.

Quitting Applications

After you load and save files, embed objects, and drag Scraps until your fingers hurt, only one task is left undone: quitting an application. Windows 95 offers three ways to shut down an application.

The first and quickest way to quit an application is to click on the Close Window button in the upper right-hand corner of the application window. This is the button that contains the little *X* and sits next to the Minimize and Maximize buttons on the window's title bar.

You can also select Exit from the application's File menu. Virtually all Windows applications include an Exit item on this menu, although on occasion a developer takes the liberty of calling it something else (like Close, which shouldn't be confused with the Close option of an MDI application) (Figure 4.30).

FIGURE 4.30
*The Exit
Menu Item*

Virtually all Windows applications include an Exit item on the File menu. Clicking on Exit tells the application to close any open data files and shut itself down.

Finally, you can double-click on the application's System menu icon. This is the one that contains a miniature of the program's icon. It's located in the upper left-hand corner of the application window, right next to the program's title in the title bar. You can also open this menu with a single click and select Close, but double-clicking is quicker.

Whatever technique you employ, the application interprets the command in the same way. It closes any open data files—prompting you to save any changes first if you haven't already done so—and then closes its application window, shutting itself down.

Summary

Several features have been added to Windows to make it easier to start programs, to run them, and to use them either by themselves or in conjunction with data contained in other programs. In other words, with its Clipboard, DDE, and OLE, the Windows 95 operating system enables you to integrate all the information on your computer, whether it was generated by DOS, Windows 3.1, Windows 95, or Windows NT. More than that, the multitasking capability of Windows 95 makes it possible for you to work on more than one program at once, so you can send messages to your home office, for example, while working on a spreadsheet. All this computing power was formerly reserved for mainframes and supercomputers, but now it is truly at your fingertips.

5

Playing with Your New Toys: Applets, Games, and On-Line Help

To succeed, an operating system needs to be witty, wise, useful, enjoyable, addictive, sexy, and stimulating. Of course, to a true nerd, an operating system is all this and more—it's a way of life. But for the rest of us, all those other qualities derive from the **programs** written for an operating system, not from the system itself. That's why Microsoft bundles a variety of little programs with Windows 95—so you can have some fun with it right out of the box. The programs range from a skeletal word processor to a paint program, a calculator, an automatic phone dialer, and a handful of games. Of course, Microsoft hopes those programs whet your appetite for full-fledged software applications, maybe even from Microsoft.

Indeed, if this offering doesn't get you hooked, you might as well go back to pen and paper. Think of this grab bag of goodies as utilities if you're an experienced Windows user, or as Windows 95 applications with training wheels if you're a beginner. The programs that come with Windows 95 are simple enough for even a novice to learn quickly. For old Windows 3.1 hacks, the programs provide a good way to get to know the new look and feel of Windows 95. And if you run into anything that stumps you, it's a good idea to learn how to use the newly revamped on-line help system of Windows 95, which offers immediate assistance not only with Windows but also with other programs that you might run.

A Lightweight Software Sampler

To turn you on to what you can do with Windows 95, Microsoft has bundled several basic programs with your package. These miniature applications, or **applets** (which Microsoft also calls accessories), lack the power and range of their full-featured, commercial counterparts but still provide some functions. You can write a memo to your boss, draw a picture of your house, or calculate how long it will take to pay off the mortgage, all while learning how to use Windows 95.

You'll find even more in this grab bag of appetizing applets: besides the word processor, the paint program, and the calculator, Microsoft has included a phone dialer, a character map, a briefcase for packing and porting your data when you're on the road, a graphics program, a multitude of enjoyable, time-wasting games, and help on an assortment of topics. Windows 95 also comes with specialized applets for data communications and multimedia; I cover those in Chapters 10 and 12.

Insider's Tip

Some of the specialized applets—for example, the Backup and the Disk Defragmenter programs—are really system maintenance utilities. You can find out more about them in Chapter 14.

How to Get There

On the Programs submenu of the Start button is a submenu called **Accessories**. Click on it once to access almost all the Windows 95 applets (Figure 5.1).

FIGURE 5.1

The Accessories Submenu

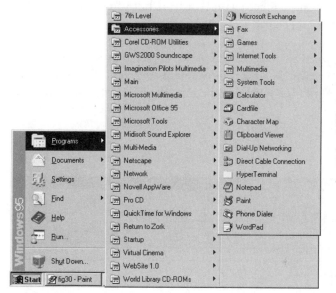

The Accessories submenu, nested within the Programs submenu of the Start button, provides single-click access to almost all the Windows 95 applets.

The Accessories submenu is also home to several submenus, including the following:

≫→ **Games.** Contains game applets.

≫→ **System Tools.** Contains system maintenance applets.

≫→ **Multimedia.** Holds tools such as the CD Player and the Sound Recorder.

≫→ **Fax.** Contains fax-related tools if you installed the Windows 95 Fax option.

The last three submenus—System Tools, Multimedia, and Fax—contain specialized applets that I discuss in Chapter 13, 12, and 11, respectively.

WordPad

Not as powerful or as full featured as a regular word processor such as Microsoft Word, Windows 95's WordPad nevertheless does what a basic word processor should do, and it's a snap to use as well. You can't run a spell checker or create a macro with WordPad, but you can create a document, save it, and print it (Figure 5.2).

Upgrade Alert

WordPad replaces the Write applet that was included with Windows 3.1. WordPad is a big improvement over Write. For example, WordPad can read Word files directly, something the old Write applet cannot do.

FIGURE 5.2
WordPad

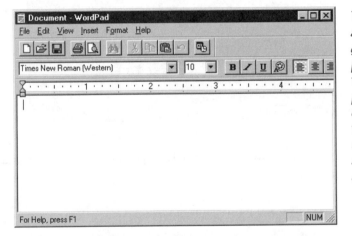

The WordPad applet is a general-purpose text-editing program that enables you to create, save, and print documents.

Formatting Text. When you format text with WordPad, the complete range of Windows 95 fonts is available to you. You can also center, justify, and perform other feats of typographic dexterity by using convenient menu commands, dialog boxes, and toolbar buttons (Figures 5.3 and 5.4).

FIGURE 5.3
*The Font
Dialog Box*

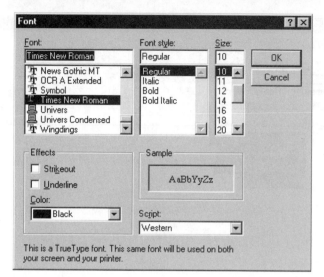

*The Font dialog
box enables you
to alter the
typeface of
highlighted
text.*

FIGURE 5.4
*The Paragraph
Dialog Box*

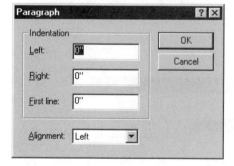

*Use this box to change
the format of a region of
highlighted text.*

WordPad also supports advanced features such as bulleted lists, and it enables you to insert the current time and date into a document (Figures 5.5 and 5.6). You can access those functions on WordPad's menus and toolbar buttons. A more limited subset of commands is available on the pop-up menu activated by the right mouse button.

••••••••••••
FIGURE 5.5
Creating a
Bulleted List

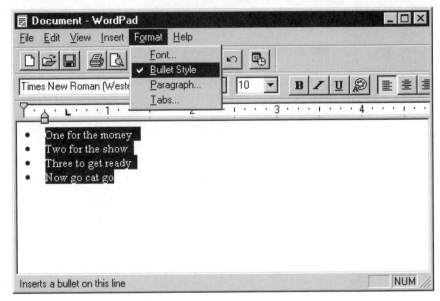

You can turn a block of text into a bulleted list by
separating individual elements with carriage returns,
highlighting the list, and clicking on the Bullet Style
button (or selecting Bullet Style from the Format menu).

••••••••••••
FIGURE 5.6
Inserting the
Date and Time

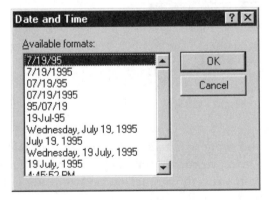

You can insert the
current date and time
into a document by
clicking on the Date/Time
button (or by selecting
Date and Time from the
Insert menu).

WordPad is also up to speed on tabs. To create new tab stops, click on the WordPad ruler bar. You see a tab stop indicator wherever you just clicked. You can drag the tab stop across the ruler bar to adjust its position precisely (Figure 5.7).

FIGURE 5.7
Tabs in WordPad

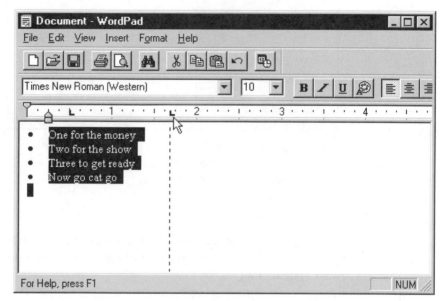

To create a new tab stop, click on the ruler bar. The tab stop indicator you just created can be dragged to any point you desire.

Clipboard Maneuvers. WordPad provides a perfect venue for practicing with the Windows 95 Clipboard. If you highlight a region of text and select Copy from the Edit menu, WordPad places a copy of the text on the Clipboard. Similarly, select Paste to insert the Clipboard's contents into a document where the cursor is positioned (Figure 5.8).

FIGURE 5.8

Copy and Paste with WordPad

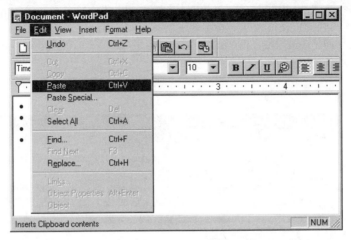

Highlight text and select Copy to place that text on the Clipboard. Select Paste to insert the Clipboard's contents at the current cursor position.

To spruce up WordPad documents, you can use the Clipboard to paste in graphics. Anything created in the Paint applet or another paint program will work (Figure 5.9).

FIGURE 5.9

Pasting Graphics into WordPad

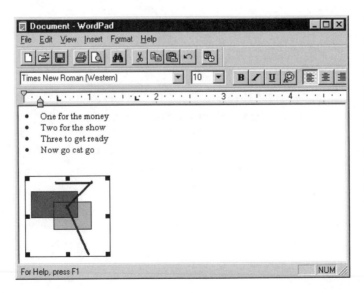

You can use the Clipboard to paste a graphics image created with the Paint applet into a WordPad document.

Insider's Tip

Because WordPad is an OLE-aware application, it can exchange OLE data with other applications and with the Windows 95 operating system. To see this feature in action, highlight a region of text in WordPad and drag it to the Windows 95 desktop. The text data is turned into an OLE Scrap, which can be dragged back into WordPad or into another OLE-aware application. You can learn more about this and other OLE techniques in Chapter 14.

Saving Data. Whenever you save a document, WordPad automatically stores it in a format compatible with Word 6.0. You can also save data in two other formats: as raw text or in Rich Text format. Saving a document as raw text—that is, as ASCII characters—means you lose all formatting and graphics but can transfer data to other programs. Rich Text format, like Word 6.0 format, retains formatting and graphics but in addition enables you to transfer information to another word-processing program. Make your format choice when you save data; use the Save As dialog box (Figure 5.10).

• • • • • • • • • • • • • •
FIGURE 5.10

The Save As Dialog Box in WordPad

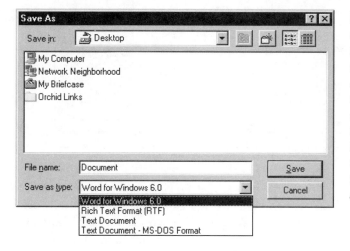

WordPad saves data in Word 6.0 format by default. However, you can override this setting by changing the entry in the Save As dialog box.

Insider's Tip

WordPad can only save formatting information—such as fonts, justification, and pasted graphics data—if you use the Word 6.0 or Rich Text format. The Text Document format produces a file with ASCII text, which drops all formatting and graphics data.

Danger Zone

If you use WordPad to edit a system file—for example, an .INI, a .SYS, or a .BAT file—be sure to save the file as ASCII text. System files often choke on the text formatting and other technical data embedded in Word and Rich Text files. If you want to avoid crashing your whole system, always double-check that system files have been saved as plain ASCII text.

Preview and Print. Once you've completed your masterpiece, WordPad makes it easy to preview and print the document. A Print Preview mode shows you exactly how your document will look on paper by providing a bird's-eye view of each virtual page, displaying the text exactly as it will appear when printed (Figure 5.11).

FIGURE 5.11

Print Preview Mode

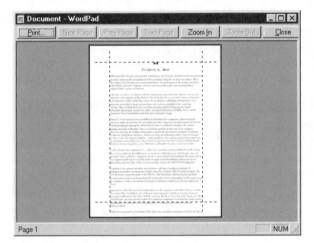

The WordPad Print Preview mode gives you a bird's-eye view of a document as it will appear on paper. To preview specific sites or roam from page to page, use the scroll bar.

You can zoom to Print Preview to see details of a particular region of a document and even to view two pages side by side. By default, Print Preview displays the current page. You can use the scroll bars to navigate around a single page or to access any other page in the document.

To bring up Print Preview, either click on the Print Preview button on the toolbar or select Print Preview from the File menu. Once you have finished previewing your document and are ready to print, WordPad offers several options.

Click on the Print button (or select Print from the File menu) to bring up the standard Windows 95 Print dialog box. From this box you can select a printer, specify the type of paper and the handling of graphics and fonts, and indicate how many copies you'd like to print (Figure 5.12).

FIGURE 5.12

*The Print
Dialog Box*

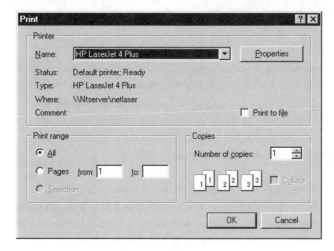

All applets that
can print include
this generic
Windows 95 Print
dialog box, which
offers an array
of printing
options.

Most of the Print dialog box items are self-explanatory. Once you've set
the number of copies, specified which pages to print, and selected a printer,
clicking the Print button sends the data to the Windows 95 print spooler and
returns you to WordPad.

A Custom Fit. As with most Windows 95 applications, you can customize
WordPad. For example, you can activate the toolbars with the View menu, and
you can control the way data from different file types is displayed by using the
Options dialog box. To open this box, click on Options on the View menu
(Figure 5.13).

FIGURE 5.13

*The Options
Dialog Box*

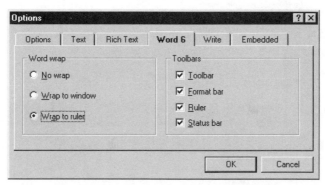

The WordPad Options dialog box enables you to
determine how the program handles different file
types and to adjust more universal settings. For
example, you can specify whether the ruler bar uses
a metric or a standard measuring system.

Paint

If you provide the inspiration, Windows 95's Paint applet provides the tools. Paint is a virtual art studio complete with easel, paints, paintbrushes, pencils, and something handy for the budding artist: an eraser. Using a mouse and Paint's tool palettes, you can create a masterpiece in mere seconds. With the help of the Clipboard (or OLE), you can export your art into other applications, such as WordPad (Figure 5.14).

Insider's Tip

Paintings and other graphic images you create in Paint are technically referred to as **bitmapped images.** With bitmapped graphics, an image is actually composed of many tiny dots, or **pixels,** just the way images are composed on your computer or TV screen. This is in contrast to **vector graphics**—used by, for example, PostScript and AutoCAD—which are images built from a series of mathematical expressions that represent the strokes, lines, and objects contained in the image.

FIGURE 5.14

The Paint Applet

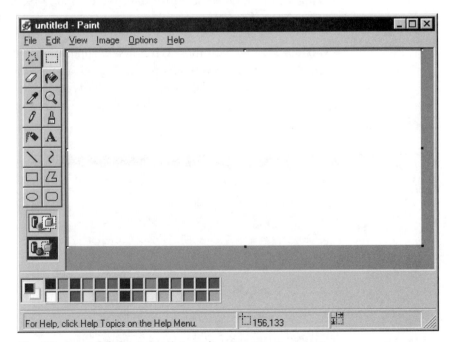

The Windows 95 Paint applet makes it easy to create bitmapped graphics. Paint provides all the tools you need to draw, edit, and manipulate images, which can be saved, printed, or copied and pasted into other applications.

Basics. When you first open the Paint applet, you see what every budding Picasso must face: a blank sheet of paper, in this case a blank sheet of virtual paper. This is your drawing surface, which you can resize and adjust as you like. To draw on this surface, you use the mouse. A typical movement is to drag a selected tool across the surface. The Paint tools are arranged in a **palette** on the left side of the application window; another palette at the bottom of the window offers you a selection of colors. If you don't like the location of the palettes, you can drag them anywhere else on the desktop (Figure 5.15).

FIGURE 5.15
Paint with
Floating
Palettes

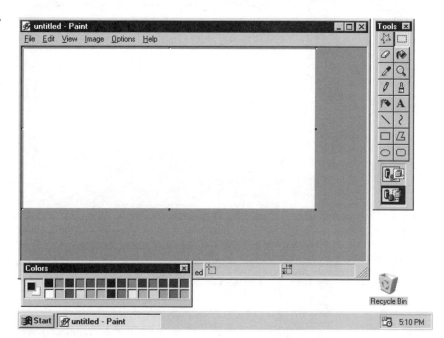

You can drag the tool and color palettes from their default locations and position them anywhere on the Windows 95 desktop. This allows you to view your art without any obstructions.

By far the most popular of the Paint tools is the brush. As its name implies, the brush is a freehand drawing tool that lets you add paint directly to the drawing surface. You select the brush icon from the tool palette and drag it across the drawing surface. Depending on your dexterity, the resolution of your mouse, and the quality of your monitor, you'll find the brush either cumbersome or elegant. With practice, you should be able to produce pleasing results (Figure 5.16).

Insider's Tip

If you are familiar with using a real paintbrush or drawing pencil, you'll probably complain that drawing with a mouse is like trying to draw with a bar of soap. Don't despair; in Chapter 7 I tell you about graphics tablets with styluses that not only feel like brushes but are pressure sensitive. The brushes splay like real ones when used with sophisticated paint programs.

FIGURE 5.16
Painting with the Brush

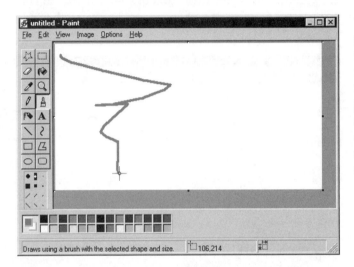

The brush tool is simple to use. Select the tool from the tool palette, then drag it across the drawing surface.

FIGURE 5.17
Changing Tools

As you change tools, the options in the lower portion of the palette change correspondingly.

You can alter brush size and shape by selecting icons in the lower portion of the tool palette. This region is context-sensitive —that is, the options change depending on what tool you have selected. For example, if you switch from the brush to the spray can, the options change from brush sizes and shapes to spray patterns (Figure 5.17).

Other painting devices include a fill tool for painting enclosed regions with a particular color; a pencil for performing precise drawing operations; an eraser for clearing a particular region of the drawing surface; a tool for drawing straight lines; shape-creation tools (for example, for rectangles, ellipses, and polygons); and a tool for adding typed text to your image (Figure 5.18).

FIGURE 5.18

Additional Tools

Paint includes a number of additional tools for creating shapes, lines, and text, as well as an eraser for clearing regions of the drawing surface.

Colors. Paint uses black as the default drawing color and white as the default background color. Changing colors is easy, though. Select a color—red, for example—from the color palette by clicking on that color with the left mouse button. From now on, all your tools will use red paint. An indicator on the left end of the color palette changes to reflect your current color selection (Figure 5.19).

You can change the background color by clicking on a color palette entry with the right mouse button. This action by itself, however, does not change the color of the background. You have to use the eraser tool next. Instead of clearing a region and replacing it with the default white background, the eraser tool replaces the background with whichever color you selected (Figure 5.20).

FIGURE 5.19

Changing Colors

To change colors in Paint, select an entry from the color palette. An indicator at the left edge of the palette changes to reflect your selection.

FIGURE 5.20

Background Color

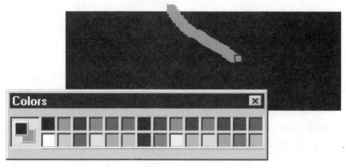

To select a different background color, click on the color palette with the right mouse button. Then when you apply the eraser tool, the region you erase turns the color you chose.

If you want to create your own colors, select Edit Colors from the Options menu. At the bottom of the Edit Colors dialog box, you'll see a large button defined Custom Colors. Pressing on this expands the dialog box to show you Paint's color mixer. You can mix your own colors using three methods. The simplest is just to click in the multicolored spectrum to select a new hue. If you'd rather mix colors by number, you can define colors with two color systems. The first lets you mix amounts of red, green, and blue (the primary colors) to create any shade. The second lets you specify the hue, the saturation, and the luminance, enabling you again to create any color. When you're done, click on the Add to Custom Colors button, and your new shade is now available on the palette (Figure 5.21).

FIGURE 5.21

Custom Colors

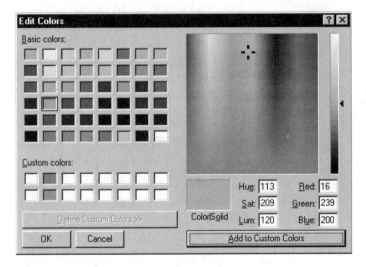

The Edit Colors dialog box includes a precision color selection tool for mixing colors to create a particular shade.

Special Tools. Paint has one special effect—a spray can—and it provides many special tools. You can, for example, magnify a part of your art or alter sections of it without affecting the rest of the drawing.

The **Magnifier** enables you to zoom in on a specific portion of your drawing. A context-sensitive portion of the tool palette displays the level of magnification. At the same time, you can look at a thumbnail view of the overall document to see how your changes affect the overall image (Figure 5.22).

FIGURE 5.22
The Magnifier

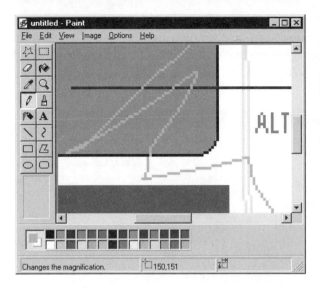

The Magnifier
enables you to
zoom in on a
particular region of
your drawing.
You can edit the
drawing pixel by
pixel to correct
mistakes and add
minute details.

The **selection tool** enables you to select a specific region of your drawing for further editing. For example, to copy part of your drawing to the Clipboard, select the region with the selection tool, then use the Edit menu's Copy command.

The normal selection tool has you drag a rectangular selection box over a particular region. But if you don't want to be boxed in, a **free-form tool** enables you to define a region using freehand drawing (Figure 5.23).

FIGURE 5.23
*Select Your
Spot*

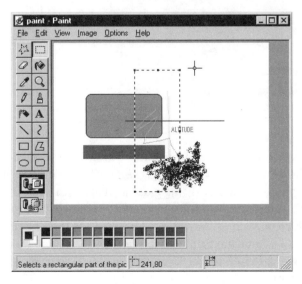

To select a region of
a drawing for further
editing, use one of
the selection tools.
The free-form tool
enables you to select
the region by means
of freehand drawing;
with the normal
selection tool, you
use a selection
rectangle that is
dragged to and
dropped over the
desired region.

Once you've selected a target region of a drawing, you can copy things to it from the Clipboard. You can also flip, rotate, stretch, and skew the region. The Image menu makes this all possible; it contains a dialog box that lists your options (Figure 5.24).

FIGURE 5.24

Stretch

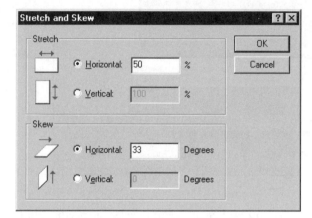

Use the stretch option to alter the size of a selected region. The Stretch/Skew dialog box gives you extensive control over the process.

To change settings that affect an entire drawing, select the Attributes option from the Image menu. You can, for example, define the exact height and width of a drawing, as well as indicate its color scheme (Figure 5.25).

FIGURE 5.25

The Image Attributes Dialog Box

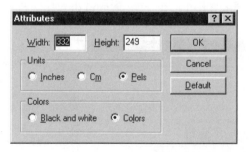

Here you can indicate the exact dimensions of a drawing, as well as define its color scheme.

Copy To on the Edit menu enables you to copy a selected region of a drawing to its own separate disk file (Figure 5.26). Similarly, the Paste From item enables you to paste an existing graphic image into your drawing.

You'll find several options on the File menu that are similar to those in other applets, such as WordPad. Those include the ubiquitous Open, Save, and Save As; Print and Print Preview; and a special item for making your current drawing the Windows 95 wallpaper (you'll learn more about wallpaper in Chapter 6).

FIGURE 5.26
Copy To

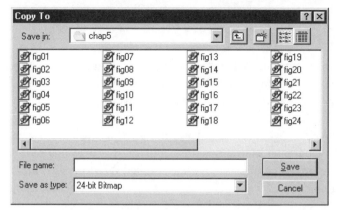

Copy To
enables you
to copy a
selected
region of your
drawing into
its own
separate
disk file.

Notepad

A holdover from Windows 3.1, Notepad is included with Windows 95 only because many applications still require Notepad for installation. To call this text editor simple would be an understatement. Not only is the program limited to working with raw ASCII text files, it offers only one font, and you can't even underline, boldface, or italicize words. Notepad does let you search for a particular text string and cut, copy, and paste. However, you're better off using WordPad whenever possible (Figure 5.27).

Insider's Tip

The reason Notepad is still hanging around is that it forces you to save every file as plain ASCII text so as not to introduce any formatting into system files, which I warned you about earlier. So use WordPad but heed my advice always to save system files as ASCII text.

FIGURE 5.27
Notepad

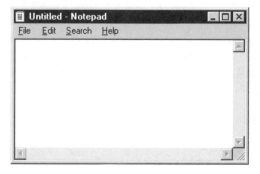

Notepad, a Windows 3.1
holdover, is included with
Windows 95 for
compatibility purposes.
Compared with WordPad,
Notepad's features are
Spartan and lacking in
sophisticated editing and
file format options.

Character Map

An applet called Character Map provides quick keyboard access to the dizzying array of fonts and characters available in Windows 95. Each typeface can include up to 255 characters; that's over twice as many as are on your keyboard. Quite a few characters—for example, the copyright symbol (©)—have no keyboard equivalents and are thus difficult to access.

Character Map solves this problem by providing point-and-click access to the entire character set of each installed Windows 95 font. The Character Map application window is a 7 by 32 grid, each space containing a character from the font you've selected. To select a character from the grid, double-click on it, then use the Copy button to place it onto the Clipboard. From there, you can paste it into another application (Figure 5.28).

FIGURE 5.28

Character Map

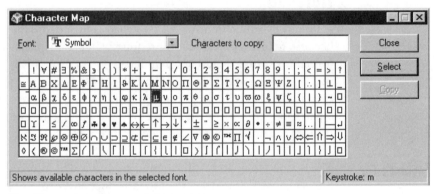

The Character Map applet provides access to characters in Windows 95 font sets.

The Character Map includes a drop-down list box for selecting fonts. Also, a status bar at the bottom of the window displays a potential keyboard equivalent for each character. For most of these equivalents, you hold down the Alt key and type a value on the numeric keypad—hardly an intuitive process, which makes the Character Map seem like an indispensable device.

Phone Dialer

Upgrade Alert

If you have a modem, your computer knows how to dial the phone. Windows 95 lets you take full advantage of this feature with a new applet called Phone Dialer (Figure 5.29). Speed dialing is easy. Start up Phone Dialer, pick a phone number, and voilà, the computer automatically dials the number. This, of course, presumes your modem is properly installed. If you're not sure, check the modem's control panel, discussed in Chapter 10.

•••••••••••••
FIGURE 5.29
Phone Dialer

The Phone Dialer applet helps automate phone dialing.

You can place a call with Phone Dialer in one of three ways. You can use the mouse to click on the numbers of an on-screen picture of a telephone keypad. Or using your keyboard, you can manually enter the telephone number into the Number To field of the Phone Dialer window. In either case, when you click on the Dial button, the program uses your modem to place the call. Once the number has been dialed, Phone Dialer prompts you with a dialog box asking whether you want to pick up the receiver and begin talking or click the Hang-up button and abort the call. As an added convenience, Phone Dialer saves the number in a list of recently dialed numbers, which extends as a drop-down list box from the Number To field (Figure 5.30).

•••••••••••••
FIGURE 5.30
My Dialer Called

When you place a call with Phone Dialer, it dials the number using the modem and then prompts you for an appropriate action. If you pick up the receiver and click the Talk button, Phone Dialer hands the call over to the telephone. If you click Hang-up, Phone Dialer aborts the call and returns you to its main window.

The most painless way to place a call with Phone Dialer is to use the speed-dial option. Phone Dialer lets you program up to ten speed-dial buttons, which provide single-click access to frequently dialed numbers. To add a speed-dial entry for your home or office, click on an unused speed-dial button and enter the number and a name in the resulting dialog box. You can also edit existing speed-dial entries by selecting Speed Dial from the Edit menu (Figure 5.31).

FIGURE 5.31

Speed Dial

Use the speed-dial function to gain single-click access to frequently dialed numbers. To add a new entry, click on an unused speed-dial button and enter a number and a name into the resulting dialog box.

Calculator

One of the most straightforward Windows 95 applets, Calculator looks a lot like its real-life counterpart. It displays a simple on-screen keypad simulating a traditional seven-function calculator with memory. You can either click on the virtual calculator buttons with the mouse cursor or enter values directly from the numeric keypad on your computer keyboard (Figure 5.32).

If you want to get fancy with your calculator and do something like convert a large number into a binary or octal numeric system, you can switch to Scientific mode from the View menu. In Scientific mode, Calculator can perform a variety of complex numeric manipulations required in scientific research (Figure 5.33).

• • • • • • • • • • • • • • •
FIGURE 5.32
Calculator

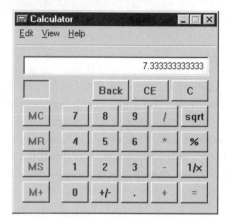

By default, the Windows 95
Calculator applet mimics a
simple seven-function
calculator with memory.

• • • • • • • • • • • • • •
FIGURE 5.33
Scientific Mode

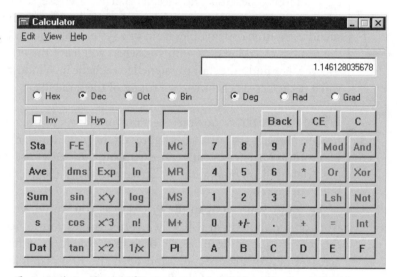

To switch to Scientific mode, select Scientific from the View
menu. Calculator's horizons expand dramatically to include
many complex numeric manipulations.

Once you've obtained your results, you can use the ubiquitous Edit menu
to copy them into the Clipboard. They can then be pasted into another
application.

The Briefcase

If you own only a desktop computer, and if it's not connected to a network, you may never need to call on the services of the Briefcase. This utility can be a lifesaver if you have both a laptop and a desktop system and want to coordinate the information you keep on both computers. Without the Briefcase, it can be all too easy to lose track of which is the most recent version of a file. You can thus commit one of the mortal sins of computing: accidentally copying an older version of a file over a newer version, wiping out any of the changes you've made to the new version.

**Upgrade
Alert**

Road warriors will love the Briefcase because it makes it easy to transfer data from laptop to desktop, and vice versa. The Briefcase is a folder for people who regularly switch between laptop and desktop and who don't want to spend extra time copying files from one system to another. Designed to ease the process of taking data with you when you leave the office, the Briefcase uses the date and time stamp assigned to each file in Windows 95 to track and when necessary synchronize two copies of the same file.

A Sample Scenario. So you're leaving for Taiwan in the morning, and you need to massage the latest sales figures on the plane out. Drag and drop those files into the Briefcase—it's called **packing** your Briefcase—and then drag the Briefcase icon onto a disk or across a network connection to your notebook computer.

En route, you can open the Briefcase as you would any folder view and work on the contents at will. When you return to your office, simply reverse the process: move the Briefcase back to the desktop, either with a disk or across a network connection, and open the Briefcase folder. Windows 95 compares the contents of the Briefcase to the original files on your desktop. If there are any changes, Windows asks you whether you want to update the originals. You can either update the originals individually or update the entire contents of the Briefcase. In either case, the original files are replaced with the revised files in the Briefcase folder.

My Briefcase. Did you notice? Even if you work with shades, this new feature would be hard to miss. When you first installed Windows 95, there was an icon on the desktop called My Briefcase. This is your **Starter Briefcase,** which you are free to rename anything you like; use the menu that pops up when you click the right mouse button. You can also create other Briefcases by selecting Briefcase from the New submenu of any folder view's pop-up menu.

Lots of people have trouble packing before a trip. To help you pack your Briefcase, Windows 95 includes a helpful **wizard** utility. If you want the Briefcase wizard to assist you in packing, double-click on My Briefcase. The wizard presents you with a series of dialog boxes that lead you through the packing process, making sure you have everything you need for the files you select and that it's neat and tidy. Clicking on the Finish button sends the wizard away and returns you to a folder view of the Briefcase's contents.

My Briefcase's folder view sports a toolbar, and the folder's contents are displayed in Details view. The Status field lets you know whether a particular Briefcase entry is current on your desktop system (Figure 5.34).

FIGURE 5.34
*Default
Briefcase
Folder View*

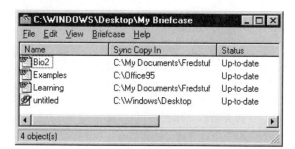

In the Briefcase folder view, you see a toolbar and the contents of the Briefcase displayed in Details view.

Danger Zone

If the Status field reads "Up-to-date," the file in the Briefcase matches the original. If the field reads "Needs updating," your Briefcase version no longer matches the original (Figure 5.35).

FIGURE 5.35
*Working with
a Briefcase*

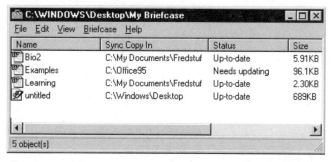

The Status field tells you whether a particular Briefcase entry is in sync with its original. If the Status field reads "Up-to-date," then the two match. If it says "Needs updating," then one of the two copies is more up-to-date.

My Briefcase   My Briefcase   Shortcut to
                                  Scsi e-drive on
                                  'Ntserver' (E)

• • • • • • • • • • • • •
FIGURE 5.36
*Moving a
Briefcase*

*To pack your Briefcase
and hit the road, stuff
it with whatever files you
need and drag it to a
disk. Then pop the disk
out of your desktop
computer and stick it
into your notebook
computer. If you have a
network or direct cable
connection, you can
forget the disk transfer.*

To add new files to a Briefcase, drag them from their folders and drop them into the Briefcase's folder view. Close the folder view, and the Briefcase is ready to travel. Typically, you drag the Briefcase to a disk icon (which moves, as opposed to copies, the Briefcase—this is normal). Then you remove the disk from your desktop PC, load it into your notebook, drag the Briefcase from the disk drive's folder view, and drop it onto your notebook's desktop. Again, Windows 95 moves the Briefcase when you drag and drop; this type of folder is almost never copied. You can also use a network or a direct cable connection to drag and drop the Briefcase into your notebook (Figure 5.36).

Synchronizing the Data. Once you're back home, it's time to unpack your Briefcase. Open the folder view and check out the Status field. If it indicates that files need to be updated, click the Update All button on the folder view's toolbar (or select Update All from the Briefcase menu). Windows 95 prompts you with a dialog box, which contains a scrolling list of all the files that need to be updated (Figure 5.37).

• • • • • • • • • • • • •
FIGURE 5.37
*Updating a
Briefcase*

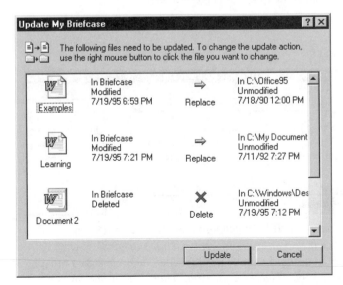

*Click the
Update All
button to bring
up a dialog box
listing all the
files that need
to be updated.
The arrows
indicate
whether the
original or
the Briefcase
version will be
updated.*

It's all one big shuffle: the left side of the dialog box contains icons for the files in the Briefcase, the icons on the right side represent the originals, and the arrows in between the icons tell you which way the update will go. If an arrow points to the original, the original will be updated, and vice versa.

Danger Zone

If one of the copies of a file has been deleted—either the original or the Briefcase version—then a red *X* is placed between the two icons. This is to warn you that your only copy will be deleted to "synchronize" with its match. Be forewarned: if you click the Update button, *both* your copies will be deleted.

Conveniently, you have the option of updating files how and when you like. Click the right mouse button while the cursor is over a particular entry to bring up a pop-up menu that enables you to change the default update action on the fly. You can change the direction of the update arrow, or if you prefer to procrastinate, you can select the Skip option to bypass synchronizing that particular file. And if a file's been marked for deletion, you can undo that command or create a new copy of the file, either in the original location or in the Briefcase (Figure 5.38).

FIGURE 5.38

Overriding Defaults

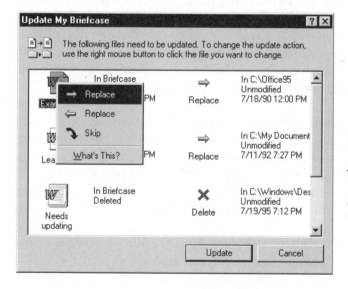

By clicking the right mouse button over a particular dialog box entry, you bring up a pop-up menu that enables you to alter the update process for each entry.

Once you're happy with the way your entries are arranged, click the Update button, and the files are automatically updated. If you're not an all-in-one-fell-swoop kind of person, you can synchronize files one at a time: select a single entry in the Briefcase folder view, then click on the Update Selection button. Once the files are updated, the Status field changes to reflect their new state.

From Port to Port. Yes, Virginia, you can use Briefcase to transport your files between any two computers running Windows 95. So anytime you need to bring your files to a remote computer and keep the copies on both systems current, use a Briefcase as your data carrier.

Insider's Tip

Oops! There is a loophole in the Briefcase system. What if you change both your Briefcase and your original files independently? You'll freak out the Update mechanism, unless the program used to create the files was OLE-aware. OLE features a revision-reconciliation mechanism that cross-checks alterations in both files against an original version. But if the application isn't OLE-aware, you get to reconcile the two files yourself—manually. (And they said computing was supposed to make life easier?)

Windows 95 Games

No operating system would be complete without some sort of distraction for the weary worker, and Windows 95 is no exception. On the Games submenu, you'll find no fewer than five unique and challenging games designed to bring out your lighter side while you're taking a break from number crunching. Some, like Solitaire, are holdovers from Windows 3.1 (and are notoriously addictive). Others, like Freecell, made their debut on Windows NT, Windows 95's big brother. All are guaranteed to entertain.

Insider's Tip

There's one serious problem with the game applets: if you get too entertained around work, your boss could accuse you of improper use of company assets or some other hideous crime against bureaucracy. Don't worry; just tell the boss that these games are actually mouse training utilities, that they are an important educational component of the system and allow you to get familiar with Windows 95 without damaging important work files.

Freecell. A highly popular (and addictive) card game, Freecell was first introduced on Windows NT. Your goal is to move all the cards to home cells, using free cells as place holders. To win, you make four stacks of cards on the home cells: one for each suit, stacked in order of rank. You are supposed to be able to achieve success with every game, but we suspect this rumor might be a plot to keep you plugging away until you, or your machine, crashes (Figure 5.39).

FIGURE 5.39
Freecell

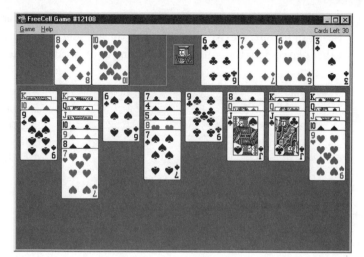

Freecell is a popular card game first introduced on Windows NT. It is believed (although not proven) that every game is winnable.

Hearts. Hearts can be played across a network by more than one player. The player with the lowest ending score wins. To play, you pass three cards to the next player. The value of the cards in your hand determines how many points you earn in each round. It's possible to gain or lose a large number of points in this game; you need to experiment to get the hang of it (Figure 5.40).

FIGURE 5.40
*Hearts
in Action*

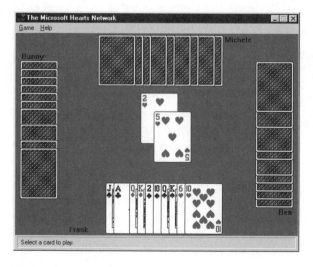

You play Hearts by passing cards to the player next to you. The player with the fewest points at the end of the game is the winner.

When you begin a game of Hearts, you can choose either to become the dealer or to join an existing game. Only one player can act as the dealer; all the other players join the game by connecting to the dealer's system (Figure 5.41).

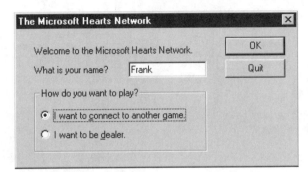

FIGURE 5.41

Starting Hearts

Want to play dealer or join an existing game? Hearts gives you an option when you first start to play.

FIGURE 5.42

Minesweeper

Click on a grid. The numbers you unearth help you predict where mines are buried. To win, you have to uncover all the "safe" squares without detonating a mine.

If you want to play the game solo against the computer, Windows 95 provides three artificial opponents. To play solo, choose to be dealer, then press F2 (or select New from the Game menu) to start a new game.

Minesweeper. No matter how many hours people play this game, it never fails to prove riveting. That's because there's always an element of surprise, and the game is challenging as well. A holdover from Windows 3.1, the object of Minesweeper is to locate all the mines in a virtual mine field without uncovering (and thus detonating) any of them. To do this, you click on the squares of a grid over the mine field. As you uncover a "safe" square, it tells you how many mines are buried in the surrounding eight squares (Figure 5.42).

The number provided by a safe square helps you guess which of the surrounding squares are most likely to contain mines. You can avoid those squares as you continue to uncover more safe squares. If you accidentally uncover a mine, however, all of the mines in the mine field detonate, and you lose. To win, you have to uncover all the safe squares without detonating a mine. You are timed, so you can rate yourself on both speed and level of difficulty.

To adjust Minesweeper's settings, including how difficult you want to make it, use the Game menu. To start a new game, click on the smiley-face icon at the top of the Minesweeper window.

Party Line. Party Line is not really a game per se. However, you could develop a game using this program, which enables you to post public comments to a group of users. The comments appear in each participating computer's Party Line window and follow one another in succession, much like a group of people sharing a conversation on a telephone party line (Figure 5.43).

FIGURE 5.43
Party Line

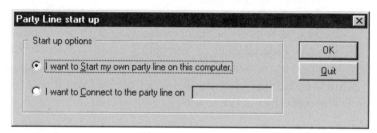

Party Line isn't so much a game as a mechanism for posting public comments that can be viewed by a group of networked users.

When you first start Party Line, you have to decide whether you will act as a Party Line **server** or connect to an existing Party Line hosted on someone else's PC. If you choose to be the server, other Party Line users can then connect to your computer and participate in the Party Line conversation.

You can set up Party Line in a number of ways. For example, you can place the Party Line window on top of your other application windows, you can display or hide the Party Line window's title bar, and you can select a small font so that you see more Party Line talk inside the program's window. A history function enables you to record previous Party Lines. To access those options and to contribute to a conversation, double-click in the Party Line application window to bring up the Start a Rumor dialog box (Figure 5.44).

FIGURE 5.44
Start a Rumor Dialog Box

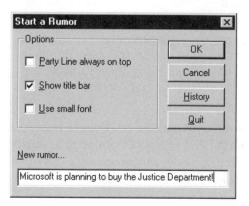

To contribute to a Party Line conversation or change some of Party Line's display characteristics, double-click on the program's application window. This brings up the Start a Rumor dialog box.

Solitaire. Few games have evoked as many strong emotions as Windows Solitaire. Another holdover from Windows 3.1, Solitaire has been the object of many a Windows user's wrath over the years because of its highly addictive nature. It's simply a hard game to walk away from. For many early Windows users, Solitaire was the only reason for having a graphical user interface, or GUI, on their computers.

As the name implies, Solitaire is a virtual version of the old single-person card game. You play Solitaire by dragging cards between stacks in an effort to produce ordered piles of alternating colors. Windows Solitaire includes a shuffle deck, as well as spaces in which to place the ace from each suit to build to foundations—solitaire-speak for the way you sort the deck in a solitaire session (Figure 5.45).

FIGURE 5.45
Solitaire

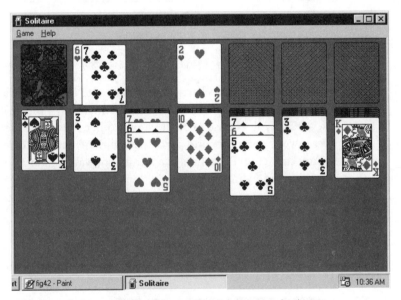

Windows Solitaire is like the real card game, which involves moving cards from stack to stack to create ordered piles of alternating colors. The game includes a shuffle deck, as well as spaces in which to place the ace from each suit to "build to foundations."

You can set up different parameters. Do you want to draw one or three cards at a time from the shuffle deck? Do you want to score Vegas style, normal style, or no style? You can even choose among a variety of colorful decks to brighten up your Solitaire display. Use the Game menu to set up any of those options.

On-Line Help

When in doubt, press F1. That's pretty much the rule of thumb for getting help with Windows. The Windows 95 help system is on line, which means help is at your fingertips. You don't have to backtrack or return to a main help menu; just hit F1 wherever you are. Windows 95 figures out what you were doing when you hit the F1 key and brings up the appropriate assistance. With plenty of tips, examples, and shortcuts to applications, Windows 95 makes it easy to get an answer to that universal question: What do I do now?

How It Works. If you're working in WordPad, for example, and need to know how to set the margins for the current document, you can press F1 (or select Help Topics from the Help menu). Up comes the Windows 95 Help dialog box, with WordPad's help file loaded and ready to answer your question (Figure 5.46).

FIGURE 5.46
Help in WordPad

To bring up WordPad's help mechanism, press F1 or select Help Topics from the Help menu.

Most Windows applications support the Windows 95 on-line help feature. In addition, most applications also provide their own help files.

The Windows 95 Help dialog box contains three index tabs, each of which brings up a page of options. The first tab, Contents, provides an eagle's-eye view of a particular help file. You can expand and contract any Contents entry by double-clicking on it, focusing on a particular section or returning to the overview (Figure 5.47).

FIGURE 5.47
*Resizing a
Contents Entry*

*You can expand
and contract
entries in the
Contents tab to
narrow or broaden
the focus of your
search.*

For example, to find out how to change a margin, expand the section on printing; this brings up the entry for setting page margins. Double-click on this entry, and you see a window with text that describes exactly how to perform the operation (Figure 5.48).

FIGURE 5.48
Getting Help

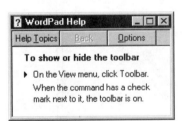

*Once you find the Contents entry for
a particular item, double-click on it to
bring up a window with directions on
how to do what you want to do.*

Each help text window itself offers additional useful features. A grab bag of great tools becomes available when you click on the Options button at the top of the window. The Annotate tool enables you to add your own comments to the help file, a boon to those who learn best by taking notes and reviewing them later. A dialog box prompts you to add an annotation, which later appears as a **paper clip** 📎 icon attached to a page of help text (Figure 5.49).

The help text windows offer other options as well. You can print the current help text, copy it to the Windows 95 Clipboard, and change the display characteristics of the help text window itself. **Help Topics** takes you back to the Contents tab, and **Back** returns you to the previously selected help topic.

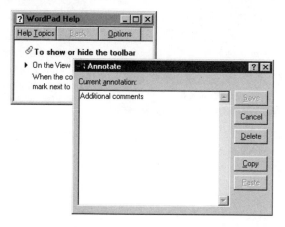

FIGURE 5.49
Annotations

You can annotate help text, adding your own notes and comments for later review.

Highlighted or underlined text has links to additional help information. For example, in WordPad the word *copy* is highlighted in the help entry about copying information between documents (located under Working with Text in the Contents dialog box tab). If you click on *copy*, you bring up a window containing a brief definition of the term and a description of how it relates to the WordPad procedure for copying information between documents (Figure 5.50).

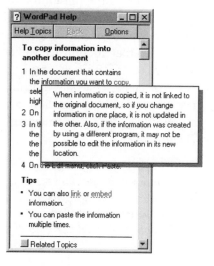

FIGURE 5.50
Help Links

When you click on a highlighted word or phrase, Windows 95 reveals additional, related information.

In some cases you see a button labeled ◻ Related Topics at the bottom of a help text window. Click on this button to bring up a dialog box with the names of other, related help topics. If you select one of those items and click on the Display button, you jump directly to the selected topic (Figure 5.51).

FIGURE 5.51
*The Related
Topics Button*

*If a help text window
contains a Related
Topics button, you
can click on it to bring
up a dialog box that
enables you to jump
directly to a related
help text entry.*

Insider's Tip

The Windows 95 help system enables live links to be created between applications and the Windows 95 operating system itself. Applications use this capability to differing degrees, but it allows for the development of much more helpful help files. For example, an application's help file could link directly to the Windows printing system and print a test page as part of teaching you how to print from within that application. Ultimately, developers will be able to create powerful Help files that not only tell you how to perform an operation but also bring up live tools within an application and step you through a tutorial using your own data. That way, finishing the tutorial also gets your job done. The help system can be an assistant to your work process rather than a separate program that shows you an example not necessarily related to your situation (Figure 5.52).

FIGURE 5.52
*Shortcuts in
Help Files*

*Windows 95 help files can include links,
or shortcuts, to parts of the Windows
95 interface or even an application
program. Clicking on one of the
shortcut icons—for example, copy—
can bring up the same function, copy,
in an application, jump-starting you
toward solving your problem.*

How to Search. Although browsing through the Contents tab of the Help dialog box is interesting if you know what you're looking for, there are faster ways to find information. Two other tabs in the Help dialog box, **Index** and **Find,** both enable you to perform keyword searches on an entire help file.

For example, using the Index tab, type a phrase—such as Print Preview—into the first field of the dialog box. The second field automatically sorts through all available help text items looking for a match. Windows 95 locates and highlights the help text item you were looking for by the time you've finished entering the phrase (unless you can type over 1,000 words per minute). Once you've located the item you were looking for, double-click on it to open its help text window (Figure 5.53).

FIGURE 5.53
*Searching for
Help Text*

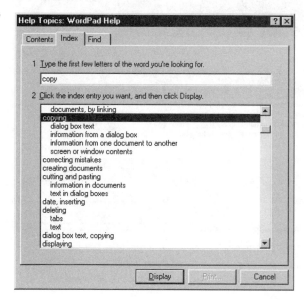

Use the Index tab to search for information on a word or a phrase. Type the phrase or term into the first field, and the second field automatically sorts through the entire help file to locate the appropriate help text.

Some subjects are covered by a help text entry but don't require a mention in the Contents or Index windows of the help file. To find those minimally mentioned subjects, use the full-text search engine provided by the Windows 95 help system. Click on the Find tab of the Help dialog box. If this is the first time you've used the Find tab, you see a separate dialog box indicating that Help needs to create a list of every word in the help file to aid in its search.

At this point Windows 95 can use one of two methods for creating the list. The Express technique creates a list of every word and phrase in the help file. This is the way you want to go, unless you're running out of hard disk space.

In that case choose the Custom option, which lets you identify—by means of another dialog box—those areas of help you want to have available for full-text searches. If you set up the basic commands this way, it consumes less of your system's free disk space (Figure 5.54).

• • • • • • • • • • • • • •
FIGURE 5.54
*Full-Text
Searches*

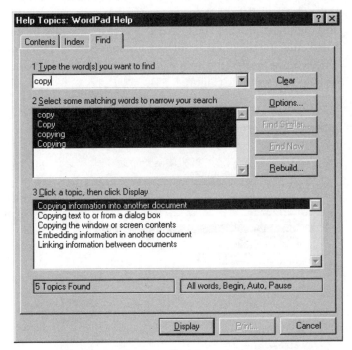

You can do a full-text search of any help file based on a keyword or phrase. Help creates a custom list of every word in the help file, using the dialog box shown here.

Pre-Windows 95 Help Files. Everything I've discussed so far about help files applies to Windows 95-compatible applications. Should you encounter a Windows 3.1-era help mechanism, expect to see a different look (Figure 5.55).

Although their interfaces vary, old-style help files operate similarly to Windows 95 help files. You see highlighted links in the text, and a Contents window for browsing the available help topics. Luckily, even old-style help files get a boost from Windows 95; if you bring up the Index or Find functions, Windows 95 uses the newer versions of the tools I described in the previous section.

• • • • • • • • • • • • • •
FIGURE 5.55
*Prehistoric
Help Files*

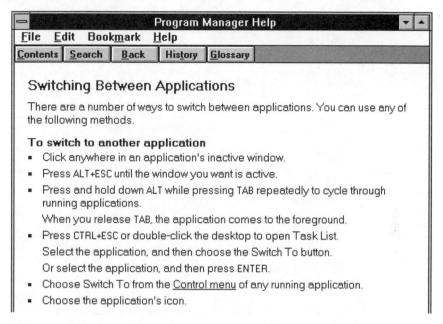

Older, pre-Windows 95 applications use a different on-line help system. Their help files look markedly different from those of Windows 95-era applications, but the way you interact with them is pretty much the same.

Summary

Everything about Windows 95 was planned to make it easy for the first-time user to adjust to computing in general. That's why miniature versions of real computer programs—for word processing, calculating, painting, and automated phone dialing—were included with Windows 95. All of those applets, as they are called, offer some benefit, although once you've gotten the hang of them, you'll realize their limitations as well. However, you may never get tired of the games Microsoft has included; Solitaire has become an addiction for millions of Windows users, and a few new games have been added to the pack. Finally, you'll find some new help features in this version of Windows, with the added benefit that they are available on line, exactly at the spot where you need help. You can also perform full-text searches for help with a particular word or phrase and design custom searches if you want to narrow your focus to a particular area. All in all, whether it's a game, a work program, or a help feature, there's something to suit every user and every mood.

6

Personalizing Windows 95

People like to customize. You pick out your own clothes, decorate your home according to your own tastes, and enjoy your right to add any amount of salt and pepper to your plate. At work you arrange your desk into your own personal chaos, placing critical elements— like the coffee mug—within easy reach. In life, your individuality shows through in everything from the colors you choose for your clothing to the order in which you organize your credit cards in your wallet.

Those fun-loving software engineers up at Microsoft made it possible for you to express your individuality by customizing the Windows 95 interface. You can, for example, change the color of your desktop from the default seaweed green to a more pleasant pastel, a shocking psychedelic, or even a graphic image (tip: you may not want to make it too graphic). You can also customize application windows by painting their elements different colors or by altering the fonts.

Although some customization options exist merely for pleasure, others have a more practical side. For example, you can modify the contents of the Windows 95 Start menu itself, placing items you use a lot within easy reach. Even the Taskbar's behavior can be customized. And in true Windows 95 fashion, you can make all those changes easily, by responding to the appropriate dialog box and moving objects with the ubiquitous drag and drop.

Designing Your Desktop

If you're like me, the first thing you'll do is run right out and substitute colors in the Windows 95 interface. Everybody's taste in colors is different, and virtually every visual element can be recolored to suit your personal taste, including the desktop, dialog boxes, and application window controls. Indeed, it almost seems as if Microsoft intentionally made the default background for Windows 95 an obnoxious shade of green to challenge users to come up with better color schemes on their own.

To change the colors of on-screen items, you use the Display Properties control panel. To view this panel, select Control Panels from the Start menu's Settings submenu, then double-click on the Display icon. You can also click with the right mouse button on any open area of the Windows 95 desktop, then select Properties from the pop-up menu. In either case, you're presented with the Display Properties control panel (Figure 6.1).

Like most control panels, the Display Properties panel presents its information in a tabbed dialog box. On each page a miniature computer screen shows you your changes before you actually apply them. Like a film director —or an omniscient digital artist—you can scroll through page after page of options, fine-tuning the image on the preview screen until you achieve the desired effect.

•••••••••••••

FIGURE 6.1

*The Display
Properties
Control Panel*

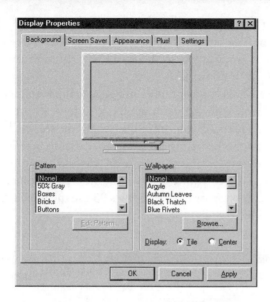

To change the appearance
of your Windows 95
environment, bring up
the Display Properties
control panel.

Background

The first page of the dialog box, Background, enables you to alter the surface
of your desktop by applying **wallpaper** or **patterns.** For example, if you select
Live Wire from the Pattern list box, Windows 95 adds a series of black, zigzag
lines over the current background color (Figure 6.2).

•••••••••••••

FIGURE 6.2

*The Live Wire
Pattern*

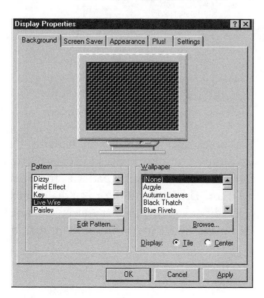

When you apply a
pattern, such as Live
Wire, shown here, Windows
95 adds the pattern's
custom specifications to
the currently selected
background color—
hence the zigzag effect
on this screen.

Similarly, if you select the Argyle wallpaper from the Wallpaper list box and click on the Tile button, Windows 95 covers your screen with an image reminiscent of a gaudy argyle sock. Yes, it's true: Beau Brummell is alive and well and living in Windows 95.

You can use virtually any graphic image as wallpaper, including anything you create yourself with the Paint applet. Windows 95 provides you with a number of wallpapers; if you don't like what you see, click on the Browse button. Up pops the Browsing for Wallpaper dialog box. You can navigate through the folders on your computer until you find a graphic design that you like (Figure 6.3). Once you've located the desired graphic, you can either center it on the desktop or have Windows 95 tile the image, filling the entire background with the design.

FIGURE 6.3

Browsing for Wallpaper

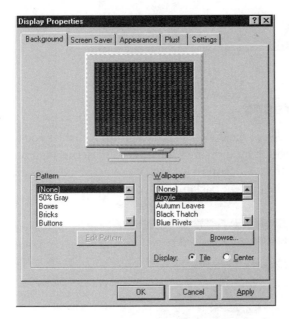

Use the Browsing for Wallpaper dialog box, which you reach by clicking on the Browse button, to select a custom graphic image for your wallpaper.

Windows 95 also provides a number of patterns for your selection. Although you can't import graphic images to act as patterns (as you can to act as wallpaper), you can alter existing patterns and even create new ones with the Pattern Editor. The Pattern Editor is a dialog box for creating and editing patterns. To edit an existing pattern, select its name from the Pattern list box and click on the Edit Pattern button. Up pops the Pattern Editor (Figure 6.4).

FIGURE 6.4
Editing a
Pattern

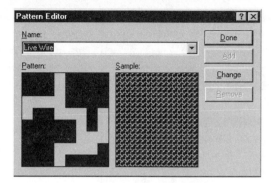

To edit an existing pattern,
first select its name from
the Pattern list box, then
click on the Edit Pattern
button to bring up the
Pattern Editor dialog box.

With the Pattern Editor, you can manipulate individual pixels in the Pattern field and preview your changes in the accompanying Sample field. Once you finish, click the Done button, and the Pattern Editor asks you if you want to save the changes. Click on Yes, and the pattern is updated. You can also save your creation as a completely new pattern by typing a new name into the Name field before clicking on the Done button.

Insider's Tip

In the Windows 95 world, wallpapers override patterns. For example, if you select the Autumn Leaves wallpaper and tile it, then select Thatches as a pattern, don't be surprised if all you see are Autumn Leaves. Because patterns are designed to work with only solid-color desktops, a pattern always takes a back seat when a graphic is in use.

Color Schemes

Wallpapers and patterns are only part of the picture. Click on the Appearance tab, and you see a dizzying array of colorization options. It's enough to make Ted Turner turn seaweed green with envy (Figure 6.5).

The first thing you notice is the Scheme list box. Windows 95 lets you either colorize each item separately or use predefined color **schemes** that alter more than one item simultaneously. Each sample scheme, like Desert or Lilac, is supposedly color-coordinated. If, like me, you find the combinations less than appealing, you can select the one that comes closest to being palatable, then customize its individual elements.

••••••••••••••
FIGURE 6.5
*The
Appearance
Page*

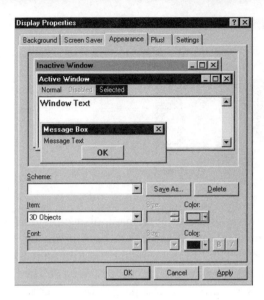

Ted Turner, watch out!
Colorization has finally
hit it big in Windows 95.
The Appearance page
provides a dizzying array
of colorization options,
which can be applied
either component-by-
component or in schemes.

For example, let's say you like the Rainy Day scheme but find the dark black background a bit depressing (no use getting suicidal—it's only Windows, after all). First select the Rainy Day combination using the Scheme list box, then select Desktop from the Item list box. Skip two spaces to the right of the Item list box to a list box called Color. Click on Color, and you're presented with a choice of 19 colors. Still not satisfied? Click on the Others button at the bottom of the list to bring up a custom color-selection dialog box. Here you can define the color of your dreams (Figure 6.6). You can perform this fine-tuning on virtually every visual element in the Windows 95 interface, from application window title bars to the background color of menu items (which is blue by default).

You can also alter the text used in specific areas of the interface; for example, you can alter icon titles. When you select a text element from the Item list box, additional list boxes become active. You can change point size, the color of some items, and other characteristics, such as boldfacing and italicizing (Figure 6.7).

Insider's Tip

Although the Appearance page previews your changes (in the form of simulated application windows and dialog boxes), it doesn't represent some items, like the text used in icon titles. To see changes to those items, either you can close the Display Properties dialog box by clicking on the OK button, or you can leave the dialog box open on the desktop and bring up the changes manually by clicking the Apply button. You can use the Apply button from all the Display Properties pages; indeed, this option is found in many other dialog boxes throughout Windows 95.

FIGURE 6.6
*Coloring Your
Desktop*

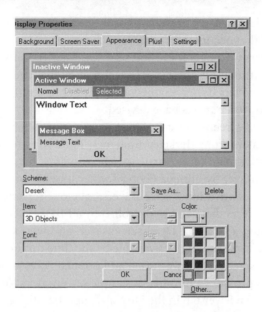

To change the color of an item, such as the desktop, first select the element in the Item list box, then click on the Color list box to choose from a number of possibilities. If you're really picky, you can define your own custom color.

FIGURE 6.7
Altering Text

When you select a text element for customization, additional list boxes become active, enabling you to change the color, the point size, and other characteristics of the text.

Screensavers

Screensavers are like stealth background designers—they take over what's on your screen when you're not at work. Basically, a screensaver is a specialty program that displays an animation sequence on your PC's screen when the computer is idle.

Originally designed to prevent phosphor etching and the subsequent "ghost images" that occur when an image stays on screen for a long period of time, screensavers no longer serve that purpose. That's because newer screens don't use the cathode-ray tube (CRT) technology that causes the problem. However, screensavers have remained a big hit because of the many creative animations that clever artists have devised.

Your choice of screensaver can reflect your personality, whether whimsical (Flying Toasters from Berkeley Systems), humorous (Opus and Bill of Bloom County/Outland fame), artistic (Microsoft's Scenes), or witty (build your own screensaver by filling a Flying Toaster module with flying quotes). You can also get motivational screensavers, religious screensavers, and psychedelic screensavers that can be controlled by a MIDI keyboard. A friend of mine is designing a Grateful Dead screensaver, and who knows, a classical composers screensaver might be available by the time this book is published. In other words, screensavers are varied and popular accessories.

Windows 95 provides a number of sample screensavers for your pleasure. Click on the Screen Saver tab in the Display Properties dialog box, and you're transported to screensaver central. Here you can also access Windows 95's screensaver controls (Figure 6.8).

FIGURE 6.8
*The Screen
Saver Page*

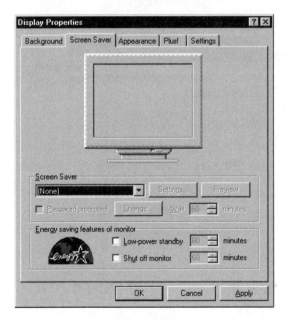

The Screen Saver page of the Display Properties dialog box enables you to control all aspects of Windows 95 screensaver operations.

The Screen Saver list box on the Screen Saver page offers a variety of sample screensavers, including the ever-popular Flying Windows. Select one of the samples, and a miniature computer screen comes to life with a preview of that screensaver in action (Figure 6.9).

FIGURE 6.9
*Screensaver
Trailers*

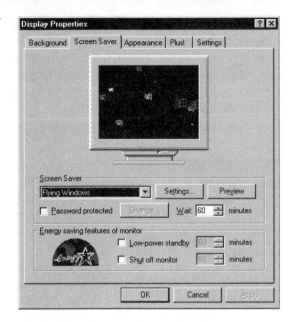

*Click on an entry in the
Screen Saver list box to
preview that screensaver.*

Want to see how the screensaver will really look on your screen? Click on the Preview button; your screen goes blank, then the animation takes over. To stop the preview, simply move the mouse or press any key on the keyboard. Indeed, to stop any screensaver—all of which monitor the mouse and the keyboard—just move the mouse or press a key. This indicates you are back at work, ready to earn that paycheck.

Another screensaver control is the Wait field, which lets you specify how long Windows 95 waits before bringing up the screensaver. If you set the value to ten minutes and don't touch your computer for that long, Windows 95 kicks in the screensaver.

Some screensavers have other controls as well. For example, with the Flying Windows screensaver, you can adjust the speed at which the windows fly across your screen, as well as the density of windows (Figure 6.10). Other screensavers include settings specific to their animation. To adjust the controls on a screensaver, select it, then click on the Settings button.

FIGURE 6.10
*Settings for a
Screensaver*

*To set the controls for a
screensaver, select it, then click
on the Settings button to bring
up the Configuration dialog box.*

If you're concerned about others snooping in your computer when you're away from your desk, you can use your screensaver as a lock. This makes it impossible for people to turn off the screensaver and see what's in your computer files unless they know your password or they shut down your system and reboot it before the screensaver can take over. To add or change a password, click on the Password Protected checkbox and then on the Change button. This brings up the Change Password dialog box (Figure 6.11).

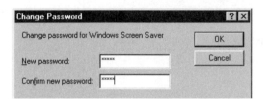

FIGURE 6.11

Adding a
Password

To add or change a password for a particular screensaver, first select the screensaver, then click on the Password Protected checkbox and the Change button.

Once you've entered and confirmed your new password, click on OK. Your password is now in effect. When you return to your PC and your screensaver is on, you are prompted with a dialog box and must reenter your password before the screensaver stops its animation sequence.

Finally, for the eco-conscious among us, Windows 95 supports the new Energy Star power-saving monitors. If you have this type of monitor, you can set up Windows 95 so that after a specific period of inactivity, the monitor goes into standby mode or shuts itself off.

Insider's Tip

Although you can use the Windows 95 Screen Saver page to control the settings of most screensavers, a few products, such as After Dark for Windows from Berkeley Systems, feature their own proprietary interfaces. We advise you to test-drive a commercial screensaver before you purchase it, to see how difficult it is to set up and change the controls.

Customizing the Taskbar

Continuing in the spirit of any-which-way-you-want, Microsoft has made sure you can customize the Windows 95 Taskbar. The Taskbar is something people tend to either love or hate. Some users will want to make the ultimate customization and get rid of the Taskbar altogether. Those who love it will want to make sure it's always available, and they'll rejoice that they can even adjust its appearance. For those who really want to tweak their Taskbar, options are available that let you control how items appear in the Start menu and whether part of the Taskbar turns into a tiny clock.

Here's how to exercise your options: Select Taskbar from the Start menu's Settings submenu (or click on the right mouse button over an unoccupied region of the Taskbar and select Properties from the pop-up menu). This opens the Taskbar Properties dialog box.

The first option you see, Always on Top, defines how the Taskbar interacts with application windows. If the checkbox is marked, the Taskbar remains visible above any open application window, even if they both occupy the same region of the desktop (Figure 6.12).

• • • • • • • • • • • • • •
FIGURE 6.12
*Taskbar and
Application
Windows*

If the Always on Top checkbox is marked, the Taskbar always remains visible, even when an application window occupies the same space on the Windows 95 desktop.

This setting also controls the way maximized application windows appear on your screen. If Always on Top is selected, maximized applications use the top edge of the Taskbar as the bottom boundary of their application windows (Figure 6.13).

If you disable the Always on Top feature by clicking on the checkbox to clear the mark, the Taskbar behaves like any other application window. If it's currently selected, it's on top; if another window is selected, the Taskbar takes second place and may be covered over (Figure 6.14). A maximized window sets its lower boundary at the very bottom of the screen, not at the top edge of the Taskbar.

••••••••••••
FFIGURE 6.13
*Taskbar and
Maximized
Windows*

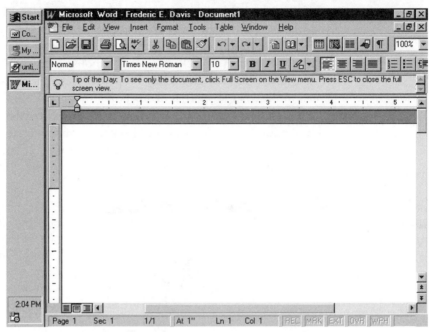

When Always on Top is selected, maximized
application windows use the top of the
Taskbar as their lower border.

••••••••••••
FIGURE 6.14
*Disabling the
Always on Top
Feature*

*If you disable the Always on
Top feature, the Taskbar
behaves like any other
application window.*

What if you can't decide whether you want the Taskbar on top all the time
or not? There's a compromise: you can choose Auto Hide, which keeps the
Taskbar hidden. You can make it reappear by moving the mouse pointer to

the bottom edge of the screen. This gives you the best of both worlds. You get to use all your desktop real estate for application windows, yet you can quickly access any of the Taskbar's riches simply by dragging the mouse to the bottom of the screen.

Insider's Tip

Normally you want to keep the Always on Top feature on because the Taskbar is such an integral part of the Windows 95 interface. If, however, you decide to disable the feature—for example, to increase the amount of window space for a maximized application—you can still view the Taskbar without having to minimize any windows. Press Ctrl+Esc on your keyboard, and the Taskbar pops up over whatever application is currently filling the screen.

Another Taskbar option, Show Small Icons, enables you to change the size of the icons that appear in the initial Start menu. When this option is disabled (the default setting), the Start menu displays large, easily identifiable icons for the first tier of entries. If you enable Show Small Icons, you get the smaller, less legible icons you see in the Start menu's nested submenus (Figure 6.15). If you don't have much screen real estate, especially if you own a laptop, this option may prove useful.

Finally, the Show Clock option enables you to control the notify area of the Taskbar. When this feature is enabled, a small digital clock is displayed showing the current time. To find out what the date is (in case you've been working too hard), position the mouse pointer over the clock.

••••••••••••
FIGURE 6.15
*Small Icons in
the Start Menu*

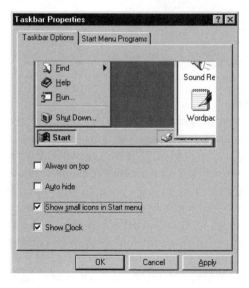

*Select the Show Small Icons
option to get smaller, less
legible icons in the first tier of
Start menu entries. This is
useful if you're working on a
notebook or another system
with a crowded screen.*

. . . .

Messing with the Start Menu

All things start with the Taskbar. So if you want to change the contents of the Start menu, go to the Taskbar's Properties dialog box, which includes a second page called Start Menu Programs.

To access the Start Menu Programs page, first bring up the Taskbar's Properties dialog box by selecting Taskbar from the Start menu's Settings submenu (or by clicking the right mouse button on the Taskbar and selecting Properties from the pop-up menu). Next click on the Start Menu Programs tab, which launches Start Menu Programs (Figure 6.16). Go to the section called Customize Start Menu. Here you see three buttons: Add, Remove, and Advanced.

· · · · · · · · · · · · · ·
FIGURE 6.16
*Messing with
the Start Menu*

To change the Start menu's contents, go to the Start Menu Programs page, which is part of the Taskbar's Properties dialog box.

Adding a Program. No doubt you'll want to add your own programs to the Taskbar. To add a new program to the Start menu, click on the Add button. A friendly Add Program **wizard** pops up. This wizard is like a tour guide; it shows you around a strange place. The first page of the wizard presents a diagram of the procedure you follow to add a new program to the Start menu. First you enter the pathname into the program's disk file (Figure 6.17).

If you don't know the pathname, click on the Browse button to bring up the standard Windows 95 Browse dialog box (Figure 6.18). Use the navigational buttons to move through the folders on your computer until you find the program's disk file.

Once you find the program, highlight it with the mouse pointer and click on Open. You're returned to page one of the Add Program wizard with the pathname automatically inserted into the Command Line field.

FIGURE 6.17
*Adding a
Program*

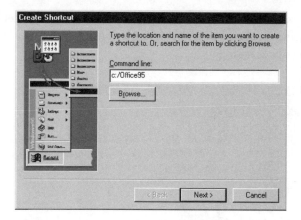

The first page of the
Add Program wizard
asks you to type in
the pathname to the
program's disk file.

FIGURE 6.18
*Browsing for a
Program*

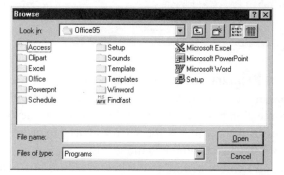

If you click on the
Browse button, you
can use the Windows
95 Browse dialog box
to navigate your
system's folder
structure until you
find a particular
program.

Now click on the Next button to move to Select Program Folder, which is page two of the wizard. You see a list of folders that looks somewhat like the tree pattern in the submenu of the Start menu. You can deposit your newly created shortcut into any of these folders by clicking on one of them, or you can create a new folder by clicking on the New Folder button.

Your new folder will be located in the currently selected folder. For example, if the Programs folder (the equivalent of the Programs submenu of the Start menu) is highlighted, clicking New Folder creates a folder within the Programs folder (and thus a new submenu under Programs), which you can rename (Figure 6.19).

After you either select or create a folder, click on the Next button to bring up a page called Select a Title for the Program. Here you get to create a name. For example, if you just added a shortcut for accessing WordPad, you could enter the title WordPad. If you want something more descriptive, however, feel free to indulge yourself and enter something like Big, Bad Text Editor. Freedom only relates to Windows programs—you can't choose your own name or icon for a DOS program.

Finally, clicking the Finish button closes the wizard and returns you to the Start Menu Programs page. Congratulations! You've just added a new program to your Start menu.

••••••••••••••
FIGURE 6.19
*Creating a
New Folder*

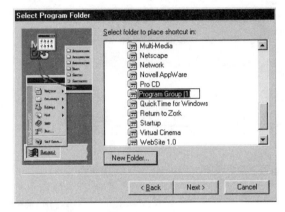

To create a new folder inside the currently selected folder, click on the New Folder button. You can rename the new folder, and it appears as a submenu under the Start menu.

Removing a Program. Of course, what is built must occasionally be torn down. Programs, once installed, tend to fall out of favor with their users. New versions come along; old versions are reinstalled into new locations. Whatever the reason, the time may come when you need to prune your Start menu, and this is when you'll need the Remove button.

Clicking on Remove brings up the Remove Shortcuts/Folders dialog box, which you can use to selectively exterminate existing Start menu entries. For example, to remove the entry for the Explorer (which is part of the Programs folder by default), highlight the entry in the provided tree view and click on the Remove button (Figure 6.20). A dialog box asks you to confirm the deletion operation; if you click on Yes, the selected shortcut or folder is removed.

••••••••••••••
FIGURE 6.20
*Removing a
Start Menu
Entry*

To remove a Start menu entry, first highlight the entry in the tree view, then click on the Remove button.

You can remove as many folders and shortcuts as you like from within this dialog box. Once you finish pruning, click on the Close button to return to the Start Menu Programs dialog box.

Danger Zone

Take care when pruning your Start menu entries. Although Windows 95 protects itself by letting you modify only entries that are part of the Programs submenu (you can't, for example, remove the Find or Help items), you can still do a lot of damage if you prune the wrong entry. You wouldn't want to have to recreate the entire contents of the Accessories submenu because of an errant mouse click.

The Advanced Button. Good things come to those who wait. If you successfully waded through the preceding material, you're in luck: there is a better way. Clicking on the Advanced button on the Start Menu Programs page brings up an Explorer view of the entire Start menu folder hierarchy (Figure 6.21).

FIGURE 6.21

Exploring the Start Menu

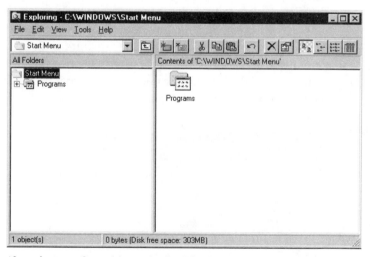

If you're comfortable with the Windows 95 Explorer, you can use this powerful tool to manipulate the Start menu's contents. Simply click on the Advanced button.

The panel on the left side of the window displays a tree view of the entire Start menu structure. On the right you see the entries in each submenu. Only the Programs submenu is displayed, but a simple click of the mouse on the Programs plus sign reveals all the other nested submenus (Figure 6.22).

FIGURE 6.22
*Revealing the
Submenus*

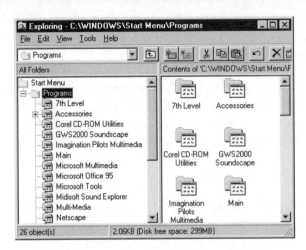

By default you
can see only
the Programs
submenu. Clicking
on the Programs
plus sign, however,
reveals all the
nested submenus
in the Start menu.

This Explorer view gives you the power to recreate your computer world.
In other words, you can directly control other folder and Explorer views. This
capability makes it easy to add a new program to a particular submenu.

For example, to add a new program to the Multimedia submenu, open the
folder view that contains the program, then click on the Advanced button to
bring up the Explorer view of the Start menu's contents. Expand the Start
menu Explorer view tree until you see the Multimedia folder, then highlight
it. Finally, drag the icon for the new program from its folder view and drop it
into the Multimedia folder (Figure 6.23).

FIGURE 6.23
*Adding a
Program with
Drag and Drop*

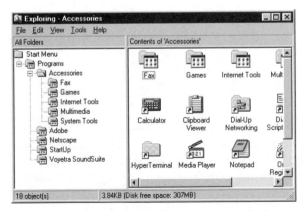

To add a program to the Start menu with drag and
drop, get to the Explorer view of the Start menu by
clicking on the Advanced button. Then drag the
program from its folder view and drop it into a folder
located on the Explorer view of the Start menu.

You've just created a shortcut to the new program by adding it to the Multimedia folder. Now when you close the Explorer view and click on OK on the Start Menu Programs page, a new menu entry for the program is added to the Start menu's Multimedia submenu.

Insider's Tip

You can also use drag and drop to add shortcuts to the top level of the Start menu itself. Just drop the icon for the program directly onto the Start button. A Shortcut to the program is added at the top of the Start menu.

Multiple Users

You can customize your Windows desktop to your heart's delight. But what if you share your computer with other people, people whose taste in wallpaper runs to argyle when you'd prefer Snoopy on a surfboard?

Microsoft has provided a solution to the problem of several people sharing the same computer: multiple desktops. This concept is based on user profiles and passwords and makes it easy to share a PC among several users. Each person who uses the system keeps his or her own, private settings for elements such as desktop wallpaper and color schemes, icon positions, and even network connections. Those settings are stored as part of a user's profile and start up when that user enters his or her password.

When you boot up a multiple-desktop system, a Logon dialog box asks you to enter your name and password (Figure 6.24). Windows 95 uses this information to identify which user profile it should load.

FIGURE 6.24

*The Logon
Dialog Box*

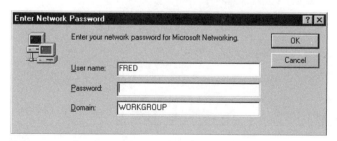

When a multiple-desktop Windows 95 system is first booted, it presents a Logon dialog box. The information you enter here—specifically, your name and password—determines which desktop gets loaded.

For example, if the name entered is Groucho, then Groucho's profile gets loaded, and the desktop is configured accordingly. If the name entered is Harpo, then Harpo's desktop gets loaded. Changes made to the desktop by one user are restricted to that particular user's profile; other desktops are unaffected. That way individuals can customize their working environments without stepping on each other's toes.

How to Set It Up

To set up a computer to run with multiple desktops, open the Control Panel folder on the Start menu's Settings submenu, then double-click on the Passwords icon to open the Passwords Properties control panel. Next, click on the User Profiles tab to forward to that page of the dialog box.

To set up multiple user profiles, click on the Users Can Customize radio button (Figure 6.25). A radio button, when selected, deactivates all the other radio buttons available. You'll notice that two other fields, Include Desktop Icons and Include Start Menu, become active.

FIGURE 6.25
*A Multitude
of Desktops*

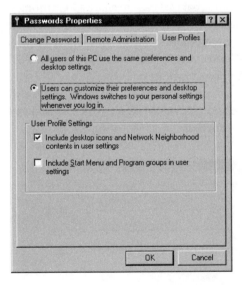

To start up a multiple-desktop operation, click the Users Can Customize radio button on the User Profiles page of the Passwords Properties control panel.

Include Desktop Icons tells Windows 95 whether to save the overall desktop arrangement—that is, icon spacing, colors, and any network connections —as part of each user profile. Include Start Menu tells Windows 95 whether subsequent changes to the Start menu affect all the desktops or only one.

When you're through defining the user profiles, click on the OK button to save the changes. A dialog box tells you you need to restart the PC before the changes take effect. Click on Yes, and the PC is rebooted automatically.

Working with User Profiles

When your PC reboots for the first time after you set up multiple desktops, you're prompted with your first Logon dialog box. Unless you were previously connected to a network, both the user name and password fields are blank. To create a new profile, simply type in a name—for example, your first name or an abbreviation of your first and last names—and a password.

If this is the first time you've logged onto the PC since setting up multiple desktops, Windows 95 asks you to confirm your password. Simply retype it and press Enter. The next thing you see is the Windows 95 desktop. Congratulations! You've created a user profile.

Insider's Tip

In reality, the password is optional. If you don't want to use one, press Enter and then Enter again when Windows asks you to confirm the password. This can speed the log-on process. Also, if you tend to forget passwords (I even lost one Internet account because I couldn't remember my password), it might be a good idea just to keep an open computer.

Now go ahead and rearrange the desktop to your heart's content. Change colors, move icons, even rename a few things. Next, select Shutdown from the Start menu, but instead of shutting down or restarting, select Logon as a Different User (Figure 6.26).

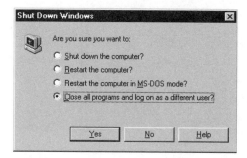

FIGURE 6.26

Log Off to Log On as a Different Personality

To switch user profiles, select the Logon as a Different User option from the Shut Down Windows dialog box.

Suddenly you're right back where you started: at the Logon prompt. Now try entering a different user name and password to log on as that user. Again you're asked to verify the password, but this time when the desktop loads, none of your changes—the ones you made when operating under the other user profile—are visible. Where'd they go?

Don't panic—this is a feature, not a bug. Windows 95 has stored your settings as part of your user profile. It then loaded a default profile for the new user you just created. Your days of multiuser desktop anguish are finally over.

Insider's Tip | The default profile for each user is based on how your system is set up before you create multiple desktops. So if you want to change any aspect of the desktop for all users—for example, if you want to set up a network connection—do it before launching the multiple-desktop option. Then when each user creates a new account, that person will have the options you've included as part of the default desktop.

Date and Time

Setting up your system's date and time is fun. That's because Microsoft designed a slick front end just for this otherwise mundane task. The Date/Time Properties control panel provides useful tools for telling time and even for planning ahead on the calendar (Figure 6.27). To bring up the control panel, select Control Panel from the Start menu's Settings submenu, then double-click on the Date/Time icon.

FIGURE 6.27
The Date/Time Properties Control Panel

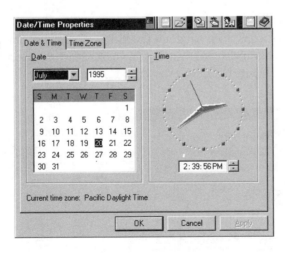

To set the system's date and time, use the Date/Time Properties control panel, located in the Control Panel folder.

A miniature calendar with manual month and year fields can be used to set the current date. If you're curious, you can examine future calendars well into the next century; simply change the year and month fields to see the desired calendar.

A large analog clock shows the current system time in minutes and seconds. To set the time, edit the field directly below the analog clock, either by typing a new entry or by selecting a region of the field and clicking on the plus and minus buttons.

Insider's Tip

You can also use the Taskbar to get to the Date/Time Properties control panel. Double-click on the digital clock at the right end of the bar.

The second page of the Date/Time Properties control panel enables you to specify your time zone. Select the zone from the drop-down list box, or easier still, click on your part of the world on the accompanying map (Figure 6.28).

FIGURE 6.28
*Setting the
Time Zone*

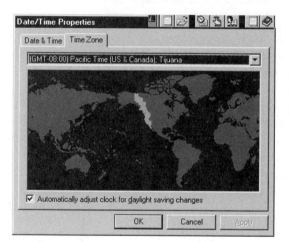

*To change your
time zone, either
select it from the
drop-down list box,
or click on your
part of the world.*

Regional Settings

If you're a transcontinental Windows user—or if you just have a pen pal in another country—check out the Regional Settings options. The Regional Settings Properties control panel enables you to localize your system to a particular country's currency and measurement standards.

The first page of the dialog box, titled Regional Settings, provides a template for settings that vary based on geographic location. Like the time zone tool mentioned previously, the Regional Settings page contains both a list box and a map of the world (Figure 6.29). Either select your location from the list or click on the appropriate map location.

FIGURE 6.29

*Regional
Settings*

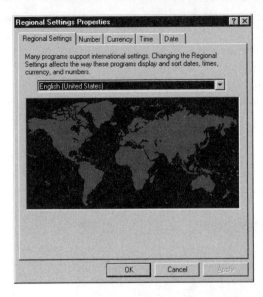

To apply a template
to settings related
to currency and
measurements, select
your country on the
Regional Settings page.

On the Number page you can specify everything from the placement of decimal points to a choice of measuring system, English or metric (Figure 6.30). Use the Currency page to choose a currency symbol—for example, a dollar or a pound sign—as well as more esoteric functions such as how many numbers comprise a digit group (Figure 6.31). Finally, the Time and Date pages enable you to define formats for numerical entries. For example, you can choose a date separator (normally a forward slash) and can specify your preferred style for *a.m.* and *p.m.*

FIGURE 6.30

*The Number
Page*

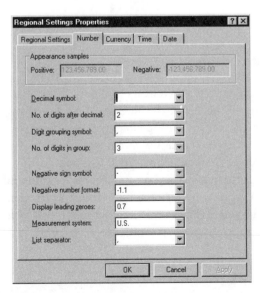

On the Number page,
you can set up the way
numerical values are
displayed.

••••••••••••
FIGURE 6.31
*The Currency
Page*

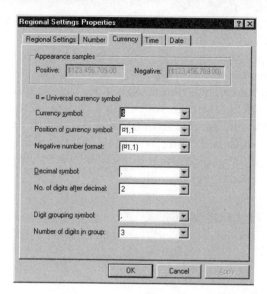

The Currency page enables
you to customize how
Windows 95 displays
currency values.

Regional Settings Properties

Regional Settings | Number | Currency | Time | Date

Appearance samples

Positive: $123,456,789.00   Negative: ($123,456,789.00)

¤ = Universal currency symbol

Currency symbol: $

Position of currency symbol: ¤1.1

Negative number format: (¤1.1)

Decimal symbol: .

No. of digits after decimal: 2

Digit grouping symbol: ,

Number of digits in group: 3

OK   Cancel   Apply

Accessibility Options

**Upgrade
Alert**

Not everyone finds Windows easy to use. This is especially true for the physically challenged. Whether it's a hearing impairment, a visual impairment, or
simply a dislike for jumpy mice, navigating a complex graphical interface like
Windows 95's can be a chore. To make life easier for anyone with a physical
challenge, Windows 95 includes Accessibility Options that change the system's
behavior. Even it you don't consider yourself specially challenged, check out
these options; you may find something useful. Everyone's challenged in some
way. The Accessibility Options control panel, which is in the Control Panel
folder, can be accessed by selecting Control Panel from the Start menu's Settings submenu, then double-clicking on the Accessibility Options icon.

Keyboard

The first page of the Accessibility Properties dialog box enables you to change
your keyboard setup (Figure 6.32). Here you can redefine the way Windows
95 interprets keyboard commands.

For example, the StickyKeys option enables you to enter multiple-key combinations—such as Alt+Enter—by pressing one key at a time. Similarly, the
FilterKeys option tells Windows 95 to ignore accidentally repeated characters

and brief keystrokes and to slow the keyboard repeat rate so that data can be entered less rapidly. Finally, the ToggleKeys option instructs Windows 95 to play audible tones when specific keys (for example, Caps Lock, Num Lock, and Scroll Lock) are pressed.

In addition, you can fine-tune those options with a Settings button, available in each section of the page. For example, click the Settings button in the StickyKeys section to launch a second dialog box, which you can use to further adjust your keyboard controls (Figure 6.33). As a nice touch, a checkbox at the bottom of the page instructs other Windows 95 programs to run any keyboard help features they might have.

FIGURE 6.32

The Keyboard Page

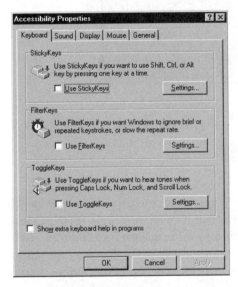

Redefine keyboard actions using the Keyboard page.

FIGURE 6.33

Fine-Tuning StickyKeys

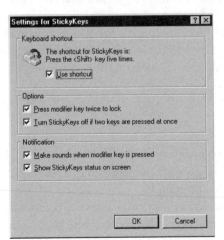

You can further adjust each keyboard option by clicking on the Settings button in whichever section you want to change.

Sound

If your hearing's off, but your sight is fine, the Sound features can help. An option on the Sound page provides visual cues whenever a specific sound occurs. The SoundSentry option produces a psychedelic light show, flashing the title bar or the border of an application window when a sound is generated (Figure 6.34). Windows 95 can flash a visual warning even when a full-screen DOS program is running. Another option, ShowSounds, instructs applications running under Windows 95 to provide caption text whenever they generate speech or other sounds.

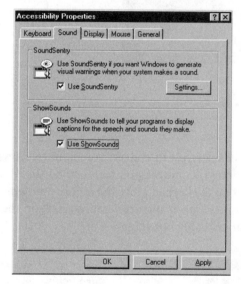

SoundSentry tells Windows 95 to provide visual cues when specific sounds occur.

Display

The Display tab of the Accessibility Properties dialog box enables you to set up a high-contrast color scheme, making the interface more legible. You can use either the default high-contrast scheme or a custom scheme that you define by clicking on the Settings button (Figure 6.35).

FIGURE 6.35
*High-Contrast
Color*

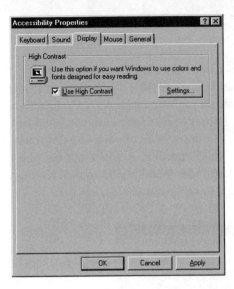

*On the Display page you can
set up Windows 95 to use a
high-contrast color scheme.*

Mouse

The Mouse page enables you to convert your numeric keypad into a controller for the Windows 95 mouse pointer. Turn on the MouseKeys feature, and the arrow keys on the keypad move the mouse pointer. To adjust characteristics such as pointer speed and acceleration, click on the Settings button to bring up a separate dialog box (Figure 6.36).

FIGURE 6.36
MouseKeys

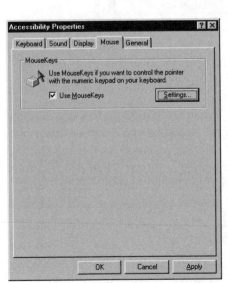

*The MouseKeys feature can
turn your numeric keypad
into a virtual mouse.*

General

Almost nothing has been left out of this panoply of accessibility features. The General page enables you to define several global controls. For example, Automatic Reset limits chosen accessibility options to the current Windows 95 session and automatically disables them after a certain amount of idle time (Figure 6.37). You can also set up audio or video alerts to let you know when certain features become active. And a SerialKey interface gives your computer access to alternative input devices through a serial port.

FIGURE 6.37
*The General
Page*

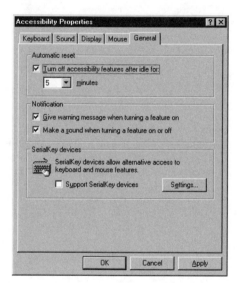

*Define global controls—
such as automatic disabling
of accessibility features—
on the General page.*

Summary

Windows 95 gives you a variety of options for dressing up your desktop to match your every mood. Some controls are even useful, providing you with shortcuts to frequently used programs and functions. For the first time, people who share a computer can customize their own desktops, designing their own backgrounds, adding wallpaper, choosing their own screensavers, and rearranging the Taskbar and other controls. Finally, Microsoft has added features for those who are specially challenged—and for anyone who finds the features handy.

7

Of Displays, Mice, and Keyboards

Computers used to be faceless, and to communicate with them you had to punch cards with binary instructions, then enter the cards through a slot in the hard drive. The Windows 95 graphical user interface puts a face on your computer. That, along with a mouse or other pointing device and a keyboard, enables you to have direct two-way communication with your computer.

This chapter presents an overview of the Windows 95 display system, including display cards, monitors, and Windows-compatible display driver software. I also cover pointing devices, predominantly mice but also trackballs, styluses, and pens. And I discuss the venerable keyboard, which has survived relatively unchanged since the invention of the mechanical typewriter in the last century.

Display Systems

A good display system shows off the Windows 95 environment and Windows applications to their best advantage. Your display system includes three components: the **monitor,** the **display card,** and the **display driver.** The display driver enables Windows to exploit the capabilities of the display card. The display card—also called the *adapter card* or the *video card*—affects the quality of your display more than the monitor itself does, because the display card controls resolution, number of colors, and amount of visible flicker. The monitor must be compatible with the display card, since output signals from the latter vary.

**Upgrade
Alert**

Not only does Windows 95 sport an improved graphics engine, it also includes a universal display driver that handles generic display tasks. This means that display manufacturers no longer need to provide complete drivers. All they need to include are minidrivers that inform Windows 95 about the capabilities of their display devices.

As a result you see better performance (because the universal driver speaks the same 32-bit language as does Windows 95), and manufacturers can write minidrivers that capitalize on the features of their display cards. (With previous versions of Windows, each manufacturer had to keep current both the generic display commands and the hardware-specific instructions for a driver. Without a universal driver, conflicts were more likely to occur among the drivers on your system.)

Windows 95 includes a slew of new minidrivers for displays that existed when Windows 95 was shipped. If your display is included, Windows automatically replaces your older driver with a new minidriver. If your display isn't included, Windows 95 loads and runs the 3.1 driver. However, for the best performance, contact the manufacturer of your display for an updated driver. If you have access to the Internet, a major on-line service, or a bulletin board service (BBS), you can probably find a forum hosted by the manufacturer of your display.

All Windows drivers that provide resolutions of at least 640 by 480 pixels can display either large or small fonts to accommodate monitors of varying sizes. Using larger fonts improves the legibility of text, whereas smaller fonts minimize the amount of room required by windows and menus on the desktop.

Because Windows 95 incorporates DOS, you don't need DOS display drivers—another improvement over earlier versions of Windows. The Windows 95 universal driver enables you to run DOS graphics programs in a window, display colors more accurately, and select fonts of different sizes for DOS windows.

Insider's Tip

If you play games on your computer, you have good reason to get excited about Windows 95. Microsoft worked closely with hardware vendors such as ATI Technologies to establish a new standard that accelerates the speed and increases the quality of games. The results of this collaboration are published in the Windows 95 Game Software Development Kit, which enables software developers to create accelerated versions of their games.

It's a two-part process, however. You also need a graphics accelerator card incorporating the proper hardware acceleration element. ATI's Graphics Xpression, WinTurbo, and Graphic Pro Turbo cards are examples of appropriate choices; all use the Mach 64 graphics accelerator chip. Those cards provide built-in support of the DirectDraw driver.

The net result? With Windows 95 games and the correct hardware, you see up to four times more detail than you see with typical DOS games run under Windows 3.1. The action is faster and the experience more like a high-end arcade game.

• •

Display Standards

Microsoft has done its best to accommodate all the major display standards in the IBM PC universe. The Windows 95 installation disks provide a wide variety of display drivers that support all but a few outdated display card standards. No driver is included, for example, for the old **CGA (Color/Graphics Adapter)** display, which can still be found on older systems, especially laptops and portables. However, you can use your CGA display with Windows 95 if you obtain a CGA display driver from the Windows Driver Library, available from Microsoft on disk, through the company's on-line support system, or on most commercial on-line services.

In the early 1980s Hercules developed its own monochrome display card to challenge IBM's display cards. The original **Hercules monochrome adapter** displayed high-quality text, as well as high-resolution monochrome graphics, so it garnered the support of most leading developers, as well as users of desktop publishing and Computer Aided Design (CAD) applications.

By the mid-1980s the IBM **Enhanced Graphics Adapter** (**EGA**) emerged as the most popular display card for the IBM PC. The standard EGA configuration included a puny 64K of display memory, which allowed only a four-color display. The display card could, however, accept up to 256K, which allowed a 16-color display at a resolution of 640 by 350 pixels. Because EGA uses rectangular pixels, and Windows 95 was designed for the square pixels of VGA (described next), Windows distorts images on EGA displays. Although most people now buy the higher-resolution VGA displays, EGA displays are still common on older systems, including 286s and even a few 386s.

The now-standard **Video Graphics Array** (**VGA**) display card emerged with the introduction of the IBM PS/2 in 1987. Unlike the earlier CGA and EGA displays, which use digital signaling techniques to control the number of colors on a monitor, VGA monitors employ analog signaling, so they can potentially display millions of colors. Most older and some current but inexpensive VGA display cards, because of data-bit limitations, manage only a fraction of this potential; they display either 16 or 256 colors. VGA cards capable of displaying 32,000 colors (called *high color*) or over 16 million colors (called *true color*) are becoming increasingly common, and many new computers come equipped with them.

Pixel resolution measures the number of spots of light on a monitor. A resolution of 640 by 480 pixels on a VGA display indicates that each line contains 640 pixels—or picture elements—and that the monitor displays 480 lines of pixels.

Color-depth resolution refers to the number of bits of color information that each pixel can display. In a 4-bit-per-pixel system, only 16 colors can be displayed simultaneously on the screen. The reason is that each bit is a binary number—that is, it can be either 0 or 1—so 4 bits yields 16 possible combinations. Similarly, 8 bits per pixel can yield 256 colors, 16 bits per pixel can yield more than 64,000 colors, and 24 bits per pixel can yield more than 16 million colors.

VGA's **standard resolution** is 640 by 480 pixels—about 30 percent higher than the resolution of a standard television set. However, a TV image often looks more realistic than the graphics on a VGA computer display, because TVs have better color-depth resolution.

Insider's Tip

To achieve a color image as realistic as a photograph, you need to use a 24-bit display, which devotes 8 bits each to the three primary colors of light—red, green, and blue. However, by optimizing a computer's color palette, you can display images on a 16-bit display with only a slight loss of color quality. Some photo-realistic images can even be squeezed onto a 256-color palette; however, the loss of color resolution results in fair quality and a less than realistic image.

The **amount of memory on a display card** affects both the pixel resolution and the number of colors that can be displayed. The display card must contain enough memory to address all the pixels on the display multiplied by the number of bits of color resolution per pixel. Thus, on a 640-by-480 pixel display, an 8-bit-per-pixel VGA card requires twice as much memory as does a 4-bit-per-pixel VGA card, and a 24-bit card requires at least three times the memory of an 8-bit card.

You can often install additional memory on display cards to produce higher resolutions, more colors, or faster screen redrawing. Most adapters require **video RAM chips**—also called **VRAM chips**—which are not the same kind of RAM you use to expand the memory of your computer system. VRAM chips run at higher speeds and are considerably more expensive than standard computer RAM. Some cards allow you to expand memory using standard RAM chips; however, performance is sometimes impaired by this trade-off.

To display resolutions higher than 640 by 480 pixels, a monitor must be able to accommodate the required **horizontal scan frequency.** To display the 800 by 600 resolution of a SuperVGA card, for example, a monitor must support at least a 35 kHz horizontal scan rate; to display a 1,024-by-768 resolution, the monitor needs to support at least a 49 kHz horizontal scan rate. Some display cards offer a range of scan rates; for example, SuperVGA is offered with horizontal scan rates ranging from 35 to 48 kHz. As a rule of thumb, the higher the horizontal scan rate, the better the quality of the display and the greater the stability of the image.

As a general guideline here are the scan rates that work best with the following resolutions:

➠ **640 by 480**. Works best with a scan rate of 31.5 kHz.

➠ **800 by 600**. Works best with a scan rate of 35 to 48 kHz.

➠ **1,024 by 768**. Works best with a scan rate of 48 to 72 kHz.

Don't confuse the horizontal scan frequency with the **vertical scan frequency**—also called the refresh rate—which is the rate at which a monitor redraws the screen image. This measure reflects the amount of flicker on a monitor. The standard vertical scan frequency is 60 Hz, which means the screen is redrawn 60 times per second. Newer display cards support higher vertical scan rates, typically 72 Hz, the standard in Europe. High-end cards support up to 200 Hz. The higher vertical scan rates reduce flicker and create a more stable image, creating a higher-quality display and helping prevent eyestrain and fatigue.

Table 7.1 summarizes the characteristics of the major PC display standards that are supported by drivers shipped with Windows 95.

TABLE 7.1

Technical Specifications for PC Display Standards

Display Standard	Pixel Resolution	Color Resolution	Number of Colors	Minimum Video RAM Required	Horizontal Scan Frequency (in kHz)
VGA	640 by 480	4-bit	16	256K	31.5
SuperVGA	800 by 600	4-bit	16	256K	35 to 48
SuperVGA	800 by 600	8-bit	256	512K	35 to 48
XGA	640 by 480	4-bit	16	512K	31.5 to 35.5
XGA	640 by 480	8-bit	256	512K	31.5 to 35.5
XGA/2	1,024 by 768	8-bit	256	1MB	48 to 69

Many of the display standards offer resolutions other than the ones listed in Table 7.1. For example, a standard VGA card can run in more than a dozen modes. Sometimes a display card or a specific combination of settings isn't supported by the drivers supplied with Windows 95. In this case contact the display card vendor for an updated driver. Some drivers also contain bugs that affect only certain applications. If you encounter unexplained problems with particular applications, make sure you have the most recent version of the appropriate display driver. Display card vendors typically distribute updated drivers in their forums on commercial on-line services, such as CompuServe and America Online, as well as on their own electronic bulletin boards.

Expanding the Desktop

Running Windows at a higher resolution enables you to work with a larger desktop. A resolution of 800 by 600 pixels—the standard for SuperVGA—increases the area of your desktop by more than 50 percent over its size with VGA's standard resolution of 640 by 480 pixels (Figure 7.1).

FIGURE 7.1

*Comparison of
SuperVGA and
VGA Displays*

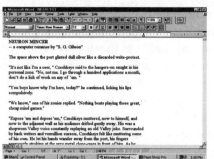

*You see considerably more detail on a SuperVGA
display of 800 by 600 pixels than on a standard
VGA screen with a resolution of 640 by 480 pixels.*

Increasing your screen resolution to 800 by 600 pixels provides additional room to display windows, icons, and other on-screen paraphernalia. With either a VGA or a SuperVGA display, Windows uses 96 pixels to display each inch of a document. Thus, on a SuperVGA display of 800 by 600, you can view almost the entire width of an 8½- by 11-inch page (800 divided by 96 is almost 8½).

As you move to a higher resolution at the same screen size, the images in your Windows display appear to shrink. On a small monitor, this shrinking can make menus, window titles, dialog boxes, and other interface components difficult to read. To compensate, you can select the Large Fonts option from the Settings tab on the Display Control Panel. A better alternative, however, is to increase the size of your monitor if you go to resolutions above 640 by 480. I recommend at least a 15-inch display for a SuperVGA at a resolution of 800 by 600; this keeps the size of the images equivalent to those on a normal VGA monitor. For a resolution of 1,024 by 768, a 17-inch or larger display is appropriate.

Insider's Tip

Monitors are measured diagonally, so increasing the size by just a couple inches adds a significant amount of area to a display. For example, stepping up to a 15-inch monitor from a 14-inch one increases the display area by around 20 percent; going from 14 to 17 inches adds 50 percent more space.

Admittedly, large displays sell for a premium price, though prices are coming down as larger monitors become the norm. Moreover, large monitors can be worth the investment, especially for desktop publishing and graphics applications. Keep in mind, though, that increasing either the pixel or the color-depth resolution of your display can hamper performance. Usually, adding colors cuts into performance more than increasing the pixel resolution, but this varies with the design of the display card.

Depending on your display card, going beyond 256 colors can substantially cut into performance. For example, a 1,024 by 768 display card capable of 16-color display runs only slightly more slowly than a standard VGA card. However, if you go beyond 256 colors—even at a resolution of 640 by 480—you can slow down your display noticeably. If you need high resolution and many colors, I recommend investing in a more advanced display card.

Graphics accelerator cards are a kind of display card that speed up graphics by providing their own video processing power. Not that long ago 32-bit models were the high end of graphics accelerator cards. Number Nine introduced the first 64-bit card, and other vendors followed suit. What do you get for your 64 bits—zillions instead of millions of colors? No, you get greater color depth at higher resolutions: 16 million colors at up to 1,600 by 1,200 dpi. You also get faster performance; the card processes 64 bits of graphics data at one time instead of 32 bits, speeding graphics drawing and the vertical scan frequency simultaneously.

You might be interested in the 64-bit cards if your work (or play) includes 3-D rendering; some cards, such as Matrox's MGA Impression Plus, offer real-time 3-D acceleration. These cards offer video capture, editing, and playback at sizes of up to full-screen and speeds of up to 30 frames per second (which is the speed at which a conventional movie plays). Number Nine has also recently introduced the first 128-bit card, the Imagine 128, once again raising the bar for video acceleration.

Danger Zone

Beware of **interlaced displays,** which can be found in monitors with resolutions of 640 by 480 or greater, especially in older models. With an interlaced display, the video gun of the monitor's video tube creates an image by writing every other line on the screen, then returning to the top of the screen to fill in the empty lines; in effect, it interlaces the empty and the written lines. Thus an interlaced 1,024 by 768 display system is really a 1,024 by 384 display that scans the face of the video tube twice. This double passage causes a noticeable flicker, which varies depending on how quickly your eyes react to images, how close you are to the screen, and whether fluorescent lighting is present (such lighting produces its own flicker, which can accentuate the screen flicker).

The flicker can be so pronounced that it causes eyestrain and headaches. Typically companies that sell interlaced displays recommend using longer-persistence phosphor in the monitors (phosphors are what cause a screen image to appear). However, the longer-persistence phosphors introduce yet another problem: they make the screen appear dim and can even leave ghostlike trails of former images when you move a window, an icon, or another object. Fortunately, most new monitors are noninterlaced, so you shouldn't have much of a problem if you buy new equipment.

If you are in the market for a display with a high screen resolution, obtain a **noninterlaced display,** which is easier on the eyes than an interlaced display. You need the following three components:

➤ A display card capable of generating a video signal that produces a noninterlaced display.

➤ A monitor that can display noninterlaced video and that has a high enough vertical scan frequency to work with the display card.

➤ A software configuration for the display card that works with noninterlaced video.

If both your display card and your monitor support noninterlaced video but are older, you may need to adjust jumpers or DIP switches on the card or even set a switch on the monitor to obtain noninterlaced video. If your card and your monitor are mismatched, you may experience flicker, distortion of images, or a short, fat display that takes up only part of the screen.

Insider's Tip

You can use a special software trick to create several virtual desktops, in effect increasing the desktop real estate available for your display. The technique works by letting you set up several desktops, complete with document icons and shortcuts to applications and folders, and then quickly switch between them. A smart way to use this feature would be to organize desktops with by project or by the type of work—personal documents on one desktop, for example, business documents on another, and games on a third.

Several commercial utilities provide this feature, incuding Norton Navigator and Dashboard 95.

Figure 7.2 shows an example of Norton Navigator's virtual desktops for your Windows display.

● ● ● ● ● ● ● ● ● ● ● ● ●
FIGURE 7.2
Virtual
Desktops

Increases the number of Windows desktops and lets you quickly switch between them. without additional hardware by using the expanded virtual desktop.

TIGA, XGA, 8514/a, and Other Obscure Standards. In the late 1980s Texas Instruments introduced a display card technology called **TIGA (Texas Instruments Graphics Architecture)** as a high-performance alternative to VGA. A number of manufacturers use TIGA to produce screen resolutions of 1,024 by 768 pixels and higher. TIGA boards include the Hercules Graphics Station card and the NEC Graphics Engine card.

Windows 95 doesn't directly support TIGA, but you can use the standard Windows 95 VGA driver or a Windows 3.1 TIGA driver. If you install Windows 95 over a previous version of Windows, Setup keeps the previous TIGA driver. If you install Windows 95 from scratch, Setup installs the standard VGA driver. Either way, you still get good results from the TIGA adapter.

In an attempt to produce a display card that would outperform VGA, in the late 1980s IBM introduced the **8514/a** as an accessory for the PS/2 series. That display card provides 256 simultaneous colors from a palette of 262,400, at a resolution of 1,024 by 768. In reality this is no more than some Super-VGA displays offer.

In addition, the 8514/a has three serious drawbacks: its displays are interlaced, it works only with the MCA bus (whereas similar cards by ATI and Paradise work with ISA and EISA buses), and it is not compatible with VGA. Thus, if you want to produce a VGA image, you need separate VGA circuitry —on either a board, an add-in card, or the motherboard—to pass the image on to the 8514/a display card and through to your monitor.

Danger Zone

If you use a VGA card to pass a VGA signal through to an 8514/a card, Windows 95 may be unable to detect the memory used by the VGA adapter. You need to keep Windows from using the memory address areas used by the VGA adapter. To do this, use the EMMExclude= statement in the [386Enh] section of your SYSTEM.INI file. For example, the statement line

```
EMMExclude=C400-C7FF
```

excludes the area that usually causes the memory conflict.

You might encounter another problem if you have an older VGA card that requires an updated RAM DAC chip. The RAM DAC is the digital-to-analog converter that changes the digital information in your computer's memory (or on the card's memory) into the analog video signal that the card sends to your display. If your RAM DAC is too old, you may have problems switching between full-screen DOS sessions run from within Windows. In some cases a blank screen appears when you try to make a switch. If this happens, update the RAM DAC or the display card.

If your screen blanks out when you are running a DOS session with an 8514/a card, you can sometimes retrieve the display by typing MODE CO80 at the invisible DOS prompt. This forces the display into color 80-column mode, sometimes causing it to reappear.

In 1990 IBM introduced its **XGA** display card, which provides 256 colors at a resolution of 1,024 by 768, as well as a high-performance 640-by-480 256-color mode. Another mode displays 65,536 simultaneous colors at a resolution of 640 by 480.

Like IBM's 8514/a card, its XGA card is interlaced and is available for only the MCA bus. Some third-party developers offer noninterlaced XGA-compatible cards for the ISA and EISA buses, but those are not nearly as prevalent as either VGA or TIGA cards. Owners of ISA and EISA systems should note that certain TIGA display cards are noninterlaced and offer resolutions and performance that rival those of XGA.

XGA was designed with bit-mapped graphics in mind, so it provides better Windows 95 performance than does the 8514/a card, which was developed for CAD packages and therefore optimized to draw lines rather than bit maps. IBM's XGA card works with only 386 and larger systems, and it is limited to two resolutions: 640 by 480 and 1,024 by 768. You need an XGA/2 card to support the useful midrange resolution of 800 by 600, which is standard with SuperVGA cards.

Graphics Accelerators

More and more Windows users are turning to display cards that provide **graphics acceleration.** Because Windows 95 is a graphical user interface, much of your system's performance depends on its ability to execute Windows graphics instructions. By using a graphics accelerator card, therefore, you can speed up much of your Windows 95 environment.

The Windows graphics kernel, called the GDI (Graphics Device Interface), is responsible for drawing all the images on your screen, both text and graphics, while you run Windows. A standard VGA card has no intelligence of its own; it serves merely as a frame buffer for your display. This means that your computer's CPU chip must perform all the GDI instructions; that is, the chip renders the graphics to send to the VGA card, which in turn stores the information in its buffer before sending it to the display. The higher the resolution of your display and the more colors in the image, the greater the work load for your CPU.

Insider's Tip

A graphics accelerator can sometimes boost performance more than an upgrade in processor speed. However, boosting processor speed does contribute to graphics performance, and graphics accelerators often perform best with high-speed CPUs.

If you decide to add a graphics accelerator, the following are some of your choices:

➤ **Accelerated graphics cards**. A modern breed of VGA card, accelerated graphics cards include circuitry that performs some of the most common Windows graphics operations. Those tasks are thereby off-loaded from the CPU chip, improving overall system performance. Examples of accelerated graphics cards include those that use the Vision 864/868 chips from S3, the Mach 32 and Mach 64 chips from ATI, and the W5086 chip from Weitek.

➤ **Coprocessor cards**. These cards contain a programmable, on-board processor chip that takes over many of the graphics operations normally performed by the CPU chip. Coprocessor cards are typified by the 8514/a, TIGA, and XGA cards discussed earlier in this chapter.

➤ **Bus-cycle acceleration**. These cards decrease the number of bus cycles that a CPU must complete to perform graphics operations. The Chips & Technologies 82C453 chip uses this approach.

➤ **Bus mastering cards**. Available only for systems with EISA or MCA buses, bus mastering video cards take advantage of the advanced capabilities of those buses.

➤ **Local bus video**. This strategy integrates the display card into the local bus of the CPU chip, bypassing the expansion bus to achieve the highest possible data transfer speeds. Examples include the VESA local bus (VL-bus) and the Peripheral Component Interconnect (PCI) bus, which is almost standard fare on Pentium systems.

Different display cards with substantially the same hardware design as each other can provide varying levels of performance, depending on the quality of the driver supplied with the card. This applies to standard and accelerated cards, including coprocessor cards. Windows video drivers can be difficult to write; hence developers seem to be tweaking and fine-tuning their drivers continuously. If you're still using a Windows 3.1 video driver, you're not getting the best performance; you might be better off using the standard VGA driver supplied with Windows 95. Be sure to contact the manufacturer of your display card to get the latest Windows 95–compatible driver.

Drivers are updated continually. When you purchase a new card, take into account how easily you can acquire a new driver. Does the manufacturer maintain a forum on CompuServe, America Online, or Prodigy? Does it have a bulletin board service that you can call anytime to download a new driver at no cost? And ask about the Internet; now that it is so accessible to so many people, companies are sponsoring home pages on the World Wide Web (WWW) and have FTP (file transfer protocol) sites for free downloading.

If you've got a web browser, you can view manufacturers' home pages to compare product specifications and prices. Many of those home pages also include links to electronic magazines (and electronic versions of printed magazines, such as *Windows Magazine*) that rate products. Use those links to compare offerings from different manufacturers.

No matter how good your Windows video driver is, its performance can be limited by your display card. The new breed of VGA cards called **accelerated graphics cards** reduce some of those limitations. The cards assume many of the graphics operations normally performed by the CPU, freeing up the CPU to perform other tasks and also speeding up the transfer of graphics information to the display card. Rather than transfer an entire image to the card, you send only the graphics instructions. A typical accelerated graphics card is the Diamond Speedstar Pro VRAM card.

The ATI Graphics Wonder and the Orchid Fahrenheit 64 cards are fixed-function cards that assume specific graphics functions, such as line drawing and bitblt (bit-block transfers). Those fixed-function cards use special chips, such as those made by S3, Weitek, and ATI. Although the chips are not programmable, they take over the toughest graphics processing tasks and are inexpensive compared with fully programmable coprocessors.

Another relatively low-cost acceleration technique is **bus-cycle acceleration,** which adds a chip to your card that can halve the number of bus cycles the CPU performs for each graphics operation. This tactic is employed by Chips & Technologies in its 82C453 chip, which is included in the Artist Graphics WinSprint 100 display card.

Graphics **coprocessor cards,** such as the TIGA, XGA, and 8514/a cards, feature programmable chips that can execute most Windows graphics operations. These chips take a greater load off the CPU than do fixed-function cards, but you pay a price; several cost more than $1,000. Coprocessor cards often offer advanced features, such as the ability to work with video signals; essentially, they provide a graphics computer on a card. However, because they are no longer supported directly by Windows 95, I'd avoid them.

Danger Zone

Although accelerator coprocessor chips on your display card can speed up system performance significantly, the computer's expansion bus still imposes a bottleneck. The ISA bus presents the worst barrier; upgrading to an EISA or MCA bus can improve the flow. However, EISA and MCA buses still cut into the performance capabilities of your display card.

The ultimate graphics acceleration option is to bypass the expansion bus altogether and tap into the CPU chip's **local bus;** this approach allows extremely high-speed transfer of information between your CPU chip and the display card (see Chapter 13). To implement this technique, however, the display card's circuitry must be built directly into the motherboard or into a direct-access slot called a **local bus slot.** If you're a speed demon, consider local bus video.

Although the local bus strategy offers the best potential for speeding up a system's graphics capabilities, it also carries the highest price: you have to buy a new system. Also, be forewarned: many systems with display cards built into the motherboard run at the same speeds as the system's expansion bus, because they don't use the local bus strategy. Therefore, buying a system with a display card built into the motherboard is no guarantee that you'll achieve higher speeds and better performance. Get a system with a local bus slot instead.

Because local bus video is a fairly young technology, the industry standards for its implementation are still evolving. However, two standouts include the **VESA local bus standard (VL-bus),** and the speedy **PCI (Peripheral Component Interconnect) bus.** You might also run into proprietary systems developed by manufacturers; avoid them if you can. Almost all newer systems—especially systems with Pentium chips—include PCI slots. And most manufacturers produce graphics cards for VL-bus and PCI slots.

· ·

Monochrome VGA

Monochrome VGA is a low-cost version of VGA that comes in two varieties: **monochrome** and **grayscale**. Monochrome VGA systems are most often found in laptop computers and display only 1-bit color. Grayscale VGA usually offers 4-bit color, which yields 16 shades of gray. Grayscale systems actually use 16-color VGA display cards, which display varying brightnesses of a single color on a monochrome monitor. For a strictly monochrome display, install Windows 95 with the driver labeled VGA with Monochrome Display. For a grayscale monochrome display, use the standard VGA driver.

Monochrome monitors cost considerably less than color monitors, but color adds information. The ability to run Windows 95 in color is worth the price of an upgrade to a VGA color monitor. Besides, monochrome VGA systems often include color VGA display cards, in which case you need to upgrade only your monitor.

When the standard VGA color palette is displayed in monochrome, many of the resulting brightnesses appear similar, making it difficult to discern individual colors. To correct this, change the Windows color scheme to Monochrome, using the Color icon in the Control Panel. You can also create your own grayscale color scheme. Don't confuse this with installing the VGA with Monochrome Display driver supplied with Windows. That driver provides 1-bit color for strictly monochrome displays, such as the kind found on laptops. Laptop users with LCD displays can also select from several color schemes created expressly for LCD screens; those choices begin with the letters *LCD*.

Display Drivers

To make the most of your hardware's possibilities, it's important to use the correct and most recent display driver available. Unlike DOS, Windows 95 doesn't require applications to directly address each type of display card. Instead, all programs address a Windows graphics kernel, called the **GDI (Graphics Device Interface)**, which remains the same regardless of what display card is installed. To make a card compatible with Windows, the manufacturer must provide a device driver that translates GDI instructions to the display card. Thus, the field of future video products is wide open; as long as you have a Windows 95 display driver, you'll be able to use any future type of display.

How Display Drivers Work. Windows cannot use any piece of hardware—a so-called device—without a software component called a **driver.** A driver translates commands between Windows and the device. If you press keys on a keyboard, for example, the keyboard driver tells Windows what command you are issuing. Similarly, a driver translates commands from Windows to the display.

This is probably familiar stuff if you've used previous versions of Windows. In fact, if you've used Windows for a while and have upgraded or added equipment, you probably have had to learn more than you really wanted to know about drivers. But Windows 95 deals with drivers a bit differently.

When you install Windows 95 over an earlier version of Windows, the Setup program examines your previous drivers, detecting the presence of hardware devices if your computer and the devices support Plug and Play. (Plug and Play is a feature that enables bidirectional communication between your computer and hardware devices. Windows 95 supports Plug and Play.) Setup then installs any updated versions of the hardware drivers that are supplied with Windows 95. If the installation disks don't contain the updated drivers it needs, Windows 95 reinstalls Windows 3.0 or 3.1 drivers. During this process Windows 95 also removes any incompatible drivers or components.

If your computer supports Plug and Play and you later add another piece of hardware, Windows 95 will know that you've connected a device. Furthermore, once Windows identifies the device, it can often choose a software driver from its collection and go on to use the device.

With the intelligence of Plug and Play, Windows 95 makes it less likely that you will have to deal with drivers, especially if you have fairly new equipment. If you've got older equipment that isn't supported by new Windows 95 drivers—what Microsoft terms "legacy" hardware—you may have to do a little more work.

Changing Display Drivers. With the generous list of display drivers it supplies, Windows 95 can work with most of the display products on the market. For example, the SuperVGA driver supports 800-by-600 16- and 256-color resolutions on most SuperVGA cards—such as those produced by ATI, Cirrus Logic, Everex, Genoa, Orchid, Paradise, STB, and Trident—and on other cards compatible with the SuperVGA standard set by VESA.

Danger Zone

The SuperVGA drivers supplied with Windows 95 work with the vast majority of standard video cards. A few cards don't work with the standard drivers; you need to obtain drivers from their manufacturers to be able to use them with Windows 95.

When you install a display, Windows usually determines what driver, fonts, and other details are necessary to complete the configuration. It's all done automatically, especially if you have newer hardware or if your driver is supported directly by Windows 95. However, you can quickly view and change the display driver if you wish. To change a display configuration manually, follow these steps:

➤ Open the Display Control Panel. (Try this shortcut: click with the right mouse button on a blank spot on the desktop, then click on Properties on the pop-up menu. Or open the Control Panel folder and double-click on Display.)

➤ Click on the Settings tab, then on Change Display Type. The Change Display Type dialog box appears (Figure 7.3). This dialog box indicates what type of display card is installed, plus what type of monitor you have hooked up. The dialog box also displays information about the display card and provides a checkbox in which you can specify whether your monitor complies with the Energy Star guidelines. (Normally Windows checks the Energy Star checkbox when Windows installs the display, but you can override this feature if you want. It doesn't work anyway if your monitor isn't compliant.)

FIGURE 7.3
The Change Display Type Dialog Box

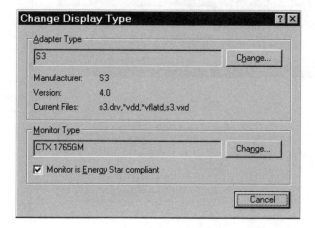

Bring up the Change Display Type dialog box to get the facts on your display card.

➤ To change display drivers, click on the Change button next to the Adapter Type field. This brings up the Select Device window, in which all the display cards supported by Windows are listed (Figure 7.4). To see a list of only those display cards that are compatible with your monitor, click on Show Compatible Devices (Figure 7.5).

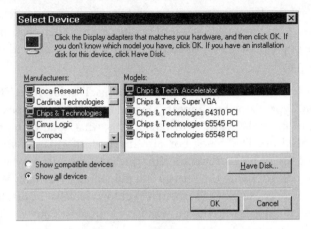

FIGURE 7.4

The Select Device Dialog Box

Like the Add Printer wizard, the Select Device dialog box lists many popular display manufacturers and the models of monitor they make. Select your display type from the list, or choose Have Disk to install an unlisted driver.

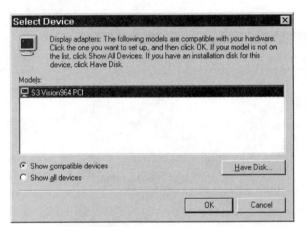

FIGURE 7.5

Only Compatible Devices Displayed

Click on Show Compatible Devices in the Select Device dialog box to see a list of only the display cards compatible with your monitor.

➸ Select a compatible device, or click on Have Disk and follow the wizard to select a driver from your floppy disk. Then click on OK to change the display driver setting.

If the driver you select is not installed on your system, Windows 95 asks you to insert one of the Windows installation disks. Windows then reads the device driver from the disk and recognizes the new display driver when you restart your system.

If your monitor and display card type aren't listed, click on the Have Disk button. Windows 95 instructs you to insert the disk containing the new driver into the floppy drive. (If the driver is stored elsewhere, use the backspace key to delete A:\. Then enter the path to the new display driver.) Once you've inserted the driver disk into drive A or indicated the path to the driver files, Windows Setup reads the files and copies them onto your hard disk.

If your display card isn't supported by the drivers included on the Windows 95 installation disks, contact the manufacturer to get an updated driver, if it's available. Most manufacturers of display cards make Windows 95 drivers. Such a driver may enable you to access special features of the card, such as support for higher resolutions or more colors. In the meantime, you can use the Windows 3.1 driver or the generic Windows 95 VGA driver.

Insider's Tip

To prevent most hardware compatibility difficulties, select display systems that are specifically designed to work with Windows 95. Be sure any display card you purchase that is not supported by a Windows 95 driver comes with its own fully optimized Windows device driver.

Display technology is constantly being improved to keep pace with the new Windows 95 environment. Keep abreast of technical changes in the following ways:

➻ Contact the appropriate manufacturer and upgrade your hardware.

➻ Visit and join your local Windows or PC user group.

➻ Read platform-specific computer publications.

➻ Hook up to on-line information services and explore their Windows forums.

Color and Resolution Changes. If your monitor can display more than one resolution, you can change the monitor's configuration. You can do this on the fly—that is, without closing the application you are in—if your display card and driver support Plug and Play. Otherwise, you need to restart Windows before making your changes.

Using the Display Control Panel, you can change the number of colors displayed on your monitor, as well as the resolution and the font size. To change a display configuration manually, follow these steps:

➻ Open the Display Control Panel. To do so, click with the right mouse button on a blank spot on the desktop and click on Properties on the pop-up menu, or open the Control Panel folder and double-click on Display.

➻ Click on the Settings tab. The options that appear enable you to set color depth, resolution, and font size (Figure 7.6).

FIGURE 7.6

*The Settings
Tab of the
Display
Properties
Dialog Box*

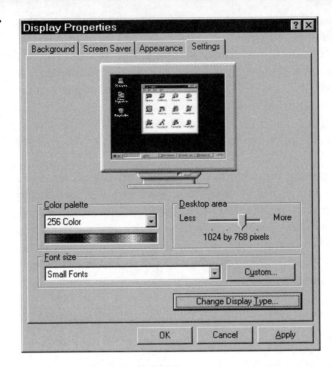

*Use this area to
change the size
of your desktop
fonts, the screen
resolution, or the
number of colors
used by Windows
95.*

➺ To change the color depth, drop down the Color Palette list and choose the number of colors you wish to display. To change the resolution, click on the Desktop Area slider bar and move it to the right or the left; the resolution you have chosen appears below the slider bar. To change the font size, choose a size from the Font Size drop-down list box, or click on Custom and specify a custom font size.

➺ Click on OK, and your changes are accepted.

Not all options may be available, because the settings are based on what kind of driver you have. If an option isn't available, it is dimmed. Also, some cards support certain color depths only at specific resolutions. For example, a card might be capable of 65,536 colors at a resolution of 640 by 480 but only be able to display 256 colors when the resolution is increased to 800 by 600.

Insider's Tip

Windows 95 offers predesigned color schemes that also incorporate increased font sizes. Choose one of the color schemes, and the size of window names and commands is automatically increased. You can find the schemes in the Appearance tab of the Display Control Panel; their names are followed by the words *large fonts* in parentheses.

. . . .

Display Ergonomics

Two factors affect how easy your monitor is to use and how safe it is: the quality of the video monitor itself and the way you set it up. When you select a monitor, go for a noninterlaced display. Be aware that some display cards are noninterlaced at lower resolutions, such as 640 by 480, but switch into an interlaced mode at higher resolutions, such as 1,024 by 768. Check the specifications and documentation of your display card to determine if this is the case.

Also pay attention to the scan rates. Your monitor should work together with your display card at **high vertical scan frequencies** to minimize flicker. Because Windows displays text as graphics, the quality of your display affects both text and graphics applications. A high-quality display minimizes flicker and distortion, both of which can lead to eyestrain and headaches.

Insider's Tip

If you're stuck with an interlaced display or a display with a low refresh rate, you can do several things to minimize the flicker. First, keep away from fluorescent lighting. Fluorescent lights emit a flicker of their own that can exaggerate the monitor's flicker. If your office is lit largely by fluorescent lights, get an incandescent desk lamp; the light from this lamp will overwhelm the fluorescent light.

Sometimes display cards and monitors can be reconfigured to work with a higher refresh rate or in a noninterlaced mode; check your manual. Another trick is to select a color scheme in the Control Panel that consists of all solid colors, rather than dithered colors or patterns. Solid colors appear more stable on a display. Dithered colors are not pure; they are made by combining tiny dots of different colors that your eyes perceive as one color.

When you buy a monitor, consider also its **dot pitch**—the size of the dots on the monitor that create the pixels. Generally, the smaller the dot pitch, the clearer and sharper the images on the display. I recommend avoiding monitors with a dot pitch that exceeds .28 millimeters.

How you position your monitor also affects the ergonomics of your system. The most troublesome problem is glare; set up your monitor to avoid light from a window or an artificial source. If you can't reposition your monitor, a so-called antiglare accessory that fits over the screen might be helpful. Quality varies widely, however, so test the screen first to be sure it allows a clear view of the monitor.

Some monitors are treated to minimize glare. One method is to etch a tiny grid into the monitor's surface, which gives it the appearance of frosted glass. I dislike this technique because it reduces the sharpness of images on the screen.

A better glare-reduction method involves treating the screen with a coating called **OCLI.** This coating is usually available only on higher-priced monitors.

Insider's Tip

The best place to position your monitor is slightly below eye level. Your eyes should rest naturally on the monitor's surface, so you don't need to crane your neck up or down. Many computer desks are designed so that the monitor is high enough only when placed on top of the system unit. If you have a tower-shaped case, or if you prefer not to place your system unit underneath your monitor, you may need a monitor stand to boost the height of your monitor. (I use old phone books.) A swivel base is a good accessory for a monitor because it enables you to fine-tune the viewing angle. However, don't use it as a substitute for placing the monitor at the proper height.

The most controversial ergonomic issue related to display systems concerns **VDT emissions.** Video monitors and television sets emit energy in various forms, ranging from electromagnetic radiation to high-pitched audio waves. The scientific jury is still out as to whether those emissions pose significant health hazards, but emotions run high on the issue. Some people feel the emissions are dangerous because potentially they could cause cancer and birth defects. Others say that less radiation is emitted than one would expect from a bedside electric alarm clock.

Personally, I think the danger from most monitors is minimal, especially from monitors of recent manufacture. The only ones I consider potentially dangerous are monitors produced in the early 1980s and some of the large-screen color monitors built before 1986. Public awareness of the potential health threat of VDT emissions and the potential onslaught of product liability lawsuits have prompted most monitor manufacturers to increase the shielding on their monitors, which reduces emissions. If emissions are a concern for you, look for monitors that adhere to the Swedish National Council for Meteorology standards, most often referred to as MPR II, which set limits on the amount of very low frequency (VLF) and extremely low frequency (ELF) radiation a monitor can emit.

I think that in the near future monitors made with materials that do not produce emissions will replace cathode-ray tube monitors. The color LCD screens used in many laptop computers are already made of such materials.

Finally, if you have a relatively new machine or are in the market for one, you can be a good citizen of the world by using a monitor that complies with the Environmental Protection Agency's **Energy Star** guidelines. If your computer is also Energy Star–compliant, it can minimize the amount of power your system consumes by powering down the monitor (and any other Energy

Star–compliant components) when the system has been idle for a while—for example, when you run off to a meeting or lunch. Windows 95 supports Energy Star; options appear in the Screen Saver tab of the Display Properties Control Panel. (If those options are dimmed, go to the Settings tab and click on Change Display Type. Make sure your monitor appears in the Monitor Type field of the Change Display Type dialog box, then check the Monitor Is Energy Star Compliant checkbox.)

· ·

What the Future Brings

Because custom device drivers can extend the breadth and power of Windows independent of VGA or any other standard, and because so many PC users now have Windows, Windows encourages the development of new graphics products for IBM PCs and compatibles. Advanced displays that can attain resolutions as high as 2,048 by 2,048 were previously unavailable to the majority of PC users. The advent of Windows changed this situation, because with the proper software driver, all Windows applications can now access this resolution. As a result, more graphics display systems are being introduced now than at any other time in the history of the PC.

New display cards are capable of displaying millions of colors and presenting realistic images of photographic quality on the screen. With Windows 95, PC owners can achieve the same level of video quality that Macintosh users have enjoyed for years. In fact, leading Macintosh manufacturers, such as TrueVision and RasterOps, have introduced high-quality PC graphics cards whose capabilities far surpass those of VGA.

Another trend is to incorporate television signals into display systems. The most common of the cards that do this are called "video in a window" cards. They are popular for multimedia applications because they enable input from a video disk player or a VCR to be displayed in a movable window (see Chapter 13). Vendors such as Matrox have begun to build TV circuitry directly into cards, either during the manufacturing process or as part of an upgrade. Couch potatoes can turn into desk potatoes as they view their favorite television shows in windows on their computer screens.

Expect improvements in display technology to go hand in hand with advances in sound compression, so that real-time video conferencing will be standard for both homes and businesses. New forms of communication are occurring—for example, real-time chat conferences and workshops at Internet sites—enabling people from around the world to discuss any topic in the world.

As for video monitors, expect them to be replaced by flat-screen color monitors, such as the active-matrix LCD monitors found on high-end laptops. Flat-panel color displays provide exceptionally sharp images and virtually no flicker, because they are based on liquid crystal rather than on the cathode-ray tube technology found in standard video monitors. Besides producing a better-quality display, LCD monitors are also lighter and easier to set up, and eliminate the potential risk of VDT emissions.

Mice and Other Pointing Devices

Pointing devices include many types of hand-held objects, from the well-known mice to trackballs, graphics tablets, pens, glidepoints, touch screens, joysticks, and (primarily on laptops) trackpoints. Most PCs are connected to mice and other pointing devices; a few years ago, fewer than 10 percent were pointer-driven. Windows, which is running on over 100 million computers worldwide at this writing, has increased the demand for mice, and Microsoft has benefited in terms of its own mouse sales. Logitech leads in mouse sales, with roughly 40 percent of the market.

Of all the types of pointing devices, the mouse is still the most commonly used. For some applications, especially graphic arts and CAD, either a graphics tablet with a stylus or a pen stylus that you use on your desk provides a natural way to work with Windows.

Pointing Device Ergonomics

Your choice of a mouse or other pointing device should be based on ergonomic concerns as well as on the functioning and features of the hardware itself. Your first decision is whether to use a mouse or another pointing device. Personally, after years of hands-on experience, I find the mouse the easiest to operate, with the trackball placing second. (I'm talking about a big, full-sized trackball, not the tiny, almost useless type that comes built into many laptops.) Pens, like their real counterparts, can cause writer's cramp. If you choose a pen, keep in mind that the thicker the stylus, the easier it is to hold for long periods. One relatively new addition to the pointer scene is a finger-activated pad called a glidepoint. Like the housing of a trackball, the pad doesn't move; instead, you slide your finger on the pad to move the cursor on screen. Tap once and you've clicked; tap twice to double-click. Glidepoints typically have two or more buttons, too.

Another new type of pointing device, this one found only on some laptops, is the trackpoint. You may have seen one; a trackpoint looks like a pencil eraser that got stuck in the middle of a keyboard. IBM pioneered those devices a few years ago in its Thinkpad laptops, and a number of other major laptop manufacturers have adopted the pointer as well, including Toshiba and Canon. You move the cursor by pushing the trackpoint in the direction you want the cursor to go. While definitely easier than trying to navigate a mouse on a tiny airplane tray, manipulating a trackpoint takes a little getting used to.

Light pens and touch screens are intended for special-purpose applications, such as information kiosks and other dedicated systems. Although those pointers work with Windows, I don't recommend them for the average user. Holding a light pen to your screen for long periods of time can tire your arm. Touch screens require you to use your finger, which is also tiring, and the screens smudge easily.

The placement of your mouse is important. Having to reach too far forward for it can strain your shoulder. Reaching up for the mouse can tire your arm; it should be level with the height of your elbow or slightly lower. If using the mouse tires your finger or wrist, you can switch the mouse to your other hand, using the Mouse Control Panel to swap the mouse buttons.

If your wrist often tires, you may want to invest in a wrist-cushioning product, which also helps prevent carpal tunnel syndrome. The WristPad, a rectangular bar of foam covered with a soft fabric, elevates your wrist to the height of the mouse. The WristSaver Mousepad, which integrates wrist support with a mouse pad, is slightly less comfortable.

Mice, Trackballs, Graphics Tablets, and Pens

The mouse was invented more than 20 years ago by Doug Englebart, a researcher at Tymenet. Englebart's first mouse was made of wood, supported by wheels, and topped by a tiny red button. The mouse didn't roar, however, until 1984, when Apple introduced the mouse-operated Macintosh, focusing both industry and user attention on the benefits of this little device.

What makes a mouse? Despite their variations, all mice are held in the hand and are moved to control the corresponding movements of a pointer on the computer screen. Most but not all have either two or three buttons. And usually each mouse has a tail—a cord connecting it to the computer— although cordless mice are scampering around on more desktops than ever.

Although mice differ widely in physical appearance, each contains an internal tracking mechanism that transmits the mouse's movements to a computer. All mice track movement by recording horizontal and vertical motions, employing either a mechanical, an optomechanical, or an optical mechanism.

A **mechanical mouse,** such as one built by Microsoft, contains a rolling ball that tracks the movements of the mouse. The ball turns two rollers that are positioned at right angles to each other; one roller records vertical motion, and the other tracks horizontal motion. Both rollers drive mechanical encoders that send the horizontal and vertical signals to the computer. The mouse driver software translates those signals into X and Y coordinates and applies those coordinates to control the movement of the pointer on the screen.

Optomechanical mice, such as those built by Logitech and Apple, contain the same type of ball as do mechanical mice. However, the rollers of an opto-mechanical mouse are connected to optical encoders, which use light to send signals to the computer and subsequently to the pointer on screen. According to Logitech, optomechanical mice are more durable than the strictly mechanical ones, with lifespans of 300 miles of mouse movement, as opposed to the 50 to 100 miles of movement provided by a Microsoft mouse.

An **optical mouse** operates only with a special, marked mouse pad. Coated with a reflective surface, this pad is printed with a grid. As you move the mouse over the pad, photosensors inside the mouse decode the reflections of the grid into horizontal and vertical movements. Mouse Systems' PC Mouse is an example of this species. Because optical mice don't contain moving parts, they are reputed to be more reliable and accurate than other types of mice. On the other hand, if you lose the special mouse pad, you're incapacitated.

Imagine turning your mouse on its back and adding a drop of growth hormone to its roller ball. Presto! You've got a **trackball.** The unit housing the trackball is stationary; to move the pointer on the screen, you roll the protruding ball with your fingers. Trackballs require less desk space than do mice, and they allow you to perform coarse operations, like menu selection, with greater speed and less hand movement. (Trackballs are used in video games for quick control over the cursor.) On the other hand, you get more precise control with a mouse, especially for drawing programs and CAD. And trackballs are not as comfortable as mice to use for long periods of time. When you're moving the ball with your fingers, you can't use them to press buttons. Even if you move the ball with your palm, you still have to lift your hand to access the buttons.

Graphics tablets, or digitizing tablets, are the most precise and also the most expensive pointing devices. A standard graphics tablet measures 8 ½ by 11 inches, but both larger and smaller models are also available. An electromagnetic sensor is embedded in the surface of the tablet. To move the pointer on your screen, you need either a stylus or a puck.

Artists find that a **pen-shaped stylus** provides the most natural drawing tool. Some sophisticated drawing programs support graphics tablets with pressure-sensitive styluses; when you press harder against one of these tablets, your brush stroke thickens as it would if you were actually painting. A new pen-shaped stylus from Wacom also includes an eraser on the top, so that you can erase and feather digital lines. In addition, the Cordless Mouse Pen from Fellowes Manufacturing combines several technologies to give you the freedom of an untethered drawing device. The **puck,** most often used with CAD applications, is shaped somewhat like a mouse and contains cross hairs for precise cursor placement.

Graphics tablets can be expensive; the cost depends on size, resolution, and options. If you're a serious graphic artist or CAD user, consider one of the Windows-compatible graphics tablets manufactured by Wacom, Kurta, GTCO, or CalComp.

Upgrade Alert

Windows 95 supports Plug and Play for mice and other pointing devices, and Windows' new drivers eliminate the need for DOS mouse drivers. In addition, you can connect your pointing devices to the serial ports (COM1 through COM4) or to the dedicated mouse port, if your computer has one.

Resolution of the Mouse

The sensitivity of a mouse tracking mechanism determines its resolution. Resolution depends on the level of movement a mouse mechanism can detect and transmit to the computer; it's measured in **points per inch (ppi).** If the resolution of a particular mouse is 200 ppi, for example, its tracking mechanism can detect movements as small as $\frac{1}{200}$ inch. That's the typical resolution of a bargain basement mouse. Microsoft's and Logitech's offerings claim resolutions of 400 ppi.

In general, the higher the resolution of a mouse, the more control you have over the behavior of the mouse. For detailed work, such as drawing, a higher-resolution mouse provides the ability to draw fine details that might be difficult with a low-resolution mouse.

In most early mice, a direct one-to-one ratio existed between the resolution in ppi of a mouse and the pixels on the screen. If your mouse device driver uses a one-to-one ratio and your mouse has a resolution of 200 ppi, the pointer on screen moves 200 pixels each time you move the mouse an inch.

By varying the resolution of a mouse, you can change the ratio of ppi to pixels from the regular one-to-one standard, either increasing or decreasing the mouse's **tracking speed.** Beginning mouse users usually prefer slower tracking speeds, because at those speeds the mouse is less sensitive to unpracticed movements. Experienced users usually prefer the higher tracking speeds, because they don't have to move the mouse as much to accomplish most tasks.

Windows 95 also provides **ballistic tracking,** also called ballistic gain. With this speed-sensitive feature, the faster you move the mouse, the farther the cursor travels on the screen. Some users find such fast tracking an impediment; they prefer an undistorted, direct correlation between mouse and pointer movements.

Pointing Device Product Overview

It's time to review the mice and other pointing devices. From the hundred or so available on the market, I've selected a few to describe. The ones I've chosen offer good performance and a wide assortment of features in a reasonable price range.

Microsoft Mouse. The Microsoft Mouse is available in serial, PS/2-style PDP (Pointing Device Port), InPort, and bus versions. It sports a clean design and fits comfortably into either palm—a plus ergonomically. The ball is positioned slightly forward of center, can be removed easily for cleaning, and grips most flat surfaces with a good amount of traction. A Microsoft Mouse should be good for 50 to 100 miles of mouse travel, which is the equivalent of about ten years of everyday use.

This mechanical mouse boasts a resolution of 400 ppi. It also offers ballistic tracking with a wide range of tracking speeds, from exceedingly fast to excruciatingly slow. With the ballistic control turned up high, you can cover an entire VGA screen using only one square inch of desk space. But don't set the ballistic control too high, or you'll have trouble controlling the cursor.

Microsoft supplies a mouse-control utility, called Mouse Manager, with the Microsoft Mouse. The utility provides mouse settings that you don't find on the standard Control Panel (Figure 7.7).

Mouse Manager enables you to change the color of a mouse pointer so that it stands out more clearly on an LCD display. You can also control the size of the pointer. A larger pointer is easier to see when you run Windows in a high-resolution mode, which shrinks objects on the screen. A "growth" setting enlarges the pointer while it's moving quickly and returns it to its normal size for doing detailed work. You can also customize the cursor and other features to help make your mousing more fun.

FIGURE 7.7

*Mouse
Manager
Utility*

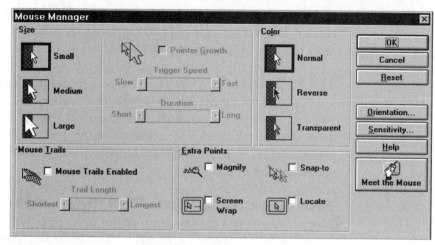

Microsoft ships this mouse-control utility with its mice.

Logitech Mice. Logitech is the overall leader in mouse sales, offering many models to fit a variety of needs and budgets. The centerpiece of Logitech's mouse line is the MouseMan, a 400 ppi ballistic mouse that comes in designer colors.

The MouseMan offers an advanced ergonomic design. Its large size makes it a handy hand rest, and because the mouse ball is positioned toward the rear, it's easy on your wrist to position the cursor. A symmetrical design lets you use whichever hand you're most comfortable mousing with, and you can easily switch hands if one hand needs a break. The MouseMan is also offered in a serial version that includes both 9- and 25-pin connectors as well as an adapter that plugs into a PDP mouse port. The MouseMan has three buttons and includes a Windows software utility that enables you to assign the buttons to macros or keystrokes.

In addition to the MouseMan line, Logitech offers the Kidz mouse, a small mouse designed for children. It even looks like a mouse. Although the Kidz mouse is cute, it's definitely for kids only, because the earlike buttons are spaced too closely for an adult to use comfortably. For families in which adults and children use the same computer, Logitech provides an extension cable that enables you to connect both the Kidz mouse and a normal mouse at the same time.

On the cutting edge of mouse design is Logitech's three-button cordless radio mouse. Most other cordless mice employ an infrared beam, which can be interrupted by objects on your desk. The radio design ensures continuous transmission to the receiver.

Logitech's 3-D mouse is at the high end of the mouse spectrum. This mouse, designed for high-end CAD applications, is the only mouse that provides full three-dimensional positioning.

IBM PS/2 Mouse. IBM introduced its only mouse in 1987 to compete with the hegemony of the Macintosh mouse. The original PS/2 Mouse, manufactured for IBM by Alps, has a basic two-button mechanical design. This mouse pales in comparison with Microsoft's offering, but because of IBM's name and marketing muscle, it has managed to win a significant percentage of the mouse market.

Mouse Systems: Optical Mouse, White Mouse, and OmniMouse. In 1982 Mouse Systems was the first company to make mice for the PC, two years before Apple introduced its mouse-centric Macintosh. Mouse Systems, now a subsidiary of KYE, is still a big cheese in the mouse market with its Optical Mouse, White Mouse, and OmniMouse. The Optical Mouse is the company's flagship product. Though it is touted by the manufacturer as "the industry's most accurate mouse," its performance is actually similar to that of the Microsoft Mouse.

One of the company's newest offerings is the ProAgio mouse, a five-button mouse that offers some snazzy features. For one thing, a small button on the side is programmed to switch between applications; it enables you to access the Task Manager without using the function keys. The ProAgio also has a unique SmartScroll feature: when you press a button while moving the mouse, the cursor scrolls at a uniform speed.

The Optical Mouse is a three-button mouse available in a serial version with a PS/2 adapter. Because it's optical, you must use it with the reflective grid-lined mouse pad, included in the package. The Optical Mouse can be made to emulate a two-button mouse in Windows by sliding a small switch on the back of the mouse.

In addition to the high-end Optical Mouse, Mouse Systems offers two less expensive models: the White Mouse and the OmniMouse. The White Mouse, a three-button mechanical mouse, and the optomechanical OmniMouse are also offered in serial versions with PS/2 adapters. Neither requires a special reflective pad.

Fellowes MousePen. The MousePen from Fellowes Manufacturing is a mouse substitute with a distinctive design. It's shaped somewhat like a pen and ends in a pea-size ball with two small buttons that are the equivalents of regular mouse buttons. The MousePen is a ballistic mouse that comes in three versions: a professional model with a third button that controls cursor speed and works with either a PS/2 or serial port, a slightly cheaper serial-only model, and a children's model called the Computer Crayon.

The MousePen is like a religious cult: either you love it or you don't know about it and don't miss it. Its small following consists mainly of laptop users, who claim you can easily use the MousePen on your leg when you are cramped into an airline seat without enough room to maneuver a traditional mouse. Some desktop users like it because it feels more like a pen—an attribute I have a hard time appreciating as a benefit. The MousePen's detractors say that using it is like trying to write with a ballpoint pen on waxed paper because the small ball doesn't always make firm contact with the surface below and tends to skip.

Fellowes does supply two additional balls with the MousePen to correct the skipping problem that occurs with the regular ball. Those other balls have a rougher, more textured surface that solves the skipping problem but creates a cleaning problem: the balls pick up dirt and dust almost as well as a small vacuum cleaner.

Creative Labs AeroDuet Three-Dimensional Mouse and Pen. If your work involves graphics, especially three-dimensional graphics, you might investigate the AeroDuet from Creative Labs (the Sound Blaster people). It contains three pieces: a base station, an infrared wireless mouse, and a wireless pen. The mouse and the pen work like conventional two-dimensional pointing devices. Switch into 3-D mode, however, and they detect motion along X, Y, and Z axes. In 3-D mode the mouse and the pen are suited for applications that support 3-D devices. The devices support a modest 265 dpi resolution but include software enhancement for an effective resolution of up to 2,000 dpi. At about $150, the AeroDuet is not cheap, but it includes bundled software, such as Kai's Power Tools and Spectre VR.

Tandy PS/2 Mouse and 2-Button Mouse. Yes, you can get a cheap mouse at your local Radio Shack or Tandy computer store. Tandy's PS/2 Mouse is a two-button mechanical mouse, available with a PS/2 connector. This mouse emulates Microsoft's, so it works fairly well with the Microsoft Mouse driver that comes with Windows 95.

Tandy's 2-Button Mouse is an optomechanical mouse designed to connect to the mouse port of IBM PS/2s and other machines with built-in mouse ports, such as Compaqs and Tandys. The 2-Button is crescent-shaped, which makes it feel awkward in the palm, but the mouse performs reasonably well. If your mouse dies on a Sunday, it's reassuring to know you're only a shopping mall away from a cheap replacement. Except for emergencies, however, I'd favor any other mouse in this roster.

ProHance PowerMouse 100 and ProMouse. In yet another attempt to build a better mouse, ProHance has designed the 40-button, 200 dpi PowerMouse 100. Two large buttons correspond to those on simpler mice, and 38 tiny buttons provide access to a variety of functions:

➤ Ten small, labeled buttons enable you to perform operations such as copy, move, and adjust width with Lotus's 1-2-3 macro package.

➤ A group of buttons labeled as a numeric keypad enable you to perform calculator functions.

➤ Some buttons provide keyboard equivalents, such as Enter, Esc, and backspace.

➤ A powerful macro program enables you to assign mouse-button combinations to 240 macros of up to 255 characters.

The PowerMouse can connect to either a 9-pin or a 25-pin serial port. ProHance supplies its own Windows driver and a Windows template that assigns macros to many of the PowerMouse keys to accomplish common Windows tasks. This is one of the most expensive mice available, and as with the MousePen, users tend to either love it or hate it. If you want to single-handedly roll around a miniature keyboard, this may be the mouse for you.

ProHance also offers the ProMouse, which is a scaled-down version of the PowerMouse. Shaped more like the Microsoft Mouse, the ProMouse has only ten buttons. You can assign macros to the buttons, or the buttons can replace frequently used keys. Although the ProMouse is more comfortable to use than the PowerMouse, the ten buttons are small and difficult to access.

Bargain Mice. You are most likely going to use your mouse frequently with Windows 95, so I suggest investing in a good-quality mouse that fits your hand. If you are budget conscious, however, bargain mice abound; some are offered for as little as $10. It might be worth keeping a couple of these mice around as spares in case your main mouse goes down for repairs.

A serviceable low-cost mouse is the Pet Mouse from IMSI in San Rafael, California. It lists for $29.95 and enables you to switch between Microsoft and Mouse Systems compatibility modes, which both run with Windows 95.

Logitech TrackMan. This is one of the most ergonomically designed trackballs for right-handed users, but the placement of the buttons makes it awkward for left-handers. The rolling ball is placed on the left side, with three buttons to the right of it, so you can keep your hand fully opened; the thumb manipulates the ball, and the fingers are free to click buttons. The TrackMan is available in both serial and bus versions and is compatible with the Logitech mouse driver included with Windows 95.

Kensington Expert Mouse. Despite its name, Kensington's Expert Mouse is actually an oversized trackball. Half of its 2-inch ball, which resembles a billiard ball, protrudes from the unit. The Expert Mouse is at the high end of the price spectrum and comes in serial, PS/2, and bus versions. The stability of the large ball and the solid feel of the unit have earned it popularity among Macintosh users.

Mouse Systems PC Trackball. In addition to making several models of mice, Mouse Systems also offers a three-button trackball. The PC Trackball has an innovative, dome-shaped design, with the buttons placed at the base of the dome, just below the ball. This makes it comfortable to move the ball with two fingers while resting your thumb on the left or right button. The PC Trackball is also one of the more economical trackballs and is available in a serial version with a PS/2 adapter.

. . . .

Keyboard and Pointer Combinations

If you've got a cluttered desk or a small computer stand that doesn't have enough room for either a mouse or a trackball, then you might be interested in a keyboard that comes with its own pointing device. One of the first keyboard combos like this was Chicony's Keyboard KB-5581. This keyboard comes with 101 keys and an integrated trackball; it requires the same amount of space as a standard 101-key keyboard. The no-frills trackball has a resolution of only 200 dpi, but the complete package costs less than either a keyboard or a trackball purchased separately. The trackball works with the Windows Microsoft Mouse driver. This product's only drawback is the design of the keyboard, which includes two horizontal rows of keys at the top. As a result, it's easy to press a function key accidentally instead of a number, and vice versa.

A newer release of the KB-5581 sports an extended keyboard with an eraser-head pointer. This type of pointer is favored by laptop manufacturers. The pointer is situated in the center of the keyboard for easy reach by either hand. Look to see more keyboard and pointer combinations—especially with split and ergonomic keyboard designs—as people become more comfortable with laptop layouts and discover how convenient an integrated pointer is.

Microsoft Ballpoint and Logitech TrackMan Portable. When PC laptops were introduced, they weren't designed with mice in mind. Then Apple introduced the PowerBook, with its small trackball located below the keyboard and now with a built-in glidepoint. PC vendors have quickly followed suit, and now most laptops include a built-in pointing device, whether a trackball, a glidepoint, or a little eraser-head pointer built into the keyboard. If you've got an earlier laptop or one without a built-in pointer, you still have some options.

The three leading alternatives are the Fellowes MousePen, mentioned earlier, and two miniature trackballs, the Microsoft Ballpoint and the Logitech TrackMan Portable, which look surprisingly similar. The semicircular devices contain a small trackball on one side. To use them, you grasp the device between thumb and palm, moving the trackball with your thumb and pressing buttons along the sides of the device with your fingers.

The Mouse Control Panel

Microsoft combined all the Windows 95 mouse configuration options into one Control Panel. It's easy to set up your mouse to suit your working style. The Mouse Control Panel has four tabs:

➻ **Buttons**. On this page you can change the configuration of the mouse buttons and set the double-click speed.

➻ **Pointers**. On this page you can change the appearance of the mouse pointer or insertion point to go with specific actions. You can also save a custom configuration.

➻ **Motion**. Here you can customize mouse speed and choose whether to display mouse trails.

➻ **General**. Here you can view or change the mouse driver.

Switch-Hitting Buttons and Adjusting Double-Click Speeds. Windows recognizes only two mouse buttons, although many mice include three and even four buttons. One button is the primary button; you use it for most of your clicking, double-clicking, and dragging. Windows 95 uses the secondary button to display a pop-up menu of commands related to whatever was clicked on and to perform special dragging operations. When you're in an application, the action of this button depends on the application. In Microsoft Word, for example, you can use the second button to see pop-up menus for selected text.

The standard Mouse Control Panel enables you to choose which button is your primary button; the left button is the default. If you're left-handed, you might want to change the Button Configuration setting in the Control Panel's Mouse Properties dialog box. Click on Left-Handed to make the right mouse button the primary button (Figure 7.8).

• • • • • • • • • • • • •
FIGURE 7.8

The Button Page of the Mouse Control Panel

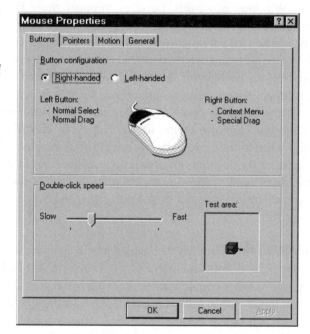

Click on Left-Handed to switch button configurations.

Another option on this page enables you to change the interval between the two clicks of a double-click. If you're a slow clicker, your computer might interpret a double-click as two separate clicks. Use the slider bar and the Test Area in the Double-Click Speed box to change the double-click speed. Move the slider bar toward Slow or Fast, then double-click in the Test Area box to try it out. If you click too slowly, nothing happens, and you should move the slider bar further towards Slow. But when you double-click at the correct speed or faster, the jack-in-the-box pops up (Figure 7.9). Double-click again, and the jack-in-the-box goes back into its box.

• • • • • • • • • • • • •
FIGURE 7.9
*The Double-
Click Speed
Test Area Jack-
in-the-Box*

*This jack-in-the-box pops up when
you successfully test a double-
click speed you have chosen.*

Scurrying for mouse supremacy, some vendors have produced mice with three and four buttons. In fact, three-button mice abound in the UNIX world. Very few Windows programs, however, support more than two buttons, although some mice include drivers that enable you to set up the third button as a function key for a frequently issued keystroke sequence or macro.

Utility programs and drivers included with third-party mice that have two or more buttons enable you to assign commands to the second and third mouse buttons. For example, assigning your third button the function of the Enter key enables you to click OK quickly in a dialog box. Some drivers, such as Kensington's Thinking Mouse driver, even allow **chording**—that is, you can assign a function to two buttons clicked simultaneously. Chording effectively increases the number of buttons on a mouse and can make short work of complicated tasks, since you can assign more than one action to a chord. For example, you can save and close a document and quit an application with only one click.

The Pointers Tab. Windows 95 enables you to change the look of pointers and cursors. The default choice is OK, but I prefer a 3-D look. To satisfy my tastes, as well as other people's tastes, three other schemes are available: a 3-D design, a scheme with standard pointer shapes in slightly larger sizes, and a scheme with extra-large standard shapes. To change the scheme of your cursors quickly, select a scheme from the Scheme drop-down list box on the Pointers page of the Mouse Properties dialog box, then click on Apply or OK (Figure 7.10).

To change the shape of one pointer, click on the name of the pointer and then click on Browse. Locate an icon file and click on Open. To make Windows truly your own, you can create images in or import them into some paint programs and save them in an icon file (with an .ICO extension). Save the file to the Windows Cursor folder so it's easy to find. Then select that file to obtain a new pointer shape.

If you change the look of your pointers or cursors, you can save them as a scheme under whatever name you like. (If you have children in the house, they might want to create their own schemes of mouse pointers using cartoon characters or original creations.)

FIGURE 7.10
The Pointers Tab of the Mouse Control Panel

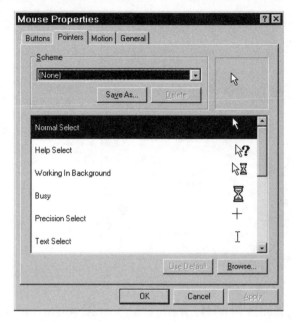

Choose a different look for your pointers and cursors for easier viewing or to make a colleague think he or she needs an eye exam.

Of Pointer Speeds and Trails. Some mouse drivers give you the ability to change mouse resolutions. To take advantage of this option, check out the Motion tab of the Mouse Control Panel. To alter the tracking speed, adjust the Pointer Speed option (Figure 7.11).

Why would you want to alter the one-to-one ppi-to-pixel ratio? Let's say you barely have any desk space in which to move your mouse around. To reduce the amount of space you need, just increase the tracking speed. Speeding up the tracking mechanism enables you to cover large distances on the screen by moving the mouse only a little. This is useful for actions such as menu selection and dialog box navigation. Slowing down the tracking speed, on the other hand, gives you more precise control over your mouse, which is useful when you perform fine detail work.

If you have a slower LCD screen, you've probably found that your pointer gets lost sometimes, especially if you move the mouse or trackball too quickly. The Pointer Trail option offers some relief. Showing pointer trails is a little like having a strobe light on as you move your pointer. When you do so, you see momentary shadows indicating where the pointer was, making your pointer easier to follow. To show pointer trails, check the Show Pointer Trails box and then use the slider bar to adjust the length of the trails. Since the changes take place immediately, you can try them out, fine-tuning the trail length to fit your liking.

• • • • • • • • • • • • • •
FIGURE 7.11
*The Mouse
Control Panel's
Motion Page*

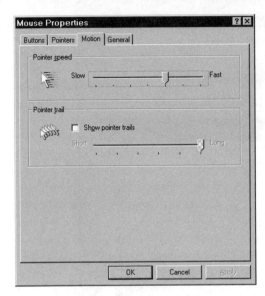

The Pointer Speed option on
the Mouse Control Panel's
Motion page enables you to
adjust the ratio of mouse
movement (in ppi) to on-
screen pointer movement
(in pixels). The Pointer Trail
option is useful with slower
LCD screens.

Changing Mouse Drivers. If you change mice, you may also need to change drivers. Most newer mice support Plug and Play, which means Windows 95 should be able to detect the type of mouse you've attached and then ask you to insert the disk that contains the driver. If not, you can choose the Add Hardware/Software wizard on the Control Panel to detect or change the driver. You can also change the driver by clicking on the Change button on the General page of the Mouse Control Panel (Figure 7.12).

• • • • • • • • • • • • • •
FIGURE 7.12
*The General
Tab of the
Mouse Control
Panel*

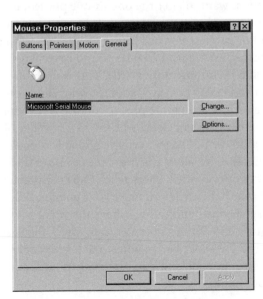

Click on the General tab
to install a new mouse
driver or change your
mouse driver.

When you click on the Change button, the ubiquitous Select Device dialog box appears. The dialog box shows only those device drivers Windows 95 assumes are compatible with the mouse or pointing device you have installed. You can also view all available drivers—Windows 95 includes drivers for Compaq, Kensington, Logitech, Microsoft, and Texas Instruments, as well as standard generic drivers—or you can click on Have Disk and insert the disk that contains the driver provided by the manufacturer.

Connecting Your Mouse. Mice and other pointing devices are attached to your system in one of three ways, depending on the type of mouse:

➡ A serial mouse is connected to a COM port.

➡ A bus mouse is connected to an add-in card that plugs into a slot inside the system. It can also be connected to a special port on a notebook computer

➡ A Pointing Device Port (PDP) mouse is connected to a mouse port on the system unit.

The serial mouse/COM port connection is the most common arrangement. Serial mice are usually less expensive than bus mice because they don't require add-in cards. The disadvantage of a serial mouse is that it uses one of your COM ports. Some systems have only one COM port, which may already be in use by a modem, a printer, or another serial device. If that's the case, you have to get either a serial card with more COM ports or a bus mouse.

Also, because both mice and COM ports can be configured for either 9-pin or 25-pin connectors, you have to match your COM port with your mouse connector pins. Most serial mice include adapters that work with either 9-pin or 25-pin adapters. If yours doesn't, you might need to get the appropriate serial port converter, available in most computer stores.

The bus mouse does not require a COM port because it attaches directly to its own connector on an add-in card. This add-in card takes up a slot inside your system. You may have an available slot, but if you have other peripherals, you may not have a free hardware **interrupt request line (IRQ),** which enables your system to communicate with hardware devices. If you run out of serial ports, add-in slots, or IRQs, you may have to disconnect something to attach your mouse. You can use the Microsoft Diagnostics utility described in Chapter 15 to investigate the status of your system's IRQs.

The InPort mouse interface card comes with the bus version of the Microsoft Mouse, which is the most common bus mouse in use. Other companies, such as MicroSpeed, also offer InPort interfaces for InPort-compatible devices. The InPort card is a small card with one chip. It contains three jumper blocks: one to configure the card for a normal slot or for the Slot 8 of XT systems, another to tell your system whether this is the primary or secondary InPort card (you can attach two), and a third to set the hardware interrupt used by the InPort card at either 2, 3, 4, or 5.

The Pointing Device Port (PDP) is the best alternative—a built-in mouse connection. The PDP is built into the motherboard of IBMs, Compaqs, and other systems. If you have a PDP, simply plug your mouse into it. It's usually located next to the keyboard connector on the back of the system unit. The PDP is gaining popularity among systems manufacturers; all PS/2s use it, and PDP input devices are manufactured by companies such as IBM, Microsoft, Mouse Systems, Logitech, Calcomp, Kensington, and MicroSpeed.

Some mice, such as the Logitech models, can be connected in more than one of the ways just mentioned. Check the documentation to see if an adapter is available that allows a mouse to be used with a different connector.

Keyboards

The keyboard still plays a major role in what is partially a mouse-controlled environment. You need a keyboard for data entry, and many commands are issued more easily and more quickly from a keyboard than from a mouse because you don't have to remove your hands from the keyboard to reach for the mouse.

In fact, you don't even need a mouse to run Windows; almost every command can be issued from the keyboard. This capability gives Windows an edge over the Macintosh, which is almost totally mouse-dependent. With Windows you can have the best of both worlds—keyboard and mouse—using each input device when it is the more efficient or merely when it suits your fancy.

Keyboard Ergonomics

The keyboard may pose the biggest health hazard associated with your computer. The link between VDT emissions from the monitor and specific health hazards is still under debate, but use of the keyboard has been proven to cause a variety of hand and wrist injuries, known collectively as **repetitive stress injuries.**

The two most common of those injuries, **tendinitis** and **carpal tunnel syndrome,** are caused by poor typing habits and an improper work setup. If you pound on the keyboard while typing or type for a long time in an awkward position, you can place too much stress on your muscles and connective tissues. You can also hurt yourself by repeating the same motion over and over without resting the tendons in your wrists and hands. Those repetitive motions can lead to chronic swelling of the tendons, or tendinitis, with symptoms ranging from numbness to severe pain.

Prolonged repetitive motion places undue stress on the tendons that pass through a small area of the wrist known as the carpal tunnel. Carpal tunnel syndrome occurs when the tendons become so swollen that they press on the nerves going to the hand. The condition can make it impossible to type or use your hands for almost anything. An operation to alleviate the pain or pressure caused by repetitive hand motion has become one of the most common surgical procedures in the United States, but it is often ineffective at eradicating the problem. That's why prevention is the best recourse.

The best prevention methods are to take frequent short breaks from typing and to position your keyboard and your body properly. You are overdoing it if your fingers remain slightly curled when your hands are at rest—a sign of tight tendons. During your breaks, stretch your fingers gently—press your hands flat against a wall—or squeeze a small ball or hand-gripper. Position your keyboard so that it is level with your wrists; typing with your wrists flexed too far forward or bent too far back can damage them.

Fortunately, many new ergonomic keyboards have built-in wrist rests, and their designs make typing more comfortable in other ways, too. A split keyboard is an especially nice improvement for those with wide shoulders, although it can take a little while to get used to the setup. Once you do, however, you may never willingly give it up and type on a standard keyboard again.

Another hazard to avoid is cradling the phone between your ear and your shoulder while you type; get a headset instead. Also, don't place your palms on the desktop and bend your wrists up so that your fingers can reach the keys.

You can adjust the height of your keyboard itself or adjust the height of your chair in relation to the keyboard. Aim to place the keyboard slightly lower than your elbow. Most desks are 29 inches tall, which is considered about 3 inches too high for comfortable typing. You can sometimes remedy this height problem by getting a keyboard drawer that attaches to the underside of the desk. (This is usually easier than sawing 3 inches off the legs of the desk.) Look for a keyboard drawer that includes a built-in wrist rest, such as the Keyboard and Mouse Support drawer offered by Wholesale Ergonomic Products.

Keyboard Device Drivers

Windows 95 provides keyboard drivers that support the following keyboards:

➡ AT-style, 84 to 86 keys.

➡ AT&T 301 and 302.

➡ Standard 101-key or 102-key (U.S. and non-U.S.).

➡ Microsoft Natural.

➡ Olivetti 101 and 102 A.

➡ Olivetti 83-key, 86-key, and M24 102-key.

➡ PC/XT-style 83-key and 84-key.

Most PC-compatible keyboards conform to the Enhanced 101 or 102 standard. If your keyboard does not, you may need a third-party device driver. In that case, contact the manufacturer.

To change the Windows device driver for a keyboard, open the Keyboard Control Panel and click on the General tab. Then click on the Change button. If your keyboard or one compatible with it isn't listed, you need to have ready the floppy disk that contains the appropriate driver.

The Keyboard Control Panel

The Keyboard Control Panel is similar to the Control Panels for other devices, such as the mouse. The Control Panel combines all the keyboard options into one tabbed dialog box. The Keyboard Properties dialog box has three tabs:

➡ **Speed**. Enables you to set the character repeat and delay speeds and specify how quickly you want the cursor to blink. (Cursors blink, for example, when you're inserting text into a word-processing application. Blinking offers a simple visual cue that helps you locate the cursor.)

➡ **Language**. Enables you to choose a keyboard language so that you can access the characters of a foreign language. Also enables you to change the layout of the keys.

➡ **General**. Enables you to change your keyboard device driver.

Speed Options. The Speed tab is the first tab of the Keyboard Properties dialog box (Figure 7.13). The Speed tab offers two character-repeat options. The Repeat Delay option enables you to set the amount of time between when you begin holding down a key and when the character it represents begins repeating. The Repeat Rate option enables you to set the rate at which the character repeats. The Cursor Blink Rate option gives you the ability to set the speed at which the cursor blinks.

FIGURE 7.13

The Speed Tab of the Keyboard Control Panel

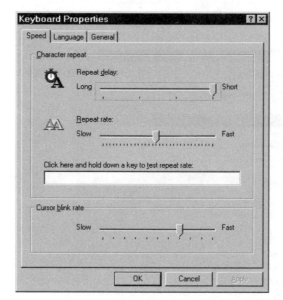

The Speed tab enables you to adjust the amount of time before a key starts to repeat itself as well as the rate at which it automatically repeats. You can also control the speed at which the cursor blinks to minimize eyestrain and edginess.

You might want to increase the interval before a key repeats if you're heavy-handed or are a novice at typing. If the key repeat delay is set at too short an interval, you're likely to type double or triple letters when you intend to enter a single letter.

To change the amount of time that elapses before a key repeats itself, drag the Repeat Delay slider bar to the left to lengthen the time delay or to the right to shorten it. To adjust the rate at which the key repeats once it gets going, use the Repeat Rate slider bar. To test your settings, click in the Test box, then press any alphanumeric key on the keyboard.

You can also change the cursor blink rate. As you type in a word-processing or other type of application, the cursor blinks to indicate where your next typed letters will go. Some people find that a cursor blinking at a fast rate makes them feel frenetic and tense, while others find that if it blinks too slowly, they lose sight of the cursor altogether. To change the rate, drag the

Cursor Blink Rate slider bar one way or the other. The cursor animation to the left of the slider bar indicates the current blink rate.

Altering Keyboard Languages and Layouts.

Windows 95 enables you to change your keyboard layout to that of another country, making available different characters and symbols. You can also change the layout from a standard QWERTY layout to the more efficient (but less common) Dvorak arrangement. Both settings are located on the second, or Language, tab of the Keyboard Properties dialog box (Figure 7.14).

FIGURE 7.14

*The Language
Tab of the
Keyboard
Control Panel*

*Once you install
additional languages,
you can have Windows
add an indicator to the
Taskbar that shows
the current language
and enables you to
switch quickly between
installed languages.*

The current keyboard language and layout are highlighted on the Language page. You can change the keyboard language to one that uses characters from another alphabet, such as Swedish or French. You can also select other versions of English, such as Canadian English. You can install more than one keyboard language, but you can use only one at a time. However, you can switch keyboard languages quickly by using your own keyboard macro or by clicking on the keyboard language indicator on the Taskbar.

To add a keyboard language, click on the Add button and select a language from the Language drop-down list box. Have your Windows 95 installation disks or CD-ROM on hand, because you will be asked to install the language from the correct disk. Follow the instructions, and Windows 95 loads the correct files automatically (Figure 7.15).

FIGURE 7.15

The Add Language Dialog Box in the Keyboard Control Panel

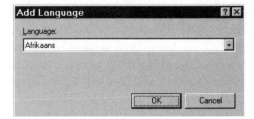

Choose a language from the list offered by Windows 95, make sure you have handy your Windows floppies or CD, and click on OK. If only it were this easy to learn the language.

Changing your keyboard layout is as easy as selecting a new keyboard language. Select the language for which you want to change the keyboard layout, then click on the Properties button to see the Language Properties dialog box. Select a layout from the Keyboard Layout drop-down list box, then click on OK. Again, be prepared with the appropriate Windows 95 disk or CD-ROM so you can install the desired layout (Figure 7.16). To remove an installed language and layout combination, select the option you want to delete and click on Remove.

FIGURE 7.16

The Language Properties Dialog Box of the Keyboard Control Panel

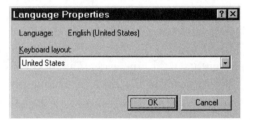

Click here to list and select the available layouts for your chosen language.

You can switch between layouts quickly either by using a keyboard shortcut (a macro) or by clicking on an indicator on the Taskbar. You can select a preset shortcut (either left Alt+Shift or Ctrl+Shift) from the Switch Languages options on the Language page. You can also choose None to disable both preset shortcuts. Some people find it handier to use the Taskbar to switch between languages.

If you check Enable Indicator on Taskbar, a square appears beside the clock on the Taskbar showing an abbreviation of the name of the keyboard language you are using. (You can find the same indicator in the Keyboard Properties dialog box under the heading Installed Keyboard Languages and Layouts.) What's more, if you position your pointer over the language indicator, you see the full name of the language, such as English (United States). Click on the indicator to bring up a list of the languages you have installed. To switch to a particular language, click on its name in the list.

For the physically challenged, the Keyboard Control Panel provides a feature to help make the screen and the keyboard more accessible. An on-screen keyboard makes it possible to use a touch screen to input data; you must install the Accessibility Options package for the Show On-Screen Keyboard option to be available. Other keyboard accessibility options include layouts designed especially for one-handed users. Display options include the ability to view data in large display fonts and high-contrast color schemes.

The Dvorak Keyboard Layout

One of the goals of Windows 95 is to boost your computing productivity. However, given the demands Windows 95 places on your system, it often seems as if the reverse were true. The standard keyboard, similarly, enhances productivity, but at quite a cost. The learning curve can be quite steep and, for some, insurmountable—or at least not worth the effort of forgoing the hunt-and-peck method. In addition, the layout of the standard keyboard that comes with most computers was intentionally designed to slow you down. In fact, the layout of your keyboard is one of the most antiquated elements of your computer interface.

Standard keyboards use what is called the QWERTY layout (named after the first six keys on the top row of the keyboard), designed in 1872 by Charles Scholes, one of the inventors of the typewriter. The cockeyed QWERTY layout was designed to prevent keys from jamming. Frequently used keys were placed at opposite ends of the keyboard, slowing typists down so that keys were less likely to jam.

Jammed keys are hardly a concern on computer keyboards, and an alternative does exist to the QWERTY keyboard: the Dvorak keyboard. Named after efficiency expert August Dvorak, the keyboard places the most commonly used letters on the so-called home row, the middle row of letters.

According to Dvorak's research, almost 70 percent of commonly used words—about 3,000—can be typed from the home row of his keyboard. By comparison, only 120 commonly used words can be typed from the home row of a QWERTY keyboard. As a result, your fingers would travel only 1 mile during a typical day of typing on a Dvorak layout, whereas the fingers of an average typist would cover 16 miles on a QWERTY keyboard. Because the fingers do less traveling, accuracy has been shown to improve by almost 15 percent, and typing speed by 20 percent.

Insider's Tip

Despite its many advantages, the Dvorak keyboard, which was patented in 1936, has remained obscure; its followers, although devoted, are few and far between. Some Dvorak proponents must have influenced Microsoft, however, because Windows 95 provides the ability to remap your keyboard to the Dvorak layout.

To do so, open the Keyboard Control Panel and click on the Language tab. Select a language, click on Properties, and then select United States-Dvorak from the Keyboard Layout section (Figure 7.17). Once you select that option, your keyboard is reconfigured in the Dvorak layout whenever you run Windows. The Dvorak layout rearranges the keyboard as shown in Figure 7.18.

FIGURE 7.17
*United States-
Dvorak Option*

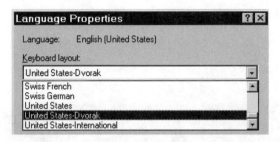

Open the Keyboard
Control Panel, click on
the Language tab, and
click on Properties.
Finally, select the
Dvorak layout.

FIGURE 7.18
*Dvorak
Keyboard
Layout*

The Dvorak layout changes the locations of most of
the letters, numbers, and punctuation marks on your
keyboard. The six QWERTY keys are now ',.PYF.

Insider's Tip

If your conversion to the Dvorak layout is permanent, you may want to rearrange the keycaps on your keyboard as well. Most keyboards allow you to pull the keycaps off directly (pull gently, or obtain a keycap-puller tool from your dealer). Then replace them according to the layout depicted in Figure 7.18.

**Dynamite
Product**

If you're just learning to type, want to learn the Dvorak layout, or want to improve your typing skills, several typing tutorial programs support the Dvorak keyboard layout as well as the QWERTY layout. My recommendation is Mavis Beacon Teaches Typing, an excellent Windows typing program for both QWERTY and Dvorak layouts from Mindscape in Novato, California. The program is both educational and entertaining and can be used by adults and kids. A clever feature is the program's ghostlike guide hands, which show you how to type correctly (Figure 7.19).

FIGURE 7.19
Ghostly
Guiding Hands

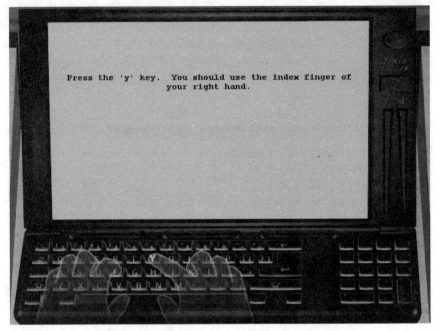

When you use the typing tutorial called Mavis Beacon
Teaches Typing, Mavis's ghost accompanies you at
the keyboard.

For more information about the Dvorak keyboard layout, contact the Dvorak International support group at P.O. Box 44, Poultney, VT 00764, (802) 287-2343 or DvorakInt@aol.com.

ANSI Characters

You may occasionally need to include special characters in a document—such as accented letters and foreign currency symbols—that are not represented by keys on the keyboard. Those characters are often referred to as **ANSI characters,** named after the ANSI character set, a set of 256 characters and symbols specified by the numbers 0 through 255.

If you need to enter a special character from the keyboard, first determine its ANSI numeric code. Table 7.2 lists the standard ANSI character codes, but because those values can vary by typeface, you may need to refer to the documentation for your font package. You can also use the Character Map to figure out which key combination to press (see Chapter 5).

TABLE 7.2
Standard ANSI Character Codes

ANSI value	ANSI character	ANSI value	ANSI character	ANSI value	ANSI character	ANSI value	ANSI character
32	(space)	66	B	100	d	134	
33	!	67	C	101	e	135	
34	"	68	D	102	f	136	
35	#	69	E	103	g	137	
36	$	70	F	104	h	138	
37	%	71	G	105	i	139	
38	&	72	H	106	j	140	
39	'	73	I	107	k	141	
40	(	74	J	108	l	142	
41	)	75	K	109	m	143	
42	*	76	L	110	n	144	
43	+	77	M	111	o	145	'
44	,	78	N	112	p	146	'
45	-	79	O	113	q	147	"
46	.	80	P	114	r	148	"
47	/	81	Q	115	s	149	•
48	0	82	R	116	t	150	–
49	1	83	S	117	u	151	—
50	2	84	T	118	v	152	
51	3	85	U	119	w	153	
52	4	86	V	120	x	154	
53	5	87	W	121	y	155	
54	6	88	X	122	z	156	
55	7	89	Y	123	{	157	
56	8	90	Z	124	|	158	
57	9	91	[	125	}	159	
58	:	92	\	126	~	160	
59	;	93	]	127		161	¡
60	<	94	^	128		162	¢
61	=	95	_	129		163	£
62	>	96	`	130		164	¤
63	?	97	a	131		165	¥
64	@	98	b	132		166	¦
65	A	99	c	133		167	§

TABLE 7.2 *(cont.)*
Standard ANSI Character Codes

ANSI value	ANSI character	ANSI value	ANSI character	ANSI value	ANSI character	ANSI value	ANSI character
168	¨	190	¾	212	Ô	234	ê
169	©	191	¿	213	Õ	235	ë
170	ª	192	À	214	Ö	236	ì
171	«	193	Á	215	×	237	í
172	¬	194	Â	216	Ø	238	î
173	-	195	Ã	217	Ù	239	ï
174	®	196	Ä	218	Ú	240	ð
175	¯	197	Å	219	Û	241	ñ
176	°	198	Æ	220	Ü	242	ò
177	±	199	Ç	221	Ý	243	ó
178	²	200	È	222	Þ	244	ô
179	³	201	É	223	ß	245	õ
180	´	202	Ê	224	à	246	ö
181	µ	203	Ë	225	á	247	÷
182	¶	204	Ì	226	â	248	ø
183	·	205	Í	227	ã	249	ù
184	¸	206	Î	228	ä	250	ú
185	¹	207	Ï	229	å	251	û
186	º	208	Ð	230	æ	252	ü
187	»	209	Ñ	231	ç	253	ý
188	¼	210	Ò	232	è	254	þ
189	½	211	Ó	233	é	255	ÿ

Once you determine the ANSI numeric code for the character you want to type, make sure your computer's numeric keypad is active. (Usually, a light on the keyboard glows to indicate that the keypad is active; and pressing Num Lock toggles the keypad on and off.) Hold down the Alt key while you type the ANSI code on the numeric keypad; using the numbers on the top row of the keyboard doesn't work. Be sure to include a zero in front of the code number.

For example, to type the copyright symbol, locate its ANSI code, which for most typefaces is 169, and hold down Alt while typing 0169. When you release the Alt key, the copyright symbol appears. If you don't use the zero, Windows interprets the code as for the computer's built-in character set, which contains many of the same characters as the ANSI set but varies by manufacturer. Sound complicated? Now you know why Microsoft created the Character Map utility.

Danger Zone

ANSI characters that are typed into a Windows document (or pasted into a document from Character Map) may not be interpreted properly if you open the document later with a DOS application. Also, remember that not every font uses the same character set.

. . . .

Summary

The display, the mouse, and the keyboard are the hardware interface between you and your computer—in other words, those elements physically enable you to interact with Windows. All three directly affect the performance of Windows 95 and of your system as well.

The display system consists of a Windows driver, a display card, and the display itself (usually a video monitor). All three components are critical to the performance of your system: the display card controls the resolution and the number of colors that can be produced, the monitor needs to match the output signal of the display card, and the Windows display driver enables you to take advantage of the display card's capabilities.

In addition, Windows graphics accelerators can take some of the graphics load off a system's CPU. The devices range from simple software drivers to fixed-function graphics cards and sophisticated graphics coprocessor cards. A promising area of graphics acceleration involves local bus systems that bypass the computer's expansion bus to provide the display card with direct access to the CPU chip.

The mouse and other pointing devices enable you to manipulate on-screen objects, issue commands, select text, and perform other functions. Although the mouse is an important part of a graphical interface, Windows 95 is not completely dependent on it; you can operate the system with a keyboard alone.

Even with a mouse, you also need a keyboard for data entry. Often a keyboard enables you to issue commands more quickly than you can with a mouse, because you don't have to remove your hands from the keyboard.

Daring folks and efficiency maniacs (and perhaps those who suffer from repetitive stress injuries or other disabilities) can also avail themselves of Windows' capacity to convert the standard keyboard layout into the more efficient Dvorak layout. However, if you do, you're breaking from the pack, and other people who use your Dvorak-configured computer might think they are on the verge of a nervous breakdown.

Inside
Windows 95

Fonts

Designed at Xerox PARC in the seventies, the graphical user interface, or GUI, made possible the first great leap forward into the field of desktop publishing: the ability to match what you see on your screen with what comes out of your printer. WYSIWYG, which stands for "what you see is what you get," first took hold on the Macintosh, which popularized the graphical user interface and spawned a second breakthrough: the **PostScript** system of computer typography.

Jointly developed in 1985 by Apple and Adobe Systems, PostScript transformed desktop publishing in the way the Gutenberg press revolutionized manuscript printing. PostScript is a computer language for describing the way a page looks. A description of a page can be sent to any output device, from a printer to a typesetting machine. PostScript also removes the "jaggies" —those ragged edges—from printed characters. As a result characters on screen and off the printer look as if they were professionally typeset. Today PostScript has become the standard for most serious desktop publishers.

Of course, Microsoft Windows also benefited from the PostScript Renaissance, which led to the development of TrueType, the typography and page-description system included with Windows 95. The GUI merged print and graphics, lifting Windows from the dark ages of print into the age of desktop publishing. Windows 95 does away with some of the font and printing problems inherent in Windows 3.1 and adds some refinements as well. Here's what you can do with some of the print and font features in Windows 95:

➼ Install fonts quickly and use them immediately (that is, without restarting Windows).

➼ View and print TrueType font samples.

➼ Control the destiny of a print job once it's in the queue.

➼ Set up as many printers as you like, including one printer with many settings.

➼ Set up a network printer directly from your PC with the touch of a mouse.

If anything can improve the quality of your time in front of the computer, it is changes in type design and printing. In this chapter I take a look at Windows fonts and typography. In the next chapter I move into the closely allied field of Windows printing, covering topics such as improvements in the Windows printing process, printer drivers, network printing, managing multiple printers, and remote printing.

Dynamite Product

TrueType offers many of the capabilities of PostScript. However, if you plan to do serious desktop publishing, you probably want to get the Windows version of PostScript, Adobe Type Manager (ATM). ATM offers the same features as TrueType and also includes the industry-standard PostScript language. Most importantly, ATM provides access to the enormous library of professional-quality PostScript typefaces. The current Windows 95 compatible version of ATM is 3.02, which I discuss in this chapter.

Typography

Confusion pervades the terminology of typography. Print shops—using the traditional lead type and printing presses—developed definitions for the terms typeface, type style, and font. Then came computers, turning everything topsy-turvy. For traditional printers, **typeface** means something different from **font;** for computer users, a typeface is a font, and both terms refer to the general design of a group of characters. For example, Arial, Courier, and Palatino are all typefaces—or fonts. Adding a new twist to the typography name game, Microsoft has coined another term, **font family,** which refers to a group of typefaces or fonts with similar characteristics.

Indeed, the universe of Windows fonts and typography continues to expand. In addition to TrueType and PostScript, third-party typography programs abound, and all enjoy a surprising breadth of support from typeface and printer vendors. Font-conversion utilities, such as **Alltype** and **Font-Monger,** translate between TrueType, PostScript, and other kinds of typefaces and fonts to help solve the compatibility problems that can arise in such a fertile profusion of products. What follows is a brief treatise on the state of the font from the Windows perspective.

All typefaces can be grouped into five font families:

➤ **Roman.** Serif typefaces, such as Times New Roman (TrueType) and Times Roman (screen). Serif typefaces have short lines—called serifs— that extend at angles from the ends of letters.

➤ **Swiss.** Sans serif typefaces, such as Arial, Small Fonts, MS Sans Serif, and Helvetica.

➤ **Modern.** Stylized fonts and typefaces.

➤ **Script.** Fonts that resemble cursive writing.

➤ **Decorative.** Highly embellished display and symbol fonts.

Windows uses those family specifications when it installs fonts and when it maps fonts to the screen and to the printer. Windows also relies heavily on the PANOSE font-matching system, which I discuss later in this chapter.

Insider's Tip

You don't need to know the following terminology to understand Windows 95, but in case you want to know the distinctions among fonts, here goes: In **fixed fonts** each character takes up an equal amount of horizontal space, whereas in **proportional fonts** each character has its own, intrinsic width (that is, an *I* is thinner than an *M*). Don't confuse this concept with that of **type width,** which describes whether a typeface has been **condensed** or **expanded** (that is, whether the width of all the characters has been shrunk or stretched for a distinctive look), or the term **type track,** which refers to whether space has been added or removed between characters. Microsoft uses the term **font style** as a synonym for **type style,** which describes characteristics such as bold, italic, and regular (also called roman). The term **font effects** refers to type attributes such as underline, strike through, and color.

· ·

A Triad of Fonts

Windows classifies fonts into three categories, based on how they are drawn for display or for printing. With **TrueType fonts,** the outline of a character is drawn first and then filled in, or rendered; this allows fonts to be scaled to any size, rotated on the screen or the printer, and filled in to the resolution of your display.

The other two types of fonts—raster and vector—are carried over from Windows 3.0. **Raster fonts** are stored as bit-mapped images in specific point sizes; they look good only in the sizes in which they are stored. Most Windows 3.0 fonts were rasters; they could not be scaled or rotated. Few people need them anymore for printing, but Windows 95 uses them for screen display. Raster fonts are sometimes used to display your work on screen if you choose a printer font that has no screen font. Windows 95 also uses raster fonts to display text in menus, toolbars, and icon titles—items that you generally don't change or pay much attention to.

Vector fonts are drawn on the screen or for the printer by means of a mathematical description of the typeface design. Originally employed by pen plotters, these fonts were used by early Windows applications (before 3.1) requiring fonts that could be resized and rotated. Again, this kind of font is rarely necessary anymore, because better options exist, but you never know when you're going to have to send output to a plotter. In any case, to provide backward compatibility, vector fonts remain.

· ·

Font Compatibility

Here's a rundown of the types of fonts and typefaces that work with Windows 95:

➣ **TrueType.** Scalable typefaces for both screen and printer. TrueType fonts are still one of the easiest ways to produce attractive printed materials, and they print out quickly on most laser printers.

➠ **PostScript**. Scalable typefaces for both screen and printer. They require the purchase of Adobe Type Manager but are the standard for professional desktop publishing.

➠ **Screen fonts**. Raster fonts of specific sizes used by Windows to display text on the screen.

➠ **Vector fonts**. Also called plotter fonts, these scalable fonts are intended mainly for use with pen plotters.

➠ **Printer fonts**. Fonts built into or loaded into a printer. You need a matching screen font to view these properly in Windows. If you don't have a matching screen font, don't expect WYSIWYG; very likely the spacing will be funky on your screen.

Windows 95 supports the following three types of printer fonts:

➠ **Device fonts**. Fonts built into a printer or plugged into it via a card or a cartridge, such as the cartridges that plug into Hewlett-Packard LaserJets.

➠ **Soft fonts**. Software-based fonts for a printer. These fonts are installed on the hard disk and downloaded to the printer as needed. Soft fonts usually must be loaded into a system with their own installation program.

➠ **Printable screen fonts**. Screen fonts that can also be printed.

Screen Fonts, Printer Fonts, and Substitutes

Whenever you use a **printer font,** try to obtain the matching **screen font.** The printer font is essential for quality output; the screen font controls the appearance of characters on screen.

What happens when your screen and printer fonts don't match? If you print matter in a particular screen font but do not have the corresponding printer font, your laser printer may react by reproducing the screen font in what resembles a crude dot-matrix style. If you're still using an old dot-matrix printer, then screen fonts and even plotter fonts may be acceptable. Your printer may also substitute one of its built-in fonts for the screen font.

If, on the other hand, you use a printer font but do not have the corresponding screen font, then Windows substitutes whichever screen font, plotter font, or TrueType font most closely matches the printer font. To determine which font to use, Windows compares characteristics such as available characters, pitch, font family, height, width, and weight. Although what you see on the screen may not exactly equal what you get on the page, Windows still tries its best to match on-screen line and page breaks and other formatting to printer output.

If you want to override Windows 95's choices of substituted fonts, open the Printers folder, select the printer in question, and choose Properties from the File menu or the pop-up menu. Click on the Fonts tab to bring it forward. Select Send TrueType Fonts to Printer According to the Font Substitution Table and click on the button labeled Edit the Table. You can edit the table no matter which option is selected in this dialog box.

The Font Substitution table lists all available TrueType fonts under the heading For This TrueType Font and lists each substituted font or other method of printing the TrueType font (for example, Send as Outline) under the heading Use Printer Font. Under the heading Printer Font For: is a list of available printer fonts. Click on the name of the font you want to replace and select a replacement from the list of printer fonts. Your selection then appears in the table.

Insider's Tip

If you plan to edit the substitution table or if you want to learn more about the characteristics of fonts, read the section titled Viewing Fonts by Similarity later in this chapter.

. . . .

TrueType Fonts

Say good-bye to the hassles of matching screen fonts and printer fonts. True-Type provides fully scalable and rotatable typefaces that appear the same on screen as on the printed page and print the same on any printer. TrueType uses a universal page-description language that is understood by almost all printers, from dot-matrix printers to high-resolution imagesetters. TrueType can convert its fonts to PostScript for printing and can convert its fonts to other formats as well, such as PCL 4, the language spoken and understood by the Hewlett-Packard LaserJet and compatible printers. TrueType does all this automatically and behind the scenes.

TrueType also bridges platforms. It offers a unified system of computer typography for both the Macintosh and Windows. If you use TrueType fonts in a Windows document, you can transfer the document to a Macintosh, or vice versa, and it looks the same.

Basic Typefaces. Windows 95 Setup automatically installs TrueType along with an all-purpose collection of 14 TrueType typefaces. As soon as Windows 95 is on your computer, you have access to the following fonts:

➤➤ **Arial**. A sans serif face that is a clone of the popular Helvetica typeface.

➤➤ **Arial Italic**. The italic version of Arial.

➤➤ **Arial Bold**. The bold version of Arial.

➤➤ **Arial Bold Italic**. An Ariallike design that incorporates both bold and italic styles.

➤➤ **Courier New**. The monospaced typewriter look lives! A nice low-tech look.

➤➤ **Courier New Italic**. The italic version of Courier New.

➤➤ **Courier New Bold**. The bold version of Courier New.

➤➤ **Courier Bold Italic**. A Courierlike design that incorporates both bold and italic styles.

➤➤ **Symbol**. A set of symbols for math, charts, games, or whatever use you can dream up.

➤➤ **Times New Roman**. A respectable serif face that is a clone of the popular Times typeface.

➤➤ **Times New Roman Italic**. The italic version of Times New Roman.

➤➤ **Times New Roman Bold**. The bold version of Times New Roman.

➤➤ **Times New Roman Bold Italic**. A Timeslike design that incorporates both bold and italic styles.

➤➤ **Wingdings**. A cool collection of icons, dingbats, and special symbols, which contains everything from telephones to computer parts to a bomb with a lit fuse.

Figure 8.1 shows a sample of each of the 14 TrueType typefaces included with Windows 95.

Arial
AaBbCcDdEeFfGgHhIiJjKkLlMmNnOoPpQqRrSsTtUuVvWwXxYyZz
1234567890!@#$%^&*()[]{}\|'":;,.?/~`

Arial Italic
AaBbCcDdEeFfGgHhIiJjKkLlMmNnOoPpQqRrSsTtUuVvWwXxYyZz
1234567890!@#$%^&()[]{}\|'":;,.?/~`*

Arial Bold
AaBbCcDdEeFfGgHhIiJjKkLlMmNnOoPpQqRrSsTtUuVvWwXxYyZz
1234567890!@#$%^&*()[]{}\|'":;,.?/~`

Arial Bold Italic
AaBbCcDdEeFfGgHhIiJjKkLlMmNnOoPpQqRrSsTtUuVvWwXxYyZz
1234567890!@#$%^&*()[]{}\|'":;,.?/~`

Courier New
AaBbCcDdEeFfGgHhIiJjKkLlMmNnOoPpQqRrSsTtUuVvWwXxYyZz
1234567890!@#$%^&*()[ ]{} \ |"':;,.?/~`

Courier New Italic
AaBbCcDdEeFfGgHhIiJjKkLlMmNnOoPpQqRrSsTtUuVvWwXxYyZz
1234567890!@#$%^&()[]{}\|"':;,.?/~`*

Courier New Bold
AaBbCcDdEeFfGgHhIiJjKkLlMmNnOoPpQqRrSsTtUuVvWwXxYyZz
1234567890!@#$%^&*()[]{}\|"':;,.?/~`

Courier New Bold Italic
AaBbCcDdEeFfGgHhIiJjKkLlMmNnOoPpQqRrSsTtUuVvWwXxYyZz
1234567890!@#$%^&*()[]{}\|"':;,.?/~`

Symbol
ΑαΒβΧχΔδΕεΦφΓγΗηΙιϑφΚκΛλΜμΝνΟοΠπΘθΡρΣσΤτΥυςϖΩωΞξΨψΖζ
1234567890!≅≠∋%⊥&*()[]{}∴|©∏:;,.?/~

Times New Roman
AaBbCcDdEeFfGgHhIiJjKkLlMmNnOoPpQqRrSsTtUuVvWwXxYyZz
1234567890!@#$%^&*()[]{}\|'":;,.?/~`

Times New Roman Italic
AaBbCcDdEeFfGgHhIiJjKkLlMmNnOoPpQqRrSsTtUuVvWwXxYyZz
1234567890!@#$%^&()[]{}\|'":;,.?/~`*

Times New Roman Bold
AaBbCcDdEeFfGgHhIiJjKkLlMmNnOoPpQqRrSsTtUuVvWwXxYyZz
1234567890!@#$%^&*()[]{}\|'":;,.?/~`

Times New Roman Bold Italic
AaBbCcDdEeFfGgHhIiJjKkLlMmNnOoPpQqRrSsTtUuVvWwXxYyZz
1234567890!@#$%^&*()[]{}\|'":;,.?/~`

Wingdings
[Wingdings symbol glyphs]

Put a face on your documents with one of these 14 TrueType fonts.

**Upgrade
Alert**

TrueType font files no longer live in your windows\system folder (*folder* being the new term for *directory*). Instead, they are located in the Fonts sub-folder of the main Windows folder, which is, predictably, called Windows, unless you changed its name during installation.

If you've been following font evolution, you may remember that each TrueType font used to require two files to make it whole—a .ttf file and a .fot file. In Windows 95, one .ttf file holds all the necessary information. Another change, important to system administrators, is that font information (such as location) is no longer stored in the win.ini file, but in the Registry. One of the few reasons you might care about that change is that you don't have to restart your computer to use newly installed fonts. For more infor-mation on the Registry, see Chapter 14.

As you can see in Figure 8.1, Arial, Courier New, and Times New Roman each has separate fonts for regular, bold, italic, and bold italic styles. Primi-tive computer typography software merely fattened a character to make it bold or slanted it to make it italic; this resulted in irregular type that was often aesthetically unpleasing. The TrueType typefaces adhere to the classic stan-dard, which calls for the creation of a typeface for each type style. Arial, for example, includes the files shown in Table 8.1 for its fonts.

• • • • • • • • • • • • • •
TABLE 8.1
*The Arial
TrueType Font
and Its Files*

File Name	Font Name
ARIAL.TTF	Arial Regular
ARIALBD.TTF	Arial Bold
ARIALI.TTF	Arial Italic
ARIALBI.TTF	Arial Bold Italic

Each application implements bold, italic, and other styles in a slightly dif-ferent way. Some applications list each style of font separately. Most applica-tions list only the regular font and provide separate commands for bold, italic, and bold italic. When you access a style command, the program checks to see whether the stylized font is available. If it is not, some applications mutate the normal font, but this results in a less attractive alternative. The outline and shadow styles, however, are almost always created by means of mutation rather than by means of a separate font file.

Dynamite Product

Hundreds of third-party TrueType typefaces are available for Windows. In addition, Microsoft sells several sets of typefaces as part of the Microsoft TrueType Font Pack for Windows. The first set contains 22 typefaces designed by Monotype Typography. Together with the 13 TrueType text typefaces included with Windows 95, these fonts closely match the 35 standard fonts included with most PostScript printers.

Table 8.2 lists the TrueType font families and their equivalent PostScript font families. Each font family includes a regular, italic, bold, and bold italic typeface.

....

TABLE 8.2
PostScript Equivalents of TrueType Fonts

TrueType Font Family	PostScript Font Family
Arial	Helvetica
Arial Narrow	Helvetica Narrow
Bookman Antiqua	Palatino
Bookman Old Style	Bookman
Century Gothic	Avant Garde
Monotype Corsiva	Zapf Chancery
Courier New	Courier
Monotype Sorts	Zapf Dingbats
Symbol	Symbol
Times New Roman	Times Roman

The design of a typeface cannot be copyrighted; only its name is protected by copyright law. Because of this, the Helvetica design is called Arial in Windows, whereas some vendors call it Swiss. Although TrueType typefaces are roughly equivalent to their PostScript counterparts, subtle design variations do exist between the two types of characters. The spacing, furthermore, can vary so much between the two typefaces that line length and therefore line breaks and page lengths are not equivalent.

What's in the Font Pack? In addition to the Monotype fonts I just mentioned, the TrueType Font Pack includes 22 Lucida typefaces developed by digital typography pioneer Chuck Bigelow and calligrapher Kris Holmes. Lucida typefaces include the following:

➻ **Lucida Blackletter.** The olde English look.

»+ **Lucida Bright**. A distinctive, easy-to-read serif typeface.

»+ **Lucida Bright Demibold**. A bold version of Lucida Bright that is not too heavy.

»+ **Lucida Bright Italic**. The italic version of Lucida Bright.

»+ **Lucida Bright Demibold Italic**. A somewhat bold, italicized version of Lucida Bright.

»+ **Lucida Bright Math Symbols**. Symbols for mathematicians.

»+ **Lucida Bright Math Italic**. An italic math font; not an italic version of Lucida Bright Math Symbols.

»+ **Lucida Calligraphy**. Resembles the calligraphic lettering on a diploma.

»+ **Lucida Fax**. A typeface optimized for legibility after fax transmission.

»+ **Lucida Fax Demibold**. A heavier version of Lucida Fax.

»+ **Lucida Fax Italic**. An italic version of Lucida Fax.

»+ **Lucida Fax Demibold Italic**. A heavier version of Lucida Fax Italic.

»+ **Lucida Handwriting**. A simulation of human handwriting, based on the handwriting of Kris Holmes.

»+ **Lucida Math Extension**. Even more math symbols for those mathematicians who aren't satisfied with Lucida Bright Math Symbols and Lucida Bright Math Italic.

»+ **Lucida Sans**. An especially readable sans serif typeface for those who think Arial is ugly.

»+ **Lucida Sans Demibold**. A heavier version of Lucida Sans.

»+ **Lucida Sans Italic**. An italic version of Lucida Sans.

»+ **Lucida Sans Demibold Italic**. A heavier version of Lucida Sans Italic.

»+ **Lucida Sans Typewriter**. A sans serif alternative to Courier, reminiscent of IBM Selectric type.

»+ **Lucida Sans Typewriter Bold**. A bold version of Lucida Sans Typewriter.

»+ **Lucida Sans Typewriter Oblique**. A slightly italicized version of Lucida Sans Typewriter.

»+ **Lucida Sans Typewriter Bold Oblique**. A bold version of Lucida Sans Typewriter Oblique.

The TrueType Font Pack fleshes out the basic selection of TrueType type-faces included with Windows 95. I recommend the Font Pack for anyone using a laser printer.

To identify which fonts are TrueType, many applications precede the names of TrueType typefaces with a TT symbol (Figure 8.2). The applets bundled with Windows, such as WordPad and Paint, also follow this convention.

FIGURE 8.2

*Font Menu
with TT
Symbols*

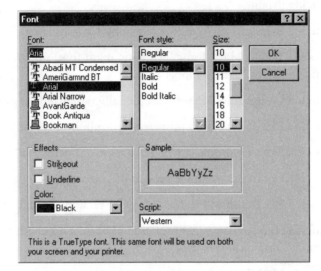

*The TT symbol tips
you off that this
is a TrueType
typeface. Use
these whenever you
can; they look good
and print quickly.*

You can also get a second Microsoft TrueType Font Pack, which includes 44 new typefaces. The fonts in this package are fully embeddable (more on that later in the chapter).

The TrueType Font Pack 2 includes the following fonts:

➠ **Augsburger Initials.** Elegant initial caps that resemble woodcuts.

➠ **Baskerville Old Face.** Slightly rounded serif letters.

➠ **Bell MT.** Another Timeslike serif face.

➠ **Braggadocio.** A big, bold headline look with a stenciled appearance (letter parts are separated by discrete spaces).

➠ **Briem Script.** A carefully hand-lettered look, rounded and not too formal.

➠ **Britannic Bold.** A serif typeface that gives the impression of being several decades old but not old-fashioned.

➣ **Castellar**. All caps with a double brush stroke (one wide, one thin); bears that official look for diplomas and other documents.

➣ **Centaur**. Another serif typeface; the bodies of the lowercase letters are slightly squat, and the horizontal strokes are angled.

➣ **Contemporary Brush**. A casual, sans serif typeface for informal notices and other announcements.

➣ **Desdemona**. Art deco, uppercase, outlined letters; think of Sarah Bernhardt.

➣ **Eckmann**. Medieval feeling, broad strokes, carefully lettered.

➣ **Edda**. Highly stylized, artistic, "witchy" or mystical letters; think of Aubrey Beardsley.

➣ **Elephant**. Brash, bold serif typeface for headlines.

➣ **Eurostile**. A no-nonsense, sans serif, rounded look.

➣ **Futura**. Good old Futura; slim, upright, sans serif respectability.

➣ **Gill Sans Ultra Bold**. That friendly, rounded typeface on steroids.

➣ **Gradl**. Tall, skinny, stylized.

➣ **Harrington**. Fussy, rounded serif typeface that seems appropriate for British tearooms.

➣ **Impact**. No nonsense here. Tall, tightly packed, no serifs. Very bold.

➣ **Mistral**. Familiar, heavy-stroked handwritten script. Casual.

➣ **New Caledonia**. Rounded serif letters, horizontal strokes unrelentingly straight.

➣ **Old English Text MT**. Very gothic and "olde."

➣ **Onyx**. Tall, skinny, tight-serifed headline.

➣ **Parade**. Casual serif typeface with a carefully handwritten look; might be the title typeface for a comic strip.

➣ **Peignot medium**. This looks a lot like the font that was used for the Mary Tyler Moore show.

➣ **Playbill**. Slightly Old West. That condensed look you see on theater programs.

➤ **Ransom.** Each letter a different style, as if it were scissored from a magazine to make up a ransom note.

➤ **Stencil.** Welcome to the Army.

➤ **Stop.** Bold but whimsical letters with distinct gaps between letter parts.

➤ **Wide Latin.** Standard serif characters put on a weight-gain diet, then stretched horizontally.

➤ **Wingdings 2.** More of the same.

➤ **Wingdings 3.** Even more of the same.

Danger Zone

The Font Pack 2 includes a great utility called Font Assistant, which enables you to categorize your fonts by groups, then activate whichever group you like at any time. It's handy and efficient, and I wish I'd known about it a long time ago. However, it doesn't work with Windows 95. But don't cry over the Font Assistant; the fonts in Font Pack 2 work well and look great, so install them and enjoy.

Printing TrueType Fonts

Earlier in this chapter I mentioned that TrueType creates a character by drawing an outline and filling it in. To accelerate the display or printing of a TrueType font, Windows 95 creates a font cache in which it stores those rendered bit maps. Each time you use a certain size of TrueType font, Windows creates a bit map of all the characters in that font. So the first time you use a particular font during a session with Windows, that font usually takes a little longer to display and print. However, because those bit maps are stored in the font cache for the remainder of the session (or until the font cache is full), you'll notice a quicker display and printing time when you reuse the same font during that Windows session.

The Windows 95 Registry handles fonts. Microsoft marketers therefore claim that an unlimited number of TrueType fonts can be active simultaneously. In theory, this means you can place as many fonts on a page as you like. In practice, you are limited to placing about a thousand fonts on a page at a time or having about a thousand fonts active simultaneously. In the real world, theory and practice amount to about the same thing.

Danger Zone

If you use a plethora of fonts and a multitude of sizes within a single document, you will probably notice a slowdown of performance and printing speed. This is because the font cache has become overloaded with rendered bit maps and hence has to be swapped out to the hard disk more often. However, this won't cause as much of a performance problem as it did with earlier versions of Windows. The problem occurs with all Windows fonts, not just True-Type. Because one TrueType typeface provides fonts of all sizes, it requires far less space than would an equivalent raster font, which usually requires a separate font file for each point size.

TrueType typefaces can be printed on any printer that supports the Windows universal printer driver. This means that the font looks the same whether it's printed on a dot-matrix printer, a laser printer, or a typesetting machine, although the quality varies.

When you upgrade from Windows 3.1, Windows 95 does not change the fonts of previously created documents. Documents should appear exactly as they did before you got Windows 95. If you find yourself using a document that was created with a program or in an environment that did not support TrueType, you can open it, select its type, and select a TrueType font for it. Some vendors offer utilities that automatically upgrade documents to True-Type; refer to the documentation to see if this feature is offered.

Danger Zone

Because each computer system tends to have a different set of fonts installed, no guarantee exists that you can print a document identically on two different computers. Although WYSIWYG provides a visual correlation between what you see on your screen and the output from your printer, this principle doesn't always apply across computers. A discrepancy typically occurs in an office, where the carefully formatted document you prepared on your own system looks as if it's been through a mangler when you print it out on your colleague's system.

Typeface troubles can also emerge when you send a disk to a PostScript service bureau for output, unless the service bureau already owns the fonts you used or you include the typefaces on the disk. Although this is a common practice, it's an added hassle and a potential copyright violation, because most commercial typefaces are licensed for only one machine.

An easier and more legal approach to the service bureau problem is to use a Print to Disk file (also called a PostScript file). You route all the information you would have sent to your printer—including graphics, and data—into one file that you can usually put on a disk and take anywhere, especially to a service bureau. Once you set up the "port" for this type of print job, it's no different than printing any other job on your computer. You can easily download the file you end up with to a printer elsewhere. This approach offers many benefits:

➻ You can proof the print file on your own PostScript printer before you send the file to the service bureau.

➺ You can save money, because service bureau staff don't have to open and print the original file.

➺ Printing to a file is easy to do with Windows 95.

➺ You don't violate copyright laws because the font information is included in your PostScript files.

To perform this useful feat, select File as the port to which you print. File, as already described, stores all the data that would have gone to the printer in the file you designate. You can print to a file by clicking on the printer icon for your usual printer, or you can create an icon specifically for the output device you want. For example, you can install a printer driver for your neighbor's color printer and target it to file, and you can do the same for your service bureau's imagesetter. Just ask them what model it is.

Once you determine which printer icon you're going to use, select the icon and choose Properties from its File menu or pop-up menu. Click on the Details tab, and select File in the Print to the Following Port dialog box.

TrueType Font Embedding. Font embedding helps solve some of the problems with document portability by including fonts as part of a document. Microsoft has devised three levels of TrueType font embedding, ranging from highly restrictive to open.

Which level of embedding to select is left up to the font developer. At the most restrictive level, developers can prevent their fonts from being embedded into documents. If **no embedding** is allowed, even applications that support font embedding don't let you embed the restricted typeface into a document. As a result the recipient is compelled to purchase the typeface or make a font substitution. Most PostScript fonts have this level of restriction. However, because it's a hassle, this restrictive choice is seldom exercised by developers. If you do find you can't embed a font, consider complaining to its developer about this heavy-handed restriction.

At the middle level of restriction, a TrueType typeface can be developed as **read-only** for the purpose of embedding. This allows a document to be viewed and printed in the proper typeface when it's transferred to another computer system. However, the typeface is only temporarily installed on the machine, and the recipient is not able to modify the document or use the typeface in any other document or application. Many vendors of large fonts sell TrueType fonts with the embedding status set to read-only. This choice allows documents to be freely exchanged while protecting the developer's ability to sell more copies of the typeface.

As a third alternative, font developers can set their font embedding status to **read-write.** With read-write embedding, a document that embeds a True-Type font contains a fully installable copy of the font itself. When a document containing a read-write TrueType font is sent to another user, the recipient can freely edit the document and view or print it. In addition, the read-write fonts can be used by other applications on the recipient's system and can usually be installed permanently on the other computer, as if that user had purchased the font.

Insider's Tip

A read-write font can be used in any Windows application that works with TrueType and is designed to support font embedding. You can even reembed the font and send it to another user. The TrueType fonts included with Windows 95, as well as the fonts in the TrueType Font Packs, are set on read-write embedding status. This read-write capability is advantageous, particularly when compared with the read-only status of many commercially available font packs.

• •

PostScript Fonts

PostScript fonts (which are a form of outline fonts) are written in a language understood by any PostScript device, from a high-end imagesetter to the low-end Apple LaserWriter. The appearance of a PostScript font varies only with the resolutions of the devices on which it is printed. Once printed, PostScript fonts can be scaled, rotated, stretched, and otherwise manipulated with no decrease in quality. In a graphics program, you can turn a typeface character into a graphic element, then add color or patterns, change the size or height of its parts, and exercise other options.

The standard family of PostScript fonts includes the following:

➺ Helvetica.

➺ Helvetica Narrow.

➺ Palatino.

➺ Bookman.

➺ Avant Garde.

➺ Zapf Chancery.

➺ Courier.

➣ Zapf Dingbats.

➣ Symbol.

➣ Times Roman.

Those fonts are built into all PostScript printers (except the earliest Apple models). Other PostScript fonts can be downloaded or stored on a hard disk in the printer to minimize print times.

PostScript fonts may not sound much different from TrueType fonts. However, they have a longer history and, as I mentioned before, are the accepted standard in the printing industry, because of their inside track with commercial imagesetters and printers.

Historically, the type of printer you used determined your choice of fonts. PostScript fonts (along with several other unsuccessful contenders) used to be the only scalable fonts. Your other choice was old PCL, or bit-mapped, fonts, which a few years back were compatible with printers such as LaserJets. People with PostScript printers could use characters of any size without thinking about it. Those with old PCL printers had to "build" or create bit-mapped versions of fonts at whatever point sizes they wanted to use—a tedious job.

Two developments in the Windows environment brought down the wall between those with PostScript printers and those without. First, **Adobe Type Manager (ATM)**—the PostScript font manager—made it possible to print PostScript fonts on a non-PostScript device. Using the scalable outlines, ATM creates bit-mapped images of each character and prints them as graphics. Second, TrueType came on the scene. TrueType does essentially the same thing as PostScript by making it possible to use scalable fonts. No longer do people have to worry whether they have the right point size or if their system has the room to store a vast number of fonts.

TrueType versus PostScript

Which is better, TrueType or PostScript? There's no easy answer, because each system has its strengths and weaknesses. TrueType is included free with Windows 95, which certainly makes it attractive. For professional desktop publishers and typesetters, PostScript is more entrenched, maintaining a clear advantage in this arena. Although TrueType works with PostScript printers by converting TrueType fonts to PostScript fonts, some applications require real PostScript fonts. To get PostScript for Windows, you need ATM, which provides scalable typefaces for your screen and printer and thereby offers roughly the same functions as TrueType.

As for performance, TrueType prints faster to non-PostScript printers such as Hewlett-Packard LaserJets, whereas PostScript soft fonts work better with PostScript printers, because the printer and system fonts are similar. Both products do an admirable but understandably slow job of printing on dot-matrix and inkjet printers.

Insider's Tip

Because of the predominance of PostScript in desktop publishing, many desktop publishing products for Windows come bundled with Adobe Type Manager. If you're already buying one of those software packages, the additional cost of ATM is usually minimal; sometimes software vendors bundle ATM as a "free" sales incentive.

Hinting. An important difference between TrueType and PostScript is how they implement **hinting,** a technique used to include information in an outline typeface. The process helps to compensate for the discrepancies that occur when gently flowing outlines are converted to gridlike bit maps. Both TrueType and PostScript are based on outline fonts, and both use some form of hinting.

Hinting adjusts the outline of a character so that the strokes that make it up are better aligned with the dots on a printer or the pixels on a monitor. This process greatly increases the legibility of the text, especially when small type is displayed on your monitor or on a 300 dpi laser printer. However, hinting becomes irrelevant on a 1,200 dpi typesetting machine, because more pixels are available for displaying each character.

Whereas TrueType incorporates its hints into the typeface file, PostScript places hinting in the font rasterizer, which draws the characters on the screen. With TrueType, each character in the typeface can contain its own hints. As a result software that displays TrueType on screen can be more efficient, because it doesn't need to calculate hinting on the fly; it just reads the hinting information contained in the typeface. The drawback with TrueType is that once the typeface is created, hinting cannot be improved.

PostScript hinting is contained in the PostScript rasterizer—the software that converts the outline of the font into a bit map for screen display or printer output. PostScript fonts come in two flavors. The older, Type 3 fonts do not contain hinting. The newer, Type 1 fonts contain hints that tell the rasterizer how much to distort the outlines of all the characters in a typeface (rather than of each character, as with TrueType) to adjust them for low-resolution output devices.

Insider's Tip

The bottom line in the TrueType versus PostScript debate is this: For professional typesetters, print shops, and desktop publishing services, hinting is irrelevant, and PostScript is the standard. If you just need a straightforward and inexpensive (often free) way to make your laser printer produce attractive documents, I recommend TrueType. Because of its approach to hinting, TrueType can look good at comparatively low resolutions—for example, on 300 dpi laser printers and 640 by 480 and 800 by 600 VGA monitors, which are still the staple of the PC market.

System Fonts

As I mentioned earlier, Windows 95 includes a selection of raster fonts for displaying the text of icons, menus, dialog boxes, window titles, and other system components. Each system and screen font appears in the Fonts folder with a red *A* on it. Unlike Windows 3.1, which uses a font called System for screen display, Windows 95 uses a variety of fonts in its display, and many of them are changeable.

The following raster fonts are included with Windows 95:

➤ **Courier**. A fixed-width serif font reminiscent of a typewriter font.

➤ **MS Serif**. A proportional font in the Times tradition.

➤ **MS Sans Serif**. A fixed-width serif font reminiscent of a typewriter font.

➤ **Small Fonts**. A proportional font designed to look good when its size is under 8 points.

➤ **Symbol**. A proportional font composed of math symbols.

➤ **System**. A font used by elements of the Windows 95 interface.

Six sizes (8, 10, 12, 14, 18, and 24 points) are provided for several types of display. The raster fonts come in six resolutions: four that match specific displays and two for use with printers. The files for those fonts are COUR(X).FON, SSERIF(X).FON, SERIF(X).FON, SMALL(X).FON, and SYMBOL(X).FON, where the *X* varies from *B* to *F* (Table 8.3).

TABLE 8.3
*Resolution and
Aspect Ratios
of Raster Fonts*

Letter	Device	Horizontal by Vertical Resolution	Aspect Ratio
B*	EGA display	96 by 72 dpi	1.33:1
C*	Printer	60 by 72 dpi	1:1.2
D*	Printer	120 by 72 dpi	1.66:1
E	VGA display	96 by 96 dpi	1:1
F	8514/a display	120 by 120 dpi	1:1

*These files are not included on the Windows 95 disks.

The name of each font includes one of the letters shown in Table 8.3; the letter indicates the resolution of the font. For example, the set of five fonts installed for a VGA display includes COURE.FON, SSERIFE.FON, SERIFE.FON, SMALLE.FON, and SYMBOLE.FON.

Windows can scale raster fonts to even multiples of the provided sizes. However, in large sizes these fonts appear jagged around the edges. You can print with raster fonts if their resolution and aspect ratios closely match those of your printer (an aspect ratio is the relationship of the height to the width of an object). You may need to refer to your printer manual to determine what horizontal and vertical ratios it's capable of producing to find the raster font that matches best.

Windows also uses two other fonts, **Fixed** and **Terminal,** to display items on screen. The Fixed font is nonproportional and was the primary system font of the ancient Windows 2.0. Fixed now provides compatibility with older applications. The Terminal font, sometimes called the OEM (original equipment manufacturer) font, is nonproportional and is used to display OEM text in the Clipboard Viewer utility. In addition, it's used by Windows applications, such as Terminal, that require a font with a fixed width. Telecommunications displays often require fixed spacing to properly display rows, columns, tables, and on-line menus on screen.

Windows Setup installs Fixed and Terminal fonts that match your computer's display. The Fixed and OEM font files are shown in Table 8.4.

TABLE 8.4
*Fixed and
OEM Fonts for
Standard
Displays*

Display	Resolution	Fixed Font	OEM Font
EGA	640 by 350 (AT&T 640 by 400)	EGAFIX.FON	EGAOEM.FON
VGA	640 by 480	VGAFIX.FON	VGAOEM.FON
8514/a	1,024 by 768	8514FIX.FON	8514OEM.FON

Although the Fixed and OEM fonts have their place in the Windows 95 Registry, their font assignments are still listed in the [boot] section of the SYSTEM.INI file. For example, the [boot] section of SYSTEM.INI on a system with a VGA display would include the following two lines:

```
FIXEDFON.FON=VGAFIX.FON
OEMFONTS.FON=VGAOEM.FON
```

Insider's Tip

The raster fonts installed on your system are listed in the Fonts folder inside the main Windows folder. You can see what point sizes are available for each font. To do so, click on the Start button, choose Settings and Control Panel, then double-click on the Fonts icon. In the Fonts folder the icons for raster fonts bear a red A, and all sizes in which they are available are listed below or next to them. If any ancient Windows fonts remain—for example, Tms Rmn or Helv—Windows 95 replaces them with the MS Serif and MS Sans Serif fonts by remapping them in the [fontSubstitutes] section of the WIN.INI file.

In addition to the raster fonts, Windows 95 includes three files of **vector fonts:** ROMAN.FON, MODERN.FON, and SCRIPT.FON. The files contain mathematical instructions for drawing the typefaces; vector fonts were originally used by pen plotters, in which a pen follows instructions to draw characters on paper.

Before TrueType and ATM, vector fonts were the only scalable fonts available for Windows, and some developers used them to create large characters and special type effects, such as rotated text. The inclusion of vector fonts in Windows 95 provides compatibility with such applications and enables you to use a pen plotter. However, I recommend using TrueType if you want scalable type on anything other than a plotter.

Table 8.5 identifies which kinds of fonts work with what printers in Windows 95.

TABLE 8.5
Printer and Font Compatibility

Printer	TrueType Fonts	Raster Fonts	Vector Fonts
HP LaserJet-compatible	Yes	No	Yes
PostScript	Yes	No	Yes
Dot matrix	Yes	Yes	Yes
Pen plotter	No	No	Yes

Changing System Fonts. Windows 95 Setup installs the fonts you need for your display. You can also print with those fonts, and you can change display fonts. Be forewarned, though, that some printers, such as pen plotters, cannot print raster fonts, regardless of resolution or aspect ratio. For such printers you need to use vector or TrueType fonts.

To change the fonts used in your system programs and listings, choose Settings from the Start menu, select Control Panel, and double-click on Display. You can change fonts using either of the following two tabs:

➻ The **Appearance** tab enables you to change the fonts in message boxes, title bars, button captions, and other parts of a window. This page is arranged by color, and you can click on individual components (such as window parts) to change them. After you change a font, the Font text window becomes active.

➻ The **Settings** tab enables you to change the font of names listed under icons and to change the size of text in areas such as dialog boxes. Select a smaller font, such as the tiny Small font, to see more items in the folder and file panes of windows. Select a larger font to make it easier to read text at a high screen resolution, which shrinks everything on your display. Be careful when playing with system fonts because some setting may cause strange effects in some applications.

Insider's Tip

If you choose a TrueType font of 8 points or smaller for display, Windows 95 automatically substitutes the Small font. At that size you can't tell the difference between the Small font and an 8-point TrueType font. In fact, you'd be hard put even to read an 8-point or smaller TrueType font in a display.

You can also customize the fonts of the Help system. Help usually includes an Options menu, which contains a Font cascading menu. Your choices need little explanation: Small, Normal, and Large. This changes the text only within the Help window.

Fonts and DOS Applications

You can select from a variety of fonts in which to display character-based DOS applications run from within Windows 95. This new feature enables you to select small type, so a full DOS display fits in a window smaller than a standard VGA display. In this way you can run several DOS applications at once in full view, or you can keep a single window open without obscuring the rest of your Windows screen.

To change the font used in a DOS window, open a windowed DOS session and select the Properties command from the DOS Windows Control menu. Click on the Font tab in the MS-DOS Prompt Properties window (Figure 8.3).

• • • • • • • • • • • • • •
FIGURE 8.3
MS-DOS
Prompt
Properties
Dialog Box

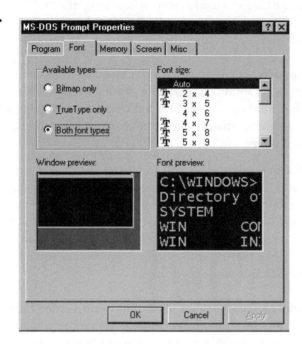

Windows 95 lets you select the font size in which to display character-based DOS applications in a window.

Another way to select a font for DOS is to click on the arrow to the right of the drop-down list box at the left of the toolbar in a DOS window. You can also click on the A, or Fonts, button on the toolbar.

Each of those options opens the Font Selection dialog box, in which you can select and preview available bit-mapped and TrueType fonts. TrueType fonts are identified by the letters *TT*.

Those fonts are based on the U.S. standard DOS character set.

Your choice of fonts depends on which video grabber file you use. Note that CGA fonts used with DOS applications can simulate a CGA display inside a window, regardless of what type of actual display you use.

• •

Installing Fonts

Windows 95 provides several methods for installing new fonts. Which method you choose depends on the font and the printer driver:

⇢ To install **TrueType, raster, and vector fonts,** you use the Fonts icon on the Control Panel.

⇢ You install **PostScript fonts** with the utilities included with Adobe Type Manager.

⇢ You install **Hewlett-Packard LaserJet soft fonts** and other types of fonts for the LaserJet on your hard disk by using the printer driver's font installer. In some cases you may also need to add the fonts to Windows by using the Fonts icon on the Control Panel. You install some third-party soft fonts on your hard disk using the utility supplied with the fonts, then install them in Windows using the Fonts icon on the Control Panel.

The Fonts Folder

To handle a font in previous versions of Windows, you had to use an installer, a font management utility, or the Fonts dialog box in the Control Panel. In Windows 95 you can see and manipulate a font directly in the Fonts folder, providing it's a TrueType, raster, or vector font. The Fonts folder doesn't handle PostScript or other kinds of fonts. To get to the Fonts folder, choose Settings from the Start menu, open the Control Panel, and double-click on the Fonts icon (Figure 8.4).

FIGURE 8.4
The Fonts Folder

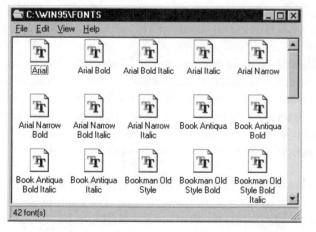

The Kingdom of Fontal Delights: view, install, or remove fonts from here.

The Fonts folder displays all installed TrueType, raster, and vector fonts. The icons for TrueType fonts are labeled TT; the icons for raster and vector fonts sport a red *A*. You can set up the window to use large icons (the default display), to list fonts alphabetically with tiny icons adjacent to each name, or to group fonts by type. All those choices are available on the View menu or the pop-up menu. The View menu also offers a Hide Variations command, which enables you to display the basic font for each family, sweeping intrafamily variations under the carpet.

The Fonts folder offers other features as well, including the following:

➤ You can see the properties of any font file by choosing Properties from the File menu or the pop-up menu.

➤ You can reverse the display order of the folder with a quick flick of the mouse.

➤ You can show a toolbar at the top of the window to make most of those tasks even easier.

If you like, you can direct Windows 95 to show only TrueType fonts. This option is similar to the one in Windows 3.1, and it still applies only to applications. Even if you enable it, all available fonts appear in the Fonts folder. If you want to enable the feature anyway, choose Options from the View menu in the Fonts folder, then click on the TrueType tab and check the option labeled Show Only TrueType Fonts in the Programs on My Computer.

Viewing Installed Fonts. Viewing installed fonts has become easier with Windows 95. You view a font directly in its folder, instead of having to use an installer, a font management utility, or the Fonts dialog box in the Control Panel.

To view a sample of a font, double-click on the font's icon. The font sample you bring up includes several point sizes, plus the name of the manufacturer, the version number, the file size, and the format. The sample includes all standard characters; the bigger your monitor and the window in which the sample is displayed, the more of the sample you see. Click on the Print button to print the sample and on the Done button when you finish.

Viewing Similar Fonts. To view fonts in order of similarity, open the Fonts folder and go to the View menu. Choose List Fonts by Similarity. You may be wondering, "similar to *what*?" In the List Fonts by Similarity To list box, you answer that question yourself; the similarity is to a font you select (which must be another font installed in and managed by your Fonts folder).

Windows 95 determines font similarity using the **PANOSE Typeface Matching System,** a font classification system developed to battle font confusion and aid in font substitution. PANOSE assigns a number to a font, based on an assessment of its design, including its serifs, proportions, contrast, stroke variations, arm type, letterform, midline, and x height.

Insider's Tip

The name PANOSE serves as a mnemonic device. The letters *P, A, N, O, S,* and *E* include most of the shapes found in standard, uppercase text characters. Those uppercase letters, along with the lowercase letters *a, b, e, g, k, m, o, q, s,* and *t,* contain the important features of any given typeface.

PANOSE data are stored as font information and control the order of entries in the similarity list. PANOSE information enables a font to be listed in the List Fonts by Similarity To box; if PANOSE information is not available, the font doesn't appear in that list. After it reviews PANOSE characteristics, Windows 95 returns a diagnosis of Very Similar, Fairly Similar, Not Similar, or No PANOSE Information Available.

Viewing fonts by similarity can be useful if you need to substitute fonts. For more information on substituting fonts, see the Typography section earlier in this chapter.

Installing TrueType Fonts. The easiest, most gratifying way to install True-Type fonts is to drag them to the Fonts folder. You can do this directly from a floppy, a CD-ROM disk, or a folder on your local computer or on a networked computer. This is preferable to copying the fonts to a temporary location on your computer before dragging them, a procedure that requires extra disk space and provides little gain in installation time.

You can also add fonts by choosing Install New Font from the File menu in the Fonts folder. Use the Folders list and the Drives drop-down list box to identify the source of the fonts, whether it's a local or a networked site. Select the fonts, pressing Ctrl to select noncontiguous fonts or holding down the mouse button and continuing to drag down to select a series. You can also use the Select All button.

Insider's Tip

If you open a folder that contains a lot of fonts, it's going to take a while for Windows 95 to recognize and display the contents of the folder. Don't panic or click wildly because you don't get an instant response. A counter on the screen indicates what percentage of the data has been retrieved.

If you install fonts from a floppy or any other medium that isn't going to be available whenever you want to use those fonts, make sure the option Copy Fonts to Fonts Folder is checked. Your system can also access fonts directly from a CD-ROM disk, but access is slower, and you have to keep the font CD in place just about all the time. It's better, if you have the space, to store the fonts on your hard disk.

The only other option in the Add Fonts dialog box is the Network button. Use this button to connect to other drives that might be a source of fonts. Of course, you should be able to see your mapped drives in the Drives drop-down list box, but other drives might not have been mapped.

Why would you use fonts stored on another system instead of dragging the font files directly into the folder? Because instead of seeing the file names of the fonts (for example, COURBI.TTF for Courier New Bold Italic), you see a more readable name with a small icon next to it. Either way, you can use and preview fonts as soon as you have installed them without having to shut down and restart your system.

Installing PostScript Fonts. PostScript fonts are still installed in the WIN.INI file and are subject to that file's 64K limit. Use Adobe Type Manager (ATM) to install and manage your PostScript fonts, as you always have. ATM 3.01 is compatible with Windows 95, although version 3.01 doesn't support the installation of PCL soft fonts in Windows 95; this is scheduled to be addressed in the next version of ATM. Once the PostScript fonts are installed, you can use them freely in your applications, unless you've set up Windows so that you see only TrueType fonts in your applications. If so, you won't be able to locate the PostScript fonts.

If you don't have ATM, you can still install your PostScript fonts manually by adding the appropriate lines to the WIN.INI file. Here's how: The WIN.INI file looks for PostScript font listings in its [Printer,Port] sections. The listings consist of one line per font and refer to the drive, the directory, and the name of the font file or files. Usually two files are listed: the PFM, for metric spacing information, and the PFB, which contains the font outlines themselves. The PFM is crucial; without it the font would not be listed in the ATM Control Panel or in any application. The PFB is not crucial if you don't print the file yourself (for example, if you send it to a commercial printer who has that font). With just the PFM file, you can select a font and get a good idea of the spacing—good enough so you can lay out your page. WIN.INI contains a reference to each style of a typeface. Table 8.6 shows a sample of lines from the WIN.INI file.

TABLE 8.6
PostScript Font Listings in the WIN.INI *File*

`[PostScript,LPT1]`	*Section heading. There's one for every port you specify.*
`softfonts=15`	*Number of fonts installed.*

```
softfont1=c:\psfonts\pfm\bhh_____.pfm,c:\psfonts\bhh_____.pfb
softfont2=c:\psfonts\pfm\bhl_____.pfm,c:\psfonts\bhl_____.pfb
softfont3=c:\psfonts\pfm\bhm_____.pfm,c:\psfonts\bhm_____.pfb
softfont4=c:\psfonts\pfm\bhb_____.pfm,c:\psfonts\bhb_____.pfb
softfont5=c:\psfonts\pfm\fuceb___.pfm,c:\psfonts\arot____.pfb
softfont6=c:\psfonts\pfm\fcebo___.pfm,c:\psfonts\hrb_____.pfb
softfont7=c:\psfonts\pfm\fucl____.pfm,c:\psfonts\mobl____.pfb
softfont8=c:\psfonts\pfm\fuclo___.pfm,c:\psfonts\mob_____.pfb
softfont9=c:\psfonts\pfm\fuc_____.pfm,c:\psfonts\mobi____.pfb
softfont10=c:\psfonts\pfm\fucb____.pfm,c:\psfonts\mods____.pfb
softfont11=c:\psfonts\pfm\fucbo___.pfm,c:\psfonts\modsi___.pfb
softfont12=c:\psfonts\pfm\fuco____.pfm,c:\psfonts\morg____.pfb
softfont13=c:\psfonts\pfm\fucb____.pfm,c:\psfonts\mosb____.pfb
softfont14=c:\psfonts\pfm\fucbo___.pfm,c:\psfonts\mosbi___.pfb
softfont15=c:\psfonts\pfm\fuco____.pfm,c:\psfonts\moi_____.pfb
```

The font names in WIN.INI aren't very intuitive, but the examples in Table 8.6 include Bauhaus (Heavy, Light, Medium, and Bold), ArchitextOne Type, Hiroshige Bold, and several flavors of Minion. For example, softfont1 is Bauhaus Heavy, and softfont2 is Bauhaus Light.

Danger Zone

The underscores following letters in the font names are crucial, because font names must contain eight characters before the extension.

Some applications, such as CorelDraw, automatically install fonts into your system and update the WIN.INI file. Because those fonts and others you've installed into Windows gobble up memory and space on your hard disk, I recommend you install only those fonts you actually use. Sure, it's tempting to have a long list of fonts just a few clicks away. However, it's better to keep your system mean and lean, and installing fonts as you need them is straightforward.

Insider's Tip

To install a large group of fonts at one time, first place them all in the same directory. You can then select the entire group all at once.

• •

Removing Fonts

To remove a font, select its icon in the Fonts folder and choose Delete from the File menu or from the pop-up menu. You can also drag the icon to the Recycle Bin or a Recycle Bin shortcut. But beware of font-deleting binges: unlike previous versions of Windows, Windows 95 doesn't give you the option of keeping uninstalled fonts on your hard disk. As soon as you empty the Recycle Bin or it empties itself, the fonts are gone. If you want to uninstall a font but keep it on the hard disk, drag (or cut and paste) it to another folder on your local or network drive.

Danger Zone

Prevent a fontal lobotomy. Don't remove the MS Sans Serif font set, because Windows uses it for system purposes. (Windows 3.0 used the Helv font, which Setup replaces when you upgrade.) If MS Sans Serif isn't available, Windows substitutes a different font, which can make some on-screen items difficult to read.

Some documents that you print may use fonts that are not installed in your system. This can happen if you receive a document from someone else or if you remove a font that was previously installed. In such cases, Windows does its best to substitute a font that approximates the missing one. If the missing font is TrueType, Windows can make a better substitution, because it can call on TrueType to render the character. And if TrueType fonts are embedded in a document, you can print it properly without having to substitute fonts.

• •

Character Map

The Character Map accessory provides a simple way to view the characters of any font installed on your system. It also enables you to cut and paste characters into a document, so you can use characters that aren't on the keyboard without having to search for and type in arcane ANSI codes. You can access the Character Map, or CHARMAP, by selecting Programs from the Start menu, then clicking on Accessories (Figure 8.5).

The Character Map window contains a grid displaying all the characters in the currently selected typeface. Above the grid is a drop-down list box labeled Font, which you can access with the mouse or by pressing Alt+F. From this list, you can select a typeface to display in the grid. Figure 8.6 depicts a Windows 95 TrueType typeface called Wingdings, which is made up of symbols, icons, and dingbats.

FIGURE 8.5

*Character Map
Window with
Times Roman
Typeface*

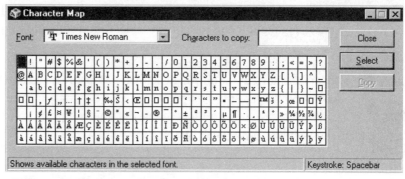

The Character Map utility provides a handy way
to view and access special character sets.

FIGURE 8.6

*Character Map
Window with
Wingdings
Typeface*

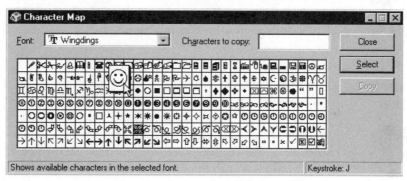

Hold down the mouse button while pointing at a
character to see an enlarged view of it.

Characters displayed in the grid are often shrunk to a less-than-optimum resolution. To see an enlarged view of an individual character, hold down the mouse button while pointing at the character.

To copy a character that you want to paste into another application, double-click on it. You can also navigate using the keyboard. Press Tab to move the cursor into the character grid, then use the arrow keys to navigate through the grid. Click on the Select button or press Alt+S to select a character. Whatever your method, the character you select is placed in the Characters to Copy field at the top of the Character Map window. When you are ready, click on the Copy button (or press Alt+C) to transfer anything in the Characters to Copy field onto the Clipboard. When the characters are on the Clipboard, switch to any document and choose the Paste command (or press Ctrl+V). Sometimes the character is transformed when you paste it; this occurs when it is in a different font from your document. To reset the character, highlight it and select the correct font from within the application.

Insider's Tip

Here's a shortcut for quitting Character Map: press Esc, and the window vanishes. Sorry, you still can't print the Character Map or, even more desirable, a list of characters with their codes. But you can print font samples from the Fonts folder, as noted earlier in this chapter.

Dynamite Product

If you're really into typefaces, you might want a commercial font utility to help you view and organize your collection. **FontShow,** by Rascal Software, is an inventory and catalog program that does the trick. It enables you to view and print entire type catalogs in a variety of formats, and yes, you can see all the characters. FontShow supports both PostScript and TrueType fonts and PostScript and non-PostScript printers.

Dynamite Product

Plus Pack, from Microsoft, contains several system tools that can help smooth and improve your computing experience. The Plus Pack includes utilities to help remove the screen "jaggies" from TrueType fonts, as well as utilities to "clean" a disk (that is, to scan and defragment it) and to set up and keep a schedule of disk maintenance. With the Plus Pack, you can create a batch file in DOS mode to run the defragmenter or other program of your choice at given intervals. You can also use the timer on yourself—to remind you to stretch every so often, for instance.

Summary

Whereas the developers of Windows 3.1 concentrated on improving computer output by introducing TrueType fonts, the developers of Windows 95 placed more emphasis on high-quality typography. Microsoft has also introduced easier and quicker ways to install fonts, print fonts, view fonts, and even remove them. Desktop publishing is as painless as it's ever been. The next chapter describes parallel improvements made to the printing process with Windows 95.

Printing

Despite talk about the paperless office, a computer without a printer is like a full coffee pot without cups. Recognizing the importance of printing, Microsoft has streamlined the printing process with Windows 95. For the first time, you can experience true background printing, two-way communication between the printer and the computer, automatic deferred printing, enhanced metafile spooling, extended capabilities port support, and Image Color Matching. Overall, setting up and using a printer is easier, faster, and more flexible with Windows 95 than it was with previous versions of Windows.

Almost everything is new about printing in Windows 95. If you don't want to think about printing, you can plug in your printer and walk through the printer setup. But then you'd be missing out on all the new features, which not only give you added control over printing but also allow you more time than before to get on with your other work.

The Printers Folder

With Windows 95 you control all print-related functions from one central location, the Printers folder. To open the folder, select Settings from the Start menu, then choose Printers (which is actually a shortcut to the Printers folder). You can also open the Printers folder by double-clicking on the Printers icon on the Control Panel, much as you would have done with Windows 3.1. The Printers folder contains an icon for each printer installed on your system, both local and networked. In addition, the folder contains the Add Printer icon; double-click on it to start the Add Printer wizard, which helps you install a new printer (Figure 9.1).

FIGURE 9.1
The Printers Folder

All Windows 95 printing functions can be controlled from the Printers folder.

You can view and change information in the Printers folder in several ways. First, if you select a printer and open the File menu, you can see whether the printer is the current default printer; the default printer has a check mark next to it. You can also see whether the printer is set to print off line. When you select Work Offline, Windows 95 stores documents as printable files—that is, with all the information a printer needs to print the files—on your hard disk. Work Offline is useful when you use a laptop away from the office. Just print documents off line, then print them on your normal printer when you return to the office. Work offline, however, only works on a network printer. For a local printer, if you want to print later, use the Pause Printing option instead.

The Set as Default checkbox also can tell you whether the printer you've selected is the default printer. If the box is unchecked and you want to make the current printer the default printer, click on the Set as Default checkbox.

You can also look at and change printer properties with the Printers folder. Select a printer and choose Properties from the File menu, or click the right mouse button on a printer icon and choose Properties from the Shortcut menu.

When you choose the Properties command, the Properties dialog box pops up. The tabs in the dialog box contain settings for the printer you have selected. It's not a bad idea to examine the settings to make sure they really correspond to your printer, particularly if your printer isn't standard. Have you added memory or another paper tray? If so, and if you don't have a newer, Plug and Play printer, you may need to update the appropriate Properties tab so Windows 95 knows about the change (see the next section of this chapter, on bidirectional communication). The Properties dialog box offers other options as well, such as paper size, time-out settings, and printer port selection. You can explore your options using the right mouse button. Choose What's This? from the Shortcut menu to learn more about any one option.

Danger Zone

If you modify printer settings, print a test page to make sure you haven't inadvertently created an incompatibility or other type of problem.

Yet another way to unearth information about a printer is to double-click on its icon to open its print queue. The queue shows any files that are waiting to print or that you've printed off line. The File menu still contains the Work Offline and Set as Default commands. A small printer icon on the Taskbar near the clock indicates that there are files waiting to print. The print queue gives you the power to rearrange documents waiting to print—handy if you want to advance your own documents in a network print queue when nobody else is looking.

Bidirectional Communication

Windows 95 talks to your printer, and your printer—if it supports bidirectional printing—now can talk back. With bidirectional printing, Windows 95 can glean information such as what fonts are available on the printer, how much memory it has, and whether it needs paper. Because the printer can communicate with Windows 95, setup is easier, and if a problem arises, the printer can identify it and let Windows know about it. If the printer also supports Plug and Play, it can provide Windows 95 even more information, making installation and configuration a snap.

Bidirectional communication works only if your printer supports Plug and Play, and no practical way exists to retrofit older printers. If you don't need a printer right now, you're out of luck until it's time to buy a new one. At that time you'll likely want to look for a Plug and Play model.

Enhanced Metafile Spooling

Windows 95 quickly spools all print jobs that do not use PostScript in a format called Enhanced Metafile (EMF). Spooling is a process by which your computer's or printer's memory (or both) temporarily stores print jobs from applications while they are being printed, releasing the application for your use. EMF information is processed in the background before being sent to the printer, so you can resume work immediately after issuing the Print command. All Windows programs benefit from EMF spooling.

Windows 95 spools print jobs from DOS programs as well, albeit not with EMF, so the process is slower. If you regularly print from both DOS and Windows programs, you may notice that Windows 95 eliminates conflicts between DOS and Windows programs trying to print simultaneously.

If you want to disable Enhanced Metafile spooling, go to the printer's Properties window, click on Details, then click on Spool Settings. Choose Raw from the Spool Data Format list to disable EMF spooling, then click on OK.

Extended Capabilities Port Support

An extended capabilities port (ECP) is a port that can accommodate various I/O ranges and IRQ and DMA settings; you can tailor the ECP to meet your needs. An ECP improves printing speed, especially when the device at the other end is also ECP. Windows 95 provides ECP support, which you set up with the Device Manager. However, you can do so only if Windows 95 has detected the ECP port on your computer. If the software has not detected the ECP port, you may be able to correct the problem by using the Add New Hardware section of the Control Panel.

Image Color Matching

Color discrepancies are often an aggravation in desktop publishing. Image Color Matching (ICM) does a great deal to relieve that problem. Developed by a consortium of hardware vendors and standards setters (including Microsoft,

Kodak, Apple, Sun, and Silicon Graphics), ICM enables applications to print the same colors as they display. It does this by establishing color profiles based on international color standards for software and hardware. The result is color that is consistent among applications, hardware devices, and platforms.

How can you take advantage of ICM? Buy software and hardware that support the standard. Because ICM is built into Windows 95, it's up to software and hardware vendors to take advantage of the standard. I expect many will, particularly manufacturers of scanners and color printers. Already many desktop publishing and graphics programs support one or more color-matching schemes.

Installing a Printer

To install a printer, double-click on the Add Printer icon in the Printers folder. The Add Printer wizard steps you through installation by asking simple questions, usually one per dialog box. The first dialog box asks how your printer is connected (local versus network). Answer the question by clicking on the appropriate radio button, then click on Next.

In the next dialog box, you choose the make of your printer from a list of manufacturers. Windows 95 includes drivers for over 800 printers. When you click on the name of a manufacturer, a list of the printers it manufactures appears. If you don't see the name of your printer, check to see whether the printer includes a disk or a CD-ROM with a printer driver. If it does, click on the Have Disk button and follow the instructions. When you select the Have Disk option, Windows 95 asks you to insert one of your printer's disks or its CD-ROM during installation.

The next dialog box asks you to select a port for your printer. You can also configure the port if you want. If your printer supports Plug and Play, you skip this step altogether.

Finally, you are requested to give your printer a name and asked whether you want to designate it as the default printer. You can also print a test page. Windows 95 then copies the appropriate files, and a new printer icon, labeled with the name you chose, appears in the Printers folder. You can print to it right away. Later in this chapter I describe tricks to speed up your send and setup times.

Insider's Tip

The name you give a printer can serve a creative as well as a pragmatic function. You can add a little office levity, or you can perform a community service by including in the name the location or resolution of the printer or information about what stationery it contains.

If Windows 95 already has a printer driver for the type of printer you are installing, a dialog box appears asking whether you want to keep or replace the existing driver. This usually happens when you reinstall a printer driver or when you add a printer that uses the same type of driver as a previously installed printer. If you're unsure of a driver file's location but you know it's somewhere on your computer or a connected computer, use the Browse button to peruse the drives and directories connected to your system.

Danger Zone

If you choose to replace a driver, be forewarned: all printers that use the driver you are replacing will switch to the new one as well.

Insider's Tip

When you install a printer, Windows 95 sets up the printer driver for the printer's default configuration—that is, the printer's configuration when it came out of the box. That's why you should check out how Windows 95 set up the printer as soon as you install the driver, particularly if you've modified the printer in any way. To see how Windows set up the printer, open the Properties dialog box by clicking with the right mouse button on the Printer icon in the Printers folder and choosing Properties from the Shortcut menu. If you've added memory to a printer, you need to specify the current amount of memory in the Properties dialog box; otherwise Windows 95 cannot take advantage of the additional memory. In addition, you may want to enable or disable certain printer features or change default settings, such as resolution and paper size. In short, examine the options whenever you install a new driver. I'll discuss available options later in this chapter, but remember that you can always extract more details about an option by clicking on What's This? with the right mouse button.

Choosing a Printer Port

If your PC is not connected to a network, your printer is probably connected to one of the LPT, or parallel, ports. Some printers, however, are connected to COM, or serial, ports, and others, such as the IBM Personal Page Printer, are connected to EPT ports (an EPT port consists of an add-in card and a driver that sets up the port with the config.sys file). If you're on a network, the method you use to connect to a printer depends on the network (see Chapter 10).

Most PC systems can accommodate up to three parallel ports and four serial ports. However, PCs usually come equipped with only one parallel port and two serial ports. If you need more—for example, so you can connect several local printers or multiple serial devices such as modems and mice—you can purchase add-in cards. Cards that supply extra ports are both inexpensive and easy to obtain. If you're unsure what ports are available on your system, check out the Device Manager, described in Chapter 17.

The following designations let Windows know where to route information to be printed:

➤ LPT1, LPT2, and LPT3 specify parallel ports.

➤ COM1, COM2, COM3, and COM4 designate serial ports.

➤ EPT refers to an EPT port.

➤ FILE tells Windows not to use a port at all but to send output to a disk file. When you select this option, Windows prompts you for the name of an output file each time you print.

Parallel Ports. Most PC systems employ standard default settings for the base I/O port and use hardware interrupts for the serial and parallel ports. The default settings for the parallel ports are shown in Table 9.1.

TABLE 9.1
*Default
Settings for
Parallel Ports*

Port Name	Default Interrupt	PC Default Address	PS/2 Default Address
LPT1	7	0378h	03Bch
LPT2	5	0278h	0378h
LPT3	7	03Bch	0278h

The Device Manager helps you find out how your ports are configured and warns you if a conflict exists or if your port setup doesn't match the defaults in Table 9.1. To access the Device Manager, open the System Control Panel and click on the Device Manager tab. Device Manager identifies a problem port with a circled exclamation mark; double-click on the name of the port to see where the problem lies. To resolve a problem with a port, click on the Resources tab and try entering different values under Settings Based On.

If you can't find a configuration that eliminates the conflict, click on Change Setting and reassign the port address range for the printer. Or change the addresses of the device that's causing the conflict with your printer. Check that device's documentation and change its I/O port addresses or interrupts accordingly.

Serial Ports. Printing through a serial port is considerably slower than printing through a parallel port. However, some printers, such as label and envelope printers, provide only serial interfaces. If your printer is connected to a serial port, the port should conform to the default I/O port and interrupt settings used by Windows 95. Although it's possible to change some of Windows' I/O port and interrupt settings, do so only if it's absolutely necessary. It's a better idea to configure your port to match Windows' default settings than to change Windows' settings to match an aberrant hardware configuration. In any case, Windows 95 usually assigns the best settings for your hardware, especially if the hardware is Plug and Play. Table 9.2 shows the default settings for the serial ports of both PCs and PS/2s.

TABLE 9.2
*Default
Settings for
COM Ports*

Port Name	Default Interrupt	Default I/O Address
COM1	4	3F8
COM2	3	2F8
COM3	4	2E8
COM4	3	02E0h

To view and change COM port settings, double-click on the System icon in the Control Panel and click on the Device Manager tab. Then choose Ports, select a device, and click on the Properties button (or double-click on the name of the device). To change settings, click on the Port Settings tab. This brings up the same COM port controls as when you install a new printer. Check your printer's documentation to see what settings the printer requires. The most common settings are 9,600 baud, no parity, 8 data bits, and 1 stop bit, with hardware handshaking. **Handshaking** (also called *flow control*) controls the flow of data to the printer and thus prevents the computer's print buffer from overflowing. Some printers use Xon/Xoff software handshaking. In any case, the driver handles handshaking settings; because print buffers can fill up quickly when you print from Windows 95, don't disable the handshaking option if you have a serial printer.

Time-Outs. Another setting for ports is time-outs. Printer time-outs specify the amount of time that elapses before you are notified of a printer problem. To set time-outs, click the right mouse button on the icon of the desired printer in the Printers folder, then choose Properties from the pop-up menu.

The first time-out setting, **Not Selected,** enables you to specify the number of seconds Windows 95 waits after sending data to a printer for the printer to respond that it is on and able to print. After the specified number of seconds has elapsed with no response, a dialog box appears, telling you that the printer is off line. The default setting of 15 seconds allows plenty of time for the printer to wake up and respond. If you see that dialog box, it may indicate that your printer is improperly connected, turned off, or suffering from some technical malady.

The second time-out setting, **Transmission Retry,** specifies the number of seconds that the printer can work without notifying Windows that it's finished processing data that has been sent to it. After this amount of time elapses with no response, you see a dialog box declaring that your printer cannot accept any more data. The default settings are 90 seconds for Post-Script printers and 45 seconds for all others. Those defaults are sufficient unless you print a complex document that contains many graphics and different typefaces. In that case, the printer can take significantly longer to process each chunk of information; this is particularly true for PostScript printers, which may require a setting of several minutes to prevent unnecessary warning messages from appearing on your screen.

Insider's Tip

Unless you print complex PostScript graphics, you probably don't need to adjust the time-out settings, particularly if your printer supports bidirectional communications. If either of the two dialog boxes I just described appears often, change the configuration of other printer settings—such as memory and font types—before adjusting the time-out settings.

Installing a Printer Twice

Even if you have only one printer, you may want to install it more than once. Additional drivers can be used for the same printer when you want it to behave differently depending on what you feed it. This is useful if your printer has more than one personality (for example, a Hewlett-Packard printer that is sometimes a PostScript printer). If you print mostly in portrait mode from your word processor and in landscape mode from your spreadsheet application, for example, you can set up two printer icons, so that you never have to change the settings.

You could also add your Hewlett-Packard LaserJet twice to the Printers folder, configuring it once for LPT1 and the second time to send output to a disk file. This trick is handy when you use a printer connected to another system. Your "second" printer could be a friend's that has better resolution or duplexing capabilities, or it could be at a service bureau, where you can get higher-resolution output, color, negatives, or other qualities you can't squeeze out of your own desktop printer.

To install a printer a second time, repeat the steps of the first installation but give the printer a different name this time. Because the drivers will have been installed already, you shouldn't be prompted to insert any disks.

Removing a Printer

To delete a printer, open the Printers folder, select the icon of the printer to be banished, and choose Delete from the File menu. You can also click with the right mouse button on the icon and choose Delete from the pop-up menu. I wish everything were this easy.

Printing from Windows Applications

With most Windows programs, you print a document directly from the File menu or by clicking on a Print button. Some programs include a separate Print menu, but most install the Print command on the File menu. Consequently, for the vast majority of Windows applications, the keyboard sequences Alt,F,P and Ctrl+P are still the easiest ways to begin a print job when you're inside the document you want to print.

However, if the document isn't open, applications designed for Windows 95 offer new tricks, expanding on the drag-and-drop printing capabilities of Windows 3.1. You can print documents by dragging them either onto a shortcut to your printer or onto a printer icon in the Printers folder; you can also use the Send To command on the Shortcut menu. (The Shortcut menu pops up when you click with the right mouse button on just about anything in the Explorer or My Computer. Shortcuts to printers and other destinations can be added to the Send To menu by dropping them into the Send To folder inside the Windows folder.) You can send multiple documents to the printer with either drag and drop or the Send To command.

Appearance

The appearance of a printed document is affected by the following factors:

➻ The fonts and formatting options you choose from within an application.

➻ The ability of your printer to print the fonts and formats you've chosen.

➻ The use of special drivers to achieve certain kinds of output. For example, many presentation graphics packages use a printer driver that redirects graphics to a modem for transmission to a slide service bureau. Fax modem software often works in a similar way; instead of sending a document to a printer, it redirects the output—fonts, graphics, and all—to a fax modem.

TrueType fonts (or PostScript fonts if Adobe Type Manager is installed on your system) provide the best match between the typeface you see on the screen and the printed version. If you don't use TrueType, it may take some tweaking to print documents the way you want them to look.

Most Windows applications provide a Printer Setup command on the File menu, which lets you choose a printer and configure that printer's driver. The command and its location vary from application to application. You might find Printer Setup on the File menu, as part of the Print command (click on Options or Printers), or under Page Setup.

Changing the printer is meant to be as easy as changing a TV channel, and on the surface it is. When you choose Printer Setup, you see a list of all installed printers. Select a printer from the list, and Windows designates it as your active printer. The catch is that that printer becomes the default printer for all applications. Switching printers is so easy, though, that it takes little effort to do so on a regular basis.

Printing from DOS Applications

DOS applications used to bypass Windows at printing time, even when you ran the DOS programs from a Windows session. When you printed from WordPerfect for DOS, for example, the job would be sent directly to the printer port that you selected from WordPerfect.

Windows 95, however, controls the printer ports for both Windows and DOS applications, even though DOS applications can't take advantage of all the printing features offered by Windows 95. An important exception is the Windows print queue, which DOS programs take advantage of to eliminate potential conflicts with Windows programs.

If you have trouble printing a DOS application, make sure it works with the type of printer you are using. You need to select the printer (and possibly install a printer driver for the printer) from the DOS application; choices made in Windows do not directly affect the DOS program.

To reformat a DOS document so it can take advantage of Windows fonts, you must first transfer it to a Windows application. Once there, the application can be reformatted in one of the following three ways:

➟ Many Windows applications, such as Word for Windows, WordPerfect for Windows, and Ami, can read the file formats of DOS word-processing applications, including formatting commands for items such as boldface and page margins. If you cannot directly open a document created by a DOS program, you may be able to save the document in another format that your Windows word processor understands, such as RTF (Microsoft's Rich Text format).

➤ The next-best choice is to save your DOS document as a text-only file, then open it in your Windows application. For example, even the bundled Write applet can open plain text files and perform a considerable amount of formatting.

➤ If all else fails, you can resort to cutting and pasting information from a DOS window into a Windows application. This option requires the most fussing and reformatting, but it may be your only choice if your DOS application doesn't let you save text only or save text at all. With this method you can bring virtually anything from a DOS application into a Windows application for formatting and printing. For more information about how DOS applications behave in Windows, see Chapter 15.

Insider's Tip

Windows 95 includes the Print Troubleshooter, a Help section for those all-too-frequent printing problems. Click on a specific question, click on a possible answer, and hopefully you'll find a solution. It's worth a try and is more convenient than calling Technical Support.

Managing Print Queues

A print queue monitors all current print jobs sent to a given printer and helps you set up "emergency" changes in printing order. If you control a variety of output needs (multiple printers, several paper sources, people who think their bad planning constitutes a crisis on your part), you will probably be happy to have control over the print queue.

Let's take a reasonably insane situation. You issue three print orders: WordPad is to print a draft document on a 24-pin printer, Paintbrush is to send a drawing to a LaserJet, and Excel is to print a graph on a plotter. You can execute all those operations simultaneously and write a memo to your boss (or play Freecell) as you wait for everything to print.

You can view any printer's queue by double-clicking on that printer's icon in the Printers folder. A small printer icon near the right side of the Taskbar indicates an active print queue; double-click on the icon to see what's in the queue (Figure 9.2).

FIGURE 9.2

*An Active
Print Queue*

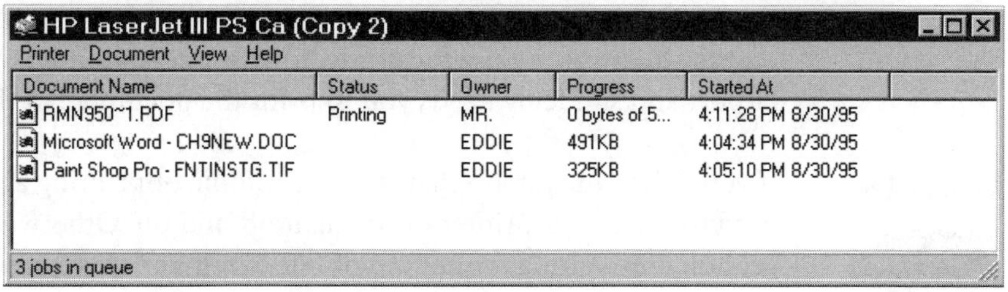

*From this view of the print queue you can keep track
of what print jobs are underway and reassign priority
to different printing tasks.*

Each entry in the print queue contains the title of a print job (usually the name of the application and the document being printed), the size of the file in kilobytes, the percentage of the file that has been printed (if it's still printing), the "owner" of the job, and the time and date it was sent to print. Jobs are listed in the order in which they will be printed.

From the menus in the Printers window you can pause or cancel a particular print job or purge all print jobs. Use the following commands from the Printer menu to change all print jobs in the queue globally:

»‣ **Pause Printing.** Temporarily stops all print jobs.

»‣ **Purge Print Jobs**. Removes all jobs from the queue permanently.

To control the print queue on a per-job basis, use the following commands from the Document menu:

»‣ **Pause Printing**. Temporarily keeps a document from printing.

»‣ **Cancel Printing**. Makes that print job go away.

A check mark next to the appropriate Pause Printing command indicates that either a job or an entire queue is paused. When you want printing to resume, click again on the command to clear the check mark.

Note that you can use the Pause Printing command only if spooling is enabled on your computer. For more on how to enable spooling, see the section later in this chapter called Changing Print Speed.

Whether you can pause a print job on a network print queue depends on the network software and the control it offers to the individual workstation. Some network software builds in limits so that individuals can't mess with another user's files; as a result the network runs more smoothly.

You can change the order of files in a queue except for the first file listed (unless that printing job has not yet commenced). To make a change, select the item, drag it to a new position in the list, and release the mouse button. It's easy to imagine a use for this feature: suppose your boss is leaving for the airport and suddenly needs you to print the document at the end of the list.

Danger Zone

If you delete a print job that is in the middle of printing a graphic, you may need to reset your printer or toggle it off and on. Otherwise the printer can get hung up waiting for an End of File command that never arrives.

Insider's Tip

The printing process creates temporary spool files. In Windows 3.1, the names of temporary spool files begin with ~SPL and end with the extension .TMP. In Windows 95, it's not always so straightforward, but because the process is carried out behind the scenes, you don't have to get involved. Here's how it works: When you print using enhanced metafile spooling (which is the default), .TMP files are created. Those files do not go to the printer; instead, they are sent to your system, telling it to process the information and keep it away from your immediate work space. This enables you to return to work immediately. Later, the same information goes into a spool, or .SPL, file, which is sent to and understood by the printer. In addition, another file, called a shadow file (.SHD), keeps a tracking record of the spooling process. If you send raw data to the printer, you get only .SPL files, no temporary or shadow files.

Spool files are located in the Windows\System\Spool\Printers folder. Temporary files are usually located in the Temp subdirectory of the main Windows folder.

Normally Windows 95 deletes spool and temporary files automatically after they have been printed. If your system crashes or is shut down in the middle of a print job, however, you may wind up with some leftover temporary files. If this happens, check for the leftover files and delete them. If you want to print them first, copy them to your printer port. For example, if your printer is connected to LPT1, go to a DOS prompt (go to the Start button, choose Programs, and click on MS-DOS Prompt) and type

```
COPY C:\WIN95\TEMP\~SPL????.TMP LPT1:
```

This assumes that the TEMP variable specifies the C:\WIN95\TEMP directory.

Changing Print Speed

At long last Windows isn't just faking it; it's actually multitasking. Multitasking has become a reality for Windows 95, unless you have some old drivers that aren't compatible with this marvelous feature. (So remove those drivers and find ones that run in protected mode!)

Processing and printing speeds partially depend on your setup. For example, if your computer spools to a network server, it's important whether that server is running Windows 95 or some other software. A server running Windows 95 usually provides networked users with good performance on their own computers while printing is taking place, because the server handles most of the processing needed for printing. On the other hand, if the server uses NetWare or Windows NT, much of the processing happens before it goes to the network—that is, on your own computer.

Other factors can affect print speed as well. To explore your options, open the Printers window, select your favorite printer, and choose Properties from the File menu. Click first on the Details tab and then on Spool Settings, and some choices appear.

Select Spool Print Jobs So Program Finishes Printing Faster if you're Type A and feel you must return to your next task within seconds. When you select this option, printing requires more time and more disk space, but you don't notice because most of the processing is taken care of in the background by enhanced metafile spooling. With this option, you also get to decide when to start the printing. Choosing Start Printing After Last Page Is Spooled gets you back to work as quickly as possible but consumes the most disk space. Selecting Start Printing After First Page Is Spooled doesn't get you back to work quite as quickly, but it doesn't require as much disk space either.

Choose Print Directly to the Printer to get pages through the printer as quickly as possible, bypassing the spooler. You won't be able to resume working with your application, however, until printing is complete.

Printer Drivers

When you first install Windows 95, the Add Printer Setup wizard asks you to enter the name of the printer or printers connected to your system, either directly or across a network. At that point Windows 95 installs the appropriate driver for each device. Software drivers contain routines that communicate between printers and Windows 95. Windows 95 includes printer drivers that support most printers available for PCs and compatibles.

The proper driver implements the concept of WYSIWYG. This means that in theory the images on a monitor are identical to those that emerge from the printer. Don't take this too literally, however. How many people who own a color monitor also have a color printer? And the sad truth is that most monitors lack the high resolution and the space to present the high-quality stuff you can print on any of the hundreds of excellent printers on the market today. That's why the concept of YWYMLTG (You Wish Your Monitor Looked This Good) more often applies.

Once your printer is successfully installed, you shouldn't have to deal with printer drivers, unless you change a printer's setup options. But given the importance of printer drivers, you might want to know a few things about their structure and their role in Windows 95.

A printer driver is key to printing a document on any Windows-compatible printer. Essentially, a printer driver translates data in a document into information the printer can use to print the document. Depending on the type of printer, a printer driver also provides other instructions to the printer, such as how many copies to print and which paper tray to use. Despite the plethora of printers available today and the variety of features they offer, printer drivers enable you to print from any Windows program to any Windows-compatible printer. Each printer driver provides its own idiosyncratic set of controls, which appear in the Printer Setup dialog box. Some drivers are specific to only one model of printer, and other drivers work with a family of printers.

· ·

Options

Although the layout of the Printer Properties dialog box varies, you still see many of the same controls from driver to driver. To open the dialog box, click with the right mouse button on the Printer icon and choose Properties from the Shortcut menu. Most printer controls allow you to choose either a portrait (vertical) or a landscape (horizontal) orientation for your documents. Portrait is the default. Tabs within the printer's Properties window (sometimes called a property sheet) contain information about the functions of the printer; click on those tabs to adjust the driver's settings.

Most Printer Properties dialog boxes offer the following selections:

➺ **Paper**. Enables you to specify paper size, source, orientation, layout (single page, two-per-sheet, and so on), number of copies to be printed, and unprintable areas.

➺ **Graphics**. Enables you to specify resolution (higher resolution yields better quality but decreases print speed), halftone options (screen frequency and angle), mirror and negative imaging options, and scaling (if applicable).

➺ **Fonts**. Varies with different types of printers but may show installed printer fonts, provide options for installing or deleting printer fonts, and offer other font options, such as how to deal with TrueType fonts when you print to a PostScript printer.

Insider's Tip

An obscure (or at least well-nested) feature found on the Fonts page of many printer drivers gives you the option of printing TrueType fonts as bit-mapped fonts or graphics. This capability comes in handy when a printer cannot handle some aspect of a TrueType job, such as a strike-through, a rotated font, or low memory. You can also use the feature for special effects, such as masking parts of letters with graphics. Be forewarned: this process is slower than printing the fonts in the usual fashion.

➤ **General**. Shows the name of the current default printer, includes a comment area, offers the option of printing separator pages between printed files, and displays the Print Test Page button.

The comment area provides space in which to enter a description of the printer. If you share a printer set up by a user on a different computer, that user's comments (if any) appear on your properties sheet. You can change the comments to suit yourself; they cannot be read by others who share the printer.

An optional separator page prints between jobs. You can choose from two preset separators: a full-page graphic (Full) and a page of plain text (Simple). Any Windows graphic can grace a separator page; click on the Browse button to locate an image to use. Separator pages are available only if the printer you use is connected directly to your computer; otherwise the option is dimmed.

➤ **Details**. Lets you know which port and driver are being used and enables you to add or change ports and drivers as necessary. The Details page also contains two buttons—Capture Printer Port and End Capture—that create a port to a network drive. Those buttons enable you to change printer time-outs, port settings, and spool settings for a printer you access through a network. The Capture Printer Port is also for use by DOS applications.

Some printers include the following additional tabs in the Printer Properties dialog box:

➤ **PostScript**. Enables you to choose a PostScript output format: regular, portable, encapsulated, or archive. You use the regular option, which is the default, when you print directly to a PostScript printer. You can use the other options to print to disk for actual printing later, or to create an Encapsulated PostScript (EPS) file that you import and print from another program. The PostScript page also enables you to bypass sending the PostScript header, which you should do only if you're printing to a local printer. An error-printing feature is helpful for diagnosing PostScript problems, if they occur, and you can boost time-out values if your document contains complex graphics or your printer is slow. The archive format saves all the PostScript data for printing the pages in a compressed format.

In addition, you can examine and modify data transmission settings by clicking on the Advanced button, which opens the Advanced PostScript Options dialog box. When you install your printer, Windows 95 optimizes the settings in that dialog box to provide the best possible performance and compatibility.

➡ **Device Options.** This page indicates how much printer memory is available. It also enables you to change settings specific to your printer, such as Resolution Enhancement Technology and duplexing.

Important differences exist among printer drivers, and adjustments may have to be made for different printers. The settings described above apply to generic printers, such as the Hewlett-Packard LaserJet. Because many new printers, especially color printers and those with other special features, contain drivers with custom options, you should inspect the adjustments and settings carefully so you can take better advantage of those features.

Insider's Tip

Just as Windows 95 itself benefits from RAM added to your computer, Windows printers can work faster if you install extra memory in them. If you have several megabytes of RAM installed in your printer, the corresponding Windows printer driver can store many TrueType fonts and other graphics on the printer, which speeds up printing. If you don't have at least 2 megabytes of RAM on a laser printer, consider adding more. The driver can also save time by monitoring the amount of free memory in the printer, retaining and reusing fonts that have already been downloaded, as space allows.

To take advantage of additional memory installed in a printer, the printer driver needs to know how much is available. If your printer is Plug and Play, the driver gets this information automatically. If it isn't, you have to enter the amount of memory in the Printer Properties dialog box. Don't overestimate the amount of memory contained in your printer; the printer driver could overload the printer with information and generate an Out of Memory error. Some people assume that all the installed memory is available, but this isn't always the case. Many printers use some of that installed memory to store drivers and other system information, so not every byte is free. Your printer's user manual can tell you how to determine the amount of available memory.

Printer Support

A two-tiered device-driver model enables Windows 95 to support almost every imaginable model of printer. The first tier is an umbrella driver, aptly called the universal driver, which covers most types of printers. The second tier is made up of a huge number of minidrivers specific to models not covered by the universal driver. The minidrivers, usually written by printer manufacturers but conveniently shipped with Windows 95, are go-betweens that speak with both the printer and the universal driver, which in turn communicates with Windows itself. (If your Windows 95 CD or disks don't contain a driver for your printer, the printer manufacturer should be able to supply you with one. If the printer doesn't already include a driver, it might be just a phone call away; most manufacturers maintain an electronic bulletin board service [BBS] so that you can download current drivers, and many have forums on one or more of the major on-line services, such as CompuServe.)

Insider's Tip

Minidrivers written for Windows 95 also work with the Windows NT 3.5 universal printer driver, so you don't need separate versions if you work in a mixed network environment.

The universal printer driver (UNIDRV.DLL) supports resolutions of up to 600 dpi. This driver also supports most non-PostScript page-description languages, covering TrueType and Intellifont scalable fonts, monochrome HP GL/2, generic text printing, ESC P/2 raster graphics, and most dot-matrix formats.

PostScript printers are another species and require a PostScript driver (PSCRIPT.DRV). The current PostScript driver supports Level 2 PostScript, Image Color Matching, control over the format of your output, version 4.2 PostScript Printer Description (PPD) files, reporting of available printer memory, and installable device options. Some older PostScript printers require a printer-specific support file ending in .WPD. Windows 95 still supports those files for the sake of compatibility, but they've been superseded by PPD files, which serve essentially the same purpose.

If you're somewhere out in the printer hinterland and can't get the correct driver for your printer, try installing the driver for a printer that's similar to yours, such as an older model of the same printer. You may not be able to take advantage of all your printer's new features, but you might get by until you obtain the correct driver. If that fails, try one of the following methods, all of which involve setting up your printer to mimic a more common variety.

➥ **PostScript printers.** A PostScript printer can often be set up as an Apple LaserWriter Plus—the mother of all PostScript printers. The LaserWriter Plus is essentially a generic PostScript printer.

➥ **Non-PostScript laser printers**. If your printer has a Hewlett-Packard (HP) LaserJet compatibility mode—sometimes called HP PCL compatibility—you can set it up as an HP LaserJet Plus or an HP LaserJet Series II. For example, I set up my OkiLaser 400 as a LaserJet Series II, and it operates flawlessly. The LaserJet Series II uses version 4 of PCL. If you happen to know that your printer emulates PCL 5, you can install the driver for the LaserJet Series III (which supports scalable PCL 5 fonts), although the Series II driver also works just fine.

➠ **Dot-matrix printers.** Most dot-matrix printers can emulate either an Epson or an IBM Proprinter. If you have a 24-pin dot-matrix printer compatible with an Epson, you can set it up as an Epson LQ-1500. If you have a 24-pin IBM-compatible printer, try it as an IBM Proprinter X24. Try an IBM-compatible 9-pin printer as a regular IBM Proprinter. Try a 9-pin Epson compatible with a narrow carriage as an Epson FX-80; if it has a wide carriage, try it as an Epson FX-100.

➠ **Pen plotters**. Most pen plotters are compatible with those made by Hewlett-Packard. You can often set them up as HP7475A plotters.

➠ **None of the above**. If you can't get anything else to work, or if you have an old daisy-wheel or text-only printer, you can set your printer up as a Generic Text Only printer. To do this you use the TTY.DRV printer driver, which simply spits out the text of your document from the printer port. Graphics, obviously, are ignored. The Help file for the TTY.DRV driver is TTY.HLP.

· ·

Bundled Drivers

The printer drivers included on the Windows 95 installation disks fall into six main categories:

➠ Hewlett-Packard LaserJet and compatibles.

➠ PostScript.

➠ Dot-matrix.

➠ Other laser and dot-matrix.

➠ Inkjet.

➠ Pen plotter.

Hewlett-Packard LaserJet and Compatible Printers. The Hewlett-Packard LaserJet and compatibles are by far the most commonly used printers with Windows. The HP LaserJet family includes printers made by Hewlett-Packard, as well as dozens of compatibles made by other manufacturers. Also included in the HP dynasty are printers that use LED displays instead of lasers to imprint images on paper. The HP LaserJet family employs

a page-description language called HP PCL, for Hewlett-Packard Printer Control Language. LaserJet and compatible printers can use TrueType fonts, font cartridges, downloadable soft fonts, and vector screen fonts. However, they cannot print raster screen fonts.

If you use an HP PCL printer, TrueType should be your first choice of font type. The universal driver is optimized to print TrueType characters, so this is one of the best ways to take advantage of the speed of Windows 95 printing. HP LaserJet printers fall into one of the following five categories, which HP compatibles usually emulate as well:

➥ **HP LaserJet.** The original HP laser printer, it used only a single font cartridge and didn't work with downloadable soft fonts. You don't find many HP LaserJets still in use, because most of them were upgraded.

➥ **HP LaserJet Plus.** An upgrade of the original LaserJet. Still limited to one font cartridge but works with downloadable soft fonts. Most LaserJet-compatible printers sold by third parties are compatible with the LaserJet Plus.

➥ **HP LaserJet II.** Improves on the LaserJet Plus design by allowing two font cartridges to be used simultaneously. Also uses slightly different escape codes for functions such as selecting the paper tray.

➥ **HP LaserJet IID** and **IIP.** Improve on the LaserJet II design by allowing bit-mapped fonts to be rotated. In addition, the IID offers two-sided printing.

➥ **HP LaserJet III series.** Improves on the previous models by adding its own set of non-TrueType scalable fonts, called Intellifonts. Adds an image-enhancement mode that prints more realistic grayscale images, such as photographs. Offers Resolution Enhancement Technology, which smooths fonts and graphics. Although you can obtain cartridge and soft font versions of the scalable Intellifonts, I recommend going with TrueType fonts because of their compatibility with many printers.

➥ **HP LaserJet 4 series.** Improves and expands printing options with true 600 dpi resolution (in some models), 120 levels of gray, many internal scalable fonts (both Intellifont and TrueType), bidirectional communications, a high-speed RISC processor, and automatic I/O switching (which is useful when you print in different formats—for example, in both Post-Script and PCL).

➥ **HP LaserJet 5 series.** The current line of LaserJets. These models offer faster processors than the equivalent series 4 models, as well as a faster print engine (six pages per minute instead of four) and a second paper tray as a standard feature. This printer's flashiest feature is an infrared port for wireless printing, which comes in handy when you can't string a printer cable. Infrared transmission depends on a direct line of sight, so your printer and your computer need to be able to see each other for this to work. Best of all, this printer is quite affordable, with bargain prices starting at around $1,000.

Downloadable Soft Fonts for LaserJets. HP and several other font vendors offer downloadable soft fonts for LaserJet and compatible printers. Again, if you want a simple, trouble-free set of typefaces, I recommend TrueType fonts. But if you want to install downloadable fonts from HP, use the Font Installer utility, which is built into Windows 95.

Using fonts from a vendor other than HP can be problematic, since you usually need a custom installation program. Sometimes soft font installation utilities create appropriate screen fonts; when they don't, Windows substitutes one of its own screen fonts. To install a soft font (or a .PCM file for a cartridge), access the Font Installer. To do so, click on the Fonts tab in the printer's Properties window, then click on the Install Printer Fonts button. The HP Font Installer dialog box appears (Figure 9.3).

- - - - - - - - - - - - - -
FIGURE 9.3
Font Installer
Dialog Box

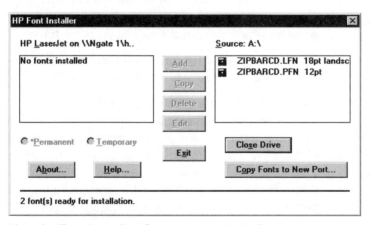

Use the Font Installer if you want to install
downloadable soft fonts for your printer.

LaserJet-compatible soft fonts can be downloaded from a storage device to a printer on either a temporary or a permanent basis. A permanent font resides in the printer's memory until you turn off the printer or restart it. A temporary font downloads only when the printer driver encounters that font in a document you are printing. Once you print the document, the soft font is deleted from the printer's memory.

Danger Zone

In some older LaserJet-compatible printers, such as the Apricot Laser, temporary soft fonts must be loaded at the start of a print job; the fonts cannot be accessed if they are encountered in a document that is printing. In a case like this, it's better to use TrueType fonts.

To download soft fonts on a permanent basis, select the Permanent option during the installation process. A dialog box appears asking if you want to download the fonts now or at start-up. If you select Now, the fonts are installed as soon as you exit; this deletes any other downloaded fonts in the printer.

If you select Startup, Windows copies a file called PCLSFOYN.EXE to your hard disk and creates a batch file called SFLPT1.BAT (assuming the printer to which you are downloading fonts is attached to an LPT1 port). At system start-up, SFLPT1.BAT asks whether you want to download the permanent soft fonts at that time. This process also adds a line to your AUTOEXEC.BAT file that causes the SFLPT1.BAT file to run during system start-up.

Danger Zone

The SFLPT1.BAT file uses the TEMP= statement in AUTOEXEC.BAT. If the TEMP= statement is not set up properly, the SFLPT1.BAT file doesn't work, and your fonts aren't downloaded. See Chapter 15 for further details on how to use the TEMP= statement in AUTOEXEC.BAT.

The Font Installer automatically creates a directory on your hard disk called \PCLFONTS. The directory stores the files that contain the soft fonts; those files use the extension .USP. The \PCLFONTS directory also contains related files, such as SFLPT1.BAT and PCLSFOYN.EXE. In addition, Windows 95 requires a printer fonts metrics file, denoted by the extension .PFM, which provides information such as the size and the spacing of the soft fonts.

If you install a third-party font that uses the same name as a font already installed on your system, you need to change the name of either the newcomer or the existing font. Keep in mind that you can't change the name of a cartridge font. To change the name of a font, select it from the list of installed fonts and click on the Edit button, which brings up the Edit dialog box (Figure 9.4). Type a new name in the Name field and click on OK.

Danger Zone

When you change the name of a font, try not to change any of the other items in the Edit dialog box, such as Font ID or Family. Such changes can confuse Windows about the font's characteristics and may prevent Windows from using the font at all.

• • • • • • • • • • • • •
FIGURE 9.4
*Edit Dialog
Box*

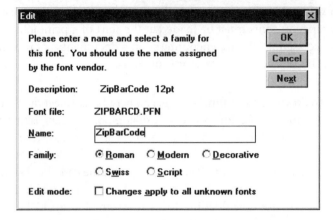

*Each font must
have a unique
name. Use this
dialog box to
rename any
duplicates.*

Creating a Font List. If you ever have occasion to reinstall multiple soft fonts for your printer, you can benefit from an undocumented timesaving feature. Normally you have to use the Font Installer to reinstall all the fonts and regenerate their associated .PFM files. With the Create Installer Directory File feature, you create a file called FINSTALL.DIR, which contains the soft font information used by WIN.INI. In this way you can recreate your soft font entries without the hassle of going through the Font Installer process.

To create an FINSTALL.DIR file, click on the Fonts tab in the printer's Properties window and click on the Install Printer Fonts button to access the Font Installer; then hold down Ctrl+Shift while you click on the Exit button. The Create Installer Directory File dialog box appears (Figure 9.5).

• • • • • • • • • • • • •
FIGURE 9.5
*Create Installer
Directory File
Dialog Box*

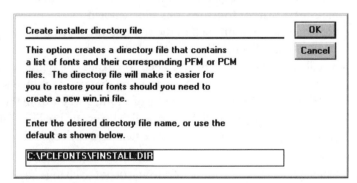

*This dialog box enables you to create a file with
information about your downloadable soft fonts.*

The Create Installer Directory File dialog box contains a text box suggesting directory and file names under which to save your soft font information. You should leave the file name FINSTALL.DIR and specify the directory in which you want to store your downloadable fonts (usually \PCLFONTS, by default). To make sure the Installer Directory file contains a current list of all your soft fonts, use this undocumented procedure to create a new FINSTALL.DIR file whenever you add or remove downloadable soft fonts.

To reinstall your soft fonts from the FINSTALL.DIR file after you've started Windows, bring up the Font Installer dialog box and hold down Ctrl+Shift while you click on the Add Fonts button. A special version of the Add Fonts dialog box appears (Figure 9.6).

FIGURE 9.6
Add Fonts
Dialog Box

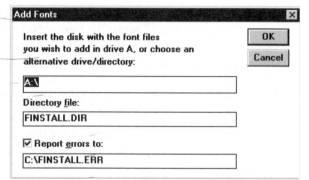

The Add Fonts dialog box enables you to reinstall soft fonts quickly from the finstall.dir file.

In the Add Fonts dialog box enter the drive, the directory path, and the file name of the FINSTALL.DIR file, then click on OK. You are returned to the Font Installer dialog box, with the soft fonts listed on the right side of the box. Select the fonts and click on the Move button; when prompted for a directory, enter the directory path that contains the soft fonts. Windows doesn't take the time to copy the fonts; it just updates WIN.INI so that you can use the fonts.

Danger Zone

Downloadable soft fonts work only when your printer is connected to the same port as when the fonts were installed. If you change the printer's port assignment, the soft fonts are no longer available. To access them, click on the Copy Fonts to New Port button, located in the Font Installer dialog box. You also need to use that button if you have more than one HP LaserJet-compatible printer, because the fonts are specific to one port.

LaserJet-compatible printers can handle only 16 downloadable soft fonts per page. If you try to print a page with more than 16 soft fonts, a dialog box pops up with the message, "PCL Printing Warning: Soft Font Page Limit: Some Fonts Will Be Substituted." If you see this dialog box, click on OK to continue with the print job. You'll get your first 16 fonts; after that it gets ugly.

Another heart attack producer is an Error 20 message. This means you are downloading more fonts than your printer's memory can handle. Don't panic. Press the Continue button on the front panel of the printer. If you think you received this message in error, ask yourself, "Did I download some permanent soft fonts into the printer?" If you committed this misdeed, those fonts may be hogging most of the printer's memory. You can clear the memory by downloading the temporary soft fonts again or, if worst comes to worst, toggling the printer off and on.

PostScript Printers. The PostScript font and printing technology, like TrueType, provides scalable outline fonts that can be printed in any size (although some applications stop at 127 points), rotated to any angle, and printed on a wide variety of output devices. The first PostScript laser printer, the Apple LaserWriter, included 17 fonts; the next version, the Apple Laser-Writer Plus, came with 35 fonts. One reason you can set up many models of PostScript printers as Apple LaserWriters Plus is that they usually include at least the same 35 fonts.

The advantage of a PostScript printer is the availability of PostScript fonts; you can download PostScript fonts from companies such as Adobe and Bitstream. However, those extra PostScript fonts have one drawback: because they include custom installation utilities, you can't use the Windows Post-Script driver to install them.

Once you do install additional PostScript fonts, you can't scale them on screen unless you purchase Adobe Type Manager. Otherwise, all you can do is install specific sizes of screen fonts; unless you have a gigabyte of memory, you should install only those sizes you plan to use. If you want to take full advantage of your PostScript fonts, I advise you to buy ATM.

You can print TrueType fonts straight to a PostScript printer, but if you want to change the looks of your fonts or speed up the printing process, you can pull some conversion tricks. To access the following options, click on the Fonts tab of your printer's Properties window:

➤ **Send TrueType Fonts to Printer according to the Font Substitution Table**. Substitutes built-in printer fonts for TrueType fonts. Although this accelerates print speed, printed output may not exactly match screen fonts.

➤ **Always Use Built-In Printer Fonts instead of TrueType Fonts**. Gives you less control but more speed; causes the same screen font discrepancies as does the previous item.

➤ **Always Use TrueType Fonts**. Sometimes you really do want to use the fonts you tell Windows you want to use. Print speed slows down, but the fonts you choose match the ones you print.

You can also control how fonts are sent to the printer. Click on the Send Fonts As button to access the following options:

➠ **Send TrueType Fonts As** offers three choices: Outlines (Type 1, scalable), Bitmaps (Type 3, nonscalable), or Don't Send. With small type sizes it's most efficient to send TrueType fonts as bit maps. With larger type sizes documents print more quickly if the fonts are sent as outlines.

➠ **Send PostScript Fonts As** gives you the option of downloading your Post-Script fonts. If you download them, they precede your document. But if you have already permanently downloaded the fonts, select Don't Send. Why waste time repeating the same process?

The Send Fonts As dialog box contains two other options. One controls when the system downloads outlines instead of bit maps. If you want outline fonts printed all the time, enter 0. The other setting, Favor System TrueType Fonts over Printer Fonts That Have the Same Name, enables you to decide which type of font has precedence if a naming conflict occurs.

Insider's Tip

Here's a way to pull a trick on your printer. Type conversion utilities such as Alltype and FontMonger enable you to convert PostScript fonts into True-Type fonts for screen display. After performing that conversion, you can use the Substitution dialog box to substitute the new TrueType font for the real PostScript font contained in your printer. This way, you can take advantage of printers with built-in PostScript fonts without adding the overhead of a PostScript screen-font utility such as ATM.

You can also play tricks on your printer by adjusting its virtual memory with the Advanced Options dialog box. Manipulating virtual memory can speed up printing, free up memory for other Windows applications, and alleviate potential printer problems.

How much virtual memory do you have? It's almost a state secret. To find out, you need to download TESTPS.TXT—usually located in the \Win95\System folder—to your printer. To do so, open a DOS window, type

```
COPY \WIN95\SYSTEM\TESTPS.TXT LPT1
```

and press Enter. Substitute the name of the port connected to your printer if it is not LPT1. TESTPS.TXT contains a PostScript program that prints a page showing how much virtual memory is in your printer.

Some PostScript printers, such as the Apple LaserWriter NTX and the Pro 630, can receive a memory transplant in the form of a hard-disk drive attached to the printer. This yields many megabytes of virtual memory.

PostScript printers include their own bug-reporting systems. If a communication problem develops between your printer and your computer, the printer driver provides a way to view error messages from the printer. To look at the error messages, check the Print PostScript Error Information checkbox on the PostScript page of the printer's Properties window. However, you may need a degree in cryptic languages to understand the error messages, or you may need to read your printer manual or your PostScript reference manual. If you resort to calling for technical support, the person you talk to should be able to decipher the error messages.

Dot-Matrix Printers. Dot-matrix printers once dominated the world of personal computers. Many have been replaced by low-priced laser printers, especially for use with Windows. But millions of dot-matrix printers are still around, and they are fully supported by Windows 95.

Dot-matrix printers print each character as a collection of small dots. Early dot-matrix printers had print heads with nine pins that created the matrix of dots. Then came 24-pin print heads, with their greater graphics resolution. Both types of printers support TrueType. The typefaces look pretty ragged on nine-pin printers, but the output from 24-pin printers almost rivals that of laser printers (it just takes longer to achieve).

My biggest complaint about dot-matrix printers is the amount of noise they generate. As the print head moves across a page, the pins are hammered through a ribbon onto the paper. If several printers are running at once in your office, you might have grounds for seeking a noise-violation inspection from OSHA. The hammering does have one advantage, though: it's useful for printing through the multipart forms commonly used in accounting software.

Dot-matrix printers work with their own built-in device fonts, which are usually limited selections of ugly typefaces. The printers also work with True-Type and with raster and vector screen fonts. Windows 95 creates the bit-mapped image of a TrueType font and sends it in graphics format to the printer. Because graphics print so slowly on some dot-matrix printers, you might try using the less pleasing but speedier built-in fonts whenever looks don't count and you've got a long document to print.

The Printer Setup dialog box for dot-matrix printers usually lets you specify your graphics resolution in dots per inch (Figure 9.7). As resolution increases, so do both the print quality and the time required to produce a page. To print drafts choose a low resolution; use the maximum resolution only for final copies. Many nine-pin dot-matrix printers support a high-resolution graphics mode, which can double the normal graphics resolution. Because Windows sends TrueType fonts to dot-matrix printers as graphics, the high-resolution mode improves the appearance of TrueType fonts and graphics. The gain in resolution, however, comes at the expense of speed.

The Printer Setup dialog box for a dot-matrix printer may also contain settings for paper size and paper feed (either tractor or single sheet). Automatic paper feed is available only on Fujitsu dot-matrix printers. If your printer supports font cartridges or soft fonts, click on the Fonts button to install them. Examples of such printers are some 24-pin models manufactured by Epson and NEC.

Some dot-matrix printers can also print in color, with a multicolored ribbon. Windows 95 supports those printers with a universal color support library, DMCOLOR.DLL. Windows installs this color library only if you tell Windows you are using a Citizen color printer, although some other brands of printer are compatible with the Citizen.

FIGURE 9.7
Dot-Matrix Printer Setup Dialog Box

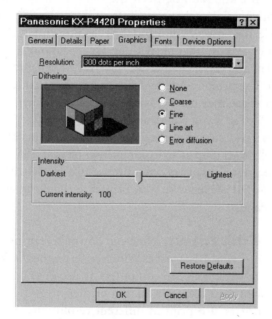

A typical dot-matrix Printer Setup dialog box asks you to describe the physical characteristics of your print job.

Danger Zone

Some dot-matrix printers—especially the IBM Proprinter X24, the Epson MX-80, and a few varieties of the Okidata 24-pin printer—are sensitive about how data flows from the Windows spooler. Short pauses can cause those printers to hiccup, which can halt the printing process or cause a printer to spew out garbage.

If that happens, turn off the spooler. Click with the right mouse button on the printer's icon in the Printers Control Panel, and choose Properties. Click on the Details tab in the resulting dialog box, click on Spool Settings, and in the Spool Settings dialog box, click on Print Directly to the Printer. Then click on OK to close the dialog boxes. If you still encounter problems, access the Connections dialog box through the Printers icon and redirect your printer output to a disk file by designating FILE as the port, as described earlier in this chapter. To print the file, copy it to a printer port (LPT1, for example) from the DOS command prompt, using the DOS COPY command.

24-Pin Dot-Matrix Printers. If you're going to use a dot-matrix printer with Windows 95, a 24-pin printer provides more attractive text and graphics than do the older, nine-pin models. However, 24-pin printers vary considerably; they print at different resolutions and with different **aspect ratios.** (An aspect ratio is the ratio between the number of vertical dots and the number of horizontal dots that constitute an image.)

For example, the Epson 24-pin and the IBM Proprinter 24 series can print at resolutions of 120 by 180 dpi (with an aspect ratio of 1:1.5), 180 by 180 (1:1), and 360 by 180 (2:1). Others, like the NEC 24-pin, provide a resolution of 360 by 360. The printer's 180 by 180 resolution is best for printing raster screen fonts because they use a 1:1 aspect ratio. A 180 by 180 screen font is available from Epson if you really need one.

If Windows 95 doesn't provide a driver for your 24-pin dot-matrix printer, you may be able to set it up as an Epson printer or as an IBM Proprinter, provided that the printer emulates one of those two models. This may require you to flip some DIP switches on your printer to change its emulation mode, so check the manual.

Nine-Pin Dot-Matrix Printers. Nine-pin dot-matrix printers are the dinosaurs of the printer world. But just as Windows 95 reaches back down the evolutionary path to work with 286 computers, it also does its best to maintain compatibility with these older dot-matrix printers.

Nine-pin printers also print at different resolutions and with different aspect ratios. The Epson nine-pin and the IBM Proprinter typically print at an aspect ratio of 1.67:1. The Epson nine-pin driver supports the following resolutions: 120 by 72 (aspect ratio of 1.67:1), 120 by 144 (1:1.2), and 240 by 144 (1.67:1). You can print raster screen fonts using the D font set (120 by 72 dpi) with the 120 by 72 and 240 by 144 printer resolutions. The D font set can also be used at half-point sizes (for example, 12.5 points) with the 240 by 144 printer resolution.

All the nine-pin dot-matrix printers supported directly by Windows 95 use the UNIDRV.DLL driver library. Citizen printers also require a DMCOLOR.DLL driver file from the color library.

Inkjet Printers. Like dot-matrix printers, inkjet printers attack the paper with ink. However, because they spray rather than hammer ink onto the paper, they produce less noise and higher resolutions, which approach those of laser printers. In addition, some inkjet printers—for example, the HP DeskJet series—support color printing by mixing ink in primary colors as it's sprayed onto the page. Inkjet printers provide an economical alternative to laser printers, with black-and-white models hovering around $300 and high-quality color models available for less than $500.

Other Printers. Although most laser and dot-matrix printers fall into one of the categories I just discussed, Windows 95 also supports a host of other printers. Table 9.3 lists the printer drivers, soft font installers, and printers supported by the Windows 95 installation disks. All the printers listed require the UNIDRV.DLL driver library file. The TTY.DRV driver is provided as a way to send plain text to the printer port and can be used as a driver of last resort.

TABLE 9.3
Printer Drivers Requiring Soft Font Installers

Printer Driver	Soft Font Installer	Supported Printer
IBM4019.DRV	SF4019.EXE	IBM Laser Printer 4019
LBPII.DRV	CAN_ADF.EXE	Canon LBP-8 II
LBPIII.DRV	CAN_ADF.EXE	Canon LBP-4
	CAN_ADF.EXE	Canon LBP-8 III
PG306.DRV	SFINST.EXE	Hermes H 606
	SFINST.EXE	Olivetti PG 306
	SFINST.EXE	Triumph Adler SDR 7706

The Canon LBP-8 Mark III and Mark IV printers use their own outline font technology. Those two printers work with Windows vector screen fonts, as well as their own internal fonts. The Canon series II and III laser printers do not directly support TrueType fonts. To print TrueType fonts on those printers, you must treat the fonts as graphics or as bit maps, both of which print more slowly than the native fonts. To convert TrueType fonts into a graphic format, open the Properties dialog box for a printer and click on the Fonts tab. Small type prints best as bit maps, the default setting. You may save time, however, by printing large type as graphics.

IBM's Laser Printer 4019 can use TrueType fonts, its own internal device fonts, vector fonts, and IBM downloadable fonts and font cards. To install the IBM fonts, use the standard font installer provided with Windows 95.

Pen Plotters. Pen plotters are often used with Computer Aided Design (CAD) programs to create schematic diagrams, architectural drawings, and other documents that it's desirable to have a pen draw. A plotter is also handy for creating overhead transparencies for presentations. Plotters work with their own built-in device fonts and with Windows vector fonts but not with TrueType or raster fonts.

When you print documents on a pen plotter, you sometimes have to experiment with margin settings from within your application. You can also try flipping on the plotter's Expand switch, which increases the plotting area but sometimes decreases the quality of the output. Refer to your plotter's documentation for more information on using hardware settings to adjust margins.

The plotters in the following list all use the HPPLOT.DRV pen plotter driver supplied with Windows 95. Many other plotters can emulate HP plotters. Refer to a plotter's documentation to see if you need to flip a DIP switch to put the plotter in HP emulation mode.

AT&T 435	HP 7470A	HP 7475A
HP 7550A	HP 7580A	HP 7580B
HP 7585A	HP 7585B	HP 7586B
HP ColorPro	HP ColorPro with GEC	HP DraftPro
HP DraftPro DXL	HP DraftPro EXL	HP DraftMaster I
HP DraftMaster II		

Network Printers: Point and Print

Windows 95 gives you the ability to point and print, reducing network printing to child's play. You can drag a printer icon from a network server to your desktop, your printer window, or another convenient location. You can also print an open or closed document to a network printer with no fuss. When you send something to print, Windows 95 knows which drivers and configurations are necessary and sets them up on the local computer.

Sharing a Printer

Windows 95 makes networked printing bidirectional. To make your printer available to someone on your network, go to your Printers folder and click with the right mouse button on a printer, then choose Sharing from the pop-up menu. In the Sharing window, set up the desired options. (If other people on your network want to share something besides your printer, see Chapter 10.)

. . . .

Printing

When a printer is properly set up on your network, you can easily access it by clicking on its icon. But to get the icon up on your screen, you first need to make a connection with the shared printer.

Use the Explorer to enter the Network Neighborhood, where you can view all the computers on your network. To see which computers have printers that can be shared, click on the View menu, then click on Details. Each computer you highlight on the left side displays its drives and any connected devices on the right side. If you want to share a printer, double-click on the icon for its computer. Then double-click on the printer icon that appears. If you are not connected to that printer, Windows 95 asks if you want to set up the printer, and if so, Windows walks you through the necessary steps.

You print to a network printer as you would to any printer; forget the schlepping of files from days of yore. If the network printer is not your default and you use the traditional Print command or Ctrl+P, you can select the printer from your application's Print dialog box. Otherwise, use the Send To command on the pop-up menu, or drag and drop the document's icon onto a network printer icon or a shortcut.

. . . .

When It's Ready

A feature called WinPopup tells you when your network print job is done by displaying a message in a pop-up window. To install WinPopup, open the Control Panel and choose Add/Remove Programs. Click on the Windows Setup tab, select Accessories, click on Details, and scroll down the resultant list until you find WinPopup. If a check mark appears next to WinPopup, it's already installed. If a check mark is not present, check the box and click on OK, and Windows 95 installs WinPopup. You must have access to your Windows 95 CD-ROM, disks, or network volume. Start WinPopup on the print server, on your computer, or on any other computer on the network.

To start WinPopup automatically every time you launch Windows, move the WINPOPUP.EXE shortcut to the Startup folders of the print server and of any other computer on the network. Choose Options from the Messages menu if you want to customize the message WinPopup generates.

Netware Print Servers

Point and print helps you connect to a printer on a Netware print server. Double-click on the Netware server icon in your Network Neighborhood. Drag and drop the printer icon from the Netware Server window to your own Printers folder. The Add Printer wizard walks you through on-line instructions, which ask you, among other things, to enter a name for the printer. Windows 95 copies the appropriate printer-related system files to your local Windows System folder.

Print It Later

Windows 95 supports deferred printing, whether you use an application designed for Windows 95, for older versions of Windows, or for DOS. The feature is designed for folks on the road who wish to travel printerless and for anyone who prefers deferred pleasures.

Go to the Control Panel and double-click on the Printers icon. Select the printer on which you wish to print later. Then choose Work Offline from the File menu or the printer's pop-up menu. The printer's icon dims. Go through the steps you normally would to print a document. The print job enters the queue; you can see it if you double-click on the dimmed icon. When you are ready to print, return to the Printers folder and choose Work Offline again from the printer's Properties menu, deselecting it. The job begins printing automatically or at least actively joins the queue. If you are not on a network printer, you need to use the Pause Printing option instead.

What to Buy

To capitalize on the Windows 95 graphical environment, you need more than a good screen display; you should also have a good graphics-capable printer. Because Windows handles everything on a page, including typefaces, as graphics, a graphics-capable printer is important.

Windows 95 works with hundreds of printers, because Microsoft wants to eliminate every excuse for not getting Windows. Early versions of OS/2 were plagued by printer drivers that didn't work properly. This delayed delivery of the system and angered users who couldn't get it to print properly. Microsoft is motivated not to repeat that mistake, for both marketing and functional reasons: you don't want to make the customer mad, and it's important for a visually oriented system to generate appropriate output.

If you're just buying into Windows 95, which calls out for a fast computer and no skimping on the RAM, you most likely won't welcome the extra expense of a new printer. But if you are in the market for a printer and know that a good percentage of your computing time will be spent using Windows, the next few sections list some pieces of advice in descending order of importance, depending on your commitment to WYSIWYG.

Get a Windows Driver

Before you buy a printer from any source, make sure it's supported by a Windows driver. At installation, Windows 95 lists hundreds of printers that it supports. You can also look at that list by double-clicking on the Add Printer icon in the Printers folder. If you are purchasing a printer to use with Windows 95, either make sure Windows lists the printer, or exact a promise from the manufacturer that a current driver is supplied with the printer.

With the overwhelming popularity of Windows, it's safe to say that the list of printers it supports includes just about any printer you'd want to buy. In fact, a printer that isn't on the list is probably either very new or very old. You take your chances with the latter. Hopefully, anyone who buys a printer at a garage sale is aware of the risks. As for newer models, a printer that does not supply either a Windows 95 driver or compatibility with an existing Windows 95 driver is probably not such a good deal.

Go Laser

Insider's Tip

I recommend a laser printer, especially with today's bargain street prices for Windows-compatible laser printers from Hewlett-Packard, Lexmark (an IBM spin-off), Texas Instruments, and other manufacturers. Those prices run at well below $1,000, sometimes closer to $500. If you like laser quality but have a tight budget and don't print large numbers of pages, an inkjet printer is a good second choice. You can get black-only models for a few hundred dollars, and I've seen more than one nice color inkjet printer for around $350.

If you're not titillated by the fancy print options offered by Windows 95, keep your old printer; you can still appreciate some improvements. But if you plan to upgrade to a printer that takes complete advantage of the new system, consider one that supports the new "bennies" in Windows 95 (bidirectional communication and an extended capabilities port). Do your homework: some printers are also fax machines, scanners, and copiers. They'd probably even answer the phone with a little prodding, but I haven't seen one yet that makes coffee.

In the computer marketplace, a component becomes affordable to most users when it dips below the $1,000 level. The modern laser printer slipped beneath that price barrier a few years back and continues to fall. If you plan to ever print graphics, consider purchasing a laser printer.

When you shop for a laser printer, look for the following features:

➻ Make sure the printer has at least **1.5MB of memory** or the ability to expand to that point. If you plan to print PostScript graphics, you need 2MB or more, depending on the printer. With any less, the printing of graphics is hopelessly slow and with complex graphics is sometimes impossible. Some newer printers from HP and other manufacturers use memory more efficiently than older printers and therefore require less of it, even for PostScript printing; look for those if you're on a tight budget.

➻ Make sure the printer has **download capabilities,** so it can load fonts from an external source, such as your PC.

➻ Seek a speed of at least **8 PPM** (pages per minute), unless you really don't mind waiting. However, 4 PPM might be fast enough for a single user who doesn't print a large volume of pages. Everybody wants faster and cheaper, but you can't always get both in the same place.

➻ **Shop around.** Laser printers don't qualify as commodity items, but they still share more similarities than differences. However, prices for similar products can vary considerably. For instance, a printer with a particular laser engine—the system's most important component—may cost several hundred dollars less than a different machine with the same engine. So before you buy a laser printer through mail order or at one of the computer superstores, research the components that go into that particular brand. You may be getting a good deal or no deal at all.

Go Color

Using Windows 95 with a standard black-and-white printer is a prescription for frustration if you're visually oriented. Your magnificent multicolored documents become monochromatic on output. The solution is to invest in a color printer or plotter. The entry price for color isn't as high as you might expect; the HP DeskJet 560C costs less than $500 (mail order).

Choosing a color printer, like other equipment decisions, is application driven—that is, it is based on the principle of WYGDOWYWTDWI (What You Get Depends on What You Want to Do with It). The two major applications that lend themselves to color printing are graphic design and desktop presentation. For design work you want a printer that can handle large pages, so you can print full-size drawings with room around the edges for instructional markings. For presentations, size is of secondary importance, but you want a printer that can create high-quality overhead transparencies.

Summary

Almost every Windows print feature has been improved in Windows 95, accelerating print speed and giving you greater control over the process. Printer control is centralized in a Printers folder, and added features include two-way communication between the printer and the computer, enhanced support for network printing, driver support, and support for almost every printer in existence. Although you don't have to fiddle anymore with the technicalities of your printer setup, Windows 95 provides a host of options in case you want to control aspects such as speed, font conversion, queue arrangements, delayed printing, and printers shared on a network.

CHAPTER

10

Networking and Communications

In computing, as in politics, there is power in numbers. The capabilities of a personal computer are multiplied when its connected to other computers through a network or by means of another type of communications link. And as in politics, if you make the right connections, you stand to gain access to information that would otherwise be unavailable to you.

In recent years, improvements in the tools for connecting computers have helped catalyze an explosive growth in the personal computer industry. With the introduction of faster modems, ISDN lines, improved cabling technologies, and better software for making connections—whether across an office or across the world—computer communications has become more accessible to a wider range of people. To connect your computer to others, all you need to do is add a cable or two and a few inexpensive network cards to your personal computer, whereas once you needed access to a minicomputer or a mainframe computer, plus a full-time network administrator to reboot that megalithic computer regularly.

Computer networks enable users to share information and equipment. Each computer can work alone or in conjunction with other computers connected to the network. At any level—from two personal computers linked together in a home office, to a vast corporate network, to the mother of all networks, the Internet—connecting your computer to others extends your reach to a larger universe. And access to on-line communities is built into Windows 95; all you need to provide is the hardware.

One of the greatest advantages of a networked environment is the ability to share resources. A **resource** is anything that can be used by people connected to the network. Typical resources are printers and hard drives; other examples are individual folders on your own hard drive and software programs stored on other people's hard drives.

The first part of this chapter describes how to use Windows 95 with a network. Windows 95 now provides support for several popular networks, such as Novell's NetWare. It also includes a new interface, the Network Neighborhood, which enables you to view and control network components. In addition, Windows 95 offers new ways to share your computers resources—for example, your printer—as well as ways to protect your networks security. In the second part of this chapter, I discuss installing and configuring a modem, the HyperTerminal software program for basic communications tasks, dial-up networking, Direct Cable Connection, and how to use Windows 95 to surf the Internet.

. . . .

Built-in Network Support

With Windows 95, Microsoft has included built-in support for the most popular commercial networks, including, of course, Microsoft's LAN Manager, Windows for Workgroups, and Windows NT. The following networks are also supported by Windows 95:

➤ Novell NetWare (3.11 and later, which can also communicate with NetWare 2.x—that is, any version of NetWare 2).

➤ Banyon Vines (5.52 and later).

➤ DEC Pathworks (installed as a protocol).

➤ SunSoft PC-NNFS (5.0 and later).

Windows 95's built-in support enables you to use those networks without having to fine-tune every network configuration file on every networked computer. Some tweaking is still required, however, to get things working right, and this chapter shows you how to set up everything with a minimum of bother.

. . . .

One on One

There's good news for small groups who want to engage in straightforward activities like sharing files, printers, and modems. If you want to connect fewer than a dozen computers, the cheapest and least complicated choice is the **peer-to-peer** network included with Windows 95. No additional software is required.

A peer-to-peer environment does not employ a central **server**—the muscle-bound computer that stores and disburses hefty programs, databases, and the like. Each computer in a peer-to-peer network is both a **client** and a server. For example, your computer is a client when you instruct it to use a network printer. It's a server when someone copies a file from a shared folder onto your hard drive. You might think of a client-server network as a wagon wheel, with one central hub (the server) and many spokes (the client workstations). By comparison, a peer-to-peer network is more like a wagon train drawn into a circle of individual, more or less equal workstations.

Setting up a peer-to-peer network involves cards and cables. First you install network interface cards in each computer and connect the cards with cable (either coaxial cable, which looks like cable-TV cable, or twisted-pair cable, which resembles phone cord). In many cases Windows 95 detects that you've installed a network card and installs the necessary software drivers for you. You can then work with the Network Control Panel to set up how you share network resources.

Not only is a Windows 95 peer-to-peer network cheap, it's also easy to install and use. However, some drawbacks do exist. What if everyone on the network wants to use a database located on your hard drive just when you're trying to work on a spreadsheet that's not even related to the database? You may find your program slowing down because of the network access taking place in the background. Despite potential problems, though, peer-to-peer networks work for most small groups. If you try one and it doesn't work, you can always buy and install traditional network software later.

Here are the basic steps for installing a Windows 95 peer-to-peer network:

➺ Install Windows 95.

➺ Install a network interface card on each computer.

➺ Connect the computers with cable, either directly or through a hub.

➺ Start Windows 95. In most cases Windows 95 detects a new network card and offers to install software for it. (If Windows 95 doesn't detect your network card automatically, you can install the appropriate drivers by using the Add New Hardware Control Panel.)

➺ In the Network Control Panel, enter a name for the new network and set the levels of sharing for everything you've connected.

Setting Up a Network

Because many users have made sizable investments in their networks, Microsoft developed Windows 95 to be compatible with older network components. Windows 95 also ensures continued support for existing network components from a variety of vendors, as well as making its new **32-bit, protected-mode** components work with older DOS and Windows applications, device drivers, and DLLs (dynamic link libraries).

Although Windows 95 is compatible with older network components, Microsoft recommends using 32-bit, protected-mode components. Protected-mode network components enable you to take advantage of a peer-to-peer system. And protected-mode components offer network administrators the ability to create system policies; you can keep certain functions off-limits to individual users while doling out programs and resources to the entire network.

If you have to use older, **real-mode** drivers, you also need the DOS network configuration files used in earlier versions of Windows. For example, you may need to use certain AUTOEXEC.BAT file settings. The safest way to install network components for Windows 95 is to make sure that any existing real-mode components are running when you start Windows 95 Setup. Setup is smart enough to identify the existing components and automatically install the corresponding support for Windows 95. The configuration settings are also forwarded to the Registry, but not in every case. You need to verify that information later.

What's in a Name? Every networked computer running Windows 95 must be part of a work group and must also be assigned a name, regardless of what is required by any existing network environment (for example, Novell Net-Ware). Windows 95 uses those names to identify computers on the network.

If you don't enter those names when you are prompted for them during Windows 95 installation, you can always do it later. In fact, you can change the names at any time (unless your network administrator has restricted this ability). Double-click on the Network icon in the Control Panel, or click with the right mouse button on the Network Neighborhood icon on the desktop, then select the Identification tab. Enter names for your computer and your work group, as well as a brief description of your computer. The description you type here appears in network lists on remote computers.

Danger Zone

When you change your computer's name and the name of its work group, other users connecting to your computer for its resources, such as a database, have to reconnect to those resources using the new names.

. . . .

Adding Network Components

For longtime Windows users, installing and configuring internal components has been akin to digging for turnips in a frost-covered field. Now, with Plug and Play, it's like waiting for the coconuts to fall from above. Even if your network adapter does not support Plug and Play, installing a network adapter has been simplified with the Add New Hardware wizard, which appears when you double-click on the Add New Hardware Control Panel. As long as Windows 95 has the dope on your peripheral—that is, if Windows knows how the peripheral needs to be set up—the wizard guides you through your choices. If your network adapter is so new that even Bill Gates doesn't know about it, you may need to get drivers from the manufacturer instead.

To avoid the installation/configuration hassle, you can install Windows 95 over an existing installation of Windows for Workgroups. If you do this, Windows 95 sets up the network adapter using settings from Windows for Workgroups.

Insider's Tip

Hardware manufacturers are constantly updating drivers to eliminate the bugs (euphemistically called features) reported by users. It's never a bad idea to check the manufacturers BBS, FTP, or Web site or a commercial network such as CompuServe, America Online, or Microsoft Network for the most recent drivers; they could be more up-to-date than those on the disk included with the network adapter.

If your network adapter is a Plug and Play device, here's what happens when you install it:

➤ Windows 95 detects the network adapter.

➤ Windows 95 automatically configures the required resources and sets up the required protocols, using each component's default setting.

➤ You are asked to reboot your system.

➤ Your network is fully functional, with nothing left to install.

Insider's Tip

For Plug and Play to work, your computer must be running only protected-mode network components, including the client, the protocols, and the network adapter drivers. See Clients, Protocols, Adapters, and Services later in this chapter for details about those components.

Windows 95 Plug and Play support applies to software as well as hardware components. If a network adapter required for an application is removed or otherwise disabled, the application switches into **off-line** mode so that you can work without interruption. If the application can't continue without the missing network adapter, the application saves all unsaved data and shuts down.

For example, if you try to print a document to a network printer when the computer used as print server is disconnected or shut down, Windows 95 automatically takes the printer off line, saving any print jobs locally until they can be printed. You can continue to use your word processor, but you can't print anything until the print server is reconnected. (To check the status of a printer, double-click on the Printers icon in the Control Panel, double-click on the printer you want to use, and open the Printer menu. If Work Offline is checked, print jobs will be queued on the hard drive until the printer is available.)

If your network adapter does not support Plug and Play, you add an extra step to the installation process. After you install the network adapter and start

Windows 95, double-click on the Network icon in the Control Panel. Click on Add on the Configuration page to bring up the Select Network Component Type dialog box, where you double-click on Adapter. The Select Network Adapter dialog box appears; if your adapter appears on the list, select it and click on OK. If it doesn't, or if you want to install a more recent driver for an adapter that does appear on the list, click on Have Disk and proceed through the installation. (Note that you can also install network components by using the Add New Hardware wizard. Double-click on the Add New Hardware icon in the Control Panel to start the wizard, then follow the instructions.) Sometimes, Windows 95 installs the wrong settings for a non–Plug and Play card, so write down the proper settings in case you need to override the default settings.

In most cases, setting up Windows 95 network components for desktop machines is truly plug and play (as opposed to plug and pray, which describes how some pundits predicted the new standard would operate). If you're not so lucky, however, Windows 95 does try to help: it detects problems, reports them to you, and allows you to continue working in **Safe** mode until the problem is resolved. If, after you install a network adapter, Windows 95 starts in Safe mode, the network adapter may not be installed properly (check your settings and try again). It is also possible that the card isn't physically attached to the network (check to make sure the network cable is attached to the card *and* properly terminated). If you're not sure what the problem is or don't need the network connection right away, let Windows 95 start in Safe mode; you can still do work, and you can reinstall network adapters at a later time.

. . . .

From the Cockpit

To view the resources and layout of your network environment, double-click on the Network icon in the Control Panel. The Network Control Panel contains three tabs. The **Configuration** tab enables you to see what network components are installed. With this tab you can install and remove network components, and you can determine whether other users can use the resources on your hard disk or connected to your computer, such as files or printers. You use the **Identification** tab to name your computer and assign it to a group, as I discussed earlier in this chapter. The **Access Control** tab enables you to control who and what on the network can access your resources (Figure 10.1).

••••••••••••••
FIGURE 10.1

*The Network
Control Panel*

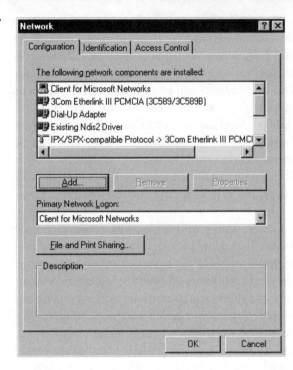

The Network Control
Panel serves as
command central for
connecting your PC to
other PCs; you can
install, configure, and
remove drivers, as well
as select options for
accessing your
computer.

Clients, Protocols, Adapters, and Services

If you install Windows 95 over Windows for Workgroups, Windows 95 Setup uses your Windows 3.1 configuration information to set up the network. And as I discussed in the previous section, Windows 95 helps you configure your network components even if you're starting from scratch. But in case you need to work with network components yourself—for example, if you need to add or update drivers or remove unneeded drivers—or you're simply curious about Windows 95 networking, here's a primer on the major network components.

To see which network components are installed, open the Network Control Panel. When you select a component, you can view a brief description of it in the Description area of the Control Panel (Figure 10.2).

The four primary types of network components are clients, adapters, protocols, and services. A **client** is a software driver on your computer that connects it to another computer on the network, enabling you to use the other computers resources. The kind of driver you install depends on the type of network that links the computers.

FIGURE 10.2

*The Network
Control Panel*

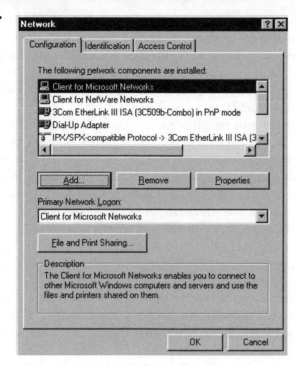

FIGURE 10.2

*The Network
Control Panel*

*Select a network
component, and
you can look in
the Description box
to see what the
component does.*

An **adapter** is a piece of hardware—most commonly a network card—that physically connects a computer to a network. The most prevalent kind of adapter is a card that plugs into a slot on the computer's motherboard. Laptops use credit-card-sized PCMCIA adapter cards (also called PC cards). Less common are parallel port adapters, which are appropriate for pre-PCMCIA laptops (you can use them with desktop machines as well). Parallel adapters are inherently slower than other adapters and as a result may not work well with some network protocols. In any case Windows 95 needs a driver to communicate with the adapter in your machine. Thus, after you install an adapter card, use the Network Control Panel to install a driver for the adapter. Or you can let the wizard do it for you.

A **protocol** is a language in which networked computers communicate with one another. Computers on a network must all run the same protocol to be able to exchange information, but a networked computer can support more than one protocol. If you connect to a Novell network, you will probably use the IPX (Internetwork Packet Exchange) protocol, which is the standard Novell protocol. TCP/IP (Transmission Control Protocol/Internet Protocol) is a family of protocols used most often by UNIX networks. NetBEUI (NetBIOS Extended User Interface) works with networks such as

Windows for Workgroups, Windows NT, and LAN Manager. (Those networks may also use protocols other than NetBEUI, however.)

A **service** is a communications tool that enables you to share resources after you connect to a network. Examples of services include file and print servers, tape backup, and Remote Registry (the latter keeps track of all the network resources available to your computer).

You can examine the properties of any component by double-clicking on the name of the component on the list in the Network Control Panel (or selecting the component and clicking on Properties). In most cases you should not change the properties; Windows 95 attempts to set up network components in the appropriate way for your system. If your network environment changes and you're not sure whether you need to change the properties of a component, the simplest solution is to reinstall the component and let Windows 95 make the appropriate adjustments to the settings. The one exception is settings for network clients, which reflect your preferences rather than the network configuration.

For example, you can specify whether a Microsoft Network client logs onto a Windows NT **domain.** (In the computer kingdom, a domain denotes a group of networked computers that share a common name. Typically, a domain corresponds to a work group, a department, or another logical unit.) You can also set up your computer so that it logs onto all its networked drives each time you restart Windows 95, or you can set up a quick log-on routine so that your system logs onto network drives only as you need them. (Quick log-on can save you valuable seconds when other network drives are unavailable, such as on weekends when everyone else shuts off their computers.) Similarly, if your computer is a Novell NetWare client, you can select which network server you want to access, assign a drive letter to the server, and decide whether to run a network log-on script provided by the network administrator.

In general, you only need to adjust client settings once. Then you can forget about them until you get a promotion and join a different work group.

Setting the Default Log-On. If you install more than one network protocol, you can tell Windows 95 which one to access when you log on. To do so, double-click on the Network icon in the Control Panel. From the Primary Network Logon drop-down list box on the Configuration page, select the client or log-on option you use most often.

Even if you're using only Windows 95 peer-to-peer networking, you can change the Primary Network Logon to log you onto your local session of Windows 95 (Figure 10.3). This feature can prove handy when your laptop computer is disconnected from the network, and you don't want Windows 95 to spend time searching for network components.

FIGURE 10.3

The Network Control Panel with Windows Logon Selected

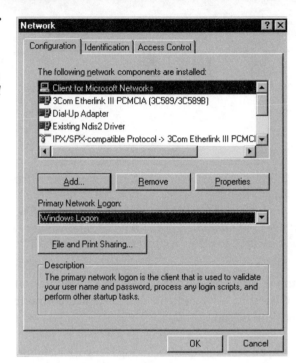

If Windows Logon is selected as the Primary Network Logon option, Windows 95 bypasses its search for network resources during start-up.

Browsing the Network

You can let your mouse do the walking from one computer to another in a Windows 95 peer-to-peer network without going through a server. That's because a new browsing feature—the Windows 95 **Network Neighborhood**—enables you to stroll through your own work group or any other work group in your organization. If you have permission, you can search another computer on your network for information or resources as easily as you can search your own hard disk.

Network Neighborhood provides a consistent interface for browsing the network, no matter what type of network you're running. The feature also enables you to place shortcuts to network resources on your desktop. For instance, if you frequently use the same network printer or repeatedly open a particular folder on a remote computer, you can set up an icon on your desktop for that resource so it is readily available.

To see what network resources are available to you, double-click on the Network Neighborhood icon. Or if an Explorer window is open, select the Network Neighborhood folder (Figure 10.4).

....

FIGURE 10.4

*Network
Neighborhood*

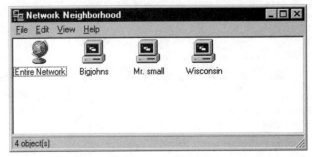

Double-click on a resource's icon in Network Neighborhood
to open a My Computer window and use that resource.
Press Shift and double-click to open an Explorer window,
as shown here (you can also click with the right mouse
button and choose Explore from the Shortcut menu).

To examine resources outside your work group, click on Entire Network.
To access the resources or contents of a particular computer or work group,
double-click on its icon.

Insider's Tip

Maybe you've noticed similarities among Network Neighborhood, My Computer, and the Explorer. It's no accident; both Network Neighborhood and My
Computer are derived from the Explorer, and I can prove it. Just press Shift
as you double-click on either Network Neighborhood or My Computer, and
the Explorer window opens. The window displays a folder view and an overall view of your computer. Personally, I prefer using the Explorer because of
that overall, hierarchical view.

Insider's Tip

If you can't find something on your network, you might be looking in the
wrong place, or you might not have access privileges for that resource. For
more information, see Searching for Network Resources later in this chapter.
You may also need to contact your network administrator or the person
whose resource you want to access.

. . . .

Connecting to Network Resources

Windows 95 has taken big leaps ahead of previous versions in terms of ease
of use. Not only is it easier to connect to a network, it's also simpler to use the
resources and information other networked computers can provide.

When your computer is wired to a network, Windows 95 can connect you
automatically each time you turn on your machine; all you need to provide is

a password. This ability, called *unified log-on,* means a network user can log onto Windows 95 and all available networks at the same time. Unified log-on also enables network administrators to coordinate use of Windows 95 with access to the network.

The first time you start Windows 95 on a network, Windows displays a log-on dialog box for each network client on your computer. Then Windows automatically stores the passwords you have entered in a password cache. Subsequent log-ons to Windows 95 unlock the cache, so you can connect to networks without having to type your passwords each time.

Once you're on the network, you can use any resources, such as printers and computers, that are connected to the network and shared, provided you have the appropriate level of security access. To use a resource, locate it and select it with Network Neighborhood (or the Network Neighborhood portion of an Explorer window). Then click on whatever computer and folder you want to open. If you want to work with a file, select it, then copy it, open it, or run it as you would any file on your computer.

If the resource is a folder or a printer, click on it with the right mouse button; this brings up the Shortcut menu, where you'll find options galore. If the resource is a folder, you can map it as a network drive so you can reach it more easily from any Explorer window. If the resource is a printer, you can open and view its print queue and even install a driver (Figure 10.5).

FIGURE 10.5

*Using a
Network
Resource*

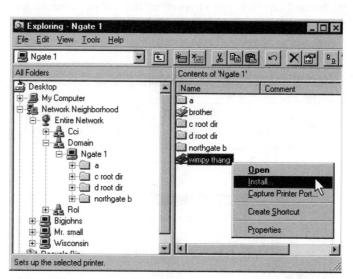

Find the network resource you want to use by traversing the Network Neighborhood, then click on the resource with the right mouse button to view your options. If the resource is a file, you can handle it as you would any file on your computer.

Insider's Tip

Computers connected to a network are available only when they are turned on. If a computer is turned off, it does not appear in the Network Neighborhood, so you cannot see or access anything on its hard drive.

Mapping Network Drives

You can always use Network Neighborhood to look at other computers on the network, but it may be more convenient to map a remote drive. (A remote drive is a hard disk on a computer attached to yours through a network. A local drive is a drive on your own computer.) Mapping a network drive assigns a letter to that remote drive. Once a drive has been mapped, you can have Windows 95 remap it whenever you log onto the network, making access more convenient when other conditions change.

Mapping a drive gives it an address on your computer, so that pre Windows 95 applications can find the drive and open files on it. (Applications built for Windows 95 have the know-how to find remote drives even if they have not been mapped.)

To map a remote drive, locate it in Network Neighborhood in the Explorer, then click on the name of the drive with the right mouse button. Choose Map Network Drive from the Shortcut menu. By default, Windows offers the first available unused drive letter for the mapped drive, but you can choose another one (Figure 10.6).

FIGURE 10.6

Mapping a Network Drive

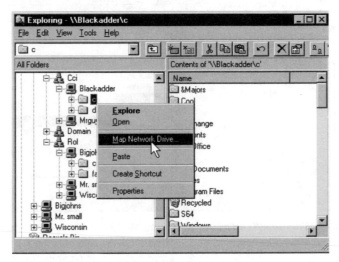

Click on a drive in Network Neighborhood with the right mouse button and choose Map Network Drive from the Shortcut menu to map the drive. Here, I'm about to map the C drive on the computer Blackadder.

You can also map a network drive by clicking on the Map Network Drive button that appears in the Explorer and on other toolbars. You type the network server name and path in the Map Network Drive dialog box and choose a letter to assign the drive. (For example, to connect to the server BABY and the shared directory FACE, you enter the name \\BABY\FACE.) If this procedure seems rather DOS-like, keep in mind the one benefit of using the Map Network Drive dialog box: it stores the pathnames of every one of your network drives, so you can quickly map a network drive by choosing it from the Path drop-down list box. This beats having to find and select the drive in the Explorer (Figure 10.7).

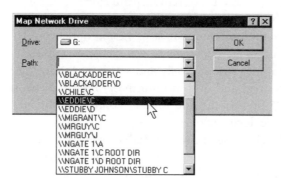

FIGURE 10.7
Mapping a Network Drive Using Buttons

You can quickly connect to a network drive you've accessed before by clicking on the Map Network Drive button and choosing the drive from the list that appears.

Map Network Drive button

Disconnect Network Drive button

You can make the mapping of any drive **persistent**—that is, you can have the mapping automatically restored each time you start Windows 95. To do so, check the Reconnect at Logon checkbox in the Map Network Drive dialog box.

Printing across a Network

The most commonly used function of any network—whether it consists of two computers or 20—is sharing a printer. Windows 95 makes it easy to switch among printers, whether you do so because one is in use or because you need one that can do color printing or some other special job.

Use the Add Printer wizard to set up a network printer. To access the wizard, open the Printers folder located in the My Computer window and double-click on the Add Printer icon. Choose Network Printer when the Add Printer wizard appears, then set up the printer as usual. (Either you need to know the network path to the printer, or you must click on the Browse button to help you locate the printer.) Once a printer is installed as a network printer, you can restrict access to it using the printers Properties dialog box. Click on the printers icon with the right mouse button to display its properties, click on the Sharing tab, and designate on the Sharing page whether you want to share the printer.

Insider's Tip

You can also use Network Neighborhood to install a network printer. Locate the printer on the network, click with the right mouse button, and choose Install from the Shortcut menu.

Windows 95 has simplified the process of using networked printers in three ways: point and print, remote print-queue control, and deferred printing. **Point and print** enables you to print to a network printer simply by selecting it. If the local computer lacks the appropriate printer drivers, Windows 95 (or Windows NT Server or Novell NetWare) copies the driver from the remote computer automatically and sets it up locally. All you have to do is drag a document and drop it onto the printer in Network Neighborhood; Windows 95 fires up the Add Printer wizard, installs and sets up the driver, and prints the document.

Remote print-queue control enables you to cancel, pause, and resume printing from a remote computer; you can even rearrange the order of print jobs in a queue. (This assumes you have the appropriate access privileges, which your network administrator determines.) You open the print queue for a network printer by opening the Printers window; to do so, choose Settings, then Printers from the Start menu (Figure 10.8). Then double-click on the icon of your selected printer. You control the printer by choosing commands from the Printer menu. To pause or cancel printing of an individual document, select it in the queue and choose the appropriate command from the Document menu. To leapfrog your document to first place in the queue, select it and drag it to the top of the list. (If any of those manipulations don't work, you may not have permission to modify the print queue.)

FIGURE 10.8

*The Print
Queue*

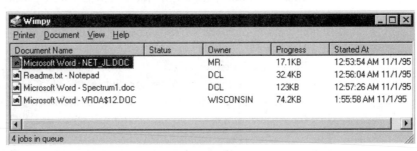

*The print queue for a printer lists all jobs waiting
to print, as well as the printer's status.*

In some cases you can receive feedback from the printer. An ECP, or extended capabilities port, enables bidirectional communications between a printer and a computer. If your system supports an ECP, your printer can notify you, for example, when the paper has jammed or when the print tray needs paper.

With **deferred printing,** you can queue print jobs when your printer is temporarily disconnected from the network. This feature is a boon for laptop users; you no longer need to rely on the limited capacity of your human memory to determine what needs to be printed once you are back in the office. Instead, you can designate at any time which documents are to be printed. If you're not connected to the network printer, Windows 95 stores the print job in a queue on your computer. When you reconnect your computer to the network, Windows 95 sends any deferred print jobs to the network printer automatically.

Searching for Network Resources

With Windows 95 Microsoft has finally made it as easy to search for folders and computers on the network as it is to find a file on your own hard drive. To search for files, folders, computers, and even services on the Microsoft Network, you can use the Find command, which is either on the Start menu or on the Tools menu in the Explorer. If you have a general idea of where something is located, it's faster to click on a drive or a folder in the Explorer with the right mouse button, then choose Find from the Shortcut menu. All of those methods open the Find dialog box (Figure 10.9).

FIGURE 10.9

The Find Dialog Box

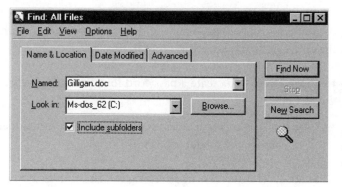

Using the Find dialog box, you can search for files, folders, and other resources in a single folder, on a computer, or across an entire network.

Once you open the Find dialog box, you can continue your search in a variety of ways. The simplest way is to enter the name of a file, a folder, or another resource; if you don't know the exact spelling, you can enter just part of the name. When you click on Find Now, Windows 95 searches the site shown in the Look In field for any file or folder whose name contains the text you entered. Click on Browse to search through a list of available folders.

Insider's Tip | If you open the Find dialog box by clicking with the right mouse button on a drive or a folder in the Explorer and then choosing Find, the Look In field points to whatever drive or folder you selected.

Folks who like how searches were conducted in older versions of Windows and DOS can still use wild-card characters to enter file names; use the asterisk (*) for any string and the question mark (?) for any character. For example, FRED*.* locates all files whose names begin with the four letters FRED, and ??FRED.MSG locates files whose names contain any two characters followed by FRED.MSG.

Powerful features for finding files and folders have been added to Windows 95. You can narrow a search based on the date of file creation or modification by clicking on the Date Modified tab. If you don't know a file's name but know a string of characters that it contains, you can have Windows 95 search each file name for the string; you enter the string on the Advanced page. If you want to find computers or Microsoft Network services, you can use similar methods, although not as many are available. If you can't find a computer, it could be that you are not networked to it or are not authorized to access it.

. . . .

Network Security

Windows 95 offers new features that protect shared resources on networked computers—including *yours*—and that also prevent unauthorized access to the entire network. Security comes in two levels:

➤ **Share level.** You create a password for each shared resource you want to restrict.

➤ **User level.** You create a password that enables individual users to access all of your shared resources.

Share-level security is like keeping information in a series of safes; a user has to know the right combination to open each one. Users type a password each time they want to access a specific resource, such as a folder or a printer. With share-level security, you determine what is shared, and you specify a password for each shared resource. (By the way, the noun *share* is used by propeller-heads to refer to a shared resource, typically a shared drive or folder on a network server. For example, I copied the graphics files from the project share on your computer, Gidget.)

User-level security is like having a security badge; you flash it once to enter a restricted area, then you're free to wander around. Assigning user-level security (sometimes called account-based security) means that a user types only one password to gain access to all the shared resources on a network. However, you can install user-level security only on a client-server network, one running on Windows NT or Novell NetWare servers. Peer-to-peer networks, which run on Windows 95 and Windows for Workgroups, are not capable of user-level security, which requires a centralized list of users along with their privileges and password validation, as well as other tools that only a client-server network is set up to offer. In other words, user-level security is network administrator territory, something outside the realm of Windows 95.

When you attempt to use a shared resource that is protected by user-level security, Windows 95 provides your password to the server. Either the server verifies that you're OK and can use the resource according to the rights assigned to you, or it tells you to get lost.

You can share resources with any combination of individuals or work groups on the network, and different computers on the same network can use different types of security. To specify which type of security you wish to use, double-click on the Network icon in the Control Panel and choose the Access Control tab (Figure 10.10).

• • • • • • • • • • • • • • •
FIGURE 10.10

The Access Control Tab

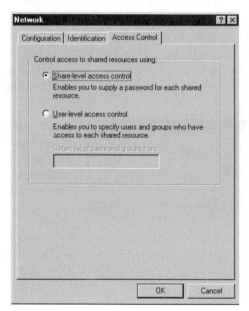

On the Access Control page you can specify whether you want to provide share-level or user-level access. To provide user-level security, you need to be on a Windows NT or Novell NetWare network.

Once you select either share-level or user-level access, you need to define what to share. If you want to share a folder using share-level security, you need to decide whether to assign a password to the folder. If you don't assign a password, anybody can use the folder. Next you define level of access: no access, read-only access, or full access. Read-only access enables users to open or copy files in a folder but not to change or delete files in the folder or add files to the folder.

With user-level security, you determine who can share a folder and what kind of access they have. You select users from the **Access Control List, or ACL,** stored on your NT or NetWare network. Windows 95 refers to the ACL automatically when you share a resource.

Insider's Tip

If you choose user-level security and run Microsoft Network, a Windows NT server or domain must be available to validate user accounts. If you choose user-level security and run NetWare, a NetWare server must be available to validate user accounts. Share-level security is not available for NetWare networks.

Sharing a Resource

To share your system's resources, you must first make sure that sharing is enabled on your computer. If you are on a large network, sharing on your computer was probably enabled or disabled by the network administrator at the time your computer was set up for the network.

To enable sharing or to check the sharing status of your computer, double-click on the Network icon in the Control Panel, and click on the File and Printer Sharing button on the Configuration page. In the File and Printer Sharing dialog box, make sure the appropriate boxes are checked (Figure 10.11).

FIGURE 10.11

File and Printer Sharing Dialog Box

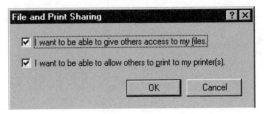

Use this dialog box to give other network users access to your files and folders, as well as to a local printer.

Once sharing is enabled on your computer, you can grant or deny access item by item. Drives and folders that you wish to share are then shared automatically until you turn off the sharing function.

Here's how to share a folder or a drive:

➤ In the Explorer, click with the right mouse button on the folder or drive you want to share, and choose Sharing from the Shortcut menu. The Properties dialog box for the resource appears with the Sharing tab visible.

➤ Click Share As, then specify how you want to share the resource. If your computer is set up for share-level security, the Properties dialog box looks like the one in Figure 10.12, enabling you to choose the kind of access you want.

➤ If your computer is set up for user-level security, the Properties dialog box looks like the one in Figure 10.13. Use this dialog box to modify your list of users and their access privileges.

FIGURE 10.12

A Folder Properties Dialog Box with Share-Level Security

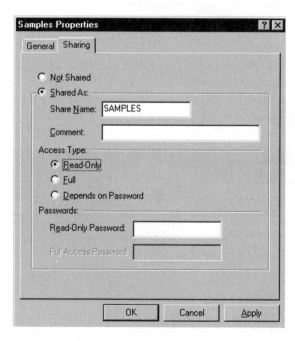

Use this dialog box to spell out what other users can do with the shared resource.

FIGURE 10.13

*A Folder
Properties
Dialog Box
with User-
Level Security*

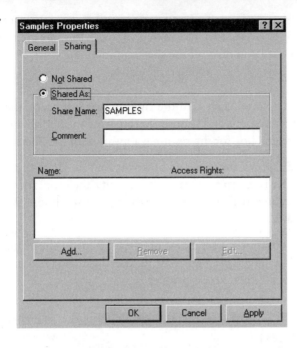

*Use this dialog
box to add or
remove users or
to modify their
privileges.*

Remember that if a drive or a folder is shared, all of its contents (including subfolders) are shared as well. You can't restrict access to a folder if its parent folder is shared. You can, however, leave the parent folder unshared but share individual subfolders (Figure 10.14).

FIGURE 10.14

*A Shared
Folder*

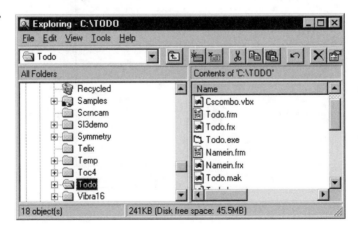

*When you
share a
resource, a
small hand
appears
beneath the
folder or the
drive in the
Explorer, as
shown with
the Samples
folder here.*

Because you can share subfolders of an unshared parent folder, the folder structure of shared resources is often different on remote computers than it is on your computer. That's because subfolders move up a level on a remote display when the parent folder is not shared. As a result, your carefully crafted hierarchy of folders and subfolders may turn into anarchy on a remote computer.

Insider's Tip

You can share a folder quietly, hiding it from the Network Neighborhood browsing list. To do so, you append a dollar sign to the end of the folder's share name; for example, Doom becomes Doom$. It's a good way to hide your games folder from the casual busybody. Others can share the folder only if they know it's there. They have to choose Map Network Drive from the Tools menu in the Explorer, then enter the exact pathname in the Map Network Drive dialog box. (For more information about mapping a network drive, see Mapping Network Drives earlier in this chapter.)

The Properties Dialog Box

Windows 95 enables you to customize your resources with handy Properties dialog boxes. A Properties dialog box stores all kinds of information about a resource and enables you to modify some attributes. Each resource, from a folder to a disk drive to a printer, has a Properties dialog box, and the dialog box contains information unique to that resource.

To look at a resources Properties dialog box, click with the right mouse button on the resource's icon in the Explorer or My Computer or on the desktop, then choose Properties from the Shortcut menu that appears. Properties dialog boxes vary from item to item. Many have two or more tabs, organized by the kinds of information they contain. A folder's Properties dialog box can also contain a Sharing tab (I discussed Sharing tabs earlier in this chapter). Besides sharing resources, you can assign the resource a descriptive name or set up a password to restrict access to the resource.

Assigning a Resource Name. When you share a resource, you can assign it a special name for sharing purposes. That name appears on remote computers when other users select Details from the View menu.

To assign a resource name, click with the right mouse button on the resource's icon in the Explorer, then choose Sharing from the Shortcut menu. On the Sharing page, type a name for the resource in the Share Name box. You can also type a brief comment that is visible to remote users when they select Details from the View menu (Figure 10.15).

FIGURE 10.15
A Shared Folder with a Share Name

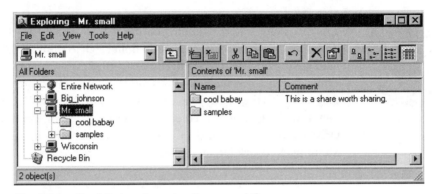

The folder Cool Babay is actually named Bruce on the computer that owns it.

Insider's Tip

Thoughtfully used, the resource-naming feature can save time and eliminate frustration for people sharing your folders. For example, while the folder name Ch1EdSch5-96 might make perfect sense to you, your co-workers would probably appreciate seeing Chap1, Editing Schedule for May '96.

Insider's Tip

You can assign a resource name to any shared resource on your computer but not to shared resources on remote computers, even if you have full permission to access those resources.

Assigning Passwords. Passwords are used for shared resources when share-level security is in place. If no password is assigned, anyone with access to the network can open a shared resource. When you assign passwords, you can narrow the field of people who can see or change your files.

You can use passwords in one of two ways. You can define one way in which a file can be used by remote users and assign a single password; anyone with the password can then use the file in the way you've specified. Or you can define two passwords—one for read-only access and one for full access.

You assign passwords using the Properties dialog box for a resource. In the Explorer, click with the right mouse button on the shared resource, then choose Properties from the Shortcut menu. Click on the Sharing tab and type the passwords you want to use.

Insider's Tip

To assign one password to several folders at the same time, drag with the right mouse button in the Explorer to select a group of folders, then choose Sharing from the Shortcut menu. The password you type on the Sharing page applies to all the folders you selected.

Insider's Tip

You can assign passwords and restrict access only to local resources—resources located on or attached to your own computer. Even if you have full access to a folder on someone else's machine, you can't change the password that permits access to the folder.

Managing Network Printing and Other Resources

With Windows 95, Microsoft has done away with the Print Manager and replaced it with the print queue. Every printer has its own queue, and you can easily look at the queues of printers on a network. It's like checking out your local printer; double-click on any network printers icon to see that printer's queue. The information in a network's print queues can give you an idea of which printer will be available first.

In addition, if you have administrative privileges for a printer, you can click with the right mouse button on any print job to pause, resume, or cancel it, and you can use the commands on the Print menu to stop or start the printing of all jobs at once. You can also rearrange the order of print jobs in a queue by highlighting jobs you want to move and pressing the up and down arrow keys to reposition those jobs.

When you print to a network printer, a printer icon appears next to the clock in the Windows 95 taskbar and remains for as long as the print job is pending or printing. When the print job is completed, the icon disappears. This little device enables you to monitor the status of a print job without getting up to check the printer.

Net Watcher

It's like a spy satellite: Net Watcher shows everything that's happening on a network, from connections with peer computers to the sharing of resources with other computers. Net Watcher is buried in the System Tools folder, inside the Accessories folder, which is in the Programs folder (Figure 10.16). (If it's not there, you can install it. Start the Add/Remove Programs Control Panel, and on the Windows Setup page, select Accessories and click on the Details button. Then check Net Watcher and install it.)

FIGURE 10.16

Net Watcher

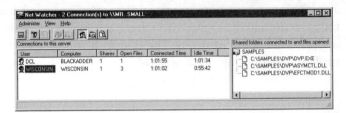

Net Watcher is your personal Control Panel for managing network connections.

Net Watcher provides three views (which you choose from the View menu): By Connection, By Shared Folders, and By Open Files. By Connection shows you which users are connected to at least one resource on your computer. If you select a user's name from the User column, you can see what resources and files that user is accessing. The By Shared Folders view enables you to select each resource you are sharing and see which users are connected to it. The By Open Files view lists all files that are open and shows who is using each file.

You can use Net Watcher to disconnect users, to share or stop sharing resources, and to modify sharing properties. Choose one of the three views from the View menu, select a resource you want to modify or a user you want to disconnect, and choose a command from the File menu.

If you are on a client-server network, you can use Net Watcher to locate and connect to servers. From the Administer menu choose Select Server and then either type in the name of the server you want to view or choose one from the Browse list.

Data Communications

Communications covers the exchange of information between two or more computers. Communications encompasses an incredible spectrum of activities, from sending and receiving mail and faxes to remote networking, from playing games over a modem with a friend across town to electronically traversing the world on the Internet. Computers can communicate by network or by telephone. When communication occurs by phone, it's known as **telecommunications.**

The most common form of communications requires a modem and telecommunications software, which together with a telephone line enable your computer to call another computer. This computer can be a personal computer, a mainframe, a large information service such as CompuServe or

America Online, or an Internet service provider. In this chapter I also discuss three other forms of communications: remote access software, which enables you to dial into a network via telephone; fax software, which enables your computer to send and receive faxes; and Direct Cable Connection, a new feature that enables you to create a network connection to another computer using just a serial or parallel cable.

Most communications software programs work with one of your computer's COM ports, although other types of software—particularly fax programs—can work with printer ports. Windows 95 has been designed to set up your COM ports automatically to work with your Windows 95–compatible software. But because the COM port plays a dominant role in communications, it's a good idea to understand how it works with Windows.

COM Ports and Windows 95

COM ports are serial communications ports that are either built into your system's motherboard or supplied on add-in cards plugged into the computer's expansion bus. Most computer systems (except notebook computers) include at least two COM ports, which are assigned the system names COM1 and COM2; a system can contain as many as four COM ports. Windows permits the use of up to nine serial ports (COM1 through COM9) and automatically assigns a modem to one of them when you install the modem.

You usually access COM ports through either 9-pin or 25-pin connectors on the back of a system unit. However, some adapter cards, such as modem cards, use the COM port internally and simply provide a standard telephone-jack connector at the back of the system unit. If you're not sure what type of connectors you have, refer to the documentation included with your hardware. You can also use the System Properties Control Panel to determine the status of your COM ports, including how the interrupts are set and which base I/O addresses the ports are using. Table 10.1 shows the standard interrupts and base I/O addresses used by the COM ports on an ISA bus system.

TABLE 10.1
Settings for COM Ports on an ISA Bus

ISA Port	Interrupt	Base I/O Address
COM1	4	03F8h
COM2	3	02F8h
COM3	4	03E8h
COM4	3	02E8h

If you use a serial mouse with Windows, I recommend that you plug it into the COM1 port. Use the other ports for your communications devices.

Windows 95 detects the proper base I/O addresses and **interrupt request lines (IRQs)** for the COM ports built into your PC by searching through your system's BIOS chips. It also detects conflicts between devices that try to use the same IRQ. Windows 95 automatically resolves such conflicts between Plug and Play peripherals. It detects conflicts between non–Plug and Play peripherals and informs you of them, but you need to reassign interrupt settings for the ports. To do so, you use the Device Manager tab in the System Control Panel. In general, however, Windows 95 demonstrates the ability to mediate conflicts.

Modem Installation

Windows 95 treats modems the same way it handles other hardware peripherals. If an internal modem is installed when you run Setup (or if an external modem is connected and turned on), Windows 95 configures the modem automatically. (Read the section on Plug and Play in Chapter 12 for details.)

If you have already installed Windows 95, adding a modem requires additional steps. Turn your computer off, install the modem, then restart the computer. You install the device driver software next. All paths lead to the Install New Modem wizard, which leads you through the steps. Here's how you get there:

➼ Double-click on the Modems icon in the Control Panel, then click on the Add button.

➼ Double-click on the Add New Hardware icon in the Control Panel. The Install New Modem wizard searches for the modem and can suggest the software that needs to be installed. However, if the wizard doesn't find the new modem, you can use the wizard to install a modem driver manually by declining the wizard's offer to search for the hardware automatically.

➼ Open the Windows 95 communications program that you intend to use. Windows 95 offers to install modem software for you.

The Install New Modem wizard can usually discern what type of modem you have; if it can't, you can select your modem from a list. If the model you've installed doesn't appear on the list, either you can install drivers from the modem manufacturer by clicking on Have Disk, or you can install generic drivers that work with most modems (Figure 10.17).

FIGURE 10.17
*The Install
New Modem
Wizard*

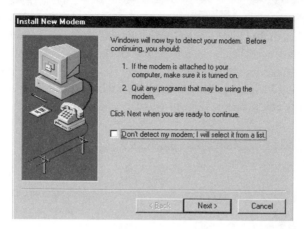

The Install New
Modem wizard
detects your modem
and installs the
appropriate software
for it. (If your modem
is external, be sure
it's connected and
turned on.)

Configuring the Modem

After your modem is installed, the Dialing Properties dialog box opens. Dialing Properties enables you to describe the phone characteristics and calling card options of whatever phone you want to use to place calls. For example, if you connect via modem from your home phone, which has Call Waiting, you might want to disable the feature for business calls. Or you might have to dial 9 from your office to get an outside line. You can set those parameters in the Dialing Properties dialog box, and they are stored in the TELEPHON.INI file. Give the parameters descriptive names of your own choice (Figure 10.18).

FIGURE 10.18
*The Dialing
Properties
Dialog Box*

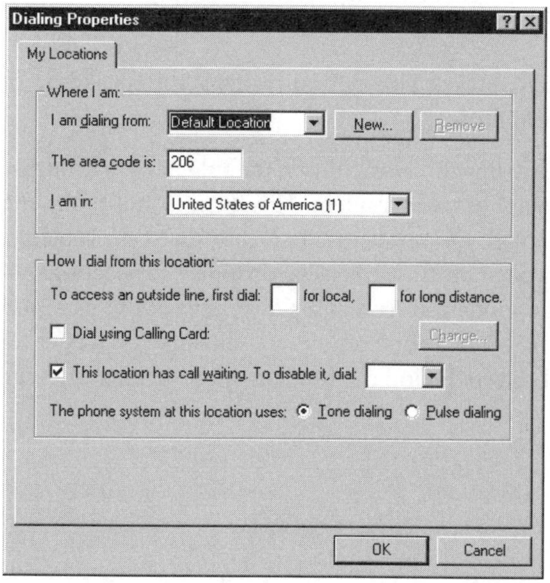

Type a descriptive
name and choose a
fitting icon for your
Connection.

To change the settings for your modem after initial setup, open the Modem Properties dialog box in the Control Panel. Here you see which modem and location are active (or selected). Click on the Properties button to change the port settings, the volume, or the baud rate of the selected modem. Click on the Dialing Properties button to change which location is selected or to add or modify any location (Figure 10.19).

FIGURE 10.19

The Modem Properties Dialog Box

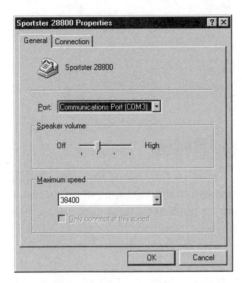

The curious among you can examine and modify modem settings in the Modem Properties dialog box.

Most of the options in the Modem Properties dialog box require no configuration, but you may need to tweak a few settings. The following are options you might want to change:

➡ **Speaker Volume.** This option controls the speaker in the modem, not in your computer.

➡ **Maximum Speed.** Normally this should be set to a number greater than the rated speed of your modem. However, if you often encounter problems when you use your modem at its fastest speed—problems such as corrupted files, garbage on the screen, or dropped connections—you may want to force the modem to run at a slower speed. I've occasionally encountered problems when I run commercial on-line services at top speed and have noticed that reducing the modem speed helps (although everything runs more slowly, of course). Note that some older Windows telecommunications programs allow you to set the modem speed from within the program.

➺ **Call Preferences (Connection tab).** The Call Preferences options can save you money on on-line telephone time. One option enables you to determine how long Windows 95 allows a phone line to ring unanswered before hanging up the phone. You can also decide how long the modem remains connected when it's idle—a useful feature when you download a long long-distance file and forget to end the session.

Once you install a modem, all your Windows 95 applications—Microsoft Fax, Exchange, HyperTerminal, and Phone Dialer—use the modem settings; you don't need to tweak the settings for each program. You may still need to adjust modem settings for applications that don't take advantage of the Windows 95 universal modem driver, such as older communications programs you used with Windows 3.1.

Insider's Tip

You may need to change connection settings to match a remote computer. However, any changes you make to those settings in the Modem Control Panel also affect the default settings for all your Connections. So if you need to change settings for a specific Connection, change them from within the telecommunications program you use to connect to the remote computer. For example, HyperTerminal saves settings for individual Connections.

. . . .

Installing a Network Fax Modem

If you have a fax modem, you can share it with other computers on your network. In this way all the computers in your work group can send and receive faxes using Microsoft Fax, the fax software included with Windows 95.

Set Up the Server. To share your fax modem—after you install it and Microsoft Fax—double-click on the Mail and Fax icon in the Control Panel to open the MS Exchange Properties Control Panel. Double-click on Microsoft Fax (or select it and click on Properties) and, on the Modem page, click on the most explicitly titled option you'll ever encounter: Let Other People on the Network Use My Modem to Send Faxes (Figure 10.20).

••••••••••••
FIGURE 10.20
*The Microsoft
Fax Properties
Dialog Box*

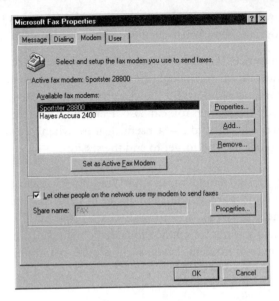

This dialog box wins the
prize for having the
longest name for an
option: Let Other People
on the Network Use My
Modem to Send Faxes.
Check this option to set
up your fax modem as a
network fax server.

Click on the Properties button next to the Let Other People option, and
set the sharing options (including security) for your fax modem as you would
for any other resource. In fact, your fax modem appears to other computers
as a shared folder on your computer. To avoid confusion, therefore, you may
want to rename the shared fax modem; you can do this by clicking on the
Properties button and typing a new name.

Insider's Tip

Although you can share a *fax* modem, you can't share a modem. That is, other
computers can't use your modem for data communications, only for faxing.

Set Up Clients. After you set up a fax server, you can set up fax clients.
(Exchange as well as Microsoft Fax must first be installed on each computer
linked to your fax server.) On the fax clients—that is, on the computers without fax modems—fire up the Exchange Inbox.

From the Microsoft Fax Tools submenu—located on the Tools menu—
choose Options. On the Modem page of the Microsoft Fax Properties dialog
box, click on Add to open the Add a Fax dialog box (Figure 10.21).

••••••••••••••
FIGURE 10.21
*The Add a Fax
Dialog Box*

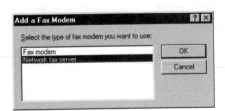

Choose the Network Fax Server
option in the Add a Fax dialog box
to add a connection to the
network fax modem.

Double-click on Network Fax Server (or select it and click on OK), and in the Connect to Network Fax Server dialog box specify the network pathname to the shared fax modem (Figure 10.22).

••••••••••••••
FIGURE 10.22

The Connect to Network Fax Server Dialog Box

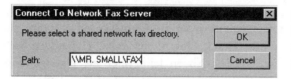

Choose the Network Fax Server option to add a connection to the network fax modem.

To share your fax modem, you need to know the exact name of the computer, as well as the share name of the fax modem; unfortunately, the Connect to Network Fax Server dialog box does not have a browse feature like the ones you find in most Windows 95 dialog boxes for shared resources. The network pathname is made up of two parts: the name of the computer that's sharing the fax modem (as shown on the Identification tab of the Network Control Panel), along with the share name of the fax modem directory. So, for example, in Figure 10.22 MR. SMALL is the name of my computer, and FAX is the share name of the fax modem directory. (FAX is the default name, and I've chosen not to change it.)

After you exit the dialog boxes, you can send a fax from one of the client computers just as you send any fax using Exchange. Remember that Exchange must be running on the fax server for client computers to be able to fax. If Exchange is not running or if the server is temporarily disconnected from the network, Windows 95 alerts each user who tries to fax something that his or her fax didn't go through. Windows then stores the fax locally (on the client computer) until the next time the fax client tries to fax something when the server is connected. For more information about faxing and Exchange, see Chapter 11.

Reach Out with HyperTerminal

HyperTerminal is a rudimentary piece of telecommunications software that enables you to communicate with another computer to exchange files or to connect to an external source of information such as an electronic bulletin board service (BBS) or the public library. The program replaces Windows 3.1's Terminal program. HyperTerminal is fully integrated with Windows 95, which means that once you install your modem (as I discussed earlier), you don't need to configure each communications program to use it. HyperTerminal supports more transfer protocols than its predecessor, but it still lacks the features of a commercial program or even of a good shareware program.

If you want to be able to use scripting language or automatic redial, or if you want to receive data automatically (rather than manually, as I discuss later in this chapter), you need a more sophisticated program, such as ProComm, WinComm Pro, Quick Link II, or Telix. HyperTerminal—like Terminal before it—seems to have been deliberately crippled by Microsoft so as not to dissuade users of Windows 95 from going out and purchasing a full-featured telecommunications program.

Insider's Tip

When you connect to a remote computer, it doesn't need to be running Windows; it can be a Macintosh system. The remote computer just needs to be able to emulate one of the terminals that HyperTerminal emulates, and the list of terminals emulated by HyperTerminal covers most any situation you'll encounter.

New HyperTerminal Connections. In HyperTerminal you create a named Connection for each location you call. To reconnect to that location, you double-click on the icon for the Connection, and you're on your way; all you have to do is choose Connect from the Call menu (Figure 10.23).

• • • • • • • • • • • • •
FIGURE 10.23
The HyperTerminal Folder

Each icon in the HyperTerminal folder represents a Connection you've created. In this example, I assigned an icon other than the default to each Connection.

The first time you open the HyperTerminal program, you create a new Connection automatically. You can define it—type a name, record the phone number, and specify other settings—and save it. To create a new Connection at any time within HyperTerminal, choose New Connection from the File menu. Either way, after you bring up the Connection Description (New Connection) dialog box, you can add a name for the Connection and, if you want, choose an icon for it. To dial the new Connection, click on Dial. To change how a Connection is set up, see Creating a Connection later in this chapter.

Connect with Another Computer. Once you've set up a Connection, here's how to dial it: double-click on a Connection icon in the HyperTerminal folder, and when the Connect dialog box appears, click on Dial. (If Hyper-Terminal is already open, click on the Open button on the toolbar or choose Open from the File menu to open a new Connection.) To redial a connection that's already open, choose Connect from the Call menu to open the Connect dialog box.

You can also enter modem commands manually. Click on Cancel in the Connect dialog box, and type the modem commands in the HyperTerminal window, just as you would with any other terminal program.

Insider's Tip

If you need to change your modem settings, or if your modem is not installed, HyperTerminal alerts you and offers to confirm settings or install the modem, as appropriate. If you've already created a number of Connections, you need to reconfirm the settings of each one the first time you open it after making changes to the modem configuration.

One drawback to HyperTerminal is the way it receives calls. To answer an incoming call from another computer, you have to use a modem command. When you're expecting a call, open the Connection for the remote computer and dismiss the Connect dialog box by clicking on Cancel. Then, in the HyperTerminal window, type

```
ATAS0=1
```

This tells the modem to pick up the line on the first ring. (Note that the *0* is a zero, not the letter *O*.) Press Enter. The modem waits until the next call and then picks up the phone.

To restore the modem so that it does not pick up the line, type

```
ATAS0=0
```

This tells the modem not to pick up the line at all. (Again, note that the *0*s are zeros, not the letters *O*.)

Alternatively, you can type the following:

```
ATA
```

In this case, when you press Enter, the modem immediately picks up the line. If you do this, you should have a phone connected to the modem so you can hear the line ring.

Send and Receive Files. When you send a file, the remote computer should be set to receive. If you are both using the Zmodem transfer protocol (which I recommend), all you have to do is send your file, and the computer on the other end detects and receives it automatically.

To send a file, choose Send File from the Transfer menu, select the file and a transfer protocol, and click on Send. To receive a file, choose Receive File from the Transfer menu, choose a transfer protocol, and click on Receive.

Insider's Tip

You can send a group of files by using wild-card characters (that is, asterisks or question marks) to specify the files in the Send File dialog box. For example, to send all the files in a directory called Upload, type \Upload*.* in the Send File dialog box. Note that the Xmodem protocol does not support multiple file uploads.

Transfer Protocols. Which transfer protocol should you use? First, it must be one that the computer on the other end supports. HyperTerminal supports four groups of protocols:

- **Xmodem and 1K Xmodem.** Older standards that are widely supported. Xmodem sends 128 characters at a time, then waits for confirmation that the data arrived intact before it sends the next chunk. 1K Xmodem is faster because it sends 1,024 characters at a time. The shortcoming of these older standards is that you can't easily send multiple files; each file must be manually assigned a name at the receiving end.

- **Ymodem and Ymodem-G.** More advanced versions of Xmodem. They support multiple file transfers. Ymodem-G is very fast because it sends one block after another without waiting for confirmation that the data arrived intact. I recommend you use Ymodem-G only when you have an error-free connection—such as over a null modem line—rather than a connection over a temperamental phone line, which could result in a broken connection.

- **Zmodem.** Zmodem is fast, has great error detection and correction, and supports multiple files. It's the protocol of choice if you have a choice.

- **Kermit.** A transfer protocol designed and implemented to allow many different computers to communicate with one another. Originally it was widely used for communicating between mainframe computers and desktop machines.

The bottom line is, use Zmodem if you can, Ymodem or Kermit as your next choice, and Xmodem only if necessary. If none of those protocols is compatible with the remote computers, you have to use a commercial telecommunications program, most of which support more protocols than does HyperTerminal.

Dial-Up Networking

Windows 95 dial-up networking enables you to connect to a network via modem and telephone lines. You can use dial-up networking when you're at home or on the road with your laptop and want to connect to your network server or office computer. You can also connect to the Internet through a dial-up service provider.

Any Windows 95 computer can be a dial-up networking client, connecting to computers configured as dial-up servers. Servers can be computers running Windows NT version 3.1 or 3.5 Remote Access Service (RAS, rhymes with *grass*), Novell NetWare Connect, or Shiva NetModem and LanRover. To communicate with the network, the client (that is, your computer) must be running the same network protocols as the server. Once you connect to the server, you can use network resources as if you were on-site.

A Windows 95 computer can also be configured as a dial-up server, but only if you install Microsoft Plus (excuse me, that's *Plus!*), which is the add-on package of goodies that some say should have been included in Windows 95. Dial-up server support is included in Microsoft Plus!, and it's the simplest and cheapest way to add dial-up capability to your network if you don't already have it. I describe how to configure your Windows 95 computer as a dial-up server later in this chapter.

To set up your computer as a dial-up networking client, dial-up networking software must be installed on your system. If Dial-Up Networking appears as an option in My Computer (or on the Accessories submenu), then dial-up networking software is installed. If the option doesn't appear in either of those places, you need to install the software.

To do so, double-click on the Add/Remove Programs icon in the Control Panel. On the Windows page of the Add/Remove Programs Control Panel, choose Communications from the list of components and click on the Details button. Choose Dial-Up Networking and click on OK.

Insider's Tip

Dial-up networking is only for connecting as a node on a network. It's not for connecting to a commercial network or to a BBS. Use HyperTerminal or another communications program to connect to those types of services.

Creating a Connection. When you install dial-up networking, the Setup wizard offers to lead you through the process of setting up a Connection for your computer. You can create additional Connections at any time with the help of the Make New Connection wizard. To use the wizard, double-click on the Dial-Up Networking icon in My Computer (or choose Dial-Up Networking from the Accessories submenu). Then double-click on Make New Connection in the Dial-Up Networking window and follow the few simple steps that the wizard leads you through, making sure to enter the phone number of the server. (If you haven't already installed modem software for your computer, the wizard helps you do that as well.)

After you save your Connection with a descriptive name, double-click on it whenever you want to connect to the server, then enter a password if necessary and click on Connect. (Of course, you need to have a modem connected and turned on.) Note that the password is assigned at the server end; you get the password from your network administrator (unless you're connecting to your own Windows 95 computer that you've configured as a server, in which case *you're* the network administrator).

After you set up a Connection, you can change the phone number or the location setting. Double-click on the Connection icon but don't click on Connect. You can change the phone number directly in the Connect To dialog box, or you can click on the Dial Properties button to change the dialing setup, including the calling card, the location, and the prefix.

Creating a Dial-Up Server. Clean up that desktop; company's coming! With Windows 95 and Microsoft Plus!, your computer can be transformed into a digital party animal, otherwise known as a dial-up server. Setting up your computer as a dial-up server enables other computer users to share your resources and theirs; it also enables you to dial into your office computer when you're on the road or at home.

Insider's Tip

You must install Microsoft Plus! before you can set up your system as a remote server. Cheapskates might want to download the Microsoft Internet Explorer and get Internet support through Microsoft Network without buying Microsoft Plus!. It's available on Microsoft's FTP site, BBS, and web page for Windows 95.

Danger Zone

If you make your computer a dial-up server, anyone can dial in and use your resources, as well as the resources of other computers on your network. That's why you need to create a password to restrict access to your server. Be sure to change the password frequently.

Before you set up your computer as a dial-up server, decide what level of security you want—user level, which requires a separate password for each user, or share level, which requires one password for each shared resource. Your decision affects some dial-up sharing options.

To set up your computer as a dial-up server, make sure Microsoft Plus! is installed, then open Dial-Up Networking. Choose Dial-Up Server from the Connections menu to bring up the Dial-Up Server dialog box. (If the Dial-Up Server command does not appear on the Connections menu, you haven't installed Plus!) Click on Allow Caller Access (Figure 10.24).

....

FIGURE 10.24

The Dial-Up Server Dialog Box

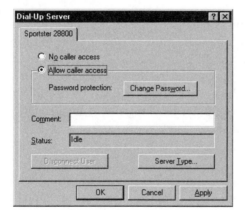

Click on Allow Caller Access in the Dial-Up Server dialog box to make your computer a dial-up server. Don't forget to add a password.

Click on Password and enter the password that will allow access to your computer. If you have user-level security on your machine, click on Add, then enter the names of authorized users. Click on OK and Server Type. The Default setting connects your computer in one of two modes: PPP for Windows 95 and Windows NT 3.5, or RAS for Windows NT 3.1 and Windows for Workgroups. (The computer calling in must use one of those modes.)

Click on OK when you're done. Any changes you've set up do not take effect in a currently open Connection. Once you enable caller access, Windows 95 monitors the modem and picks up calls.

You can disconnect a user in one of two ways. Either you can click on Disconnect User in the Dial-Up Server dialog box, or you can unplug the phone line into your modem.

Direct Cable Connection

Direct Cable Connection, or DCC, is the poor person's network adapter. It enables the pauper to network two Windows 95 computers by connecting them with parallel or serial cable. Once connected, the two computers can share resources, although more slowly than through a modem connection. DCC is handy when you don't have a modem or a PCMCIA card for connecting a portable computer to a desktop or another portable.

Insider's Tip

DCC came in handy for installing software for a PCMCIA network adapter from my Windows 95 CD-ROM. DCC let me access a shared CD-ROM drive containing the Windows 95 disc, even though my network adapter was not yet working.

To use DCC, you assign one computer host status and the other computer guest status. Both computers must be running one or more similar network protocols (such as NetBEUI or IPX/SPX) and must have different names. Once you connect the computers, the guest computer can access other computers on the host's network using NetBEUI or IPX/SPX protocols, but not TCP/IP. The guest computer can also print to any network printer if the host has enabled printer sharing.

Take the following actions to set up a DCC:

➡ Install Direct Cable Connection on both the host and guest computers. If the Direct Cable Connection command does not appear on the Accessories submenu, it's not installed. (To install DCC, double-click on the Add/Remove Programs icon in the Control Panel. On the Windows Setup page select Communications from the list of components and click on the Details button. Choose Direct Cable Connection, and click on OK.)

➡ Enable file and printer sharing on the host computer. (Open the Network Control Panel and click on File and Printer Sharing.)

➡ Connect the two computers using a parallel or a serial cable. Parallel cables are faster but are limited to 15 feet in length. Serial cables can be longer, but the connection is slower than a parallel connection.

➡ Share the resources that you want to make available to the guest computer.

In addition, if you want to print from the guest computer to a network printer, you must install the appropriate printer drivers on the guest computer.

The first time you open Direct Cable Connection, the Direct Cable Connection wizard helps you specify and configure both the host and the guest computers. You need to run the wizard on both computers.

When you're ready to connect, start DCC on the host computer by choosing Direct Cable Connection from the Accessories submenu. Click on Listen, then start DCC on the guest computer. The two machines should connect. (If they don't, check your cables to make sure you have plugged them into the correct ports.) Later, if you need to make changes in the DCC configuration of either the host or the guest, click on the Change button in the Direct Cable Connection dialog box. When you're finished working with the two computers, click on Close to disconnect them.

Surfing the Internet

Unless you've been at some digitally disconnected site for the past year, you've probably heard more than you ever wanted to know about the Internet (and O. J. Simpson). Microsoft—in preparation for an assault on its hegemony by the unknown, on-line masses—has designed Windows 95 with the Internet in mind.

To get you onto the Internet at the click of a button, Windows 95 includes the Microsoft Network (MSN), an on-line service intended to compete with CompuServe, America Online, Prodigy, and GEnie. At the time of this writing, MSN hasn't made a dent in its competitor's ratings, but with the development of content—such as a new on-line magazine promising sophisticated writing on a variety of topics—MSN may prove a worthy contestant among the on-line services.

Microsoft includes a simple World Wide Web **browser**—a program that helps you navigate and interact with the Web—with Microsoft Plus! You can use the browser with your own Internet service provider or with MSN. Version 2 of the browser supports live audio in Real Audio, software from Progressive Networks that enables sound for Internet sites that use audio. Of course, other browsers, such as the popular Netscape Navigator, are also available.

Most people connect to the Internet using a service provider—a person or a company who sets up your connection with the phone company and provides a browser configured to work with that entity's own network server. If you have a problem, you can always call up your service provider. If you want to choose a different browser, however, you can set up your own TCP/IP connection to the Internet and still work with your service provider. (TCP/IP is a commonly used protocol.)

Here's how to use TCP/IP to connect to the Internet:

➤ Install a modem, preferably one that is V.34 and 28.8K bps. Anything slower turns your information flow into a trickle.

➤ Install TCP/IP on your computer.

➤ Configure TCP/IP either for your modem or for the network Internet server, if you have one.

➤ Acquire and install whatever Internet software you want to use. Options abound; some packages bundle a predetermined set of protocols together, whereas others let you mix and match.

➤ Contact your Internet service provider and find out how to set up TCP/IP for that provider. If you do not coordinate settings with your service provider, you can waste hours—if not days—experimenting with config- uration settings.

➤ Get connected!

Insider's Tip

All the major commercial on-line services (including MSN, CompuServe, America Online, and Prodigy) offer Internet access. Most have basic plans that offer a certain amount of cheap time each month (usually ten hours per month for $8.95). However, going beyond that amount of time is no bargain. You can be billed around $3 per hour plus surcharges for file transfers for any- thing over your basic-plan time, whereas most Internet service providers charge $20 per month for unlimited time, with no surcharges for file trans- fers. Use commercial on-line services for what they do well: providing orga- nized repositories of information. But don't use them to fritter away hours on the Internet.

· ·

Installing TCP/IP for Internet Access

The UNIX networks that form the backbone of the Internet use TCP/IP pro- tocols for Internet communications. Unless you connect to the Internet exclusively through an on-line service such as MSN, you need to install TCP/IP to connect to the Internet. If you use an Internet service provider, you dial its PPP or SLIP server, which is connected directly to the Internet (more on PPP and SLIP later in this section). You can also use TCP/IP to commu- nicate with a network server that is directly connected to the Internet.

Did you install TCP/IP when you installed Windows 95? You can check by opening the Network Control Panel. Scroll down the list of installed components on the Configuration page. If TCP/IP appears on the list with an arrow pointing to the Dial-Up adapter or to another network adapter, then TCP/IP is installed on your computer.

If TCP/IP is not on your system, install it by clicking on Add in the Network Control Panel to open the Select Network Component Type dialog box (Figure 10.25). Select Protocol and click on Add to open the Select Network Protocol dialog box (Figure 10.26). Select Microsoft and TCP/IP for Manufacturer and Network Protocol, respectively. Then click on OK. You may need to have your Windows 95 installation disks or disc on hand.

• • • • • • • • • • • • • •
FIGURE 10.25
The Select Network Component Type Dialog Box

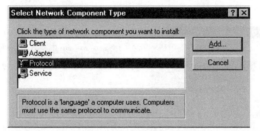

Select Protocol and click on Add to open the Select Network Protocol dialog box.

• • • • • • • • • • • • • •
FIGURE 10.26
The Select Network Protocol Dialog Box

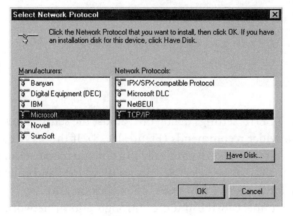

Select Microsoft and TCP/IP, then click on OK. You may need your Windows 95 installation disks or disc at this point.

After you install the protocol, scroll through the list of network components to verify that the protocol appears on the list. Windows 95 automatically configures TCP/IP to work with any network adapters on your system, including Dial-Up Networking if it was previously installed. You see a TCP/IP entry for each of the network adapters you have installed. However, you need to configure each adapter with its own TCP/IP settings.

Configuring TCP/IP. Before you connect to the Internet, you may need to set up your computer to recognize Internet domain names. The Internet's **Domain Name System (DNS)** matches a database of domain names to the address of your Internet service provider. Because some providers assign your Internet provider, or IP, address "dynamically"—that is, automatically—you may not need to assign it yourself. Contact your provider to determine whether you need to set up your address.

You must set up addresses separately for each Dial-Up Networking Connection. Open the Dial-Up Networking window, select the Connection for your Internet service provider, click with the right mouse button, and choose Properties from the Shortcut menu. Click on Server Type in the dialog box for the Connection. In the Server Type dialog box, check TCP/IP as the Allowed Network Protocols option, then click on TCP/IP Settings (Figure 10.27).

• • • • • • • • • • • • • •
FIGURE 10.27
*The Server
Type Dialog
Box*

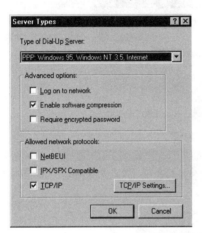

*Make sure TCP/IP is checked
in the Server Type dialog box,
then click on TCP/IP Settings.*

In the TCP/IP Settings dialog box, adjust the settings to match what your service provider recommends (Figure 10.28). If the service provider assigns an IP address that links dynamically to a domain name, select Server Assigned IP Address. Otherwise, select Specify an IP Address and enter the address. Do the same for the server addresses. Then click on OK.

If you connect to the Internet through a local network server, you can adjust the IP and DNS settings by using the Network Control Panel. Open the Control Panel, select the TCP/IP protocol, and click on Properties. Enter the DNS IP address and your IP address if needed. If your LAN assigns those addresses dynamically, you don't need to set them yourself. Internet servers that include Dynamic Host Configure Protocol (DHCP), for example, assign those addresses dynamically. You enter the DNS IP address on the DNS Configuration page by clicking on Enable DNS, entering the host and domain names, and entering the address of the DNS server.

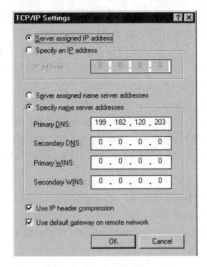

• • • • • • • • • • • • • •
FIGURE 10.28
The TCP/IP Settings Dialog Box

Adjust the settings in the TCP/IP Settings dialog box to match your Internet service provider's recommendations.

If your network includes more than one DNS server, click on Add and then enter the information for the second DNS server. If the primary server is unavailable, Windows 95 automatically tries to use the secondary one.

If you encounter trouble, contact your service provider. The provider might be able to download or fax a help file to you.

Cruising the Internet

The Internet is a large, expanding world much like planet Earth except that it exists on line. The Internet connects millions of computers and billions of people to the thousands of sites that exist and to the hundreds of new sites that spring up like weeds each day (not to mention each night). Anarchic in nature, the Internet does have a structure that can be described as follows, at least for now:

➤➤ **World Wide Web (WWW).** The newest and fastest-growing part of the Internet, the Web is the graphical face of the Internet, with formatted text, graphics, sound, video, and animation all available on a single page. Microsoft Plus! includes a Web browser based on the Mosaic program written at the University of Michigan, although you may prefer other browsers, such as Netscape Navigator or AIR Mosaic.

➤➤ **FTP.** Short for file transfer protocol, FTP enables you to log onto remote servers and download files. If you have permission from the FTP site administrator, you can also upload files to an FTP site. Web browsers routinely connect with and download files from FTP sites, both from within Web pages and as FTP site terminals as well. Windows 95 includes an FTP utility that you run from a DOS command line; just type FTP to start the utility. When the FTP prompt appears, type HELP for a list of commands. Then type HELP followed by the name of a command to obtain information about that particular command. Archie is a system for finding files on FTP sites.

➤➤ **Usenet newsgroups.** Hundreds of newsgroups congregate on Usenet. Each focuses on a particular interest, such as hang gliding, and offers members electronic bulletin boards for posting and replying to messages as well as sending files. You can use a retail or a shareware newsgroup reader to connect to newsgroups via an Internet service provider; many Web browsers include Usenet compatibility as well.

➤➤ **Telnet.** Telnet is a terminal utility that enables you to connect to a Telnet server. Windows 95 includes a Telnet utility, which you can unearth by going to TELNET.EXE in the Windows 95 directory and double-clicking on the Telnet file.

➤➤ **Gopher.** A search tool that burrows itself into the Internet in search of whatever contents you want. Veronica is a tool that searches Gopher lists for particular text content.

Most on-line services include electronic mail. To send and receive mail, you need to have a mail application, be an SMTP (Simple Mail Transport Protocol) client, and have access to an SMTP Internet server. Most service providers include mail in their basic services.

In addition to those basic tools, a cornucopia of Internet utilities and programs can help you navigate the Information Superhighway and can enrich your experience sensually. Many Web browsers, for example, include Helpers, utilities that handle everything from electronic mail to FTP to setting up other utilities automatically. Add-on tools called Helper applications enable your Web browser to play multimedia files.

Summary

Windows 95 incorporates many new features that make networking and data communications as seamless as possible. Setup hassles are minimal for most telecommunications and network hardware and software, and Windows 95 adds new options for controlling communications.

Still, installing and maintaining a network is not a trivial task. In addition to local access, the number of worldwide connections has expanded due to the popularity of the Internet. Windows 95 provides compatibility with the Internet, which, after all, is one of the few things in the computing world that's far, far bigger than Windows and even Microsoft itself.

11

Microsoft Exchange

Microsoft has revamped your e-mail system by introducing a single program—Microsoft Exchange—that deals with everything you send or receive, whether it's on a local area network, a commercial on-line service like America Online, or Microsoft's own Microsoft Network. If you are just starting to use a personal computer, you may never appreciate the advantages you reap from Microsoft Exchange. However, imagine a world with different postal systems for city mail, state mail, national mail, and international mail. That's the way it was before Exchange.

Of course, progress introduces one drawback: you have to learn how to use a new system. Read this chapter if you want to understand how to take advantage of Exchange to create and manage electronic mail and exchange it between your computer and other computers, whether over a network or over a commercial on-line service.

What It Is

Technically, Microsoft Exchange is a series of programs that exchange messages and information between computers. Some of this software (called Exchange Message Server) sits on one or several host computers. The part that resides on your machine is known as the **Exchange Inbox,** which is also called either Exchange or Inbox. When the difference is important, I say whether it is called Exchange or Inbox, and why.

Sending and receiving messages are only a small part of electronic mail. Managing a glut of addresses and messages can steal the fun (and the practicality) out of e-mail. The problem is compounded by every additional mail service you use. For this reason, the Microsoft Exchange Inbox funnels Mail and Faxes from a variety of sources into a single "information store." Exchange also offers a rich message editor, several customizable address books, and a set of folders in which you can organize incoming Mail and Faxes from all sources.

Exchange mail is considered **rich text,** because many layout features (font, point size, style, and color) can be applied to the text. The Exchange editor resembles a word processor and includes a spell checker and many formatting options. The editor also supports OLE, which means you can place linked or embedded data into your mail. For example, you can attach a spreadsheet containing a report to an e-mail note by dragging the spreadsheet's icon and dropping it into the window that contains the e-mail.

Exchange can work with any mail or fax service as long as you have a suitable driver for that service. Windows 95 includes drivers for the work-group version of Microsoft Mail, for Microsoft Fax, and for the Microsoft Network on-line service. Microsoft Plus! adds drivers for CompuServe and Internet mail. Drivers for other mail systems are available from third parties.

The work-group version of Microsoft Mail enables you to exchange messages within a single work-group on a local area network. If you have installed Dial-up networking, you can also use the work-group version of Microsoft Mail to post and receive messages over telephone lines.

Insider's Tip

Exchange is a work-in-progress. Later in 1996 Microsoft will launch the Microsoft Exchange Message Server, an advanced electronic mail system. You must upgrade your version of the Exchange Inbox to use the many features new to Exchange Server.

During 1996 many software publishers will produce Exchange-compatible programs. For example, Microsoft includes a WordMail Options command in Word 95 that enables you to use Word rather than the Exchange editor to edit your e-mail messages. Although some specifics may change, the basic information in this chapter will still apply to the Exchange Inbox.

Installing and Running Exchange

If you've installed Microsoft Exchange, an icon labeled Inbox should appear on your desktop, and an item called Microsoft Exchange should appear in the Programs section of your Start menu. If you haven't yet installed Exchange, perform the following steps:

➤ Click on Settings on the Start menu, then click on the Control Panel.

➤ In the Control Panel double-click on Add/Remove Programs, then click on the Windows Setup tab (Figure 11.1).

➤ Select Microsoft Exchange, then click on the Details button.

➤ Select the checkbox for Microsoft Exchange, as well as the checkboxes for any mail services you plan to use (such as Microsoft Mail). Then click on OK.

➤ If you're also going to use Microsoft Fax, select its checkbox.

➤ Click on OK to begin the installation.

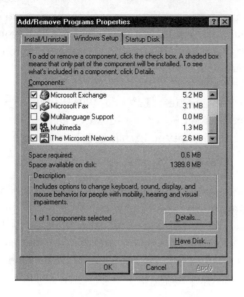

•••••••••••••
FIGURE 11.1

The Add/Remove Programs Properties Dialog Box

The Add/Remove Programs Properties dialog box is where you add Microsoft Exchange and Microsoft Fax, as well as the Microsoft Network.

Once you have installed Exchange, you can run it either by double-clicking on the Inbox icon on the desktop or by choosing Microsoft Exchange from the Programs section of the Start menu.

Insider's Tip

If you use a local area network e-mail system, check with your network administrator before installing Exchange to see if you will need additional information to set up your mailbox.

Insider's Tip

If you use a network e-mail system, such as Microsoft Mail, consider putting Exchange in the Startup section of your Start menu. When you create the shortcut, use the file name EXCHNG32.EXE, which is normally located in the \Program Files\Microsoft Exchange folder.

Working with Profiles

Before you can use Exchange, you must create a **profile**—a collection of settings that contains the following information:

➡ The name and the location of at least one personal folders file.

➡ The name and the location of a personal address book.

➡ The configuration details for each mail service you use.

Immediately after you install Exchange, a wizard guides you through the creation of a profile. If you have already installed Exchange, your profile is already set up, and Exchange is ready for use. If you do not have a working profile or wish to establish an additional profile, create one by double-clicking on the Mail and Fax icon in the Control Panel.

Although most users find one profile enough, you can set up as many as you want. If you do have multiple profiles, the profiles can use the same personal address books and personal folders file.

Your personal folders file is the repository for incoming and outbound messages. This file is subdivided into several folders, which hold your messages. For example, incoming messages are stored in a folder called Inbox. Messages to be sent are stored in a folder called Outbox. If you like, messages you have sent can be stored in a folder called Sent Items. You can create additional folders anywhere, including folders within folders, to help you organize your mail.

All messages in a personal folders file are stored in a single disk file with the extension .PST. This file is similar to the .MMF files used by earlier versions of Microsoft Mail, except that the messages in a .PST file may have been sent or received over a variety of mail systems, not just Microsoft Mail. Your profile can include more than one personal folders file, although most users find that one is enough.

If you're upgrading from a previous installation of Microsoft Mail or another network-based mail system, you may be able to import messages you sent and received with the previous system. To do this, choose Import from Exchange's File menu.

An **address book** holds the names and the e-mail addresses of the people and the companies you contact, as well as other details about them. Depending on your setup, you may have several address books. For example, you may notice a global address book for everyone using mail on your network. Regardless of what other address books exist, you will always have one active **personal address book,** a place to store information on the people you contact most often.

Insider's Tip

Your profile can accommodate only one active personal address book at a time. However, you can create multiple personal address books and switch among them whenever you want.

The Microsoft Exchange Profiles dialog box lets you know what profiles have been set up on your computer, and helps you manage those profiles (Figure 11.2). Double-click on the Mail and Fax icon to access the dialog box. The dialog box includes three tabs: Services, Delivery, and Addressing. The Services tab lists three mail services (Microsoft Fax, Microsoft Mail, and the

• • • • • • • • • • • • • •
FIGURE 11.2
*The Exchange
Profiles
Window*

*Double-click on the Mail
and Fax icon to bring up
the Microsoft Exchange
Profiles window, which
helps you manage
profiles. Most users
find one profile
sufficient.*

Microsoft Network on-line service), a personal address book (Personal Address Book), and a personal folder. Although mail services, address books, and personal folders may seem like apples, oranges, and lemons, Exchange sees them all as installable "services," which is why they are all listed in this box.

Creating a New Profile.
To create a profile, follow these steps:

➡ Click on Settings on the Start menu, then click on Control Panel.

➡ Double-click on the Mail and Fax icon in the Control panel. The Exchange Settings Properties dialog box appears (Figure 11.3).

➡ Click on the Show Profiles button.

➡ Click on the Add button. This brings up the Inbox Setup wizard (Figure 11.4).

➡ Select the checkbox for each mail service you plan to use. Click on Next and follow the rest of the wizard's instructions.

Modifying an Existing Profile.
To modify an existing profile, follow these steps:

➡ Choose Settings from the Start menu, then choose Control Panel.

➡ Double-click on Mail and Fax in the Control Panel.

➡ Click on the Show Profiles button.

➡ Select the name of the profile you want to modify, then click on the Properties button.

Click on Show Profiles and
then on Add to bring up
the Inbox Setup wizard.

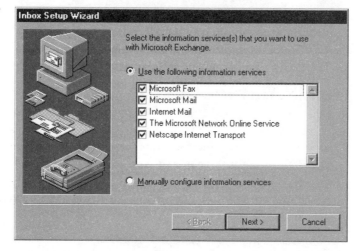

To add
services
to your
Exchange
Inbox, use
the Inbox
Setup
Wizard.

Adding or Removing a Mail Service. To add a new mail service, click on the Add button on the Services page of your profile's Properties dialog box, then choose the service you wish to add from the pop-up list. After you select the service, Exchange prompts you for additional information, which varies with the service. To remove a mail service, simply select its name on the Services page of your profile's Properties dialog box, then click on the Remove button.

Modifying a Mail Service's Properties. To adjust the options of a mail service—for example, your account name or number, a password, or the phone number used to connect to the service—use the service's Properties dialog box.

First display the Properties dialog box for your profile (choose Settings from the Start menu, choose Control Panel, double-click on Mail and Fax, and click on Show Profiles). Then, on the Services page of the profile's Properties dialog box, select a service. Finally, click on the Properties button. The choices available to you depend on the service in question. Figure 11.5 shows the Properties dialog box for the Microsoft Mail service.

• • • • • • • • • • • • •
FIGURE 11.5
*Changing the
Properties of a
Mail Service*

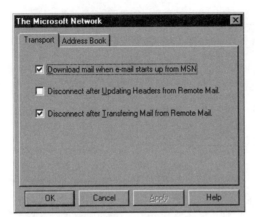

*To change the properties of
a mail service—Microsoft
Mail, in this example—
select the desired profile
and service, then choose
the Properties button that
appears.*

Protecting Your Personal Folders File. You can protect your personal folders file from unwanted snooping by setting up a password. To establish or change the password for your personal folders file, display the Properties dialog box for your profile, following the instructions presented earlier in this section. Next, select the name of your personal folders file and click on the Properties button. A Properties dialog box appears (Figure 11.6). Click on the Change Password button, then fill out the dialog box shown in Figure 11.7.

• • • • • • • • • • • • •
FIGURE 11.6
*The Properties
Dialog Box for
Personal
Folders*

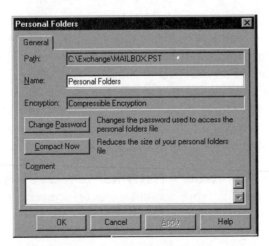

*The Change Password
button enables you to
create or change the
password for your
personal folders file.*

FIGURE 11.7
*The Microsoft
Personal
Folders Dialog
Box*

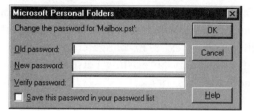

Use this dialog box to add or
change a password for your
personal folders file.

To change the password you use for a specific mail system, visit the Properties dialog box for that mail system. To do so, either choose Services from Exchange's Tools menu or double-click on Mail and Fax in the Control Panel. Then select the mail service and click on the Properties button.

Changing Your Personal Address Book.

As I mentioned earlier, a profile can have only one personal address book active at a time. However, you can create several personal address books and switch among them. You might, for example, want to keep separate books for professional contacts, personal interest groups, and friends.

To change personal address books, first display the Properties dialog box for your profile, following the instructions I presented earlier in the chapter. Then, on the Services page of the dialog box, select Personal Address Book. Finally, click on the Properties button. A dialog box appears in which you can add or change personal address books (Figure 11.8).

FIGURE 11.8
*The Personal
Address Dialog
Box*

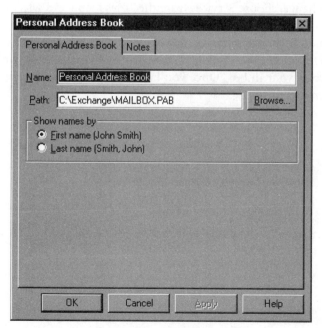

Add personal
address books
or change
address books in
the Personal
Address Book
dialog box.

To switch to a different personal address book, enter a new file name in the Path field (or click on the Browse button and point to a new file name). If you specify a file that doesn't exist, Exchange creates a new, empty personal address book. If you specify an existing personal address book, Exchange makes that the active address book.

Sending and Receiving Mail Periodically

Electronic mail systems are usually based on a store-and-forward principle. Mail sent to you goes to a "post office" on some computer—for example, on a server on your network or on a series of computers maintained by MCI Mail. The mail waits for you to collect it. Conversely, mail you send from your computer waits in the service's post office computer until the recipient collects it. This process of delivery and pickup is called **polling.**

The interval at which polling occurs depends on the mail service; it can be performed anywhere from every few minutes to once a day. You can establish a regular pickup and delivery schedule on the Delivery page of the service's Properties dialog box.

By default Microsoft Mail polls for mail every ten minutes. You can change that interval on the Delivery page of the Microsoft Mail Properties dialog box. (To see the Properties dialog box, double-click on Mail and Fax in the Control Panel, select Microsoft Mail, and click on the Properties button. From within Exchange, choose Services from the Tools menu and select Properties.)

Insider's Tip

When Exchange retrieves new mail for you, an envelope icon appears in the events area of the Taskbar (Figure 11.9). You can double-click on this icon to display your in box. Once you have opened all new messages, the envelope icon disappears.

FIGURE 11.9
Mail Alert

An envelope (the first icon on the right) appears in the events area of the Taskbar when you have unread incoming mail. Double-click on the icon to open your mailbox.

Sending and Receiving Mail on Demand

If your mail service doesn't offer scheduled polling times, or if you want to transfer mail immediately, choose Delivery Now Using from the Exchange Tools menu. A submenu pops up, listing each of your mail services. When you choose a service, Exchange immediately polls it.

You can also poll every service available by choosing All Services from this submenu (or by pressing Ctrl+M). When you do so, Exchange polls each service in the order specified in your profile's Properties dialog box. To change the order in which mail services are polled, double-click on Mail and Fax in the Control Panel. Then click on the Show Profiles button, select the name of your profile, and click on Properties. In the Properties dialog box, click on the Delivery tab (Figure 11.10). To move a service up or down in the polling order, select it on the list and click on the up or down arrow.

FIGURE 11.10

The Delivery Page

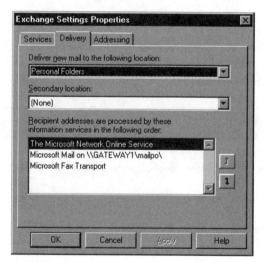

The Delivery page of your profile enables you to specify the order in which services are polled, when you choose to have all services polled at once.

Creating Mail

To create a new message, either press Ctrl+N, click on the New Message tool on the Exchange Toolbar (Table 11.1), or choose New Message from the Compose menu. A New Message window appears (Figure 11.11).

FIGURE 11.11

Composing a Message

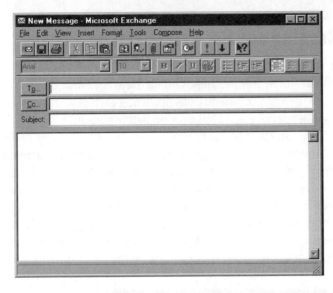

This form appears when you want to compose a new message.

In the top portion of the New Message window, you enter the names of your addressees, the names of those to whom you want a courtesy copy (Cc) sent, and a subject heading for your message. You type your message in the large space at the bottom of the window.

TABLE 11.1

The Exchange Toolbar

The Exchange toolbar offers the following tools (from left to right):

➤ Moves you up one level to the parent of currently displayed folder.

➤ Displays (or hides) the folder list.

➤ Creates a new message.

➤ Prints the selected message.

➤ Moves the selected message.

➤ Deletes the selected message.

➤ Replies to the sender of the selected message.

➤ Replies to the sender and all recipients of the selected message.

➤ Forwards the selected message.

➺ Opens the address book.

➺ Opens the Inbox folder.

➺ Displays the Help pointer; Exchange displays help about the next item you click.

Addressing a Message

You can include as many names as you please on both the To and the Cc lines in the New Message window. The easiest way to specify this information is by picking names from a personal address book. Click on the To or the Cc button to bring up an Address Book window (Figure 11.12).

FIGURE 11.12
The Address Book Window

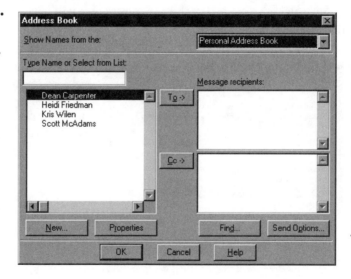

You can easily address messages by using the To or the Cc buttons in the New Message window. Doing so brings up this list, from which you can select the recipients of your message.

Insider's Tip

The To addressees are the primary recipients of a letter. The Cc, or "courtesy copy," addressees receive the same message, but Cc recipients are not usually expected to act on a message. Also, some mail systems will exclude the Cc addressees when a recipient replies to mail.

To address a message, select names from the left side of the Address Book window, then click on the To or the Cc button. If the names you need are in a different address book, select the correct address book from the drop-down list box in the upper-right corner of the window.

Insider's Tip

Which address book appears first in the Address Book window is determined by the Properties dialog box for your profile. You can change the order of address books by going to the Addressing page of your profile's Properties dialog box (Figure 11.13).

To select an addressee's name quickly from the list in the Address Book window, start to type the name in the Type Name field near the upper-left corner of the window. As you are typing, Exchange scrolls through the list to the entry that most closely matches what you've typed.

Another way to address a message is to select the addressees before starting the message. First, display your address book (click on the Address Book tool, press Ctrl+Shift+B, or choose Address Book from the Tools menu). In the address book select one or more names (hold down Ctrl while clicking to select multiple names), then click on the New Message tool (or press Ctrl+N) to open the message form. The name or names you have selected appear in the To field.

FIGURE 11.13
Changing the Order of the Address Book Listings

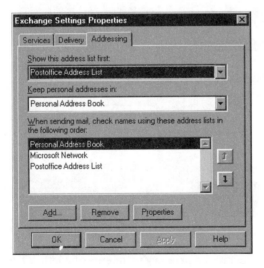

You can change the order of address book listings in the Address Book window by going to the Addressing page of your profile's Properties dialog box.

Sending a Message to a Distribution List

If you regularly send messages to the same group of recipients, a distribution list is an invaluable time-saver. You specify the name of the list on your To or Cc line and Exchange generates a message for all the addressees in the list.

To set up a distribution list, select New in the Address Book (or choose New from the File menu, or select the first icon on the left side of the window).

Choose Personal Distribution List from the list that appears to bring up the Distribution List page (Figure 11.14).

················

FIGURE 11.14

The Distribution List Window

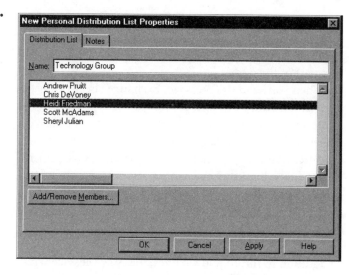

Use this window to build a distribution list. You can get here by selecting Personal Distribution List from the Address Book's New Entry form.

To add a person to an established distribution list or to remove someone from the list, click on Add/Remove Members. The Edit New Personal Distribution List Members window appears (Figure 11.15). To add a name, either select the name and click on the Members button or double-click on the name. To remove a name, select it and press the Delete key on your keyboard or click on the mouse button and select Cut from the Properties menu.

················

FIGURE 11.15

Customized Distribution Lists

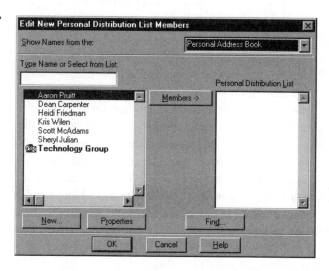

You can add addresses from more than one address book to a distribution list by selecting the new address book from the drop-down list box in the upper-right corner of this window.

Entering Recipients' Names by Hand

You can also address a message manually by typing the names of your recipients on the To and Cc lines, using semicolons to separate multiple recipients. If you're not sure of the spelling of an addressee's name, you can type only the first part of the name.

When you send the message, Exchange checks your address lines against all available address books. If what you've typed is sufficient to identify your addressees uniquely, Exchange finishes the typing for you. If not, Exchange presents a list of candidates and lets you choose the recipients. If you type only the letter *M* on the Cc line, for example, Exchange presents a list of everyone in all address books whose name starts with *M*.

Sending Blind Courtesy Copies

In addition to the To and Cc lines, the New Message window can include an optional Bcc (blind courtesy copy) line. Each recipient you specify on the Bcc line receives a copy of your message, but other recipients (those on the To and Cc lines) do not see the names of the Bcc recipients.

To display the Bcc line in the New Message window, choose Bcc Box from the window's View menu. You can fill in the names of Bcc recipients the same way you do the names of To and Cc addressees.

Customizing Exchange's Toolbars

Two of Exchange's toolbars—the one directly below the menu bar in the Exchange window and the one in the New Message window—can be customized. Tailor either of those toolbars by choosing Customize Toolbar from the Tools menu. The Customize Toolbar dialog box appears (Figure 11.16).

The right-hand window of the dialog box shows the toolbar's current layout, including the separators between groups of tools. The left-hand window shows the tools that can be added to the toolbar.

To add a tool, select it in the left-hand window and click on the Add button. To remove a tool, select it in the right-hand window and click on the Remove button. To move a currently available tool to the left on the toolbar, select the tool in the right-hand window and click on the Move Up button. To move a tool to the right, select it and click on Move Down. To restore the default toolbar arrangement, click on Reset.

FIGURE 11.16

*The Customize
Toolbar Dialog
Box*

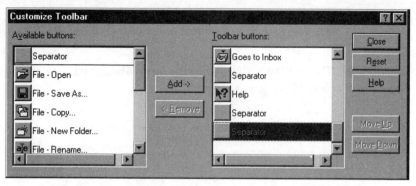

*You can customize Exchange toolbars by using this dialog box.
To get here choose Customize Toolbar from the Tools menu.*

Insider's Tip

All of Exchange's toolbars include tool tips. If you're not sure what a tool does, rest the pointer over the tool for about a half second and read the description that pops up.

Composing a Message

To compose a message, type it in the text box in the lower half of the New Message window. As I mentioned earlier, this window acts like a word processor and provides you with many formatting options.

The default message font is 10-point Arial regular, in black. To change the default font, color, or style, choose Options from Exchange's Tools menu. Click on the Send tab in the Options dialog box, then click on the Font button.

Some keyboard shortcuts are available. The shortcuts for boldface, italic, and underline are Ctrl+B, Ctrl+I, and Ctrl+U, respectively.

The Formatting Toolbar. As you type your message, you can take advantage of the tools on the New Message window's formatting toolbar (Table 11.2). You can also apply those options by choosing commands from the Format menu. The Format menu's Font command includes a strike-through option, which does not have a toolbar equivalent.

TABLE 11.2
*Exchange
Formatting
Toolbar*

The formatting toolbar in the New Message window includes the following tools (from left to right):

➡ Changes the font (typeface) of the selection.

➡ Changes the font size of the selection.

➡ Toggles the selection to boldface (or if the selection is already boldface, changes it back to normal).

➡ Toggles the selection to italic (or if the selection is already italic, changes it back to normal).

➡ Underlines the selection (or if the selection is already underlined, removes the underline).

➡ Changes the color of the selection.

➡ Changes the selected paragraphs into an indented, bulleted list (or if the selection is already bulleted, removes the bullets and indents).

➡ Decreases left indent.

➡ Increases left indent.

➡ Left-aligns the selected paragraphs.

➡ Centers the selected paragraphs.

➡ Right-aligns the selected paragraphs.

Rearranging Text. You can rearrange text with the usual cut-and-paste methods. Alternatively, you can move a block of text by selecting it and dragging the block to a new location. To copy a block of text instead of moving it, hold down the Ctrl key while you drag.

Using Find and Replace to Edit Text. Exchange's Find and Replace commands work like their counterparts in most word-processing programs. Both commands are located on the Edit menu; their keyboard shortcuts are Ctrl+Shift+F for Find and Ctrl+H for Replace.

Inserting Text from Another File into a Message. Exchange offers several ways to place text from different applications or in existing disk files into your messages. One simple method is to copy the text to the Clipboard and paste it into the message. You can also insert the text of an entire file using the Insert File command, which brings up the Insert File dialog box (Figure 11.17).

• • • • • • • • • • • • • •
FIGURE 11.17
*The Insert File
Dialog Box*

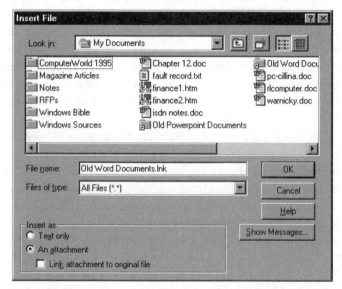

You can insert a complete file into a message using the Insert File dialog box. The Insert As option enables you to embed only the text of the file, the entire file, or a link to the file.

Choose the name of the file you want to insert as you would with any other file dialog box. In the bottom part of the dialog box, click on the Text Only button. Click on OK, and the file's text appears in the message window.

Attaching a Document. An **attachment** is a document or other file either embedded into or linked to an electronic mail message. Attachments are used to send nontextual data such as spreadsheets, pictorial images, or program files via electronic mail or fax. The recipient of a message sees an attachment as an icon, which can be opened and viewed by double-clicking on it. Additional file-processing options may appear when the recipient clicks with the right mouse button on the icon.

If an attachment is embedded, the recipient must have a copy of an application that can display (**render**) the embedded data. Typically, that application is the program that created the original document, but sometimes other programs can work as well. For example, you read a Microsoft Excel worksheet in Lotus 1-2-3. Alternatively, the Windows 95 Quick View feature makes many types of data visible, eliminating the need for the application.

If an attachment is linked into a message, the recipient must have access to the original data. Typically you link documents, rather than embed documents, when the recipient is another user on your own local area network who doesn't need a separate copy of the file. Linking is also preferable to embedding when you send the same data to a large number of recipients. Embedding a copy of the attachment for each recipient consumes a lot of disk space.

To attach a file to a message, follow the procedure I described earlier in this chapter for inserting the text of a file into a message (Figure 11.17). In the bottom part of the dialog box select An Attachment. To link rather than embed the entire file, select the checkbox labeled Link Attachment to Original File. If you want to embed the attachment instead, be sure this checkbox is cleared. You can also embed an attached file by dragging it from a folder or an Explorer window and dropping it into your message window.

Insider's Tip

You can attach several files at once by holding down the Ctrl key while you select the files.

Embedding or Linking an Object. You can also embed or link a portion of a file (an object) into a message, provided the file was created by a program that supports OLE. To embed or link this type of object, copy it from its source application (which sends the object to the Clipboard). Return to the message window and choose the Paste Special command from the Edit menu.

Forwarding Messages. You can forward messages to other recipients. A message you forward can include comments from you in addition to a copy of the original message you received. You can also forward a message by creating a new message, then embedding or linking into it the message you want to forward. Choose Message from the Insert menu. In the dialog box that appears, select the message you want to attach.

Printing an Outbound Message. To create a printed copy of a message you're about to send, choose Print from the message window's File menu. Or if you prefer, you can click on the Print tool.

Spell-Checking Your Messages. To check the spelling of a single message, choose Spelling from the Tools menu (or press F7) while the message is displayed. To have Exchange check the spelling of a number of messages before they are posted, do the following:

➤ Choose Options from the Tools menu.

➤ Click on the Spelling tab.

➤ On the Spelling page, select the checkbox labeled Always Check Spelling Before Sending (Figure 11.18).

➤ Select any other desired options, then click on OK.

FIGURE 11.18

Spell Checking

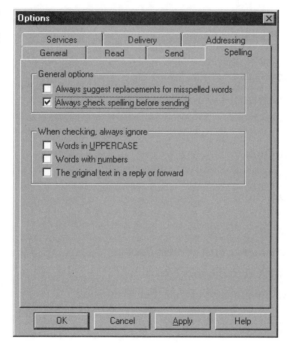

To force spell checking for all outgoing messages, check the option labeled Always Check Spelling Before Sending on the Spelling page of the Options dialog box.

Posting a Message

When you finish composing a message, you can **post** (send) it using any of the following methods:

➤ Click on the Send tool, the first tool on the left on the New Message window's default toolbar (Table 11.3).

➻ Choose the Send command from the File menu.

➻ Press Ctrl+Enter.

When you post a message, it is stored temporarily in your Outbox folder. When Exchange polls the mail system on which you want to send the message and transmits the message, the message is removed from the Outbox and added to your Sent Items folder, unless you have asked Exchange not to retain copies of mail that has been sent.

TABLE 11.3
*New Message
Toolbar*

The tools on the New Message window's default toolbar include the following (from left to right):

➻ Sends message.

➻ Saves message in a disk file.

➻ Prints message.

➻ Cuts selection.

➻ Copies selection.

➻ Pastes selection.

➻ Opens address book.

➻ Checks names against address book.

➻ Inserts a file into the message.

➻ Displays the message's Properties dialog box.

➻ Requests a receipt.

➻ Sets importance to high.

➻ Sets importance to low.

➻ Displays the Help pointer, which provides help about the next item you click.

If Your Message Cannot Be Delivered. Occasionally an outbound message cannot be delivered. Sometimes a recipient's e-mail address changes, or a mailbox is closed. A link in the chain of delivery (such as a gateway or a server) may not be working, or you may abort a message in midtransmission.

When a message cannot be delivered locally, Exchange usually assumes the guise of system administrator and sends you a message about the failure. The specifics of the message (and whether you even receive one) depend on your mail system.

If the error message originates with Exchange, the message includes a Send Again button so you can resend the message easily. This button can be used at any time. If you don't want to resend the message immediately, save the System Administrator message in your in box and reopen it at a later date.

. . . .

Setting a Message's Priority

Exchange can send mail at three levels of **importance** (more frequently known as **priority**): high, normal, and low. Messages sent with high importance are marked with a red exclamation point in your recipients' in boxes. Messages sent with low importance are marked with a downward-pointing black arrow. Messages of normal importance are not marked.

You can select the importance level of any message with tools on the New Message window's Toolbar (Table 11.3). Click on the exclamation point to set the importance level at high; click on the down arrow to set the importance of the message at low. You can also set the importance level on the Properties dialog box, which you can access on the New Message window's File menu.

The default importance level is normal, which is what you should probably use most of the time; always setting levels to high or low makes you like the boy who cried wolf (or wimp). However, if you want to, you can change the default importance value on the Send page of the dialog box you reach by choosing Options from the Tools menu.

Insider's Tip

Many mail systems have their own priority systems. If a mail service offers its own priority options, you should ignore Exchange's options and use the service's. To change the priority level in this case, choose Send Option from the File menu before posting a message. Click on the tab for your mail service, then choose the priority option from that dialog box. To set a new default priority level for all messages sent by a particular mail service, choose Options from the Tools menu, click on the Services tab, select the name of the service, and click on Properties.

• •

Sensitivity Options

Exchange offers four mutually exclusive **Sensitivity** (privacy) options: Normal, Personal, Private, and Confidential. Messages designated personal, private, or confidential are marked as such in the Sensitivity column of the recipients' personal folders files, provided the recipients choose to display the Sensitivity column. (For information about displaying particular columns, see Customizing the Column Layout later in this chapter.)

Recipients also see a description of each message as personal, private, or confidential in the status bar of their message windows, assuming they have chosen to display the status bar. Additionally, messages sent with Private or Confidential sensitivity arrive in read-only mode.

Normal is the default sensitivity setting. To send a message with a different setting, choose Properties from the New Message window's File menu (or click on the Properties tool). In the message's Properties dialog box, choose one of the options in the Sensitivity drop-down list box (Figure 11.19). To change the default sensitivity setting from Normal to Personal, Private, or Confidential, choose Options from the Tools menu, then click on the Send tab. On the Send page, choose an option from the Set Sensitivity drop-down list box (Figure 11.20).

• • • • • • • • • • • • • •

FIGURE 11.19

Setting the Importance and Sensitivity of a Message

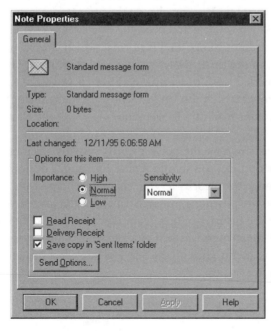

Use the General tab of the Note Properties dialog box to send the message's Importance and Sensitivity.

FIGURE 11.20

*Changing the
Default
Settings for
Sending Mail*

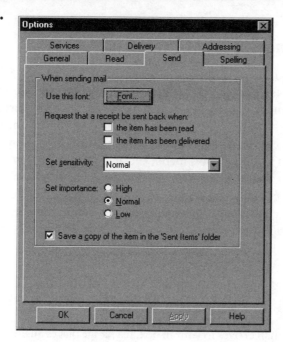

Set the default
importance and
sensitivity levels for all
outgoing messages on
the Send page of this
dialog box.

Receipt Options

You can request two types of receipts for messages you send. A **delivery receipt** is sent to your in box when a message arrives at the recipient's in box. A **read receipt** is returned when the recipient opens the message. You can request either or both types of receipts for particular messages or for all messages.

To request either type of receipt for a particular message, choose the Properties command from the File menu. Select either or both of the receipt checkboxes near the bottom of the Note Properties dialog box (Figure 11.19).

To request receipts of either type for all outgoing messages, choose Options from the Tools menu, click on the Send tab, and select either or both of the receipt checkboxes on the Send page (Figure 11.20). Some commercial mail systems charge extra for receipts, so requesting receipts for all messages could turn out to be costly.

No visual clue or alert is displayed with a message you are creating to indicate that a receipt has been requested for it. To see whether a receipt has been requested, check the message's Properties dialog box. You can open the dialog box by pressing Alt+Enter in the New Message window or by selecting the message and clicking on the Properties tool.

Retaining Copies of Posted Messages

By default, copies of outbound messages are retained in the Sent Items folder after the messages are delivered, so you have a record of everything you've sent. You can copy or move posted messages from the Sent Items folder to any other folders you have set up for organizing your correspondence.

If you prefer not to retain copies, you can turn this option off by choosing the Options from the Tools menu, clicking on the Send tab, and deselecting the checkbox labeled Save a Copy of the Item in the 'Sent Items' Folder (Figure 11.20). You can still retain copies of individual messages by choosing Properties from the File menu before a message is sent. At the bottom of the Properties dialog box select the checkbox labeled Save Copy in 'Sent Items' Folder (Figure 11.19).

Reading and Replying to Mail

When new mail arrives in your in box, Exchange places an envelope icon in the events area of your Taskbar. Double-click on the envelope to open your in box, where new messages are listed in boldface type. To read a message, double-click on its entry in the in box (or in any other folder), or select it and press Enter. To close a message, press Esc or click on the New Message window's Close button.

Insider's Tip

After you read a message, you can move to the next message in the current folder by pressing Ctrl+> or clicking on the Next tool on the toolbar. To move to the previous message, press Ctrl+< or click on the Previous tool.

Notification Options

Exchange has several more forceful, albeit playful, ways to notify you that new mail has arrived. Exchange can beep, play a tune, or pop up a message in the center of your screen. To change the notification method, choose Options from Exchange's Tools menu. In the top section of the dialog box that appears, choose how you want to be notified (Figure 11.21).

If you choose the Play a Sound option, Exchange plays whatever wave, or sound, file you've assigned to the New Mail Notification event in the Sounds section of the Control Panel. If you don't have a sound board in your computer, you hear a simple beep when new mail arrives. If you select Briefly Change the Pointer, Exchange turns your customary mouse pointer into an envelope for a second or so.

FIGURE 11.21
*Modify the
Messenger*

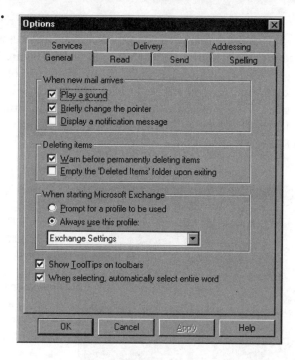

*To change how Exchange
reminds you about
events such as new
mail, deleting items, or
which profile to use,
choose Customize from
the Tools menu and use
the General tab.*

If you need an intrusive announcement, choose Display a Notification
Message. When new mail arrives, a dialog box appears in the center of the
screen. You can go directly to the first new message by clicking on Yes. If you
wish instead to return to the work you are doing, click on No.

Replying to Mail

To reply to a message, click on either the Reply to Sender or Reply to All tool
on the message window's toolbar. You can also choose those commands from
the Compose menu.

Exchange opens a new message window with the To line filled in. If you
choose Reply to All, your reply goes to all the original To and Cc recipients.
Unlike other mail programs, Exchange also sends another copy to your in box.
If you don't want to avail yourself of this privilege, find and select your name
on the To line of the reply and press the Delete key on your keyboard.

Including the Original Message with Your Reply.   Exchange automatically
adds the text of the original message to the end of your reply. A line separates
your reply from the original message, and the original text is indented. Including the original message in your reply can help both you and your correspon-
dents follow the thread of the discussion, although it can make for hefty e-mail.

If you prefer not to include the original message in your reply, choose the Options from the Tools menu, click on the Read tab, and deselect the checkbox labeled Include the Original Text When Replying (Figure 11.22).

During a long e-mail discussion, you may wish to turn off the automatic indenting of original text; otherwise the early messages may be crammed into the right side of the message window. To turn off indenting, deselect the checkbox labeled Indent the Original Text When Replying in the dialog box shown in Figure 11.22.

FIGURE 11.22
Reply Controls

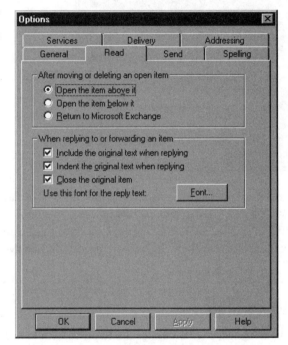

Choose Options from the Tools menu, then use the Read page of the resulting dialog box to determine how original messages are handled in your replies to correspondence.

Choosing a Default Reply Font. To distinguish your reply from the original message, you can choose a default reply font, which is normally a blue font so bright you almost need shades to read it. When you collaborate with others, choose a font that's different from what others in the pack use. You can choose a font that's different in color, typeface, or size. To choose a new default reply font, click on the Font button in the dialog box shown in Figure 11.22.

Forwarding Messages

To forward a message, do one of the following things:

➠ Click on the Forward tool in either a message window or the Exchange window's toolbar.

➠ Choose Forward from the Compose menu.

➠ Press Ctrl+F.

   Exchange opens a new message window with the text of the original message displayed below a separator line. Fill out the address portion of the window, add your comments (if any) above the separator line, and click on the Send tool (or press Ctrl+Enter).

Editing Messages

You can edit any message you receive, unless its sensitivity has been set to Private. When you close the message window, Exchange asks whether you want to preserve or discard your changes.

Saving Attachments

If a message contains an embedded file (or attachment), you can view the embedded file by double-clicking on its icon. In many cases you will want to detach the attachment—that is, save it as a separate file. To do so, follow these steps:

➠ Choose Save As from the File menu.

➠ Click on the Save These Attachments Only button near the bottom of the Save As dialog box.

➠ If your message has more than one attachment, select the ones you want to save in the list that appears below the Save These Attachments Only button.

Printing Messages

To print a message, either press Ctrl+P, choose Print from the File menu, or click on the Print tool on the toolbar. Messages can be printed from within a message window or from any Exchange folder. To print several messages at once, select the ones you want to print (hold down the Ctrl key while you select the messages), then issue the Print command.

Moving or Copying Messages to Other Folders

After you read a message, you might want to move or copy it from your Inbox folder to another folder. From the message window choose the Copy or Move command from the File menu to copy or move a message to a new folder. (The keyboard shortcuts are Ctrl+Shift+C and Ctrl+Shift+M, respectively.) An outline of your folder structure appears, enabling you to point to the folder you prefer as the destination for your message. You can also use drag and drop to move and copy messages between folders.

Deleting Messages

To remove a message, either click on the Delete tool on the toolbar, press Ctrl+D, or choose Delete from the File menu. Your message is relocated to the Deleted Items folder, where it remains until purged from the computer.

If you want to purge the Deleted Items folder each time you quit Exchange, choose Options from the Tools menu. On the General page, select the checkbox labeled Empty the 'Deleted Items' Folder upon Exiting (Figure 11.21).

If you do not select that checkbox, your deleted mail remains in the Deleted Items folder until you purge the folder yourself. You do so by selecting items in the folder and deleting them again.

Managing Addresses and Address Books

The number of address books available to you at any one time via Exchange depends on your mail services and your connections. Although you normally have access to your personal address book, other address books may come and go.

If you use Microsoft Mail and are connected to your network's post office, you normally have access to the Postoffice Address List. This address book, maintained by your Mail administrator, contains entries for everyone with an account at your Microsoft Mail post office. The address book is not available to you when you work off line.

If you use Microsoft Network (MSN), its address book is available to you only when you are connected to the service; MSN doesn't provide an address book for your machine. When you send mail to another MSN member, Exchange uses the on-line service's member-search facility. However, you can circumvent this by adding the names of regular MSN addressees to your personal address book in Exchange.

. . . .

Displaying Address Books

To display an address book, either click on the Address Book tool on Exchange's toolbar, press Ctrl+Shift+B, or choose Address Book from the Tools menu. You see a window similar to the one shown in Figure 11.23.

. . . .
FIGURE 11.23
*Exchange
Address Book*

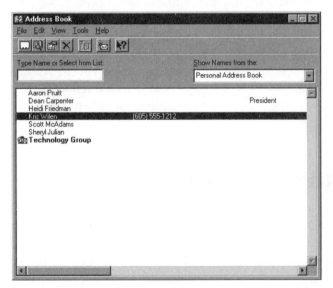

To see an address book, select the Address Book tool. In this window you can then select a particular address book and whatever names you need from it.

The drop-down list box in the upper-right corner of the window tells you which address book you're looking at and enables you to switch to a different one. The text box in the upper-left corner provides **speed search** capability, which I describe in the next section.

Finding an Addressee

To move quickly to a particular name in the current address book, begin typing that name in the text box in the upper-left corner of the Address Book window. As you type, the list scrolls to the item that most closely matches what you've typed.

Speed search works well when you know the first characters of the entry you want. The Find command works well when you know a string of characters within a name or when you want to locate a groups of entries that have letters in common. You can access the Find command either by clicking on the Find tool on the Address Book's toolbar, by choosing Find from the Edit menu, or by pressing Ctrl+Shift+F.

In the Find dialog box, type any character or group of characters. Like the Find command on the Start menu, this Find command locates all entries that contain the specified character string.

Insider's Tip

The Find command searches only the currently displayed address book. If you cannot locate an addressee, you may need to change address books and search again.

Starting a New Message from within the Address Book. As I mentioned earlier, you can start a new message while you are using the address book. Select the names of the recipients, then click on the New Message tool or press Ctrl+N. The New Message window opens with the selected names on the To line.

Maintaining a Personal Address Book

The personal address book is intended to give you quick and reliable access to commonly used addresses. Generally, using the personal address book is quick because the list is smaller than a companywide list or an on-line service's directory. The list, which sits on your own hard disk, is always accessible, which makes your personal address book more reliable than lists that are susceptible to network or remote connection failures.

You can add entries to your personal address book by entering new names manually, by copying entries from other address books, or by capturing an address from incoming mail. With so many sources of address information possible, Exchange wisely protects your phone book from duplicate entries.

If you copy a name that already exists in your personal address book, Exchange ignores the addition.

Creating New Addresses. To create a new entry in an address book, first display any address book. Then click on the New Entry tool or choose New Entry from the File menu. In the New Entry dialog box, choose the type of address you want to add and the address book to which you want to add the address. Exchange then displays a Properties dialog box for the new addressee, enabling you to enter the new address, as well as other pertinent details.

Copying Addresses from Other Books. To copy an entry into your personal address book from any other address book, first select the desired entry in the other address book. Then click on the Add to Personal Address Book tool or choose Add to Personal Address Book from the File menu.

Capturing Addresses from Messages You Receive. When you receive a message from a new correspondent, you can easily add the sender's address to your personal address book. To do so, perform the following steps:

➠ Select a name from the From, To, or Cc line of the message.

➠ Click with the right mouse button and choose Add to Personal Address Book. Or choose Recipient Object from the Edit menu, then choose Add to Personal Address Book from the submenu that appears.

Creating Personal Distribution Lists. As I mentioned earlier, a **distribution list** is a named collection of addressees. Distribution lists take the drudgery out of sending the same piece of mail to many people at once. Entering the distribution list's name on the To or Cc line is the equivalent of entering the name of each member of the list separately.

You can add people to your distribution list from any available address book. For example, you can add people whom you contact on your local area network, through Microsoft Network, and even by fax. When you send a message, Exchange takes care of the details, using the appropriate type of "mail" for each addressee.

To create a new personal distribution list, follow these steps:

➠ Display any address book.

➠ Choose New Entry from the File menu or click on the New Entry tool. The New Entry box appears (Figure 11.24).

FIGURE 11.24

Creating a New Distribution List

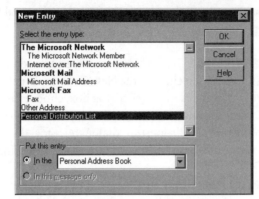

To create a new distribution list, select New Entry from the address book and choose Personal Distribution List from the drop-down list box at the bottom of the New Entry dialog box.

➤➤ In the drop-down list box at the bottom of the New Entry dialog box, select Personal Address Book. In the top part of the dialog box, select Personal Distribution List. Click on OK. A Properties dialog box for your new distribution list appears (Figure 11.25).

FIGURE 11.25

Building a Distribution List

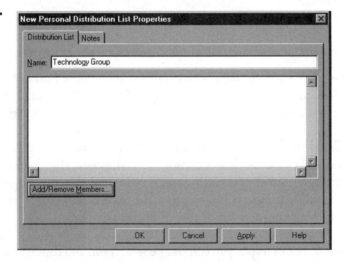

Construct a new distribution list by naming it, then clicking on Add/Remove Members to add addresses.

➤➤ Type a name for your new list, then click on the Add/Remove Members button.

➤➤ In the subsequent dialog box, add names to the distribution list by double-clicking on or selecting names from the list on the left, then clicking on the Members button (Figure 11.26). The names move to the list on the right. To select names from a different address book, choose an address book from the drop-down list box in the upper-right corner of the dialog box.

➤➤ To remove a name from the distribution list, select it on the list on the right and press the Delete key on your keyboard.

••••••••••••••
FIGURE 11.26

*Changing a
Distribution
List*

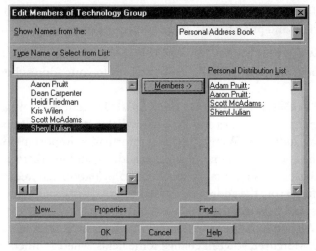

Add a member to a distribution list by selecting an address
book, then double-clicking on or selecting the desired name
from the list on the left and clicking on the Members button.
Remove a name from the list by selecting it from the list on
the right and pressing the Delete key on your keyboard.

➻ When your list is complete, click on OK to return to the Properties dialog
box, then click on OK again to return to your address book.

The name of the new distribution list appears in boldface type in your
address book with an icon of two faces over an envelope, the symbol for a
distribution list.

Maintaining Distribution Lists. You can add or remove names from a distribution list at any time by following these steps:

➻ Display the address book that contains the distribution list.

➻ Double-click on the name of the distribution list or select it and click on
the Properties tool. The Properties dialog box for the distribution list
appears.

➻ Click on the Add/Remove Members button.

➻ In the subsequent dialog box , add a new name by double-clicking on it on
the list on the left or selecting it and clicking on the Members button
(Figure 11.26). To select names from a different address book, choose the
address book you want in the drop-down list in the upper-right corner of
the dialog box.

➠ To remove a name from the distribution list, select it from the list on the right and press the Delete key on your keyboard.

➠ When your list is complete, click on OK to return to the Properties dialog box, then click on OK again to return to your address book.

The Properties of Address Book Entries.

Address books and the entries in them have properties and Properties dialog boxes. The Properties dialog box for an address book entry includes information important for Exchange, such as the addressee's name, electronic address, and mail service. The Properties dialog box also contains space for information ignored by Exchange but useful to you: the addressee's postal address, work and home telephone numbers, and personal data, such as a birth date.

What specific information on an addressee is tracked varies by mail service. Moreover, you can change some fields, whereas others are designated as read-only (and are displayed in gray).

To display an addressee's Properties dialog box, select the addressee's name in an address book or from any address line of a message (that is, from the From, To, or Cc line). Then click on the Properties tool, press Alt+Enter, or choose Properties from the File menu. (You can also click with the right mouse button on the addressee's name and choose Properties from the Object menu.)

Using an Addressee's Properties Dialog Box as a Phone Dialer.

If your addressee's Properties dialog box includes fields for telephone numbers, you can use the dialog box as a phone dialer. Click on the Dial button beside any telephone number.

Checking the Properties of Address Books.

Address books also have Properties dialog boxes, though they are generally less elaborate than the Properties dialog boxes of address book entries. To display the Properties dialog box for an address book, first display that address book. Then click with the right mouse button on the entry in the drop-down list box in the upper-right corner of the Address Book window, and choose Properties from the Object menu that appears.

Managing Folders

Whenever you create a new personal folders file (or first install Exchange), Exchange supplies you with four standard folders. New mail arrives in the **Inbox** folder; outbound mail stays in the **Outbox** folder until it's delivered to the appropriate mail systems. Copies of messages you send are (optionally) retained in the **Sent Items** folder, and deleted messages move to the **Deleted Items** folder.

After a period of time, you may find that four folders are not enough. As the Inbox or Sent Items folder fills with too many messages to find or remember easily, you can create new folders to organize your messages. You can organize folders by addressee, by topic, or any other way you please. You can also create folders within folders to accommodate your organization or to parallel the way your disk is organized.

To create a new folder, select the new folder's parent folder, then choose New Folder from the File menu. To create a folder within your personal folders file, select Personal Folders in the left pane, then choose the New Folder command. To create a folder within your Inbox folder, start by selecting Inbox in the left pane, then choose the New Folder command.

To rename a folder, click on it with the right mouse button and choose Rename from the pop-up Properties menu. Or select the folder and choose Rename from the File menu.

You can move or copy a folder by dragging it from either pane and dropping it in its new parent folder. (To copy the folder, hold down the Ctrl key when you select the folder.) You cannot move the Inbox, Outbox, Sent Items, and Deleted Items folders.

To delete a folder, select it and either click on the Delete tool, press the Delete key on your keyboard, or click with the right mouse button and choose Delete from the pop-up Properties menu.

Insider's Tip | If you inadvertently delete a folder, you can move it back from the Deleted Items folder, as long as you do not close Exchange before the folder is recovered.

Managing Exchange Windows

An Exchange window displays information in two panes. The left pane outlines the organization of your folders. The contents of the selected folder appear in the right pane. If your Exchange window has only a single pane, click on the Show/Hide Folder List tool (second tool from the left) or choose Folders from the View menu to expose the left pane.

You can adjust how much space each pane is given by dragging the vertical bar (the "split" bar) that divides the window. To adjust the width of columns in the right-hand pane, drag the vertical bar at the right side of the column heading. (You can also adjust a column's width via the keyboard by choosing the Columns command from the View menu. In the right side of the dialog box, select the column you want to adjust, then enter a number in the Width box.)

Boldface type in either pane designates a folder holding unread messages. A plus sign in the left pane indicates an entry that can be expanded. To expand the list and see the subentries, click on the plus sign. A minus sign in the left pane indicates an entry that can be collapsed. Click on the minus sign to collapse the entry. To expand an entry with the keyboard, select it and press the right arrow key. To collapse an entry, select it and press the left arrow key.

Managing Mail Among Folders

You can copy, move, or delete messages using drag and drop or commands. To move a message to a different folder, drag the item from the right pane and drop it in the destination folder in the left pane. To copy an item from one folder to another, hold down the Ctrl key while you drag the item to its destination. You can also move or copy multiple messages. To do so, select the messages first (use the Shift key to pick a range of messages or the Alt key to toggle individual messages). Then drag the entire group of messages to the new folder.

To copy or move an item without using drag and drop, select the item, then choose Copy or Move from the File menu. (You can also click on the item with the right mouse button and choose Move or Copy from the pop-up Properties menu.) Exchange displays your folder hierarchy in a new dialog box, enabling you to point (or navigate with the keyboard) to the destination folder.

To move or copy multiple messages from the same folder, hold down the Ctrl key while you select each message. Then drag and drop, or choose commands from the File or pop-up Properties menu.

To delete a message or a group of messages, select the messages you want to delete, then either click on the Delete tool, press the Delete key on your keyboard, or click with the right mouse button and choose Delete from the Object menu. Remember, you can safely restore a deleted message if you move it from the Deleted Items folder to another folder immediately.

Sorting Messages

It happens to everyone at least once: the pettiness of bureaucracy engulfs your soul, and you decide you are going to sort the items in a folder so you can easily identify messages. If you feel so moved, you can use the contents of any column as the basis of the sort by clicking on the column heading. For example, to sort by correspondent, click on the From column. To sort by date (the default), click on the Received heading.

When you sort by clicking on a column heading, Exchange follows a default sorting order. For example, the Received column is normally sorted with the most recently received messages at the top. The Subject and From columns are sorted in alphabetical order. When you sort by Subject, Exchange ignores the *RE*s and *FW*s that appear in the Subject field to indicate replies and forwarded messages.

You can reverse the normal sorting order by holding down the Ctrl key while you click on the column headings. You can also click on the column heading with the right mouse button and select Sort Ascending or Sort Descending from the pop-up Properties list.

You can also choose Sort from the View menu. In the dialog box that appears, select a column name from the drop-down list box and choose either the Ascending or Descending option.

Like a good mother, Exchange reminds you which column was last used to sort. A gray triangle shows which heading was used to sort the messages. An upward-pointing triangle denotes an ascending sort, and a downward-pointing triangle denotes a descending sort.

Customizing the Column Layout. Like the Seven Pillars of Wisdom, new mail folders are organized into seven columns: Importance, Item Type, Attachment, From, Subject, Received, and Size. You can change the order of the columns, add or remove columns, and change the widths of column by choosing Columns from the View menu. This produces the dialog box shown in Figure 11.27.

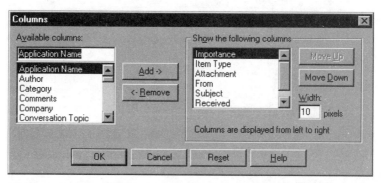

You can use the Columns dialog box to select which columns to display and to determine the order in which they are displayed.

To rearrange the columns, begin by selecting an item in the right-hand list (the list under the heading Show the Following Columns). Then click on the Move Up button to move the column to the left or the Move Down button to move the column to the right. To change the width of a column, enter a new number in the Width field (to indicate either pixels or characters).

You can remove a column by selecting it in the right-hand list and clicking on the Remove button. To add a new column, select that column in the left-hand list and click on the Add button.

To restore the default column layout, click on Reset. You can also alter column widths using the pointer. Refer to the section earlier in this chapter called Managing Exchange Windows.

Finding Messages with the Find Command.

Remember that memo your boss sent you saying you've been downsized? You can locate that message and any other message using Exchange's Find command. When Find locates a message (or a group of messages), you can also read it, reply to it, forward it, and perform other operations on it directly from the Find window. Find can be customized in the same way as other Exchange folders are.

To start Find, either select Find from the Tools menu, type Ctrl+Shift+F, or click on a folder with the right mouse button and choose Find from the Properties dialog box. The dialog box shown in Figure 11.28 appears. It's like the Start menu's Find command: fill in the desired search criteria and click on Find Now. Messages that meet your criteria appear in a list at the bottom of the box.

•••••••••••••••
FIGURE 11.28

*Finding
Messages*

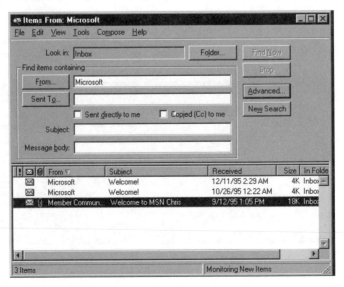

*You use this
dialog box
to locate
messages
that meet
certain
criteria.*

Find usually searches all your personal mail folders. You can search parts of your folder hierarchy by clicking on the Folder button. Select the folder or folders you wish to search. To search the entire tree represented by those folders, check the Include All Subfolders option.

You can use as many Find windows as you need. The search criteria appear on the window's title bar and on the Taskbar. For example, if you search by sender, the sender's name appears on Find's title bar as well as on the Taskbar.

When you leave Exchange, it automatically closes any open Find windows. When you restart Exchange, it automatically reopens those Find windows.

Archiving Items in Your Personal Folders File.
With a personal computer and Windows 95, you too can act like a spy agency and archive your messages. Although Exchange lacks an Archive command, you can use Find to achieve the same results. Follow these steps:

»→ Create a separate personal folders file to hold your archived messages.

»→ Select the Find command and click on the Advanced button. The Advanced dialog box appears (Figure 11.29). Fill in both Received fields with the same date. The From date refers to messages you have received, and the To date refers to messages you have sent. Find locates all messages sent or received on or before the date you enter.

FIGURE 11.29

*Archiving
Messages*

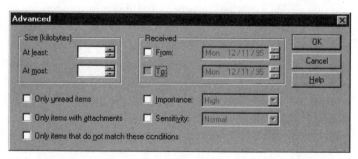

*To archive messages, click the Advanced button and fill in
the Received fields so that Find searches for messages
sent or received on or before a specified date. Then move
those messages to your archive file folder.*

»→ In the Find window choose the Select All command from the Edit menu.

»→ Choose Move from the File menu and point to your archive folder file.

Choosing the date can be slightly confusing. Remember that Find locates files whose date is on or before the given date. So to pick files more than 30 days old, use the date of 31 days ago. For example, to find items more than 30 days old on June 1, 1997, use the date May 1, 1997.

Adding or Removing a Mail Service. To add a new mail service, click on the Add button on the Services page of your profile's Properties dialog box, then choose the service you wish to add from the list that appears. After you select the service, Exchange prompts you for additional information needed to set up the new service. The information needed varies by service. To remove a mail service, select its name on the Services page of your profile's Properties dialog box, then click on the Remove button.

Dial-Up Networking with a Local Area Network Mail System

It's never been so easy to play hooky. If you use a local area network (LAN) mail system and need to access your mail when you're out of the office, Exchange can make the connection for you. Your LAN needs a remote-access server with a modem or other suitable communications device. Your computer needs a modem or other suitable communications device, an installed version of the Windows 95 Dial-Up Networking software, and a properly configured Exchange and Dial-Up Networking.

First make sure Exchange is configured properly. Choose Services from Exchange's Tools menu, select the name of the mail system you're using, and click on Properties. If you're working with Microsoft Mail, you can find dial-up options on the Connection tab (Figure 11.30).

Microsoft Mail can handle the PC-to-post office connection in several ways. If you choose the LAN option, mail is exchanged only through the local area network. If you select the option labeled Remote Using a Modem and Dial-Up Networking, Exchange always brings up Windows 95's Dial-Up Networking to establish a connection with Microsoft Mail. If you select Offline, Exchange lets you post messages to your Outbox but holds the messages until you choose another connection option. If you select Automatically Sense LAN or Remote, Exchange calls on Dial-Up Networking when the network is unavailable.

For a dial-up connection to your LAN mail system, you also need to install Dial-Up Networking. Check with your mail or LAN administrator to find out which settings to use.

FIGURE 11.30

Microsoft Mail's Connection Page

The Connection page controls the way you connect to a service (in this case Microsoft Mail) when you start Windows 95.

You also need to inform Exchange of the changes. The Properties dialog box for your mail system contains a place to enter the name of your Dial-Up Networking Connection. You may also find scheduling options, options for using remote preview, and other details such as redial and time-out settings. For Microsoft Mail, those matters are all handled by the Remote Configuration, Remote Session, and Dial-Up Networking pages of the Properties dialog box. Again, your mail or LAN administrator can give you the specific settings.

Using Remote Mail with Local and Dial-Up Connections.

Are you getting weighed down by rich text and attachment-heavy mail? If your system is suffering from mail arteriosclerosis, check out the remote preview option provided by some mail services. Remote preview enables you to download only the message headers; a header contains the name of the sender, the subject of the message, its date, and its size. You can examine the headers (either on line or off line), mark the ones you want, and download the marked messages to your machine to be read.

Depending on your mail system, you can also use remote preview to screen network mail. For example, Microsoft Mail's remote preview feature is turned on by default when you use a dial-up connection. However, you can turn the preview feature off when you are working on line. This option is handy when you're using a slow network or when you want to screen messages before you receive them.

To turn on remote preview for on-line connections to Microsoft Mail, choose Services from the Tools menu, select Microsoft Mail, click on Properties, and click on the LAN Configuration tab (Figure 11.31). Select the Use Remote Mail checkbox. When you make any change to the mail system, you need to exit and restart Exchange for the change to take effect.

FIGURE 11.31

The LAN Configuration Page

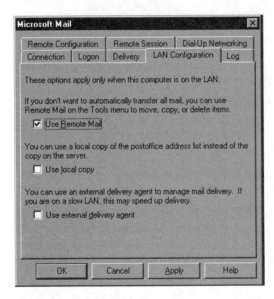

The LAN Configuration page of the Microsoft Mail service enables you to use Remote Mail to preview a message header before downloading the entire message.

To use remote preview with a mail service, choose Remote Mail from the Tools menu. If you have more than one eligible service, choose a service from the menu that appears. Exchange opens a Remote Mail window for the selected service (Figure 11.32).

FIGURE 11.32

Previewing Remote Mail

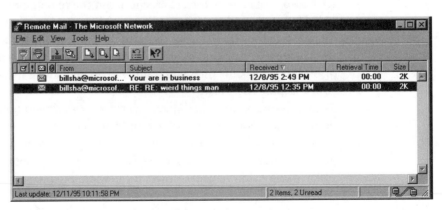

The Remote Mail window enables you to preview your messages by checking their headers, giving you the opportunity to download only what you want to read.

To connect to the service and retrieve headers, choose Connect and Update Headers from the Tools menu or click on the Update Header icon— third tool from the left on the toolbar (Table 11.4). After the system has retrieved your headers, you will probably remain on line, although some systems disconnect you after getting your messages. You can immediately disconnect at this point by choosing Disconnect from the Tools menu or by clicking on the second tool from the left on the toolbar. Or you can stay on line and read the headers.

For each header, you can choose one of three marking options from the Edit menu: Mark to Retrieve, Mark to Retrieve a Copy, and Mark to Delete. To transfer a message from your mail service to your Exchange Inbox and remove the message from the service, choose Mark to Retrieve. To transfer a message to your Inbox but leave a copy with your mail service, choose Mark to Retrieve a Copy. To remove a message from your mail service without reading it, choose Mark to Delete. Tools for those options are located in the middle of the toolbar, and a menu version of each command is located on the Tools menu.

To help you decide which messages to handle and which to defer, Exchange not only tells you the sender's name, the subject matter of the message, and the file size but also gives you an estimated retrieval time for downloading the message. This information might influence whether you mark a message for retrieval or wait until you connect to the LAN.

After you mark the message, choose Connect and Transfer Mail from the Tools menu, or click on the Transfer Mail tool. Your messages are handled as marked, and any messages waiting in your Outbox for the service are transferred.

Mail-Enabled Applications. A **mail-enabled application** is an application that enables you to send messages directly to other users on your LAN mail system without starting Exchange. Many major desktop applications have this capability. For example, Microsoft Mail has a Send and Routing Slip option for mail in its File menu. If a program has a Send, Send File, Routing Slip, or other comparable command, the program fits into this category. Any program that uses **MAPI** (Microsoft's mail application programming interface) should work with Exchange.

The mail features of programs vary, but generally when you use the Send command or another similar command, a program creates a new mail message using its own custom form rather than the typical Exchange message form. Typically, the program then places the current file into the message as an attachment. Some programs provide the option of mailing a selection of the current file rather than the entire file. Some programs also offer to send the file to a distribution list.

Many applications operate independently of Exchange. Exchange does not have to be running for you to use the mail features of those applications. If an application needs a component of Exchange, Exchange runs that component automatically.

· · · · · · · · · · · · · ·
TABLE 11.4
Remote Mail
Toolbar

The Remote Mail toolbar includes the following tools (from left to right):

➨ Connects to remote mail service.

➨ Disconnects from remote mail service.

➨ Updates the list of message headers, connecting to the service if necessary.

➨ Retrieves marked messages from the remote service and sends outgoing messages.

➨ Marks selected messages for retrieval.

➨ Marks selected messages for retrieval of copies, leaving the original messages on the remote service.

➨ Marks selected messages for deletion.

➨ Unmarks all messages.

➨ Displays the Help pointer, which enables Exchange to display information about the next item you select.

Microsoft Fax

If the media is the message, the messenger is the fax. For over two decades, the most popular piece of digital office equipment has been the fax machine. Worldwide, fax machines still outnumber personal computers and their printers combined. The designers of Windows 95 acknowledged that a complete communications solution must provide facsimile transmission.

Making the computer-to-fax link is easier than ever. Spurring the proliferation of computer-generated faxes has been the steep decline in the cost of **fax modems**—modems that can send faxes between computers and that can "print" pages to fax machines. Virtually all brand-name modems sold today can send and receive faxes.

As digital creations, fax machines have advanced in several ways. They include more features for customizing messages, and some fax machines can be connected to networks, as well. Newer standards require that faxes be sent as complete binary files, so that they can be stored on disk and printed later.

Modem **faxware**—the software that controls a computer's ability to handle faxes—operates on the principle that whatever you print can also be sent as a fax. And if you can receive a fax, you can store it on disk for later viewing, editing, and printing. Faxware and fax machines are incorporating more security measures to ensure that the right person receives the fax and that the contents cannot be viewed by the wrong parties.

Managing a glut of faxes offers the same challenges as managing an avalanche of electronic mail. As I discussed earlier in this chapter, Windows 95 was designed to host a single Exchange Inbox that holds all electronic mail and faxes. Microsoft Fax offers tools that enable you to view, print, store, and forward faxes as easily as you can handle electronic mail.

. . . .

New Features

Windows 95's Microsoft Fax offers a comprehensive set of features that support fax communications. If you have a fax modem attached to your computer (or have access to a shared fax modem on a network), Microsoft Fax enables your computer to double as a fax machine.

You can send faxes in a variety of ways. You can choose the Compose New Fax option from the Start menu and let the wizard guide you through the steps of addressing and formulating a message. Alternatively, you can use the Print command from any application and send a printed document to the fax "printer" installed by Microsoft Fax. If an application offers a mail feature, you can fax a document by using the Send command (or its equivalent) and specifying a fax addressee. You can send faxes by composing messages in Exchange's message window and sending them to fax addressees chosen from an address book. Any faxes you receive appear as messages in your Exchange Inbox.

Exchange Fax supports **Binary File Transfer (BFT),** a method of sending faxes as binary files. If you send a fax to a system that also supports BFT, the receiving system can store the fax on disk, treating it as if it were an editable electronic message. If the receiving machine doesn't support BFT, the fax is sent in a standard Group III format that all fax machines recognize. By default, Exchange Fax sends a message in the "best available" format, meaning it sends a fax as Group III unless BFT is available, in which case BFT is used instead.

Exchange Fax supports RSA encryption for security and works with fax-on-demand systems. Exchange Fax also includes a fax viewer, which displays faxes on screen, and a cover letter designer.

Setting Up Microsoft Fax

To make Microsoft Fax fully functional on your computer, you first need to install the software and configure it. This section covers installing the software. If you followed the instructions earlier in this chapter, you set up the Exchange Inbox and Exchange Fax at the same time, and you can skip this section.

If you did not install the Inbox, return to the section entitled Installing and Running Exchange early in this chapter and follow the instructions there. You must install the Inbox to use Windows 95's Fax features.

If you installed the Exchange Inbox but did not install Exchange Fax, follow these directions:

➠ From the Start menu, start the Control Panel.

➠ Double-click on Add/Remove Programs. Pick the Windows Setup tab.

➠ Locate and click on the Microsoft Fax checkbox. A checkmark should appear in the box, as shown in Figure 11.33.

FIGURE 11.33
*Installing
Microsoft Fax*

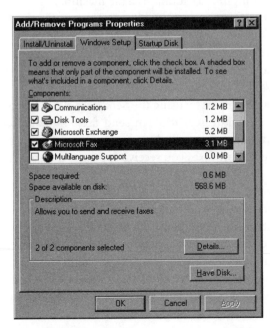

To install the Microsoft Fax software, select the appropriate line from the Windows Setup tab in the Add/Remove Programs Properties dialog box of the Control Panel.

➤ Click on OK, and follow the directions if Setup asks for the Windows 95 distribution files.

In addition to installing both Exchange and Fax, you need to add the fax service to your Exchange profile. For details about how to do this, see Adding or Removing a Mail Service earlier in this chapter.

• •

Configuring Microsoft Fax

After installing Microsoft Fax, you should see a new submenu called Fax in the Accessories folder of the Start menu. This folder holds menu items that enable you to send and receive faxes and design your fax cover pages.

You also see a new device in your Printers folder, a printer called Microsoft Fax. This is actually a printer driver that converts the output from applications into fax format and sends that output to the fax modem.

If you have not configured this device, click with the right mouse button on the Microsoft Fax printer and select Properties. Figure 11.34 shows how you probably want to fill out the Details page, providing your fax modem is owned by your computer. Note that the "printer" port should be Fax: (Unknown Local Port). Do not select a communications port, such as COM1 or COM2, even if your fax modem is connected to one of those ports.

• • • • • • • • • • • • • •
FIGURE 11.34
The Details Page

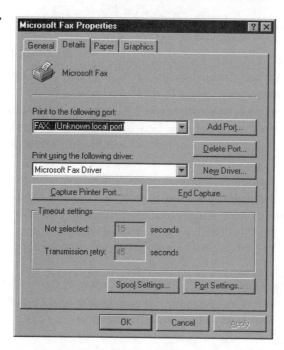

Set up the Details page for Microsoft Fax as shown in this figure.

Also check the User and Message pages. On the User page make sure that your name, fax number, and mailbox (if you are on a network) are correct (Figure 11.35). You may want to fill out the remainder of this page, because it provides the information fed onto fax cover pages.

••••••••••••
FIGURE 11.35
The User Page

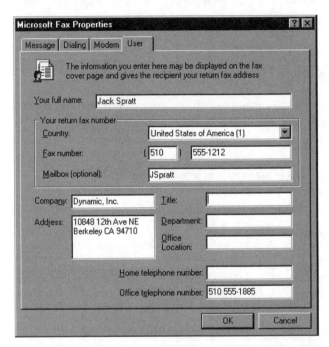

Enter personal and work information about a user on the User page.

Examine the Message page, too (Figure 11.36). Here, you can spell out when your faxes are sent: immediately or at a particular time. You can enter other information on various pages of the Microsoft Fax Properties dialog box. For example, you can change the dialing parameters (including the number of retries and the amount of time between retries when Fax cannot connect), enter the name of the modem Fax uses, and input facts about yourself.

Insider's Tip

If you are working on the road or using your portable computer at home, make sure the dialing location is correct. Click on the Dialing Properties button in the Control Panel's Modem applet and choose or set your current location in the I Am Dialing From drop-down list box.

Insider's Tip

Because many cover sheets print your fax number based on the information in the Microsoft Fax Properties dialog box, use your company's fax number unless you want faxes sent to your machine.

FIGURE 11.36

The Message Page

On the Message page you control when faxes are sent, how they are sent (in binary or Group III format), and what the cover page says.

Insider's Tip

You can create a desktop shortcut for Microsoft Fax in your Printers folder. Doing so enables you to send faxes by dragging documents and dropping them onto the shortcut. To create the shortcut, drag the Microsoft Fax icon from the Printers folder to the desktop and answer Yes to the dialog box.

Adding Fax Recipients to Your Personal Address Book

Microsoft Exchange uses one address book—your personal address book—for both faxing and e-mail. To add a new recipient, follow these steps:

➡ In Exchange click on the Address Book tool or choose Address Book from the Tools menu. With any address book displayed, click on the New Entry tool (the first tool on the left side of the toolbar) or choose New Entry from the File menu.

➡ In the drop-down list box at the bottom of the New Entry dialog box, select Personal Address Book. In the top part of the dialog box, under the Microsoft Fax entry, select Fax. Then click on OK. The New Fax Properties dialog box appears (Figure 11.37).

··············
FIGURE 11.37
*New Fax
Entries*

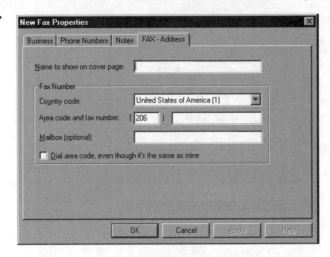

For each new
Fax recipient
you want to
enter into your
personal
address book,
enter a name
and a phone
number on the
FAX-Address
page of the New
Fax Properties
dialog box.

➤ Fill in the name and phone number boxes on the Fax-Address page. All the other fields on this page and the other pages of this dialog box are optional. Click on OK to record the new entry.

Insider's Tip

Although most of the information you can enter in the New Fax Properties dialog box is optional, any information you enter on the Business page can be used to prepare cover sheets.

Insider's Tip

You don't need to create an address book entry for every person you fax, but it's convenient to have an entry for someone you fax repeatedly.

· ·

Sending a Fax

Windows 95 offers several ways to create and send a fax. One method is to choose New Message from Exchange's Compose menu and specify a fax address. Because Exchange treats Microsoft Fax the way it does any other installed mail system, you can compose faxes just as you create e-mail.

You can also use the Compose New Fax wizard to send a fax. This wizard guides you through the entire process, from entering text to selecting options.

You can print from an application to the Microsoft Fax pseudoprinter, too. Select Microsoft Fax from a program's printer-selection menu, which you can often access by selecting Print or Printer from the File menu. Then print the file to send. If your application includes a mail feature, you can send the document to a fax recipient.

Two shortcuts can help you fax a document in a disk file while you are using the Windows Explorer. One method is to select the file and click on it with the right mouse button. In the menu that pops up, choose Send To and select Fax. The second method is to drag the file from the Explorer to the Microsoft Fax icon in the Printers folder (or a shortcut on the desktop).

Insider's Tip

You can send a fax by any of the methods I just described, but if you drag and drop a fax onto the Microsoft Fax printer icon, the fax you send cannot be edited by the recipient as can faxes sent by the other methods.

The Compose New Fax Wizard

For help in creating and sending a fax, you can call up the Compose New Fax wizard. To access the wizard from the Start menu, choose Programs, then Accessories, and then Fax, then choose Compose New Fax. The wizard appears (Figure 11.38).

FIGURE 11.38

The Compose New Fax Wizard

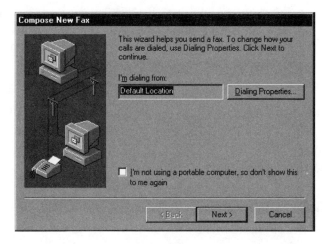

The initial screen of the Compose New Fax wizard provides a space in which to enter the current dialing location.

The first item of business is confirming your dialing location. If you are traveling, make sure the dialing location shown in this initial screen is correct. If it's not, click on Dialing Properties and choose your current location from the I Am Dialing From drop-down list box.

If you have not defined multiple dialing locations, the wizard's screen includes the checkbox shown at the bottom of Figure 11.38. If the computer is stationary, select this checkbox. The next time you compose a fax, the wizard skips this screen. (If your situation changes and you define new calling locations, the screen reappears.)

When you click on Next, the Recipient dialog box appears (Figure 11.39). You can choose addressees either by clicking on Address Book and selecting names from the lists or by entering names and phone numbers and clicking on the Add to List button.

• • • • • • • • • • • • •
FIGURE 11.39
*The Recipient
Dialog Box*

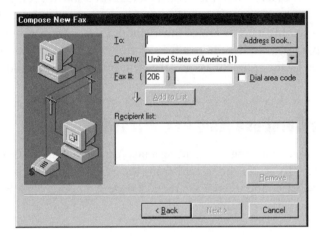

*Enter recipient
information or pick
an addressee from
the address book
in the Recipient
dialog box.*

The dialog box displays the area code from which you are dialing. If you're faxing to someone with the same area code, Fax will not dial the area code unless you select the Dial Area Code checkbox.

Insider's Tip

You can send a "fax" to other users by adding them to the recipient list in your address book. Those addressees receive your message as ordinary e-mail.

When you finish identifying recipients, click on Next. The Cover Page dialog box (Figure 11.40) appears.

• • • • • • • • • • • • •
FIGURE 11.40
*Options,
Options*

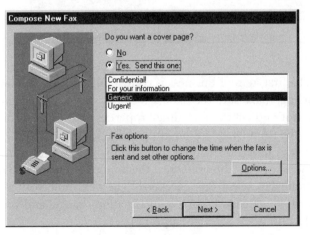

*This dialog box
enables you to
select a cover
page for your fax
and to choose
other options.*

If you want a cover page, click on Yes, Send This One and select a cover page. If you have created a cover page that doesn't appear on the list, click on Options. In the Options dialog box, click on the Browse button and navigate to the cover page you want. If you don't want a cover page, click on the No button. You can also click on Options if you want to change any of the defaults defined in your Microsoft Fax Properties dialog box.

Click on Next and complete the Subject line, add any note, and specify whether the note should start on the first page (Figure 11.41). If your cover page includes a Subject field, the subject you type appears in that field.

• • • • • • • • • • • • • •
FIGURE 11.41
Just the Facts

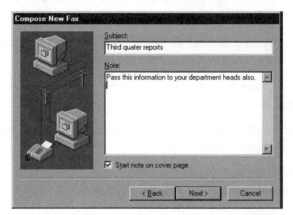

On this screen you enter the subject of a fax, add a note if you want, and determine where the note starts.

Clicking on Next again brings up the dialog box shown in Figure 11.42. If you want to attach a disk file, enter its full name or use the Add File button to bring up a File dialog box, then select the file. If the recipient's system supports BFT and you decide to have Microsoft Fax send an editable message, the file arrives as an embedded object. Otherwise, Fax renders the document and transmits its image.

• • • • • • • • • • • • • •
FIGURE 11.42
Attaching Files

Use this dialog box to attach files to a fax.

After clicking on Next one more time, click on Finish. The fax message is sent, either immediately or at the end of whatever period of time you selected.

· ·

Options for Sending Faxes

By clicking on the Options button in the dialog box shown in Figure 11.40, you can adjust the settings for a fax in the following ways:

➤ You can send the message immediately, or you can send it later, either when discount telephone rates take effect or at another time.

➤ You can set the number of times Windows tries to send a message to a recipient and the amount of time between tries.

➤ You can choose the paper size, the image quality, and the orientation of a rendered fax.

➤ You can locate and use a cover page that did not appear in the earlier dialog box (see Table 11.6).

➤ You can ask that a message be held if the addressee cannot receive it as an editable document.

➤ You can send a fax in rendered form (that is, in a form that is not editable), even if an addressee has the capability of receiving it in editable form.

➤ You can determine whether security measures are applied to the message.

The next section covers the more complex options.

Telling Fax When to Send. Microsoft Fax can transmit messages either immediately, during telephone rate discount hours, or at a specific time. To set a specific send time, click on the Set button in the Send Options for This Message dialog box (Figure 11.43). Then use the spinner in the dialog box that appears (Figure 11.44).

Discounted telephone rates are available from 5:00 P.M. to 8:00 A.M. daily. If you want to change those hours (you might want to change the discount starting time to 11:00 P.M., for example, when rates are usually discounted more), use the Microsoft Fax Properties dialog box to change the default.

••••••••••••
FIGURE 11.43
Send Options

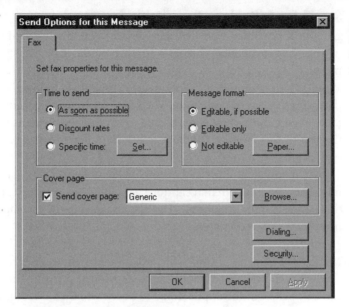

Use this dialog box to adjust how and when to send a fax.

••••••••••••
FIGURE 11.44
The Timer

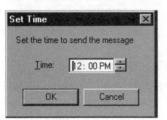

Use the spinner in the Set Time dialog box to set a fax's transmission time.

Setting Retry Options. By default, if Fax cannot connect the first time, it retries three times, waiting five minutes between tries. To specify different retry settings for the current message, click on the Dialing button in the Send Options for This Message dialog box (Figure 11.43).

Specifying Paper Size, Image Quality, and Orientation for Rendered Faxes.

By default, faxes are composed in standard letter-size dimensions (8 ½ by 11 inches), in portrait mode, and at the best image quality available. You can override any of those defaults by clicking on the Paper button in the Send Options for This Message dialog box (Figure 11.43) and choosing the desired options.

Specifying Editable or Noneditable Format. By default, faxes are sent as Editable If Possible (faxes sent this way are sometimes described as being sent in the "best available" format). In this mode, Fax transmits an editable message to any addressee whose system supports BFT. Machines running Windows 95, Windows for Workgroups 3.11, and Windows NT and machines that support the Microsoft at Work fax platform, for example, can receive faxes in editable form. Files attached to a message appear as icons along with the text of the message. To view an attached file, the recipient double-clicks on its icon.

When you send a fax as Editable If Possible to a standard Group III fax machine or to a system that cannot accept BFT, Microsoft Fax transmits a rendered image of the document. Any files attached to the message are also transmitted as rendered images.

Insider's Tip

Microsoft Fax cannot send a file attachment with a rendered fax unless the sending computer has an application capable of printing the file, and the file can be opened in the application. To check whether a document can be sent in rendered form, click with the right mouse button on the document's icon in a folder or in the Explorer window. If Print appears on the Object menu, the document can be sent as an attachment to a rendered fax.

If you must send an editable message, choose Editable Only in the Send Options for This Message dialog box (Figure 11.43). Fax then returns an error notification if one or more of your recipients cannot receive editable messages. If you want your recipients to receive a rendered message regardless of what kind of system they use, choose Not Editable.

Specifying an Unlisted Cover Page. The Send Options for This Message dialog box (Figure 11.43) lists all the cover pages (that is, files created with Cover Page Editor) stored in the Windows directory. To choose a cover page stored elsewhere, click on the Browse button.

Security Options. To keep unauthorized recipients from reading an editable fax, you can encrypt it or assign it a password. You can also attach a "digital signature" to files enclosed in your message. The recipient can verify your signature to ascertain that the enclosures originated from you and were not modified after you signed them. For information about security features, see the section Providing Security for Your Faxes later in this chapter.

Inspecting the Queue of Outbound Faxes. When one or more faxes are waiting to be sent, a document icon surrounded by animated lines that appear to be moving pops up in the events area of the Taskbar. To see how many faxes are in the queue, rest your mouse on this icon. You can examine the queue by double-clicking on the icon (Figure 11.45).

FIGURE 11.45

The Fax Queue

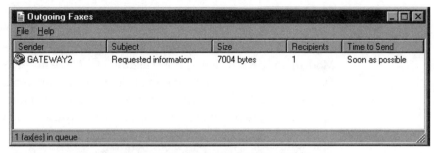

To see a list of outgoing faxes, double-click on the fax machine icon in the events section of the Taskbar.

If you decide not to send a fax that's scheduled for transmission, select it in the Outgoing Faxes window and choose Cancel Fax from the File menu. Or delete the fax from your Exchange Outbox folder.

When Fax Cannot Send Your Message. If Microsoft Fax cannot send a fax to one or more of your recipients, your Exchange Inbox folder receives an administrative message stating who didn't get the message and in some cases why they didn't get it. The administrative message appears in a format that includes a Send Again button. Click on Send Again to send the fax back to the output queue.

Receiving Faxes

Microsoft Fax is a bidirectional product, capable of both sending and receiving faxes. By default, Microsoft Fax answers incoming calls automatically whenever Exchange is running. This can have positive and negative side effects.

Fax is a "TAPI-aware" program, meaning it uses the Microsoft telephony applications programming interface to handle the communications port. Fax and other TAPI-aware programs can share your communications port, actively monitoring and using it. For example, Fax can monitor for incoming fax calls while another communications program, such as Procomm for Windows 3.0, communicates with another service.

Without this sharing, programs block access to the communications port. For example, the non-TAPI-aware Procomm for Windows 2.1 is stymied in its attempts to reach the communications port when Fax is active. Communications programs that don't use TAPI cannot cooperate successfully with

Fax. To accommodate non-TAPI programs, Fax releases its communications port. In most cases you can continue without shutting down Fax.

In some cases, however, you need to suspend Fax manually from answering the phone. To do so, first double-click on the fax machine icon in the events area of the Taskbar to bring up the Microsoft Fax Status dialog box (Figure 11.46). Click on Options and then Modem Properties to open the Fax Modem Properties dialog box (Figure 11.47). Switch Fax temporarily to Don't Answer and try the program. If it can "open" the serial port for use, the procedure works. Note that if you have only a single phone line and a single modem, you are not able to receive a fax while you are on line.

FIGURE 11.46

How's My Fax?

To access the Microsoft Fax Status window, double-click on the fax machine icon in the events area of the Taskbar.

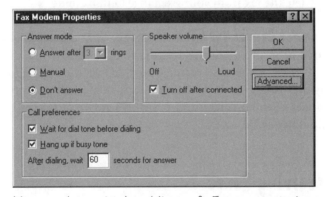

FIGURE 11.47

*The Fax
Modem
Properties
Dialog Box*

You can determine how Microsoft Fax reacts to incoming calls and change other properties by using the Fax Modem Properties dialog box. To bring up the dialog box, click on Options and then Modem Properties in the Microsoft Fax Status dialog box (Figure 11.46).

Changing the Answer Mode and Other Modem Settings. When Fax is running (that is, when you are using Exchange and Fax is in the current profile), an icon of a fax machine appears in the events area of the Taskbar. To verify that Fax is running in Auto Answer mode, rest the mouse pointer on this icon for a moment and read the message that pops up.

To switch to Manual Answer mode or to change other settings that affect your modem's behavior, double-click on the fax machine icon. When a Status window appears (Figure 11.46), choose Modem Properties from the Options menu to open the Fax Modem Properties dialog box (Figure 11.47).

If you switch the answer mode to Manual, Fax continues to monitor your communications port but does not answer an incoming call until you instruct it to. To make Fax answer a call, display the Status window (double-click on the fax machine icon in the events area of the Taskbar if the window isn't visible) and click on the Answer Now button.

If you switch the answer mode to Don't Answer, the icon remains in the events area, but Fax "releases" the communications port. With Fax in this mode, you can use a non-TAPI-aware communications program.

Reading and Replying to Incoming Faxes

Depending on how they are sent to you, faxes you receive are either editable messages or rendered images. When either kind of fax arrives in your Exchange Inbox folder, you are notified, according to the options selected on the General page of Exchange's Options menu (Figure 11.21).

Editable messages appear as ordinary e-mail and are indistinguishable from electronic mail you receive over your network e-mail program, Microsoft Network, CompuServe, and other services.

You can view any fax by using the Windows 95 Fax Viewer to display rendered messages (Figure 11.48). Table 11.5 describes Fax Viewer's toolbar buttons.

FIGURE 11.48

*Print and
Display Faxes*

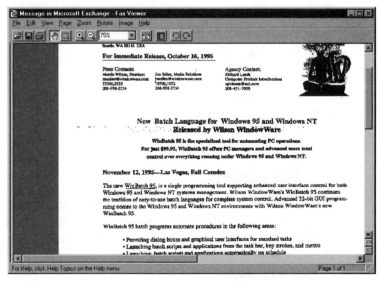

The Fax Viewer displays and prints received faxes.

To reply to or forward an editable or rendered fax message, use the same Exchange tools and commands as you use for electronic mail. However, you cannot reply to or forward a rendered fax from within Fax Viewer.

TABLE 11.5
*The Fax
Viewer Toolbar*

The tools on the Fax Viewer toolbar include the following (from left to right):

➡ Opens a fax document.

➡ Saves a fax to a disk file.

➡ Prints a fax document.

➡ Selects Drag mode; the mouse pointer changes into a hand, and you can move an image within the window by dragging it.

➡ Chooses Select mode; the mouse pointer changes into cross hairs, and you can select part of an image for copying.

➡ Zooms in.

➡ Zooms out.

➡ Zooms a predefined or entered amount.

➡ Changes the size of an image so its page width is the same as the width of the Fax Viewer window.

➡ Shows or hides the thumbnail images of all pages in Fax Viewer's left pane.

➡ Rotates an image 90 degrees to the left.

➡ Rotates an image 90 degrees to the right.

The Fax Viewer

The Fax Viewer—like a combination microscope, telescope, and printer—gives you the ability to perform several operations. To print a message, choose Print from the File menu or click on the Print button on the toolbar. (You can also choose Print Preview from the File menu, then choose Print from the Preview window.)

To save a message as a separate file, choose Save a Copy As from the File menu. Fax Viewer gives the file the extension .AWD. To reopen an .AWD file, click on the Open button on the toolbar or double-click on the .AWD file in a folder or the Explorer window.

To enlarge or reduce the image of a document, choose commands from the Zoom menu or click on the magnifying-glass tool with the plus sign (to zoom in) or the magnifying-glass tool with the minus sign (to zoom out) on the toolbar. Alternatively, you can choose from the preset percentages in the toolbar's drop-down list box or enter a percentage. (The size of the original document is 100 percent.)

To change the position of the image in the Fax Viewer window, click on the hand icon on the toolbar, then drag the image. (You can also change the image's position with the scroll bars.) To rotate or flip an image, choose commands from the Rotate menu or use the toolbar's Rotate Left or Rotate Right button.

To invert the colors of an image, choose Invert from the Image window. White characters on a black background can make low-resolution text easier to read.

To display thumbnail sketches of each page in a message, choose Thumbnails from the View menu. Choose this command again to turn off the thumbnails.

Providing Security for Your Faxes

It's difficult to provide tight security for faxes. Fax machines are usually kept in public areas so that any passerby can glance over a received fax. And without a widely used authentication method, someone sending a fax can impersonate someone else.

If your recipient can handle binary file transfers (that is, can receive editable faxes), several methods are available to you to secure your faxes:

➤ Assigning a password. The recipient must enter the password to open the fax.

➤ Using an encryption scheme developed by RSA Data Security to encode a message. To be able to read the fax, a recipient has to use a "public key" that you publish.

➤ Using a "digital signature" that authenticates any attachments included with a fax. By using your public key, the recipient can verify that the attachments were sent by you and are unaltered originals.

Using a Password to Protect a Fax. To send a password-protected fax, first prepare the fax in the usual manner. If you're using the Compose New Fax wizard, click on the Options button in the dialog box shown in Figure 11.40, which concerns the cover page and fax options. The Message Security Options dialog box appears (Figure 11.49). Select the Password Protected button, enter a password in the dialog box, and click on OK twice to continue.

• • • • • • • • • • • • •
FIGURE 11.49
Fail-Safe

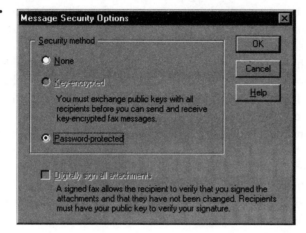

The Message Security Options dialog box enables you to set up security for a fax.

If you're creating a fax by using the New Message command, choose Send Options from the File menu in the message window. Click on the Security button on the Fax page of the Options dialog box, and the Message Security Options dialog box appears. Select the Password Protected button, enter a password, and click on OK twice to continue.

Receiving a Password-Protected Fax. When you receive a password-protected fax, the message is identified in your Inbox as encrypted. To read the message, double-click on the message header as you normally would to open the message. Exchange prompts you for the password. After you successfully enter the password, an unprotected copy of the original message is created, leaving the password-protected original in place.

After you read the unprotected copy of the fax, you can delete it to protect the contents of the message. You must also open the Deleted Items folder (where the message has moved from the Inbox) and delete the message again.

Sending an Encrypted Fax. RSA security works using a two-key system, called a private-public encryption system. One key is private and is maintained by you. You use this key to encrypt (encode) messages. The other key is called a public key and is given to anyone who needs to decode (decrypt) your messages. Before you can send an encrypted fax, you must prepare those two keys and send the public key to those who will receive your encrypted faxes.

Insider's Tip

What some can create, others can duplicate. RSA provides a relatively secure means of protecting messages. However, RSA security is fallible and can be defeated by determined individuals. Additionally, RSA security can be compromised by poor security habits, such as leaving your private key on a non-secured computer.

Insider's Tip

Longer passwords create longer keys, which are more difficult to break. The easiest way to maintain a good password is to use a memorable sentence, such as "The thing I like most about my computer is. . . ."

Creating Private and Public Keys.

To create a set of private and public keys, follow these steps:

➺ Choose Microsoft Fax Tools from Exchange's Tools menu, then choose Advanced Security. The Advanced Fax Security dialog box appears (Figure 11.50).

• • • • • • • • • • • • • •
FIGURE 11.50
More Security

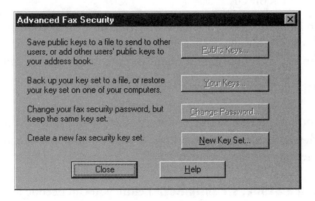

The Advanced Fax Security dialog box enables you to maintain your public and private keys.

➺ Click on the New Key Set button.

➺ In the dialog box that appears, enter and reenter a password phrase. This phrase is the basis of your private and public keys and prevents other users from tampering with your key set.

➺ Click on OK and wait while Exchange creates your new key set.

If your own computer is completely secure, you can save your password on the computer by selecting the checkbox labeled Save the Password in Your Password List. For more complete security, however, do not select this checkbox.

Exchange stores your key set as part of the Registry. You never see the keys, but you can now send your public key to your trusted fax recipients.

Sending Your Public Key to a Fax Recipient.   The next step in using private-public key security is to send your public key to a trusted recipient as an unencrypted fax or e-mail message. Afterward, the recipient can decrypt any fax you send, as long as you don't change the key set.

Take the following steps to send your public key:

➤ Select Microsoft Fax Tools from Exchange's Tools menu, then choose Advanced Security.

➤ Click on the Public Keys button.

➤ If you are requested to do so, enter your password phrase.

➤ Click on the Save button to store your public key in a file.

➤ In the Fax Security dialog box, select your name, click on the To button, then click on OK.

➤ Exchange displays a standard Save As dialog box, proposing to save the file in your Windows folder as YOURNAME.AWP (where YOURNAME is your name). Accept the default name or enter a new name, and click on Save.

➤ Click on Close twice to return to Exchange.

Compose a new fax or e-mail message using standard procedures, then attach your newly created .AWP file. If you're faxing, you can password-protect the message for extra security.

Adding a Sender's Public Key.   Before you can decode an encrypted message, you must add the sender's public key to his or her entry in your personal address book. Follow these steps:

➤ After you receive a sender's public key as an attachment to a fax, open the message and save the attachment as a separate file. (To do so, select the attachment, choose Save As from the File menu, click on the button labeled Save These Attachments Only, and enter a file name.)

➤ Choose Microsoft Fax Tools from the Tools menu, then choose Advanced Security.

➽ In the Advanced Fax Security dialog box, click on the Public Keys button.

➽ If you are requested to do so, enter your password phrase.

➽ In the Managing Public Keys dialog box, click on the Add button.

➽ Select the name of the attachment containing the public-key file to add it to your address book, then click on Open.

Handling a Received Encrypted Fax. When an encrypted fax arrives, Exchange identifies it in your Inbox as encrypted. Double-click on the message header to create an unencrypted copy, leaving the original intact. If the message must remain secure, delete the unencrypted copy when you have finished reading it, then delete the copy of it that was moved from the Inbox to the Deleted Items folder.

Assigning a Digital Signature to Attachments. Digital signatures are an offshoot of private-public key encryption. They enable a recipient to confirm that an attachment was created by the sender and was not altered by anyone else.

Exchange provides one digital signature option. Open the Message Security Options dialog box (select New Message from Exchange's Compose menu, then choose Send Options from the File menu in the message window and click on the Security button.) Select the Digitally Sign All Attachments checkbox and click on OK. Exchange embeds a digital signature in all attachments. This all-or-nothing action carries a small overhead, and anyone without the public key can ignore the digital signature.

Verifying a Digital Signature. With a sender's public key, you can authenticate attachments to the sender's fax messages. To verify the digital signature assigned to a fax attachment, follow these steps:

➽ Display the message text and select the attachment.

➽ Choose Microsoft Fax Tools from the Tools menu.

➽ Choose Verify Digital Signature.

Exchange notifies you as to whether it has verified the attachments. Remember that you must have the sender's public key in your personal address book to verify a digital signature.

. . . .

Cover Page Editor

You can add a personal touch to your faxes by designing your own cover pages with Cover Page Editor, which is included with Microsoft Fax. The application offers a full range of text and graphics features that enable you to draw and type text onto a cover sheet. You can also use the editor to insert clip art from multiple sources.

To start the editor, choose Programs from the Start menu, then choose Accessories, Fax, and Cover Page Editor from the subsequent menus (Figure 11.51). (You can also start the editor from the Microsoft Fax Properties dialog box shown in Figure 11.36. Click on either Open or New.)

. . . .
FIGURE 11.51
*Customized
Cover Sheet*

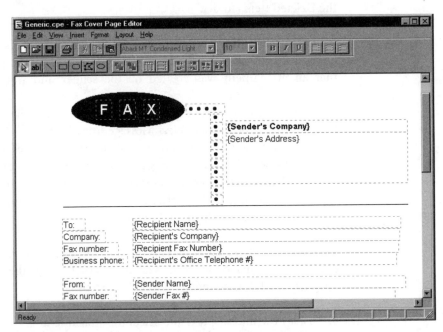

The Cover Page Editor gives you the opportunity to
personalize cover sheets for your faxes.

TABLE 11.6

The Cover Page Editor Toolbar

The tools on the Cover Page Editor toolbar include the following (from left to right):

Upper Bar	Lower Bar
Enables you to create a new cover page.	Activates pointer.
	Inserts text.
Opens an existing page.	Draws a line.
Saves the current page.	Draws a rectangle.
Prints the current page.	Draws a round-cornered rectangle.
	Draws a polygon.
Cuts the selected item.	Draws an ellipse.
Copies the selected item.	
Pastes the selected item.	Brings to the front.
	Sends to the back.
Changes the text font.	
Changes the font size.	Equally spaces horizontally.
	Equally spaces vertically.
Changes the text to bold.	
Changes the text to italic.	Aligns left.
Underlines text.	Aligns right.
	Aligns top.
Left-justifies text.	Aligns bottom.
Centers text.	
Right-justifies text.	

Inserting Fields. Fields on Exchange cover pages contain strings that are replaced by information you have entered elsewhere—for example, information you entered while setting up a fax or entered in an address book. Subject, Sender's Name, and Note are examples of cover page fields.

To choose what information to include on a cover page, choose Recipient, Sender, or Message from the Insert menu. A submenu shows what information can be inserted into the cover page.

Each field originally contains its own name, enclosed in braces. For example, the field that will contain the subject of a message originally reads {Subject}. When you use the cover page for a specific fax, text in each field is replaced by the appropriate data. Whatever appears on the subject line of your message, for example, replaces {Subject} on the cover page.

Text on the cover page that does not appear within braces is fixed—that is, it does not change when you insert information into the corresponding fields. The Cover Page Editor includes on each cover page both the fixed text and the information entered into the fields you have chosen. Since you often want to use every field, this feature reduces the time it takes to create a cover page.

Adding Text Frames. To add fixed text to a cover page, click on the Text tool (the second tool from the left on the lower bar of the Cover Page Editor toolbar). The mouse pointer turns into a plus sign. Position the pointer where you want the new text to appear and create a rectangular frame to hold the text by holding down the mouse button and dragging the mouse. Release the mouse button when the lower-right corner of the frame is in approximately the right place. After the frame is created, type the fixed text into the frame.

Insider's Tip

The text tool has no menu equivalent.

To edit fixed text, first select it. Then type new text or delete the existing text, just as if you were using a word processor.

Insider's Tip

You can select an object by pressing the Tab key repeatedly until the object you want is selected.

Formatting Text and Frames. To format a text object on a cover page, first select the object. Next choose the formatting you want to apply from a menu or the toolbar.

Choosing Font from the Format menu enables you to change the font, the point size, and other characteristics of the type. Choosing Align from the

Format menu enables you to change the text's alignment to left, center, or right. Line, Fill, and Color, also on the Format menu, gives you control over the text's color. Because of the limitations of traditional fax machines, you choice of color is restricted to white, black, and three shades of gray.

To format the frame surrounding a text object, select the frame and choose the Format menu's Line, Fill, and Color command. You can add lines in various weights and colors and provide a background color. As with text, the color choices are black, white, and three shades of gray.

Note that all menu commands, except color, have toolbar equivalents.

Inserting Clip Art and Other Graphics. You can insert virtually any registered OLE object onto a cover page. This includes clip art, bit-mapped graphics, pictures, Excel spreadsheets, and other objects. Obviously, inserting a movie or a MIDI clip onto a static page may not have the intended result, but just about anything else can go on the page.

To insert an object, choose Object from the Insert menu, which pops up the Insert Object dialog box (Figure 11.52). Select an object type. To create a new image of that type, click on OK. To insert an existing object, click on Create from File, then click on OK. The File Open dialog box appears; select the file whose contents will be copied onto the page.

FIGURE 11.52

Graphics for the Cover Page

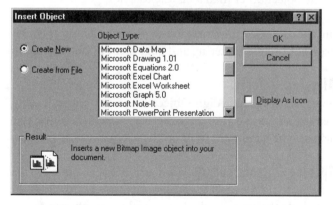

Choosing Object from the Insert menu brings up a list of registered graphics types that can be inserted on a cover page.

You can also insert an object by copying it onto the Clipboard from the original application. Then simply paste the object onto the cover page.

Insider's Tip

You can format more than one object at a time by selecting the desired objects (hold down Ctrl and click on the objects) or using the Select tool to draw a rectangle around the objects. Then you apply the formatting commands.

Adding a Freehand Drawing. The Cover Page Editor offers five freehand drawing tools: Line, Rectangle, Rounded Rectangle, Polygon, and Ellipse. Except for the Polygon tool, you use all tools as you do the Text tool: you click on a starting position, drag the pointer to the ending position, and release the mouse button.

You can create a square by holding down the Shift key while you drag with the Rectangle or Rounded Rectangle tool. To create a circle, hold down Shift while you drag with the Ellipse tool.

The Polygon tool creates a closed shape with any number of vertices. To use this tool, click on the location of the first vertex. Continue clicking at the locations of subsequent vertices. Double-click on a final location to close the shape and finish the drawing.

Formatting Graphics. To change the border or background color of a graphic, select the Format menu's Line, Fill, and Color command. You use the command in the same way as you use it to format text frames.

Resizing and Repositioning Objects. To change the size of any object on a cover page, select the object and drag the desired handle until the shape is the size you want. To change the position of an object, select it and drag any part of the object other than a handle to a new position.

You can use an alignment grid to help position objects. To turn the grid on, choose Grid Lines from the View menu. The grid is a visual aid only, however. For precise centering and alignment of objects, use the Layout menu.

Aligning Objects. You can align one or more objects at a time. Select the objects and choose Align Objects from the Layout menu. Then choose the desired alignment (top edge, bottom edge, left edges, right edges). You can also use the alignment tools on the toolbar.

Spacing Objects Evenly. To distribute space evenly among three or more objects, select the objects and choose Space Evenly from the Layout menu. To distribute the space in the horizontal plane, choose Across. To space objects evenly in the vertical plane, choose Down.

Centering Objects. To center objects between the left and right edges of a cover page, select the objects, choose Center on Page from the Layout menu, and then choose Width. To center objects between the top and bottom edges of a page, select the objects, choose Center on Page from the Layout menu, and then choose Height.

Adjusting Overlapping Objects. You can adjust the order in which objects overlap, which is called the **z order.** The z order reflects the order in which the objects are stacked.

To move an item forward in the stack, either select the object and press the plus key to move it up one level, choose Bring to Front from the Layout menu, or use the Bring to Front tool on the toolbar. To move an item back through the stack, either select the object and press the minus key, choose Send to Back from the Layout menu, or use the Send to Back tool on the toolbar. Note that z order changes have no apparent effect on transparent objects.

Previewing and Printing. You can preview or print a cover page to help you perfect its look. However, all fields appear in their original (nonreplaced) form.

To preview a page, choose Print Preview from the File menu. In the Preview window you can zoom in and out to inspect small and large sections of the page. You can also click on the Print button to generate a hard copy of the cover page. Alternatively, you can choose Print from the File menu to generate a hard copy.

Saving a Cover Page. To save a cover page so that you can use it with your fax messages, choose Save from the File menu. The page is saved with the extension .cpe. If you want Microsoft Fax to find the cover page automatically, save the file in the Windows 95 directory.

Using a Fax-on-Demand Service

You can use Microsoft Fax to dial up a fax-on-demand service and download either all documents waiting for you or a particular document. To do this, choose Microsoft Fax Tools from Exchange's Tools menu. Then choose Request a Fax. The Request a Fax wizard appears (Figure 11.53).

Select Retrieve Whatever Is Available or Retrieve a Specific Document. Complete the rest of the dialog box as required if you are downloading one or more specific documents. The title of a document is usually a number, and you generally insert commas between entries.

After you have filled in the dialog box correctly, click on Next. The wizard works like the Compose New Fax wizard described earlier in this chapter. Enter the name and number of your fax service and follow the rest of the wizard's instructions so that Fax can connect and retrieve your faxes.

FIGURE 11.53

*Fax on
Demand*

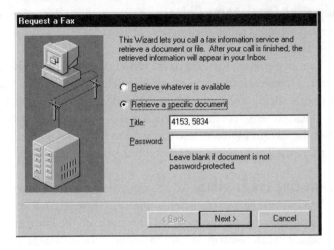

*You can use
the Request
a Fax wizard
to retrieve
information from
a fax-on-demand
service.*

Using a Shared Fax Modem

You can use Fax with a fax modem anywhere on your network, provided the modem is set up to be shared. Transmitting faxes via a shared modem is identical to sending faxes via a local fax modem. Messages for you received on a shared modem, however, are stored in the Inbox folder on the server. Either the server manager or additional software is required to reroute the messages to your local mailbox.

Sharing a Fax Modem. Setting up a shared fax modem or changing your setup so you can use a shared fax modem requires little work. To set up a server so that its modem can be used by others, follow these steps:

➼ Start Exchange.

➼ Choose Microsoft Fax Tools from Exchange's Tools menu.

➼ Choose Options.

➼ Click on the Modem tab.

➼ Select the checkbox labeled Let Other People on the Network Use My Modem to Send Faxes.

➼ A pop-up window enables you to determine which disk drive will contain the queue of outgoing faxes. You can accept or change the drive letter that is displayed. This dialog box appears only when you have more than one hard-disk drive.

➤ In the Share Name field, accept or alter the proposed share name.

➤ Click on the Properties button.

➤ From the group of options under the heading Access Type, choose Full. However, if you want to assign a password restriction to the fax modem, enter a password in the Full Access Password field.

➤ Click on OK twice to return to Exchange.

To Use a Shared Modem. To set up your system so that it uses a shared modem, take the following steps:

➤ Start Exchange.

➤ Choose Microsoft Fax Tools from the Tools menu.

➤ Choose Options.

➤ Click on the Modem tab.

➤ Click on the Add button.

➤ Select Network Fax Server and click on OK.

➤ Enter the network path to the shared modem. By default, the share name is Fax. For example, if the modem is shared on a computer named Server, you would type \\server\fax.

➤ Click on OK.

➤ Select the shared modem from the Available Fax Modems list, then click on Set As Active Fax Modem.

➤ Click on OK to return to Exchange.

Summary

Finally, all your mail—whether it comes from a LAN server or a commercial on-line service such as CompuServe—can be handled in one stop. Microsoft Exchange, an electronic mail package built into Windows 95, unifies your connections to local networks and dial-up services.

Exchange maintains one or more profiles for your computer. Each contains information on your personal folders files and your personal address book and configuration details for each mail service you use.

Exchange sports the hallmarks of a good word processor: a feature-rich editor for creating and editing messages, and a spell checker. Text can be cut and pasted into messages, and files can be inserted, linked, or embedded into messages.

Exchange also features qualities that would guarantee its success in a first-class spy agency: it provides methods of securing messages from unauthorized viewing (passwords), offers barometers of change, and lets you designate the importance of a message. In addition, you have all the powers of a congressional archivist at your fingertips. Received messages can be read, stored, or forwarded. The Find command can search for messages, and when you connect to your LAN from a remote site, you can preview your mail before downloading the messages.

For those who want to be organized, Exchange maintains one or more personal address books, as well as address books from other services. Most address books list names and electronic contact information, and some also contain space for entering personal information or additional professional data. You can also expedite distribution to a group of folks by using the distribution-list feature provided in the address book.

You can now send and receive faxes using Microsoft Exchange and Microsoft Fax. You can create a fax either with the help of a wizard, by using the Exchange Inbox, or by printing from a software program. Faxes can be password-protected, and RSA security can be applied to a fax. The origin of an attachment can be verified, and an attachment can also be checked for unauthorized alteration.

Faxes can be sent as files using Binary File Transfer if the recipient machine is capable of receiving a fax in that format. Faxes can also be sent as standard Group III faxes or as prerendered pages.

You can custom design cover pages for your faxes using Microsoft Fax's Cover Page Editor. In addition, Microsoft Fax can retrieve messages from fax-on-demand services and can use shared fax modems on a network.

3

Advanced Windows 95 Techniques

12

Multimedia

During the past year a new dimension has been added to the way people use computers. Multimedia—a technology that was still in swaddling clothes just a few years ago—has come of age. Multimedia components are all but standard on computer systems sold today, and Windows 95 has been designed to make the most of them.

Strictly defined, **multimedia** simply means more than one medium. In the computer world, multimedia has come to describe the use of sound and graphics together in applications. Graphics include still images, animation, and video. Sound encompasses recorded sounds, synthesized sounds, and speech.

The emergence of multimedia has dramatically increased the usefulness of the computer as a learning tool and a reference source. Multimedia encyclopedias, reference books, on-line magazines, and other learning tools pack the shelves of computer stores, not to mention bookstores. With more than 60,000 CD-ROM titles available at the time of this writing and with development and sales of game software booming, any operating system worth its salt needs to deliver on the promise of multimedia. The new 32-bit architecture of Windows 95 does just that; it makes for bigger and bolder sound and video, transforming your PC into a more exciting platform for entertainment and education.

Multimedia has had its greatest impact on the way people use computers at home, but it has affected all areas of computing. Business applications include software for creating presentations, training programs, and multimedia databases. Scientists use multimedia to create simulations, add voice annotations to their work, and analyze phenomena that have critical sound or movement components. Educational uses span kindergarten through graduate school; multimedia software is revolutionizing our educational system. And multimedia fits naturally into the entertainment industry; interactive movies and TV and virtual reality adventure games are visible on the horizon, and other, as yet unimagined recreational pastimes are coming in this century.

Multimedia is often associated with **interactivity** and CD-ROMs. The term *interactivity* refers to the exchange of information between a user and a program. Such interaction can be as simple as playing and rewinding an animated sequence or answering questions on a history quiz, or as complex as experiencing a computerized simulation of space flight. Numerous studies have shown that interactive presentation of information in a format that includes audio and visual elements provides an effective and entertaining method of learning. CD-ROMs play a role because multimedia data, such as sound files and video sequences, take up large amounts of storage space. A standard CD-ROM disc can store more than 600 megabytes of information, providing an inexpensive way to distribute multimedia information.

Although CD-ROM and multimedia are often thought of as synonymous, a CD-ROM is simply a storage device. Other methods of delivering multimedia information are quickly becoming feasible and will soon be ubiquitous. In particular, information available on commercial network services as well as on the World Wide Web increasingly includes elements associated with multimedia, such as graphics, links to media events and other sites, and even real-time audio and video. The advantage of on-line information, whether it is multimedia or not, is that it can be revised frequently by its authors; in fact some Web pages are updated daily. While the graphics, audio, and animation available on line are usually simple so that downloading times remain within reasonable limits, the amount of information immediately available on line boggles the mind.

Insider's Tip

Multimedia, like many hot topics, has become the sole subject of several magazines, including *New Media, Electronic Entertainment, Multimedia World, PC Graphics and Video,* and *Multimedia Monitor.* Those magazines offer technical information and news in a rapidly changing arena. *Multimedia Today,* published on a quarterly basis by IBM, contains up-to-date listings of multimedia-related hardware and software (from all vendors, not just IBM).

The Mechanics of Multimedia

Multimedia works better than it used to, now that Windows has undergone a 32-bit make-over. (I covered some of the benefits of the Windows 95 32-bit architecture in Chapters 1 and 4.) For multimedia applications, 32-bit architecture means bolder sound, faster display of graphics, and smoother integration of sound and video. A move to Windows 95 provides an instant multimedia upgrade for your PC, even if you do not upgrade any of your hardware. If you do upgrade your hardware, Plug and Play takes the hassle out of configuring new components.

The multimedia extensions included with Windows 95 provide a variety of features and benefits:

➤ You can play standard **digital audio** files from applications.

➤ The **Sound Recorder** utility enables you to record and edit, as well as play, digital audio files.

➤ The **CD Player** utility enables you to play audio CDs. You can also customize your collection by creating individual playlists for each CD.

➤ Support for **Audio Video Interleave (AVI),** also known as Video for Windows, is built into Windows 95. AVI files contain video data and sound data, coordinated so that their playback is synchronized. (Apple Computer offers a similar system called QuickTime, originally designed for the Macintosh but now available for Windows as well.)

➻ A software control system, **MCI (Media Control Interface),** provides Windows applications with a standard method of controlling a wide range of external devices, such as audio CD players, videodisc players, VCRs, MIDI instruments, scanners, and anything else that includes an MCI-compatible device driver.

➻ A simple utility called **Media Player** enables you to control MCI devices and play sound and video files as well as CDs.

➻ You can play standard **MIDI** music files—or parts of the files that you select—from applications. The MIDI tab in the Multimedia Control Panel enables you to remap MIDI instruments so that files created on one MIDI hardware setup will play the proper instruments on another MIDI setup.

➻ You can easily upgrade multimedia components. With **Plug and Play,** Windows 95 can find, install, and configure most CD-ROM drives, sound cards, and other multimedia devices as soon as you connect them to your computer. The Add New Hardware wizard walks you through the installation of non–Plug and Play devices.

➻ The **Device Manager** in the System Control Panel makes it easy to install and configure multimedia device drivers. (Windows 95 can set up many device drivers for you, particularly if the devices are Plug and Play.)

➻ You can use a **joystick** in addition to the mouse.

Graphics

Three main forms of graphics are used in multimedia:

➻ **Still images.**

➻ **Video.**

➻ **Animation.**

Still Images

Computers use two main types of still images:

➤ **Bit-mapped graphics.** Composed of small dots called pixels. Each pixel's color and intensity are defined by one or more bits in the computer's memory. Bit-mapped graphics are best for images that contain much detail, shading, and subtle color. The resolution of a bit-mapped image is determined by the number and the layout of the pixels that make up the image.

➤ **Vector graphics.** Composed of drawing instructions that describe the dimension and shape of every line, circle, arc, or rectangle. Vector graphics are best for line art. The resolution of a vector image is determined by the resolution of the output device.

A bit-mapped graphic is stored at a fixed resolution. You can edit the image at that resolution, but if you shrink, stretch, or enlarge the graphic, it may suffer from distortion and loss of image quality. Vector graphics, in contrast, can be enlarged, reduced, and otherwise edited without affecting resolution or image quality, because the image is redrawn each time it is displayed or output.

Bit maps require more disk space than vector graphics, because bit maps contain information about each pixel displayed on the screen, whereas vector graphics are stored as commands that create the images. Vector graphics, however, take longer to render because they have to be drawn by the processor, whereas bit maps are simply loaded directly into memory.

Examples of bit-mapped graphics are .BMP, .DIB, and .PCX files, which you can edit with Paint, and the TIFF files used by desktop publishing software. Examples of vector graphics are Windows metafiles, encapsulated PostScript files, and files created by Computer Aided Design (CAD) programs.

You can acquire still images for a multimedia application from a variety of sources:

➤ Use a graphics application to create images from scratch. Paint programs are best for creating bit-mapped images, and drawing programs are best for creating vector images. 3-D programs are best for creating rendered three-dimensional objects.

➤ Download art from an Internet site or from a commercial bulletin board service (BBS) or on-line service (such as America Online, CompuServe, or Microsoft Network).

➤ Purchase computer clip art and edit or modify it if needed. Both bit-mapped and vector clip art are available. Many word-processing, desktop publishing, presentation, and drawing programs now come with libraries of clip art suitable for common uses (for example, holiday art and office art).

➦ Scan in bit-mapped images with a flatbed or hand-held scanner. Both color and black-and-white scanners are available.

➦ Take film (transparencies or negatives) to a photographic processor and have the images transferred onto a Photo CD, which stores them as high-quality color bit-mapped images.

➦ Use a video digitizer (also called a frame-grabber) to capture an image from a video camera or a VCR.

One important note: if you acquire multimedia art from a BBS, scan in existing art, or capture video or sound, keep in mind that the work you're using may belong to someone else. If you intend to redistribute the work or make use of it for commercial purposes, you may be subject to copyright laws. If so, get the copyright holder's permission before using the work.

Video

Video has already established itself as a major medium, making it a natural for multimedia. The most prevalent product in consumer electronics is the television, followed by the VCR and the camcorder. Creating your own video is so easy, it's become a major American pastime. It's not surprising that video production, like publishing, has made its way to the desktop. Windows 95 enables you to play videos on your desktop and incorporate them into other programs. And with the right equipment, you can create videos digitally, on your desktop.

Because the video market is so large, it provides a readily available source of existing video segments and film clips that can be used to create multimedia software titles. And like desktop publishers, desktop video producers can concoct almost anything the high-end video industry can offer, including promotional videos, training demos, sales presentations, special effects and animation, and even TV shows.

Two types of video work with personal computers:

➦ **Analog video.** Uses the same standard video signals as do TVs, VCRs, laser-disc players, and camcorders. Analog video is typically stored on videotape or videodisc and is the form of video transmitted by television stations and cable companies. With the right hardware you can capture analog video and translate it into digital video.

➤+ **Digital video.** A digital form of video that can be stored as computer files. Digital video is convenient because Windows 95 can run it without special hardware or software. When a video is digitized, each frame is stored as a series of pixels, much like a bit map, so that resizing the video window can result in distortion. In addition to the picture information, a digital video file can contain digital audio data that's synchronized with the video, just like the sound track of a movie. AVI is the standard format for Windows 95 digital video, although you can use other formats—such as QuickTime —if you first install the appropriate drivers.

To work with analog video, you need the type of display card known as a video-in-a-window, or video capture, card. Those cards are capable of displaying an analog video image in an on-screen window. The source of the signal can be a laser disk, a VCR, a TV, a cable converter, a camcorder, or another compatible device.

Once you have the hardware to view analog video, you can use a video capture card to digitize the video (turning it into files readable by Media Player, for example). Once prohibitively expensive, the process of digitizing video has now become a possibility for a broad range of users. You can buy a solid, albeit basic, video capture card that digitizes video at up to 30 frames per second (the same rate at which television shows are broadcast) for about $500, including digital video editing software. Additional options, of course, increase the cost. For example, if you need to convert your digital video to analog—say you want to copy a video to videotape—you need a card that can output analog video, which can run upwards of $1,000.

Another, growing source of digital video files is animation programs, such as Autodesk Animator and Asymetrix 3D F/X. You create animation differently than you do digitized video (more on this later). However, once animations are created, you often work with them in exactly the same way as you work with AVI clips.

Digital video requires that your computer be able to transfer huge amounts of data. Think of digital video as a series of bit maps, which your computer must read from a hard disk or a CD-ROM and display at up to 30 pictures per second. Your computer works like a flip book, except that it also has to draw each picture as it flips past. This means your computer needs a fair amount of horsepower to access and display video, not to mention any accompanying audio. For that reason, digital video is a hardware salesperson's dream; you're going to need more, faster hardware. Or at least you're going to want it.

Video Compression. Digital video file formats are designed to minimize the amount of hard-disk space required for a file by reducing the amount of data necessary to render a video. For example, not every frame in a video file is a complete snapshot. Instead, video capture and compression software can designate every fifth or tenth frame as a **key frame**—that is, as a complete frame. Frames between key frames contain only data representing changes between frames—for example, a bird flying across the sky.

In addition to supporting those file formats, Windows 95 supports a number of video **codecs** (compression and decompression utilities). These vary in effectiveness and speed but share one purpose: to reduce file sizes by eliminating unnecessary information.

Which compression scheme you use depends on the type of video you're creating or editing (for example, animation versus live video capture), the quality required for playback, file size limitations, and the time required to compress the video. For each video format, you can control the tradeoff between file size and quality; in general, the more compressed a file, the more you give up in quality. The following are video compression methods supported by Windows 95:

➳ **Video 1.** A Microsoft compression method used most often with AVI files. It doesn't support 24-bit color but does let you control the color palette, unlike other compression schemes. For example, Cinepak and Indeo automatically dither 24-bit color when they play back at 8 bits.

➳ **Cinepak.** A compression method created by SuperMac Technologies (now Radius) that produces highly compressed, high-quality 24-bit video. It typically requires well over an hour to compress each minute of finished video.

➳ **Indeo.** Any of several compression schemes created by Intel. The latest version rivals Cinepak in quality and, like Cinepak, uses a 24-bit format. However, it requires much less time to compress files than Cinepak does.

➳ **RLE.** An 8-bit format from Microsoft that's best used for video or other media of relatively uniform color. Quality suffers and file sizes increase if you use RLE on live video with continuous-tone colors.

If you have a video capture card, you may need to obtain extra compressor drivers in addition to the codecs included with Windows 95.

Danger Zone

Don't apply more than one compression method to a video sequence. Most methods result in some loss of quality, and the loss is compounded if multiple techniques are applied. Before experimenting with compression settings, save the original, uncompressed version of your video sequence.

If you need to capture or play back full-screen video, you should get **MPEG** hardware and software. MPEG is a video format that's been gathering support in the past year or two. The scheme radically compresses motion video so that it can be played back on a typical PC at full-screen sizes. Because compressing video and saving it in the MPEG format is processor-intensive and requires special hardware, most people until recently sent their videos to a dedicated service bureau for MPEG encoding. Now the price of MPEG hardware, although still relatively high, has dropped dramatically, and at least one software-only MPEG encoding program is on the market. Although not included in the initial Windows 95, Microsoft has since released MPEG for Windows 95, a software add-in that decompresses MPEG if you have a fast Pentium or equivalent system. This software-only approach doesn't provide as good result as the dedicated MPEG chips.

Checklist for a Video Capture Card. In the process of deciding which video capture card to purchase, determine whether the card captures still frames, check the resolution and pixel depth of the images, and find out if the card can double as a video output card. Some cards come with bundled software, such as Adobe Premiere or Asymetrix Digital Video Producer. You can use those programs to edit raw video, using features such as the following:

➣ **Graphic overlay.** This gives you the ability to overlay computer-generated images onto video images, enabling you to superimpose animation, titles, and special effects onto video.

➣ **Chroma key.** With this technique you can replace the background color in one video with a second video image. Television newscasts use chroma key to insert the weather map behind the weather reporter, who is really standing in front of a blank blue wall.

➣ **Transition effects.** This technique enables you to blend one image into another to create a smooth transition between two scenes.

➣ **Audio.** With audio you can edit one or more audio tracks within the video, making adjustments or adding a narration or a music track.

In addition to video editing programs, other multimedia programs offer powerful features for refining video files as well. Macromedia Director, long the most popular multimedia program on the Macintosh and more recently available on Windows, enables you to add animation special effects to AVI files.

Another peripheral you may want to get is a **video switch box.** One of these enables you to choose from several analog video sources, such as a TV broadcast, a camcorder, and a VCR.

Insider's Tip

If you plan to create or edit digital video, a good A/V hard drive might be a useful purchase. Created specifically to meet the demands of video, A/V drives eliminate common problems such as frames being dropped when the hard drive can't keep up. Leaders in the digital video world include Avid, FWB, MicroNet, Micropolis, and Radius; all of those companies make A/V drives.

Animation

Most people associate animation with cartoons. With Windows 95, however, animation can assume a more businesslike demeanor. It's easy to assemble simple, animated presentations in which you move images and text around on the screen. You can also animate a chart or a bulleted list so that it goes through its paces automatically.

Two types of animation software for Windows are available:

➡ **Presentation software.** Broad-based products, such as Action, Power-Point, and Compel, designed for businesspeople, educators, and anyone else who has to make a presentation.

➡ **Animation software.** Professional-level packages, such as Animator Pro and Macromedia Director, that simulate the traditional animation process to provide a cartoon artist's or animator's version of desktop publishing. To create this type of animation requires a system with a fast processor, a fast disk, fast video, and lots of RAM.

Several companies sell clip animation libraries; check the back pages of your favorite multimedia or animation magazine. With clip animation, you can quickly add an artistic, if not original, element to business or other material. Clip animation is offered in FLC/FLI format, which is Autodesk Animator's native format, as well as in AVI, QuickTime, and other formats.

Sound

A primary force in human communication, sound encompasses both speech and music. Sounds can inform, entertain, and evoke emotion. The ability to use sound with your computer adds an important dimension to its role as a communications tool.

Sound capabilities are fast becoming a standard component of computer systems. Windows 95 supports two forms of sound: **digital audio** (.WAV) and **MIDI.** Digital audio enables you to record and work with speech and other natural sounds. MIDI is a format for recording, editing, and playing music on electronic instruments.

Digital Audio

Digital audio software works by turning a hard disk into a virtual tape recorder. To connect a microphone or other source of sound to the computer, you need a sound card (the most popular are Sound Blaster and its compatibles). The circuitry inside a sound card enables you to record sound by converting analog sound waves into a digital form, which your computer can use.

To convert natural sound waves into a digital format that can be stored on your hard disk, digital audio software takes a series of measurements, or "samples," of the sound. Because of this, digital audio is sometimes referred to as sampled sound. The frequency of sampling is called the sample rate, and the accuracy with which the samples are taken (either 8-bit or 16-bit accuracy) determines the overall quality of the sound. High-quality recording (such as on audio compact discs) requires frequent sampling at 16-bit resolution and thus uses a greater amount of storage space than does lower-quality recording.

The following are the most common file formats for digital audio files on the PC:

➡ **.WAV.** The standard format used by the Windows multimedia extensions.

➡ **.VOC.** The Sound Blaster format. Conversion utilities can translate .voc files into .wav format if necessary.

The quality of a digital sound depends on the capabilities of your sound card, the quality of the microphone or other sound source, the accuracy of the sample, and the sampling rate at which the sound was digitized. Table 12.1 shows how storage requirements vary by type and rate of sampling.

· · · · · · · · · · · · · ·
TABLE 12.1
Storage Requirements for Digital Sound Based on Type of Sample and Sampling Rate

Sample Type	Sampling Rate	Storage Requirements
8-bit, mono	11.025 kHz	0.6MB/minute
8-bit, mono	22.05 kHz	1.3MB/minute
8-bit, stereo	22.05 kHz	2.6MB/minute
16-bit, mono	44.1 kHz	5.3MB/minute
16-bit, stereo	44.1 kHz	10.6MB/minute

As a guideline for evaluating output, 8-bit, mono, 11.025 kHz sampling produces quality roughly equivalent to that of AM radio and is fine for most business purposes. The 8-bit, stereo, 22.05 kHz sampling is comparable to FM radio quality, and 16-bit, stereo, 44.1 kHz sampling provides outstanding quality, equivalent to that of an audio compact disc.

In addition to those common .WAV types and rates, Windows 95 supports a 4-bit compressed .WAV format called **ADPCM.** Samples created in this format take up half the disk space of equivalent samples of 8-bit audio and sound as good as or better than 8-bit audio. However, keep in mind that this is strictly a Windows 95 format; ADPCM sound files don't play in Windows 3.1.

If you have an older sound card, it may be 8-bit. However, most sound cards on the market today support 16-bit audio.

You can compare the differences in sound produced by different combinations of settings. Record a sample file, then choose Save As from the File menu, click on Change, and choose an audio format. (Choose the highest quality you want to sample first.) Save the file and give it a descriptive name, create additional versions of the file using other settings, and then compare the results.

Insider's Tip

If you're creating audio for public consumption, go for better-quality sound, even though it requires more disk space. If your audio will be reproduced in a group setting (such as over loudspeakers in a classroom or an auditorium), use 16-bit audio. Why? Because the degradation in quality when you use 8-bit sound can be amplified glaringly through large speakers. If possible, preview the audio using the same type of equipment your audience will have available.

CD-ROMs

The audio **compact disc,** or **CD,** has become the primary medium for selling music and other recorded material, making the phonograph record obsolete. CD sound is digitally recorded in 16-bit stereo at 44.1 kHz. The information is stored on the disc as a series of microscopic pits on an otherwise polished surface, which is then covered with a transparent coating. The CD player projects a laser beam that scans the surface of the CD and interprets the pits as binary data. This digital audio is converted back to an analog waveform for listening. Because only light touches the surface of a CD, it is less subject to the distortion resulting from wear that affects the quality of a phonograph record.

Each audio CD can store more than 600 megabytes worth of binary data —the equivalent of 100 copies of *The Windows Bible,* or more than a quarter-million pages of text. Because CD audio is so popular, the technology has become relatively inexpensive; CDs can be produced in quantity for less than a dollar per unit. Because of the availability of CD technology, it has been adopted as a data storage medium by the computer industry in a form called **CD-ROM.**

The ROM part of CD-ROM stands for read-only memory, which reflects the fact that you cannot usually write data onto a CD-ROM. However, it's becoming more common for individuals and corporations to create their own CDs, using CD-ROM recorders (sometimes called CD-ROM burners) and specialized software (like Corel's CD Creator). In addition, it's not hard to find a service bureau that will produce a single CD-ROM from your data to create a demo disc or to permanently archive a large amount of data.

CD-ROM technology enables you to stuff hundreds of megabytes of data into a format that is far less expensive than a hard disk—$7 to $8 per disc, with burners starting at $1,200. CD-ROM discs are more convenient and permanent than magnetic or digital backup tapes, and you can immediately access any file on a CD-ROM, just as you would be able to do with a hard disk. Because multimedia data requires so much space, and because unlike hard disks, CD-ROMs are removable, CD-ROMs often provide the only practical way to distribute multimedia information. You can store many gigabytes of data in a library containing only a few CD-ROM discs.

A double-speed CD-ROM drive—the standard speed—costs around $200, and often the drive includes an assortment of starter software. The standard speed for CD-ROM drives has increased fourfold from earlier days. It's possible to buy even faster drives, up to sextuple-speed. However, those CD-ROM drives are still not nearly as fast as a hard drive, which can run a program, search a database, or play a digital video file more quickly than a CD-ROM drive can.

CD-ROM drives are commonly classified by their speed relative to the first generation of CD-ROM drives, which were capable of transferring 150 kilobytes per second. Double-speed drives can transfer 300 kilobytes per second, quad-speed drives can transfer 600 kilobytes per second, and so on.

In most cases Windows 95 sets up a CD-ROM drive automatically. (In the old days you had to find a DOS device driver to support a CD-ROM drive.) If Windows 95 doesn't configure your CD-ROM drive automatically, apply the Add New Hardware wizard. Click on the Start menu, choosing Settings and then Control Panel. Double-click on the Add New Hardware icon, and the wizard walks you through setup.

. . . .

Other CD-ROM Formats

Photo CD, a format for storing digital images on a CD-ROM, is becoming an increasingly important way to archive photographs. Photo CDs contain several versions of each graphic, stored at different resolutions. You can use a lower-resolution version for draft versions of a file, then plug in the high-resolution, space-munching version when you're finished.

When first introduced by Kodak a few years ago, Photo CD was supposed to become the next Polaroid camera; in other words, Kodak expected Photo CD to appeal to a broad market. It didn't happen at first because you need a player to view Photo CD-ROMs, and people weren't all that interested in looking at their snapshots on a TV set.

Desktop publishers are now being drawn to Photo CD because it gives them the ability to print multiple resolutions of an image and because it does a better job of color translation than was previously possible. (The quality of printed Photo CDs has improved since the major software companies discovered better methods of translating Kodak's color definitions into those used for printing.) In addition, almost every CD-ROM drive sold nowadays is Photo CD compatible. (If you are buying a new drive, do make sure it is Photo CD compatible.)

CD Plus, a new format developed by Sony, Philips, and Microsoft, combines the music tracks of a traditional audio CD (in the Red Book audio format) with data tracks (in the Yellow Book data format). This technology enables recording artists to create multimedia CDs, incorporating photos, music videos, recorded interviews, or lyrics that are synced to the music on the CD. You can play a CD Plus in any audio CD player, just as you would a traditional audio CD. You can also pop a CD Plus into a compatible CD-ROM drive under Windows 95 and play the multimedia information on the disc as well as the music. Many CD-ROM drives are already capable of playing CD Plus, but others, including those from NEC and Toshiba, are not. If you're in the market for a new CD-ROM drive, make sure it supports this exciting new format.

The MPC Standard

In the beginning, multimedia technology for Windows suffered from a lack of standards. As a result multimedia software usually worked with only a narrow selection of hardware products, which made integrating products difficult. To address this problem, Microsoft developed two related items: standard **multimedia extensions** to Windows and the **MPC (Multimedia Personal Computer)** standard.

The good news is that multimedia has grown up. In the past couple of years, multimedia titles have been racing each other to the shelves, and titles for Windows have led the pack. As for hardware, you can use Plug and Play to install hardware with a minimum of hassle whenever you upgrade your multimedia components. Look for the Windows logo on hardware or software to ensure compatibility.

The MPC standard was conceived by Microsoft, along with Tandy and several other companies, as a way to develop a consistent hardware and software standard for Windows multimedia software. A Multimedia PC Marketing Council works to establish minimum hardware standards for multimedia PCs. The MPC logo on a computer system signifies that it can play Windows multimedia software that also bears the MPC logo. This is analogous to VHS in the video world; the VHS trademark on a video recorder means it can play videotapes that also bear the VHS label. By defining the minimum hardware requirements for playing sounds and displaying graphics, and by defining fundamental hardware compatibility standards, Microsoft has provided a hardware standard that software developers can target when developing multimedia software.

In 1993 the original MPC standards were upgraded and called MPC II. Now we're looking at another upgrade to the standards; MPC III is due to take effect any minute. The new specifications for MPC III computers and peripherals take into account the huge improvements made in audio and video technologies over the past couple years.

For a computer system to qualify as an MPC III machine, it must meet the following requirements:

Processor:	Pentium/75 mHz
Memory:	8MB
Storage:	540MB
CD-ROM drive:	Quad-speed
Audio:	16-bit; wavetable recommended
Video:	640 by 480; MPEG1

As with any other system requirements, such as those for running a software title, the MPC standards cover the minimum requirements for running programs. Your multimedia titles might run better on a machine that is more muscular than one described by the standards. If you develop your own multimedia titles, you will almost certainly need a more robust setup. Most new PCs are configured as MPC machines or can easily be upgraded by adding a sound card or a CD-ROM drive. If you are technically competent, have access to an in-house technician, or know a dealer who sells and installs upgrade kits, it's not difficult to upgrade a non-MPC computer. Indeed, once your hardware is in place, Windows 95 can help you install the necessary software.

Insider's Tip

The biggest potential hassle of upgrading to Windows 95 is lack of support for aging hardware. If you have an old sound card, for example, Windows 95 may not recognize it. Hardware vendors, however, are eager to jump on the Windows 95 bandwagon. If you run into trouble with your multimedia hardware, ask your vendor for instructions and updated Windows 95 drivers. Most vendors have a BBS, a presence on the Internet, or a forum on one or more commercial on-line services where you can obtain updated drivers and information.

With MPC, everything you buy should work right out of the box. And if it doesn't, you need to call only one vendor—the one who sold you the computer—rather than the people who sold you the separate components, such as the sound card or CD-ROM drive.

An MPC upgrade kit usually contains two main components:

➤ **A sound card.** Provides digital audio, a MIDI synthesizer, and an external MIDI port.

➤ **A CD-ROM drive.** This drive can be either internal or external.

The sound card may also feature an SCSI connector for the CD-ROM, but sometimes only a single SCSI device may be attached to that connector. Other upgrade kits provide a separate SCSI adapter card, which can usually handle up to seven SCSI devices.

CD-ROM drives are offered in either internal or external models. An external CD-ROM drive is easier to install, because it hooks up by means of a cable. Internal drives often require special mounting brackets or rails, which differ from system to system and are often not included with upgrade kits.

Multimedia takes its toll on hardware performance, so buy as powerful a system as you can. In addition to the MPC III standards just described, the following are considerations in putting together a multimedia system:

➤ **Processor.** Get a fast 486 for playback-only machines. If you plan to create multimedia materials, get the fastest processor available.

➤ **Memory.** You need 8 megabytes for playback, 12 megabytes to create multimedia.

➤ **Storage.** A gigabyte is a good idea anyway, but if you'll be creating multimedia, get at least that amount.

➤ **CD-ROM drive.** These drives are bundled with most systems nowadays, and it's generally less expensive to buy a CD-ROM drive as part of a system than as part of an upgrade kit. Get at least a quad-speed drive.

Insider's Tip

If you plan to enter the multimedia maelstrom by purchasing individual devices or a multimedia upgrade kit rather than a completely new system, save yourself a headache: make sure the kit or any device displays the Designed for Windows 95 logo on the box. This logo means that the device —whether it be a sound card, a CD-ROM drive, or another type of device— supports Plug and Play. If all your system components meet the Plug and Play requirements, installation is a snap. But if they don't, you may need to jump through a few hoops to get everything running.

Multimedia Applets

Windows 95 includes four multimedia applets: CD Player, Media Player, Sound Recorder, and Volume Control. To open any of those applets, click on the Start menu and choose Programs, Accessories, then Multimedia.

. . . .

CD Player

Windows 95 provides a built-in player for audio CDs that works much like a good CD player. To open CD Player, insert a CD into your CD-ROM drive. Windows 95 detects it automatically and starts playing it. Alternatively, click on the Start button. From the menus that appear, choose Programs, Accessories, Multimedia, and finally CD Player (Figure 12.1).

FIGURE 12.1

CD Player

CD Player works like a conventional audio CD player, except that you can specify a playlist for each CD.

If you've used a standard CD player or a VCR, the CD Player window will look familiar to you. To discover the function of a button, rest your mouse pointer on it; a short description appears.

On its Options menu, CD Player includes many of the features you find on regular CD players, such as random order (also called shuffle play) and continuous play. Using Intro Play, you can play just the first few seconds of each song until you find the one you want. In addition, the Windows 95 CD Player has a few bells and whistles all its own. CD Player remembers every CD you play, and you can create a separate playlist for each one. To skip a particular song, exclude it from a playlist you create for the CD; then replay the expurgated CD whenever you like.

To create a playlist for a CD, insert the CD and wait for the CD Player icon to appear on the Taskbar. Click on the icon to maximize CD Player, then choose Edit Play List from the Disc menu. CD Player opens the Disc Settings dialog box, in which you can name artists and titles, selecting tracks for the playlist (Figure 12.2).

By default, all tracks on a disc are on the playlist. To remove a track, select it on the playlist and click on the Remove button.

You can also change the order in which tracks are played. To rearrange the play order, click to select the track or tracks you want to move, then release the mouse button. Next click on the highlighted tracks and drag them to a new location in the playlist. The changes take place immediately. If you want to change the playlist only for a single session, choose Preferences from the Options menu, then click to deselect Save Settings on Exit.

•••••••••••••
FIGURE 12.2
Making a Playlist

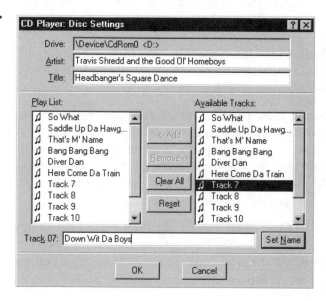

Because each CD contains a unique identifying code, Windows 95 will use the playlist you create next time you play your Travis Shredd CD.

Media Player

Media Player is a tool for playing multimedia data files and audio CDs. (In case you didn't read the previous section, note that Windows 95 also provides a separate CD Player.) The Windows 95 Media Player offers two substantial improvements over the Windows 3.1 version: you can play AVI files, and you can copy selections from a CD or a multimedia file to the Clipboard, then paste them into another document.

Media Player presents a simple application window, reminiscent of the controls on a tape deck, a VCR, or a CD player (Figure 12.3). You can use the control bar in the Media Player window to scroll through a multimedia file. Nine buttons are available for manipulating files. The title bar of the window reports what device or file is active and whether it is playing, paused, or stopped.

•••••••••••••
FIGURE 12.3
Media Player

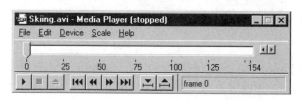

Media Player enables you to control multimedia devices and play multimedia data files.

To operate a device or play a file with Media Player, open the file with the File Open command or with one of the commands on the Device menu. The Device menu lists the multimedia file types available on your system. In addition to audio CDs, Media Player works with three types of multimedia files:

➤ **Audio Video Interleave files (AVI files).** These files are combinations of sound and video and can be created with Video for Windows, which is included with Windows 95.

➤ **Sound files.** Digital audio sound files (both .WAV and .VOC) contain sounds that have been converted into a digital format. When you record a sound using a microphone and the Sound Recorder utility, you create a .WAV file. Windows includes several of those files containing an assortment of possible system sounds. (For example, you can replace that annoying error beep with jungle sounds.)

➤ **MIDI files.** MIDI files are like sheet music for a computer: they contain the instructions for creating sounds, but they don't provide the sound itself. MIDI has become the standard interface between musical instruments, synthesizers, and computers. Windows 95 includes several sample MIDI files.

To play a media file, choose a device from the Device menu. A dialog box appears enabling you to select the file you want to play. To play subsequent files on the currently selected device, you can use the Open command on the File menu.

The scroll bar provides further control over multimedia files. When you load a file, a numeric scale appears above the scroll bar (Figure 12.4). The scale displays one of two measurements, Tracks or Time. The Tracks scale applies to simple devices that organize information into tracks. For example, an audio CD player displays the number of cuts on a compact disc. You can move the scroll button to a particular track to start playing it.

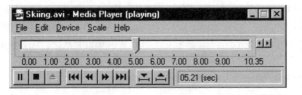

FIGURE 12.4
Media Player's Time Scale

A scale over Media Player's scroll bar displays either Tracks or Time; the Time scale is shown here.

The Time scale is divided into time intervals, which vary according to the length of the media file. You can adjust the position of the scroll button to start playing the file at a particular time.

Sound Recorder

Sound Recorder works only if you have a Windows-compatible sound card. With such a card and Sound Recorder, you can record sounds directly to files on your hard disk, then edit and play back the files. You can even add simple effects to the sounds, making them louder or faster, adding echoes, or mixing two or more sounds together.

Insider's Tip

Sound Recorder is handy but limited in its capabilities. For serious sound-editing work, try a more full-featured shareware or commercial program, such as Voyetra's AudioWave.

Sound Recorder works with the standard Windows digital audio files, denoted by the .wav extension. If your digital audio files are in the .wav format, Sound Recorder can play them, regardless of what sound hardware was used to record them. Since Sound Recorder is an OLE server application, you can use it to embed sound files into or link sound files to compound documents.

If you used Sound Recorder in Windows 3.1, you'll notice that it's still pretty much the same handy little tool. The only additions are the Properties and Audio Properties commands, which provide—and enable you to provide —information about .wav files.

Sound Recorder contains five buttons that control the recording and playing of sound files (Figure 12.5). You operate the buttons much as you would the buttons on a tape deck or a VCR. Familiar symbols denote Rewind, Fast Forward, Play, and Stop; the button with the red circle is Record.

FIGURE 12.5

Sound Recorder

Sound Recorder is an OLE-compatible utility that enables you to record, edit, and play back sound files.

To play a file, open it and click on the Play button. As the file plays, the sound's waveform is displayed graphically in the Sound Recorder window. Click on the Stop button to halt play, and click on Play again to resume playing where you left off.

You can also use the scroll bar to move to a specific place in a sound file. Slide the scroll button to move through the file. For greater precision, click on the scroll arrows to move in .1-second increments, or click on the scroll bar to take 1-second steps. As you scroll or step through a sound file, the **Position** box reports your current position in the file, expressed in seconds. The **Length** box reports the total length of the file in seconds.

The Rewind and Fast Forward buttons operate instantaneously; a single click takes you to the beginning or the end of a file. Keyboard shortcuts for Sound Recorder are shown in Table 12.2.

· · · · · · · · · · · · · ·

TABLE 12.2

*Sound
Recorder
Keyboard
Shortcuts*

Keyboard	Sound Recorder Button
End	Fast Forward
Home	Rewind
Right and left arrow keys	Scroll arrows; each depression of the key moves you .1 second through file

Recording. Sound Recorder can either record a new file, record over an existing file starting in the middle of it, or record new material starting at the end of an existing file. To record a new sound file, choose New from the File menu and click on the Record button. (The Record button is dimmed if you do not have a successfully installed sound card.) When you finish, press Stop, then save the new sound file. The maximum length of the recording is affected by the amount of memory your system has available; you may be cut short if the program runs out of memory.

To start recording in the middle of a sound file, scroll to the desired location in the file and press Record. The new material records over and erases the remainder of the original file. You can also scroll to the end of the original sound file and append a new recording to that file. Note that some sound hardware does not support the ability to record over an existing file.

Insider's Tip

If you have a CD-ROM drive, you can use Sound Recorder to record samples from your favorite music CDs. Insert a music CD into the CD-ROM drive. When the CD gets to the part you want to record, click on the Record button. Sound Recorder records about 6 seconds of audio at a time; you can continue to record by clicking again on Record. You can also edit the sample you've captured and save it as a .wav file. Using the Sound Control Panel, you can attach the .wav file to a Windows action, such as exiting a program. Pretty clearly, opportunities for fun are limited only by your imagination.

Editing a Sound File. Even if you lack the hardware to record sounds, you can use Sound Recorder to edit and play sound files. You do need some type of sound-output hardware, such as an add-in card.

Sound Recorder provides sound-editing controls on its Edit and Effects menus. Make changes to a sound file, then audition it by pressing the Play button. If you like the new sound, save the changes. If you aren't happy with the audition, you can undo the changes you've just made by choosing the Revert command from the File menu.

Sound Recorder's Edit menu offers the following commands:

➺ **Insert File.** Inserts a second sound file anywhere into the current sound file. The inserted file increases the length of the current file, because the second sound does not overlap the first sound.

➺ **Mix with File.** Mixes a second sound file with the current file, dubbing the sounds in the two files together.

➺ **Delete before Current Position.** Erases from the beginning of the sound file up to the current playing position, as specified in the Position box.

➺ **Delete after Current Position.** Erases from the current playing position to the end of the sound file.

To insert the contents of a sound file into the current file, scroll to a location in the current file and choose Insert File from the Edit menu. The Insert File dialog box appears; it is a standard file-browsing dialog box. You may insert as many files as available memory permits.

To mix the contents of two files, move the scroll box to the location in the current file where you want to begin mixing in the new sound. Then choose the Mix with File command to bring up the Mix with File dialog box, which enables you to choose a file to mix in. You can mix several sounds together by choosing this command for each sound file you want to add.

To delete a portion of a file, first scroll to a position in the file. Then choose the Delete before Current Position command to zap everything up to that point, or choose Delete after Current Position to erase everything after that point.

Sound Recorder's Effects menu offers several other commands for manipulating sound files:

➺ **Increase Volume.** Increases the volume of the sound by 25 percent.

➺ **Decrease Volume.** Decreases the volume of the sound by 25 percent.

➤ **Increase Speed.** Speeds up the playback of the sound by 100 percent.

➤ **Decrease Speed.** Slows down the playback of the sound by 50 percent.

➤ **Add Echo.** Produces a simple digital reverb effect that adds an echo to the sound.

➤ **Reverse.** Reverses the sound so that it plays backward.

To use any of those commands, open a file and choose the command you want from the Effects menu. The command applies to the entire file. Except for Reverse, you can layer the effect of a command by choosing it two or more times. If you want to add an effect to just a portion of a file, you have to copy the sound file, chop it up into smaller files, and apply the effect to one file at a time.

Volume Control. Windows 95 provides two utilities for adjusting the volume on your computer. The first is a simple master volume control scroll bar that adjusts the volume level of your entire system. The second is the Volume Control applet, which acts like a universal remote, controlling the volume and balance of each sound component on your system individually.

To access the master volume control, click on the Speaker icon in the Taskbar. By default, this icon is in the bottom right-hand corner of the screen, next to the clock (Figure 12.6).

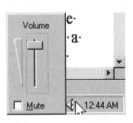

FIGURE 12.6
*Volume
Control*

Click once on the Speaker icon in the Taskbar to make the master volume control appear; you can use it to turn down all the noise at once.

The master volume control scroll bar provides a quick way to adjust the volume of whatever happens to be making noise on your computer. It's a handy way to mute your computer quickly when the phone rings, for example.

The Volume Control applet gives you control over individual components that record or play sound. Use it to control the volume and balance of sound input devices, such as microphones, and of playback devices, such as a CD-ROM drive. The applet also includes a master control.

To open Volume Control, double-click on the Speaker icon in the Taskbar. You can also click on the Start button and choose Programs, then Accessories, then Multimedia, and finally Volume Control.

The exact appearance of the Volume Control window depends on what devices you have installed and on the capabilities of those devices. The window of a standard multimedia system looks something like the window shown in Figure 12.7.

FIGURE 12.7

The Volume Control Applet

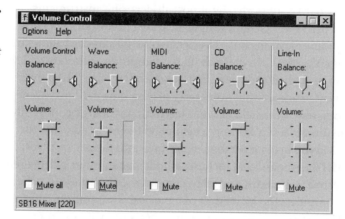

Double-clicking on the Speaker icon in the Taskbar opens the Volume Control applet, which enables you to adjust the volume and the balance of each device individually.

The Volume Control window displays controls like the ones on a stereo tuner. Move a horizontal slider to the left, and more sound comes from the left speaker. If the sound is in stereo, you may hear only parts of it. The volume controls are vertical; the higher the slider, the louder the sound. If you want to mute a device completely, click to check its Mute box. When you uncheck the box, the sound comes back at the level determined by the volume slider.

To determine which of your installed devices appear in the Volume Control window, choose Properties from the Options menu. Once you set up a device the way you like it, you may want to remove it from the Volume Control window so that its settings aren't changed inadvertently.

Danger Zone

The Volume Control applet may have compatibility problems with other mixers on your computer. Most likely a mixer was included with your sound card, and you may have other mixers on your system as well. You might want to look at all the mixers you have, choose the one you like best, and delete the others (or at least plan not to use them).

. . . .

MIDI

The **Musical Instrument Digital Interface,** or **MIDI,** was born as a development tool for musicians. The MIDI standard was jointly established in 1982 by makers of electronic instruments. Their goal was to create a simple, low-cost way to connect pieces of equipment, such as synthesizers, keyboards, and computers. MIDI has since blossomed into a multibillion-dollar industry, and the standard is supported by almost all electronic instruments and music software.

MIDI works like a simple local area network (LAN) that runs over a serial communications link. The original MIDI standard allows up to 16 devices to be connected in a daisy chain configuration with standard MIDI cable. Once connected, the devices can send and receive MIDI messages that define events, such as what notes were played, how hard they were pressed, and how long they were held down. Electronic keyboards commonly send this information to a synthesizer, which plays the notes accordingly.

If you bring a personal computer into the act, or if you use a professional MIDI keyboard that includes a built-in computer called a sequencer, you can record, save, edit, and play computer MIDI files. In other words, you can manipulate the MIDI data of a musical composition. Music software for PCs, Macintoshes, and some sequencers supports a common data file format known as the Standard MIDI file format; files in this format often end in the extension .SMF or .MID.

When you play a MIDI file, the computer sends the information in the file to a MIDI instrument, which converts the information into the sound of a specific instrument and into specific pitches and durations. To acquire MIDI files, you can purchase preprogrammed MIDI music, hire a MIDI music studio, record your own compositions, or download other people's compositions from Internet sites, BBSs, and commercial on-line services. (You'll also find those on-line sites a good place to exchange information with other people interested in MIDI.) Software products range from programs that enable you to record and edit MIDI compositions, to music education, to applications that transcribe what you play into professional-looking musical scores.

Major hardware support for MIDI includes the following product categories:

➪ **MIDI adapters.**

➪ **Synthesizers.**

➪ **Samplers.**

➪ **Controllers.**

A **MIDI adapter** enables you to connect your computer to external MIDI devices, such as keyboards, synthesizers, and samplers. Sophisticated MIDI adapters enable you to connect more than one MIDI network if you need more than 16 MIDI channels. MIDI adapters are supplied either on their own add-in cards or as part of a multifunction sound card, such as the Sound Blaster.

Synthesizers use electronics to artificially create the waveforms of sounds. Some synthesizers simulate natural sounds quite realistically. Synthesizers can be located inside a computer on add-in cards or can be external units connected via MIDI. External MIDI synthesizers sometimes come as stand-alone units, called modules, which resemble stereo system components; they also often come with piano-style keyboards.

Samplers play natural sounds that have been digitally recorded, including music and other sound. Like synthesizers, samplers are available as add-in cards, as external boxes, or combined with keyboards. Sampled sound generally sounds more realistic than synthesized sound. When you're shopping for a good sound card, look for a 16-bit card with sampled sound.

Controllers are devices that generate MIDI signals. The most common type of MIDI controller is a piano-style keyboard. Often those keyboards contain fewer than a piano's 88 keys, and some less-expensive models have smaller-than-normal keys (I suggest avoiding the latter). Other types of MIDI controllers include electronic drum pads and breath controllers; the latter are similar to reed instruments, such as clarinets and saxophones.

With the right software your computer can also serve as a MIDI controller. If a MIDI instrument is connected to your system, you can use Media Player to play a MIDI composition. Or you can use other music software to play an on-screen keyboard, to program the notes of a song, and to generate MIDI data in other ways.

MIDI files are smaller than audio files because of the way the data is stored. An audio file contains complete recorded sounds and requires no interpretation. A MIDI file is more like sheet music; it contains the instructions for playing sounds but not the sounds themselves. When you play a MIDI file, the interpretation of the music depends on the quality of your sound card, much as the playing of a Mozart concerto depends on the musicians and on the quality of the instruments on which the composition is played.

Because MIDI files are smaller than audio files, playing them places less of a burden on your processor. For example, a 5-minute musical composition could consume as much as 5 megabytes if stored as a digital audio file. The same composition stored as MIDI information might require only 50 kilobytes.

With Windows 95, MIDI files place even less of a burden on your system. Using a new technology called **polymessage MIDI support,** Windows 95 can play multiple MIDI instructions simultaneously with other system events, allowing MIDI instructions to be processed at the same time as graphics and other data. With polymessage MIDI support, even a complex sequence uses only a small percentage of the CPU's resources. Polymessage MIDI support makes MIDI tantalizing to game and application developers, because rich, complex sound can be added without taking a big hit on disk space and your system's throughput capability.

How Windows 95 Uses MIDI. Microsoft has developed guidelines for how Windows applications should handle MIDI information. The Windows MIDI guidelines are based on a MIDI standard called **General MIDI,** which sets forth a standard way to configure MIDI output devices, such as synthesizers, so they all play similar sounds when sent the same MIDI data.

Before General MIDI, almost every synthesizer worked with MIDI but in a slightly different way. Although MIDI defined program codes for up to 128 sounds for each sound bank in a MIDI instrument, the sound and the arrangement of the sounds were left undefined. As a result, almost every synthesizer arranged its sounds differently, so that playing a certain note might trigger a tuba on one system, a piano on another, and a gunshot on a third. Musicians had to keep track of what devices played which sounds in response to certain MIDI messages. Most MIDI files, in fact, sounded right only when played on the type of synthesizer used to record the sounds.

To define a standard configuration for MIDI instruments, several hardware and software companies established General MIDI, which is a standard way to arrange the 128 sounds in a bank of synthesizer sounds. If a synthesizer supports General MIDI, a note that is supposed to play a violin always produces a violin sound. The Roland Sound Canvas is an example of a General MIDI synthesizer.

Windows defines two more levels of synthesizer performance in addition to the General MIDI standard:

»+ **General MIDI synthesizers** can simultaneously play up to 16 notes on 15 melodic instruments and up to 8 notes on 8 percussion instruments.

»+ **Base-level synthesizers** can simultaneously play up to 6 notes on 3 melodic instruments and up to 3 notes on 3 percussion instruments.

»+ **Extended-level synthesizers** can simultaneously play up to 16 notes on 9 melodic instruments and up to 16 notes on 8 percussion instruments.

To enable software developers to create a single MIDI file that could be played on both base-level and extended-level synthesizers, Microsoft developed a method for splitting up the 16 instrument channels allowed by MIDI. According to the Microsoft guidelines—known as the **MPC MIDI**—base-level synthesizers use channels 12 through 15 as the melody channels and 16 as the percussion channel; extended-level synthesizers use channels 1 through 9 as the melody channels and 10 for the percussion channel.

Configuring MIDI. With Windows 95, the MIDI tab in the Multimedia Properties dialog box replaces the Windows 3.1 MIDI Mapper. Because Windows 95 has built-in support for General MIDI, configuring MIDI instruments is a more streamlined procedure than it was with previous versions of Windows. Unfortunately, this streamlining makes it less flexible than the scheme used in Windows 3.1. If you are using MIDI equipment that does not support General MIDI, you will need to get third party configuration utilities to use MIDI properly in Windows 95.

To configure a MIDI instrument for your machine, click on the Start button, then choose Settings and Control Panel. In the Control Panel double-click on the Multimedia icon to view the Multimedia Properties dialog box, then click on the MIDI tab (Figure 12.8).

• • • • • • • • • • • • • •
FIGURE 12.8

The MIDI Page of the Multimedia Properties Dialog Box

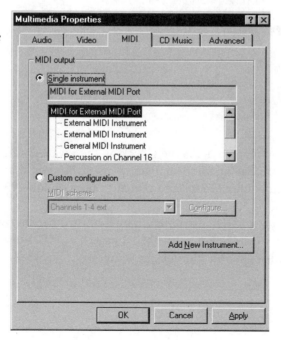

To add instruments with the help of the MIDI Instrument Installation wizard, click on Add New Instrument.

On the MIDI page, you can choose to use a single instrument, or you can select a configuration of several instruments on different channels. Windows 95 automatically configures the instruments according to the General MIDI specifications that I just mentioned.

For most uses you should stick with the General MIDI mappings to ensure that your MIDI files play the way they were designed to. However, if you do want to change the channels to which specific instruments are mapped, click on the Configure button on the MIDI page. This opens the MIDI Configuration dialog box, which you can use to change the channel mappings for your system (Figure 12.9).

FIGURE 12.9

The MIDI
Configuration
Dialog Box

You can design and save MIDI instrument schemes by clicking on Save As, and you can add or remap instrument assignments by clicking on Change.

Once you map your channels, click on the Save As button and name the configuration. Saving MIDI configurations enables you to switch among several custom configurations and return to the Windows 95 default without remapping.

To add a new MIDI instrument, plug the instrument into a port, then click on Add New Instrument on the MIDI page. The MIDI Instrument Installation wizard walks you through the setup, which generally takes less than a minute.

Summary

With multimedia a standard feature of PCs today, Windows 95 provides an instant, inexpensive upgrade for any multimedia system. Its 32-bit architecture makes the most of sound and video, and because it is 100 percent backward-compatible, your 16-bit applications will work even better than they did with Windows 3.1.

The multimedia applets included with Windows 95 give you control over your multimedia devices. With the Windows Media Player utility, you can play multimedia files, such as sound files and animation, and you can also control external devices, such as VCRs, laser-disc players, and MIDI music synthesizers. CD Player enables you to play and keep track of your audio CDs. It also enables you to develop your own playlists so that you can hear the songs you like in the order you want.

The Sound Recorder applet enables you to record, edit, and play back digital audio, provided you have the required sound hardware. The sound files you create can be embedded or linked into OLE applications and can also be assigned to system events, such as Windows start-up or exit.

By enabling you to combine graphics and sound, multimedia technology broadens and transforms the computer's role as a communications tool. Multimedia software and hardware products are a powerful force today in many arenas, including business, education, publishing, and entertainment.

13

Optimizing Windows 95 Resources

The performance and capabilities of your Windows 95 environment ultimately depend on the selection and configuration of your hardware. The most important hardware components reside inside your computer's main system unit—you know, the big box that you connect everything else to. The three things inside that mysterious box that most

473

affect the performance of Windows are the processor; the memory chips, or RAM; and the hard-disk drive.

Those three components work synergistically with Windows 95 to overcome many of the limitations still found in today's PCs because of their DOS origins. For example, Windows 95 lets you extend your computer's memory beyond what is available on its RAM chips with a special trick called virtual memory. This involves converting space on your hard disk into what appears to Windows to be additional RAM.

Although Windows 95 does its best to optimize itself during the installation process, you still might find it helpful to understand how the three main components of your computer system work together. You can learn to optimize your computer's hardware to best meet the significant demands made by Windows 95.

The Compatibility Myth

Although Windows 95 runs on IBM PC and compatible systems, no standard really exists for IBM PC compatibility. Not surprisingly, almost every PC manufacturer claims that its system is 100-percent IBM compatible. Indeed, the industry appellation for the IBM market is "the IBM PC and compatibles market." But profound differences exist among the systems described as IBM PC compatible. Even IBM itself has produced machines that are in many ways incompatible with one another, from the old PC, XT, and AT to the newer PS/2 and PS/1 machines. The only real tie that binds those systems is their ability to run the DOS operating system.

What makes IBM PC compatible products so prevalent is the wide acceptance of Windows and DOS applications, along with a cornucopia of third-party accessory hardware designed to work with those programs. Accessory hardware includes add-in cards, processors, video displays, and memory. Confusion enters the picture here as well, because the term "IBM PC compatible" applies to many kinds of hardware accessories incorporating an enormous array of components.

The good news is that most incompatibilities can easily be resolved. Once they are, most Windows applications share a level of compatibility not possible with DOS alone. Windows 95, by means of device drivers and virtual devices, makes different hardware devices look the same to your applications. This means you no longer have to go through the agony of configuring each application to run on your hardware setup, as is often the case with DOS.

Because of the wide spectrum of PC-compatible hardware, almost every computer system is configured differently, making it difficult to identify hardware incompatibilities. In general, however, the following hardware items pose most of the compatibility problems:

➤ **ROM BIOS chips.** These are the personality module of your system, providing it with the ability to run DOS. They vary by manufacturer; makers include Compaq, AMI, and IBM.

➤ **Memory configuration.** Knowing how much RAM you have isn't enough. You also have to know whether to configure any of it as either expanded or extended memory to support certain DOS applications.

➤ **Disk drive and controller card.** Is it IDE, SCSI, or something weird like ESDI?

➤ **Bus.** Your bus is based on one or more one of these standards: ISA, EISA, MCA, VL, or PCI.

Although I'll present ways to avoid many incompatibility and performance pitfalls, I can't promise you all the answers. Some of your problems may be insurmountable; you might even have to purchase a new piece of hardware before you can run Windows 95. But that seems a small price to pay for the opportunity to select from so many configuration options offered by so many manufacturers.

Unlike DOS, Windows 95 provides a compatibility buffer between your computer's hardware and your Windows applications. When you install Windows 95, it becomes easier to run Windows programs and add peripheral devices.

The Central Processing Unit

The **central processing unit,** or **CPU,** is your computer's brain. Because the CPU chip actually runs your programs and operating system, it has the most impact on your system's overall capabilities and performance.

CPU chips are distinguished from other, less powerful chips by the fact that CPUs can do the following:

➤ Perform arithmetic and logical operations.

➤ Decode special instructions.

➤ Issue electrical signals that control other chips.

IBM PCs and compatibles presently include the following six types of CPUs:

➺ **8088.** An almost antique 16-bit processor limited by an 8-bit bus (buses communicate with memory and periphals). This chip was in the original IBM PC.

➺ **8086.** A close cousin of the 8088, used in early PCs and PC clones.

➺ **80286, or 286.** Introduced in the IBM AT.

➺ **80386, or 386.** The first 32-bit processor and the smallest that runs Windows 95.

➺ **80486, or 486.** This is just a fast 386 with a math coprocessor chip, but it's what you need to get Windows 95 going at normal speed.

➺ **Pentium.** A souped-up 486 that can run two instructions at the same time. Serious Windows users will appreciate the zippy performance.

All of those processors were designed by Intel Corporation, although other companies—notably AMD, IBM, and Cyrix—also produce some of the chips. The Intel family of chips is referred to as the Intel 80X86 family. The *X*, like the variable in algebraic equations, is a number that changes sequentially to indicate each new member of the family. Starting with the 286, these chips are commonly referred to by their last three numbers, which is the convention I'll also use.

This series of six CPU chips represents more than 15 years of development, which Intel plans to continue for the rest of the 1990s. Intel is already well along in planning the next several generations of chips, although the names will change. Each chip in the series retains compatibility with its predecessor but also performs new functions. Thus, programs written for the 8086 can run on a 286, although the 286 offers new features; similarly, programs designed for the 8086 and the 286 run on the 386, although the 386 adds capabilities that the 8086 and the 286 do not have.

The latest member of this series—named the Pentium—has become the processor of choice for Windows users over the past few years. The Pentium has the horsepower required to run a sophisticated and complex graphical operating system such as Windows 95. The Pentium also inches toward a 64-bit CPU standard by including a math coprocessor that is accurate to 64 bits. Another important step toward a full 64-bit processor is Intel's next chip, code-named the P6. The P6 will be a must-have item for Windows 95 power users, because that beast of an operating system can consume all the processor horsepower you can feed it.

Standard versus Enhanced Mode

Intel CPUs have gone through a long period of evolution. The CPU chips used in the original PC—the 8088 and the 8086—operated in what is called **real mode.** In real mode the operating system can directly access only 1 megabyte of memory, and DOS was originally designed to work only in this mode. The limitations of real mode haunt DOS to this day and cause many of the memory-management headaches you experience when you configure Windows.

With the introduction of the 286 chip came protected mode, which protects memory addresses above 1 megabyte from the conflicts that result when several applications try to access that memory at the same time. Thus, a processor running in protected mode can safely address memory above 1 megabyte. Windows 3.0 offered a special real mode that allowed it to operate using an 8088 or 8086 chip's real mode. Windows 3.1 did away with real mode; it runs only in the processor's protected mode.

Along with the 386 CPU chip, another processor mode, called **virtual mode,** was introduced. Virtual mode creates almost any number of self-contained virtual machines that appear to be individual 8086-based systems, each with its own 640K of memory. Starting with Windows 386 enhanced mode, and now with Windows 95, you can tap the processor's virtual mode to run multiple DOS sessions, each in its own window. Windows 95 also uses virtual mode to run existing 16-bit Windows applications as part of its System Virtual Machine. Likewise, 32-bit Win32 applications run in their own virtual machines under Windows 95.

The Best Processor for Your Needs

How much processor is enough for you? There's no simple answer, but here are some recommendations about processor selection based on what kinds of applications you plan to use:

» **386SX and 386DX.** Yup, you can run Windows 95 on a 386. It says so right on the box. But do yourself a giant favor: upgrade that thing to at least a 486. That way you won't spend most of your time in front of the computer staring at that cute hourglass icon.

» **486SX, various speeds.** When AMD cloned the 386, Intel struck back with the 486SX series. Although SX designates a 16-bit bus in the 386 series, 486SX chips have a full 32-bit bus processor. The 486SX is actually a 486DX without the math coprocessor. Intel is offering clock-doubled 486 chips that plug into the upgrade socket found on most 486SX-based systems. (A clock-doubled chip runs at twice its internal speed.)

➻ **486DX/25 MHz.** This 486 chip combines a 386 processor, a 387 math coprocessor, and 8K of on-chip processor RAM cache (which provides a high-speed buffer between the chip and the computer's main RAM). For the average user, this is the minimum for a Windows machine. This processor can easily be upgraded with the 486DX2/50, a clock-doubled chip that boosts performance to 50 MHz.

➻ **486DX/33 MHz.** An even faster version of the 25 MHz 486DX. Intel provides a clock-doubled version of this chip, the DX2/66, that boosts performance to 66 MHz, providing an inexpensive way to extend the life span of this system.

➻ **486DX/50 MHz and 486DX2/66 MHz.** At the time of this writing, the DX2/66 is the most popular of the 486 line and provides good all-around performance for Windows applications. Beware of systems built around the 50 MHz DX (not DX2) chip; numerous compatibility hurdles exist, especially with VL-bus peripherals. The 50 MHz DX chip is a rarity.

➻ **486DX4/100 MHz.** A relatively new design, the 486DX4 boosts clock speed to 100 MHz, providing triple the performance of a typical 486DX/33 MHz. Not as powerful as the higher-end Pentium chips, the DX4 is ideal for power users of notebook computers.

➻ **Pentium 60 MHz and 66 MHz.** These chips have become the mainstream platform for mid-range PC systems over the last year. They combine an on-board memory cache with the ability to execute more than one instruction at a time. A good value, these entry-level Pentiums support excellent Windows 95 performance.

➻ **Pentium 90 MHz, 100 MHz, 120 MHz, and 133 MHz.** As the numbers imply, these are even faster versions of the Pentium. At this writing, 90 and 100 MHz systems are relatively inexpensive, and even the faster ones will come down to reasonable prices by the time you read this.

My general recommendation is that you buy a 486DX2/66 MHz system or better if you can afford it. Those systems provide good performance at reasonable prices, and many 486 systems can be upgraded easily by replacing their processor chips with faster models (like the DX4/100 or even the new Pentium OverDrive processor).

Upgrade Alert

Although the list of chips I just gave you was current when this book was written, the field is evolving rapidly. AMD is introducing its own Pentium clone, and Intel has already announced its successor to the Pentium—the P6—which seems destined to become the chip you'll want if you're a Windows power user.

Processor Cache

Windows 95 uses a variety of complex memory-management techniques, which cause your system to access RAM frequently. Ordinary RAM chips can't keep up with the pace of your Windows environment and its applications, but you can prevent a slowdown by installing or beefing up your **processor RAM cache**.

The processor RAM cache (also referred to as a Level 2 cache) is a type of RAM that can significantly affect system speed. It is usually found only on high-speed 386 or larger systems. Basically, your processor uses the processor RAM cache to store information that's being transferred either to or from the regular RAM chips. The processor RAM cache itself contains a type of high-speed memory that decreases the time lag between the operations of high-speed CPU chips and the slower system RAM.

The processor RAM cache supplies the processor with data quickly while receiving information from the slower system RAM. Thus the processor RAM cache fools the processor into thinking that your system memory runs at the higher speed of the processor RAM cache while you rely on lower-cost RAM to run your system memory.

Typically, processor RAM caches range from 256K to 1MB in size, with some systems offering the potential for an even larger capacity. The processor RAM cache serves as a high-speed holding area for the processor; it does not add to the amount of RAM available to your programs.

The location—or existence—of your processor RAM cache depends on what kind of system you're using. In 386 systems, the processor RAM cache consists of separate chips. Those high-speed static RAM chips are either soldered directly onto the motherboard or placed in sockets. This type of cache is known as an **external processor cache.** Some RAM caches provide extra empty sockets for RAM cache expansion. Other PCs lack a RAM cache altogether and contain only empty sockets for installing normal RAM.

With the 486, Intel placed a small RAM cache directly onto the chip; this is known as an internal processor cache. Although the standard 486 chip contains only 8K of internal cache, it operates at higher speeds than do caches located on supplementary chips because the cache is built right into the chip.

IBM also produces a version of the 386 chip that contains an internal cache to increase speed. The chip is used in certain models of the PS/2 line of computers, such as the PS/2 Model 57SLC.

Even if your 486 or other CPU chip already contains an internal RAM cache, you may also want a secondary RAM cache to further enhance your system's performance. Years of benchmark testing have shown that the combination of an internal and an external RAM cache yields the best overall performance.

One thing to consider when you purchase a computer system is the size of its processor RAM cache. The rule of thumb is the bigger the better. Also, not all processor RAM caches work equally well, since different manufacturers use different schemes for caching memory. You may want to test the systems or refer to published tests to see which systems offer the best performance for Windows 95. In general, RAM caches do offer Windows 95 a significant performance boost, and I recommend using a processor cache of at least 256K.

Some systems are set up to allow up to 1MB of external processor cache. In the 16-bit world of Windows 3.1, a 256K cache was noticeably better than a 64K cache, but expanding the cache to 512K didn't offer as much of a performance boost—that is, at 512K you reached a point of diminishing returns. However, Windows 95 makes heavy use of 32-bit code, and this in turn places a heavier burden on the memory subsystems of your PC than Windows 3.1 did. As a result, larger caches—from 512K to 1MB—tend to have more of a positive impact. When in doubt, go with the biggest cache you can afford.

Upgrading Your Processor

Depending on your pocketbook, plenty of means are available to upgrade from a slower CPU. Some computer systems are designed with processors that can be upgraded. The CPU chip in one of these **upgradable systems** typically resides on a small circuit board that plugs into the motherboard. To upgrade the processor, you simply replace the small circuit board.

Applying a different technology, Intel offers direct chip replacement for upgrading 486 processors. This technology, called **OverDrive**, is the easiest way to upgrade a system. The OverDrive chips are 486 chips that incorporate a clock-doubling or tripling process, which allows a chip to run at twice or three times its normal speed. To upgrade your system, just pop out the old 486 chip and replace it with a new, faster one. Some 486 systems contain an upgrade socket that accepts an OverDrive chip without requiring you to remove the original chip. At the time of this writing, Intel has announced but not yet shipped Pentium OverDrive chips that will allow some 486 systems to be upgraded to Pentium machines.

Another way to upgrade your system is to **replace the entire motherboard;** Hauppage, Micronics, and American Megatrends are all well-known manufacturers of motherboards. Although replacing the motherboard can be more expensive than adding a plug-in processor card, it reduces the possibility of compatibility hassles. Replacement motherboards from no-name companies are offered at surprisingly low prices, with discounters selling 486 boards for well under $500 and Pentium motherboards for less than $1,000.

At those prices, some of the motherboards are competitively priced with the plug-in processors. If you do buy a new motherboard, make sure it fits inside the case of your current system and works with your power supply, disk drive, and other elements. Some motherboard vendors perform the transplant for you at a nominal additional charge. Although this approach allows you to replace your motherboard, you may still be left with a slow, outdated disk controller, hard disk, display adapter, or power supply.

An enterprising solution—and the one I recommend most often to 386 users—is simply to **replace your entire system.** You can sell your old system to someone who doesn't need or want Windows. Or take a tax write-off and donate the system to a local school or nonprofit organization. In the long run it may be cheaper—and a lot less hassle—to replace your system altogether.

The Math Coprocessor Chip

A **math coprocessor chip**—also called a **floating point unit,** or FPU— boosts the speed of math calculations. Unless you plan to use an application that requires intensive number crunching, such as a spreadsheet or a CAD or graphics program, you probably don't need to invest in a math coprocessor chip. Whereas a CPU handles all types of instructions, a math coprocessor is specifically designed to handle mathematical computations, which it performs more quickly than the CPU.

Long ago Intel designed a family of math coprocessors that pair up with Intel's CPUs. For example, the 287 coprocessor was matched up with the 286 CPU, and the 387 was mated with the 386 CPU. Cyrix also produces Intel-compatible math coprocessors that it offers at a significantly lower price. No corresponding Intel math coprocessor exists for the 486DX or Pentium chip series, however, because both chips already perform the math coprocessor function. In essence, the 486DX is a souped-up 386 combined with a 387 math coprocessor and 8K of additional on-chip cache, while the Pentium is a souped-up 486 with dual instruction pipelines, which process two software instructions at once.

Insider's Tip

I recommend against using a 486SX chip, because it is really a 486DX without the math coprocessor. Intel sells a 487, which it represents as a way to add math coprocessor functions to the 486SX. But in truth the 487 is just a 486DX; when you install it into the so-called 486SX upgrade socket, you effectively turn off the 486SX. If you bought the 486SX and the 487, then you've been hornswoggled by Intel into buying two redundant processor chips for your system.

The design of your motherboard determines whether you can take a math coprocessor on board, because you need an additional socket. Many boards provide that additional socket, usually situated near the CPU socket.

The System Bus

The **system bus** provides an electrical highway over which the CPU transmits instructions. You access the system bus by means of slots that accept add-in cards for memory, peripherals, and other hardware options.

With IBM PCs and compatibles, CPU data handling and bus structure are characterized by the number of lanes—that is, the number of data groups the computer can transfer to the bus in a single operation. The 8088 is limited to 8 lanes, or 8 bits per transfer, and the 286 and the 386SX are limited to 16. The 386DX, 486, and Pentium CPUs provide 32- or 64-lane superhighways (Figure 13.1).

FIGURE 13.1

Bus Scheme for Intel Processors

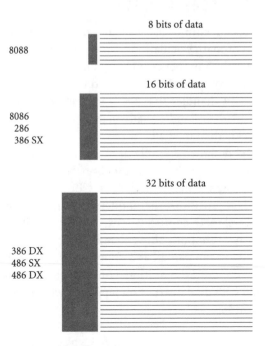

An Intel processor uses either an 8-, a 16-, a 32-, or a 64-bit bus.

In addition to the processor bus, PCs contain a peripheral bus that accepts add-in cards. The peripheral bus is also called the I/O bus, because it's the traffic hub of most input and output activity. Just because your system comes with a 32-bit processor and a 32-bit processor bus, don't assume it also includes a 32-bit peripheral bus. Indeed, most 386 systems were shipped with a 16-bit ISA peripheral bus. The following are types of PC peripheral buses:

➤ **8-bit ISA bus.** The original peripheral bus for the PC and the XT; not used in today's systems.

➤ **16-bit ISA bus.** Introduced with the IBM PC AT, it remains the most prevalent bus in PC systems.

➤ **16-bit MCA bus.** The low-end PS/2 bus.

➤ **32-bit MCA bus.** The high-end PS/2 bus.

➤ **32-bit EISA bus.** The high-end ISA-compatible bus.

➤ **32-bit VL-bus.** The low-end local bus.

➤ **32-bit PCI bus.** The low-end bus for Pentium systems.

➤ **64-bit PCI bus.** The high-end bus for Pentium systems.

The bus for the original PC and the AT is referred to as the **ISA,** or **Industry Standard Architecture**, bus—a name that reflects the popularity of this bus among manufacturers of PC compatibles. The **EISA (Extended Industry Standard Architecture)** bus retains IBM PC compatibility while extending the capabilities of the ISA bus. **MCA,** or **Micro Channel Architecture,** was developed by IBM for the PS/2. **VL-bus** was developed by **VESA (the Video Electronic Standards Association)** as a way to boost video performance in graphical environments like Windows. **PCI** was developed by Intel to provide high-speed input and output, or I/O, for its new Pentium CPUs and other high-speed processors, such as the PC6 and Power PC chip. Apple Computer has just introduced Power Macintosh systems based on the PCI bus, providing an important new level of compatibility between PC and Macintosh systems; in fact many PCI cards now work in both Intel and Macintosh systems.

Although both the 8088 and the 8086 CPU chips are considered 16-bit processors, the 8088 can transfer data over the processor bus only 8 bits at a time. Therefore, computers with the 8088 chip, such as the original PC and many of its clones, are restricted to an 8-bit I/O bus.

The first PC to use a 16-bit peripheral bus was the IBM PC AT. The AT bus combines an original PC 8-bit bus connector with a smaller connector at the end of the original PC slot. The smaller connector contains the additional circuitry needed to carry a full 16 bits of data across the bus (Figure 13.2).

FIGURE 13.2
*PC and AT
Slots*

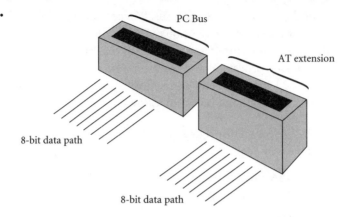

PC Bus

AT extension

8-bit data path

8-bit data path

An 8-bit PC slot and the small extension connector that turns it into a 16-bit AT slot.

The 16-bit AT-style bus has become the prevalent one in the industry. Most IBMs and compatibles, add-in cards, and peripherals use this bus. When people speak of an ISA bus these days, they are generally referring to the AT-style bus. Although the ISA bus works with both 8- and 16-bit cards, Windows 95 users should use 16-bit cards whenever possible. This is especially important with disk controller, memory, and video cards, because Windows 95 places heavy demands on those components.

Alternative Bus Architectures: MCA and EISA.
With the PS/2 series in 1987, IBM launched a new bus architecture: the Micro Channel Architecture, or MCA. MCA was actually a new type of connector for add-in cards and was designed in both 16-bit and 32-bit versions. IBM had noble aspirations: to extend the AT's bus capabilities from 16 to 32 bits and provide a more advanced bus architecture. However, the hardware giant also introduced one major drawback: MCA was incompatible with all IBM's own add-in cards for the PC, the XT, and the AT. MCA, therefore, was also incompatible with the thousands of non-IBM add-in cards that worked with the PC and AT buses.

When the AT and its 16-bit capabilities were launched, compatibility with earlier models was maintained. Owners of ATs could still use add-in cards designed to work with the 8-bit bus of the PC and the XT. The older, 8-bit cards still worked in the 16-bit bus slot of the AT because the 8-bit portion of the AT bus maintained the same bus architecture as the PC and XT 8-bit slot. Therefore you could add new memory boards and disk controllers requiring the 16-bit bus but still use inexpensive, 8-bit cards for printers, modems, and other comparatively low-throughput devices. This "backward compatibility" allowed people to upgrade from the PC to the AT and take their boards with them.

The new MCA architecture stymied the ability to upgrade. Boards developed for the PC or AT bus wouldn't function with the MCA bus. Instead, IBM counted on the development of MCA add-in cards and MCA-compatible machines, all designed to work with the improved capabilities of the 32-bit MCA bus.

However, those hopes went unfulfilled. Although IBM sold millions of PS/2 systems, the MCA bus didn't garner popularity among third-party developers. And users were dissatisfied because they couldn't use boards designed for the PC and AT buses with MCA machines. As a result, most manufacturers and users continued to use AT-bus machines. In fact, the AT bus, with its 16-bit data path, addresses the capabilities of 286 and 386SX systems perfectly, because their chips have only 16-bit processor buses.

The advent of the 386DX, 486, and higher-level chips, however, called for 32-bit I/O capabilities. With those more powerful chips, the 16-bit AT bus created an I/O bottleneck. IBM offered to license the MCA bus, with its 32-bit I/O capabilities. However, manufacturers found IBM's fee unacceptably high relative to their costs to produce the AT-style bus.

Indeed, IBM's announced licensing fees backfired. Led by Compaq, a group of computer manufacturers designed an alternative 32-bit bus, dubbed the EISA, for Extended Industry Standard Architecture. The EISA provides backward compatibility with the 8-bit boards from the original PC and with the 16-bit boards made for the AT bus.

EISA also broke the ranks with an important technical advance. A new type of add-in card designed specifically for the EISA bus could take advantage of the full 32-bit capabilities of the 386DX and 486 processors. EISA systems rival 32-bit MCA systems as the top performers on the market today.

In counterattack to the EISA assault, IBM set up offensives on two fronts. First, it lowered its MCA licensing fees and requirements to encourage the manufacture of PS/2 clones. Second, IBM increased the performance of the MCA bus to rival that of EISA. IBM also provided add-in card manufacturers with the chip sets they needed to optimize performance of cards for the MCA bus.

As of today, the ISA standard still dominates the bus battlefield. IBM has retreated and now offers some PS/2 models with the ISA bus. The MCA bus lags far behind ISA in acceptance, and newcomer EISA also remains in the rear ranks, although it has gained widespread acceptance in the server marketplace. In price, EISA machines far exceed machines based on the other two standards, and the same goes for corresponding add-in cards. This fact, coupled with the trend toward local bus systems, will likely restrict EISA from becoming anything but a niche player in the bus wars.

Local Bus. In addition to ISA, EISA, and MCA, proprietary buses are available from some systems vendors for use with memory boards and high-speed video adapters. For example, a system with a 16-bit ISA bus may also include a proprietary 32-bit slot into which you can plug additional RAM; this setup enables your system to access memory directly in 32-bit mode without the bottleneck imposed by a 16-bit bus. The drawback to this type of proprietary bus is that you can obtain cards only from one system vendor if you want to add RAM, high-speed video, or whatever else works in the slot.

More recently, in an attempt to supplant some of the proprietary buses, VESA and Intel each developed a new standard for so-called local bus implementations. In general, local buses operate at the speed of the processor and improve performance for add-in hardware, such as display adapter cards and disk drive controllers.

VL-bus is the VESA standard and has gained strong support over the past few years. Local bus video dramatically speeds Windows 95's graphics operations, so no new 486 system should be purchased without a VL-bus video controller.

Intel's local bus initiative, PCI (Peripheral Component Interconnect), is even more ambitious than VL-bus. Designed to provide a high-speed I/O path for the Pentium CPU, PCI can deliver data to and from peripheral devices either 32 or 64 bits at a time. Because of its high overall clock frequency (typically 66 MHz as opposed to VL-bus's 33 MHz) and its ability to perform I/O operations independently of the CPU's own local bus, PCI is the bus of choice for high-end Windows 95 systems. And now that PCI has gained support from Apple Computer, it probably will gain the support of workstation manufacturers to become a prevalent multiplatform standard over the next few years.

Ranking the Buses. The 16-bit ISA bus is the most prevalent PC bus today and works with the widest selection of add-in cards. Modern PCs supplement this bus with VL-bus or PCI implementations. The hybrids offer the best of both worlds: compatibility with existing ISA peripherals and the ability to exploit the faster local bus peripherals.

The 16- and 32-bit versions of the MCA bus can be found in the PS/2, as well as in an emerging group of MCA clones. MCA systems are fine for Windows 95; I strongly recommend the 32-bit version. The downside to the MCA bus is that because of limited availability, add-in cards are often more expensive than their ISA equivalents. Therefore MCA machines are my third choice, after ISA/VL-bus or ISA/PCI and EISA.

My favorite choice is the ISA/PCI combination. When used in conjunction with a Pentium CPU, this combination provides backward compatibility while letting your Pentium strut its stuff with the latest peripherals. If you're looking at a 486 system, then PCI is probably overkill. Go with an ISA/VL-bus combination, which is adequate for systems ranging from the lowly 486/33 MHz all the way up to the scorchingly fast 486DX4/100 MHz.

Plug and Play

An exciting new development in PC bus technology is **Plug and Play.** Initiated by Microsoft and Intel, Plug and Play defines a series of extensions to the major bus architectures, enabling peripheral devices to configure themselves automatically as soon as you install them.

Before the advent of Plug and Play, you often had to struggle with hardware configuration parameters—such as interrupt, I/O port address, and shared memory ranges—to install a new peripheral properly. With Plug and Play, in contrast, your peripherals gain a level of intelligence that lets them negotiate with your system for specific configuration resources (like an interrupt number). This negotiation takes place automatically when you start your PC.

Windows 95 includes built-in enhancements to support Plug and Play. When Windows 95 detects that a Plug and Play "event" has occurred—let's say you installed a new printer—it automatically identifies the printer and in some cases even installs supporting software (such as device drivers) with no intervention on your part. Gone are the days of plug and pray. You can learn more about Plug and Play, as well as other aspects of Windows 95's installation process, in Chapter 16.

Memory

Memory ranks second only to the CPU as the most important influence on the performance of your system. Memory chips take one of two forms: RAM or ROM.

ROM, or **read-only memory,** chips are a basic form of solid-state memory (*solid-state* refers to the fact that unlike disk drives and other memory technologies, chips have no moving parts). ROM chips contain the built-in instructions, including BIOS (the basic input/output system), that control the input and output of computer hardware, along with other functions such as start-up routines and diagnostic programs. Most modern versions of BIOS (those produced within the past few years) are compatible with Windows 95 and therefore don't pose any operating problems. ROM chips are found on the motherboard and on the add-in adapter cards that control devices such as disk drives and video displays.

Another type of solid-state memory chip is the processor RAM cache, discussed earlier in this chapter. Other RAM caches can be found on add-in or peripheral cards, such as disk controllers and video adapters. Those dedicated RAM caches are available only for the devices and cannot be used by your computer as general-purpose memory. Peripheral cards can also include processors, RAM, and other chips, making them much like small, self-contained computers.

In most cases the term **RAM (random-access memory)** describes the memory chips—whether on your computer's motherboard or on its add-in memory boards—that serve as the main memory available to your system. This system RAM is the computer's main work space. Applications are usually stored on the hard disk but are transferred into the system RAM to run. Data that you enter or recall from a storage device is stored in RAM while you manipulate it.

The RAM chips in your computer's system memory are known as **dynamic RAM,** or **DRAM**. This kind of memory is called **volatile memory** because it clears itself of data every time you turn off the computer. Some systems offer static RAM chips, which are nonvolatile and very fast and retain their information if the power is turned off. At the present time, static RAM chips are much more expensive than DRAM chips and are therefore relegated to special applications where the price can be justified.

With Windows 95, RAM and hard-disk space both provide applications with memory. The amount of RAM not only affects the speed of Windows but also determines how many applications you can run at one time. Windows 95 can use a technique called *virtual memory* to fool your system into thinking it has more RAM than it really does.

. . . .

RAM

RAM is your most important memory resource. Like all good things in life— friends, wealth, leisure time, and computer games—you can never have too much RAM. Here's what specific amounts of RAM can do for Windows:

➤ **4 megabytes.** This is the minimum amount of RAM needed for running Windows 95. Crawling is a more accurate description of your operating speed when you are limited to 4 megabytes.

➤ **8 megabytes.** This is what I consider an adequate amount of RAM for running Windows 95. It's definitely the minimum for multitasking Win32 applications. Eight megabytes puts you in the RAM comfort zone.

➤ **16 megabytes.** Now you're running laps. This is the amount of RAM I recommend for running Windows 95. You can usually fit this amount of RAM onto a 386 or 486 system board or an add-in memory card. Sixteen megabytes gives you plenty of RAM for your applications.

➤ **More than 16 megabytes.** Nirvana. If you can afford it, you can use as much RAM with Windows 95 as your system can accommodate with most 486 or larger systems. Traditionally, only servers and graphics workstations are configured with more than 16 megabytes, but a trend among Windows power users is to go for 32MB or even more to run Photoshop and other RAM-ravenous applications.

Adding RAM. It's not only a matter of how much RAM you need; where you put it also counts. To add RAM, you can insert either chips or what are known as SIMMs into sockets on the motherboard. A SIMM, or Single Inline Memory Module, is a bunch of chips welded together into one easy-to-install unit. Another way to add RAM is to plug it into a memory card that accepts chips, SIPPs (Single Inline Pin Packages), or SIMMs. Or you can replace existing chips with higher-density RAM chips.

Plugging In a Memory Card. Add-in cards, which plug into either a proprietary slot or the expansion bus, contain DRAM chips, SIPPs, or SIMMs. I recommend that you insert memory directly into the motherboard whenever you can. However, sometimes you have to use an add-in card because the motherboard does not provide space for expansion.

When selecting a memory board, choose the kind that uses proprietary slots; this type is usually faster than the type that plugs into the peripheral bus, especially if it's an ISA bus. Many 32-bit memory expansion slots allow RAM to perform as well as does RAM that is inserted directly into the motherboard.

Installing Higher-Density Chips. You can also increase the amount of RAM on your system board by replacing existing chips or SIMMs with higher-density RAM chips, which contain more bits per chip. Older systems use 256-kilobit chips, but 1-megabit chips are now the norm, and 4-megabit chips are available, albeit expensive. Since most systems have a limited number of open SIMM sockets, you may want to move to 4-megabit components sooner rather than later.

Assume, for example, that your system has 4 megabytes (4MB) of RAM, and this RAM consists of four 30-pin 1MB SIMMs, each made up of eight 1-megabit chips (8 bits make up 1 byte). You're thinking of increasing the amount of RAM in your system to 8MB. Instead, you may want to bite the bullet now and go all the way to 16MB. This is because most 30-pin SIMM-compatible motherboards have only eight SIMM sockets. If you go to 8MB by filling the rest of the eight sockets with 1MB SIMMs, you may find yourself shelling out additional cash down the road when you wish to go beyond this level. The only way to upgrade such a motherboard beyond 8MB is to pull all the 1MB SIMMs and start over from scratch with the more expensive 4MB SIMMs, each of which is made up of eight of the 4-megabit chips. These 4MB SIMMs are gaining in popularity.

Be careful to check the manufacturer's specifications before upgrading the memory in your system, because many system boards address memory idiosyncratically. Part of the price we pay for freedom of choice in the PC-and-compatibles universe is having to deal with system boards made by a variety of manufacturers. The number of existing system boards extends well into the thousands.

When upgrading your memory with higher-density RAM chips, you may have to expand in multiples of 2 or 4 megabytes, depending on the number of memory banks available on your motherboard. Table 13.1 shows scenarios for a typical system that accommodates eight banks of SIMMs.

· · · · · · · · · · · · · ·

TABLE 13.1
Possible RAM Configurations in a System with Eight SIMM Sockets

Total Megabytes	Number of Banks	Type of SIMMs
4	4	1 MB
8	8	1 MB
8	2	4 MB
8	1	8 MB
16	4	4 MB
16	2	8 MB
16	1	16 MB

Danger Zone

In many older systems, you can't mix and match different densities of SIMMs. Even in systems that permit different densities of chips to be mixed, restrictions usually apply as to which banks can receive certain densities. Those restrictions also apply to some systems that use SIPPs for expansion. So investigate your system to determine what kind of chips you need if you want to upgrade.

Parity Checking and RAM. In theory, it takes eight RAM chips to create 1 byte of RAM, because there are 8 bits to a byte. Although some computers, including many Macintosh models and a few PC systems, contain eight RAM chips per bank or SIMM, most PCs require nine chips per bank or SIMM. The additional, or ninth, bit—called the parity bit—is used for error detection. A crude form of error checking, parity checking uses the ninth bit like a traffic light to warn of a possible error. If any of the 8 bits is damaged electrically by the computer or accidentally changed by some hardware or software failure, the ninth bit changes from red to green, or vice versa (that is, its numerical value changes from odd to even, or vice versa). Parity-bit checking is so primitive, however, that if 2 bits are changed in the same way, the ninth bit doesn't reflect the change, because the two bits balance each other out.

A parity-check error message sometimes appears after you start your computer. As part of its start-up routine, almost every PC first checks the RAM by writing information to it, reading it back, and checking the parity bits to ensure that the data was correctly written and read. If the routine finds a problem in a chip (usually resulting from a manufacturing defect, old age, or a power aberration), you see a message that reads something like "Parity check one" if the problem is on your system board, or "Parity check two" if the problem is on an add-in board.

On IBM PS/2 systems, numerical error codes appear: 110 is the equivalent of "Parity check one," and 111 stands for "Parity check two." If those messages or codes appear after you start your computer, turn it off and try to solve the problem, either with diagnostic software or by getting your unit serviced.

Another all-too-familiar parity error message may appear on your screen as a group of numbers that ends with the three digits 201. The digits that precede 201 are four hexadecimal numbers that suggest exactly where the computer thinks your system contains a failed RAM chip. If you get a parity error message at start-up or reboot, fix it without delay so it doesn't disturb you in the middle of a session.

Parity errors are more troublesome when they occur during a work session. A parity error can halt your system altogether and force you to restart it. If you fall victim to this disaster, any information in RAM is lost.

Some PC clones allow you to disable parity checking. This prevents a parity error from halting the operation of your system, but the integrity of your data is not ensured. If only one character somewhere off in a stray file is affected, a parity error may not cause you much grief. But the wrong character in a letter to a client could prove embarrassing, and a single incorrect number in a spreadsheet or a formula could dramatically alter a financial report.

Windows 95 and RAM. Windows 95 employs various tricks to take advantage of available memory. In fact, total RAM often falls short of what's required by the combined sizes of application files you've loaded. Windows and many of its applications load only part of a program into memory at a time. A spreadsheet program, for example, might load only the data-entry portion of the program while you're entering numbers, leaving the graphics portion unloaded until you switch to constructing charts. Or the spreadsheet application might load only a particular section of the data file you're handling rather than load the entire data file. To facilitate this memory conservation, Windows programming languages are designed to create programs that load only part of themselves into memory at a time.

Those software manipulations, however, trade speed for memory. When a program swaps part of either itself or the data it's handling between memory and a disk drive, the slower speed of the disk drive can decelerate the program. The program's performance would be better if the system contained enough RAM to store the entire program and data file. Most programs designed for memory swapping are smart enough to detect an ample supply of RAM. A few, however, swap no matter how much memory a system contains.

To understand the chicanery involved in swapping files to and from memory, as well as other techniques that Windows employs to make the most of system resources, it helps to be familiar with the three types of RAM used by PCs: conventional memory, extended memory, and expanded memory. Conventional memory technically refers to the 1 megabyte of RAM that can be addressed by DOS, but the term is commonly used to designate the user RAM area, or the first 640K of this 1 megabyte. In addition, there's UMA, or upper memory area, and HMA, or high memory area. To make things even more confusing, the UMA is sometimes called UMB, for upper memory blocks. If all this is more than you can fit into your memory, here's a brief rundown of what the terms mean:

➤ **Conventional memory.** The first 640K of RAM installed in your machine. To run Windows 95, you must have a full 640K of conventional memory.

➤ **Extended memory.** The RAM in your machine beyond the initial 1 megabyte. You must have some extended memory to run Windows 95, at least 3,072K.

➤ **HMA, or high memory area.** The first 64K of extended memory.

➤ **UMA, or upper memory area.** Also known as UMB, or upper memory blocks. The memory between 640K and the 1-megabyte limit of DOS.

➤ **Expanded memory.** An older method of increasing RAM. Uses empty memory locations between the end of the 640K of conventional memory and the 1,024K (1 megabyte) of base memory, the area normally used by ROM and system software. Windows 95 doesn't use expanded memory, but DOS applications run from within Windows 95 may need expanded memory.

Figure 13.3 shows how those memory areas are addressed by your system.

FIGURE 13.3
The Layout of
Memory Areas

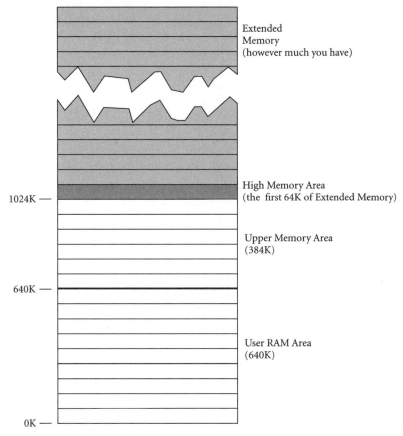

Extended
Memory
(however much you have)

High Memory Area
(the first 64K of Extended Memory)

1024K —

Upper Memory Area
(384K)

640K —

User RAM Area
(640K)

0K —

Conventional memory, upper memory, and extended
memory are arranged in this fashion so they can be
accessed by the system.

What's a Hexadecimal Memory Address?

Computer memory locations are often identified by their hexadecimal values, or in nerd parlance, their **hex values.** A hex value is a number expressed in base 16, or hexadecimal, rather than the everyday base 10 or the computer base 2.

Base 10, the decimal system, uses ten digits, 0 through 9. Base 16 employs 16 digits; 0 through 9 retain the same values as in the decimal system, and the additional six numbers, 10 through 15, are represented by the letters *A* through *F*. Sometimes a lowercase *h* is placed after a hexadecimal value to avoid confusion with decimal numbers. Table 13.2 compares selected hexadecimal numbers with their corresponding decimal numbers.

TABLE 13.2
*Equivalent
Hexadecimal
and Decimal
Numbers*

Hexadecimal	Decimal	Hexadecimal	Decimal
0	0	A	10
1	1	B	11
2	2	C	12
3	3	D	13
4	4	E	14
5	5	F	15
6	6	10	16
7	7	11	17
8	8	FF	255
9	9	100	256

As you may be able to deduce from Table 13.2, a single-digit number in hex can be larger than a single-digit number in the decimal system. And the last double-digit number in hex (FF) is larger than the last two-digit number in decimal (99). This allows large numeric values to be expressed with fewer digits.

Also, because computer memory is based on multiples of eight, hex is a more convenient numbering system for programmers than the decimal system. However, as is often the case in computing, what's easier for programmers can cause grief for the average user. To help you get oriented, Figures 13.3 and 13.4 show both hex and decimal values for memory addresses. If you need to convert between the two systems, you can use the Calculator's Scientific mode, which I describe in Chapter 5.

Conventional Memory

It's the Methuselah of RAM. **Conventional memory** is found in all PC-compatible computers. The original PC contained an 8088 CPU chip, which could address only 1 megabyte of RAM. In other words, it could keep track of a million 1-byte locations within RAM. This 1-megabyte limit, imposed by the design of the original PC, is the maximum amount of memory that can be addressed by DOS. In those days, with many systems containing a measly 64K ($\frac{1}{16}$ megabyte) of RAM, a full megabyte seemed like megamemory. That's why it was originally thought that power users would be more than satisfied with 256K RAM ($\frac{1}{4}$ megabyte).

Most PCs today are shipped with the maximum amount of conventional memory, 640K. Although DOS can address 1 megabyte at a time, only 640K of that megabyte is available to applications. Technically, the entire 1 megabyte is conventional memory. However, the remaining 340K is more commonly called upper memory and is reserved for device drivers and other system software.

Why this division of conventional memory? Because of the design of the 8088 processor, IBM decided to divide the available megabyte of addressable RAM into 16 segments of 64K each. Six of the blocks were set aside for the ROM chips—which contain low-level instructions for the computer and the computer BIOS—and for the display adapter and ROM extensions, which were used for hard-disk controllers and their additional BIOS. That left ten segments of 64K each, or 640K total RAM, that could be used by the operating system and by applications and data. Figure 13.4 depicts the segments of the megabyte of conventional memory.

Each 64K segment is divided into roughly 4,000 subsections, which IBM calls paragraphs, and each paragraph is 16 bytes long. Programmers identify a specific memory address by naming the segment and then referring to the beginning paragraph within that segment.

FIGURE 13.4

Memory Addresses in Upper Memory and Conventional RAM

	Decimal Address (in K)	Hex Address		
1024K (1 megabyte)	1023	FFFF		
	960	F000		
	959	EFFF		
	896	E000		
	895	DFFF		Upper Memory Area (384K)
	832	D000		
	831	CFFF		
	768	C000		
	767	BFFF		
	704	B000		
	703	AFFF		
640K	640	A000		
	639	9FFF		
	576	9000		
	575	8FFF		
512K	512	8000		
	511	7FFF		
	448	7000		
	447	6FFF		
	384	6000		
	383	5FFF		User Ram Area (640K)
	320	5000		
	319	4FFF		
256K	256	4000		
	255	3FFF		
	192	3000		
	191	2FFF		
	128	2000		
	127	1FFF		
	64	1000		
	63	0FFF		
0K	0	0000		

The first megabyte of RAM is divided into 16 segments of 64K each. Ten of those segments, or 640K, constitute the user RAM area, or conventional RAM.

Upper Memory Area

The **upper memory area** includes memory addresses 640K through 1,023K. In hex, this range is A000 through FFFF.

The upper memory area did not originally contain physical RAM. Instead the region's addresses were used as reference points that specified the location of ROM and RAM on adapter cards plugged into the system's expansion bus, as well as the location of the ROM chips in the system motherboard that contain the computer's BIOS. For this reason the upper memory area is also called the **adapter segment.**

ROM chips were later remapped to upper memory area addresses in a process called ROM shadowing. This provides DOS with a standard method of accessing ROM without knowing where it is physically located.

The upper memory area is divided into 24 blocks of 16K each. Those blocks are called the **upper memory blocks,** or **UMBs.** Although the acronym UMB is often used interchangeably with UMA, UMBs are actually subunits of the UMA (Figure 13.5).

Figure 13.5 shows some of the common uses for the upper memory area. To determine how your system uses its upper memory area, run the Microsoft Diagnostics Program or a similar utility that analyzes and maps memory. It is useful to know how your upper memory area is used, because Windows 95 can exploit the unused memory areas to provide additional conventional memory for DOS sessions. In addition, system crashes and other failures commonly result when an adapter card and your system software both try to use the same area of upper memory.

To further familiarize you with the critical upper memory area, here's a brief rundown on how some of the common addresses are used:

➺ **A000-AFFF.** This 64K section of upper memory is used by the RAM on VGA and EGA display adapter cards. Those cards place information from the RAM they contain into this memory area to make it accessible to your system.

➺ **B000-B7FF.** Monochrome display adapter (MDA) cards and Hercules monochrome cards make use of this 32K memory area.

➺ **B800-BFFF.** This 32K memory area is used by CGA, EGA, Hercules monochrome, and VGA text cards.

➺ **C000-C7FF.** This 32K area is used by non-PS/2 VGA cards as the address space for their ROM chips. Some cards use only 24K of this area, while others consume the entire 32K. This address space is also used by EGA cards and 8514/a adapters.

➺ **C000-CBFF.** This 48K area is used by 8514/a adapters.

➺ **CC00-DFFF.** This 80K area is often unused, although the address range beginning at D000 is often used by expanded-memory managers to begin a 64K page frame.

➺ **E000-EFFF.** This 64K memory area is not available on most systems. IBM PS/2s use this address space for an extra ROM BIOS chip.

➺ **F000-FFFF.** This 64K address space is used by PCs for the ROM BIOS chips that control the computer's basic I/O functions, such as disk access.

FIGURE 13.5

Upper Memory Area

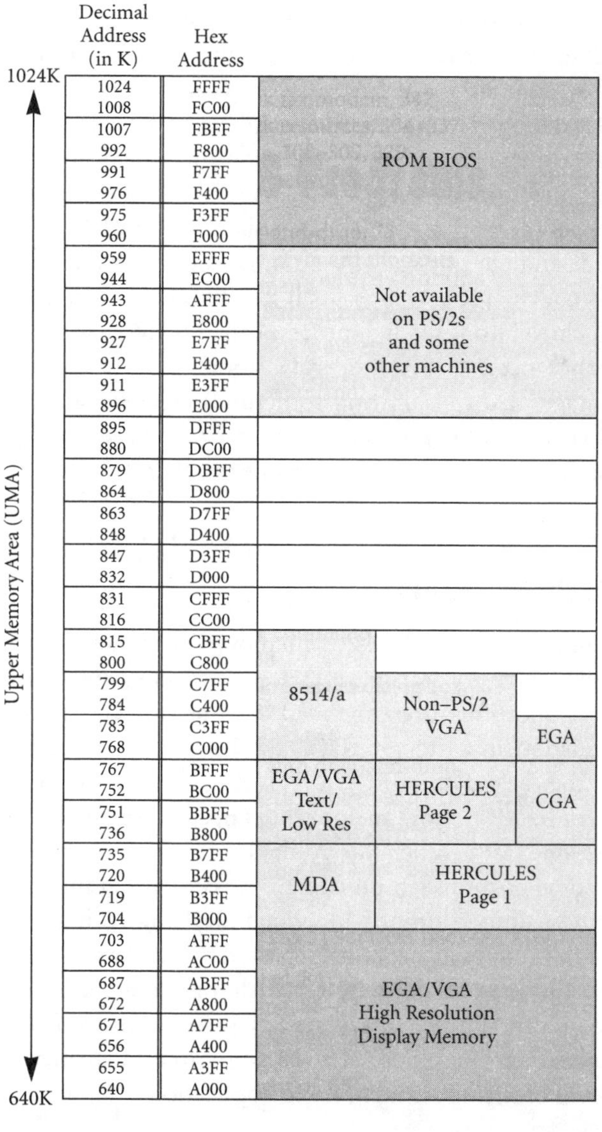

The upper memory area spans the memory addresses between the end of the 640K of conventional memory and the end of the 1 megabyte of memory that DOS can address.

Decimal Address (in K)	Hex Address			
1024	FFFF	ROM BIOS		
1008	FC00			
1007	FBFF			
992	F800			
991	F7FF			
976	F400			
975	F3FF			
960	F000			
959	EFFF	Not available on PS/2s and some other machines		
944	EC00			
943	AFFF			
928	E800			
927	E7FF			
912	E400			
911	E3FF			
896	E000			
895	DFFF			
880	DC00			
879	DBFF			
864	D800			
863	D7FF			
848	D400			
847	D3FF			
832	D000			
831	CFFF			
816	CC00			
815	CBFF			
800	C800	8514/a	Non–PS/2 VGA	
799	C7FF			
784	C400			
783	C3FF			EGA
768	C000			
767	BFFF	EGA/VGA Text/Low Res	HERCULES Page 2	CGA
752	BC00			
751	BBFF			
736	B800			
735	B7FF	MDA	HERCULES Page 1	
720	B400			
719	B3FF			
704	B000			
703	AFFF	EGA/VGA High Resolution Display Memory		
688	AC00			
687	ABFF			
672	A800			
671	A7FF			
656	A400			
655	A3FF			
640	A000			

1024K (top) ... Upper Memory Area (UMA) ... 640K (bottom)

You can use the EMM386 memory manager, described later in this section, or a third-party memory manager to load device drivers and memory-resident software into unused addresses in the upper memory area. This increases the amount of 640K user RAM available on your system.

When you start Windows 95, it inspects the upper memory area for free space that it can use to further optimize its own performance. Sometimes Windows inadvertently grabs memory that appears to be free but is actually required by another device. For example, if a video card isn't using a particular area of memory, Windows assumes that area is free. When the video card later tries to use that memory, the screen may look garbled, or your system may crash.

By setting parameters in your CONFIG.SYS, SYSTEM.INI, and other files, you can designate areas of upper memory to be either available or off-limits to Windows and memory managers. This maximizes the use of upper memory while avoiding potential memory conflicts. I briefly describe how to do this later in this chapter and explain the technique in more detail in Chapters 14 and 15.

As I mentioned earlier, in the original IBM PC design of the early 1980s, the upper memory area did not consist of physical RAM. Most newer systems provide enough physical RAM so that the upper memory area can be composed of actual RAM chips. Such systems enable you to copy the contents of ROM chips into RAM in a process called RAM shadowing. This boosts performance because RAM operates more quickly than ROM. Despite this advantage, RAM shadowing sometimes creates compatibility problems. If you experience memory conflicts, first try to see whether temporarily disabling RAM shadowing alleviates the problem.

Expanded Memory

PCs employ two methods of memory expansion: expanded memory and extended memory. Windows 95 itself uses only extended memory, but many DOS applications use expanded memory, and Windows 95 can provide expanded memory to your DOS applications that require it.

In the early days of PCs, a typical user would quickly consume the first 640K of RAM. If more memory was needed for constructing larger spreadsheets, one last frontier was available: upper memory, reserved by IBM but with some portions left unused. Some early programs employed schemes to grab those unused areas of upper memory; unfortunately, each program went about the grab in its own way, so a system crash was likely to occur when two or more of the programs made a rush for the upper frontiers of memory.

To prevent the conflicts created by an upper-memory free-for-all, **memory managers** were developed. Those programs act like software referees, allocating areas of the upper memory to applications that need the extra RAM.

The first major development to break the 1-megabyte restriction of DOS —spearheaded in 1985 by Lotus Development Corporation in conjunction with Intel—was called expanded memory. Expanded memory involves a scheme called **bank switching**. To implement this scheme, the computer switches four 16K blocks of RAM—referred to as pages—back and forth between the conventional memory and an area of expanded memory (Figure 13.6). These four 16K pages form one 64K page frame. You need an expanded-memory manager to keep track of what is switched.

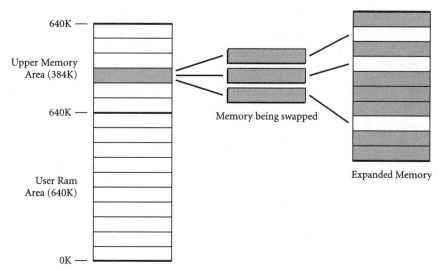

FIGURE 13.6

Bank Switching

To perform bank switching, the computer swaps several small areas of memory in and out of RAM. This makes expanded memory accessible to the CPU.

Lotus and Intel, the developers of bank switching, sought assistance from Microsoft in developing compatibility with DOS. The three companies together developed the Lotus/Intel/Microsoft Expanded Memory Specification 3.2, better known as the LIM EMS 3.2, or simply LIM 3.2. LIM 3.2 was limited to bank switching a single 64K page frame (composed of four 16K pages) at a time; this took its toll on system performance.

In a typical high-tech leapfrog, AST—then one of the leading suppliers of add-in memory boards—developed its own enhancement to that standard, the Enhanced Expanded Memory Specification, or EEMS. Later AST met with the LIM group to consolidate their schemes into a new standard: the LIM EMS 4.0, or simply EMS 4.0.

EMS 4.0 sped up the operation of expanded memory with a technique called backfilling, which enables the expanded-memory manager to handle more than four 16K pages of memory. Backfilling works by rotating groups of 16K pages into the conventional memory area. By rotating a pool of memory pages, a larger amount of memory can be swapped between conventional memory and expanded memory.

EMS 4.0 provides a maximum of 32 megabytes of expanded memory and also includes programming tools. Most DOS applications that use expanded memory use EMS 4.0, although some older programs still use LIM 3.2. You can check a DOS application to identify which version of EMS it uses.

Expanded Memory and Windows. Because expanded memory is required by many DOS applications, such as spreadsheets and CAD software, you may need to use expanded memory even though Windows 95 doesn't require it. Windows 95 automatically converts extended memory to expanded memory for DOS programs; this is a function of Windows 95 itself rather than a function of a memory-management utility, such as HIMEM.SYS or EMM386.EXE under DOS. In Chapter 15 you can learn how to configure Windows 95 to supply expanded memory to DOS programs.

Expanded-Memory Managers. Expanded-memory managers that run on 386 or larger systems—for example, EMM386, Netroom, QEMM, and 386MAX—can all be used to place Terminate and Stay Resident DOS programs (TSRs), device drivers, and other memory-resident software into the upper memory area. But beware: this memory space can get crowded quickly. To view a map of your system's memory, use the Microsoft Diagnostics program (MSD.EXE) To control how EMM386 uses your system's upper memory, you can use memory option switches when you install EMM386.

Space conflicts can also occur because Windows 95 uses part of the upper memory area as a buffer that translates DOS and network API calls from protected mode into real mode, which is the only mode DOS understands. All too often there isn't enough free memory for both expanded memory and this translation buffer.

The solution is either to relocate the translation buffer to conventional memory or to remove the expanded-memory page frame. Windows 95 allocates space to the page frame first; if there's no room left over, Windows tries to relocate the buffer to upper memory or to the 640K conventional-memory area. If you are running a large DOS application, however, you may run into a shortage of conventional memory.

To reverse the order in which Windows 95 allocates the page frame and translation buffer into upper memory, you can change the [386Enh] section of SYSTEM.INI by adding the line

```
ReservePageFrame=false
```

This setting tells Windows to allocate the translation buffer first, then the page frame memory if space is available. If it isn't, your expanded-memory manager may not be able to find a page frame, in which case your DOS programs won't be able to access the expanded memory they need to run.

You can further tweak where Windows 95 places translation buffers and expanded-memory page frames. Use the following commands in the [386Enh] section of SYSTEM.INI:

- EMMExclude=

- EMMInclude=

- EMMPageFrame=

- EMMSize=

- IgnoreInstalledEMM=

- NoEMMDriver=

- ReservedHighArea=

- UsableHighArea=

Because Windows 95 already attempts to use all available free areas of upper memory, you probably won't have to use the three commands that would instruct Windows to do just that: EMMInclude=, EMMPageFrame=, and UsableHighArea=. If no space is available in upper memory, you can always use the line

```
NoEMMDriver=YES
```

in [386Enh] to tell Windows 95 to disable expanded memory altogether and drop the search for a 64K page frame in upper memory.

If you're having trouble starting Windows 95, a hardware adapter may be in conflict for space with the translation buffer. To solve this problem, specify that the memory range E000 through EFFF not be used by either expanded memory or the translation table buffer; because no convention applies as to how this area should be used by add-in cards, conflicts can occur and prevent Windows 95 from starting. To exclude this area, add the following line to [386Enh]:

```
EMMExclude=E000-EFFF
```

This line often takes care of the upper-memory conflicts that can prevent Windows 95 from starting.

Many of the statement lines that start with EMM in the [386Enh] section of SYSTEM.INI control placement of the translation buffer as well as expanded memory.

. . . .

Extended Memory

Expanded memory offers a kludgy approach to providing more than 1 megabyte of memory to applications. Bank-switching segments in and out of the upper memory area consumes software overhead, vitiates performance, and creates conflicts in the upper memory area. But at the time it was developed, no alternative existed that could maintain compatibility with the 8088 and the 8086.

The advent of the 286 and protected mode enabled systems to directly address many megabytes of memory, which in turn led to extended memory. Extended memory is an extension of continuously addressable memory beyond 1 megabyte; no bank switching or other software tricks are needed to access it.

For many years extended memory had little practical value because the technology that would allow it to work with DOS had not been invented. You could allocate extended memory for use as a disk cache or a print spooler, but it could not be used to run DOS applications. Windows 3.0 changed this by introducing Microsoft's **Extended Memory Specification (XMS)** and **DOS Protected Mode Interface (DPMI).**

The first 64K of extended memory is called the **high memory area (HMA).** The HMA is located at memory addresses 1,024K to 1,088K. Microsoft discovered a trick to make the HMA appear to the computer to be part of the system's conventional memory. This enables you to load part of Windows 95's DOS code into the HMA, freeing part of the 640K of conventional memory. Other programs, especially network software drivers, can also make use of the HMA; however, only one program at a time can use the HMA, even if that program uses only a small portion of the HMA's memory. By default, Windows 95 reserves the HMA for use by DOS code during MS-DOS sessions.

Extended memory is an expansion past the 1-megabyte limit; however, for purposes of using Windows 95, you can envision extended memory as an extension of the 640K of conventional memory. In the Windows 95 environment, extended memory plays as important a role as does conventional memory—in fact, you can't run Windows 95 without at least some extended memory. If you have an add-in memory card that can be configured either as extended memory or as expanded memory, configure it as extended memory. If your DOS applications need expanded memory, Windows 95 can use the extended memory to emulate expanded memory.

With Windows 3.1, Microsoft's HIMEM.SYS memory manager controls extended memory using the XMS standard. The HIMEM.SYS utility is an extended-memory manager that acts as a referee, controlling the system's extended memory and making sure that Windows and applications don't try to grab the same area of extended memory at the same time—a sure way to crash a system.

With Windows 95, the functions of HIMEM.SYS have been rolled into the hidden WINBOOT.SYS file that is loaded when you first start your PC. The file's function is basically the same; the file has just been combined with other files, such as IO.SYS, for simplicity.

Now for a detour back into kludge technology. To access extended memory with DOS, it was necessary to develop utility programs called **DOS extenders,** which were either sold separately or embedded into applications. Unfortunately, the DOS extenders sometimes used conflicting methods of accessing extended memory, which caused system incompatibilities and crashes. This conflict haunted earlier versions of Windows.

Subsequently, two software protocols were developed to regulate how all applications use extended memory. The first was the Virtual Control Program Interface (VCPI), developed by several companies, including Quarterdeck, Phar Lap, and Rational Systems.

The VCPI protocol enables programs that use DOS extenders on 386 systems to run with 386 expanded-memory managers, such as QEMM and 386MAX. Windows 3.0 did not support the VCPI specifications, which caused incompatibilities with third-party expanded-memory managers that did support the specifications.

Windows 95 supports the VCPI protocol, but only in MS-DOS mode. The VCPI protocol is incompatible with the normal operating mode of Windows 95 as well as with most other multitasking operating systems, such as Windows NT, OS/2, and UNIX. That means DOS-extended programs that use VCPI cannot run in a Windows 95 DOS session; they must have total control of the PC, which means Windows must be in MS-DOS mode for them to run.

DOS Protected Mode Interface (DPMI) was developed as a group effort by Microsoft, Rational Systems, Phar Lap, and several other companies. The DPMI specifications provide DOS applications with a standard protocol for switching the processor into protected mode, thereby accessing extended memory. The DPMI standard works with Windows 95, and most applications that use DOS extenders have been upgraded to support the DPMI standard.

Hard-Disk Storage

Any graphically oriented operating system, like Windows 95, consumes your computer's memory resources—both RAM and hard disk—more quickly than does a character-based system like DOS. With a character-based system, a screen of information might have a capacity of 2,000 characters, whereas a Windows 95 screen with a 256-color VGA display can contain 2,457,600 bits of data.

Data storage affects memory requirements, and in the Windows 95 environment, data consumes the most storage space. In DOS, not only is the screen display composed mostly of characters, so is the data stored on hard disk. In Windows 95, data files more commonly contain graphics in addition to characters. Add multimedia capabilities, and your data storage requirements skyrocket. Animation files can consume 10 to 30 screens of graphics for every second of animation, and sound files can require a megabyte or more of storage space for a brief passage of digitized speech or music.

Windows 95 applications can far exceed the 640K RAM limitation of DOS applications by taking advantage of Windows 95's memory-management capabilities. On top of the added requirements of data storage, applications, and screen displays, Windows itself includes a cadre of software components that must work together to create the environment. All those factors place demands both on your system's RAM and on storage devices.

What I said earlier about RAM applies to hard-disk storage as well: get as much as you can afford for now, and you'll probably want to save up to buy more later. To give you an idea of how quickly Windows 95 consumes hard-disk space, the full Windows 95 installation itself can take more than 25 megabytes of hard-disk space, and even a Spartan installation requires at least 15 megabytes. Full-fledged Windows 95 applications, such as Word and Excel, can each consume 30 to 40 megabytes or more. When you add data and virtual-memory paging files, it becomes apparent why the 100- or 200-megabyte hard disk that was adequate for Windows 3.1 seems skimpy for Windows 95.

Insider's Tip

Buy the fastest hard disk possible. The speedier the disk, the faster Windows 95 can manipulate virtual memory, and the faster the overall performance of Windows. And get a fast connection for your fast hard disk; I recommend an SCSI hard disk and an SCSI interface card that plugs into the computer's local bus, preferably a PCI bus. A fast SCSI drive plugged into a PCI bus is the best way to meet the excruciating demands of Windows 95.

You can find many types of hard-disk drives in the loosely affiliated group of computers known as PC compatibles. The controller card that operates the drive, rather than the drive itself, determines whether the drive is compatible with Windows 95. The following are the major PC controller card technologies:

➤ **ST506** This was one of the most frequently used controllers during the early to mid-1980s.

➤ **WD1003.** This controller, based on chips produced by Western Digital, replaced the ST506 and remains a major standard.

➤ **ESDI.** The Enhanced Small Device Interface is a high-speed controller found in many Compaq DeskPro and other high-performance systems.

➤ **IDE.** The Integrated Drive Electronics standard places most of the controller circuitry on the drive; this reduces the amount of hardware needed inside the PC. IDE drives often plug directly into the motherboard and are common in portable computers. IDE hard disks are far and away the most prevalent type, and this standard has now been extended with the Enhanced IDE specification, which provides better performance and enables you to use larger hard disks than was previously possible.

➤ **SCSI.** The Small Computer System Interface controller provides its own expansion bus, which allows seven SCSI devices to be connected to a single controller card. Those devices can include disk drives, tape drives, CD ROM players, and even nonstorage devices such as scanners. I recommend SCSI not only because it enables you to connect multiple devices to a single card but also because inexpensive PCI SCSI cards provide terrific performance at a reasonable price.

All of the aforementioned controllers are compatible with Windows 95. However, the 32-bit file access features, described in the next section, generally require a third-party hard-disk driver to work with ESDI and SCSI drives.

• •

Getting More

Because the speed of your hard disk has a significant impact on system performance, Windows 95 provides four options that accelerate hard-disk operations:

➤ A built-in disk-defragmenting program that arranges the contents of your hard disk so that data can be accessed more quickly.

➤ A 32-bit disk driver that enables Windows to control your hard disk directly.

➺ A 32-bit file system driver that makes reading and writing disk files quicker than with previous versions of Windows.

➺ A built-in system cache program that dynamically allocates system RAM for caching file system I/O.

Those four features work together to improve overall disk I/O performance under Windows 95.

Defragmenting Your Hard Disk. The first step toward improved performance is to defragment your disk on a regular basis. Because of the way Windows 95 interacts with disk drives, a single file is not always written into one continuous space on a disk. As a result, files are fragmented. After prolonged use of your hard disk—that is, after you rewrite and erase many files—many small file fragments can become scattered on your disk.

Defragmenting your disk regroups those fragments, allowing them to be read more quickly and creating a larger area of continuous free space on your hard disk. Windows 95 includes its own Disk Defragmenter utility, which can be found on the System Tools submenu of the Start menu.

Insider's Tip

It's a good idea to delete any unnecessary files before you defragment your hard disk. This frees up some of your system's disk space, making it easier for Disk Defragmenter to do its job. Good candidates for deletion are temporary files left accidentally on your system; those files usually end with the .TMP extension. You can also delete backup files, often identified by the .BAK extension.

When you first start Disk Defragmenter, you are prompted to select the hard disk you wish to defragment. You can let Disk Defragmenter select your boot drive, or you can select a different drive in the drop-down list box (Figure 13.7).

• • • • • • • • • • • •
FIGURE 13.7
Selecting a
Drive to
Defragment

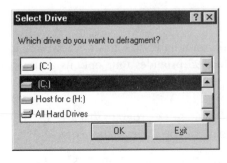

When you first start Disk
Defragmenter, you are asked
to select a drive to defragment.

Once you've selected a drive, click on the OK button to bring up a second dialog box containing four options: Start, Select Drive, Advanced, and Exit. Clicking on Start tells Disk Defragmenter to begin defragmenting the contents of the selected drive. You can monitor Disk Defragmenter's progress by watching the status bar labeled % Complete. Or you can watch the defragmentation process: click on the Show Details button, and an animated map of the disk's contents is displayed in living color (Figure 13.8).

FIGURE 13.8

Viewing Disk Defragmenter's Progress

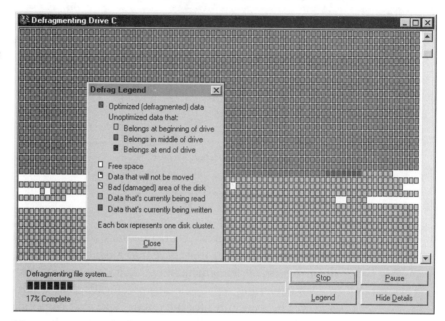

You can see a colorful, animated display of Disk Defragmenter's progress by clicking on the Show Details button.

You can ask Disk Defragmenter to pause at any time by clicking on the Pause button. To abort the defragmentation process—for example, if you need to send an e-mail message immediately—simply click on the Stop button. The Disk Defragmenter warns you if it hasn't finished and asks you to confirm your choice (Figure 13.9). Don't worry—you can stop Disk Defragmenter at any point during the defragmentation process without ill effects.

FIGURE 13.9

Stopping Disk Defragmenter

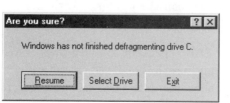

To stop Disk Defragmenter before it has finished, click on the Stop button and verify your choice in the resulting dialog box.

If you click on the Advanced button before clicking on the Start button, Disk Defragmenter brings up its Advanced Options dialog box, which presents you with defragmentation choices. For example, in the Defragmentation Method area, you can choose one of three defragmentation techniques: Full, Defragment Files, and Consolidate Free Space (Figure 13.10).

FIGURE 13.10
The Advanced Options Dialog Box

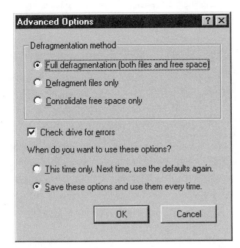

Clicking on the Advanced button brings up the Advanced Options dialog box, which enables you to choose Disk Defragmenter options.

Selecting Full tells Disk Defragmenter both to defragment your disk files and to consolidate any free space into a continuous block. This is the most effective form of defragmentation, but it's also the most time-consuming.

Defragmenting only your files is quicker than a full defragmentation. However, because only files and not free space are consolidated, disk files that you save in the future will probably be even more fragmented.

Consolidating only free space creates a similar problem. While areas of free space are consolidated into contiguous blocks, Disk Defragmenter doesn't concern itself with how this affects existing disk files. As a result, files may actually become more fragmented.

My recommendation? Whenever possible, do a full defragmentation; you'll achieve the most dramatic improvement in disk I/O performance. If you need only a performance boost when you access files, then go ahead and defragment only your files. If what you need is a block of free disk space—for example, so you can install a new program without its files becoming fragmented—use the Consolidate Free Space option.

Danger Zone

The Check Drive for Errors checkbox should always be marked. Disk defragmentation is serious business; lots of data is moved around, and even a minor error in your disk's allocation tables can cause Disk Defragmenter to turn your hard data into digital Jell-O.

· ·

Virtual Memory

The RAM in your PC is a finite resource. With only so many megabytes to go around, sooner or later you're going to run out of system memory. Windows 95 prepares for this inevitability by using a portion of your hard disk as a temporary scratch pad, ready for those times when the amount of memory required by a program exceeds the amount of physical RAM available.

By means of a process known as **virtual memory**, Windows 95 temporarily swaps portions of code and data to and from the hard disk, freeing RAM for use by programs. As a result, you can run more applications and load bigger data files than would be possible given the amount of physical RAM.

How Virtual Memory Works. Windows 95 automatically provides virtual memory for all running applications. The applications themselves are oblivious to the entire virtual-memory process; they simply ask for memory, and Windows 95 gives it to them. The operating system itself deals with how and where to get the memory—whether to allocate it from free physical RAM or to swap code and data from an idle program to disk, creating free physical RAM that in turn can be allocated.

The scheme used to create virtual memory is an ingenious one. Windows 95's virtual-memory system is based on a **Least Recently Used (LRU)** algorithm that determines which programs should be swapped to disk first. Typically, the least active program—for example, a spreadsheet program that has been minimized to the Windows 95 Taskbar and is not receiving any input—is the first to go. Windows 95 copies the program's memory **pages** (the locations in physical RAM that the program occupied) to a paging file on the hard disk, then marks those memory locations as free and usable. Windows can then allocate those pages to another program, satisfying that program's request for more memory.

But what happens when the swapped program becomes active again and needs its pages back? Simple: Windows 95 swaps those pages back into memory from the paging file. If necessary, Windows swaps other pages to disk to make room for the pages it is swapping into memory. This happens over and over again as applications gain or lose favor with the LRU algorithm, based on the amount they are used.

Insider's Tip

As you might imagine, the paging file sees a lot of action on a heavily taxed system. This is one good reason to invest in a speedy hard-disk drive and to maintain it by regularly running the Disk Defragmenter utility.

Changing Virtual-Memory Settings. With prior versions of Windows, you had to be an expert in virtual memory to tune it up properly. Fortunately, Windows 95 features a much-improved virtual-memory subsystem, one that requires almost no tuning. If you keep your disk defragmented and use the ScanDisk utility to keep your hard disk in good health, Windows 95 takes care of the rest.

If, however, you simply can't resist the urge to tinker, an interface to the Windows 95 virtual-memory subsystem is located in the Performance tab of the System Control Panel. To access the interface, open the Control Panel window, then double-click on the System icon and select the Performance tab. Finally, click on the Virtual Memory button to bring up the Virtual Memory dialog box (Figure 13.11).

• • • • • • • • • • • • •
FIGURE 13.11
*The Virtual
Memory
Dialog Box*

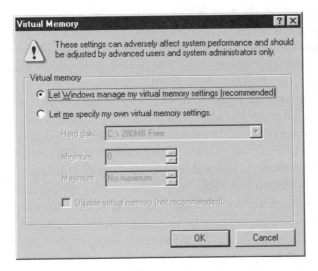

*Virtual-memory
settings are
found in the
Virtual Memory
dialog box,
located in the
Performance tab
of the System
Control Panel.*

This dialog box features a nasty warning, saying that when it comes to configuring virtual memory, Windows 95 usually knows best. Unless you're absolutely certain you want to tinker with this feature, you're better off leaving the Virtual Memory field set to its default position, which is "Let Windows manage my virtual memory settings (recommended)."

Here's one reason you might want to change your virtual-memory settings: what if the hard disk that boots up your computer isn't the fastest drive in your system? Your boot drive is the target for Windows 95's paging file. If this drive isn't your fastest, you may not be using all of your system's virtual-memory potential.

For example, let's say you normally boot from an IDE drive, yet you have also attached a high-performance SCSI disk drive to your system. In this case, you may want to tell Windows 95 to target its paging file to the SCSI drive.

You'll reap the rewards of better virtual-memory performance by virtue of the SCSI drive's higher overall throughput.

To change the target drive for the Windows 95 paging file, click on the radio button labeled "Let me specify my own virtual memory settings." Then select the desired drive from the Hard Disk drop-down list box (Figure 13.12).

FIGURE 13.12

Selecting a
Paging Drive

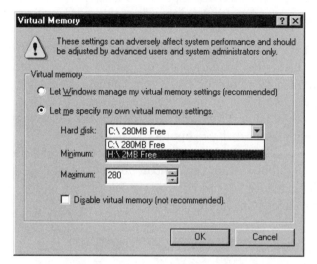

To select a different drive as the target for the Windows 95 paging file, click on the Hard Disk drop-down list box.

You may also want to fine-tune the size of your system's paging file. For example, if you want to force Windows 95 to allocate a certain amount of paging file space at start-up, enter a value into the Minimum field. This ensures that Windows 95 grabs that amount of space automatically instead of expanding the paging file dynamically as demand dictates. The net result can be better overall virtual-memory performance, especially in RAM-starved systems.

Danger Zone

If you want to, you can shut down the Windows 95 virtual-memory system altogether, whether for diagnostic purposes or to conserve power on a notebook computer by minimizing disk activity. To do so, click on the Disable Virtual Memory checkbox. Usually this isn't a good idea because you severely limit Windows 95's flexibility to deal with tight memory situations. In extreme cases Windows 95 can even crash due to a lack of virtual-memory capabilties, so use this setting with caution.

Insider's Tip

Overall, Windows 95 does a good job of managing its virtual-memory settings. In practice, little advantage is gained by manually reconfiguring the way virtual memory works under Windows 95. My recommendation: don't fix what isn't broken.

File System Settings

Previous versions of Windows relied on a DOS-based file system to organize data on storage devices, such as hard and floppy disks. Windows 95 does away with this reliance on DOS, implementing its own powerful 32-bit file system, which is faster than DOS and features additional benefits, such as the ability to use long file-name aliases.

As with virtual memory, Windows 95 itself does a good job of configuring its new file system for optimal performance. However, in some situations, you might want to adjust the file system configuration—for example, if your computer is a file or print server on a network. In such a scenario, you can configure Windows 95 to favor disk and network I/O over other system tasks, improving network throughput for attached clients.

To access the Windows 95 file system settings, load the System Control Panel by double-clicking on its icon in the Control Panel folder, then select the Performance tab and click on the File System button. Up pops the File System dialog box (Figure 13.13).

FIGURE 13.13

The File System Dialog Box

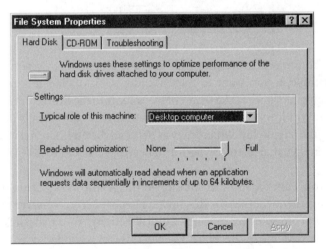

To access the Windows 95 file system settings, click on the File System button on the System Control Panel's Performance page.

The first field, Hard Disk Optimization, enables you to tell Windows 95 how you use your PC. If it's a desktop computer, select Desktop PC. This tells Windows 95 to balance disk I/O demands with other tasks. It is the optimal configuration for a stand-alone system and provides the best overall performance for applications you run from your own hard disk.

If your system is acting as a file and print server on a network, select Network Server to instruct Windows 95 to favor disk and network I/O requests over the requests of local applications. If many other workstations rely on your system for file storage and shared printer access, this option yields the best network throughput.

Finally, if your system is a notebook PC, selecting Mobile or Docking tells Windows 95 to tune its disk I/O activity to minimize battery drain. Few things put more of a strain on notebook batteries than disk I/O, so the fact that the operating system can adjust its behavior to minimize this strain is a real benefit.

The second field of the File System dialog box, CD-ROM Optimization, enables you to determine how Windows 95 caches your CD-ROM drives. A slider control allows you to adjust the size of the cache, in kilobytes. The more memory you set aside, the faster your CD-ROM drive operates. The Optimize Access Pattern list box enables you to tell Windows whether your CD-ROM drive operates at single, double, triple, or quad-speed. The Windows 95 CD-ROM file system can then optimize the way it seeks individual sectors on your CD-ROM drive.

Caching

Windows 95 doesn't just include its own built-in system cache to speed access to file system devices; it also includes an even better feature. In the 32-bit world of Windows 95, a file system device isn't necessarily a hard disk. Network connections and CD-ROM drives are also file system devices—they have their own file system drivers—and so they too are cached by the same, systemwide caching mechanism that speeds disk access. In fact, Windows 95 includes a complete, installable file system interface, so third parties can write their own file system drivers, exploiting the caching capabilities of Windows 95.

Another winning feature of the new caching mechanism is that it can grow to meet your system's needs. That's because the cache size is determined in part by the level of activity in your virtual-memory subsystem. For example, if your PC is suddenly barraged with disk I/O requests from a hungry database program, Windows 95 can adjust the size of its system cache, expanding it on the fly to compensate for the increase in file system activity. Similarly, if the amount of network I/O activity suddenly jumps, the system cache grows to deal with the flood from the wire.

Finally, the system cache in Windows 95 includes a feature commonly referred to as lazy writing. This means the operating system occasionally postpones writing data to disk to improve the responsiveness of applications running in the foreground. Later, when Windows 95 detects that the system is idle or when a predefined time limit is reached, Windows writes the data to disk in the background, letting you continue to work in the foreground without interruption.

Insider's Tip

> Because the Windows 95 caching subsystem is completely self-tuning and is installed automatically, you never need to fiddle with configuration switches. It's one of the nicer no-brainer attributes of Windows 95.

DriveSpace

It's inevitable. With the advent of Windows 95 and all those feature-rich Win32 applications, some of us are going to run out of disk space. It's as unavoidable as death and taxes, and running out of disk space can leave you unable to finish that already delayed presentation—a fate worse than death.

Fortunately, just as you can sometimes defer death and taxes, Windows 95 can help you delay a disk-space crisis with **DriveSpace**, Microsoft's home-grown and now patent-infringement-free disk compression technology. In a nutshell, DriveSpace compresses a portion of your hard disk so that it can hold more data. The new, compressed portion of the disk appears to the computer to be another mass storage device, complete with its own drive letter and directory structure. In reality, the DriveSpace "drive" is nothing more than a hidden file stored on the original, or host, hard disk. Windows 95 creates the illusion that the DriveSpace volume is a real drive to make it easier for applications to interact with it.

For example, to copy files to a DriveSpace volume, you use the same drag-and-drop techniques as you do when you copy between real hard disks. The DriveSpace volume appears as another hard disk in My Computer, and you can manipulate it as you would a genuine disk. Similarly, the File Open dialog boxes in application programs can't tell the difference between a DriveSpace drive and a real hard disk; to the dialog boxes, the DriveSpace drive looks just like the real McCoy.

When you copy files to a DriveSpace volume, they are automatically compressed by means of an algorithm that removes redundant characters and blank spaces in the file's contents. Those redundant items are replaced by more-compact **symbols** (code characters that represent larger constructs), and the new, **compressed file** is stored in the DriveSpace volume.

As a result of this compression process, a DriveSpace volume can store more data within its confines than a real hard disk drive of equivalent size. For example, a 250MB DriveSpace volume can often store 350MB or more of data, whereas a real 250MB hard disk is limited to its stated capacity. So by compressing a region of a disk, or even the entire disk, you effectively add to its net capacity. It's like getting a bigger hard disk for free.

Insider's Tip

Because the capacity of a DriveSpace volume depends on its ability to compress incoming data, and because different file types—for example, documents, programs, and worksheets—vary in their compressibility, no way exists to determine exactly how much data a particular DriveSpace volume can hold. It all depends on the type of files you store there. For this reason Windows 95 offers an estimate instead of a hard number when reporting how much room you have on a specific DriveSpace volume. In practice, you may or may not get that much data to fit on the volume.

Make a DriveSpace Volume. You can create and manage DriveSpace volumes with the DriveSpace applet, which is located on the System Tools submenu of the Start menu. If this is the first time you're running DriveSpace, you're presented with a window similar to the one in Figure 13.14.

FIGURE 13.14

*The
DriveSpace
Applet*

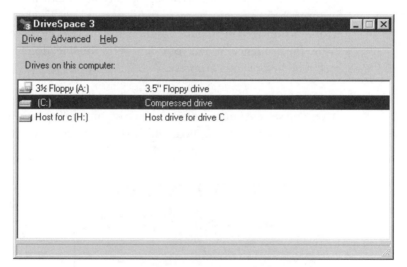

You create and manage DriveSpace volumes with the
DriveSpace applet, which is located on the System
Tools submenu of the Start menu.

The Drives listing includes all available disk drives on your PC. Notice that only physical hard disk drives are listed; DriveSpace cannot create a compressed volume on a network drive or on what it considers a simulated volume.

At this point, you must decide whether you want to compress the entire contents of a drive or create a new, empty DriveSpace volume that occupies only part of a drive. To compress an existing disk drive, the drive's entire capacity is devoted to the DriveSpace volume. As DriveSpace compresses the drive, it moves existing file and directory information onto the new Drive-Space volume, compressing the information in the process. DriveSpace then swaps drive letters around so that the newly created DriveSpace volume appears to be the original hard disk, only fatter, while the original drive acquires a new drive letter.

For example, if you compress drive D, the newly created DriveSpace volume is assigned the drive letter D. The original, or host, drive is assigned a different drive letter, such as H or I, and for all practical purposes it ceases to exist as a storage volume. You can still access it if you like, but it will appear to be completely full, which is exactly the case: the DriveSpace volume's hidden file is occupying almost every megabyte of the original drive.

Danger Zone

Before compressing an existing disk drive, you should first back up your data and run ScanDisk on the drive. DriveSpace automatically checks your drive for errors before compressing it and is particularly good at recovering from errors encountered during the compression process. However, there's no substitute for prudence. When your data is on the line, don't take any chances: back it up before you compress.

To compress an existing drive, simply highlight it in the list of available drives and select Compress from the Drive menu. You are presented with the Compress a Drive dialog box, which shows before and after shots of your drive's capacity characteristics (Figure 13.15).

FIGURE 13.15
The Compress a Drive Dialog Box

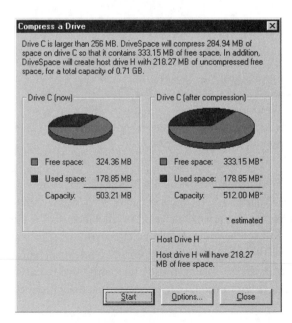

The Compress a Drive dialog box presents you with pictures of your drive's capacity characteristics before and after compression.

Be forewarned: the so-called after shot represents DriveSpace's estimate of how much free space you can expect. Compression is an inexact science, so don't be surprised if you find that DriveSpace's promise of 100MB turns out to be more in the range of 60 to 70MB. DriveSpace tends toward the optimistic when it estimates potential free disk space.

Clicking on the Options button brings up the Compression Options dialog box. This dialog box allows you to fine-tune the DriveSpace process (Figure 13.16)

· · · · · · · · · · · · · ·
FIGURE 13.16
*Compression
Options*

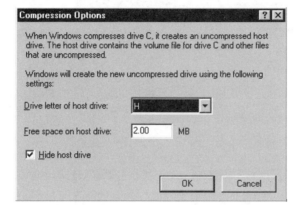

*To make detailed
adjustments to
DriveSpace
compression, bring
up the Compression
Options dialog box.*

For example, the Drive Letter of Host drop-down list box lets you assign a drive letter to the uncompressed, or host, drive. In the same way, the Free Space on Host Drive field enables you to specify how much of the original drive should be left uncompressed. By default DriveSpace leaves 2MB uncompressed, but you can increase this value.

Finally, the Hide Host Drive checkbox tells DriveSpace to hide the original drive from application programs and My Computer. If you've compressed an entire hard disk, this completes the illusion that the new DriveSpace volume is indeed the original and diminishes the chance you might accidentally access the host drive instead of the new DriveSpace volume.

When you're ready to begin the compression process, click on the Start button. DriveSpace displays a progress indicator while it's working. When DriveSpace has finished, it tells you to reboot your system so that the new Drive-Space configuration can take effect.

Creating a New DriveSpace Volume.   Whereas compressing an existing drive moves that drive's data onto a new DriveSpace volume, creating an empty DriveSpace volume does exactly the opposite; it allocates some of your hard disk's free space to a new, empty DriveSpace volume. This volume is assigned its own drive letter independent of the original, and you can access it just as you would any other drive.

To create a new, empty DriveSpace volume that occupies only part of an existing drive, highlight the name of the appropriate drive, then select Create Empty from the Advanced menu. You are presented with the Create New Compressed Drive dialog box, which lets you specify the exact dimensions of the new volume (Figure 13.17).

••••••••••••••
FIGURE 13.17
The Create New Compressed Drive Dialog Box

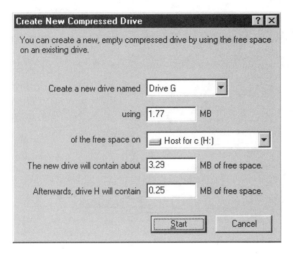

To create a new DriveSpace volume in an area of free space on an existing drive, select Create Empty from the Advanced menu.

For example, to create a 50MB DriveSpace volume on disk drive D, select a new drive letter from the Create a New Drive Name list box, specify 50 in the Using field, and then select the D drive icon from the Free Space On list box. The other fields—The New Drive Contains About and Afterwards, Drive D Will Contain—are completed automatically with information based on DriveSpace's own estimates. Click on the Start button, and DriveSpace creates a volume to your specifications.

Maintaining DriveSpace Volumes. Once you've created a DriveSpace volume, you can use the DriveSpace applet to perform maintenance tasks. For example, to keep track of the volume's compression ratio—that is, how much DriveSpace has been able to compress the data in that volume—double-click on its entry in the Drives on This Computer field (or select Properties from the Drive menu). This brings up the volume's Compression Properties sheet (Figure 13.18). Other interesting bits of information in the Compression Properties sheet include the physical location of the DriveSpace hidden file, the amount of free and used space in the volume, and a checkbox indicating whether DriveSpace is hiding the host drive.

FIGURE 13.18

Viewing the Properties of a Compressed Drive

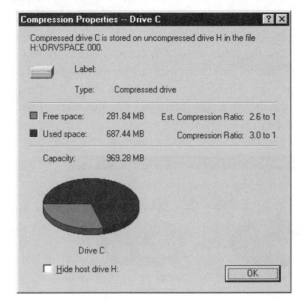

To view the compression ratio of a DriveSpace volume, double-click on its entry in the Drives on This Computer field to bring up the volume's Compression Properties sheet.

You can also adjust the estimated compression ratio for a particular Drive-Space volume. This governs how much free space Windows 95 reports for that volume when you browse in My Computer or the Explorer. To change the estimated compression ratio—for example, if you know you're going to store highly compressible data on the volume and thus can make the estimate more optimistic—highlight the volume in the Drives field and select Change Ratio from the Advanced menu. This brings up the Change Ratio dialog box (Figure 13.19). To adjust the ratio, move the slider control in the desired direction.

FIGURE 13.19

Changing the Estimated Compression Ratio

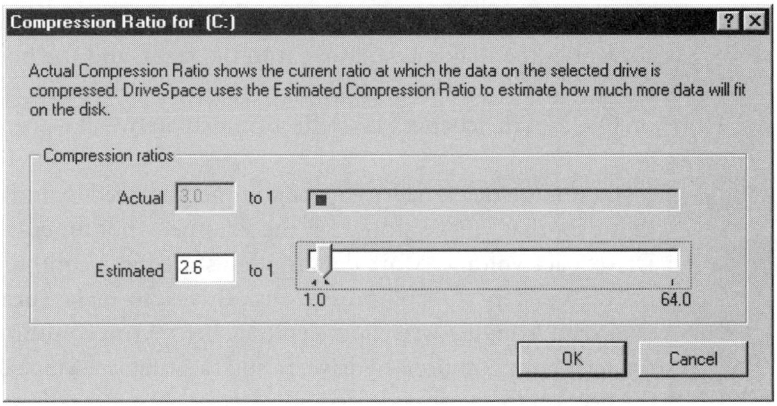

> **Compression Ratio for (C:)**
>
> Actual Compression Ratio shows the current ratio at which the data on the selected drive is compressed. DriveSpace uses the Estimated Compression Ratio to estimate how much more data will fit on the disk.
>
> Compression ratios
>
> Actual `3.0` to 1
>
> Estimated `2.6` to 1   1.0 ___ 64.0
>
> OK   Cancel

To change the estimated compression ratio, select Change Ratio from the Advanced menu and adjust the slider as needed.

You might sometimes need to adjust the size of a DriveSpace volume—for example, when you require more free space on the host drive and thus need to shrink the volume's hidden file. As long as you have enough free space in a DriveSpace volume to compensate for a loss in overall size, you can adjust the volume's size. Highlight the volume in the Drives field and select Adjust Free Space from the Drive menu to open the Adjust Free Space dialog box (Figure 13.20).

• • • • • • • • • • • • • •
FIGURE 13.20
The Adjust Free Space Dialog Box

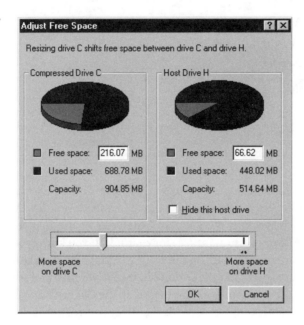

To adjust the size of a DriveSpace volume's hidden file, simply move the slider control in the dialog box.

To adjust the size of a DriveSpace volume's hidden file, move the slider control in the dialog box. Move it to the right, and the host drive gains free space. Move it to the left, and the DriveSpace volume increases in size. Click on OK, and the changes take effect immediately.

Danger Zone

If you want to delete a DriveSpace volume, you need to find a place for important data that you've stored on the volume—not an easy task with a large DriveSpace volume. More data is often stored in a compressed volume than fits on a system's uncompressed disk drives, so make sure you can transfer your data from the DriveSpace volume before you commit to creating a particularly large compressed drive. In such a situation, a tape drive or a network connection to a well-endowed file server can be a real lifesaver.

Once your data is safe, you can delete a DriveSpace volume by highlighting it in the Drives field and selecting Delete from the Advanced menu. DriveSpace displays a dialog box warning you of the dire consequences of your action: once you delete a DriveSpace volume, any data stored on the volume is lost forever. Be absolutely certain you've transferred anything important before proceeding.

Three final options—Mount, Unmount, and Change Drive Letter—enable you to activate, deactivate (hide), and change the drive letter of a volume. All three options are located on the Advanced menu.

· ·

Heap Space in Windows 95

I saved the bad news for last. Just when you thought Windows 95—with its virtual memory, 32-bit file systems, and dynamic disk caching—could provide deliverance from the 16-bit memory limitations imposed by Windows 3.1, here come the final holdovers, creating barricades to greater memory use: the **GDI heap** and the **USER heap.** Those heaps are two 64K chunks of RAM that limit the number of Windows applications you can run at one time— particularly applications containing lots of graphics or interface components. If you try to run more applications than either of the two heaps can hold, your system can freeze or crash.

The Windows 95 Graphics Device Interface module (GDI.EXE) uses the GDI heap to store the handles and pointers to graphics objects such as brushes, pens, bit maps, buttons, and other graphic regions that make up the Windows graphical interface. GDI.EXE also manages certain printing functions. Programs that use complex toolbars or perform many graphics manipulations can quickly consume this 64K.

The USER heap is used by the window-management module (USER.EXE) to store components of the user interface, such as the windows themselves. Thus each time you open a window, you consume some of the USER heap.

The About command on the Help menu of most Windows 95 applications contains a report, called System Resources, that lists the percentage of free memory available to your GDI and USER heaps. When you first start Windows, your free system resources are reported as somewhere between 90 and 100 percent, depending on how many windows and icons are displayed. Each application you start usually consumes between 5 and 10 percent of your free system resources, and each open folder or Explorer view also consumes a few percentage points. To see how much of your free system resources an application consumes, check the About box, then open the application and check the percentage in the About box again.

The 64K heap limitation is imposed by the underlying System Virtual Machine design that has been held over from Windows 3.1; you have to buy Windows NT to escape from this constraint. Even if your system has 32 megabytes of RAM and tens of megabytes of virtual memory, you can use only a fraction of it if you run applications that consume too much of your GDI and USER heap space.

Windows 95 does improve heap space problems considerably over previous versions by moving many of the interface components into newer, 32-bit heaps. However, compatibility with existing 16-bit applications has mandated that Windows 95 retain some of the heap characteristics of Windows 3.1. In practice you'll find that you can do a lot more with Windows 95 than you could with Windows 3.1 before you run out of system resources. Still, the limitation exists, and if you run many concurrent programs, it's a good idea to keep an eye on your available system resources.

Summary

The performance of Windows 95 and the applications you run within it ultimately depends on the quality of your hardware. Key among hardware components are the processor, memory, and the hard-disk drive. Microsoft has attempted to make its operating system compatible with as much as possible of the varied hardware available today, but you must learn how to tweak your hardware to achieve optimum performance.

When you select a processor, you should consider the types of applications you use and base your decision on the performance criteria your system needs to meet. I suggest a fast 486 as a minimum for serious Windows users.

Memory is the second most important factor in determining system performance. Internal memory is stored in either RAM or ROM chips. Although it's never possible to have too much RAM, where you place your RAM chips can also have a marked effect on operation. Windows 95 operates best with extended memory. Windows 95 can also use some of your hard disk to create virtual memory, which fools your system into thinking you have extra RAM.

Because Windows 95 makes greater demands on your system's memory resources than previous versions did, you want to have the fastest hard disk you can afford to accelerate your access to virtual memory. Windows 95 introduces new features for expanding memory, including virtual memory, high-speed caching, and DriveSpace—Microsoft's very own compression technology. Most of those memory expanders work automatically, so little tinkering is left for the user; in fact, I advise you to keep your hands off the workings of Windows 95 except in a few special cases. Finally, although Windows 95 removes many of the problems caused by an archaic DOS carryover that imposes 640K limitations on key system resources, you still have to be careful when you run many programs at the same time. The ghost of DOS still lingers in Windows 95.

14

Integrating Applications with DDE and OLE

Without becoming a programmer, you can now integrate information created by one program into a document created by another program. To accomplish this legerdemain, Windows 95 offers three tools: the Clipboard, DDE, and OLE. As the primary mechanism for transferring information from one program to another, the **Clipboard** enables you to use the cut (or copy) and paste commands to capture information from one program and shuttle it to another. Once transferred to another program, the original information abandons all ties to its program of origin and becomes incorporated into the new document in a static form. The Clipboard works with most Windows applications and even enables you to exchange a limited amount of information with DOS programs.

DDE (Dynamic Data Exchange) is a rung higher on the ladder of data-sharing techniques. DDE not only enables programs to communicate with each other through Windows 95, it also includes a standard language in which Windows applications can send messages directly to each other. For example, you can use DDE to link numerical information in a spreadsheet to data in a word-processing document; as the data in the spreadsheet changes, the corresponding numbers in the word-processing document are updated automatically.

OLE (Object Linking and Embedding, pronounced "oh-lay") combines the functions of the Clipboard and DDE, enabling applications to share information in an even more powerful way. Information from one document can be either embedded into or linked to another document. For example, you can embed a picture into a word-processing document, double-click on the picture to bring up the graphics application that created the picture, then use that application to edit the picture. With linking, the actual data is stored only in the source file.

This chapter demonstrates how the Clipboard, DDE, and OLE work together to help you integrate information from multiple applications. I also describe how to use a utility called **Object Packager** to manage OLE links.

. . . .

The Clipboard

The Clipboard plays an integral role in Windows 95 operations. With the Clipboard, you can easily cut or copy information from a document created in one application, switch to another application, and transfer the information by pasting it. Together with DDE and OLE, the Clipboard also enables you to cut and paste together data from multiple applications to create a document. Furthermore, if all those applications support OLE, the data in your final document can be linked to the program that created it. This lets you call on that program in case you need to edit or alter the data.

The ability to cut and paste information easily among documents from different applications gives Windows 95 a distinct advantage over DOS. In addition, when you run a DOS program from Windows 95, the Clipboard provides a bridge between Windows 95 and DOS. You can paste text and sometimes graphics from DOS programs into Windows documents and, under certain conditions, paste text from a Windows document into a DOS application.

The Clipboard accepts data in a variety of formats, which enables it to work with almost every Windows application. However, the receiving application may not always understand the data you try to transfer in. For example, Notepad accepts text but not graphics. The common forms of data that the Clipboard can handle are described in Table 14.1.

• • • • • • • • • • • • •
TABLE 14.1
What the
Clipboard
Accepts:
Data in
Many Formats

Data Format	Description
Text	Unformatted text. Text is transferred as standard ANSI character values. Characters change appearance (but not ANSI values) when the original and receiving documents use different fonts. You can reselect the original font to restore the document's previous appearance. Text is displayed in the Clipboard Viewer in the font specified in the FONTS.FON= statement in SYSTEM.INI.
OEM text	Unformatted text composed of OEM characters (rather than ANSI characters). OEM text is displayed in the Clipboard Viewer in the font specified in the OEMFONTS.FON= statement in SYSTEM.INI.
RTF text	Text stored in Microsoft's Rich Text format. RTF text includes formatting, such as typeface, font size, bold, italic, and underline.
Display text	Provides information about the data on the Clipboard but does not actually display the data. For example, identifies a region of an Excel spreadsheet.
SYLK data	Tabular data—for example, from a spreadsheet or a database—that uses Microsoft's SYmbolic LinK format.
WK1 data	Tabular data from a spreadsheet that uses the Lotus 1-2-3 WK1 format.
CSV data	Tabular data that uses the Comma Separated Values format.
DIF data	Tabular data that uses the Data Interchange Format.
BIFF data	Tabular data that uses Microsoft's Binary Interchange File Format. This is the file format used by Excel.

· · · · · · · · · · · · · · ·
TABLE 14.1 (*cont.*)
What the
Clipboard
Accepts:
Data in
Many Formats

Data Format	Description
Bit-map graphics	Bit-mapped graphic images of specific resolutions, composed of many small pixels. A color palette must accompany an image for it to be displayed in its original colors. The images are device-dependent; that is, each graphic can be displayed only on one type of device, such as a VGA monitor.
Palette	A color palette. Most palettes in Windows contain 256 colors, even if the display cannot show that many. A palette determines which colors create an image and can vary from image to image.
DIB graphics	Bit-mapped graphic images saved in the Device Independent Bitmap format. These are 256-color images and are not device-dependent.
TIFF graphics	Bit-mapped graphic images that conform to the Tagged Image File Format. TIFF files often contain their own color (or grayscale) information, so you don't need to coordinate color palettes when you transfer files between computers.
Picture	Windows Metafile graphic images. Metafile images are independent of particular devices and resolutions because they are stored as GDI graphics instructions, not as bit maps.
Wave audio	Digitized sound files compatible with the .wav files used by Windows 95's multimedia extensions.
Owner	A format available in either a text or a graphics mode. The Owner format relies on the source application to display data; if the source application is not running, the data cannot be displayed in the Clipboard Viewer.
Native	The source application's native data format. This is often the binary format in which the application saves data to files.
Link	A data format used by applications that support DDE. Supplies receiving applications with information on how to link data to its source files.
ObjectLink	A data format used by OLE server applications to provide client applications with the information needed to create linked objects.
OwnerLink	A data format used by OLE server applications to provide client applications with the information needed to create embedded objects.

The Clipboard can also accept unique data formats from specific applications. Applications sending information to the Clipboard in such formats instruct the Clipboard on how to deal with the data, and the Clipboard stores the data as raw bits. If it doesn't recognize or understand the information, the Clipboard still accepts and stores the data until you either save it or paste it into another location.

When you cut or copy information to the Clipboard, the **source application** determines how to format the data. Occasionally the source application uses a single data format, such as text. More often the application sends the image to the Clipboard in more than one format—for example, in text, RTF, and Owner formats.

The **destination application** determines which format to use when the application accepts data from the Clipboard. For example, Notepad accepts only the unformatted text version of plain text, whereas Microsoft Word might use the RTF version, which includes formatting. The Clipboard Viewer's Display menu lists the data formats used by an application to place information on the Clipboard (Figure 14.1).

The Display menu for Excel shown in Figure 14.1 includes some items that are dimmed. Data can be pasted into an application in those formats, but they cannot be viewed. To view any of the other formats, select them from the menu. The destination application determines which format to accept from among the formats that Excel provides to the Clipboard. For example, the Paint applet can accept only a bit-mapped image of an Excel spreadsheet, whereas WordPad can accept the same spreadsheet in a variety of formats, ranging from unformatted text to a bit map, a picture, or even a complete spreadsheet.

Some formats, such as Owner, are available only if the source application is running. Other formats are supplied only if the destination application requests them, in which case the source application must also be running to translate the data into the requested format. If you quit Excel, for example, only the formats listed in the Display menu are available for transfer (Figure 14.2). Indeed, the data you select in Excel before you quit it determines which formats remain on the Clipboard.

FIGURE 14.1

Display Menu with Excel Data

The Clipboard Viewer's Display menu lists the formats in which the source application (in this case, Excel) places its data onto the Clipboard.

FIGURE 14.2
*Display Menu
After You Quit
Excel*

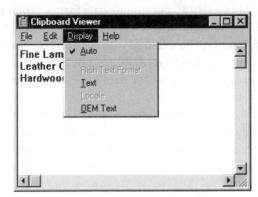

*When the source
application isn't
running, fewer
formats are available
on the Display menu.*

Dynamic Data Exchange

Dynamic Data Exchange, or DDE, enables applications to exchange information interactively. DDE is a two-headed beast. One head enables programs to
communicate with one another within the operating system—that is, within
Windows 95. The other head provides Windows 95 applications with a standard language in which to send messages to each other. Those two elements
combine to form a powerful yet flexible system for integrating applications.

The version of DDE that came with Windows 3.0 lacked stability. To
Windows 3.1 Microsoft added DDEML, the DDE Management Library,
which provides programming tools that help DDE work more consistently
from application to application. Software developers can use this library
rather than develop a DDE implementation from scratch. The library resides
in the Windows 95 \SYSTEM subdirectory inside the DDEML.DLL file. If that file
is damaged or missing, DDE may not work properly with applications that
require it.

What DDE Can Do

DDE goes beyond linking data; it enables applications to work together on a
variety of tasks. Basically, DDE enables one program to take advantage of the
services that another program has to offer. For example, Windows 95 Setup
uses DDE to communicate with the desktop to create new Start menu submenus and icons. In a more sophisticated scenario, DDE could be used to log
onto Dow Jones, extract the latest financial data about selected companies,
transfer the data into an Excel spreadsheet, then transform the data into a

summary table. The table in turn could be pasted into a memo, then faxed to some people and e-mailed to others.

With a macro language, such as Word Basic in Microsoft Word, you can automate the entire process—as long as your Windows applications support DDE. In the Dow Jones scenario, one message could tell Windows 95 to carry out all the following tasks:

➡ Run a telecommunications program, log onto the on-line service, download the financial data, and save it in a data file.

➡ Send DDE messages to start the spreadsheet, open the data file, perform calculations on the downloaded data, and create the summary table.

➡ Send DDE messages to select the summary table and paste it into the word-processing document.

➡ Use DDE to open the fax program, transfer the memo into the program, select from the dialing directory who will receive the faxes, and send the faxes.

➡ Use DDE to open the e-mail program, transfer the memo into it, look up e-mail addresses, and send the e-mail.

To work with such a macro, applications must provide solid support for DDE. Applications with robust DDE and internal macro support offer the most power for integrating and automating applications. Unfortunately, DDE support is difficult to implement and varies from application to application, ranging from nonexistent to static cut-and-paste operations to extensive implementation with access to most of the functions of the application. You have to check an application's documentation to determine exactly what level of DDE support is provided and how it is implemented.

How DDE Works

DDE involves the cooperation of two programs, the **client** and the **server.** The client application uses DDE to request information or services, and the server application provides the requested information or services. A Windows application can be designed as a client, a server, or both.

In a typical DDE session, the client sends a request to the server, which responds by either performing a function or sending the requested data. This process is called a **conversation.** A DDE conversation usually involves three elements:

➤ **An application.** Normally the name of the program acting as server.

➤ **A topic.** The class of data or service that the server provides. Often the topic is one of the server's documents.

➤ **An item.** The data or service provided.

Here's an example. The client is Word, which requests a table from an Excel spreadsheet file named BIGMONEY.XLS. Excel is the server, and the DDE conversation breaks down as follows:

➤ The application is EXCEL.EXE.

➤ The topic is BIGMONEY.XLS.

➤ The item is the range of cells that contains the table.

The DDE conversation can also include other messages, which sometimes go by different names. For example, if an application uses the DDE Memory Library, the application is called the service.

Normally DDE conversations are carried out unheard and unseen between the client and the server. All you have to do is select the information in the server, copy it to the Clipboard, and use Paste Link or Paste Special to place the data into the client. However, you need to understand the semantics of a DDE conversation if you want to use DDE with another macro or batch language.

When you link information from a server to a client, you choose between two types of software links: **hot links** and warm links. If you link information between two applications that are both running hot links, the client is updated as soon as server data changes. With warm links, in contrast, changes are made to client data only when the client requests an update. If the server is running but the client document is closed, the client's information is not updated.

➤ **Hot links.** Automatically updates clients whenever server data is changed.

➤ **Warm links.** Makes changes only if the client requests an update from the server.

To prevent obsolescence of linked data, a dialog box appears whenever you open a client document to ask whether you want to update the links in that document. If you respond in the affirmative, both warm and hot links are updated. Since server applications must be running to update links, the client starts them up.

Object Linking and Embedding

Object Linking and Embedding is a powerful way to share information among applications. It combines the cut, copy, and paste functions of the Clipboard with the interactive capabilities of DDE. By embedding or linking data into a document with OLE, you can build a document that contains data from a variety of applications. Such a document is called a **compound document.**

OLE enables you to view or edit data in a compound document without knowing what applications created the original data. When you double-click on data in a compound document, the application used to create the data starts up automatically, ready for you to edit the data. When you finish editing, you close the application to return to the compound document.

OLE represents a major step in the evolution of computing. No longer are you limited to a single application that works with only a single type of data, such as words or graphics. OLE frees you to create and work with documents that incorporate many kinds of data from various applications. Compound documents can even assume a multimedia dimension, incorporating sound, animation, and digital video.

Uses for OLE

OLE enables you to create your own integrated software. Traditional integrated software, such as Microsoft Works, will become obsolete, because you'll be able to combine whatever software you like, from general-purpose to specialized, to create custom packages. This ability to combine programs will allow people to personalize their PCs into a countless number of configurations.

OLE makes it easy for organizations to develop in-house applications. A business can tap off-the-shelf applications for the key functions of a custom system. Only a small program then needs to be written to meet the unique needs of the organization.

You can put OLE to work in a variety of ways. At one end of the spectrum, you can create a "smart" Clipboard that remembers which applications created the data you have pasted into a document. At the other end, you can build complex, interlinked compound documents, which can form the core of an entire management information system.

You can stuff vast quantities of information into a tiny OLE package, which can be represented on screen as an icon or as another type of simple graphic image. Such packages can contain documents that in turn contain icons linked to other documents. In this way, OLE enables you to build a hypertext—or more accurately, a hypermedia—information system, which you navigate by clicking on linked icons.

OLE Terminology

As an emerging standard, OLE has spawned its own vocabulary:

- **Object.** A self-contained unit of information. An object can encompass a single cell of a spreadsheet, an entire data file, or a complete application. Objects can usually be edited or played.

- **Edit.** To edit the data represented by an object, using the server application that created the data.

- **Play.** To activate the data represented by an object, using the server application. Play can involve, for example, displaying a graphic image, playing an audio file, showing an animation, or playing a video sequence.

- **Package.** An iconic or graphic representation of an object. Packages are created by the Object Packager, often as a way to encapsulate data created by a non-OLE application.

- **Embed.** To place both the native and presentation data of an object into an OLE client.

- **Link.** To place the presentation data for an object into an OLE client, along with a pointer to the file that contains the object.

- **Broken link.** The result when a link to a source file is moved, deleted, or intentionally broken with the Links dialog box.

- **Link maintenance.** Use of the Links dialog box to repair broken links, change links, or break links.

- **Server.** Any Windows application that can create OLE objects to embed or link into client documents.

- **Client.** Any Windows application that can accept, display, and store objects pasted into it by an OLE server application. Only clients can create compound documents.

- **Verb.** Describes the actions that a server can perform on its data. The most common verbs are edit and play.

➻ **Native data.** Information you can edit or play, stored in the server's native data format. Typically, this is binary data that the application would save in a disk file.

➻ **Presentation data.** Information that a client uses only to display an object. Presentation data cannot be played or edited.

➻ **Source.** The data file in the server application that contains the original object.

➻ **Destination.** The document file into which you paste an object. Also called a compound document.

➻ **Registry.** A series of files that contain information about all the OLE server applications installed in your system. Windows uses this information to determine how to manipulate data objects for both OLE and drag-and-drop operations. The Registry Editor utility enables you to view and edit the Registry.

➻ **Visual editing.** The process by which an OLE client application takes on the personality of the server application, enabling the user to edit an embedded or linked object in place within a compound document.

How OLE Works

Information from a **source document** can be embedded in or linked to a **destination document.** The information itself is the object and can be almost any type of data, instructions, or software. The application used to create the information is the server, and the program into which the object is pasted is called the client.

To capture an object for embedding or linking, select the desired data in the source document and use either the Copy or the Cut command in the server application to place the information onto the Clipboard. The Copy command enables you both to link and to embed data, whereas the Cut command enables you only to embed data. To embed an object, use the Paste Special command in the client application to place the contents of the Clipboard into the destination document. To link the object, use either the Paste Link or the Paste Special command.

Embedding an object places a copy of the data into the client that includes both native and presentation data. The native data can be played or edited, whereas the presentation data serves merely as a visual placeholder in the destination document.

When you double-click on an embedded object, one of two things happens. If the OLE applications are old (that is, if they are based on the pre–Windows 95, OLE 1.0 specification), then the server application appears in its own window with the object already loaded and ready to edit or play. If the OLE applications are relatively current (that is, if they are based on the OLE 2.0 specification), then the client takes on the personality of the server. The client's menus and toolbars change to reflect the capabilities of the server, and you can edit the object in place within the compound document, a process known as *visual editing*. In either case, if you do edit the object, its original (the one in the server's source document) is not updated.

Linking an object inserts a **software pointer** into the client. The pointer directs the client to the server application and to the file that contains the object. Native data is not placed in the destination document. A linked object includes presentation data so that the client document can display the linked data.

As with embedding, double-clicking on a linked object brings up the server with the object ready to edit or play. The difference between embedding and linking is that changes made to a linked object automatically affect all the documents that contain linked copies of that object. In addition, visual editing, which is a popular option for embedded objects, is not available for editing linked objects; the source application itself is launched in its entirety in a separate window, and you edit the data in the context of its source document.

A package is a type of object that can be represented by an icon or almost any other graphic element. A package can contain an OLE object from a server application, data from a non-OLE application in the form of a file, and even DOS command lines.

OLE Clients and OLE Servers

An OLE client bears the burden of managing compound documents, whereas the server maintains the responsibility for editing and playing embedded and linked objects. Because a client can accept information that it knows nothing about, current OLE client applications will retain compatibility with future OLE servers.

According to software developers, it's fairly straightforward to create OLE server applications, and most applications that support OLE will likely do so as servers. An OLE client application is harder to develop because it has to create complex compound documents, as well as deal with the intricacies of visual editing.

An OLE server can create an OLE object and can also edit or play that object when you select it in a client. To create an object, select the information in the source document, then capture the object with either the Copy or the Cut command on the Edit menu.

If you use Copy, the information is transferred to the Clipboard in the broadest range of formats. A client can almost always use data that has been copied to create an embedded object, and a client can often use copied data to create a link to the source document. If you use Cut, the data is removed from the source document and placed on the Clipboard in a more limited range of formats. Because the data is removed from the source, a client cannot link to it; however, a client can create an embedded object with cut data.

Once you have copied or cut an object from the server onto the Clipboard, you can use the Clipboard Viewer's Display menu to see which data formats the server has provided for the object. The Clipboard section earlier in this chapter lists the most common data formats. A server usually provides the following formats for data objects:

➤ The native format of the server.

➤ The presentation format, in which the client to displays the object.

➤ Other standard formats (such as bit-map, picture, or text) with which the server can work.

➤ The OwnerLink format necessary for embedding. This format identifies the application that created the object, and the class to which the object belongs.

➤ The ObjectLink format necessary for linking. This format identifies the class to which the object belongs and the document that contains the linked object.

If the OwnerLink or ObjectLink format isn't in the Viewer, you can paste only a static copy of the data into the destination document—that is, the data cannot be linked or embedded. If the ObjectLink format isn't available, you can embed the object but cannot link it.

The Client Side of OLE

You realize the benefits of OLE when you use client applications. With a client you can build compound documents, assembling, organizing, and viewing information created by a diverse assortment of applications. When you have copied or cut information from an OLE server, you can switch to a client and paste the OLE object into a compound document. The nature of the data you paste into a destination document depends on which form of the Paste command you select from the client's Edit menu:

➻ **Paste.** The client checks which Clipboard data formats are available for the object, using the first compatible data format it locates.

➻ **Paste Special.** A dialog box lists the data formats available for information currently on the Clipboard. Depending on which formats are listed, you can choose either to embed or link the object or to paste the data in one of the raw data formats without creating an object.

➻ **Paste Link.** If the ObjectLink format is available on the Clipboard, a linked object is placed in the destination document.

The Paste Command. Use the Paste command when your goal is to embed an object. If the OwnerLink format is available, the Paste command usually embeds the object into the destination document. When an object is embedded, the client stores its raw data, a presentation data format for the object, and additional information, such as the object's printing requirements and the identity of the server that created the object.

Insider's Tip

In some cases you can embed an object even if the OwnerLink format isn't available. If the Paste Special menu option isn't dimmed, select it and see if the dialog box lists an appropriate object type for embedding or linking.

The Paste Special and Paste Link Commands. You use the Paste Special command to control how the information on the Clipboard is pasted into the destination document. Issuing this command brings up the Paste Special dialog box (Figure 14.3).

FIGURE 14.3
Paste Special Dialog Box with Multiple Formats

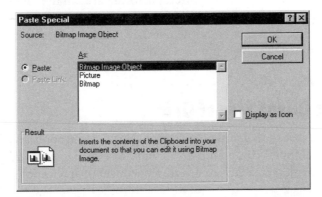

The Paste Special command in OLE clients brings up this dialog box, which enables you to control how information is pasted into a destination document.

The As: box inside the Paste Special dialog box lists the data formats available for the information currently stored on the Clipboard; the default format is highlighted. You can replace the default by selecting an alternative format.

To embed or link the information, select a format that ends with the word *object,* such as Paintbrush Picture Object. Then select the Paste radio button if you want to create an embedded object or the Paste Link radio button, if it's available, if you want to create a linked object. Clicking on OK completes the operation.

Some OLE clients include a Paste Link command on the Edit menu. However, if you want to use this command, either the OwnerLink or the Link data format must be present on the Clipboard. If only the Link format is available, the information is inserted as DDE data instead of OLE data.

To create a static copy of the information, select a format from the As: list that does not end in the word *object*—for example, Bitmap, Picture, or Text. Then click on the OK button to place the unattached copy of the data into your destination document.

Embedded Objects.

When you use the Paste or Paste Special command to embed an object along with all its native data, the embedded object does not maintain any connection to its server. Therefore any changes you make to an embedded object have no effect on the original data in the server document, and any changes to the server document do not affect the embedded object.

The client receives from the Clipboard three types of data, which together form the embedded OLE object:

➤ The **native data** that is understood only by the server.

➤ **Display data** (such as text or a bit map) that the client uses to display the object on screen. If the embedded object is a package, the display data can be an icon or other graphic image.

➤ Information contained in the OwnerLink format that identifies the data by its **object class**—for example, Bitmap Image Object or Excel Worksheet Object.

To activate an embedded object, double-click on it. This causes the client to search the OLE entries in the Registry for the associated server. OLE then opens the server, either by launching the program (in the case of an older OLE application) or by altering the client's personality for visual editing (in the case of newer OLE applications). OLE loads the native data contained in the object into the server and instructs the server to perform its primary verb on the data. The most common OLE verbs are edit and play.

If the server is an older OLE application and its primary verb is edit, then a modified version of the server appears with the tools for editing the data. Two commands are added to the server's File menu (Figure 14.4):

➳ **Update.** Updates the data in the embedded object without quitting the server.

➳ **Exit and Return.** Updates the data in the embedded object and quits the server, returning you to the client's compound document.

∙∙∙∙∙∙∙∙∙∙∙∙∙∙
FIGURE 14.4
*Editing an
Object Created
by an Older
OLE
Application*

When you edit an embedded
object created by an older
OLE application, the server
is launched into its own
application window with two
new commands added to its
File menu.

If the server is a newer OLE application, its tools temporarily replace the client's normal menus and toolbars (Figure 14.5). When you finish editing the object, click anywhere outside it, and the server updates the object. The client's toolbars and menus then revert to their normal configurations.

If the server's primary verb is play—for example, in the case of sound files, animation, and other multimedia data—then the server plays the data contained in the object. Often the server does not appear on screen when the data is played.

FIGURE 14.5
Visual Editing

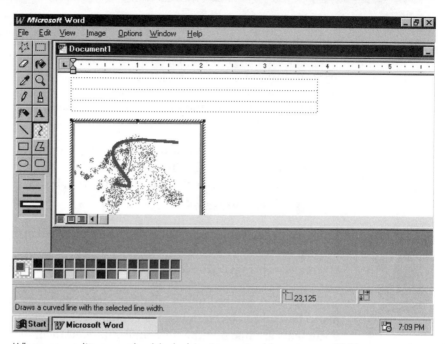

When you edit an embedded object created by a newer OLE
application, the client takes on the personality of the server,
and you edit the object in place within the compound document.

Linked Objects. The Paste Link command places a visual representation of
the data—not the data itself—into a document. The linked object's data
remains in the source file. OLE simply places a software pointer in the destination document that provides the path to and the file name of the source
file. The pointer serves as the link to the source file.

When you Paste Link an object into a client, two items are transferred from
the Clipboard:

➺ The **presentation data** that the client uses to display the object.

➺ The **ObjectLink format** that contains the pointer to the source file.

After placing those items into the compound document, the client attaches
a notice to the source file telling OLE that the file contains information linked
to a specific compound document. The source data must be in a saved file for
a client to attach a note to the file. Therefore, when you create a document,
you must save it before you can link any data it contains to another document.

One object can appear in many compound documents. When you edit the source document, your changes are reflected in all the linked documents.

Once a linked object is in place, you can edit the information it represents in one of two ways:

»→ Start the server, open the source document, and edit the data as you normally would.

»→ Double-click on the linked object and edit it as if it were an embedded object. Provided the link hasn't been broken, the server automatically starts up (or comes to the foreground if it's already running) with the source file already loaded.

Insider's Tip

Unlike embedded objects, linked objects must be edited in the context of their original source file. As a result, they can't be edited visually; editing a linked object always brings up the complete server application in a separate window.

As you edit a linked object, all other identical objects are updated automatically. Linked objects in open documents are updated in real time; closed documents are updated the next time you open them. For example, if you place an object from a spreadsheet into several compound documents, any changes you make to the pertinent part of the spreadsheet—from any of its linked objects—appear in the source document and in any other documents that contain that linked object.

Embedding versus Linking. The biggest decision you face when you use OLE is whether to embed or link an object you paste into a compound document. An embedded object is freestanding and contains all its data. When you copy a compound document with embedded objects to another system, all the information contained in the objects is moved with the document. To transfer a compound document with linked objects to another system, in contrast, you must gather all the source documents linked to the objects.

Linking, however, saves disk space and reduces network traffic by not creating redundant information. Embedded OLE objects are duplicates of existing information. If you work with large data files, such as high-resolution graphics, animation, or sound files, replicating them can waste hard-disk space and network resources.

Assume, for example, that a megabyte of color graphics and a 500-kilobyte sound file are embedded in a memo and that the memo is sent to 100 people. You guessed it: the 1.5-megabyte memo has now consumed a whopping 150 megabytes of hard-disk space and network load. Had that same memo used linked objects that all pointed to the same source document, the memo could have been distributed at a fraction of the cost in resources.

Linking, therefore, is an important technique for network users. Because all the copies of a linked object reflect the information in the source file, distributing documents with linked objects is a good way to provide a large group of people with information that can be automatically updated from time to time.

For example, you could paste a production schedule, sales goals, and sales results into a spreadsheet and distribute a document that contained objects linked to the spreadsheet. Then, as the schedule, goals, and results changed, you would have to update only the source spreadsheet file to update the recipients of the original document.

However, be forewarned that network support for OLE leaves much to be desired. Because OLE uses DDE to transport its messages, and because DDE does not work well across networks, both the OLE client and the server must be running on the same machine to work with compound documents. However, OLE does allow the data files used by linked objects to be stored on networks.

Normally, linked objects are updated automatically by the OLE server whenever the source document is changed. However, some objects may be linked manually. In this case, the client must request an update, rather than receiving it automatically. Manual links are useful for data that needs only periodic updating. Constant updating of automatic links can clog a network and take a toll on a system's performance. Using manual links helps conserve system and network resources. To discover whether a link is set to update automatically or manually, you use the Links dialog box, which I describe in the next section.

Link Maintenance. When you use linked objects, you may need to perform some link maintenance tasks. A link between an object and its source file is based on the path to and file name of the source. If that file is renamed or moved, the link breaks, and the object does not work properly until you update the information about the source file. To perform this operation and other link maintenance tasks, choose the Links command from the Edit menu, which brings up the Links dialog box (Figure 14.6).

With the controls in the Links dialog box, you can perform the following link maintenance tasks:

➡ Update the links of manually linked objects.

➡ Switch links from automatic to manual, or vice versa.

➡ Repair broken links.

➡ Break links you no longer want.

➡ Edit or activate linked objects.

FIGURE 14.6
*Links Dialog
Box*

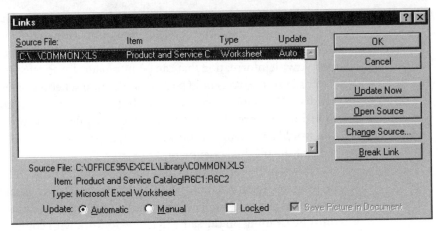

The Links dialog box is your link maintenance
control center.

The Links dialog box lists all the links to a compound document. To work on a particular link, select it from this list.

A linked object can be updated either manually or automatically. When a linked object is set up to be updated automatically (the default), the graphic representation of the object in the compound document is changed by the server whenever changes are made to the source document.

To change to manual updating, select a link and click on the Manual button. With a manual link, the image that represents the linked data is not updated in the compound document unless you request an update. You do this by selecting a link and clicking on the Update Now button. Updating affects only the graphic representation of the object in the compound document. The data itself is stored in the source file and is updated whenever that information is changed. This setting, therefore, is irrelevant if the linked data lacks a graphic representation, as with a linked package.

Because linking relies on an exact path and file name, any changes to the name or location of the source file break its links to any linked objects. Repairing those broken links is a tedious process: you open every compound document that contains an object linked to that source file and manually change the information.

To fix a broken link, open the compound document that contains the linked object in question and select Links from the Edit menu to bring up the Links dialog box. Then click on the Change Source button, which summons the Change Source dialog box (Figure 14.7).

The Change Source dialog box, like many Windows 95 dialog boxes, enables you to search through your volumes and folders. When you locate the source

••••••••••••••
FIGURE 14.7
*Change Source
Dialog Box*

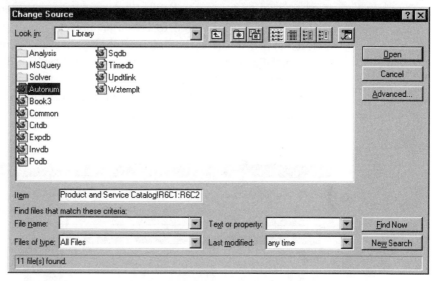

*The Change Source dialog box inside the Links dialog box
enables you to repair a broken link or change an existing link.*

file that contains the data for the linked object, click on OK to return to the
Links dialog box. The new link information is reported in the dialog box.

You can also change the link to point to a different file. The procedure is
the same as for repairing a broken link. When you move the link to a new
source file, you essentially select a new object. This object then appears in your
compound document.

When you deliberately break a link, only the presentation data—that is,
the graphic representation of the object in the file—remains in the client, as
if you had used the Clipboard without OLE. To break a link, select the object,
choose Links from the Edit menu to access the Links dialog box, then click on
the Break Link button. To break other links, select them while you're in the
Links dialog box, pressing the Break Link button to break each link.

To remove a linked object altogether, select it in the client and choose Cut
or Clear from the Edit menu. This removes both the link and its presentation
data from the client.

Other OLE Client Commands. In addition to the Paste, Paste Special, Paste
Link, and Links commands, OLE clients often include other OLE commands
in their Edit menus. Because OLE is an evolving standard, those commands
are not always consistent from application to application. Two common additional OLE commands are Insert Object and Object.

The Insert Object command brings up a dialog box that enables you to choose a server from which to create an object (Figure 14.8). The Insert Object dialog box lists all the classes of objects that can be created by the OLE servers installed on your system. Select an object type, and a server that can create that type of object automatically starts up, either in its own window or as a new client personality for visual editing. (**Insider's mini-tip:** you can select Package from the list to run the Object Packager.)

FIGURE 14.8
*Insert Object
Dialog Box*

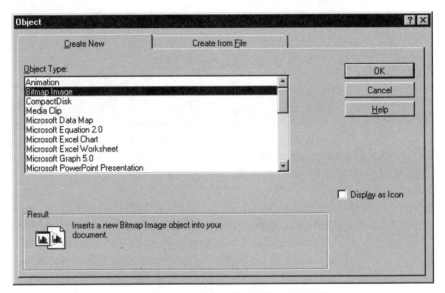

The Insert Object dialog box provides a quick way to insert an OLE object into a compound document.

The Insert Object dialog box lists an OLE object type only if the associated server is properly listed in the OLE Registry. The Registry (which can be viewed with the Registry Editor utility) contains the names of servers and the types of objects they can create. Some servers can create more than one type of object; Excel, for example, can create both a Worksheet Object and a Chart Object.

After you create new data, copy or cut the information. You can then return directly to the client to insert the object into your compound document.

The Object command runs the server associated with a linked or embedded object so that you can quickly edit or play the object. First select an object. The name of the Object command changes on your Edit menu, depending on what type of object is selected. For example, when no object is selected, the command is listed simply as Object and is dimmed on the menu (Figure 14.9). However, if you select a graphic object created by Paint, the Object menu item changes to Bitmap Image Object (Figure 14.10).

FIGURE 14.9
Edit Menu with Dimmed Object Item

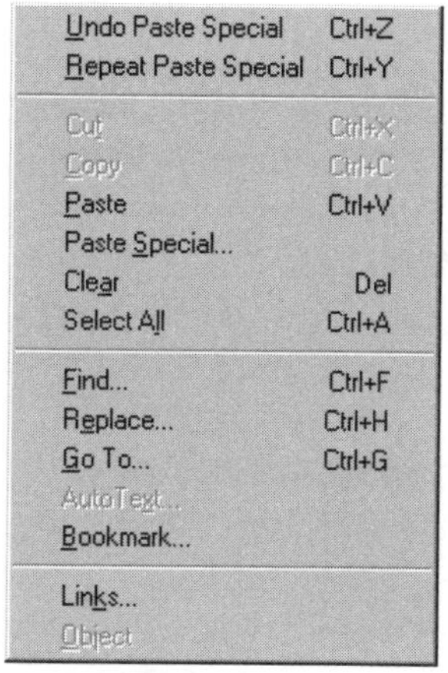

Undo Paste Special	Ctrl+Z
Repeat Paste Special	Ctrl+Y
Cut	Ctrl+X
Copy	Ctrl+C
Paste	Ctrl+V
Paste Special...	
Clear	Del
Select All	Ctrl+A
Find...	Ctrl+F
Replace...	Ctrl+H
Go To...	Ctrl+G
AutoText...	
Bookmark...	
Links...	
Object	

The Object command is dimmed when no objects are selected.

FIGURE 14.10
Edit Menu with Bitmap Image Object Item

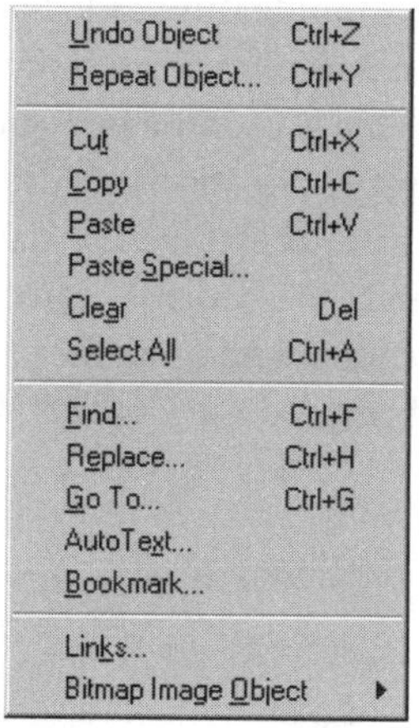

Undo Object	Ctrl+Z
Repeat Object...	Ctrl+Y
Cut	Ctrl+X
Copy	Ctrl+C
Paste	Ctrl+V
Paste Special...	
Clear	Del
Select All	Ctrl+A
Find...	Ctrl+F
Replace...	Ctrl+H
Go To...	Ctrl+G
AutoText...	
Bookmark...	
Links...	
Bitmap Image Object	▶

The Object command changes to Bitmap Image Object when such an object is selected.

If you select an object for which more than one action is possible, a cascading menu lists the actions (that is, the OLE verbs) that can be performed on the object. For example, if you select a Sound Object in a compound document, the Object item changes to Sound Object and contains a cascading menu that lists two choices: Play and Edit (Figure 14.11).

•••••••••••••

FIGURE 14.11

*Edit Menu
with Sound
Object Item
and Cascading
Menu*

Because more than one action can be
performed on a Sound Object, this
menu item provides a cascading menu
that lists both Play and Edit.

Insider's Tip

Newer OLE applications offer an important feature called **object conversion.**
Object conversion enables an OLE client application to convert an embedded
object's data into a different format. This is useful when you distribute compound documents to users whose server applications are different from yours.
Those people can use object conversion to change the data's format into a
compatible one. To check which formats are available, select the object in the
compound document, open the Edit menu, and open the cascading menu for
the object. Finally, select Convert to bring up the Convert dialog box.

••••••••••••••••••••••••••••••••

The Object Packager

The Object Packager utility is an OLE client and server program, so it can
both create OLE objects and accept them from other servers. Packager can
work with a variety of data, including an entire file from almost any program
and even a DOS command line. Object Packager enables you to encapsulate
data from both OLE and non-OLE applications and control the graphic
presentation of objects in compound documents. You can package entire
files created by either OLE servers or non-OLE applications. However, if a
package is to contain only part of a file, the file must be created by an OLE
server.

Insider's Tip

Object Packager is not listed on the Start menu. To find it, open the Windows 95 folder (typically called WINDOWS or WIN95) and locate the PACKAGER.EXE file. You can start it directly from the folder by double-clicking, or you can create a shortcut to it on the Windows 95 desktop.

The Object Packager enables you to encapsulate information into a package. A package is an OLE object represented by an icon or other graphic image that you select. For example, an OLE object consisting of a large section of a spreadsheet would normally be represented by presentation data that resembles the portion of the spreadsheet. The Object Packager enables you to substitute an icon or another graphic image for the presentation data. Thus you can make a packaged object appear as an icon, a button, a drawing, or whatever other graphic you can copy to the Clipboard.

Packages are also automatically used to represent objects that do not provide presentation data. For example, a Sound Object is displayed as a Sound Recorder icon, because no graphic representation of the sound file is provided by the Sound Recorder.

You can package non-OLE data, but you can place a package only into an OLE client. Although packages can be embedded only into compound documents, a package can contain a linked object. When such a package is embedded into a document, it behaves as if it were a linked object, with a few exceptions. When you double-click on the package, it loads the source file into the server as with a normally linked object. However, if you select such a package in a document, the Links command is not available on the client's Edit menu. To perform link maintenance on the package, you need to edit the package from within the Object Packager.

To edit the package, select it in the compound document. Then choose Package Object from the client's Edit menu, which reveals two choices:

➤➤ **Activate Contents.** Loads the package into the server program and either edits or plays the data, depending on the nature of the data.

➤➤ **Edit Package.** Loads the package into the Object Packager.

To perform link maintenance, choose Edit Package; the Object Packager appears, displaying the linked object. Choose Links from the Packager's Edit menu to access the Links dialog box and perform any necessary maintenance.

Packaging a File. A package may contain an embedded file or only a link to that file. The file can be either a data file or an application. To create a package that contains an embedded file, start the Packager and make sure the Content window is selected (Figure 14.12).

• • • • • • • • • • • •
FIGURE 14.12
*Object
Packager
with Content
Window
Selected*

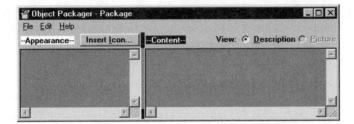

*This is what
the Object
Packager
looks like
when it's
empty.*

If the Content window is not selected, click inside it or press Tab. Then choose the Import command from the File menu, which brings up the Import dialog box. Use this box to browse through your drives and directories and to select a file to embed into the package. When you locate the file you want, click on OK to return to the Packager. The name of the file now appears in the Content window, and the icon of the application associated with that file is displayed in the Appearance window (Figure 14.13).

• • • • • • • • • • • •
FIGURE 14.13
*Packager with
Embedded File*

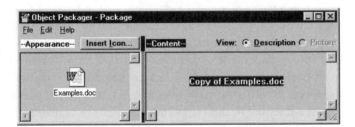

*The Object
Packager
containing an
embedded file.*

To change the icon that represents an embedded file, click on the Insert Icon button in the Appearance window. This brings up the Insert Icon dialog box, which contains the name of the application associated with the file type in the package, along with any icons contained in that application. If more than one icon is displayed in the Current Icon section of the dialog box, you can select one of them. To use an icon not in that application file, click on the Browse button and select another source file for your icons. This process is similar to the process by which you select an icon in File Manager. You can use program files, DLLs, and .ico files as icon sources.

To make the package resemble something other than an icon, select the Appearance window. Then switch to a graphics program, copy in an image from that program, switch back to the Packager, and paste the image into the Appearance window.

An icon that represents a package contains a default label that describes what the document contains. The exact label depends on the data. For example, if the package contains a graphic created with Paintbrush, the default is Paintbrush Picture. To change the label, choose the Label command from the Edit menu; the Label Edit dialog box appears. Enter a new label, then click on OK.

When you paste a graphic other than an icon into the Appearance window, the package lacks a label. To make one, create a title for the image in the graphics program before you paste it into the Appearance window. When you're satisfied with the Appearance window, select Copy Package from the Packager's Edit menu. Then switch to a compound document and issue the Paste command from the client's Edit menu.

Using Drag and Drop to Create Packages.

Want a shortcut for creating packages that contain embedded or linked files? Use drag and drop. However, this technique works only with clients that support all OLE conventions, which excludes some OLE clients.

Newly created packages use the icon associated with the extension of their source file, and the icon label bears the name of the source file. To change the icon or label, highlight the icon in the document. From the client's Edit menu choose the Package Object cascading menu, then choose Edit Package to call up the Object Packager.

From My Computer select the source file with the mouse. Then use the right mouse button to create a shortcut to the file by selecting Create Shortcut from the pop-up menu (Windows 95 treats packages as a form of shortcut). Finally, drag and drop the new shortcut into the application window in which you'd like to embed the package (Figure 14.14).

. . . .
FIGURE 14.14
Embedding a
Package

List

Shortcut to Fig

Shortcut to Fig

To embed a packaged file into a compound document, create a shortcut to the file in My Computer, then drag and drop the shortcut into the document.

Packaging a Portion of a File.

To create a package with only a section of a file, you must have created the file with an OLE server. The following technique also enables you to package an OLE object that you have already created, whether it is linked or embedded.

Open the document that contains either the source data or an existing object. Then select the information or object and issue the Copy command. Run the Packager and make sure the Content window is selected. To create an embedded object, choose Paste; to create a linked object, choose Paste Link. After making adjustments to the appearance of the package, choose Copy Package from the Edit menu. Next switch to a compound document and issue the Paste command to place the package into that document.

· ·

The Registry

The Windows 95 Registry is fundamental to OLE. It is also part of other Windows 95 operations, such as storing hardware and software configuration settings. The Registry provides Windows 95 with information about every OLE server installed on a system.

The Registry consists of a series of binary files that Setup installs in the main Windows 95 directory. The Registry contains information about the paths to and file names of OLE servers, the file name extensions of data files and their associated applications, the class names of OLE objects that servers on the system can edit, and the OLE verbs and other protocols used by objects in the system.

Although OLE doesn't rely on the information in the WIN.INI file, information in the Registry corresponds to information in the [embedding] and [extensions] sections of WIN.INI. Information in those sections may be altered when new applications are entered in the Registry.

Updating Registry Entries. When you install an OLE application, its setup program usually updates the Registry automatically. If it doesn't, look in the application's folder for a file that ends with .REG. Files with this ending are Registry update files; double-click on one to update the Windows 95 Registry.

If the application fails to update the Registry upon installation, you can also perform a limited update manually by selecting Options from the View menu of any Windows 95 folder view. Click on the File Types tab to bring that page of the dialog box to the front (Figure 14.15).

For example, to add a new Registry entry for Excel, first identify the file name extension used by the program's data files; in this example, it's .XLS. Now enter this information, along with a name for the type of file, into the Add New File Type dialog box, which you bring up by clicking on the Add New Type button (Figure 14.16).

••••••••••••
FIGURE 14.15
*The File Types
Page*

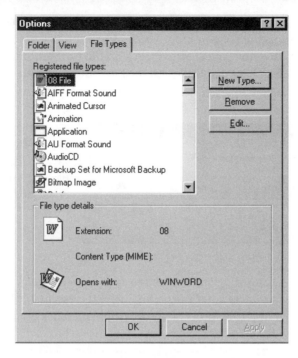

You can manually
update some OLE
information in the
Options dialog box of
any folder view.

••••••••••••
FIGURE 14.16
*Adding a New
File Type*

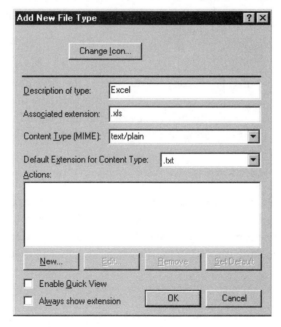

To add a new file type,
click on the Add New
Type button and fill in the
fields of the Add New File
Type dialog box.

Once you name the file type and its data file extension, you're ready to define actions for the new type. The most common actions are New, Open, and Print. To define a new action, click on the New button. To edit an existing action, highlight it and click on the Edit button. In either case you're presented with a dialog box like the one in Figure 14.17.

• • • • • • • • • • • • •
FIGURE 14.17
Editing an
Action

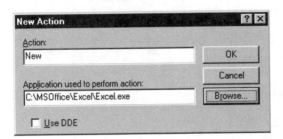

To add a new action, click the New button. To edit an existing action, highlight it and click on the Edit button.

In the Action field, name an action such as New, Open, or Print. Next, in the Application field enter the pathname to the executable file for the application program. If you don't know the pathname, click on the Browse button to bring up the Windows 95 file-browsing dialog box.

Most modern Windows applications support DDE commands for the most basic functions, such as opening a file or printing. To edit a program's DDE commands, check the Uses DDE checkbox. The dialog box expands to show the DDE command fields.

Some applications, like the Paint applet included with Windows 95, use command line arguments instead of DDE commands to tell the program what actions to take. For those programs, leave the DDE checkbox unchecked and add the appropriate command line arguments to the end of the path information in the Action field. For example, you would use the argument /P %1 to tell Paint to print a file; the complete Action field entry would read

```
"C:\WIN95\PAINT.EXE" /P "%1"
```

Insider's Tip

The quotation marks around the preceding example are deliberate. Windows 95 uses quotation marks to differentiate long file names from short file names. If your application is stored in a folder with a long (greater than 8.3 characters) file name, use quotation marks when you enter path information.

. . . .

Summary

Windows 95 provides three features that enable you to share information among applications: the Clipboard, DDE, and OLE. Using the Clipboard, you can copy or cut data from one program and paste it into another. At its basic level, the Clipboard serves merely as a holding area for information in transit. This cut-and-paste capability is common to almost all GUIs.

DDE (Dynamic Data Exchange) is a software mechanism that enables one Windows application to communicate with another. Software messages do the communicating. Some of the messages are common to almost all DDE applications, and others are intrinsic to specific applications. Applications automatically implement DDE for certain functions, but sometimes you must initiate DDE yourself by incorporating DDE messages into a macro or other programming language.

To increase the power and accessibility of DDE, Microsoft has developed an implementation of it called OLE (Object Linking and Embedding). OLE enables you to use the Clipboard to copy information from one application and embed or link it into a compound document, which contains information created by more than one application. OLE server applications provide data to OLE client applications, which can accept the data to create a compound document. When OLE is used to embed data, a copy of the original data is placed in the compound document. When OLE is used to link data, the original data remains with the source file, and only a visual representation of it is placed in the compound document.

Windows provides a utility called Object Packager to help you work with OLE. Object Packager enables you to encapsulate data from both OLE and non-OLE applications and place it in a compound document.

15

Windows 95 and DOS

Since its genesis, Windows has had a symbiotic relationship with DOS. Windows and DOS used to be sold separately, but starting with Windows 95, the two have been combined into a single product. Although Windows 95 includes both Windows and DOS in the same box, the two operating systems are not integrated seamlessly; instead they maintain their codependency.

555

DOS came first. Years later Windows was built on top of the DOS foundation. The first few versions of Windows could not run without DOS, which Windows needed to access the computer's hardware. As Windows has evolved over the years, Microsoft has worked quietly in the background to lessen Windows' dependence on DOS. With each successive release, Windows has gained more power to control PC hardware directly by means of device drivers.

To wean Windows from DOS, Microsoft systematically replaced DOS-based functions with native Windows **virtual device drivers (VxDs)**, which are a key component of Windows. A VxD creates a virtual device that always looks the same to Windows and Windows applications.

For example, the virtual display driver—the VxD that controls the computer's display adapter card—provides Windows with a virtual display on which to draw windows, dialog boxes, icons, and other graphic components. Because the virtual display replaces a physical display, Windows 95 and Windows applications don't need to know the characteristics of your actual monitor or display card. Virtual displays mean you don't have to tweak Windows or Windows programs to support a specific type of monitor, display, or resolution. Instead, the manufacturer of the display card creates a driver that translates the technical features of the hardware into a form compatible with the Windows VxD.

Windows 95 contains VxDs for more types of hardware than did previous versions of Windows. The VxDs control everything from mice to CD-ROM drives to sound cards, improving compatibility and helping make Windows 95 hardware-independent. Think of Windows 95 and its applications as running on a giant virtual computer system, rather than on any particular hardware configuration. Device drivers translate your specific configuration into the virtual computer system. Now you know why it's so important to get the right drivers for specific hardware devices.

In addition to lessening Windows 95's dependence on DOS by using VxDs, Microsoft uses a few other tricks to keep DOS out of your interface. For example, when you boot up your PC, the screen reads "Starting Windows 95" as opposed to "MS-DOS." With previous versions of Windows, you had to boot DOS first and then load Windows from the command line by typing "win." With Windows 95, the system automatically boots into Windows when you turn the computer on.

Don't be fooled, however, by Microsoft's misleading description of Windows 95 as a "completely new, 32-bit operating system." Although the marriage of convenience between DOS and Windows has changed dramatically over the years, DOS is still there, lurking under the covers of Windows 95. That's why I've devoted a chapter to the integration of DOS and Windows 95. Yes, it's true: just when you thought it was safe to throw away all those old utilities, DOS rears its ugly head from under the sheets of the Windows marriage bed.

The Big Picture

Before you dive into the complexities of DOS configuration and tuning, here's an overview of how DOS works with Windows. As with previous Windows incarnations, DOS still boots your PC when you first turn it on. DOS starts the computer in real mode and prepares it to run Windows 95. Once Windows 95 is running, it still keeps DOS hanging around in memory to serve as a kind of subsystem of Windows 95. The DOS code executes in a **virtual DOS machine (VDM)** while Windows 95 manipulates it to achieve certain goals, mostly related to compatibility with other Windows and DOS applications.

After Windows 95 is loaded onto your PC, it pretty much assumes total control. For compatibility reasons, DOS does stay around, albeit in the background. However, it is Windows 95—or more accurately, the **Virtual Machine Manager (VMM)**—that holds the keys to your PC's processor and hardware. VMM itself is a 32-bit, protected-mode operating system. Once it takes charge, it creates a number of virtual DOS machines, which emulate complete 8086-based PCs. **Protected mode** is the full 32-bit mode available on 386 and larger processors. **Real mode** is the 16-bit processor mode used by DOS and was designed for 286 and older chips. In protected mode you can run 32-bit programs in a large memory space, whereas real mode runs 16-bit programs in the awful, segmented-memory architecture typified by the 640K application space of DOS.

By creating the lean and mean VMM 32-bit protected-mode operating system, Microsoft has developed a way to further liberate Windows 95 from its reliance on DOS. At the same time, important DOS compatibility is provided by the virtual DOS machines, which are tailored to run DOS applications (Figure 15.1).

FIGURE 15.1

How Windows 95 Views Your PC

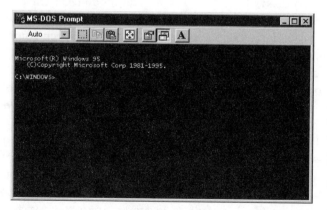

Windows 95 consists of a number of virtual DOS machines (VDMs), all managed by a 32-bit, protected-mode operating system called Virtual Machine Manager (VMM).

One of those virtual machines, the **System VM,** contains the 16-bit portions of Windows 95's window management (USER) and graphics (GDI) subsystems; 16-bit Windows programs operate inside this VM. VMM can also create additional VDMs—one for each DOS program—so you can run multiple DOS applications simultaneously. You can even multitask them.

VDMs are based on the state of the computer after DOS has booted up the PC but prior to VMM taking control. This means that if you load older DOS device drivers or Terminate and Stay Resident (TSR) programs that take up part of the 640K of DOS application memory, the reduced amount of memory is reflected in any VDM. However, each VDM also gains the benefits of whatever driver or TSR program consumed the memory. In any case, you can still use your old device drivers, but they need to be loaded during the initial, real-mode phase of start-up. The effect those drivers have on the memory configuration and capabilities of your system is reflected in any VDMs you create to run DOS applications during Windows sessions.

Boot Action

With previous versions of Windows, DOS booted your PC. A small program, called a bootstrap loader, initialized your PC's hardware and then loaded the three pieces of DOS: IO.SYS, MSDOS.SYS, and COMMAND.COM. The first two programs are the core of DOS; they contain the low-level I/O handling and file system routines that make DOS run. COMMAND.COM provides a shell program for the DOS user interface: the ubiquitous C:> prompt.

With Windows 95, the boot process works much the same way: a small bootstrap loader initializes the PC and then loads the equivalent of IO.SYS and MSDOS.SYS to create a simple, real-mode DOS environment. After this, Windows 95 deviates slightly from the original DOS/Windows norm.

In Windows 95, IO.SYS and MSDOS.SYS have been combined into a new, more powerful IO.SYS. In addition, Windows 95 includes a few Windows 95 specific device drivers, which pave the way for the protected-mode VMM. Those device drivers are loaded automatically as part of IO.SYS and include HIMEM.SYS and IFSHLP.SYS, both of which provide Windows 95 with critical links to the real-mode world of DOS.

Unlike previous versions of DOS, this new real-mode operating system doesn't automatically load COMMAND.COM. Instead it searches for an AUTO-EXEC.BAT file. If it finds one in the root directory of your hard disk, it loads COMMAND.COM (a command interpreter script) and uses COMMAND.COM to process the file. If it fails to locate an AUTOEXEC.BAT file, it doesn't load

COMMAND.COM. Windows 95 doesn't need a command interpreter because VMM takes over directly after IO.SYS preps the system.

Windows 95 makes the start-up process more automatic than previous versions did. You used to have to load Windows manually, either from a command prompt or as part of AUTOEXEC.BAT. Windows 95 hard-codes this process into IO.SYS, creating the illusion of a seamless operating system.

Despite its disappearing act, however, DOS is still very much a part of Windows 95. Although Microsoft has integrated the two operating systems without sacrificing compatibility either with DOS or with older Windows programs, the relationship isn't compromise-free. As with previous versions of Windows, the quality of your overall Windows environment depends as much on how DOS is configured before Windows 95 is loaded as on the performance of applications and device drivers specifically designed for Windows 95.

Insider's Tip

Here's the technical skinny on how Windows 95 pulls off its DOS compatibility. When Windows 95 runs in protected mode, it is in constant communication with a virtual copy of DOS running in a VDM. Most of the time Windows 95 transmits commands from running applications to this virtual DOS. For example, Windows 95 transmits to DOS any API calls made to DOS's Int21h interface. Once DOS has processed a request, Windows 95 receives and interprets the results. In other cases Windows 95 relies directly on DOS—for example, when Windows receives a request to create and manage the critical PSP (Program Segment Pointer) structures used by all DOS and Windows applications.

- -

Egad! CONFIG.SYS and AUTOEXEC.BAT Still Live

DOS is still part and parcel of Windows. Unfortunately, so are its twin configuration files: CONFIG.SYS and AUTOEXEC.BAT. Indeed, to configure the DOS portion of Windows 95, you may need to fiddle around with CONFIG.SYS and AUTOEXEC.BAT, using techniques eerily similar to those used with Windows 3.1.

Real-Mode Device Drivers and TSRs. To add a DOS device driver to Windows 95, you add a DEVICE= entry to CONFIG.SYS. Similarly, to make a specific TSR program available to all your DOS applications and command prompts, you add a reference to it to AUTOEXEC.BAT. Once in protected mode, Windows 95 uses the pre-Windows real-mode environment—the one created by IO.SYS and any items specified by CONFIG.SYS and AUTOEXEC.BAT—as the model for each new VDM it creates. Thus every DOS application or command prompt can gain access to those device drivers and TSRs from within

Windows 95. However, as I mentioned before, each VDM also loses the RAM consumed by those DOS drivers and TSR programs.

Insider's Tip

If you're familiar with Windows 3.1, you'll see that previous Windows versions handled DOS configuration in exactly the same way. Although the boot process for Windows 95 has been altered cosmetically, many of the DOS configuration techniques, such as memory management, remain the same.

Caveats about VDMs. Although the ability to define global VDM parameters at boot time can be a blessing, it can also be a curse. That's because you cannot load a DOS device driver into only a single VDM. To change one VDM, you have to make a global entry in the CONFIG.SYS file, which affects all your VDMs.

This poses a problem if not all your drivers coexist peacefully. As any seasoned DOS/Windows veteran knows, getting more than a few DOS device drivers to cohabit on a system can prove an exercise in frustration. Memory conflicts, load-order discrepancies, and other weirdness are par for the course with DOS memory management. Because Windows 95 uses the same DOS model as Windows 3.1 does, you may have to spend extra time tuning CONFIG.SYS to make a complex configuration sing harmony on your PC. The same is not true, however, for TSRs, which you can load into specific VDMs.

Virtual Device Drivers. Before you start worrying about how your existing DOS driver will work or digging through your closet for that tried-and-true third-party memory manager, take heart: the situation isn't quite so grim. Although Windows 95 doesn't eliminate either DOS or its configuration issues, it does the next best thing: it supplies 32-bit virtual device drivers (VxDs) that replace most common drivers and TSRs.

A VxD is a native 32-bit Windows device driver. VxDs are the cornerstone of the Windows 95 operating system. They are particularly flexible because they support both Windows and any DOS applications running under Windows. Windows 95 replaces the following popular drivers and TSRs with VxDs:

➤ MSCDEX.EXE

➤ MOUSE.COM

➤ MOUSE.SYS

➤ NET.COM

VxDs improve performance and use less memory than the equivalent drivers and TSRs. Because VxDs are 32-bit and run in protected mode along with Windows 95's own code, they are faster than real-mode DOS drivers, which must be run in a VDM. In addition, because VxDs exist in protected mode (except for a few specialty drivers), they consume little or no conventional, or 640K DOS, memory.

VxDs also provide Expanded Memory Specification (EMS) memory support and DOS Protected Mode Interface (DPMI) services. Those VxDs are the core of the Windows 95 VMM. In fact, VMM is itself a collection of VxDs, ranging from the arcane, like the Virtual Programmable Interrupt Controller (VPIC), to the more obvious, like the Virtual Communications (VCOMM) driver, which handles serial port I/O.

Insider's Tip

Unlike DOS device drivers and TSRs, VxDs are installed automatically when you add a new hardware device. The installation is handled either by a third-party setup program or by Windows 95 itself. Typically, hardware supported by Windows 95 relies on corresponding VxDs on the Windows 95 CD or disks, whereas devices supported by third-party software include their own VxDs on disks provided by the manufacturers.

The Windows 95 Command Prompt

Past and present DOS users may appreciate a command prompt, but they shouldn't be alarmed that COMMAND.COM is gone. Designed to simplify the interface, GUIs such as Windows don't necessarily improve speed for those already familiar with DOS commands. When it comes to raw speed, few GUI users can rival a touch-typist who is knowledgeable about DOS. Lots of folks, not just DOS users, appreciate a command line interface to perform certain tasks.

Aware of this, Microsoft has always included some form of command prompt shell with Windows so you could interact directly with the underlying DOS. This Windows command prompt could be run either full-screen or in a window. In addition, the command prompt acquired features specific to Windows, such as the ability to copy and paste data between a windowed command prompt and the Clipboard—something you couldn't do with DOS alone.

In Windows 95 the command prompt has been taken to new heights. Toolbars, TrueType fonts, and a new Start command add flexibility to the prompt.

• •

The Toolbar

If you work with DOS applications on a regular basis, you'll likely come to love the Windows 95 toolbar. This simple extension of the VDM interface gives you the ability to quickly access common functions like mark, copy, and paste, as well as to control how an application behaves when it is in the background. The Windows 95 command prompt toolbar resembles the toolbars in Windows 95 folder views (Figure 15.2).

• • • • • • • • • • • •
FIGURE 15.2

The Windows 95 Command Prompt Toolbar

The Windows 95 command prompt toolbar provides quick access to a variety of functions, including mark, copy, and paste.

Each item on the toolbar features a pop-up description of itself, which you can bring up by pointing to the item's button. To integrate data from a DOS application into a Windows application, use the mark, copy, and paste commands. The Mark button switches the DOS window into **mark data** mode. Click on the button to change the window's cursor into a block, which enables you to highlight a region of text or graphics by dragging the mouse (Figure 15.3). Once the data is highlighted, you can copy it to the Clipboard by clicking on the Copy button.

• • • • • • • • • • • •
FIGURE 15.3

Marking Data

Click on the Mark button, located on the toolbar, and drag the mouse pointer across the data you want to mark. Copy the highlighted data to the Clipboard by clicking on the Copy button.

You can also paste data into a DOS program or command prompt by clicking on the Paste button. This instructs Windows 95 to paste the contents of the Clipboard into the window at the location of the cursor. Although most DOS programs and command prompts work with the Windows 95 paste mechanism, you can paste only text, not bit-map or other graphic data formats.

Insider's Tip

Some older DOS programs are incompatible with the Windows 95 method of pasting. For those troublesome applications, Windows 95 provides an alternative pasting method that is compatible, albeit slower. The method is discussed later in this chapter in the section titled Advanced DOS Configuration Topics.

You can access all the DOS button commands from a DOS application window's System menu. Like Windows applications, DOS applications include System menus when they run as windows. Menu items include the standard Minimize, Maximize, and Restore, as well as a nested submenu structure with the Mark, Cut, and Paste commands (Figure 15.4).

• • • • • • • • • • • • • •
FIGURE 15.4
Viewing a
DOS Program's
System Menu

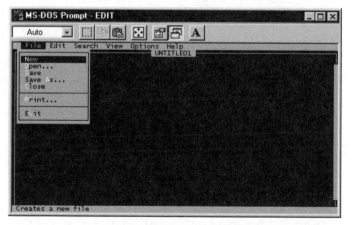

Like Windows applications, DOS applications feature System menus when they run in desktop windows.

Three other handy buttons are the Full-Screen, Properties, and Background buttons. The Full-Screen button enables you to switch between windowed and full-screen operations (Figure 15.5). You might want to use this button to switch a windowed text or graphics application into full-screen mode, so you can see the image in its original format.

*Click on the Full-Screen button to switch an application
into full-screen mode. To return the application to a
window, press Alt+Enter.*

The Properties button brings up the Properties dialog box for a DOS application or command prompt. Using this box, you can tell Windows 95 precisely how to run a DOS application, including how to set up its appearance and multitasking characteristics. You can learn more about the properties of DOS programs later in this chapter.

The Background button controls the multitasking behavior of DOS programs. When you click on this button to place it in its "down" position, it tells Windows 95 to keep running a program even when its window is in the background and another program is running in the foreground (Figure 15.6). If the Background button has not been "pressed," Windows 95 suspends the program's execution when the program is in the background. With the button in this position, you conserve your computer's processing power, because you suspend the application when it isn't in use.

*Click on the background button to toggle between two
types of DOS multitasking. If the button is "depressed," a
program continues to run even when it isn't in the topmost
window. If the button is in the up position, the application
stops running whenever it's in the background.*

Changing Fonts. Windows 95 includes a feature that could be characterized as cool—at least by DOS diehards. You can use scalable, TrueType fonts to display DOS programs on the desktop. This TrueType support gives considerable flexibility to how you display DOS data. A long list of font sizes enables you to fine-tune the text display, and an auto-sizing feature takes advantage of the scalable nature of the fonts to match text point size to window size.

Activating the Font button brings up the Font page of a program's Properties dialog box (Figure 15.7). Select the type of font you want to use—bitmap, TrueType, or both—as well as a default font. If you leave the Font Size list set to Auto, Windows 95 automatically adjusts font size to match the size of a DOS program's window. If you expand the window, the font size increases to reflect the new window size.

FIGURE 15.7
The Font Page

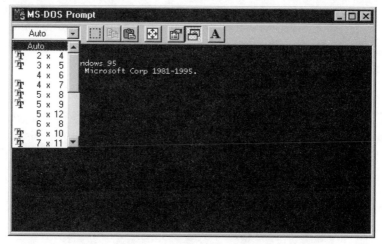

Select Auto from the Font Size list on the Font page
to tell Windows 95 to scale fonts automatically to fit
the size of the window.

Starting Programs from a Command Prompt

You can start both DOS and Windows programs from a Windows 95 command prompt. To do so, enter the DOS path to the file you want to run, and press Enter. When you launch a DOS program, it takes control of the command prompt's window, switching it to full-screen mode if necessary. A Windows program, on the other hand, loads into its own application window, leaving the DOS prompt running, ready to respond to other commands. To launch a DOS program in its own window, you can use the Windows 95 Start command, which I discussed in Chapter 4.

Configuring DOS Program Properties

Windows 95 maintains a properties sheet for each DOS application in a system. The property sheets are roughly analogous to the Program Information Files (PIF) found in Windows 3.1, but with a few new twists. The breadth and depth of the configuration options have been expanded, and you now access information by means of the right mouse button pop-up menus rather than via a separate PIF editor program.

To access the properties of a DOS application, highlight the program's icon in a folder view, then click on the right mouse button and select Properties from the resulting pop-up menu. This brings up the Properties dialog box (Figure 15.8).

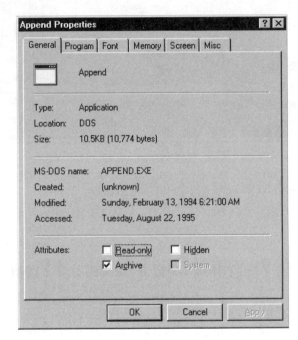

You access the Properties dialog box via the right mouse button pop-up menu.

The first page of the dialog box, General, provides basic statistics about the file itself, such as its size, the date it was last accessed, and the date it was last modified. The General page also includes checkboxes for setting the four DOS file attributes: archive, hidden, system, and read-only.

The Program Page. The second page of the Properties dialog box, Program, enables you to define the most basic configuration parameters of a DOS program (Figure 15.9). You assign a title to the program in the first field, the one next to the icon. The title identifies the program when it's running and appears in both the program's title bar and its Taskbar entry.

• • • • • • • • • • • • • •
FIGURE 15.9
*The Program
Page*

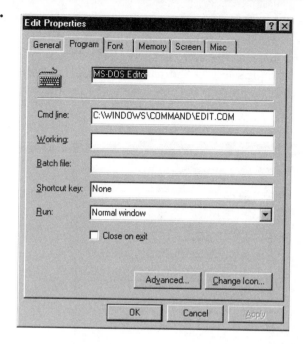

*You set the most
basic configuration
parameters, such as
the path to a file, on
the Program page.*

The Cmd Line field contains the DOS path to the program file. For example, the Cmd Line field for the Windows 95 EDIT program reads

```
C:\WIN95\COMMAND\EDIT
```

(The actual entry varies depending on the directory name you gave Windows 95 during setup.)

In the Working field, you specify a working directory for the program. This becomes the DOS current directory value, a DOS variable that determines where default file actions take place. If you know you will be accessing files from a specific directory while you are using a program, setting its Working field to the desired directory points the program's file open and close functions in the right direction.

The Batch File field—a new option with Windows 95—enables you to run a batch file after a program's VDM is created. The feature enables you to load a series of TSRs into a VDM before the application is loaded. For example, to load DOSKEY (the Windows 95 command line recall mechanism) into a VDM, you create a batch file that calls DOSKEY and then puts a reference to the batch file into the Batch File field. This tells Windows 95 to load DOSKEY into the VDM when it is first created, before Windows loads the application or command prompt.

Using the Shortcut Key field, you can assign a keyboard shortcut to a DOS program. Typically shortcuts combine Alt, Shift, and Ctrl with alphanumeric characters. To assign the shortcut Ctrl+Alt+E to the Windows 95 EDIT program, for example, select the Shortcut Key field and hold down those three keys simultaneously. This adds the new combination to the field (Figure 15.10).

FIGURE 15.10

The Shortcut Key Field

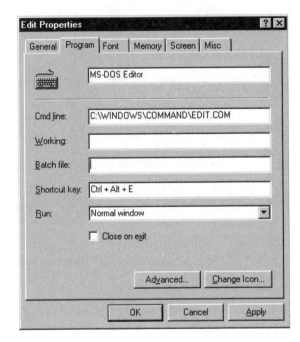

To assign a keyboard shortcut to a DOS program, select the Shortcut Key field and enter the desired key combination.

The Run drop-down list box enables you to specify how a program's window is displayed. For example, if you select Minimized, only the program's Taskbar is displayed at start-up. Select Maximized, and the program launches in a maximized window. The default setting is Normal Window, which displays the program in a nonmaximized window.

The last checkbox, Close on Exit, tells Windows 95 to close the program's window when the program stops running. Usually you want to keep the default setting, but you may occasionally want to remove the check mark from this box. For example, if you want to take a snapshot of the results of a DOS batch program after it has finished running, clearing the Close on Exit checkbox saves the last screenful of information in the window (Figure 15.11).

• • • • • • • • • • • • • • •
FIGURE 15.11

*Freezing the
Output from a
DOS Program*

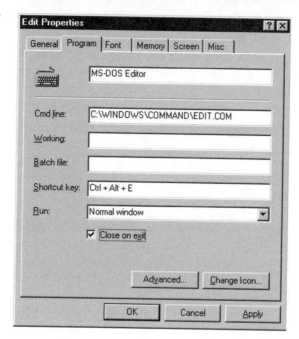

To freeze the last
screenful of
information from
a DOS program,
clear the Close
on Exit checkbox.

The Advanced Button.
This button is for folks who like to configure *really* technical parameters like whether to run a program in MS-DOS mode. Watch for a discussion of those goodies later in this chapter in the section called Advanced DOS Configuration Topics.

The Change Icon Button.
Since version 3.0, Windows has enabled users to assign icons to DOS programs. Those icons represent the DOS programs in shortcuts on the desktop and when the programs are running; the icons appear on a program's Taskbar and System menu. To get you started, Windows 95 provides a number of predefined icons in the PIFMGR.DLL file.

To select an icon for a program, click on the Change Icon button to bring up the Change Icon dialog box. Select a new icon from the scrolling list and click on OK. To look through an icon library other than the default PIFMGR.DLL, click on the Browse button and navigate Windows 95 folders until you find another file containing icons.

The Memory Page.
As I warned you earlier, the 640K memory barrier still lurks in Windows. However, now you can tweak VDMs to help alleviate the problem. To define the memory characteristics of a DOS program's VDM,

mess around with the Memory page of the Properties dialog box (Figure 15.12). You can specify what kind of memory to give the VDM: conventional, environment, EMS, XMS, or DPMI. You can also define the level of memory protection the VDM uses and specify whether the program accesses the high memory area (HMA).

· · · · · · · · · · · · · ·
FIGURE 15.12
The Memory Page

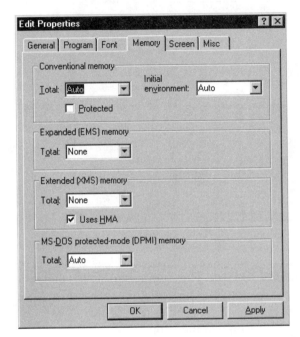

You use the Memory page of the Properties dialog box to determine what amount of memory Windows 95 makes available to a DOS program's VDM.

The Total field for each type of memory is set to Auto, which means Windows 95 determines how much of each memory type an application requires. Usually you should leave those parameters alone; Windows 95 does a good job of estimating how much memory an application requires by monitoring the application's behavior as it loads.

Some situations call for change, however. An older DOS program may be set to use all available EMS (Expanded Memory Specification) memory. In this case, Windows 95 tries to service the DOS program's request, providing it with as much as 16MB of EMS memory. This can force Windows 95 into a virtual-memory frenzy. The operating system tries to compensate for the demand by paging portions of other programs to disk; this in turn causes the system to slow to a crawl as Windows 95 frantically shuffles data from memory to disk.

If you notice a significant slowdown, a frenzy of disk activity, or both when you load an EMS DOS application, assign a limit of from 2MB to 8MB of EMS memory to the program. To do so, change the value in the EMS Total field.

The same procedure can be applied to XMS and DPMI memory values. If you notice an application is taking a long time to load or causing a lot of disk activity, set limits on the appropriate memory values.

Conventional memory values are less manageable. As I mentioned earlier in the chapter, the amount of available conventional memory in a Windows 95 DOS VDM is directly affected by the number of TSRs and device drivers you load at boot time. On a "clean" system, one that has few or no real-mode drivers, you can expect roughly 605K of conventional memory to be available. To see how much conventional memory is available on your system, use the MEM command (Figure 15.13).

• • • • • • • • • • • • •

FIGURE 15.13

*Checking
Memory Values
with MEM*

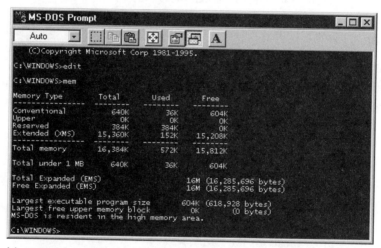

You can check how much conventional, EMS, and XMS
memory is available on your system by using the MEM
command from within a DOS command prompt.

Because the conventional memory Total field cannot compensate for memory lost to device drivers and TSRs loaded in CONFIG.SYS and AUTOEXEC.BAT, you can't increase the amount in that field to a value above what the MEM command reports. In other words, DOS and your pre-Windows DOS configuration, not Windows 95, determine the upper limit on VDM conventional memory. My rule of thumb: leave the conventional memory Total field set to Auto.

Insider's Tip

If your applications need more than 605K or if you load several real-mode device drivers via CONFIG.SYS (which consumes conventional memory space before Windows 95 loads), try a third-party memory manager. See Advanced DOS Configuration Topics later in this chapter for more information.

Like conventional memory, the Initial Environment field is tied to the pre-Windows DOS configuration. Environment space is the amount of "scratch" memory made available to the DOS command interpreter, COMMAND.COM. COMMAND.COM uses this memory to store environment variables such as the DOS path and the SET statements defined in batch files like AUTOEXEC.BAT.

If the Initial Environment field is set to Auto, Windows 95 bases the VDM's environment size on the size of the environment in the pre-Windows DOS configuration. If you know this value is insufficient for some task, you can increase it; the value is expressed in bytes. You may want to do this, for example, when you launch a DOS command prompt planning to assign new SET variables as part of a batch file or other DOS task.

Danger Zone

Some DOS programs behave erratically when they lack sufficient free environment space. If a DOS program crashes frequently or displays "Out of Environment Space" error messages, increase the value for free environment space. You should provide at least 1,024 bytes of environment space to any questionable DOS program. The maximum value for this field is 4,096 bytes.

The Uses HMA field is available only if you deliberately force Windows 95 to load DOS into conventional memory. Windows 95 usually loads the bulk of DOS into the HMA (the first 64K of extended memory). However, if you add the line DOS=LOW to your CONFIG.SYS file, Windows 95 loads DOS into the 640K of conventional memory. This in turn leaves the HMA free for use by other programs. Checking the Uses HMA field tells Windows 95 to let a program access the HMA.

Few programs use the HMA (some older Novell requesters that could load into the HMA are an exception). Hence, you should leave this parameter alone. The loss of conventional memory that results from loading DOS low is not worth the trade-off.

The Protected checkbox tells Windows 95 to prohibit a program from modifying sensitive areas of the VDM's DOS environment. Many programs play tricks on DOS, modifying its structure to boost performance. Those modifications can undermine Windows 95's stability, so if you know that a program changes DOS directly, activate this checkbox. Be forewarned: checking the box can slow down a program, so it's best to leave the box cleared unless you're sure a program undermines DOS.

The Screen Page. Whereas the Memory page enables you to set up DOS programs behind the scenes, the Screen page enables you to design the on-screen appearance of the same programs (Figure 15.14). You use the first set of values, grouped under the heading Usage, to define how Windows 95 displays a program overall. The Full-Screen radio button, when selected, displays the program in full-screen mode. Likewise, the Window radio button displays the program in a window on the desktop. In either case, the Initial Size field determines how many lines of text the DOS program's VDM displays at a time—25, 43, or 50.

FIGURE 15.14

The Screen Page

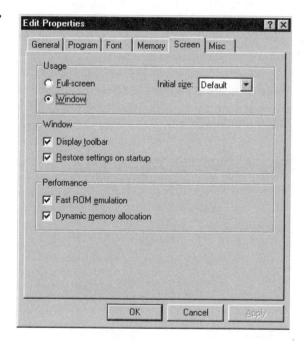

You define the display characteristics of a DOS program on the Screen page.

You can control the appearance of a DOS program running in a window by using the two options under the heading Windows. Display Toolbar controls whether Windows 95 displays its toolbar across the top of the window. Restore Settings at Startup tells Windows 95 to restore the original DOS window configuration when a program ends. This changes details such as the number of lines and the font back to their original values at start-up.

Under the heading Performance are two parameters that control how a program interacts with video hardware. Fast ROM Emulation tells Windows 95 to emulate your display adapter's ROM code in RAM. This boosts the performance of programs that write large amounts of text to the screen. However, the feature does not work with some older DOS applications. If you notice that a program has trouble writing text to the screen, disable this feature.

Dynamic Memory Allocation controls how Windows 95 handles video memory. When this feature is activated, Windows 95 allocates video memory to the program as needed. When the program switches from text to graphics mode, Windows 95 steals memory from other processes to satisfy the program's need for more video memory. When the program switches back into text mode, Windows 95 makes the "borrowed" memory available to other programs.

This feature usually should remain activated because it enables Windows 95 to manage your memory pool efficiently. However, if you notice a performance drag in programs that switch back and forth between text and graphics modes, or if you notice display corruption when a program switches from one mode to the next, disable this function.

The Misc Page. The Misc page is a holding site for miscellaneous parameters, from the mundane, such as Mouse QuickEdit, to the more arcane, such as Idle Sensitivity (Figure 15.15).

● ● ● ● ● ● ● ● ● ● ● ● ● ●
FIGURE 15.15
The Misc Page

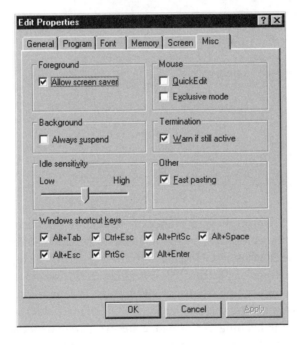

Microsoft dumped all the miscellaneous parameters that didn't merit their own Properties pages onto the Misc page.

The Allow Screensaver checkbox, when checked, allows Windows 95 to start its screensaver when a DOS program is running in the foreground. If you have problems with video or other corruption in a program when the screensaver comes on, disable this function.

Listed under the heading Mouse are the QuickEdit and Exclusive modes, both turned off. If you activate QuickEdit, any mouse action applied to the contents of a DOS program's window marks the contents for subsequent copying to the Clipboard. Use this function when you're doing lots of marking and copying, but keep in mind that you disable mouse support for the DOS application. If your DOS program requires a mouse, keep this function turned off.

Exclusive mode does just the opposite. When this feature is activated, only the DOS program receives mouse input. This means you can't use the mouse with Windows 95 or any other interface.

Always Suspend is located under the heading Background. The feature suspends a program's execution when the program is in the background.

Warn if Still Active, situated under the Termination heading, controls whether Windows 95 warns you if you try to close a DOS program with the Close Window button or the System menu's Close command. Unlike previous versions, Windows 95 can safely close a DOS command prompt in this way (with Windows 3.1, you have to type EXIT and press Enter). However, Windows 95 cannot close a DOS program that is running windowed on the desktop; you must exit the program using its own menu or keyboard commands.

When Warn if Still Active is activated and you try to close a windowed DOS application improperly, Windows 95 displays a dialog box instructing you to close the program directly. If the option is not activated, Windows 95 attempts to close the program by terminating its VDM. Most DOS programs don't appreciate having their virtual machines pulled out from under them, so I advise you to leave the Warn if Still Active option activated. If you don't close your DOS programs with their own menus or keyboard commands, you risk losing data.

Insider's Tip

Microsoft has modified some of the DOS utilities that it ships with Windows 95—most notably the EDIT program—so they directly support the Windows 95 Close Window function. You can use the Close Window button safely to exit these utility programs and terminate their VDMs. To determine whether you can safely close a program in this way, try to close it with the Close Window button. If the program closes normally, it's safe. If you see the warning dialog box, it's not safe.

A new feature of Windows 95, Idle Sensitivity, enables you to control how the operating system handles idle DOS programs. A DOS program is idle if it is waiting for keyboard input to continue processing. Such a program, however, isn't really idle; it's continually polling the keyboard for input. To avoid allocating valuable CPU time to a program that is merely polling the keyboard, Windows 95 detects programs running in an "idle loop" and reduces the amount of CPU time devoted to them.

How aggressively Windows 95 pursues such programs is determined by the Idle Sensitivity slider. Move it toward High, and Windows 95 clamps down on such programs the moment it detects they're in a loop. Move the slider toward Low, and Windows 95 is more generous, letting programs execute in a loop for a while before lowering their CPU priority.

Insider's Tip

Lowering the Idle Sensitivity value can improve the performance of some CPU-demanding DOS programs, like games. If you notice such programs running sluggishly, try cranking down the Idle Sensitivity slider. This forces Windows 95 to provide as much CPU time as possible to the program, improving overall performance. Be advised, however, that other programs in the system may suffer. As the favored DOS application gobbles up CPU cycles, other tasks may slow down or stop altogether for periods of time. In other words, use this parameter judiciously.

Under the ultimate tribute to miscellany, the heading Other, you find the Fast Pasting option. When this feature is activated, Windows 95 uses its faster technique to paste data into a DOS application. However, as I mentioned earlier in the chapter, some older DOS programs are incompatible with this technique. If you have trouble pasting Clipboard data into a particular DOS program, disable this option.

With the Windows shortcut keys, you can define which Windows 95 keyboard commands to reserve exclusively for Windows 95 while a DOS program is running. For example, if a program uses Alt+Tab to bring up a function, check the Alt+Tab checkbox if you want to reserve the combination for Windows 95 exclusively. To allow DOS to use certain commands, clear the appropriate checkboxes.

Advanced DOS Configuration Topics

Everything in this chapter so far has concerned the basics of DOS program configuration. If you want to see the frills, click on the Advanced button at the bottom of the Program page to bring up a panoply of other choices (Figure 15.16).

Prevent MS-DOS Programs from Detecting Windows gives you the ability to work with older DOS programs that have been programmed to quit running when they detect Windows. When activated, this options tells Windows 95 to disguise itself so that a DOS program believes it is running in a straight DOS environment.

Suggest MS-DOS Mode as Necessary requires more explanation. Keep reading for more on this feature.

• • • • • • • • • • • • • •
FIGURE 15.16
The Advanced Program Settings Dialog Box

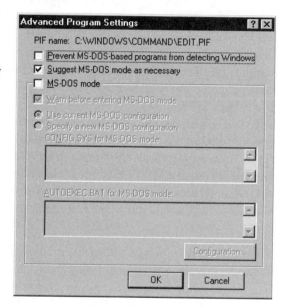

Click on the Advanced button on the Program page to bring up a challenging array of choices.

What Is MS-DOS Mode?

In creating Windows 95, Microsoft set itself a Herculean task: to design a protected-mode, 32-bit operating system that would replace both DOS and Windows in the marketplace. Not only would Microsoft have to support the installed base of Windows applications and drivers, it would also have to provide a compatible environment for every existing DOS application. This is a difficult task because not all DOS programs can run in a VDM, and some DOS applications insist on being the only program running on a PC—a throwback to the days of one application at a time.

Early 32-bit operating systems, such as Windows NT and OS/2, meet this challenge by providing a dual-boot mechanism. First you load DOS onto the PC, then you install the 32-bit operating system over it. At your request the 32-bit operating system can reset the machine for DOS, rebooting into a real DOS environment. The dual-boot solution works but is far from elegant. In fact, booting between two operating systems could be described as downright kludgy.

Armed with its Windows NT experience, Microsoft set out to develop a more seamless solution to the DOS problem. The result was MS-DOS mode, a kind of dual-boot without the booting. Selecting MS-DOS mode causes Windows 95 to unload itself from the system's memory and replace itself with a real-mode copy of DOS. Your finicky old DOS program is then free to run amok in the system. Once the program finishes, Windows 95 reloads, and you're back to square one. Even if the program hangs up, crashes, or just plain fails to terminate properly, you're no worse for the wear; simply reboot your system, and you're back in Windows 95.

In a nutshell MS-DOS mode offers a more elegant form of dual-booting. You no longer need to reboot the system completely and search for a particular DOS program. Instead you click a checkbox and let Windows 95 take care of the details. Activating Suggest MS-DOS Mode as Necessary in the Advanced Program Settings dialog box streamlines the process even further; Windows 95 evaluates the program and tells you whether it requires MS-DOS mode.

Danger Zone

Don't let the simplicity of Windows 95's MS-DOS mode fool you. When your PC enters this mode, it really has rebooted into DOS. This means that any running applications are shut down, and any network connections or on-line communications sessions are terminated. Once in MS-DOS mode, Windows 95 is nothing more than a memory, and you have to restart, reload, and reconnect when you return to the Windows 95 desktop.

When should you use MS-DOS mode? Windows 95 automatically tries to detect when a program requires MS-DOS mode, but it doesn't always make the right call. Because the type of VDM failure that forces a program to use MS-DOS mode can also hang up your entire PC, it's best to err on the side of caution. You should run a program concurrently with other programs only when you're confident it runs reliably in a normal Windows 95 VDM.

How to Set Up MS-DOS Mode. To configure a program for MS-DOS mode, check the MS-DOS Mode checkbox. Also check the Warn Before Entering MS-DOS Mode checkbox so that Windows 95 reminds you what is about to occur when you launch the program. When the latter option is activated, a dialog box gives you the chance to consider your actions before continuing (Figure 15.17).

Once you are in MS-DOS mode, an application can be run as usual. Of course, you can't operate the program in a window; Windows 95 is no longer

FIGURE 15.17

*Warning about
MS-DOS
Mode*

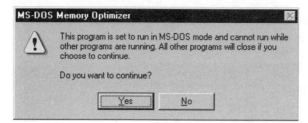

*If the appropriate checkbox is checked, Windows
95 warns you that a program requires MS-DOS
mode when you try to launch the program. You
can continue to load the program or abort the
operation and return to the desktop.*

running. When you finish working with the program, exit it normally, and in
theory you return to the Windows 95 desktop. Too often, though, as DOS programs exit, they leave the PC in such poor condition that Windows 95 fails
to reload, and you need to reboot. If you exit a program and don't see the
Windows 95 desktop (or any disk activity), chances are you must reboot. To
return to Windows 95, press Ctrl+Alt+Del (or press the PC's reset or power
switch).

Caveats about MS-DOS Mode. Few things in life are free, and MS-DOS
mode is no exception. The reason this mode works so well is also its undoing:
when you're in MS-DOS mode, you're really running under DOS. Windows
95 is no longer loaded, and unfortunately neither are any of those helpful
VxDs. Thus, to maintain many basic functions—for example, CD-ROM support—you have to use real-mode device drivers. Yes, it's true: you've come all
the way to 32-bit nirvana only to find that to play your favorite game, you
need to dive back into the DOS configuration quagmire.

For just those occasions, Windows 95 provides a number of basic DOS real-
mode device drivers. When you activate MS-DOS mode for an application,
you can choose to use your existing pre-Windows DOS configuration information or create new CONFIG.SYS and AUTOEXEC.BAT files for the program.

The Advanced Program Settings dialog box features two multiline fields
for this purpose. A Configuration button brings up yet another dialog box,
which you can use to set up the basic functions of your application (Figure
15.18). Windows 95 interprets your requests and adds the appropriate lines
to the CONFIG.SYS and AUTOEXEC.BAT fields.

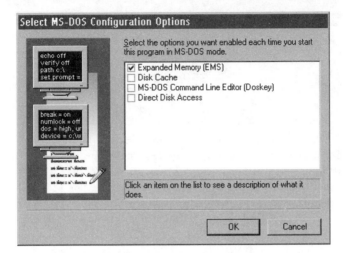

FIGURE 15.18

*Configuring
MS-DOS
Mode*

*Windows 95
streamlines the
creation of an
MS-DOS mode
environment by
providing a
series of
checkboxes
that are
translated into
appropriate
config.sys and
autoexec.bat
entries.*

After you customize and fine-tune your CONFIG.SYS and AUTOEXEC.BAT files, you're ready to give the new environment a test run. Click on OK to close the dialog boxes, then launch the program. Your configuration goes into effect, just as if you were booting a DOS system. And because you really are booting DOS, you can feel free to substitute custom third-party drivers for the basic drivers provided with Windows 95. To do so, modify or add the appropriate lines to the CONFIG.SYS and AUTOEXEC.BAT fields.

Windows 95 and DOS Memory Managers

It's a subject you probably wish you could avoid. After all, Windows 95 was supposed to do away with all this nonsense, wasn't it? Alas, memory management—in particular, DOS memory management—remains a sticky issue with Windows 95.

As I mentioned earlier in this chapter, Windows 95 uses the pre-Windows DOS configuration as a model for each VDM it creates. And although VxDs alleviate some of the real-mode driver jam that plagued Windows 3.1, in some situations only a DOS driver or a TSR can solve the problem.

With previous versions of Windows, you bought a third-party memory manager to optimize your pre-Windows DOS configuration. This kind of a product used gaps in the 384K region of real-mode memory between 640K and 1MB on Intel PCs—the region known as the upper memory blocks, or UMBs—as storage space for device drivers and TSRs. The manager optimized the load order and location of each driver or TSR in an effort to create as much free conventional memory as possible. The more memory available before Windows loaded, the more was available to its VDMs.

With few exceptions, the same situation exists with Windows 95. As with previous versions of Windows, Microsoft includes a rudimentary DOS memory manager—EMM386—as part of the Windows 95 package. However, Microsoft fails to include a companion utility, Memmaker, which automates the optimization process (Memmaker was included with all versions of DOS 6 prior to Windows 95). In other words, you're on your own when you work with EMM386. You can find documentation for this utility in your Windows 95 package.

Insider's Tip

When you use EMM386, don't forget to include the RAM statement if you intend to use EMS memory for your VDMs. Like Windows 3.1, Windows 95 is unable to access memory that is under the control of a DOS memory manager. Unless you set aside an EMS page frame by including the RAM parameter as part of your pre-Windows DOS configuration, you won't be able to use EMS for your VDMs. This practice also applies to third-party memory managers.

If you really need to optimize your pre-Windows DOS configuration, invest in a third-party memory manager. When shopping around, look for products designed specifically for Windows 95 that automate the entire installation and optimization process.

. . . .

Summary

Windows and DOS are still very much intertwined, even in this incarnation of Windows. Although it's a big step up from Windows 3.1, Windows 95 still makes you delve into the arcane world of DOS configuration from time to time to optimize your PC's operation. You may have to edit CONFIG.SYS and AUTOEXEC.BAT files or work with DOS memory managers. Microsoft did automate some features, however; for example, Windows 95 automatically keeps track of configuration information for each DOS program. To access the configuration options for a DOS program, you use the right mouse button to bring up the program's Properties sheet. This capability, coupled with numerous virtual device drivers designed to replace popular DOS drivers and TSR programs, makes working with Windows' DOS side a less intimidating experience than it was in the past.

16

Inside the Windows 95 Installation Process

Like stagehands assembling the props and the scenery of a play, setup programs work behind the scenes to get Windows 95 in place. Pausing briefly to get directions, the Setup program, its wizards, and the Control Panels work their magic in two acts.

The first act takes place when you start the Setup program. If the Windows 95 Setup program is started from MS-DOS, OS/2, or Windows NT, Setup first installs a limited version of Windows 3.1.

In the second act, Setup checks your hardware and copies the Windows 95 files to your computer. During this performance, Setup starts Windows 95, customizes files, installs additional services and drivers on the computer, and readies the system for your use.

Backstage, the Windows 95 Setup program directs an assortment of files and programs that install and configure Windows 95. The Setup program, in turn, follows its own scripts, which are contained in Setup's .INF files. If you learn to customize those scripts, the installation process can be partially or fully automated, saving hundreds of hours of your time. Customizing scripts is particularly useful when you install Windows 95 on several machines.

The Starting Players

The Windows 95 Setup programs are found on the Windows 95 installation floppy disks or CD-ROM. Setup and the Windows 95 files can be placed on a network and shared directly by several users, or Windows 95 can be installed from the network.

The SETUP.EXE program is a protected-mode, 16-bit, Windows application. The switches for SETUP are shown in Table 16.1. You can run Setup from Windows 3.1 or Windows for Workgroups. If you run Setup from MS-DOS, a real-mode stub in the program is called and executed.

SUWIN.EXE is the protected-mode Setup component run by Setup and responsible for calling all other DLLs used in Setup. SETUPX.DLL is the primary DLL used during the Copy Files phase to perform most of the installation procedures. This module reads the .INF files to handle disks and copy files. To install network services, the Setup programs call NETDI.DLL.

Setup creates a temporary directory called WININSTX.400 to hold a minimal set of files. At its peak, this directory holds about 6 to 7 megabytes worth of files. After Windows 95 is successfully installed, Setup removes the directory and its contents.

The scripts for Setup's activity are found in the following files:

SETUP.INF   The primary reference file for Windows 95, whether you start it from Windows or DOS. The information in SETUP.INF directs Setup to install Windows 95 based on your hardware, the configuration of your Windows files, and initial desktop settings.

WRKGRP.INI	Controls work-group membership. (Similar to the file with the same name in Windows 3.x.)
NETDET.INI	Detects and reacts to NetWare TSRs. (Replaces the network-detection portion of Windows 3.1's CONTROL.INF. The remainder of Windows 3.1's CONTROL.INF is now built into Windows 95's Setup program.)
APPS.INF	Contains information that Windows 95 uses to create PIFs for applications. (Same as the file by the same name in Windows 3.1, except that the file format is different.)
MSBATCH.INF	A customizable file with which you can select default actions for Setup (such as Portable rather than Typical setup) or override information in the Windows-supplied .INF files. This text file can be constructed from other files or created by means of the BATCH.EXE file supplied with the Windows Resource Kit.

• • • • • • • • • • • • • •
TABLE 16.1
Setup Switches

/?	Provides help on Setup's syntax and command-line switches.
/C	Instructs Windows 95 Setup not to load the SmartDrive disk cache.
/d	Instructs Windows 95 Setup not to use the existing version of Windows for the early phases of Setup. Use this switch if you cannot run Setup because of a damaged Windows installation.
/id	Instructs Windows 95 Setup to skip check for the minimum disk space.
/ih	Runs ScanDisk in the foreground so that you can see the results. Use this switch if the system stalls during the disk check or if an error results.
/iL	Loads the Logitech mouse driver. Use this option if you have a Logitech Series C mouse.
/iq	Instructs Windows 95 Setup to skip the ScanDisk quick check when starting Setup from MS-DOS. Use this switch if you use compression software other than DriveSpace or DoubleSpace.
/is	Instructs Windows 95 Setup to skip the ScanDisk quick check when you start Setup from Windows. Use this switch if you use compression software other than DriveSpace or DoubleSpace.

/nostart	Instructs Windows 95 Setup to copy a minimal set of Windows 3.x DLLs used by Windows 95 Setup, then to exit to MS-DOS without installing Windows 95.
<script>_<filename>	Instructs Windows 95 Setup to use settings in the specified script to install Windows 95 automatically; for example, setup msbatch.inf specifies that Setup should use the settings in MSBATCH.INF.
/t:tempdir	Specifies the directory into which Setup is to copy its temporary files. This directory must already exist, and any existing files in the directory will be deleted.

With previous versions of Windows, the only way to automate custom setups was to edit the .INI and .INF files. Microsoft now provides several utilities that enable you to control setup and the finished installation without editing those files. I discuss the utilities at the end of the chapter.

Starting the Setup Process

You trigger an avalanche when you start Setup. The preferred method is to run Setup 95 from Windows 3.1 or Windows for Workgroups. Setup should be started from MS-DOS, though, in either of the following two situations:

»+ When Windows 3.1 or Windows for Workgroups is not installed.

»+ When Windows 3.0, OS/2, or Windows NT is installed on the computer.

The start-up sequence depends on how you start Setup:

»+ If you start Windows 95 Setup from MS-DOS, Setup searches the hard disk on the computer for previous versions of Windows. If a version is found, the program requests that you quit and rerun Setup from Windows. This message can be bypassed.

➻ Regardless of the type of start-up, Setup runs ScanDisk to check for disk problems. Setup also performs the necessary checks to confirm that the computer is capable of running Windows 95—for example, making sure there is a powerful enough CPU and enough memory and disk space, and making sure that the correct version of MS-DOS is running. Setup informs you of any resource problem.

➻ If you start Windows 95 Setup from MS-DOS, Setup checks for an extended-memory specification (XMS) provider, installing its own if one is not present already. If no disk cache is found, Windows 95 Setup automatically loads SmartDrive. The cache size varies, depending on available XMS memory.

➻ Regardless of the type of start-up, Setup checks for TSR applications and device drivers known to cause problems. If any of those applications are running, Setup issues a warning.

➻ If you start Windows 95 Setup from MS-DOS, Setup installs a minimal number of Windows 3.1 files and starts them by using the shell=SETUP.EXE command. The Windows graphical user interface and welcome dialog box appear. When you Setup from Windows, this is the first thing you see.

➻ If you start Windows 95 Setup from MS-DOS, Setup switches the processor to standard mode and makes extended memory available.

Setup then starts gathering information to determine which Windows 95 components to install. The elements in question include the directory for Windows 95 files, user information, and specifics about the devices and software to be installed.

Danger Zone

Before running Setup, remove all unnecessary TSRs and close all unnecessary Windows applications. TSRs can prevent Setup from detecting aspects of your setup correctly. Setup restarts the computer several times during the installation process, closing down any running Windows applications. Also close all DOS windows. Setup will be interrupted if a DOS session or an application is running.

TSRs required to partition or control the hard disk, network drivers, or device drivers for CD-ROMs usually should remain. In some cases Windows cannot detect equipment unless the TSRs are loaded.

Danger Zone

Don't try to run Setup from a DOS window. If you do, Setup detects the situation, issues an error message, and exits.

Insider's Tip

If you are using disk-partitioning software, such as On-Track Disk Manager, and have just upgraded your BIOS to run large hard disks (larger than 512 megabytes) and Windows 95, it is usually easiest to back up your hard disk, remove the partitioning software, and restore your old Windows installation before upgrading. If you must reformat the disk, you need a startable copy of MS-DOS, your Windows 3.x disks, and a copy of your backup software. See the directions included with your hard disk.

How Long Does It Take?

The time required to install Windows 95 depends on many factors. It usually takes between 30 minutes and an hour (Figure 16.1). Prominent factors influencing installation time are CPU type and speed, amount of RAM, disk speed, media type (floppy disk versus CD-ROM), and the complexity of your current Windows 3.x setup.

FIGURE 16.1

The Setup Welcome Screen

This screen greets you and notifies you that a routine system check will be performed when you install Windows 95.

On a "clean" 120 MHz Pentium with 16 megabytes of RAM, a 1.6-gigabyte hard disk, a quad-speed CD-ROM, and a fresh Windows 3.1 setup, Windows 95 can be installed in less than 15 minutes. Contrast that installation with one on a 100 MHz 486DX/4 with 16 megabytes of RAM, Windows 3.1 on a 500MB compressed hard disk with over 6,500 files, and a double-speed

CD-ROM. This installation took 80 minutes. A similar 100 MHz 486DX/4 installation with only 1,200 files on an uncompressed disk took less than 40 minutes.

Thus, compression and a large number of files significantly slow the installation process. You may want to spruce up your Windows 3.1 installation before you convert to Window 95—for example, removing unneeded groups and files and defragmenting the disk.

Choosing the Directory for Windows 95

During setup, you are asked where to locate your Windows 95 files. You can either enter a location manually or let the automated script choose the location for you. This decision has side effects. Your choice of directories not only affects your new setup but also determines whether you can use your old version of DOS or Windows.

Setup detects whether Windows 3.1 or any version of Windows for Workgroups is installed on the computer. If so, Setup offers to install Windows 95 in the same directory as the previous version of Windows.

If you choose to install Windows 95 in the same directory as the previous version, Setup moves the configuration settings in SYSTEM.INI, WIN.INI, and PROTOCOL.INI, plus file associations from the Windows 3.x Registry, into the Windows 95 Registry. All applications and networking settings work automatically in the new Windows 95 environment. Windows 3.x Program Manager groups are converted into subdirectories of the PROGRAMS directory, so that they can be displayed on the Windows 95 Start menu. Additionally, some external commands, such as CHKDSK, from the previous version of DOS are removed from the disk.

The side effect of installing Windows 95 in the same directory as a previous version of Windows is that you will not be able to dual-boot from your system. That is, you will be able to start Windows 95 but not your old versions of DOS and Windows.

If you wish to have the option of starting your computer either under Windows 95 or under your old version of DOS or Windows, you must specify a different directory. Setup then installs the Windows 95 files into the new directory and moves the values from SYSTEM.INI, WIN.INI, and PROTOCOL.INI, as well as the Windows 3.x Registry, into the Windows 95 Registry. However, Windows 3.x program groups are not converted to Windows 95. Also, you may need to reinstall most of your Windows applications before they will function with Windows 95.

Danger Zone

If you wish to create a dual-boot system, you must not start Setup using the copy of Windows you wish to preserve. If you do, Setup does allow you to install Windows 95 in any other directory.

Insider's Tip

Setup always stores the location (the names of the disk drive and the directory) of Windows 95 distribution files in the Registry. The location can be a floppy disk drive, a CD-ROM drive, or a directory on a network server. Windows 95 returns to this location automatically whenever you add a device or additional support files.

Normally, this practice speeds the installation of new files, but it can cause confusion when the device (or network directory) becomes available. This can happen when you add or remove disk drives or when the network directory changes or is not available. Windows 95 complains about the missing files and allows you to enter the new location of the files. See the section on the Registry later in this chapter for information on how to permanently change the default location of the distribution files.

Creating a Dual-Boot System

To create a dual-boot system, select Other Directory from the dialog box shown in Figure 16.2. The Change Directory dialog box appears (Figure 16.3). Enter the name of the directory that will hold the Windows 95 files, and click on Next.

FIGURE 16.2

Choose a Directory

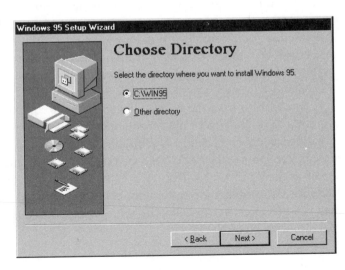

The screen enables you to choose where to install Windows 95. Select Other Directory to set up a dual-boot system.

FIGURE 16.3

Moving Orders

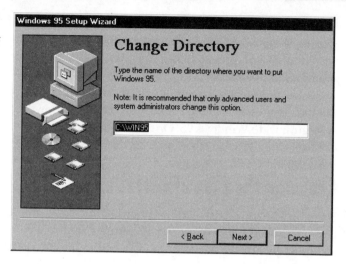

Specify the new directory for Windows 95 in this dialog box.

After Windows 95 is installed, you must change a value in the Windows 95's MSDOS.SYS file to complete setting up the dual-boot capabilities. To do so, take the following steps:

»+ After Windows 95 is installed, open the Windows Explorer and select the file MSDOS.SYS in the root directory of your boot drive. (If your drive is compressed, you must edit MSDOS.SYS on the host drive.)

»+ Click with the right mouse button on the file and select Properties from the pop-up list.

»+ Turn off the System, Hidden, and Read-Only attributes.

»+ Click the on the OK button.

»+ Choose Accessories from the Start menu, and start WordPad (or Notepad).

»+ Select Open from the File menu. In the Files of Type list, choose All Documents (*.*). Move to the root directory of the correct drive and select the MSDOS.SYS file.

»+ Find the line that reads BootMulti=0. Change the 0 (zero) to a 1 (one).

»+ Save the file and exit WordPad.

»+ Return to the Windows Explorer and click on the MSDOS.SYS file with the right mouse button.

»+ Click on the System, Hidden, and Read-Only properties.

»+ Click on the OK button.

Your system is now ready to dual-boot. When you start the computer, the Starting Windows 95 message appears. To start your computer with the old operating system, press F4. You must do so before the initial Windows 95 graphics screen appears.

Several third-party programs can transfer the remaining program groups and the required files for all applications from Windows 3.x (or Windows for Workgroups) to Windows 95. One such program is Remove It from Vertisoft.

Choosing the Type of Installation

Setup provides four installation options (Table 16.2). Your choice of installation type affects which Windows 95 features are installed on your computer and subsequently the size of Windows and the amount of control you have in customizing the installation.

TABLE 16.2

*Types of
Installations*

Setup Type	Description
Typical	The default installation, recommended for most users with desktop computers. Creates a standard Windows 95 installation with minimal interaction. You confirm the directory where Windows 95 files are to be installed, provide the user and computer identification information, and specify whether a start-up floppy disk should be created.
Portable	Recommended for most portable computers. Creates a smaller Windows installation appropriate to a portable computer. This option installs the Briefcase for file synchronization and the software for Direct Cable Connections.
Compact	Recommended for those with limited disk space. Creates the minimum Windows 95 installation.
Custom	Recommended for experienced users who want control over aspects of the Windows 95 setup. This option gives you the opportunity to select which application and network components to install, and to confirm the configuration settings for devices. The files installed by Setup reflect your choices.

In all cases Setup installs the same set of core Windows 95 files and the device drivers required by the computer. The installation types differ in which optional files are installed (Table 16.3).

TABLE 16.3

Components Installed in Typical, Portable, Compact, and Custom Installations

Optional Component	Typical/ Custom*	Portable	Compact
Accessibility Options	Yes	No	No
Audio Compression	No	No	No
Backup	No	No	No
Briefcase	No	Yes	No
Calculator	Yes	Yes	No
CD Player	No	No	No
Character Map	No	No	No
Clipboard Viewer	No	No	No
Desktop Wallpaper	No	No	No
Dial-Up Networking	No	Yes	No
Direct Cable Connection	No	Yes	No
Disk Compression Tools	No	Yes	No
Disk Defragmenter	Yes	Yes	No
Document Templates	Yes	No	No
Games	No	No	No
HyperTerminal	Yes	Yes	No
Media Player	Yes	No	No
Microsoft Exchange	No	No	No
Microsoft Fax	No	No	No
Microsoft Mail	No	No	No
Microsoft Network	No	No	No
Mouse Pointers	No	No	No
Net Watcher	No	No	No
Object Packager	Yes	No	No
Online User's Guide	No	No	No
Paint	Yes	No	No
Phone Dialer	Yes	Yes	No

TABLE 16.3 *(cont.)*

Optional Component	Typical/ Custom*	Portable	Compact
Quick View	Yes	Yes	No
Screensavers	Yes	Yes	No
Sound and Video Clips	No	No	No
Sound Recorder	No	No	No
System Monitor	No	No	No
Video Compression	Yes	Yes	No
Volume Control	No	No	No
Windows 95 Tour	Yes	No	No
WordPad	Yes	No	No

*The default choices for Custom are identical to those for Typical.

The **Typical** and **Portable** setups are similar to Windows 3.1's Express Setup. Most of the control of the transferred files rests in the MSBATCH.INF file. The Typical setup uses more disk space than does Portable, principally for tutorial and help information. The Portable setup adds transportability accessories (such as the Briefcase and dial-up networking) to help you connect to another computer. The **Compact** setting, unlike Typical and Portable, does not install any optional files.

Custom is the only option that gives you greater control over the installation process. You can be more selective about which files are loaded and can immediately change starting settings.

The Hardware Detection Phase

During the hardware detection phase, Windows 95 Setup analyzes installed computer components and attempts to detect installed hardware devices and connected peripherals. Setup examines the hardware resources that are available (IRQs, I/O addresses, CPU ports, and DMA lines), identifies the hardware resources used by the installed components, and builds the hardware tree in the Registry.

Setup uses several mechanisms to detect installed hardware devices. On a non–Plug and Play computer (called a **legacy** computer), Windows 95 attempts to identify known hardware devices by checking for I/O ports and memory addresses known to be used by the hardware. Windows 95 also checks for Plug and Play peripherals, which return their own device identification codes.

On a computer with a Plug and Play BIOS, Windows 95 checks for installed components and their configuration. Windows 95 also checks for connected Plug and Play peripheral devices connected to the computer.

During this phase Windows 95 Setup tries to identify and resolve any hardware conflicts. Setup searches for hardware using the detection module of Windows 95. The resources used by any detected Plug and Play devices are added to the Registry, and any required device drivers are installed based on the Registry settings.

Windows 95 uses the same hardware detection procedures as it uses during setup when you run the Add New Hardware option in the Control Panel, when you use the PCMCIA wizard to enable protected-mode support, and the first time you start a computer in a new docking state. Windows 95 detects computer components, such as communications ports and processors, and detects a wide range of standard equipment, such as display adapters, pointing devices, hard-disk controllers, floppy-disk controllers, and network adapters.

During the detection process, lockups can occur when Setup comes into contact with "nonexistent" or "resource-sensitive" equipment. To avoid such lockups, Windows 95 employs a safe-detection method that receives hints from configuration files, read-only memory (ROM) strings, and drivers in memory. If no such hints are found, the detection process skips detecting an entire class of equipment. If hints are found, then the detection process seeks information from specific I/O ports.

Windows 95 also reads CONFIG.SYS looking for hints about devices. And Windows 95 loads detection modules based on information in the MSDET.INF file, which lists the hardware to be detected and points to specific .INF files for each device class (for example, SCSI.INF for SCSI host adapters). Device information from the .INF files is written to the Registry.

Windows 95 also avoids touching certain resources based on particular CONFIG.SYS device= lines. For example, the detection process could lock up a fax modem by scanning the I/O ports covered by the drive. Windows 95 can read the device= line in CONFIG.SYS for the equipment and protect the associated I/O region from other detection modules.

Setup confirms which classes should be skipped in the detection process. However, if you know that a computer has a device in one of those classes, you can force Setup to detect that device class.

Safe detection is offered for the following four classes of devices:

➻ Network adapters.

➻ SCSI controllers.

➻ Proprietary adapters for CD-ROM.

➻ Sound cards.

Controlling Detection. The type of setup affects your control over detection. Using the Typical setup, you can choose to skip detection for certain types of hardware, such as CD-ROM or multimedia devices, depending on what Setup finds during its safe-detection examination of the hardware. If Setup incorrectly proposes to skip detection of certain hardware (that is, if you know the computer has the type of device Setup proposes to skip), you can override Setup's suggestion and ask it to detect the devices. Otherwise, skipping detection for the devices as suggested by Setup saves time during installation.

With Custom setup, you can specify whether Setup should skip detecting any specific devices attached to your computer. You should normally let Setup do its work unless you know that the computer has devices that cause problems during hardware detection. For example, you should skip detection of a SCSI card that caused Setup to fail during its detection process, but which Safe Recovery still tried to detect when you ran Setup again (see Figure 16.4).

FIGURE 16.4
Restarting
Setup

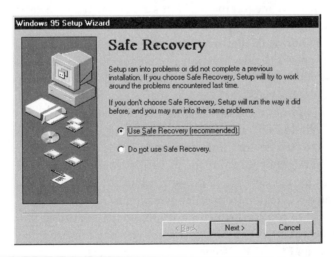

The Safe Recovery dialog box appears when you need to restart Setup due to a problem with a previous setup.

To modify the list of hardware to be detected during Custom setup, take these steps:

➤ On the first Analyzing Your Computer screen, click on the option named No, I Want to Modify the Hardware List, then click on the Next button. The second Analyzing Your Computer screen appears, containing lists of the components that Windows 95 Setup proposes to detect.

➤ To avoid detecting a specific class of hardware, clear the check mark for that hardware class from the Hardware Types list.

To avoid detecting a specific make and model of hardware device (while detecting other devices in that class), make sure that the related hardware type is checked and that the item you want to skip in the Manufacturer and Model list is not checked. If a hardware type is dimmed (but not checked), you cannot change how Windows 95 Setup detects that class of hardware.

Insider's Tip

The list of CD-ROM drives shows only proprietary drives that require special consideration during installation. All other CD-ROM drives, such as those that connect to SCSI or Enhanced IDE adapters, are detected automatically.

To begin hardware detection, click on the Next button, then click on it again.

The Roll of Logs in Safe Recovery. Windows 95 Setup creates several log files to aid in diagnosing a successful or failed installation: BOOTLOG.TXT, DETLOG.TXT, NETLOG.TXT, and SETUPLOG.TXT, plus DETCRASH.LOG if Setup fails. If Setup fails before the hardware detection phase, Windows 95 Setup recovers by reading SETUPLOG.TXT to determine where the system stalled, what to redo, and what to skip. If Setup fails during the hardware detection phase, the DETCRASH.LOG file is created. It contains information about the detection module that was running and the I/O port or memory resources it was accessing when the failure occurred.

When the detection process finds DETCRASH.LOG, Setup automatically invokes the Safe Recovery mode to verify all the devices already in the Registry and skips all detection modules up to the failed module. To make sure installation doesn't fail again, Safe Recovery skips the detection of and the attempt to configure the failed module. Safe Recovery continues the detection process, starting with the next module. If the detection process is completed successfully, DETCRASH.LOG is deleted. DETCRASH.LOG can be read only by Setup.

The procedure also works when the detection process causes a device to quit working (such as a CD-ROM drive or a network connection). Setup's Safe Recovery recognizes that the detection process was completed successfully and assumes that all the necessary hardware information has been placed in the Registry. Upon rerunning Setup, the detection process for the device in question is considered completed and is skipped, and Setup continues the installation process.

Continuing If Setup Stops. If the computer freezes during the hardware detection phase of Setup (that is, if you don't see any computer activity, and the progress meter does not change for more than 30 seconds), follow these steps:

➤ Press F3 or click on the Cancel button to quit Setup.

➤ If the computer does not respond to the Cancel button, restart the computer by turning it off and then back on again.

➤ Run Setup again. Setup prompts you to use Safe Recovery to recover the failed installation.

➤ Click on Use Safe Recovery, then click on the Next button.

➤ Repeat your installation choices. Hardware detection runs again, but Setup skips the portion that caused the initial failure.

➤ If the computer stops again during the hardware detection process, repeat the above procedure until the hardware detection portion of Setup is completed successfully.

The File Copy Phase

After you identify and confirm what components to install, Setup copies files from the Windows 95 installation disks or CD-ROM or the network server (whichever was specified). After the files are copied to the computer, you are prompted to remove any disks in floppy-disk drives and restart the computer to proceed with the final phase of Setup. If you choose to create a start-up disk, that disk is created before the files are copied.

Creating the Start-up Disk. A start-up disk is a bootable floppy disk that you can use to start and troubleshoot a malfunctioning computer. The start-up disk loads the operating system and offers the MS-DOS command line.

When it creates the disk, Windows 95 formats the floppy disk in drive A and copies a number of files, shown in Table 16.4.

TABLE 16.4
*The Files
Copied to the
Windows 95
Startup Disk*

Filename	Description
ATTRIB.EXE	File attribute utility.
COMMAND.COM	Core operating system file.
DRVSPACE.BIN	Disk compression driver.
EBD.SYS	Utility for the start-up disk.
EDIT.COM	Text editor.
FDISK.EXE	Disk partition utility.
FORMAT.COM	Disk format utility.
IO.SYS	Core operating system file.
MSDOS.SYS	Core operating system file.
REGEDIT.EXE	Real-mode Registry editor.
SCANDISK.EXE	Disk diagnostics and repair utility.
SCANDISK.INI	Configuration file.
SYS.COM	System file transfer utility.

In general, the start-up disk does not provide real-mode support for disk-management software such as Stacker 4.0, access to the network or CD-ROM, or access to compressed disk drives using software from third parties.

To have the start-up disk serve double-duty as a recovery disk, copy the following files into a subdirectory on the disk: SYSTEM.DAT, CONFIG.SYS, AUTOEXEC.BAT, WIN.INI, and SYSTEM.INI. Also copy any CD-ROM or other device drivers into the subdirectory.

Copying the Distribution Files. After creating a start-up floppy disk (if one is desired), Setup creates a list of files to copy based on the information gathered earlier. Various Setup DLLs run to install the network and other components. Those DLLs determine exactly which files should be copied from which source and what additional directories should be created.

Filling Out the Registry. After the files are copied, the Setup DLLs that install the system components also create appropriate entries in the Windows 95 Registry and change .INI file settings as required. (The Registry is created during the hardware detection phase.)

The SYSTEM.1ST file in the root directory is a copy of the Registry created when Setup completes its task. You can restore a damaged Registry by replacing the SYSTEM.DAT file with SYSTEM.1ST.

. . . .

The Final Configuration Phase

During the final phase, Setup upgrades the existing Windows configuration to Windows 95 and replaces the existing version of MS-DOS with the new Windows 95 operating system. During this process, Setup restarts the computer to run Windows 95.

When Windows 95 Setup completes this phase, a message is displayed indicating that the installation was successful and prompting you to restart the computer. After you click on OK but before Setup restarts the computer, Setup modifies the boot sector of the boot drive by adding a new system file (IO.SYS) that takes the place of the MS-DOS files IO.SYS and MSDOS.SYS. The old files are renamed IO.DOS and MSDOS.DOS.

The Final Touches. The first time Windows 95 Setup restarts the computer during the final configuration phase, Setup updates the configuration files by performing the following steps:

➤ WININIT.EXE processes three sections in WININIT.INI to combine all the virtual devices (VxDs) into a single file—VMM32.VXD—and renames files initially used by Setup, including ARIAL.WIN, USER32.TMP, and LOGO.SYS.

➤ The SYSTEM.DAT Registry file is renamed SYSTEM.DAO, and SYSTEM.NEW is renamed SYSTEM.DAT.

➤ Setup places a flag in the Registry indicating that Windows 95 is running the first time after a new installation. Hardware manufacturers sometimes add entries to the Run-Once Registry key.

➤ The Run-Once module is run to complete the initial configuration of PCMCIA and MIDI devices, to set up printers (if you are not installing Windows 95 in an existing Windows directory), and to run setup programs provided by custom hardware manufacturers.

Insider's Tip

If the system fails when it is running these first-time programs, restart Windows 95 rather than rerunning Windows 95 Setup.

➤ The Program Group Converter (GRPCONV) adds existing Windows 3.x .GRP files to the PROGRAMS directory and renames the files using long file names.

➤ Windows 95 copies the real-mode operating system files named IO.SYS, MSDOS.SYS, and COMMAND.COM into the root directory of the computer's start-up drive. Real-mode network files also are placed on the same drive. Windows 95 detects boot drives and compression drivers and writes start-up files to the boot device.

After Windows 95 restarts and reconfigures itself, Setup offers wizards to guide you in configuring the peripheral devices (such as printers and modems) connected to the computer. Additional files may be copied to your disk, and you may need to restart the computer again.

Adding New Hardware

When you add a new device to a computer, you can bring up Windows 95's hardware detection to detect and configure the device. The same hardware detection used during the initial setup of Windows 95 is reused when you add new hardware.

With a Plug and Play device, first connect the component to the computer. Windows 95 should detect the presence of the device automatically. If the device is listed in the Windows 95 database of hardware (compiled from files in the .INF directory), Windows loads the necessary software. If Windows 95 does not have the correct driver, you are asked to insert a disk containing the appropriate driver.

With legacy (non–Plug and Play) devices, use the Add New Hardware applet in the Control Panel. To install a card, for example, start Windows 95, run Add New Hardware, and click on the option labeled Automatically Detect Installed Hardware. If the applet detects and recognizes the device, it directs you on how to install drivers and configure the device.

If Windows 95 cannot detect a device, answer No when Windows 95 asks whether it should detect the device automatically. Manually select the device class, then select the device manufacturer and the specific device. Click on Next and follow the directions that appear.

If you know that Windows 95 requires the software provided with a device, select the device class and click on the Have Disk button. Follow the directions for installing the card.

The same procedures apply to adding modems, printers, and network devices. Connect a device, run the wizard, and allow the wizard to discover the device. If the device is not detected properly, manually select the device. If you know Windows 95 requires the software provided with the device, use the Have Disk button and follow the directions.

Custom-Design Your Own Installation

To write your own custom script—and thereby override SETUP.INF, the primary script responsible for installing Windows 95 and its accessories—you need to tinker with the elements that make up the MSBATCH.INF file.

Table 16.5 lists the main sections of the MSBATCH.INF file, which I will examine one by one.

TABLE 16.5
*The Main
Sections of*
MSBATCH.INF

Section	Description
[Setup]	Sets the parameters for the setup process.
[System]	Sets the parameters for modifying the system settings.
[NameAndOrg]	Defines the name and organization.
[InstallLocationsMRU]	Specifies which directory locations Setup offers when it is looking for files.
[OptionalComponents]	Controls the installation of optional components.
[Network]	Contains options for networks.
[netcard_ID]	Generic name for the identifier for the network adapters.
[NWLink]	Sets the parameters for IPX/SPX protocol.
[NWRedir]	Sets the parameters for the client of a NetWare network.
[NWServer]	Sets the parameters for file and printer sharing on a NetWare network.
[VRedir]	Sets the parameters for a client of a Microsoft Network.
[VServer]	Sets the parameters for File and Printer Sharing on a Microsoft Network.
[Printers]	Sets the parameters for installable printers.
[Strings]	Sets the user-defined strings expanded by Setup.
[Install]	Sets the parameters for additional files copied by Setup.

The [Setup] Section

The [Setup] section sets parameters for control of the Setup process. An asterisk (*) after a number indicates a default value.

Devicepath   Controls whether Windows 95 checks a source installation path for .INF files rather than looking only in the Windows .INF directory when Windows installs devices. Ensures that .INF files you add after installation are used, providing the most up-to-date setup. Use Devicepath only if the installation source files are in a network directory (not on floppy disks or CD-ROM).

Note that **Devicepath=1** causes the entire .INF database to be rebuilt each time a user changes a network component or changes drivers for any device.

Values   0* = Do not add a source directory path for .INF files.

1 = Add the installation source directory to the path for finding .INF files.

EBF   Controls whether an emergency start-up disk is created during Setup. If you are developing a hands-free installation, consider using ebd=0 so that the user isn't prompted to insert or remove a floppy disk. If you need to specify ebd=1, you can also add a reboot=0 entry so that Setup does not attempt to restart the computer while the floppy disk is in the drive.

Values   0 = Do not create an emergency start-up disk.

1 = Create an emergency start-up disk.

Express   Controls whether you can provide input during Setup. If Express=1, Windows 95 Setup uses only the settings specified in MSBATCH.INF and built-in defaults without confirmation. This setting disables most of the user interface for Setup.

Values   0* = Allow user input.

1 = Run Setup using only values in MSBATCH.INF.

InstallType   Specifies the Windows 95 Setup installation type.

Values   0 = Compact.

1* = Typical.

2 = Portable.

3 = Custom.

InstallDir   Specifies the directory in which Windows 95 is installed; in the case of shared installations, specifies the directory of the machine.

Values   Directory names.

Default   The Windows directory, if present.

PenWinWarning   Specifies whether to display a warning if an unknown version of Pen Windows is installed.

     Values   0* = Do not display the warning.

                  1 = Display the warning.

ProductID   Specifies the product ID for your site, printed on the Windows 95 compact disc or your Certification of Authenticity.

     Values   Strings.

     Default   None.

SaveSuBoot   Specifies whether to save the Suboot directory for server-based Setup.

     Values   0* = Delete Suboot directory.

                  1 = Save directory.

TimeZone   Specifies the time zone for the computer.

     Values   Strings (Table 16.5).

     Default   The time zone currently set on the computer.

TABLE 16.6
Time Zone Strings

Afghanistan	China	Israel	Saudi Arabia
Alaskan	Czech	Lisbon Warsaw	South Africa
Arabian	Dateline	Mexico	Sydney
Atlantic	E. Europe	Mid-Atlantic	Taipei
AUS Central	E. South America	Mountain	Tasmania
Azores	Eastern	New Zealand	Tokyo
Bangkok	Egypt	Newfoundland	US Eastern
Canada Central	Fiji	Pacific	US Mountain
	GFT	Romance	W. Europe
Cen. Australia	GMT	Russian	West Asia
	Greenwich	SA Eastern	West Pacific
	Hawaiian	SA Pacific	
Central Asia	India	SA Western	
Central Pacific	Iran	Samoa	

Uninstall   Specifies whether Setup creates a compressed backup version of the Windows and MS-DOS files, which are used to uninstall Windows 95. If you specify Uninstall=5, you also must add a value for BackupDir=path that specifies the directory in which Setup should place the compressed backup files.

Values 0 = Do not allow user to specify Uninstall options, and do not create backup files for uninstalling Windows 95.

1* = Show Uninstall options for user to choose.

5 = Do not show Uninstall options, but create backup files for uninstalling Windows 95 automatically.

Verify   Provided principally for use by OEMs; specifies whether to run Setup in Verify mode. This parameter is not the same as the MS-DOS Verify command. If Verify=1, you cannot prevent Uninstall in all cases, even if Uninstall=5 is in the setup script.

Values 0* = Do a full installation.

1 = Run Windows 95 Setup in Verify mode.

VRC   Specifies whether Setup overwrites existing files automatically, even if the date of the file on the disk is more recent than the date of the distribution file.

Values 0* = Prompt user to confirm before overwriting more recent files.

1 = Overwrite all without prompting for confirmation.

· ·

The [System] Section

The [System] section concerns system- and hardware-related items, such as the display, location, and use of Pen Windows. The section contains two types of entries. One type includes parameters that follow the conventions used in the other sections of the MSBATCH.INF file.

The second type of entries selects the default item from a group by naming the item or its associated section. Depending on the details of Setup, the new default may be changed by the user or will be installed automatically by Setup.

For example, the following line picks the MicronPnpBIOS14 as the default machine type:

```
Machine=MicronPnpBios14
```

The following entries use sections from the named .INF file. The choice must exactly match the section's name.

➠ **Locale=.INF_section_name** in LOCALE.INF.

➠ **Machine=.INF_section_name** in MACHINE.INF.

➠ **PenWindows=.INF_section_name** in PENWIN.INF.

➠ **Power=.INF_section_name** in MACHINE.INF or similar file (for advanced power management support).

➠ **Tablet=.INF_section_name** in PENDRV.INF or similar file.

The following entries use .INF descriptions. An .INF description must be in the pertinent list of compatible devices.

➠ **Display=.INF_description** in MSDISP.INF or a similar file.

➠ **Keyboard=.INF_description** in KEYBOARD.INF.

➠ **Monitor=.INF_section_name** in MONITOR.INF.

➠ **Mouse=.INF_section_name** in MSMOUSE.INF or a similar .INF file.

➠ **SelectedKeyboard=.INF_section_name** in MULTILNG.INF (specifies the keyboard layout).

The following are additional parameters for the section:

DisplChar	Sets the initial display characteristics.	
	Values	ColorDepth, x, y (where ColorDepth = bits per pixel, x = horizontal resolution, y = vertical resolution)
	Default	4,640,480
MultiLanguage	Sets what type of multilanguage support is installed for Windows 95.	
	Values	**English*** = Installs support for English and Western European languages.
		Greek = Adds support for Greek.
		Cyrillic = Adds support for Cyrillic.
		CE = Adds support for Eastern European languages.

Insider's Tip

If Express=1, you cannot add parameters that override safe detection for network adapters, SCSI controllers, or sound cards. This means that if Setup's software detection process does not find the hardware installed in the computer, Setup does not run its hardware detection to install support. In this case, you must run Add New Hardware in the Control Panel later to install support.

You can force the installation of certain hardware devices when Express=1 by adding specific entries in the [System] section. Otherwise, specify Express=0 in MSBATCH.INF, and you can manually specify hardware detection in the Analyzing Your Hardware dialog box.

The [NameAndOrg] Section

The [NameAndOrg] section defines the name and organization of the user for Windows 95 Setup and specifies whether the user is to be shown the Name and Organization dialog box.

Name   Specifies the full name of the user of this installation.

        Values String.

        Default None.

Org   Specifies the registered organization of the user of this installation.

        Values String.

        Default None.

Display   Specifies whether the Name and Organization dialog box appears during Windows 95 Setup.

        Values 0 = Do not display name and organization.

                  1* = Display name and organization.

The [InstallLocationsMRU] Section

The [InstallLocationsMRU] section specifies a list of directories from which the user can choose whenever Windows 95 Setup prompts for a path. Each directory is listed on a separate line of the drop-down list box.

In the following example, Setup offers the user the choice of A:\, C:\, or \\Server\Win95 as the location of files in the drop-down list box:

```
[InstallLocationsMRU]
mru1=a:\
mru2=c:\
mru3=\\server\win95
```

The [OptionalComponents] Section

The [OptionalComponents] section determines which descriptions appear in the Optional Components dialog box of Windows 95 Setup. Each entry in this section is a description enclosed in quotation marks, followed by an equal sign and either a 1 to install the component or a 0 not to install it. For example, the entries to install Briefcase and Net Watcher are as follows:

```
[OptionalComponents]
"Briefcase"=1
"Net Watcher"=1
```

Each description is defined in an .INF file. Table 16.7 lists the strings for the optional components defined in the Windows 95 standard .INF files. Additional strings are defined by other application developers.

Another way to define entries for this section is to copy the [OptionalComponents] section in SETUPLOG.TXT from a computer that already has all the optional components installed that you want defined in the Setup script.

TABLE 16.7
The Strings for Optional Components

Accessibility Options	Document Templates
Accessories	Flying Through Space
Audio Compression	Games
Backup	HyperTerminal
Blank Screen	Jungle Sound Scheme
Briefcase	Media Player
Calculator	Microsoft Exchange
CD Player	Microsoft Fax
Character Map	Microsoft Fax Services
Clipboard Viewer	Microsoft Fax Viewer
Communications	Microsoft Mail Services
Curves and Colors	The Microsoft Network
Defrag	Mouse Pointers
Desktop Wallpaper	Multimedia
Dial-Up Networking	Musica Sound Scheme
Direct Cable Connection	Mystify Your Mind
Disk Compression Tools	Net Watcher
Disk Tools	Object Packager

TABLE 16.6 *(cont.)*

Online User's Guide	Sound Recorder
Paint	System Monitor
Phone Dialer	System Resource Meter
Quick View	Utopia Sound Scheme
Robotz Sound Scheme	Video Compression
Sample Sounds	Volume Control
Screen Savers	Windows 95 Tour
Scrolling Marquee	WordPad

The [Network] Section

You can best understand network parameters if you break them down into six types:

➤ Installation parameters.

➤ Network card drivers.

➤ Shared installation parameters.

➤ Computer identification.

➤ Security parameters.

➤ User interface options.

Installation Parameters.

Clients   This parameter specifies the network client or clients to be installed. Each client is represented by a list of the device IDs used in the .INF files. Those IDs are not limited to the ones in the Windows 95 .INF files (NETCLI.INF and NETCLI3.INF).

A site that has an .INF file from another vendor can use any device IDs listed in that .INF file. However, if you are installing a client not listed in a Windows 95–provided .INF file, obtain an updated Windows 95 .INF file from the vendor.

When you install multiple clients, those clients are started in the order in which they appear. Multiple networks can be specified in a comma-separated list.

If the list contains two network clients or lists multiple networks with a primary-only network (such as IBM OS/2 LAN Server), Setup gives an error message and displays the Network Configuration Properties dialog box so you can change the selection. Setup, however, starts its verification process.

Values   Comma-separated list of client device IDs (Table 16.8).

Default   Defaults in NETDEF.INF.

Valid device IDs for network clients as specified in NETCLI.INF and NETCLI3.INF (the Windows 95–supplied .INF files).

·············
TABLE 16.8
*Valid
Device IDs*

Device ID	Network
lant5	Artisoft LANtastic version 5.x and 6.x.
netware3	Novell NetWare version 3.x.
netware4	Novell NetWare version 4.x.
nwredir	Microsoft Client for NetWare Networks.
pcnfs50	SunSoft PC-NFS version 5.x and greater.
vines552	Banyan Vines version 5.52 and greater.
vredir	Client of Microsoft Network.

Network Card Drivers.

netcards   This parameter specifies the drivers to be installed for network adapters as a list of the device IDs used in the .INF files. Those IDs are not limited to the ones included in the Windows 95 .INF files. A site that has an .INF file from another vendor can use any device IDs listed in that .INF file.

In general, I recommend that you rely on detection in Windows 95 Setup to install the correct driver and define the correct configuration settings. When a network adapter is listed, the usual verification takes place. Windows 95 Setup chooses an NDIS 3.1 driver, if available; otherwise, it uses an NDIS 2.x driver.

Values   Comma-separated list of network adapter device IDs.

Default   The results of Setup's detection.

The following entries, for example, would install drivers for Intel EtherExpress 16 or 16TP plus 3Com EtherLink II or IITP:

```
netcards=*PNP812D,*PNP80F3
```

IgnoreDetectedNetCards   Specifies what information Setup uses to configure network adapters: the detected information or the values specified by the netcards parameter in the Setup script.

Values   0* = Do not ignore detected adapters.

           1 = Ignore the detected network adapters and use the values specified for netcards=deviceID.

Protocols   Specifies the protocols to be installed as a list of the device IDs used in the .INF files. Those IDs are not limited to the ones in the Windows 95 .INF files; device IDs in .INF files from other vendors can also be used. Note that if you are installing a protocol other than those listed in the Windows 95 .INF files, you need to obtain an updated Windows 95 .INF file from the vendor.

Setup verifies the settings, and if a client is without a particular protocol, Windows 95 Setup chooses the protocol. For example, if you specify Clients=pcnfs50, then Windows 95 Setup adds NFSLINK.

Values   Comma-separated list of protocol device IDs (Table 16.9).

Defaults Defaults specified in NETDEF.INF.

TABLE 16.9
The Device IDs for Protocols in the Windows 95 NETTRANS.INF *File*

Device ID	Protocol
dec40	DECnet version 4.1 Ethernet protocol.
dec40t	DECnet version 4.1 token-ring protocol.
dec50	DECnet version 5.0a Ethernet protocol.
dec50t	DECnet version 5.0a token-ring protocol.
ipxodi	Novell-supplied IPXODI protocol.
msdlc	Microsoft DLC (real mode).
mstcp	Microsoft TCP/IP.
ndisban	Banyan Vines NDIS Ethernet protocol.
ndtokban	Banyan Vines NDIS token-ring protocol.
netbeui	Microsoft NetBEUI.

Device ID	Protocol
nfslink	Sun PC-NFS protocol.
nwlink	IPX/SPX-compatible protocol.
nwnblink	NetBIOS support for IPX/SPX-compatible protocol.

DefaultProtocol   Specifies the default protocol (assigned as LANA 0), which is bound to a specified network adapter (if the computer has more than one network adapter). If no adapter is specified, the default is the first instance of the specified protocol.

Since the only protocol bonded to LAN Adapter number 0 (LANA 0) is the default protocol, you must use this command if the computer's software expects a specific bonded protocol for LANA 0.

If netbios=1, you must set DefaultProtocol=nwnblink if you want to specify IPX/SPX-compatible protocol as the default.

Values A protocol device ID as defined in protocol= and, optionally, a network adapter device ID, as defined in netcards=.

Default 0 (zero).

The following example sets the default protocol as an instance of TCP/IP bound to a particular adapter:

```
DefaultProtocol=mstcp,*pnp812d
```

RemoveBinding   Removes the binding between two devices. This parameter is used to tune bindings in a Setup script.

Values Comma-separated list of device IDs.

Default None.

Services   Specifies the network services to be installed as a list of the device IDs from associated .INF files. Those device IDs can come from a Windows 95 or vendor-supplied .INF file, although any service listed in a Setup script is still subject to the usual verification.

The only service installed by default by Windows 95 is VServer (File and Printer Sharing for Microsoft Network). It is installed only if peer sharing services for Windows for Workgroups is enabled on the computer.

Values Comma-separated list of service device IDs (Table 16.10).

Default Windows 95 Setup defaults, depending on the value of InstallType.

TABLE 16.10
Valid Service Device IDs and Associated .INF files

Device ID	Service	.INF file
bkupagnt	Arcada Backup Exec Agent	BKUPAGNT.INF
cheyagnt	Cheyenne ARCserve Agent	CHEYENNE.INF
jadm	HP Network Printer Service for Microsoft	HPNETPRN.INF
janw	HP Network Printer Service for NetWare	HPNETPRN.INF
nmagent	Microsoft Network Monitor Agent*	NMAGENT.INF
nwserver	File and Printer Sharing for NetWare Networks	NETSRVR.INF
pserver	Microsoft Print Service for NetWare Networks	MSPSRV.INF
remotereg	Microsoft Remote Registry Service*	REGSRV.INF
snmp	Microsoft SNMP Agent*	SNMP.INF
vserver	File and Printer Sharing for Microsoft Networks	NETSRVR.INF

*Available in the Admin directory of the Windows 95 CD-ROM

Computer Identification Information.

ComputerName This parameter sets the computer's network name.

Values String of up to 15 alphanumeric characters and no blank spaces. The name must be unique on the network and can contain any of the following special characters:

! @ # $ % ^ & ( ) — _ ' { } . ~

Default Generated from the first eight characters of the user name.

Description Provides a description of the computer. Used mainly by peer servers such as File and Printer Sharing for Microsoft Networks.

Values 48 characters long; commas may not be used.

Default User name from licensing information.

Workgroup   Identifies the work group of the computer.

Values   String of up to 15 alphanumeric characters and no blank spaces. The name must be unique on the network and can contain any of the following special characters:

! @ # $ % ^ & ( )—_ ' { } . ~

Default   The previously specified work group; otherwise, a new name is generated from the first 15 permitted characters of the organization name. For example, an organization name of Microsoft Corporation results in MicrosoftCorpo as the default work group name. Workgroup is also affected by the System Policy concerning Microsoft Client for Windows Networks.

Shared Installation Parameters.

HDBoot   Specifies whether a computer running a shared copy of Windows 95 from a server is configured to start from the local hard disk or the network (HDBoot stands for hard disk boot).

Values $0^* =$ Start from the server or the floppy disk if WorkstationSetup=1.

$1 =$ Start from the hard disk and run from the network.

Table 16.11 shows the effects of the HDBoot and RPLSetup parameters for Windows 95.

TABLE 16.11
HDBoot and
RPLSetup
Parameters

Windows 95 location	HDBoot	RPLSetup
Hard-disk boot, Windows 95 on a server	1	0
Floppy-disk boot, Windows 95 on a server	0	0
Remote boot, Windows 95 on a server	0	1

RPLSetup   Controls whether Setup creates a disk image on the network server for a remote-boot workstation during workstation setup. This parameter is ignored if a corresponding WorkstationSetup value is not defined. You must set WorkstationSetup=1 to enable this feature.

Values $0^* =$ Don't do a remote-boot setup.

$1 =$ Do a remote-boot setup if WorkstationSetup=1.

WorkstationSetup Specifies whether Setup configures a client computer to run Windows 95 locally or from a shared copy on a server.

When WorkstationSetup is set to zero (0), Windows 95 Setup runs normally. When WorkstationSetup is set to one (1) and Setup is running from a server, Setup asks if the user wants to install Windows 95 as a shared copy or on the local hard disk. (See also the information on the HDBoot parameter earlier in this section.)

Values 0* = Allow a standard setup (local files).

1 = Allow a shared workstation setup (run from a server).

DisplayWorkstationSetup Determines whether the Setup user interface appears while Setup installs a shared copy of Windows 95 on a workstation.

Values 0* = Do not display user interface.

1 = Display user interface.

Security Parameters

Security Specifies the type of security and, for user-level security, the type of pass-through validation agent. These values have no effect if the installed client does not have a security provider.

Values **share*** = Share-level security.

nwserver = User-level security, validated by a NetWare server.

domain = User-level security, validated by a Windows NT domain.

msserver = User-level security, validated by a computer running Windows NT Workstation.

System Policy User-level access control settings (under policies for access control).

PassThroughAgent	Specifies the pass-through agent for user-level security. This value is ignored if share-level security is in place. The system policy for user-level access control affects this setting.
	Values Server or domain name.
	Default The value of Workgroup if Security= domain, the value of PreferredServer if Security=nwserver, or no value.

User Interface Options.

Display	Controls whether any of the Network Configuration dialog boxes appear during Custom Setup.
	Values 0 = Do not display.
	1* = Display.
ValidateNetCardResources	Specifies whether to bring up a resource conflict-resolution wizard to validate the network card resources if a partial configuration is detected or if there is an IRQ conflict for a network adapter.
	Values 0 = Do not display a wizard page.
	1* = Display a wizard page to resolve resource conflicts.

. . . .

The Network Cards Section

The actual name for this section is the network adapter's identifier as defined in the related .INF file. This section sets parameters for a specific network adapter, as defined in the [NETCARD.NDI] sections of the network device .INF files provided with Windows 95.

The entries in [netcard_ID] sections vary, depending on the adapter. The actual parameters and settings are found in the adapter's .INF file in the Windows .INF directory.

Generally, you should let Windows 95 Setup detect the adapter, install the correct driver, and define the correct configuration settings.

This section sets parameters for Microsoft TCP/IP, which was discussed in Chapter 10.

DHCP   Specifies whether TCP/IP should use DHCP for dynamic TCP/IP configuration.

                         Values   0 = Don't enable DHCP.

                                          1* = Enable DHCP.

DNS   Enables DNS name resolution. You must set DNS=1 if you plan to use LMHOST for name resolution.

                         Values   0* = Disable DNS.

                                        1   = Enable DNS.

DNSServers   Lists DNS servers in the order they should be accessed.

                         Values   Comma-separated list of DNS server names.

                         Default None.

Domain   Sets the DNS domain for the computer.

                         Values   String.

                         Default None.

DomainOrder   Lists DNS domains for host name resolution in the order they should be used.

                         Values   Comma-separated list of DNS domains.

                         Default None.

Gateways   Lists IP gateways (sometimes called IP routers) in the order they are to be used.

                         Values   Comma-separated list of IP addresses.

                         Default None.

Hostname   Sets the DNS host name for this computer (usually the same value as ComputerName).

                         Values   String.

                         Default None.

IPAddress   Sets the computer's IP address if DHCP is not enabled.

                         Values   Internetwork Protocol (IP) address (###.###.###.###).

                         Default None.

LMHOSTPath   Sets the path and file name of the LMHOST file.

                         Values   A valid path.

                         Default None.

PrimaryWINS   Sets the primary WINS name server.

                 Values   IP address (###.###.###.###).

                 Default   None.

SecondaryWINS   Sets the secondary WINS name server.

                 Values   IP address (###.###.###.###).

                 Default   None.

ScopeID   Sets the scope ID.

                 Values   String.

                 Default   None.

IPMask   Sets the IP subnet mask for TCP/IP if DHCP is not enabled.

                 Values   IP address (###.###.###.###).

                 Default   None.

WINS   Enables WINS for NetBIOS computer name resolution.

                 Values   0 = Disable WINS.

                              1* = Enable WINS resolution.

                       DHCP = Enable WINS but get parameters from the DHCP server.

. . . .

The [NWLink] Section

The parameters in the [NWLink] section specify settings for the IPX/SPX protocol. The settings are valid only if protocols=nwlink is also specified in the Setup script.

Frame_Type   Specifies the default frame type for IPX.

                 Values   0 = 802.3.

                              1 = 802.2.

                              2 = Ethernet II.

                              4* = Auto.

                              5 = Token ring.

                              6 = Token-ring SNAP.

NetBIOS Specifies whether NetBIOS support for IPX/SPX should be installed.

Values 0* = Don't install NWNBLINK.

1 = Install NWNBLINK.

· ·

The [NWRedir] Section

The parameters in the [NWRedir] section set the value for Client for NetWare Networks.

FirstNetDrive Specifies the first network drive to attach for log-in scripts for Client for NetWare Networks. This parameter overrides the equivalent setting in NET.CFG.

Values Drive letter (*A* and *A:* are equivalent).

Default F:.

PreferredServer Specifies the NetWare preferred server. This parameter does not override the equivalent setting in NET.CFG. PreferredServer settings are affected by the system policy under Microsoft Client for NetWare Networks.

Values String.

Default None.

ProcessLoginScript Specifies whether log-in script processing is enabled when Microsoft Client for NetWare Networks is running.

Values 0 = Disable log-in script processing.

1* = Enable log-in script processing.

SearchMode Specifies the NetWare search mode. The values are the same as those in NET.CFG for Novell NetWare. SearchMode settings are affected by the system policy for Microsoft Client for NetWare Networks.

Values 0 to 7

Default 0 (zero).

The [NWServer] Section

The [NWServer] section sets the parameters for File and Printer Sharing for NetWare networks.

BrowseMaster   Determines whether a computer configured with File and Printer Sharing for NetWare Networks can be selected as browse master.

Values 0 = This computer cannot be a browse master.

1* = This computer can be a browse master.

2 = This computer is the preferred browse master.

USE_SAP   Specifies whether a computer configured with File and Printer Sharing for NetWare Networks uses Server Advertising Protocol (SAP) browsing. Enables SAP browsing by any NetWare client but not in the Network Neighborhood.

Values 0* = Disable SAP browsing (use the workgroup style of browsing).

1 = Use SAP browsing.

The [VRedir] Section. The [VRedir] section sets the redirector parameters for Client for Microsoft Networks.

ValidatedLogon   Specifies whether log-ons are validated on a Windows NT domain. LogonDomain should also be set if ValidatedLogon=1.

Values 0* = Don't validate log-ons.

1 = Validate log-ons.

LogonDomain   Specifies the Windows NT domain to use for log-on validation. This parameter can be set regardless of the value of ValidatedLogon. If ValidatedLogon=1, you must set a correct value for LogonDomain to ensure that Windows 95 Setup has access to the required protected network files and to ensure that the user can log on successfully. This parameter is affected by the Log On to Windows NT settings in the Microsoft Client for Windows Networks system policy.

Values   String.

Default   Value of Workgroup in [Network].

. . . .

The [VServer] Section

The parameters in the [VServer] section control features of File and Printer Sharing for Microsoft Networks.

Announce   Specifies whether a computer configured with File and Printer Sharing for Microsoft Networks announces its presence to computers running LAN Manager on the network. Turning on Announce increases network traffic but also speeds up browsing.

> **Values**   0 = Don't announce VSERVER to the network.
>
> 1* = Announce VSERVER to the network.

MaintainServerList Specifies how a computer configured with File and Printer Sharing for Microsoft Networks behaves in a browse master election.

> **Values**   0 = Disabled (this computer cannot be a browse master).
>
> 1 = Enabled (this computer is the browse master).
>
> 2* = Auto (the computer can be a browse master if required).

. . . .

The [Printers] Section

This section controls the installation of one or more printers during Setup. Each printer has a separate entry in this section. The entry consists of a user-defined name for identifying the printer (such as a nickname or the printer's location), the model name, and the printer port, in the following format:

```
PrinterName=DriverModel,Port
```

The following restrictions apply to the entry:

➡ The length of the name for the printer cannot exceed 32 bytes (31 characters plus a null character). Setup truncates longer names.

➡ The model name must be recognized by Windows 95, by means of either a Windows or a third-party .INF file.

➡ Strings cannot contain a comma or a quotation mark.

The lines in the following example install a local printer and a network printer:

```
[Printers]
"My BJC600"="Canon Bubble-Jet BJC-600",LPT1
"LJ-VIi Next Door"="HP Laserjet
VIi",\\Server_1\Laser_2
```

Note that if the Setup script contains a [Printers] section with no entries, Setup skips the process of asking the user to select a printer the first time that Windows 95 runs.

PrinterName   Specifies the name, model, and port of a printer to be installed. The printer's name (the first parameter) appears in the Printers folder. The model name must match exactly the name of a printer driver supported by Windows 95; otherwise, Setup skips this entire section.

> **Values**   **PrinterName=** is the 32-byte string holding the printer's name; it cannot contain the following characters:
>
> \ , ; =
>
> **DriverModel=** The exact name of the driver for a printer supported by Windows 95.
>
> **Port=** The port to which the printer is attached (for example, LPT1) or a UNC pathname to a network print queue.

> **Default**   None.

The [Strings] Section

The [Strings] section contains key strings that are expanded into defined strings and used by Setup. In other sections placing percent signs (%) around a string key causes Setup to replace the string key with its corresponding value. The strings are in the form

String_Key=Value

where **String_Key** is a unique name made up of letters and digits, and **Value** is the letters, digits, and other printable characters that String_Key should become when it is expanded. Use quotation marks around this parameter if it will be an entry in a file that requires double quotation marks.

The following are three examples of string keys:

```
[Strings]
MSFT="Microsoft"
AD="AMCE DRIVERS"
DevDesc=APEX DRIVERS SCSI II Host Adapter
```

The [Install] Section

The [Install] section sets parameters for copying additional files as part of Windows 95 installation. The format of this section is identical to the format of the [Install] section of general .INF files.

Choosing a Work Group

The WRKGRP.INI file specifies a list of work groups that a user can choose to join. The WRKGRP.INI file also restricts the choices of work group available to a user, reducing the proliferation of work groups on the network. The file can also specify the defaults for a NetWare preferred server or a Windows NT domain on a per-work group basis.

The WRKGRP.INI file is stored in the Windows directory of the server containing the Windows 95 source files. Windows 95 Setup uses the values defined in WRKGRP.INI to set Registry values pertaining to the work group, the log-on domain, the preferred server, and other entities. The same values affect the options available to users in the Network section of the Control Panel.

The WRKGRP.INI file contains the following two sections:

➻ [Options] specifies the recognized options for work groups.

➻ [Workgroups] contains a list of available work groups.

You can set up each member in a work group with a domain, a preferred server, and other qualities, depending on the capabilities of your network.

Insider's Tip │ If Windows 95 Setup finds the WRKGRP.INI file in the Windows 95 source files, it copies the file to the shared Windows directory.

The [Options] Section

ANSI
: Specifies whether the work groups need to be converted from an OEM character set to ANSI.

  Values   True* or false.

Required
: Specifies whether users can type their own work-group names or must choose from a given listing.

  Values   True or false.

ForceMapping
: Specifies whether users can change the work group, the log-on domain, or the preferred server that has been mapped.

  Values   True or false.

Mapping
: Specifies the network providers to which work groups can be mapped. Also specifies the order in which values are listed in the [Workgroups] section. Implicitly, this parameter specifies where in the Registry to store settings. This parameter is optional. By default, work groups map to the domain or the preferred server.

  Values   A comma-separated list of network providers (NP1, NP2, NP3, and so on).

Default
: Specifies the default mapping for all work groups listed in the [Workgroups] section that have not been mapped. This enables you to add a single entry to an existing Windows for Workgroups WRKGRP.INI file to map all the work groups on the network. The format for Default entries is the same as for Workgroups entries (see the next section).

  Values   NP1_default, NP2_default, NP3_default, and so on.

The [Workgroups] Section

workgroup=optional_mapping Specifies a work group that users can choose. The associated mappings are applied automatically in the order specified in Mapping= (see the previous section). You can set up a workgroup= entry in the file for each work group that users can choose. The name of each work group must be followed by an equal sign (=) for the name to be interpreted correctly.

The entry that defines the network providers for each work group has the following format in the [Workgroups] section:

workgroup_name=mapping1,mapping2,mapping3, . . .

By default, work groups can be mapped to both Windows NT domains and NetWare preferred servers. If a WRKGRP.INI file exists, the Workgroup field in Windows 95 Setup and the Network option in the Control Panel both show all the work groups listed in WRKGRP.INI. Users can choose a work group from the list or type a work-group name. If Required=true in WRKGRP.INI, the user must choose from the list.

Installing Custom DOS Programs

To install custom DOS applications to run with Windows 95, you may need to modify the APPS.INF file, which contains the information for creating PIFs and assigning icons. During installation Setup places the APPS.INF file in the system directory, and Setup refers to this file when it builds the Start menu.

Note that the APPS.INF file in Windows 95 has changed substantially from its Windows 3.x counterpart. To add a new DOS application to APPS.INF, you must create an entry for the application in the [PIF95] section. The entry must be placed in the correct position alphabetically in the list. Afterward, a **Title** entry for the [Strings] section and a section that defines the application information must also be created. The Title entry must also be inserted in the correct position alphabetically in the [Strings] section. The application section can appear anywhere.

The [PIF95] Section

APPS.INF contains a section named [PIF95] that acts as a master list of settings for MS-DOS applications. Each line in this section corresponds to an entry in APPS.INF that contains information about running a specific application.

Each entry in the [PIF95] section uses the following syntax:

app file=%title%, icon file, icon num, set working, section, other file, set pif

The elements of a [PIF95] entry are as follows:

app file The file name, with extension, of the application's executable file.

title The name that appears in the application's title bar. Usually the title is a string identifier that appears in the [Strings] section of the .INF file and is set to the quoted name of the application.

icon file The file from which to extract the application's icon.

icon num The number of the desired icon from the icon-extraction table. The default is 0.

set working Automatically sets up the directory containing the executable file as the working directory (0, the default) or prevents Windows from doing so (1).

section The name of the corresponding section in APPS.INF that contains details about the application.

other file The key file within a directory for this application; used when two app file entries are identical.

set pif Allows (0, the default) or prevents (1) the creation of a .PIF file for this application.

All the entries in this section are alphabetized.

The [Strings] Section of APPS.INF

Inside the APPS.INF file is a [Strings] section, which contains entries in the same form as entries in the [Strings] section of MSBATCH.INF. The string key is the title from the [PIF95] section, and the value is the name of the application that appears in the title bar, placed within quotation marks. The entries in this section are alphabetized.

The Application Sections

Each section block as named by the **section** parameter in a [PIF95] entry defines parameters, required memory, and other options needed for the .PIF file. It also controls which options are enabled or disabled in the .PIF file (Table 16.12).

The following is an example of the syntax of the section parameter (note that you use commas to separate multiple entries):

```
[WORD.EXE]
LowMem=384
Enable=cwe
Disable=win,bgd,asp
```

• • • • • • • • • • • • •
TABLE 16.12
Abbreviations for Enabled and Disabled Entries in the Section Parameter

Entry	Meaning	Entry	Meaning
aen	Alt+Enter	**eml**	EMS memory locked
aes	Alt+Esc	**ems**	EMS memory
afp	Allow fast paste	**emt**	Emulate ROM
aps	Alt+Print Screen	**exc**	Exclusive mode
asp	Alt+Spacebar	**gmp**	Global memory protection
ata	Alt+Tab	**hma**	Use HMA
awc	Automatic window conversion	**lml**	Low memory locked
bgd	Background	**mse**	Mouse
cdr	CD-ROM	**net**	Network
ces	Ctrl+Esc	**psc**	Print Screen
cwe	Close on exit	**rvm**	Retain video memory
dit	Detect idle time	**rwp**	Run Windows applications
dos	Real mode	**win**	Run in a window
dsk	Disk lock	**xml**	XMS memory locked

Customizing Setup Scripts

You can specify custom settings for Windows 95 installations by creating a custom file in MSBATCH.INF format. This Setup script is then used for installation. The default Setup script is stored with the source files on the server. Custom Setup scripts can be stored in users' home directories or in other central locations.

You can create a custom Setup script in several ways:

➤ Use the server-based Setup program (NETSETUP.EXE) to create a script with most of the available custom settings.

➤ Use the batch Setup program (BATCH.EXE) to create a script with many settings.

➤ Create or edit a file in MSBATCH.INF format to specify all possible custom settings.

➤ Use the .INF file generator (INFGEN.EXE) to add and maintain customized scripts.

Use the server-based NETSETUP.EXE to produce a custom script that can be edited with a text editor to create the MSBATCH.INF file. Since NETSETUP.EXE adds entries for most sections, and since any changes to this file must be made by hand, this method of creating a script is the most comprehensive but also the most labor-intensive. NETSETUP.EXE also offers little help and is cryptic in the way it operates.

You can also use the BATCH.EXE program to create an editable MSBATCH.INF file. Because you fill in dialog boxes for most options, using BATCH.EXE is less labor-intensive than using NETSETUP.EXE, and the subsequent MSBATCH.INF file can be used directly.

The .INF Generator—a free Microsoft add-on—edits, combines, and adds other Windows 95 features that can be customized through scripts. NETSETUP.EXE and BATCH.EXE are provided on most CD-ROM versions of Windows 95 in the Admin\Nettools\Netsetup subdirectory. (This subdirectory and its programs are on the upgrade version of Windows 95 but have been omitted from some OEM versions of Windows 95.)

You can obtain these two files by purchasing the Microsoft Windows 95 Resource Kit (ISBN 1-55615-678-2) or by downloading the Resource Kit Utilities (a 3.2 megabyte file) from any of a number of sources, including America Online, CompuServe, the Microsoft Network, and Microsoft's World Wide Web and FTP sites. The .INF Generator (usually in a file called IG.EXE) can also be downloaded from many on-line services and from Microsoft's World Wide Web and FTP sites on the Internet.

You can also find several generic sample scripts that can be examined and edited in the Admin\Reskit\Samples\Scripts subdirectory of the Windows 95 CD-ROM and in the Windows 95 Resource Kit.

Danger Zone

Although you can edit .INF and other Setup script files with any text editor, make sure that you save a file as plain ASCII text by choosing the text (TXT) option in the File Type list. Some word processors can damage the files, because the programs insert their own formatting information into a file or change the ASCII values of certain characters. (Initialization files and scripts cannot contain characters with ASCII values above 127.)

Windows 3.1's Notepad utility, which you can keep, edits system files well, because it doesn't change the ASCII values or add formatting codes. However, Notepad doesn't work with files like APPS.INF, which exceed the puny 54K limit of what Notepad can handle. You can use Windows 3.1's Write or Windows 95's WordPad utility if you save files with the Text File option. If you have upgraded from MS-DOS 5.0 or a more recent version of MS-DOS, you can also use the MS-DOS Editor to edit Setup script files safely.

To be safe, always make a backup copy of an .INF or script file before you edit it. Discarding mistakes can be easier than trying to fix them.

Creating Your Own Setup Script with NETSETUP.EXE

You can use the Make Script button in a server version of Setup to create a default Setup script. This option can be used only to create a Setup script, not to edit an existing script. To edit an existing script, you must use a text editor.

To create a custom Setup script using a server-based version of Setup, take the following steps:

➤ From Windows 95, start NETSETUP.EXE by using the Windows Explorer or by choosing Run from the Start menu.

➤ In Server-Based Setup, click on the Make Script button.

➤ In the Save As dialog box, specify a file name for this Setup script, then specify the path to where the script is to be stored, and click on OK.

➤ Use the Server Based Setup Default Properties dialog box to adjust the custom settings. Check the corresponding boxes to turn on Setup functions or to enter values (Figure 16.5).

• • • • • • • • • • • • • •
FIGURE 16.5
*Setup for
Servers*

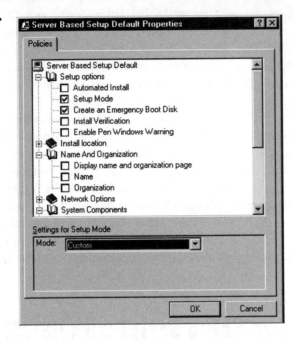

*Filling out the
checklist to produce
an .INF file for Server-
Based Setup (SBS)
or standard setups
using NETSETUP.EXE*

➤ Click on OK to save the new script file.

➤ Exit the program.

You can use the resulting script to guide an installation, or you can edit the script to refine its features.

Using BATCH.EXE to Make a Script

You can use the BATCH.EXE program to create a default Setup script. Like NET-SETUP.EXE, BATCH.EXE creates scripts but does not edit them (Figure 16.6). To edit an existing script, you must use a text editor.

To create a custom Setup script using a server-based Setup program, take the following steps:

➤ From Windows 95, start BATCH.EXE using the Windows Explorer or by choosing Run from the Start menu.

➤ Fill in the initial screen as desired.

➤ Click on the Network, Installation, and Optional Components buttons and fill out the corresponding forms as desired.

FIGURE 16.6

Installation Options

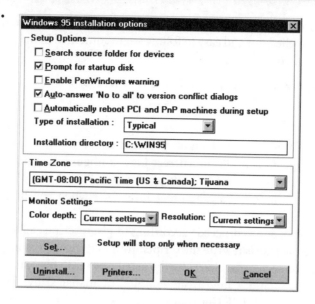

The Installation Options form from BATCH.EXE to construct a script file for Setup.

➻ Click on Done to name and save the new script file.

➻ Exit the program, or change options and save a new script.

The resulting script can guide an installation, or you can edit it to refine its features.

About the .INF Generator

The Setup Batch .INF Generator (.INFGEN.EXE) is a wizard that combines the best of BATCH.EXE and NETSETUP.EXE to enable you to create variations on Setup script files for individuals or groups with a minimum of hassle. For example, you can create a script with your company's standard settings and options and also develop separate scripts for work groups that have different security, network cards, or optional accessories. The standard script can be merged with the individualized scripts to produce unique Setup scripts for each work group.

.INF Generator includes options not available in NETSETUP.EXE or BATCH.EXE. For example, you can remove the Microsoft Network or the Microsoft Exchange Inbox from the desktop, disable the Online Registration wizard, and enable an option related to user profiles (Include Start Menu and Program Groups in User Settings).

The directions for installing and running the .INF Generator—which are clearly spelled out and easy to follow—are contained in the INFOGEN.DOC file within the IG.EXE file.

Summary

Setup of Windows 95 is a multiprogram effort to sniff out the correct hardware, copy and install the correct files, configure the setup, and aid in the migration of programs and settings from an established Windows 3.x installation to Windows 95. The procedure starts when you bring up the Setup program.

Because Setup proceeds according to given scripts, all you have to do to change the play is rewrite the scripts. Your best bet is to change MSBATCH.INF, an add-on script that overrides the usual .INF setup files. MSBATCH.INF can be created by hand, edited from samples, or managed by the NETSETUP.EXE, BATCH.EXE, and .INF Generator programs. BATCH.EXE is the friendliest program and the best for customizing most Setup actions, whereas .INF Generator provides options not available in the other programs.

Index

$ (dollar sign), share name and, 337
* (asterisk), wild-card character, 332
+ (plus sign)
   Explorer, 73
   Microsoft Exchange, 400
1K Xmodem, 350
3D Pinball, 15
   See also Microsoft Plus!
32-bit disk driver, 505
32-bit file system driver, 506
32-bit operating systems, 94
8086 processors, 476
8088 processors, 476
8514/a display card, 200–201
80286 (286) processors, 476
80386 (386) processors, 476
   system replacement and, 481
   Windows 95 and, 477
   See also processors
80486 (486) processors, 476
   DX, 478
   SX, 477–478
   See also processors
(–) minus sign
   Explorer, 73
   Microsoft Exchange, 400
" " (quotation marks), long file names and, 552
… (ellipses), 36, 41
? (question mark), wild-card character, 332

A

accelerated graphics cards, 203
   defined, 202
   examples, 203
   See also graphics accelerators
Access Control List (ACL), 334
Accessibility Options icon, 54, 185
Accessibility Properties dialog box, 185–189
   audio/video alerts, 189
   Display tab, 187–188
   FilterKeys, 185
   General tab, 189
   Keyboard tab, 185–186
   Mouse tab, 188
   opening, 185
   SerialKey, 189
   Sound tab, 187
   SoundSentry, 187
   StickyKeys, 185
   ToggleKeys, 186
Accessories submenu
   Dial-Up Networking command, 352
   Fax submenu, 123, 411, 415, 430
   Games submenu, 123
   illustrated, 123
   Multimedia submenu, 123, 457, 458
   opening, 123

   System Tools submenu, 123, 506, 515
adapter cards. *See* display cards
adapter segment. *See* upper memory area (UMA)
Add a Fax Modem dialog box, 346–347
Add Fonts dialog box, 272, 301
Add Language dialog box, 235
Add New File Type dialog box, 550–551
Add New Hardware icon, 54, 319, 342, 454
Add New Hardware wizard, 319, 454
Add Printer wizard, 182, 329
Add Program wizard, 174–175
Add/Remove Program Properties dialog box, 365–366
   opening, 365
   Windows Setup tab, 365–366, 410
Add/Remove Programs icon, 54, 351, 365
Address Book window, 375–376
   New Entry tool, 395
   Object menu, Properties command, 398
   Properties tool, 398
   toolbar, 394
   See also Microsoft Exchange
address books, 392–398
   displaying, 393

address books *(cont.)*
entry properties, 398
finding addresses in, 394
MSN, 393
Postoffice Address List, 393
properties, 398
starting message from, 394
See also Microsoft Exchange;
personal address book
Adjust Free Space dialog box, 520
Adobe Type Manager. *See* ATM
(Adobe Type Manager)
ADPCM sound files, 452
Advanced dialog box, 403
Advanced Fax Security dialog
box, 427–429
illustrated, 427
New Key Set button, 427
Public Keys button, 428, 429
See also Microsoft Fax
Advanced Options dialog box, 303
Advanced Options dialog box
(Disk Defragmenter), 508
Advanced Program Settings
dialog box, 576–577
alert boxes, 42
Alltype, 247, 303
Alt key. *See* keyboard shortcuts
analog video, 446, 447
defined, 447
working with, 447
See also video
animation, 450
clip libraries, 450
software, 450
See also graphics; video
Annotate dialog box, 155
annotating, help text, 155
ANSI characters, 238–241
codes, 239–240
defined, 238
interpretation of, 241
typing, 240
See also keyboards
Apple Macintosh, 8
applets
Briefcase, 144–148
Calculator, 142–143
CD Player, 458–459
Character Map, 140
defined, 122
DriveSpace, 515–521
game, 148–152
Media Player, 459–460

multimedia, 457–470
Notepad, 139
Paint, 132–139
Phone Dialer, 141–142
Sound Recorder, 461–464
Volume Control, 464–465
WordPad, 124–131
application icons, 37–38
defined, 37
illustrated, 38
moving, 38
See also icons
application menus, 33
application windows, 23, 24
applications
destination, 527
DOS, 95, 267–268, 287–288
installing/removing, 54
integrating, 523–553
mail-enabled, 407–408
older, running, 6
OLE, 534
OLE support, 104
opening multiple, 110
Programs submenu listing, 97
quitting, 119–120
simultaneous operation of, 110
source, 527
Start menu
adding, 174–176
removing, 176–177
starting, 96
from folder view, 98–99
from MS-DOS prompt,
100–101
from Run dialog box,
101–103
from Start menu, 96–98
switching between, 110–111
Win16, 94, 95
Win32, 94, 96
See also applets
APPS.INF file, 625–627
[PIF95] section, 625–626
section parameters, 626–627
[Strings] section, 626
archiving, personal folder file
messages, 403–404
ASCII text, 129, 130
asterisk (*), wild-card character,
332
ATM (Adobe Type Manager), 246
bundling of, 263
defined, 262

font installation and, 272
See also PostScript fonts
attachments, 381–382
defined, 381
digital signatures in, 429
embedded, 382
fax, 417
linked, 382
process, 382
saving, 391
See also mail
Attributes dialog box (Paint), 138
audio. *See* sound
audio alert, 189
AudioWave, 461
AUTOEXEC.BAT file, 559–560
MS-DOS mode and, 579–580
upper memory area and, 498
See also CONFIG.SYS file
A/V drives, 450
AVI (Audio Video Interleave)
files, 443
playing, 460
See also video

B

background, 162, 163–165
See also desktop
ballistic tracking, 218
bank switching, 499
BATCH.EXE
for creating Setup script,
630–631
defined, 628
illustrated, 631
batch files, 567
bidirectional printing, 279–280
BIFF data format, 526
Binary File Transfer (BFT), 409
bindings, 612
BIOS
Plug and Play, 595
ROM chips, 475
bit-mapped graphics, 132, 445
data format, 526
defined, 445
examples, 445
See also graphics
boot process, 558–561
Briefcase, 144–148
danger, 148
as data carrier, 148
defined, 144

entry arrangement, 147
folder, 144
icon, 144
moving, 146
My Briefcase, 144–146
packing, 144, 146
red X and, 147
Starter, 144
Status field, 145, 146
synchronizing data, 146–147
updating, 146–147
wizard, 145
working with, 145–146
See also applets
Browse dialog box, 102–103, 174, 175
illustrated, 102, 103
Look in drop-down list box, 102
uses, 102
Browsing for Wallpaper dialog box, 164
bulleted lists (WordPad), 125, 126
bus mastering cards, 202
bus mouse, 229–230
bus-cycle acceleration, 203
defined, 202
examples, 203
See also graphics accelerators
buses, 482–487
AT-style, 484
compatibility, 475
defined, 482
EISA, 483, 485
ISA, 483, 484, 486–487
local, 486
MCA, 483, 484–485, 486
PC peripheral, 483
PCI, 483, 486–487
Plug and Play, 487
ranking, 486–487
scheme for Intel processors, 482
VL (VESA), 483, 486, 487
See also processors

C

caches
external processor, 479
font, 258
processor RAM, 479
size of, 513

caching, 513–514
features, 513
self-tuning, 514
Calculator, 142–143
defined, 142
illustrated, 143
pasting results with, 143
Scientific mode, 142, 143
See also applets
Call Status dialog box (Phone Dialer), 141
carpal tunnel syndrome, 231
CD Player, 458–459
defined, 443, 458
illustrated, 458
opening, 458
Options menu features, 458
playlist, 458–459
See also multimedia
CD Plus, 454–455
CD-ROM drives, 453–454
internal/external, 457
setting up, 454
Setup detection of, 597
speed of, 453–454
CD-ROM versions, Windows 95, 13
CD-ROMs, 453–455
auto-play, 5
CD Plus, 454–455
defined, 453
formats, 454–455
multimedia and, 442
PhotoCD, 454
technology, 453
See also CD-ROM drives
CGA (Color/Graphics Adapter), 193
Change Display Type dialog box, 207
Change Password dialog box, 170
Change Ratio dialog box, 519
Change Source dialog box, 542–543
Character Map, 140
copying characters from, 275
defined, 140, 274
illustrated, 140, 275
opening, 274
quitting, 276
resetting characters in, 276
viewing characters in, 275
See also applets

Chicony's Keyboard KB-5581, 223
child document icons, 38–40
cycling through, 49
defined, 38
illustrated, 39
moving, 39
opening, 39–40
See also icons
child document windows, 22, 28–32
Control menu commands, 29
defined, 28–29
maximized, 30
menu bar, 29
minimizing, 39
viewing, 31
See also windows
chording, 226
chroma key, 449
Cinepak compression, 448
clients, 317, 322
DDE, 529–530
defined, 322, 532
device IDs, 610
dial-up, 351
installation, 609–610
linking to, 530
network fax modem setup, 346–347
OLE, 534–535
software pointer, 534
See also servers
client-server networks, 317
clip art, 433
Clipboard, 111–113, 524–528
data characteristics, 115
data formats, 525–526
data storage, 527
defined, 111, 523–524
destination application, 527
placing data on, 112–113
saving data, 115
source application, 527
uses, 112, 524
viewing, 114–115, 537–538
WordPad and, 127–128
Clipboard Viewer, 114–115, 527–528
defined, 114
Display menu, 535
display methods, 115
illustrated, 114, 115

clock, Taskbar, 173
Close button, 26, 27
Color icon, 205
color mixer (Paint), 136
color palettes, 135
    data format, 526
color printers, 312–313
color schemes, 210
color-depth resolution, 194
colors
    depth of, 210
    desktop, 162–167
    dithered, 211
    high-contrast, 188
    monitor displayed, 209–210
    Paint, 135–136
    performance vs., 198
    solid, 211
columns, 401–402
    rearranging, 402
    removing, 402
    restoring, 402
    types of, 401
    See also mail, folders
Columns dialog box, 401
COM ports, 229, 282, 283, 341–342
    COM1, 341
    COM2, 341
    connectors, 341
    default settings, 284
    defined, 282, 341
    I/O addresses, 342
    IRQs, 342
    settings on ISA bus, 341
    speed of, 284
    viewing settings, 284
    See also ports
COMMAND.COM prompt, 558–559, 572
command prompt, 561–576
    starting programs from, 565
    toolbar, 562–565
        Background button, 564
        button command access, 563
        Copy button, 562
        display, 573
        Font button, 564
        Font size list, 564–565
        Full-Screen button, 563
        illustrated, 562
        Mark button, 562
        Paste button, 563
        Properties button, 564

Windows 95 additions, 561
    See also DOS; DOS
        applications
communications, 340–355
    COM ports, 341–342
    defined, 340
    dial-up networking and, 351–353
    Direct Cable Connection
        (DCC) and, 354–355
    HyperTerminal and, 347–351
    remote access software, 341
    See also modems
Compact installation, 592–594
compatibility, 474–475
    IBM PC, 474
    problems, 475
Compose New Fax wizard, 414, 415–418
    Attach Files screen, 417
    Cover Page screen, 416–417
    initial screen, 415
    Recipient screen, 416
    Subject screen, 417
compound documents, 531
    objects in, 540
    See also OLE
Compress a Drive dialog box, 516
compression
    hard-disk drive, 514–521
    properties, 518–519
    ratios, 518, 519
    video, 448–449
Compression Options dialog box, 517
Compression Properties dialog box, 518–519
computers
    compatibility, 474–475
    description of, 613
    as dial-up server, 353
    finding, 69
    finding objects on, 71–72
    legacy, 594–595
    network name, 319, 613
    object-oriented view, 57–58
    rebooting, 57
    restarting in Setup, 598, 600
    work group of, 614
CONFIG.SYS file, 559–560
    DOS=LOW line, 572
    MS-DOS mode and, 579–580
    upper memory area and, 498
    See also AUTOEXEC.BAT file

configuration parameters, 83
Connect dialog box, 349, 352
Connect to Network Fax Server
    dialog box, 347
Control menu, 26–28
    accessing, 27
    Close command, 28, 29, 33
    document window, 29
    double-clicking on, 120
    Edit command, 28
    Maximize command, 28, 29
    Minimize command, 28, 29
    Move command, 24, 28, 29
    Next command, 29
    Restore command, 28, 29, 30
    Settings command, 28
    Size command, 24, 28, 29
control menus, 33
Control Panels, 53–56
    Accessibility Options, 54, 185
    Add New Hardware, 54, 319, 342, 454
    Add/Remove Programs, 54, 351, 365
    Color, 205
    Date/Time, 54, 182
    defined, 53
    Display, 54, 162, 207, 267
    Fonts, 54, 269
    Keyboard, 54, 232
    Mail and Fax, 54, 345, 368
    Microsoft Mail Postoffice, 54
    Modems, 55, 342
    Mouse, 55, 224
    Multimedia, 55
    Network, 55, 319, 321
    Passwords, 55
    Printers, 55, 278, 292, 320
    Regional Settings, 55, 183
    Sounds, 55
    System, 55, 510
    third-party, 53
    Windows 3.0/3.1, 56
controller cards, 504–505
    defined, 504–505
    technologies, 505
    See also hard-disk drives
conventional memory, 494–495
    addresses, 495
    changing, 571–572
    defined, 492
    device drivers and, 571
    division, 495
    DOS in, 572

maximum, 494
segments, 495
TSRs and, 571
See also memory; RAM
  (random-access memory)
conversations
DDE, 529–530
object, 546
Convert dialog box, 546
coprocessor cards, 203–204
defined, 103
nonsupport of, 203
See also processors
copying, 535
data to Clipboard, 112,
  127–128
with DDE, 113
DriveSpace and, 514
folder messages, 400
mail messages, 392
Microsoft Exchange folders,
  399
objects, 78
See also Clipboard
Cover Page Editor, 430–435
defined, 430
File menu
  Print command, 435
  Print Preview command,
    435
  Save command, 435
Format menu
  Align command, 432–433
  Color command, 433, 434
  Fill command, 433, 434
  Font command, 432
  Line command, 433, 434
illustrated, 430
Insert menu
  Message command, 432
  Object command, 433
  Recipient command, 432
  Sender command, 432
Layout menu
  Align Objects command, 434
  Bring to Front command,
    435
  Center on Page command,
    434
  Send to Back command, 435
  Space Evenly command, 434
opening, 430
toolbar, 431
  freehand drawing tools, 434

Select tool, 433
Text tool, 432
View menu, Grid Lines
  command, 434
See also Microsoft Fax
cover pages, 417
adding freehand drawing to,
  434
adding text frames to, 432
adjusting overlapping objects
  in, 435
aligning objects in, 434
centering objects in, 434
formatting graphics in, 434
formatting text and frames in,
  432–433
inserting clip art/graphics in,
  433
inserting fields on, 432
lists of, 420
previewing, 435
printing, 435
resizing/repositioning objects
  in, 434
saving, 435
spacing objects in, 434
unlisted, 420
See also Cover Page Editor;
  faxes
CPUs, 474, 475–487
defined, 475
See also processors
Create Installer Directory File
  dialog box, 300–301
Create New Compressed Drive
  dialog box, 518
Create Shortcut dialog box, 175
Creative Labs AeroDuet, 221
CSV data, 525
Ctrl key
in copying objects, 78
in moving/copying folder
  messages, 400
See also keyboard shortcuts
cursors
blink rate, changing, 233–234
defined, 20
illustrated examples, 20
Custom installation, 592–594
skipping detection in, 596
See also installation, Windows
  95; Setup program
custom-designed installation,
  601–623

customization
desktop, 162–167
multiple user, 179–182
network resource, 337–339
Start menu, 174–179
Taskbar, 170–179
Customize Toolbar dialog box,
  378–379
cutting, 524
data, 113
See also Clipboard; pasting

D

data
Clipboard, 115
copying, 112
cutting, 113
formats, 525–526
native, 533
pasting, 112
presentation, 533, 539
synchronizing (Briefcase),
  146–147
data communications. *See*
  communications
data files. *See* document files
date, 126
properties, 182–183
system, 54
Taskbar, 173
WordPad, inserting, 125, 126
See also time
Date/Time icon, 54, 182
Date/Time Properties dialog box,
  182–183
Date & Time tab, 182–183
illustrated, 182
opening, 182
Time Zone tab, 183
DDE (Dynamic Data Exchange),
  113–114, 528–550
client, 529–530
commands, editing, 552
conversations, 529–530
DDEML (Management
  Library), 528
defined, 113, 524
functioning of, 529–530
functions, 528–529
illustrated, 114
links, 113
server, 529–530
support, 529

DDE *(cont.)*
  using, 113
  See also OLE
deferred printing, 310, 331
defragmentation, 506–508
  benefits of, 506
  file, 508
  full, 508
  viewing, 507
  See also Disk Defragmenter
deleting
  distribution list names, 397,
    398
  DriveSpace volumes, 520–521
  folder messages, 400
  fonts, 54, 274
  linked objects, 543
  mail, 374, 392
  mail services, 369, 404
  Microsoft Exchange folders,
    399
  print jobs, 290
  printers, 286
  Start menu applications,
    176–177
  temporary files, 290
desktop, 17, 58
  application shortcuts on, 98
  colors, 162–167
    changing, 162
    defining, 166–167
    schemes, 165–167
    selecting, 166
  defined, 18, 58
  designing, 18, 162–163
  expanding, 196–201
  global user changes, 182
  illustrated, 23
  multiple, 180
  as object, 76
  patterns, 163–165
  personalized, 7
  text, modifying, 166
  virtual, 199
  wallpaper, 163–165
  See also graphical user
    interface (GUI)
Desktop Themes
  defined, 15
  See also Microsoft Plus!
destination document, 533
Details view, 61–62
DETCRASH.LOG, 597

device drivers. *See* drivers
Device Manager, 444
device objects, 66–67
  defined, 66
  pop-up menu, 82
  properties, 67, 81–82, 83–84
  See also objects
Dialing Properties dialog box,
  343
dialog boxes, 19–20, 41–43
  alert boxes, 42
  defined, 19
  illustrated, 20, 42
  tabbed, 19–20, 42–43
  See also specific dialog boxes
dial-up networking, 351–353
  clients, 351
  connections, creating, 352
  defined, 351
  dialing properties, 352
  with LAN mail system,
    404–408
  password, 353
  servers, 352–353
  software installation, 351
  See also networks
Dial-Up Networking window,
  352, 353
Dial-Up Server dialog box, 353
DIB graphics format, 526
DIF data format, 525
digital audio, 451–452
  ADPCM format, 452
  formats, 451
  storage requirements, 452
  See also sound
digital signatures
  assigning to attachments, 429
  defined, 425
  verifying, 429
  See also faxes
digital video, 447, 448
  compression, 448–449
  defined, 447
  See also video
DIP switches, 199
Direct Cable Connection (DCC),
  354–355
  defined, 354
  setting up, 354
  starting, 355
  uses, 354
  using, 354

  wizard, 355
  See also communications
directory, Windows 95
  installation, 589–590
Disk Defragmenter
  defined, 506
  monitoring progress, 507
  pausing, 507
  starting, 506–507
  stopping, 507
  See also defragmentation
disk-partitioning software, 588
display cards, 192
  32-bit, 198
  64-bit, 198
  8514/a, 200–201
  defined, 192
  DIP switches, 199
  EGA, 194
  graphics accelerators, 198,
    201–204
  memory, 195
  Super VGA (SVGA), 197
  TIGA, 200
  VGA, 194
  "video in a window," 213
  video RAM (VRAM) chips, 195
  XGA, 201
  See also display systems;
    displays
display drivers, 192, 205–210
  CGA, 193
  changing, 206–209
  color changes, 209–210
  defined, 192
  DOS, 193
  functioning of, 205–206
  list of, 206
  resolution changes, 209–210
  resolutions, 193
  Super VGA, 206
  versions of, 196
  VGA, 204, 209
  Windows 95, 192, 209
  See also display cards
Display icon, 54, 162, 207, 267
Display Properties dialog box
  Appearance tab, 165–167, 267
  Background tab, 163–165
  computer screen, 162
  illustrated, 163, 164
  opening, 162
  Screen Saver tab, 168

Settings tab
  Change Display Type
    option, 207, 213
  Color Palette drop-down
    list, 210
  Desktop Area slider bar, 210
  Font Size drop-down list,
    210, 267
  Large Fonts option, 197
display systems, 192–214
  components, 192
  television in, 213
display text format, 525, 537
displays
  Accessibility Options, 187–188
  colors vs. performance, 198
  configuring, 54
  ergonomics of, 211–213
  future of, 213–214
  interlaced, 198–199
  LCD, 205, 212
  non-interlaced, 199
  size of, 197
  standards of, 193
  technical specifications, 196
  technology improvements, 213
  See also display cards; monitors
distribution lists, 376–377
  adding names to, 396
  creating, 395–397
  maintaining, 397–398
  removing names from, 397,
    398
  See also mail; Microsoft
    Exchange
document files, 58
  attaching, 381–382
  closing, 108
  compound, 531
  creating, 99
  DOS, reformatting, 287–288
  dragging and dropping to, 99
  list of in Documents submenu,
    103
  opening, 106
  renaming, 99
  saving, 107–108
  types of, 99
document icons. See child
    document icons
Documents submenu, 50,
    103–104
  defined, 50

document list, 103, 104
  illustrated, 50, 104
dollar sign ($), share name and,
    337
Domain Name System (DNS),
    357–358
  defined, 357–358
  IP address, 358
  servers, 358–359
  See also Internet
domains, 324
DOS
  in conventional memory, 572
  display drivers, 193
  document reformatting,
    287–288
  extenders, 503
  file attributes, 566
  full-screen mode, 95
  mark data mode, 562
  overview, 557–558
  Setup program from, 586, 587
  Setup program from window,
    588
  toolbar, 95
  Windows 95 and, 555–581
  Windows 95 compatibility, 94,
    559
  Windows history with, 556
  See also command prompt
DOS applications, 95
  batch files and, 567
  closing with Window button,
    575
  custom, installing, 625–627
  expanded memory and, 500
  fonts and, 267–268, 564–565
  free environment space and, 572
  full screen mode, 563–564, 573
  icons for, 569
  idle, 575–576
  keyboard shortcuts to, 568
  mouse and, 574–575
  MS-DOS mode detection, 578
  multitasking behavior of, 564
  pasting data into, 563, 576
  printing from, 287–288
  properties, 564, 565–576
  screensavers, 574
  starting, 565
  System menus, 563
  titles for, 566
  video hardware and, 573–574

window configuration, 573
window detection, 576
window display, 568, 573
working directory, 567
See also command prompt;
  DOS
DOS commands, 100
  CD, 100
  MEM, 571
  START, 101
DOS Protected Mode Interface
    (DPMI), 502
  VxDs and, 561
dot pitch
  defined, 211
  See also monitors
dot-matrix printers
  9-pin, 306
  24-pin, 306
  color, 305
  defined, 304
  drivers, 304–306
  emulation, 296
  noise, 304
  paper options, 305
  Printer Setup dialog box for,
    304–305
  Windows spooler and,
    305–306
  See also printers
double-clicking, 20
  click interval, 225
  test area, 225–226
  See also mouse (mice)
drag-and-drop, 20, 77–78
  across volumes, 78
  to add shortcuts, 179
  adding Start menu program
    with, 178
  Ctrl key and, 78
  to data files, 99
  defined, 77
  embedding, 117–118
  illustrated, 77
  onto icons, 79
  for package creation, 549
  right mouse button and, 85
  Shift key and, 78
drivers
  32-bit disk, 505
  32-bit file system, 506
  conventional memory and, 571
  defined, 205

drivers *(cont)*
  display, 192, 205–210
  keyboard, 232
  minidrivers, 295
  modem, 342
  mouse, 228–229
  Plug and Play, 206
  printer, 282, 291–308
  real mode, 318, 559–560, 579
  updating of, 203
  virtual, 556, 560
DriveSpace 3
  defined, 15
  See also Microsoft Plus!
DriveSpace, 514–521
  compression capabilities, 514
  compression ratios, 518, 519
  copying files and, 514
  defined, 514
  hiding original drive, 517, 518
  illustrated, 515
  opening, 515
  volumes, 515–521
    adjusting size of, 520
    creating, 515–517
    creating new, 517–518
    deleting, 520–521
    empty, 515, 517
    hidden file, 520
    maintaining, 518–521
  See also hard-disk drives
dual-boot system, 590–592
  booting with, 592
  creating, 590–592
  MSDOS.SYS file and, 591
  See also installation, Windows 95
Dvorak keyboard layout, 236–238
  advantages, 236
  defined, 236
  further information, 238
  illustrated, 237
  typing program, 237
  See also keyboards
Dynamic Host Configure
    Protocol (DHCP), 358
dynamic RAM (DRAM), 488
  See also RAM (random-access
    memory)

E

Easter eggs
  activating, 16
  defined, 16

Edit Colors dialog box (Paint), 136
Edit dialog box, 299–300
Edit menu, 33
  Copy command, 112, 113, 127,
    137
  Copy Package command, 550
  Copy To command, 138–139
  Cut command, 113
  Insert Object command,
    543–544
  Label command, 549
  Links command, 541, 543
  Object command, 544–546
  Package Object command, 547
  Paste command, 112, 127, 536,
    550
  Paste Link command, 113,
    536–537, 539
  Paste Special command, 116,
    533, 536–537
Edit New Personal Distribution
    List Members dialog box,
    377
EDIT program, 575
editing
  colors (Paint), 136
  DDE commands, 552
  embedded objects, 116, 538
  Exchange profiles, 368
  in-place, 116–117
  linked objects, 540
  mail, 391
  mail services, 369–370
  patterns, 164–165
  personal address book, 371
  Setup scripts, 629
  sound files, 463–464
  source documents, 540
  visual, 533, 534, 539
EISA (Extended Industry
    Standard Architecture) bus,
    485
  defined, 483
  ranking, 486
  See also buses
ellipses (...), 36, 41
e-mail
  Internet, 360
  See also mail; Microsoft
    Exchange; Microsoft Mail
embedded objects
  activating, 538
  defined, 116
  editing, 116, 538

Object Packager and, 548
  updating, 538
  See also linked objects
embedding
  drag-and-drop, 117–118
  linking vs., 534, 540–541
  objects, 382, 533
  packages, 549
  with Paste/Paste Special
    commands, 537–538
  TrueType fonts, 260–261
  See also linking; OLE
EMM386 memory manager, 581
Encapsulated PostScript (EPS)
    files, 293
encrypted faxes, 426–429
  receiving, 429
  sending, 426–427
  See also faxes
Energy Star
  compliant, 212–213
  display settings, 207
  guidelines, 212
  monitors, 170
Enhanced Graphics Adapter
    (EGA), 194
Enhanced Metafile (EMF), 280
EPT ports, 282, 283
Esc key, 24
ESDI (Enhanced Small Device
    Interface) controllers, 505
Exchange Settings Properties
    dialog box
  Delivery tab, 373
  Services tab, 369, 404
  Show Profiles button, 368
expanded (EMS) memory, 492,
    498–502
  bank switching, 499
  changing, 570
  DOS applications and, 500
  EMS 4.0, 499–500
  history of, 499
  memory managers, 500–502
  VxD support, 561
  Windows and, 500
  See also memory; RAM
    (random-access memory)
Explorer, 46, 49, 72–88
  defined, 12, 72
  Disconnect Network Drive
    button, 329
  folder view window, 74
  illustrated, 12, 73

Map Network Drive button, 329
minus sign (–), 73
plus sign (+), 73
Start menu view, 177–178
toolbar, 76
Tools menu, 331, 337
tree, 73–74
    collapsing/expanding, 73
    contents, 74
View menu, Details command,
    337
viewing resources in, 73
views, changing, 76
extended (XMS) memory,
    502–504
    changing, 571
    defined, 492
    DOS access, 503
    DOS Protected Mode Inter-
        faces (DPMI), 502, 503
    high memory area (HMA),
        492, 502
    software protocols, 503
    Virtual Control Program
        Interface (VCPI), 503
    See also memory; RAM
        (random-access memory)
extended capabilities port (ECP),
    280, 331
Extended Memory Specification
    (XMS), 502
extremely low frequency (ELF)
    radiation, 212

F

F10, 34, 35
Fax Modem Properties dialog
    box, 422
fax modems, 408
    answer mode, 422–423
    network, 345–347
    settings, changing, 422–423
    sharing, 436–437
    See also faxes; modems
fax queue, 420–421
    viewing, 421
    See also faxes
Fax Security dialog box, 428
Fax submenu, 123, 411
    Compose New Fax command,
        415
    Cover Page Editor command,
        430

Fax Viewer, 423–425
    changing fax position in, 425
    enlarging/reducing faxes, 425
    inverting image colors, 425
    thumbnail view, 425
    toolbar, 424
    using, 424–425
    See also faxes; Microsoft Fax
faxes
    attachments, 417
    composing, 415–418
    cover pages, 417, 420
    dialing location, 415
    digital signature and, 425, 429
    Editable If Possible format,
        420
    encrypted, 425, 426–429
    forwarding, 423
    managing, 409
    orientation of, 419
    outgoing, 421, 422
    paper size, 419
    password-protected, 425–426
    printing, 424
    receiving, 421–423
    recipients, 416
    replying to, 423–424
    saving, 424
    security options, 420, 425–429
    sending, 414–415
        again, 421
        cannot send, 421
        encrypted, 426–427
        options, 418–421
        password-protected,
            425–426
        retrying options, 419
        when to send and, 418
    sizing, 425
    viewing, 423–424
    See also fax modems; fax
        queue; Fax Viewer;
        Microsoft Fax
fax-on-demand service, 435–436
Fellowes MousePen, 220–221
File and Printer Sharing dialog
    box, 334
file icons, 40–41
    defined, 40
    illustrated, 40
    types of, 41
    See also icons
File Manager. See Explorer;
    Windows 3.1

File menu, 33–34
    Close command, 108
    Exit command, 119
    Open command, 105, 591
    Print command, 286
    Printer Setup command, 287
    Properties command, 250
    Rename command, 84
    Save As command, 107, 108,
        115
    Save command, 107
    Update command, 538
file names. See long file names
file objects, 81
    folder view, 98
    See also files; objects
File System Properties dialog box,
    512–513
    CD-tab, 513
    Hard Disk tab, 512–513
    opening, 512
file system, settings, 512–513
file types
    action definitions for, 552
    adding, 550–552
    naming, 552
files
    ADPCM, 452
    attaching, 382
    AVI, 443
    batch, 567
    Briefcase, 147
    closing, 108
    document, 99
    EPS, 293
    finding, 68, 69–71
    help, 156–158
    MIDI, 444, 460, 466–470
    opening, 99, 104–105
    packaging, 547–549
    paging, 511
    PIF, 565
    PPD, 295
    Print to Disk, 259–260
    RTF, 288
    saving, 107–108
    shadow, 290
    SHD, 290
    sound, 460, 462–464
    spool, 290
    text-only, 288
    VOC, 451, 460
    WAV, 451, 460
    See also folders

FilterKeys, 185
Find: Computer dialog box, 72
Find dialog box, 69–71
  Advanced tab, 71
  Date Modified tab, 70–71
  Name & Location tab, 69–70, 332
  opening, 331
  search results window, 70
Find submenu, 51, 68–72
  Computer command, 51, 71
  defined, 51
  Files or Folders command, 51, 69
  illustrated, 51, 68
  On the Microsoft Network command, 51, 69
Find utility, 68–72
  defined, 68
  opening, 68
FINSTALL.DIR file, 300–301
Fixed fonts, 265
flicker, 198
  minimizing, 211
  See also displays; monitors
floppy-disk versions, 13
flow control. *See* handshaking
folder icons, 26, 40, 59
  defined, 40
  illustrated, 40
  See also icons
Folder Properties dialog box, 335–336
folder views, 59–63
  changing style, 61–63
  custom-designed, 61
  default, 61
  defined, 59
  file object, 98
  illustrated, 60
  My Briefcase, 145
  OLE aware, 118
  opening, 60
  toolbar, 63–66
  of volume root directory, 60
  See also folders; views
folder windows, 25–26
  defined, 25–26
  Explorer, 74
  Find dialog box, 70
  illustrated, 26
folders
  Briefcase, 144

  creating, 175, 176
  defined, 26, 59
  finding, 68, 69–71
  Fonts, 253, 269–273
  hiding from browsing list, 337
  HyperTerminal, 348
  Microsoft Exchange, 398–399, 400
  network, 327
  parent, 336–337
  passwords for, 339
  Printers, 278–279
  properties, 335
  Recycle Bin and, 79
  removing from Start menu, 176–177
  renaming, 176
  Send To, 286
  sharing, 334–337
  System, 84
  See also files; folder views; folder windows
font caches, 258
Font dialog box, 125
font effects, 248
font families
  defined, 247
  list of, 247
  PostScript, 254, 261–262
  TrueType, 254
Font Installer dialog box, 298–299
  Add button, 301
  directory, 299
  illustrated, 298
  Installer Directory File, 300–301
  opening, 298
  Permanent option, 299
Font Selection dialog box, 268
font style, 248
Font Substitution Table, 250
FontMonger, 247, 303
fonts, 245–276
  changing, 266–267
  cover page, 432
  default reply, 390
  device, 249
  DOS applications and, 267–268, 564–565
  features, 246
  Fixed, 265–266

  Help system, 267
  hinting, 263–264
  installing, 54, 268–273
    PostScript, 272–273
    TrueType, 271–272
  "jaggies," 276
  Lucida, 254–255
  monotype, 254
  MS Sans Serif, 274
  OEM, 265–266
  organizing, 276
  PostScript, 249, 261–264
  printable, 249
  printer, 249, 292–293
  printing
    PostScript, 262
    TrueType, 258–261
  raster, 248, 264–267
  removing, 54, 274
  screen, 249
  selecting with Character Map, 140
  soft, 249, 298–300
  styles of, 253
  substituted, 249–250
  system, 264–267
  Terminal, 265–266
  TrueType, 248, 250–261
  TrueType Font Pack 2, 256–258
  TrueType Font Pack, 254–255
  vector, 248, 249, 266
  viewing, 270–271
    installed, 270
    similar, 270–271
  See also font families
Fonts dialog box, 270
Fonts folder, 253, 269–273
  dragging fonts to, 271
  features, 270
  File menu
    Delete command, 274
    Install New Font command, 271
  getting to, 269
  illustrated, 269
  View menu
    List Fonts by Similarity command, 270
    Options command, 270
  See also fonts
Fonts icon, 54, 269
FontShow, 276

formatting text (WordPad), 124–127
.FOT files, 253
FPU (floating point unit). *See* math coprocessor
Freecell, 148–149
    defined, 148
    illustrated, 149
    See also games
FTP (file transfer protocol), 360
full versions, 13
full-screen mode, DOS, 95

G

games, 148–152
    development, 193
    Freecell, 148–149
    Hearts, 149–150
    Minesweeper, 150
    Party Line, 151
    Solitaire, 152
    See also applets
Games submenu, 123, 148
GDI (Graphics Device Interface), 201, 205
    heap, 521
General MIDI
    configuration, 470
    defined, 468
    synthesizers, 468
    See also MIDI
glidepoints, 214
    See also pointing devices
Gopher, 360
graphic overlay, 449
graphical user interface (GUI), 5, 17–43
    customizing, 162
    design of, 18
    history, 8–9
    illustrated, 6
    SAA CUA, 9
    Windows 3.1, 10
    See also desktop
graphics, 444–450
    animation, 450
    bit-mapped, 445
    in cover pages, 433–434
    pasting, 128
    still images, 444–446
    vector, 445
    video, 446–450
    See also multimedia

graphics accelerators, 198, 201–204
    accelerated graphics cards, 202, 203
    bus mastering cards, 202
    bus-cycle acceleration, 202, 203
    coprocessor cards, 202, 203–204
    defined, 198, 201
    drivers and, 203
    local bus video, 202, 204
    performance, 202
    types of, 202
    See also displays; display cards
graphics tablets, 216–217
    cost, 217
    defined, 216
    pen-shaped stylus, 217
    puck, 217
    See also pointing devices
grayscale
    color scheme, 205
    VGA, 204
    See also displays

H

handshaking, 284
hard-disk drives, 474
    accelerating, 505–506
    A/V, 450
    compressing, 514–521
    controller cards, 504–505
    defragmenting, 506–508
    IDE, 510
    SCSI, 510–511
    size of, 504
    speed of, 504
    See also DriveSpace
hardware
    adding new, 601
    database of, 601
    installing, 54
    Setup program detection, 594–598
heap space, 521–522
    GDI heap, 521
    improvements, 522
    limitation, 521–522
    USER heap, 521
Hearts, 149–150
    defined, 149
    illustrated, 149
    solo, 150

starting, 150
    See also games
help, 52, 153–159
    annotations, 155
    content entries, resizing, 154
    Express technique, 157
    fonts, 267
    getting, 154
    links, 155, 156
    options, 154
    paper clip icon, 154
    related topics, 155–156
    searching for, 157–158
    shortcuts, 156
    text windows, 154
    topics, 154
    WordPad, 153
    See also help files
Help dialog box
    Contents tab, 153–156
    Display button, 155
    Find tab, 157–158
    illustrated, 153, 154
    Index tab, 157
help files, 156–158
    express search, 157
    full-text search, 158
    links, 156
    pre-Windows 95, 158–159
    searching, 157–158
    See also help; Help dialog box
Hercules monochrome adapter, 193–194
Hewlett-Packard
    DeskJet printers, 307
    PCL (Printer Control Language), 297
    See also LaserJet printers
hexadecimal addresses, 493–494
hierarchical windows, 22
high color, 194
high memory area (HMA), 492, 502
    defined, 492
    freeing, 572
    See also memory
HIMEM.SYS, 503
hinting, 263–264
    defined, 263
    PostScript, 263–264
    TrueType, 263, 264
    See also fonts
horizontal scan frequency, 195
hot links, 530

HyperTerminal, 347–351
  call reception with, 349
  Connection icon, 349
  Connections, 348–349
    creating, 348
    dialing, 349
  defined, 347
  folder, 348
  limitations, 348
  sending/receiving files with, 350
  transfer protocols, 350–351
  See also communications

I

IBM PC compatibility, 474–475
IBM PS/2 mouse, 220
icons, 18, 37–41
  activating, 37
  application, 37–38
  Briefcase, 144
  child document, 38–40
  Control Panels, 54–55
  defined, 19
  for DOS applications, 569
  drag and drop onto, 79
  envelope, 372
  file, 40–41
  folder, 26, 40, 59
  illustrated examples, 19
  MS-DOS prompt, 49
  My Briefcase, 144, 146
  My Computer, 59, 72
  Network Neighborhood, 325
  Network server, 310
  object, 77
  package representations, 549
  paper clip, 154
  Scraps, 118
  shortcut, 84
  Start menu, 173
  substituting for graphic image, 547
  types of, 37
  volume, 40, 59
IDE (Integrated Drive Electronics) controllers, 505
Image Color Matching (ICM), 280–281, 295
  defined, 281
  using, 281
Indeo compression, 448
independent document windows, 23–24

.INF Generator, 631–632
  defined, 628, 631
  installing/running, 632
  uses, 631
inkjet printers, 307
in-place editing, 116–117
  advantages of, 117
  defined, 116
  process of, 116–117
InPort mouse interface cards, 229–230
Insert File dialog box, 381
Insert Icon dialog box, 548
Insert Object dialog box, 433, 544
[Install] section, 623
  See also MSBATCH.INF file
Install New Modem wizard, 342–343
installation
  custom DOS programs, 625–627
  disks. *See* Windows installation disks
  font, 268–273
  Microsoft Exchange, 365–366
  modem, 342–343, 345–347
  over Windows for Workgroups, 322
  peer-to-peer network, 318
  printer, 281–286
  Windows 95, 583–632
    Compact, 592–594
    Custom, 592–594
    custom-designed, 601–623
    directory, 589–590
    dual-boot system and, 590–592
    file copy phase, 598–599
    final configuration phase, 600–601
    hardware detection phase, 594–598
    Portable, 592–594
    time for, 588–589
    type, choosing, 592–594
    Typical, 592–594
    See also Setup program
[InstallLocationsMRU] section
  defined, 607
  See also MSBATCH.INF file
interface. *See* graphical user interface (GUI)
interlaced display, 198–199

Internet, 355–360
  connecting to, 355
  cruising, 359–360
  Domain Name System (DNS), 357–358
  e-mail, 360
  FTP (file transfer protocol), 360
  Gopher, 360
  servers, 358–359
  Telnet, 360
  Usenet newsgroups, 360
  World Wide Web (WWW), 355, 359, 360
  See also Microsoft Network (MSN); TCP/IP
Internet Explorer
  defined, 15
  See also Microsoft Plus!
Internet Extensions
  defined, 15
  See also Microsoft Plus!
Internet Setup Wizard
  defined, 15
  See also Microsoft Plus!
Introducing Microsoft Windows 95, 14
I/O addresses
  COM ports, 342
  port, 283
IO.SYS, 600
IPX (Internetwork Packet Exchange), 323
IRQs (interrupt request lines), 229
  COM ports, 342
ISA (Industry Standard Architecture) bus, 484
  defined, 483
  ranking, 486–487
  See also buses

K

Kensington Expert Mouse, 223
Kermit, 350
Keyboard icon, 54, 232
Keyboard Properties dialog box, 232–236
  contents of, 232
  General tab, 232
  Language tab, 232, 234–236
  opening, 232
  Speed tab, 232, 233–234

keyboard shortcuts, 19, 88–91
    Alt+minus+M, 39
    Alt+minus+N, 39
    Alt+minus+R, 39
    Alt+minus+X, 30, 40
    Alt+minus, 29
    Alt+C, 275
    Alt+F+C, 33
    Alt+F+P, 286
    Alt+F+X, 27, 34
    Alt+F4, 27
    Alt+N, 65
    Alt+S, 65
    Alt+spacebar+N, 27
    Alt+spacebar+X, 27
    Alt+spacebar, 27
    Alt+Tab, 24
    Ctrl+<, 388
    Ctrl+>, 388
    Ctrl+B, 379
    Ctrl+Esc, 35, 173
    Ctrl+F4, 33
    Ctrl+F, 391
    Ctrl+I, 379
    Ctrl+M, 373
    Ctrl+N, 373, 376, 394
    Ctrl+P, 286, 309
    Ctrl+Shift+B, 376, 393
    Ctrl+Shift+C, 392
    Ctrl+Shift+F, 394, 402
    Ctrl+Shift+M, 392
    Ctrl+Tab, 29, 39
    Ctrl+U, 379
    Ctrl+V, 275
    to DOS programs, 568
    list of, 89–91
    scrolling, 25
    Sound Recorder, 462
keyboards, 230–241
    Accessibility Options, 185–186,
        236
    ANSI characters, 238–241
    Chicony's Keyboard KB-5581,
        223
    commands for, 21
    configuring, 54
    drawers for, 231
    drivers, 232
    ergonomics, 230–231
    height of, 231
    key repeat intervals, 233
    keycaps, changing, 237
    languages, 234–236
        adding, 234–235
    switching, 234
    Taskbar indicator, 234, 235
    layouts
        changing, 235
        Dvorak, 236–238
        QWERTY, 236, 237
        switching between, 235
    pointer combination, 223–224
    properties of, 232–236
    repeat rate, 233
    repetitive stress injuries and,
        230–231
    speed options, 233–234

L
Label Edit dialog box, 549
languages, keyboard and,
    234–236
LANs (local area networks),
    404–408
laser printers, 311–312
    features, 312
    prices, 311
    speed of, 312
    See also printers
LaserJet printers, 296–302
    categories, 297–298
    downloadable soft fonts,
        298–300
    HP PCL, 297
    See also Hewlett-Packard
LCD displays, 205
    color, 212
    future of, 214
    See also displays; monitors
legacy computers, 594–595
legacy devices, 601
light pens, 215
Link format, 526, 537
linked objects, 539–540
    deleting, 543
    editing, 540
    updating, 541, 542
    See also embedded objects
linking, 382
    disk space and, 540
    embedding vs., 534, 540–541
    objects, 534
    See also embedding; OLE
links
    breaking, 543
    broken, 532
    help, 155, 156

hot, 530
list of, 542
maintenance of, 532, 541–543
OLE, 532
repairing, 542
updating, 530
warm, 530
Links dialog box, 541–542
    Change Source button, 542
    illustrated, 542
    link list, 542
    maintenance tasks, 541
    opening, 541
List view, 62
local area networks. See LANs
local bus, 486
    defined, 486
    slot, 204
    See also buses
local bus video, 204
    defined, 202
    PCI, 204
    VESA, 204
    See also graphics accelerators
local drive, 328
Logitech
    3-D mouse, 220
    cordless radio mouse, 219
    MouseMan, 219
    TrackMan, 222–223
    TrackMan Portable, 224
logon
    default, 324–325
    unified, 327
Logon dialog box, 179, 181
long file names, 94
    aliases, 512
    quotation marks ("") and, 552
LPT ports, 282, 283
    default settings, 283
    defined, 282
    See also ports
LRU (Least Recently Used)
    algorithm, 509
Lucida typefaces, 254–255

M
Macromedia Director, 450
Magnifier (Paint), 136–137
mail, 364
    addressing, 375–376
    attaching documents to,
        381–382

mail *(cont.)*
  attachments, saving, 391
  blind courtesy copies, 378
  composing, 379–383
  copying, 392
  courtesy copy (Cc), 374, 375
  creating, 373–375
  deleting, 374, 392
  editing, 391
  folders, 398–399, 400–404
    column layout, 401–402
    copying, 399
    copying messages, 400
    deleting, 399
    deleting messages, 400
    finding messages in,
      402–403
    layout customization,
      401–402
    moving, 399
    moving messages, 400
    renaming, 399
    sorting, 400–404
    See also personal folders file
  formatting toolbar and,
    379–380
  forwarding, 374, 382, 391
  moving, 374, 392
  notification options, 388–389
  OLE and, 382
  polling, 372, 373
  posting, 383–385
  printing, 374, 382, 392
  priority, 385
  reading, 388
  receipt options, 387
  recipient name, 378
  replying to, 388, 389–390
    font, 390
    with original message,
      389–390
  retaining copies of, 388
  sending to distribution list,
    376–377
  sending/receiving, 372–373
  sensitivity options, 386–387
  spell checking, 383
  text
    finding/replacing, 380
    formatting, 379–380
    inserting, 381
    rearranging, 380
  undeliverable, 384–385
  See also Microsoft Exchange

Mail and Fax icon, 54, 345, 368
mail services, 369–370
  adding, 369, 404
  deleting, 369, 404
  editing, 369–370
  remote preview with, 406
  removing message from, 407
  transferring message from, 407
  See also Microsoft Exchange
mail-enabled applications,
  407–408
Make New Connection wizard,
  352
Managing Public Keys dialog
  box, 429
Map Network Drive dialog box,
  329, 337
MAPI (mail application programming interface), 407
mapping
  persistent, 329
  remote drives, 328–329
  See also Network
    Neighborhood
mass storage devices, 60
math coprocessor, 481–482
  defined, 481
  types of, 481–482
  See also processors
Mavis Beacon Teaches Typing,
  237–238
Maximize button, 26, 27, 30, 31
MCA (Micro Channel
  Architecture) bus, 484–485
  defined, 483
  ranking, 487
  upgrading and, 485
  See also buses
MCI (Media Control Interface),
  444
MDI (Multiple Document
  Interface), 22
mechanical mice, 216
Media Player, 459–460
  defined, 444, 459
  files compatible with, 460
  illustrated, 459, 460
  Time scale, 460
  Track scale, 460
  using, 460
  See also multimedia
memory, 487–503
  area layout of, 493
  configuration, 475

  conventional, 492, 494–495,
    571–572
  display card, 195
  expanded, 492, 498–502,
    569
  expansion methods, 498
  extended, 492, 502–503, 571
  hex values, 493–494
  high memory area (HMA),
    492, 502, 572
  printer, 294, 312
  ROM, 487
  solid-state, 487
  swapping, 492
  upper memory area (UMA),
    492, 496–498
  virtual, 509–511
  volatile, 488
  See also RAM (random-access
    memory)
memory managers
  defined, 498
  EMM386, 500–502, 581
  HIMEM.SYS, 503
  third-party, 571, 581
  Windows 95 and, 580–581
  See also memory
menu bar, 29, 34
menu structure, 98
menus, 33–36
  accessing, 34–35
  advantage of, 33
  application, 33
  cascading, 36
  check marks, 36
  closing, 35
  control, 33
  defined, 18
  deselecting, 35
  dimmed items, 35
  ellipses (…) and, 36, 41
  highlighting, 35
  keyboard shortcuts, 19
  pulling up/down, 34–35
  selecting, 34
  triangles and, 36
  underlined letters in, 34
  See also specific menus and
    submenus
Message Security Options dialog
  box, 421, 425–426
messages. *See* Microsoft Exchange
Metafile format, 526
Microsoft Ballpoint, 224

Microsoft Exchange, 363–438
  address books, 392–398
  Compose menu
    Forward command, 391
    New Messages command,
      373, 414
    Reply to All command, 389
    Reply to Sender command,
      389
  defined, 364–366
  distribution lists, 395–398
  Edit menu
    Find command, 380
    Paste Special command, 382
    Replace command, 380
  editor, 364
  faxes. See Microsoft Fax
  features, 437–438
  File menu
    Copy command, 392, 400
    Delete command, 392
    Move command, 392, 400
    New Folder command, 399
    Print command, 392
    Properties command, 387
    Save As command, 391
    Send command, 384
  folders, 398–399, 400
    column layout, 401–402
    copying messages, 400
    deleting messages, 400
    finding messages, 402–403
    layout customization,
      401–402
    managing, 398–399
    moving messages, 400
    renaming, 399
    sorting messages, 400–404
  formatting toolbar, 379–380
  Inbox, 364, 398
  Insert menu, Message
    command, 382
  installing, 365–366
  mail, 364
    addressing, 375–376
    attachments, saving, 391
    blind courtesy copies, 378
    copying, 392
    courtesy copy (Cc), 374, 375
    creating, 373–375
    deleting, 374, 392
    document attachment,
      381–382
    editing, 391

    forwarding, 374, 382, 391
    moving, 374, 392
    notification options,
      388–389
    OLE and, 382
    polling, 372, 373
    printing, 374, 382, 392
    priority, 385
    reading, 388
    receipt options, 387
    recipient name, 378
    replying to, 388, 389–390
    sending to distribution list,
      376–377
    sending/receiving, 372–373
    sensitivity options, 386–387
    spell checking, 383
    text, 379–381
    undeliverable, 384–385
  mail services
    adding, 369
    deleting, 369
    editing, 369–370
  Message Server, 364, 365
  message window, 409
  Outbox, 384, 398
  personal address book, 367
    capturing addresses, 395
    copying addresses, 395
    creating addresses, 395
    editing, 371
    fax recipients, 413–414
    properties, 371
    switching between, 372
    using, 375–376
  personal folders file, 367
    archiving items in, 403–404
    managing, 398–399
    password, 370–371
    properties, 370
    Sensitivity column, 386
  profiles, 54, 366–372
    contents of, 366
    creating, 368
    defined, 366
    editing, 368–369
    multiple, 367
  running, 366
  toolbar
    Address Book tool, 393, 413
    customizing, 378–379
    Delete tool, 392, 400
    Forward tool, 391
    illustrated, 374

    New Message tool, 373, 376
    Print tool, 392
    Reply to All tool, 389
    Reply to Sender tool, 389
    Send tool, 383
    tool list, 374–375
    Update Header tool, 407
  Tools menu
    Address Book command,
      376, 393, 413
    Connect and Transfer Mail
      command, 407
    Connect and Update
      Headers command, 407
    Customize Toolbar
      command, 378
    Deliver Now Using
      command, 373
    Find command, 402
    Microsoft Fax Tools
      command, 427, 428
    Options command, 383, 387
    Services command, 371, 404
  windows, 399–400
Microsoft Exchange Profiles
    dialog box, 367–368
Microsoft Fax, 345–346, 365,
    408–437
  answer mode settings, 422–423
  BFT and, 409
  configuring, 411–413
  Cover Page Editor, 430–435
  feature, 409–410
  Outgoing Faxes window, 421,
    422
  printer, 411
  pseudoprinter, 414
  RSA encryption and, 410
  setting up, 410–411
  shortcut, 413
  TAPI-aware, 421–422
  See also faxes; Microsoft
    Exchange
Microsoft Fax Properties dialog
    box
  Details tab, 411
  Message tab, 412–413
  Modem tab, 345–346
  opening, 345, 411
  User tab, 412
Microsoft Mail, 372
  Connection tab, 405
  polling, 372
  Postoffice Address List, 393

Microsoft Mail *(cont.)*
  Postoffice icon, 54
  remote preview feature,
    405–406
  work-group version, 365
  See also Microsoft Exchange
Microsoft Mail Properties dialog
    box, 372
Microsoft Mouse, 218–219
Microsoft Network (MSN), 49,
    355–356
  address book, 393
  defined, 355
  finding on, 69, 331–332
  prices, 356
  World Wide Web browser, 355
  See also Internet
Microsoft Plus!, 14–15, 351
  contents, 15
  defined, 15, 351
Microsoft Windows 95 Resource
    Kit, 628
MIDI
  adapters, 467
  configuring, 469–470
  controllers, 467
  defined, 460, 466
  files, 444, 466–470
    playing, 467–468
    size of, 467
  General, 468, 470
  MPC, 469
  polymessage support, 468
  product categories, 466
  samplers, 467
  synthesizers, 467, 468
  Windows 95 and, 468–469
  See also multimedia; sound
MIDI Configuration dialog box,
    470
MIDI Instrument Installation
    wizard, 470
Minesweeper, 150
  illustrated, 150
  playing, 150
  See also games
minidrivers, 295
Minimize button, 26, 27
minus sign (–)
  Explorer, 73
  Microsoft Exchange, 400
Modem Properties dialog box,
    344–345
  Connection tab, 345

General tab, 344–345
  opening, 344
modems, 342–347
  autodetection of, 342–343
  configuring, 55, 343–345
  connection settings, 345
  drivers, 342–343
  fax, 408
  faxware, 409
  installing, 342–343, 345–347
  network fax, 345–347
  properties, 344–345
  See also communications
Modems icon, 55, 342
monitors, 192
  color, 205
  colors, number displayed,
    209–210
  display size, 197
  dot pitch, 211
  Energy Star, 170
  flicker, 198
  future of, 214
  glare and, 211–212
  LCD, 214
  monochrome, 205
  positioning of, 211, 212
  prices, 197
  refresh rates, 195–196
  resolutions, 209–210
  scan rates, 195, 211
  size, 197
  VDT emissions, 212
  See also displays
monochrome VGA, 204–205
  types of, 204
  See also displays; monitors
motherboard, 481
mouse (mice)
  Accessibility Options, 188
  ballistic tracking, 218
  bargain mice, 222
  bus, 229–230
  button assignments, 226
  chording, 226
  click interval, 225
  connecting, 229–230
  Creative Labs AeroDuet, 221
  DOS applications and,
    574–575
  double-clicking, 20
  drag-and-drop, 20
  drivers, 228–229
  ease of operation, 214

Fellowes MousePen, 220–221
  IBM PS/2 mouse, 220
  InPort interface card, 229–230
  invention of, 215
  Logitech mice, 219
  mechanical, 216
  Microsoft Mouse, 218–219
  Mouse Systems mice, 220
  optical, 216
  optomechanical, 216
  PDP, 229, 230
  placement, 215
  Plug and Play, 217
  points per inch (ppi), 217
  ProHance mice, 222
  properties, 224–229
  resolution, 217–218
  right button, 21
  right/left-handedness, 55, 215,
    225
  serial, 229
  tails, 215
  Tandy PS/2 mice, 221
  tracking mechanism, 215–216
  tracking speed, 55, 218
  uses, 20
  Windows button recognition,
    224
  wrist cushion, 215
  See also mouse pointer;
    pointing devices
Mouse icon, 55, 224
mouse pointer, 20
  appearance of, changing,
    226–227
  four-headed, 24
  numeric keypad as, 188
  speed of, 227–228
  trails, 227–228
  See also mouse (mice)
Mouse Properties dialog box,
    224–229
  Buttons tab, 224, 225–226
  contents, 224
  General tab, 224, 228–229
  Motion tab, 224, 227–228
  Pointers tab, 224, 226–227
Mouse Systems mice, 220
MousePen, 220–221
moving
  application icons, 38
  Briefcase, 146
  child document icons, 39
  folder messages, 400

mail, 374, 392
Microsoft Exchange folders, 299
shortcuts, 86
Taskbar, 47
windows, 23–24
See also drag-and-drop
MPC (Multimedia Personal Computer) standard, 455–457
MIDI, 469
MPC II, 455
MPC III, 455–456
upgrade kit, 456
See also multimedia
MPEG video format, 449
MPR II (Swedish National Council for Meteorology) standards, 212
MSBATCH.INF file
[Install] section, 623
[InstallLocationsMRU] section, 607
[NameAndOrg] section, 607
[netcard_ID] section, 616–618
[Network] section, 609–616
[NWLink] section, 618–619
[NWRedir] section, 619
[NWServer] section, 620
[OptionalComponents] section, 608–609
[Printers] section, 621–622
section list, 602
[Setup] section, 602–605
[Strings] section, 622–623
[System] section, 605–607
[VRedir] section, 620
[VServer] section, 621
See also Setup scripts
MSDOS.DOS, 600
MS-DOS mode, 57, 569
AUTOEXEC.BAT file and, 579–580
automatic detection for, 578
CONFIG.SYS file and, 579–580
defined, 577–578
dual-booting, 578
exiting, 579
function of, 578
real-mode device drivers and, 579
setting up, 578–579
warning, 578–579
See also DOS applications

MS-DOS prompt, 49
launching programs from, 100–101
See also command prompt
MS-DOS Prompt Properties dialog box, 268
MSDOS.SYS file, 591
MSN. *See* Microsoft Network
multimedia, 441–471
applets, 457–470
CD-ROMs and, 442, 453–455
defined, 442
graphics, 444–450
hardware performance and, 457
impact of, 442
interactivity, 442
magazines, 443
mechanics of, 443–444
MPC standard, 455–457
Plug and Play and, 444
sound, 451–452
system recommendations, 457
World Wide Web and, 442–443
Multimedia icon, 55
Multimedia Properties dialog box, 469–470
Multimedia submenu, 123, 457
CD Player command, 458
Volume Control command, 465
multiple users, 179–182
See also user profiles
multitasking, 108–111
defined, 108
DOS programs and, 564
illustrated, 109, 110
opening multiple applications and, 110
switching applications and, 110–111
task list and, 111
usefulness of, 109
Musical Instrument Digital Interface. *See* MIDI
My Briefcase, 144–146
folder view, 145
icon, 144, 146
See also Briefcase
My Computer, 10–11, 46, 58–72
defined, 10, 59
Dial-Up Networking icon, 351, 352
folder views, 59–63

icons, 59
illustrated, 11, 59
toolbar, 63–66
View menu
Details command, 61
Options command, 65

N

[NameAndOrg] section, 607
See also MSBATCH.INF file
Native format, 526
navigating, 45–91
Net Watcher, 339–340
defined, 339
illustrated, 340
location of, 339
uses, 340
views, 340
NetBEUI (NetBIOS Extended User Interface), 323–324
[netcard_ID] section, 616–618
defined, 616
parameters, 617–618
See also MSBATCH.INF file
Netscape Navigator, 15, 355
NETSETUP.EXE
creating Setup scripts with, 629–630
defined, 628
illustrated, 630
obtaining, 628
NetWare
network security levels, 334
print servers, 310
network adapters, 322
defined, 323
driver installation, 610
installing, 319
non–Plug and Play, 320–321
PCMCIA, 323
Plug and Play, 320
setup configuration, 319, 611
network components
adding, 319–321
compatibility, 318
properties, 324
setting up, 321
types of, 322
viewing, 322
See also networks
Network Control Panel
Access Control tab, 321, 333

Network Control Panel *(cont.)*
   Configuration tab, 321
      Description area, 322
      File and Printer Sharing
         button, 334
      illustrated, 323
      Primary Network Logon list,
         324
   Identification tab, 319, 321
network fax modems, 345–347
   client setup, 346–347
   server setup, 345–346
   sharing, 347
   See also modems
Network icon, 55, 319, 321
Network Neighborhood, 74
   defined, 325
   Entire Network icon, 326
   icon, 325
   illustrated, 326
   for mapping network drives,
      328–329
   Netware server icon, 310
   for network printer
      installation, 330
   opening Explorer from, 326
   selecting resource with, 327
network parameters, 609–616
   computer identification
      information, 613–614
   installation parameters, 609–610
   network card drivers, 610–613
   security parameters, 615–616
   shared installation parameters,
      614–615
   types of, 609
   user interface options, 616
network printers, 308–310, 327
   checking status of, 320
   deferred printing, 310, 331
   installing, 329–330
   managing, 339
   Netware print server, 310
   point and print and, 330
   printing with, 309
   remote print-queue control,
      330–331
   restricting access to, 330
   setting up, 329
   sharing, 308–309, 329
   WinPopup and, 309
   See also printers
network resources
   connecting to, 326–328

customizing, 337–339
managing, 339
naming, 337–338
passwords, 338–339
searching for, 331–332
shared, 333
sharing, 334–337
using, 327
viewing, 74–75
See also networks
network security, 332–334
   definitions, 334
   levels, 332
   share-level, 332–333
   user-level, 332, 333
   See also security
networked computers
   availability of, 328
   names for, 319
[Network] section, 609–616
   Clients parameter, 609–610
   ComputerName parameter,
      613
   DefaultProtocol parameter,
      612
   Description parameter, 613
   Display parameter, 616
   DisplayWorkstationSetup
      parameter, 615
   HDBoot parameter, 614
   IgnoreDetectedNetCards
      parameter, 611
   netcards parameter, 610
   PassThroughAgent parameter,
      616
   Protocols parameter, 611–612
   RemoveBinding parameter,
      612
   RPI.Setup parameter, 614
   Security parameter, 615
   Services parameter, 612–613
   SystemPolicy parameter, 615
   ValidateNetCardResources
      parameter, 616
   Workgroup parameter, 614
   WorkstationSetup parameter,
      615
   See also MSBATCH.INF file
networks, 316–340
   advantages of, 316
   browsing, 325–326
   client-server, 317
   hardware/software
      configuration, 55

logon
   default, 324–325
   unified, 327
OLE support, 541
passwords, 332, 334
peer-to-peer, 317–318
printing across, 329–331
services, 612–613
setting up, 318–319
uses, 316
Windows 95 support, 316–340
See also dial-up networking;
   network components
New Action dialog box, 552
New Entry dialog box, 396, 413
New Fax Properties dialog box,
   413–414
New Message dialog box,
   373–374, 378
   default toolbar, 384
   formatting toolbar, 379–380
New Personal Distribution List
   Properties dialog box,
   376–377, 396
non-interlaced display, 199
non-PostScript laser printers,
   295–296
Norton Navigator, virtual
   desktops, 199
Note Properties dialog box, 386,
   387
Notepad, 139
   defined, 139
   illustrated, 139
   See also applets
notify area
   defined, 53
   illustrated, 53
   See also Taskbar
numeric keypad, as mouse
   pointer, 188
[NWLink] section, 618–619
   defined, 618
   Frame_Type parameter, 618
   NetBIOS parameter, 619
   See also MSBATCH.INF file
[NWRedir] section
   defined, 619
   parameters, 619
   See also MSBATCH.INF file
[NWServer] section
   defined, 620
   parameters, 620
   See also MSBATCH.INF file

O

object conversations, 546
Object Packager, 546–550
    Appearance window, 548
    Content window, 548, 550
    defined, 546
    with embedded file, 548
    opening, 544, 547
    packaging files, 547–549
    uses, 547
    See also OLE; packages
ObjectLink format, 526, 535
object-oriented interface, 57–58
objects
    configuration parameters, 83
    copying, 78
    in cover pages, 434–435
    desktop, 76
    device, 66–67, 81–82
    document, 58
    embedded, 116, 537–538
    embedding, 382, 533
    file, 81, 98
    finding, 68–72
    icons, 77
    linked, 539–540
    linking, 382, 534
    manipulating, 76–81
    name of, 70
    off limits, 84
    OLE, 532
    pop-up menus, 82
    properties, 77
    recovering, 80
    in Recycle Bin, 79
    renaming, 83
    Scraps, 118–119
    title, changing, 84
    volume, 59
    See also folder views
OEM fonts, 265–266
OEM text format, 525
OLE, 115–119
    applications, 534
    clients, 534–535
    compound documents, 531
    defined, 58, 115, 524
    destination document, 533, 534
    drag-and-drop embedding,
        117–118
    folder views and, 118
    functioning of, 533–534
    functions, 531

in-place editing, 116–117
links, 532
mail messages and, 382
network support, 541
object classes, 544
object conversations, 546
Object Packager, 546–550
objects, 532
packages, 532
program support for, 104
Registry, 533, 538, 544,
    550–552
    contents, 550
    defined, 550
    updating entries, 550–552
    viewing, 544
Scraps, 58, 118–119
servers, 534–535
source document, 533, 534
terminology, 532–533
uses, 531–532
visual editing, 533, 534, 539
WordPad and, 129
See also DDE (Dynamic Data
    Exchange)
on-line help. *See* help
Open dialog box, 105–106
    File of Type drop-down list
        box, 106
    folder view, 105
    fully configured, 106
    Look in drop-down list box, 105
    toolbar, 105
optical mice, 216
[OptionalComponents] section,
    608–609
    defined, 608
    strings, 608–609
    See also MSBATCH.INF file
Options dialog box (Microsoft
    Exchange)
    General tab, 388–389, 423
    Read tab, 390
    Send tab, 387, 388
    Services tab, 385
    Spelling tab, 383
Options dialog box (OLE), 550,
    551
Options dialog box (WordPad),
    131
optomechanical mice, 216
orientation
    of faxes, 419
    printing, 292

OS/2 operating system, 9
OverDrive, 480
Owner format, 526
OwnerLink format, 526, 535
    data information, 537
    Paste command and, 536

P

packages, 532
    creating, 547–550
        with embedded files, 547
        using drag-and-drop, 549
        using file portion, 549–550
    defined, 534
    editing, 547
    embedding, 549
    icon representations, 549
    labels for, 549
    loading, 547
    non-OLE data, 547
    uses, 547
    See also Object Packager;
        OLE
packing (Briefcase), 144, 146
paging file, 511
Paint, 132–139
    bitmapped images, 132
    color mixer, 136
    colors, 135–136
        background, 135
        changing, 135
        creating, 136
        editing, 136
        palette, 135
    Copy To command, 138–139
    defined, 132
    illustrated, 132, 133, 134, 137
    image attributes, 138
    Image menu, 138
    painting in, 134
    stretch option, 138
    tools
        additional, 135
        brush, 133–134
        changing, 134
        fill, 134
        free form, 137
        Magnifier, 136–137
        palette, 133
        pencil, 134
        selection, 137
        shape creation, 134
    See also applets

palettes (Paint)
  color, 135
  tools, 133
PANOSE Typeface Matching
  System, 271
Paragraph dialog box, 125
parallel ports, 283
  See also LPT ports
parity checking, 490–491
  defined, 490–491
  error messages, 491
  See also RAM (random-access
    memory)
Party Line, 151
  defined, 151
  setup, 151
  starting, 151
  See also games
password-protected faxes,
  425–426
  receiving, 426
  sending, 425–426
  See also faxes
passwords
  changing, 170
  dial-up networking, 353
  faxes and, 425–426
  folder, 339
  for network resources,
    338–339
  personal folder file, 370–371
  properties, 180
  screensaver, 170
  setting, 55
  user profile, 179
Passwords icon, 55
Passwords Properties dialog box,
  180
Paste Special dialog box, 114,
  536–537
  As: box, 537
  illustrated, 536
  opening, 536
  Paste radio button, 537
pasting, 524–525
  Calculator results, 143
  data from Clipboard, 112,
    127–128
  with DDE, 113
  graphics, 128
  into DOS programs, 563, 576
  See also Clipboard; cutting
Pattern Editor dialog box,
  164–165

patterns, 163–165
  creating, 164–165
  editing, 164–165
  pixels in, 165
  wallpaper and, 165
  See also desktop
PCI (Peripheral Component
  Interconnect) bus, 204
  defined, 483
  ranking, 486–487
  support for, 486
  See also buses
PCMCIA adapters, 323
peer-to-peer networks, 317–318
  installing, 318
  See also networks
pen plotters, 308
  emulation, 296
  list of, 308
  See also printers
Pen Windows, 605
Pentium processors, 476
  clones, 479
  motherboards, 481
  speed version of, 478
  See also processors
performance
  colors vs., 198
  components, 474
  graphic accelerator, 202
  improvement, 6
  multimedia and, 457
  printing TrueType fonts and,
    258–259
  VxDs and, 561
  Windows 95, 473–522
personal address book, 367
  addresses
    capturing, 395
    copying, 395
    creating, 395
    defined, 394
    editing, 371
    fax recipients, 413–414
    maintaining, 394
    properties, 371
    switching between, 372
    using, 375–376
    See also Microsoft Exchange
personal folders files, 367
  archiving items in, 403–404
  managing, 398–399
  password, 370–371
  properties, 370

Sensitivity column, 386
  See also Microsoft Exchange
Phone Dialer, 141–142
  adding speed dial entries, 142
  call placement methods, 141
  defined, 141
  illustrated, 141, 142
  recently dialed numbers list, 141
  speed dial option, 142
  See also applets
PhotoCD, 454
PIF (Program Information Files),
  565
[PIF95] section, 625–626
  defined, 625
  elements, 626
  See also APPS.INF file
pixels
  defined, 132
  in patterns, 165
  resolution, 194
Plug and Play
  BIOS, 595
  buses, 487
  defined, 206
  drivers, 206
  mice, 217
  multimedia and, 444
  network adapters, 320
  printers, 280, 294
  support for, 206
Plus Pack, 276
plus sign (+)
  Explorer, 73
  Microsoft Exchange, 400
Pointing Device Mouse (PDP),
  229, 230
pointing devices, 214–230
  AeroDuet 3D mouse and pen,
    221
  bargain mice, 222
  defined, 214
  ergonomics, 214–215
  glidepoints, 214
  graphics tablets, 216–217
  IBM PS/2 mouse, 220
  Kensington Expert Mouse, 223
  keyboard combination,
    223–224
  light pens, 215
  Logitech mice, 219–220
  Logitech TrackMan, 222–223
  Logitech TrackMan Portable,
    224

Microsoft Ballpoint, 224
Microsoft Mouse, 218–219
Mouse Systems mice, 220
MousePen, 220–221
PC Trackball, 223
PowerMouse, 222
product overview, 218–223
ProMouse, 222
Tandy mice, 221
touch screens, 215
trackballs, 216
trackpoints, 215
See also mouse (mice)
polling, 372, 373
polymessage MIDI support, 468
pop-up menu. *See* Shortcut menu
Portable installation, 592–594
ports
COM, 229, 282
conflicts, 283
designations, 283
ECP, 280, 331
EPT, 282
LPT, 282
parallel, 283
serial, 284
time-outs, 284–285
PostScript fonts, 249, 261–264
defined, 246, 261
drawback, 302
families, 254, 261–262
hinting, 263–264
installing, 272–273
with ATM, 272
manually, 272–273
manipulation of, 261
printing, 262
TrueType vs., 262–264
WIN.INI file listings, 273
See also fonts
PostScript Printer Description (PPD), 295
PostScript printers, 262
drivers for, 295, 302–304
emulation, 295
options, 293–294
output format, 293
TrueType fonts with, 262–263
See also PostScript fonts; printers
PowerMouse, 222
presentation format, 535, 539

previewing
cover pages, 435
screensavers, 168–169
in WordPad, 130
Print dialog box, 131, 309
Print Preview mode (WordPad), 130
print queues, 288–290
active, 288–289
defined, 288
Document menu, 289
entries, 289
illustrated, 289, 330
managing, 288–290
network, 339
opening, 279
print jobs
changing order of, 289, 330
deleting, 290
monitoring, 339
pausing, 289, 330
Printer menu, 289
remote control, 330–331
Taskbar icon, 339
viewing, 288
Print to Disk files
benefits, 259–260
creating, 260
defined, 259
Print Troubleshooter, 288
printer drivers, 282, 291–308
bundled, 296–298
buying printers and, 311
categories, 296
defined, 291
differences between, 294
dot-matrix, 34–36
function of, 292
information, 293
LaserJet, 296–302
mimicking, 295–296
PostScript, 295, 302–304
replacing, 282
soft font installers, 307
two-tiered support, 294–295
universal (UNIDRV.DLL), 295
Windows, 311
See also printers
printer fonts, 249–250
defined, 249
types of, 249
printer port, 279
choosing, 281, 282–285

information, 293
See also ports
Printer Properties dialog box
Details tab, 291, 293
Device Options tab, 294
Fonts tab, 250, 292–293
Always Use Built-In Printer Fonts option, 302
Always Use TrueType Fonts option, 302
Install Printer Fonts button, 298, 300
Send PostScript Fonts As option, 303
Send TrueType Fonts As option, 303
Send TrueType Fonts to Printer option, 302
General tab, 293
Graphics tab, 292
opening, 292
Paper tab, 292
PostScript tab, 293–294
Sharing tab, 330
tabs, 279
Printer Setup dialog box, 304–305
Fonts tab, 305
Paper tab, 305
[Printers] section, 621–622
defined, 621
entry restrictions, 621
PrinterName parameter, 622
See also MSBATCH.INF file
printers
buying, 310–313
changing, 287, 329
color, 312–313
comment area, 293
default, 278, 279, 281, 293
default configuration, 282
dot-matrix, 296, 304–306
download capabilities, 312
ECP support, 280
EMF spooling, 280
fonts, 292–293
handshaking, 284
ICM, 280–281
inkjet, 307
installing, 281–286
laser, 311–312
list of, 281
managing, 55
memory, 294, 312

printers *(cont.)*
  Microsoft Fax, 411
  naming, 281
  network, 308–310, 327
  non-PostScript laser, 295–296
  paper size, 282, 292
  pen plotters, 308
  Plug and Play, 280, 294
  PostScript, 262, 263
  properties, 279, 291
  removing, 286
  resetting, 290
  resolution, 282, 292
  sharing, 308–309
  support, 294–296
  TrueType fonts and, 259
  virtual memory, 303
  See also printer drivers;
    printing
Printers folder, 278–279
  Add Printer icon, 281
  File menu
    Delete command, 286
    Properties command, 291
    Set as Defaults command,
      279
    Work Offline command,
      279, 310
  icons, 278
  illustrated, 278
  opening, 278
  printer icons, 288
  See also printers
Printers icon, 55, 278, 292, 320
printing, 277–313
  across networks, 329–331
  appearance, 286–287
  bidirectional, 279–280
  canceling, 289, 330
  capabilities, 277–278
  cover pages, 435
  deferred, 310, 331
  from DOS applications,
    287–288
  faxes, 424
  mail, 374, 382, 392
  with network printer, 309, 310
  offline, 278
  orientation, 292
  pausing, 289, 330
  PostScript fonts, 262
  separator pages, 293
  speed, changing, 290–291
  test page, 279

TrueType fonts, 258–261
  from Windows applications,
    286–287
  in WordPad, 130–131
  See also print queues
private keys, 426–427
  creating, 427–428
  See also RSA encryption
processor cache, 479–480
  external, 479
  internal, 479–480
  RAM, 479
processors
  buses, 482–487
  choosing, 477–478
  defined, 475
  functions of, 475
  math coprocessors, 481–482
  motherboard, 481
  OverDrive, 480
  real mode, 477
  speeds, 477–478
  types of, 476
  upgrading, 480–481
  virtual mode, 477
  See also Pentium processors
profiles, 54, 366–372
  contents of, 366
  creating, 368
  defined, 366
  editing, 368–369
  multiple, 367
  See also Microsoft Exchange
Program Group Converter, 600
Programs submenu
  Accessories submenu, 123
  application listing, 97
  Explorer command, 49
  illustrated, 49, 97
  Microsoft Network command,
    49
  MS-DOS prompt command, 49
ProHance mice, 222
properties
  address book, 398
  address book entry, 398
  compression, 518–519
  date/time, 182–183
  device object, 67, 83–84
  dialing, 343
  DOS application, 564, 566–576
  folder, 335
  keyboard, 232–236
  modem, 344–345

mouse, 224–229
network component, 324
object, 77
password, 180
personal address book, 371
personal folders file, 370
printer, 279, 291
Recycle Bin, 80–81
shortcut, 86
Taskbar, 171–175
Volume Control, 465
Properties dialog box (DOS),
  564, 565–576
  General tab, 566
  Memory tab, 569–572
    Conventional memory area,
      571–572
    Expanded (EMS) memory
      area, 570
    Extended (XMS) memory
      area, 571
    Initial Environment field,
      572
    Protected check box, 572
    Uses HMA field, 572
  Misc tab, 574–576
    Allow Screensaver box, 574
    Always Suspend option, 575
    Fast Pasting option, 576
    Idle Sensitivity option,
      575–576
    Mouse options, 574–575
    Warn if Still Active option,
      575
    Windows shortcut keys
      options, 576
  Program tab, 566–569
    Advanced button, 569, 576
    Batch File field, 567
    Change Icon button, 569
    Close on exit box, 568
    Cmd Line field, 567
    Name field, 566
    Run drop-down list, 568
    Shortcut Key field, 568
    Working field, 567
  Screen tab, 572–574
    Display Toolbar option, 573
    Full-Screen button, 573
    Initial Size field, 573
    Performance area, 573–574
    Restore Settings at Startup
      option, 573
    Window button, 573

Properties dialog box (resources), 335–339
  opening, 335, 337
  Sharing tab, 335–336, 338
Properties dialog boxes
  defined, 81
  file objects, 81
  illustrated, 82
  viewing, 82
  See also specific Properties dialog boxes
Properties dialog boxes (device objects), 67, 81–82
  defined, 81–82
  illustrated, 83
  working with, 83–84
protected mode, 577
protocols, 322
  default, 612
  defined, 323–324
  as list of device IDs, 611–612
  transfer, 350–351
  types of, 323–324
public keys, 427
  adding sender's, 428–429
  creating, 428
  sending to fax recipient, 428
  See also RSA encryption

Q

question mark (?), wild-card character, 332
quitting applications, 119–120
quotation marks (""), long file names and, 552
QWERTY keyboard layout, 236, 238
  defined, 236
  typing program, 237
  See also keyboards

R

RAM (random-access memory), 195, 474, 488–493
  add-in cards, 489
  adding, 489
  configurations, 490
  defined, 488
  dynamic (DRAM), 488
  higher-density chips, 489–490
  mixing, 490
  parity checking and, 490–491

printer, 294
processor cache, 480, 481
quantities, Windows 95 and, 488–489
requirements, 13
SIMMs, 489, 490
types of, 492
Windows 95 and, 491–493
See also memory
RAM DAC (RAM digital-to-analog converter), 200
raster fonts, 264–267
  aspect ratio, 265
  defined, 248, 249
  Fixed, 265
  location of, 266
  OEM, 265–266
  point sizes, 266
  resolution, 275
  sizes, 264
  Windows 95, 264
  See also fonts
real mode, 477
  defined, 557
  device drivers, 318, 559–560, 579
  operating system files, 600
  TSRs, 559–560
  See also DOS
rebooting, 57
Recycle Bin, 10, 79–81
  defined, 79
  folders and, 79
  hard disk space for, 80
  illustrated, 79
  object recovery from, 80
  object status, 79
  properties, 80–81
  schedules, 80
Recycle Bin Properties dialog box, 80–81
refresh rates, 195–196
  high, 211
  See also displays; monitors
regional settings, 183–185
  country selection, 18
  currency symbol, 184, 185
  decimal points, 184
  measurement system, 184
  numerical format, 184
Regional Settings icon, 55, 183
Regional Settings Properties dialog box, 183–185
  Currency tab, 185

  Number tab, 184
  Regional Settings tab, 184
Registry, 550–552
  contents, 550
  defined, 550
  OLE and, 533, 538, 550–552
  restoring, 599
  Setup creation, 599
  updating entries, 550–552
Registry Editor, 544
Remote Access Services, 53
remote drives
  defined, 328
  mapping, 328–329
Remote Mail toolbar, 408
remote preview (Microsoft Mail), 405–406
  defined, 405
  with mail services, 406
  turning on, 406
  window, 406
  See also Microsoft Mail
remote-boot workstation, 614
Remove Shortcuts/Folders dialog box, 176–177
repetitive stress injuries, 230–231
  carpal tunnel syndrome and, 231
  tendinitis and, 230–231
  See also keyboards
Request a Fax wizard, 435–436
resolution
  color-depth, 194
  desktop size and, 196
  display driver, 193
  monitor, 209–210
  mouse, 217–218
  pixel, 194
  printer, 282, 292
  raster fonts, 265
  standard, 194
Resource Kit, 628
resources
  exploring, 74–76
  network, 74–75
Rich Text Format (RTF), 129, 288, 525
right mouse button, 21
  drag-and-drop and, 85
  See also Shortcut menu
RLE compression, 448
ROM (read-only memory), 487
ROM BIOS chips, 475

RSA encryption, 410, 426–429
  drawbacks, 427
  private key, 426–427
  public key, 427
  See also encrypted faxes
Run dialog box, 52, 101–103
  drop-down list box, 102
  illustrated, 101
  launching applications from, 101–103
  opening, 101

S

SAA CUA (System Application Architecture Common User Access), 9
Safe mode, 321
Save As dialog box, 107
  in WordPad, 129
saving
  in ASCII text format, 129, 130
  attachments, 391
  Clipboard data, 115
  cover pages, 435
  faxes, 424
  files, 107–108
  MIDI configurations, 470
  in Rich Text Format (RTF), 129
  in Word 6.0 format, 129
  in WordPad, 129–130
scan rates, 195
  high, 211
  See also displays; monitors
Scheme list box, 165
Scraps, 118–119
  advantage of, 119
  defined, 58, 118
  icon, 118
  illustrated, 118
  uses, 118–119
  See also OLE
screen fonts, 249–250
  defined, 249
  substitutions, 249–250
  See also fonts
screensavers, 167–170
  availability of, 168
  choosing, 168
  defined, 167
  DOS application, 574
  Energy Star monitors and, 170
  as locks, 170

passwords, 170
previewing, 168–169
sample, 168
setting controls on, 169
speed controls, 169
testing, 170
waiting time to begin, 169
scroll bars, 24–25
  defined, 24
  horizontal, 24
  using, 25
  vertical, 24
scrolling, 25
SCSI (Small Computer System Interface) controllers, 505
searching
  criteria, 69, 71
  files, 70, 71
  for help, 157–158
  by modified date, 70–71
  by name and location, 69–70
  network computers, 71–72
  for network resources, 331–332
  results window, 70
  shortcuts, 86–87
  by size, 71
  by text, 71
  by type, 71
  wild-card characters and, 332
secondary windows, 22
security
  fax, 420, 425–429
  network, 332–334
  share-level, 332–333
  specification, 615
  user-level, 332, 333
Select Device dialog box, 207–208, 229
Select Drive dialog box, 506
Select MS-DOS Configuration Options dialog box, 580
Select Network Component Type dialog box, 321, 357
Select Network Protocol dialog box, 357
Select Program Folder dialog box, 175, 176
selecting
  colors, 166
  fonts, 140
  menus, 34
  resources, 327
  wallpaper, 164
  windows, 24

Send Fonts dialog box, 303
Send Options for the Message dialog box, 418, 419
Send To folder, 286
serial mouse, 229
serial ports, 284, 341
  See also COM ports
SerialKey, 189
Server Type dialog box, 358
servers, 317
  copying/cutting objects from, 535
  data object formats, 535
  DDE, 529–530
  defined, 532
  dial-up, 352–353
  Internet, 358–359
  linking from, 530
  network fax modem setup, 345–346
  OLE, 534–535
  verbs, 532, 538
  See also clients
service bureaus, TrueType fonts and, 259
services, 322
  defined, 324
  device IDs, 613
Set Time dialog box, 418, 419
Settings for StickyKeys dialog box, 186
Settings submenu, 50–51
  Control Panel command, 50, 162, 267, 368
  defined, 50
  illustrated, 51
  Printers command, 50
  Taskbar command, 51, 171
Setup program
  before running, 587
  CD-ROM drive detection, 597
  Change Directory screen, 591
  Choose Directory screen, 590
  Compact installation, 592–594
  Custom installation, 592–594
  defined, 584
  detection control, 596–597
  disk problems and, 587
  disk-partitioning software and, 588
  DLLs, 599
  from DOS, 586, 587
  DOS version replacement, 600
  from DOS window, 588

failure, 597
file copy phase, 598–599
final configuration phase, 600–601
hardware detection phase, 594–598
installation directory, 589–590
installation options, 592–594
on legacy computers, 594–595
lockups, 595
network components and, 319
on Plug and Play computer, 595
Portable installation, 592–594
Program Group Converter, 600
Registry creation, 599
restarting computer and, 598, 600
safe detection devices, 596
Safe Recovery mode, 596–597
    detection process and, 597
    logs in, 597–598
Safe Recovery screen, 596
scripts, 584–585
starting, 586–587
start-up disk creation, 598–599
switches, 585
temporary directory, 584
TSRs and, 587
Typical installation, 592–594
Welcome screen, 588
Windows detection, 589
See also installation, Windows 95
Setup scripts, 627–632
with BATCH.EXE, 628, 630–631
creation methods, 628
default, 627
editing, 629
.INF Generator and, 528, 631–632
with NETSETUP.EXE, 628, 629–630
See also MSBATCH.INF file; Setup program
[Setup] section, 602–605
Devicepath parameter, 603
EBF parameter, 603
Express parameter, 163
InstallDir parameter, 603
InstallType parameter, 603
PenWinWarning parameter, 604
ProductID parameter, 604
SaveSuBoot parameter, 604

TimeZone parameter, 604
Uninstall parameter, 605
Verify parameter, 605
VRC parameter, 605
See also MSBATCH.INF file
SFLPT1.BAT file, 299
shadow files, 290
shared fax modems, 436–437
    setting up, 436–437
    using, 437
See also fax modems
share-level security, 332–333
sharing
    enabling, 334
    fax modems, 436–437
    folders, 334–337
    network fax modem, 347
    network resources, 334–337
    printers, 308–309, 329
See also networks
Shift key
    in drag-and-drop, 78
See also keyboard shortcuts
Shortcut menu
    Create Shortcut command, 85, 549
    defined, 21
    Delete command, 286
    Find command, 331
    Map Network Drive command, 328
    Properties command, 80, 162, 171, 207, 250, 279, 337, 358
    Rename command, 84
    Send To command, 286, 309
    Sharing command, 308, 335, 338
Shortcut Properties dialog box, 86–87
shortcuts, 84–88
    adding with drag-and-drop, 179
    creating, 85
    defined, 84
    on desktop, 98
    finding, 86–87
    help, 156
    icons, 84
    illustrated, 84
    managing, 86–87
    Microsoft Fax, 413
    moving, 86
    placement of, 85

properties, 86
recreating, 88
removing from Start menu, 176–177
repairing, 87–88
tracing, 86
Shutdown dialog box, 56–57, 181
    choices, 57
    Close all programs option, 171
    illustrated, 56
SIMMs, 489
    configurations, 490
    mixing, 490
    replacing, 489
See also RAM (random-access memory)
Small Icons view, 62, 63
SMTP (Simple Mail Transport Protocol), 360
soft fonts
    defined, 249
    downloadable, for LaserJets, 298–300
    limit per page, 301
    reinstalling, 301
See also fonts; printers
software. See applications
software pointers, 534
Solitaire, 152
    illustrated, 152
    playing, 152
    setting up, 152
See also games
sound, 451–452
    Accessibility Options, 187
    digital, 451–452
    files, 460
        editing, 463–464
        mixing, 463
        recording, 463
See also multimedia
Sound Recorder, 461–464
    alternative, 461
    buttons, 461
    defined, 443
    Edit menu commands, 463
    editing files with, 463
    Effects menu commands, 463–464
    illustrated, 461
    keyboard shortcuts, 462
    playing files with, 461
    recording with, 462
See also multimedia

Sounds icon, 55
SoundSentry, 187
source document, 533
 editing, 540
 updating link to, 542–543
 See also OLE
special characters, 238–241
speed dialing. *See* Phone Dialer
spell checking, mail messages, 383
spool files, 290
Spool Settings dialog box, 306
spooling, 280
ST506 controllers, 505
Start a Rumor dialog box (Party Line), 151
Start button, 11, 46, 47–52
 defined, 47
 See also Taskbar
START command, DOS, 101
Start menu, 47
 customizing, 174–179
 Documents submenu, 50, 103–104
 Find submenu, 51, 68–72
 Help command, 52
 hierarchy Explorer view, 177–178
 icon size, 173
 illustrated, 48, 97
 maneuvering, 48
 programs
  adding, 174–176
  adding with drag-and-drop, 178
  removing, 176–177
 Programs submenu, 49, 97
 Run command, 52
 Settings submenu, 50–51, 162, 267, 278, 368
 Shutdown command, 56
starting applications
 from folder view, 98–99
 from MS-DOS prompt, 100–101
 from Run dialog box, 101–103
 from Start menu, 96–98
 See also applications
start-up disk, 598–599
 defined, 599
 files, 599
 as recovery disk, 599
 See also installation, Windows 95; Setup program

Status dialog box (Microsoft Fax), 422
StickyKeys, 185
still images, 444–446
 sources for, 445–446
 types of, 445
 See also graphics
Stretch and Skew dialog box (Paint), 138
[Strings] section, 622–623
 defined, 622
 example string keys, 623
 See also MSBATCH.INF file
subdirectories, 60
submenus. *See* menus; *specific menus and submenus*
Super VGA (SVGA), 197
 drivers, 206
 See also displays; monitors
SYLK data, 525
synthesizers
 defined, 467
 performance levels, 468
 See also MIDI
System Agent
 defined, 15
 See also Microsoft Plus!
system bus. *See* buses
System Control Panel, 283, 342, 512
system date/time, 54
System folder, 84
System icon, 55, 510
SYSTEM.INI file, [386Enh] section, 500–502
System menu. *See* Control menu
system requirements, 13
System Tools submenu, 123
 Disk Defragmenter command, 506
 DriveSpace command, 515
System VM, 558
[System] section, 605–607
 defined, 607
 See also MSBATCH.INF file

T

tabbed dialog boxes, 19–20, 42–43
 defined, 42
 illustrated, 43
 See also dialog boxes
tabs (WordPad), 127
Tandy PS/2 mice, 221

task list, 52–53
 in switching between applications, 111
Taskbar, 11–12, 46–57
 auto-hiding, 172–173
 clock, 173
 customizing, 170–179
 date, 173
 defined, 46
 envelope icon, 372
 illustrated, 12, 46, 47
 initial prompt, 48
 keyboard language indicator, 234, 235
 locations, 46, 47
 moving, 47
 notify area, 53
 properties, 171–175
 Speaker icon, 464
 Start button, 11, 46, 47–52
 task list, 52–53, 111
 unhiding, 173
 vertical, 47
 visibility of, 171
Taskbar Properties dialog box, 171–175
 Add button, 174
 Advanced button, 177
 Always on Top option, 171–172
 Auto Hide option, 172–173
 Customize Start Menu section, 174
 illustrated, 171, 172, 173, 174
 opening, 171
 Remove button, 176
 Show Clock option, 173
 Show Small Icons option, 173
 Start Menu Programs tab, 174–175
TCP/IP, 323
 configuring, 357–359
 defined, 355
 installing, 356–359
 using, 356
 See also Internet
TCP/IP Settings dialog box, 358–359
telecommunications, 340
 See also communications
Telnet, 360
temporary files, 290
tendinitis, 230–231

Terminate and Stay Resident
    programs (TSRs), 500, 558
    conventional memory and, 571
    real mode, 559–560
    Setup program and, 588
text
    cover page, 432–433
    desktop, modifying, 166–167
    format, 525
    formatting (WordPad),
        124–127
    help, 154–155
    mail, 379–381
    OEM, 525
    RTF, 525
    saving in, 129, 130
text-only files, 88
TIFF graphics format, 526
TIGA (Texas Instruments
    Graphics Architecture), 200
time
    properties, 182–183
    system, 54
    WordPad, inserting, 125, 126
    zone, 183
    See also date
time-outs, 284–285
    Not Selected option, 284–285
    Transmission Retry option,
        285
    See also ports
title bar, 26–27
    buttons, 26
    illustrated, 27
    X button, 119
    See also Control menu
ToggleKeys, 186
toolbars, 63–66
    Address Book, 394
    command prompt, 562–565
    Copy tool, 65
    Cover Page Editor, 431
    Cut tool, 64
    Details tool, 65
    Disconnect Net Drive tool, 64
    displaying, 63
    DOS application, 95
    drop-down list box, 64
    Explorer, 76
    Fax Viewer, 423
    illustrated, 63
    Large Icons tool, 65
    List tool, 65
    Map Network Drive tool, 64

Microsoft Exchange, 374–375,
    378–379
New Message window,
    379–380
Paste tool, 65
Properties tool, 65
Remote Mail, 408
Small Icons tool, 65
Undo tool, 65
Up One Level tool, 64
WordPad, 131
Topics Found dialog box, 156
touch screens, 215
trackballs, 216
    Kensington Expert Mouse, 223
    Logitech TrackMan, 222–223
    Mouse Systems PC Trackball,
        223
    See also pointing devices
tracking
    ballistic, 218
    mechanism, 215–216
    speed, 55, 218
    See also mouse (mice)
trackpoints, 215
    See also pointing devices
transition effects, 449
Transmission Control
    Protocol/Internet Protocol.
        See TCP/IP
true color, 194
TrueType Font Pack, 254–258
    Font Pack 2 fonts, 256–258
    Lucida typefaces, 254–255
    recommendation, 256
TrueType fonts, 248
    Arial, 253
    basic list of, 251
    conversion of, 250
    defined, 246
    embedding, 260–261
    families, 254
    file location, 253
    files for, 253
    functions of, 250
    hinting, 263–264
    identifying, 256
    illustrated list of, 252
    installing, 271–272
    "jaggies," 276
    maximum allowed, 258
    PostScript equivalents of, 254
    PostScript printers and,
        262–263

PostScript vs., 262–264
printing, 258–261
    performance and, 258–259
    printers, 259
    service bureaus and, 259
read-only, 260
read-write, 261
styles of, 253
third-party, 254
TT symbol, 256
universal page-description
    language, 250
See also fonts; TrueType Font
    Pack
.TTF files, 253
typefaces, 247–248
    defined, 247
    type track, 248
    type width, 248
    See also fonts
Typical installation, 592–594

U

unified log-on, 327
Update My Briefcase dialog box
    (Briefcase), 146–147
upgrade version, 13
upper memory area (UMA),
    496–498
    addresses, 496
    common addresses, 496–497
    defined, 492
    free space, 498
    illustrated, 497
    loading into, 498
    UMBs (upper memory
        blocks), 496
    uses, 497
    working with, 498
    See also memory
Usenet newsgroups, 360
user account feature, 57
USER heap, 521
user profiles, 179–182
    creating, 181
    default, 182
    global changes, 182
    multiple, 180
    name, 179
    options, 180
    password, 170
    setting up, 180–181
    working with, 181–182

user-level security, 332, 333
    access control settings, 615
    pass-through agent, 616
    See also security

V

VDT emissions, 212
vector fonts, 266
    defined, 248, 249
    Windows 95, 266
    See also fonts
vector graphics, 132, 446
versions, 13
vertical scan frequency, 195–199
very low frequency (VLF)
        radiation, 212
VESA (VL-bus), 204
VGA (Video Graphics Array),
        194
    color palette, 205
    display card, 201
    display drivers, 204, 209
    grayscale, 204
    modes, 196
    monochrome, 204–205
    resolutions, 194
    Super VGA vs., 197
    See also displays; display cards
Video1 compression, 448
video, 446–450
    analog, 446, 447
    A/V hard drives and, 450
    codecs, 448
    compression, 448–449
    conferencing, 213
    digital, 447, 448
    DOS applications and, 573–574
    key frames, 448
    MPEG, 449
    types of, 446–447
    See also graphics
video alert, 189
video capture cards
    checklist of, 449–450
    defined, 447
    purchasing, 447
video cards. See display cards
Video for Windows, 443
video switch box, 450
viewing
    installed fonts, 270
    print queues, 288
    similar fonts, 270–271

views
    changing, 65–66
    Details, 61–62
    Explorer, 76
    folder, 59–63
    List, 62
    Small Icons, 62, 63
Virtual Communications
        (VCOMM), 561
Virtual Control Program
        Interface (VCPI), 503
virtual desktops, 199
virtual DOS machine (VDM),
        557
    benefits, 558
    defining memory
            characteristics of,
            569–570
    environment size, 572
    global parameters, 560
    See also virtual memory
Virtual Machine Manager
        (VMM), 557
virtual memory, 511–512
    changing settings of, 510
    defined, 509
    disabling, 511
    functioning of, 509
    LRU algorithm, 509
    pages, 509
    paging file, 511
    printer, 303
Virtual Memory dialog box,
        510–511
    illustrated, 510, 511
    opening, 510
virtual mode, 477
Virtual Programmable Interrupt
        Controller (VPIC), 561
visual editing, 533, 534
    defined, 533
    illustrated, 539
    See also OLE
Visual Enhancements
    defined, 15
    See also Microsoft Plus!
VL (VESA) bus, 486
    defined, 483
    ranking, 487
    See also buses
.voc files, 451, 460
Volume Control, 464–465
    master, 464
    mixer compatibility and, 465

opening, 464
properties, 465
window, 465
See also applets
volume icons, 40, 59
    defined, 40
    illustrated, 40
    See also icons
volumes
    drag-and-drop across, 78
    DriveSpace, 514–521
    navigating, 60
VRAM (video RAM), 195
[VRedir] section
    defined, 620
    parameters, 620
    See also MSBATCH.INF file
[VServer] section
    defined, 621
    parameters, 621
    See also MSBATCH.INF file
VxDs (virtual device drivers),
        556, 560–561
    defined, 560
    DPMI and, 561
    EMS memory support, 561
    performance and, 561
    replacement for, 560
    Windows 95, 556

W

wallpaper, 163–165
    patterns and, 165
    selecting, 164
    See also desktop
warm links, 530
.wav files, 451, 460
wave audio format, 526
WD1003 controllers, 505
Win16 applications, 95
    defined, 94
    using, 95
    See also applications
Win32 applications, 96
    defined, 94
    using, 96
    See also applications
WIN.INI file, 272–273
Windows 1.0, 8
Windows 3.0, 8
Windows 3.1
    control panels, 56
    File Manager, 12

Help button (F1), 108
help files, 158–159
interface, 10
starting computer from, 589
Windows 95 vs., 10–13
Windows Setup, 56
Windows 95
applications, 96
capabilities of, 7–8
CD-ROM versions, 13
command prompt. See
command prompt
DOS and, 555–581
DOS compatibility, 94, 559
floppy-disk versions, 13
full versions, 13
Game Software Development
Kit, 193
history, 8–9
installation, 583–632
Compact, 592–594
Custom, 592–594
custom-designed, 601–623
directory, 589–590
dual-boot system and,
590–592
file copy phase, 598–599
final configuration phase,
600–601
hardware detection phase,
594–598
Portable, 592–594
time, 588–589
type, choosing, 592–594
Typical, 592–594
See also Setup program
manuals, 14
media and, 3, 4
navigating, 45–91
optimizing, 473–522
personalizing, 161–189
pre-installed, 14
prices, 14
RAM and, 491–493
release of, 3–4
requirements for running, 13
running older software with, 6
secrets, 8
shutting down, 56–57
upgrade versions, 13
what runs on, 94–96
what's new in, 5–6
Win16 application support, 95

Windows 3.1 vs., 5, 10–13
Windows NT vs., 9
windows, 22–33
application, 23, 24
child document, 22, 28–32
closing, 33
Control menu, 26–28
cropped, 32
corner, grabbing, 24
cycling through, 24
defined, 18
expanding, 27
folder, 25–26
help text, 154
hierarchical, 22
independent document, 23–24
Microsoft Exchange, 399–400
minimizing, 27
moving, 23–24
open, 52
rearranging, 18
resizing, 23–24
scroll bars, 24–25
secondary, 22
selecting, 24
tiling, 31–33
title bars, 26–27
Windows installation disks, 14
Windows NT, 9
applications, 96
upgrading to, 16
Windows 95 vs., 9
The Windows 95 Bible
reasons for using, 6–8
what this book is about, 5
WinPopup, 309
wizards
Add New Hardware, 219, 454
Add Printer, 281, 329
Add Program, 174–175
Briefcase, 145
Compose New Fax, 414,
415–418
Direct Cable Connection, 355
Install New Modem, 342–343
Make New Connection, 352
MIDI Instrument Installation,
470
Request a Fax, 435–436
Setup. See Setup program
WK1 data, 515
WordPad, 124–131
bulleted lists, 125, 126

Clipboard maneuvers, 127–129
copying data with, 127–128
customizing, 131
date/time, inserting, 125, 126
defined, 124
formatting text, 124–127
help, 153
illustrated, 124, 126, 127, 128
OLE and, 129
pasting data with, 127–128
pasting graphics with, 128
previewing in, 130
Print Preview mode, 130
printing in, 130–131
saving data in, 129–130
tabs, 127
toolbars, 131
Write vs., 124
See also applets
work groups, 614
choosing, 623–625
workstations
remote-boot, 614
Windows 95 shared copy on,
615
World Wide Web (WWW)
browser, 355, 360
defined, 359
multimedia and, 442–443
See also Internet
Write, 124
WRKGRP.INI file, 623–625
defined, 623
[Options] section, 624
[Workgroups] section,
624–625
WYSIWYG, 245, 259, 291

X

X button, 119
Xerox PARC, 8
XGA display card, 201
Xmodem, 350

Y

Ymodem, 350
Ymodem-G, 350

Z

Zmodem, 350

More from Peachpit Press

25 Steps To Safe Computing

Don Sellers

With planning, many computer-related health problems can be avoided. *25 Steps to Safe Computing* tells you how to reduce your risk with simple, easy-to-follow advice. It contains ergonomic tips on setting up work areas, as well as sections on backache, headache, tendinitis, radiation, pregnancy, carpal tunnel syndrome, and much more. $5.95 *(72 pages)*

Clip Art Crazy, Windows Edition

Chuck Green

Here's everything you need to incorporate sophisticated clip art into your desktop-created projects. *Clip Art Crazy* offers tips for finding and choosing clip art, along with a vast array of simple designs showing how to incorporate clip art into your documents and presentations. The CD-ROM includes almost 500 reproducible samples, culled from the archives of leading clip art design firms. $34.95 *(384 pages w/CD-ROM)*

Jargon: An Informal Dictionary of Computer Terms

Robin Williams with Steve Cummings

Finally! A book that explains over 1,200 of the most useful computer terms in a way that readers can understand. This book is a straightforward guide that not only defines computer-related terms but also explains how and why they are used. It covers both the Macintosh and PC worlds. No need to ask embarrassing questions: Just look it up in *Jargon!* $22 *(688 pages)*

Head for the Web: Your Windows Connection to the World Wide Web

Mary Jane Mara

Head for the Web provides you with all you need to tap the World Wide Web, from browsing to HTML coding to setting up a Web server. The book includes in-depth tours of the three leading Windows-based browsers: Netscape, Mosaic, and Microsoft Network's Internet Explorer. The accompanying CD-ROM contains Netscape 2.0 (for Windows 3.1 and Windows 95), Eudora Lite (the leading Internet email program), and an easy-to-use program that gives you dial-up access to the Web via Earthlink, a national Internet service provider. Covers both Windows 3.1 and Windows 95. $24.95 *(312 pages, w/CD-ROM)*

The Little PC Book, 2nd Edition: A Gentle Introduction to Personal Computers

Lawrence J. Magid with *Kay Yarborough Nelson*

Wouldn't you love having a knowledgeable, witty, endlessly patient pal to coach you through buying and using a PC? Well, you do. Popular columnist and broadcaster Larry Magid's expertise is yours in *The Little PC Book*, described by THE WALL STREET JOURNAL as "the class of the field." This edition includes the latest on Windows 95, the Internet, CD-ROMs, and more. Includes a handy Windows 95 Cookbook section. $17.95 *(384 pages)*

The Little Windows 95 Book

Kay Yarborough Nelson

Your guide to Windows 95. This easy, informative and entertaining volume spotlights the essentials so you can get to work quickly. Short, fully-illustrated chapters explore the Windows interface in detail, offering numerous tips and tricks. Each chapter includes a handy summary chart of keyboard shortcuts. $12.95 *(144 pages)*

The Non-Designer's Design Book

Robin Williams

Robin Williams wrote this one "for all the people who now need to design pages, but who have no background or formal training in design." Follow the basic principles clearly explained in this book and your work is guaranteed to look more professional, organized, unified, and interesting. You'll never again look at a page in the same way. Full of real-life design examples and quizzes. Runner-up for "Best Introductory Systems How-to Book" in the 1994 Computer Press Awards. $14.95 *(144 pages)*

The PC Bible, 2nd Edition

Edited by Eric Knorr

The PC universe is expanding, and the second edition of *The PC Bible* has grown along with it. Twenty industry experts collaborated on this definitive guide to PCs, now updated to include Windows 95 and Internet access. Whether you're a beginning or advanced PC user, you'll benefit from this book's clear, entertaining coverage of fonts, word processing, spreadsheets, graphics, desktop publishing, databases, communications, utilities, multimedia, games, and more. Winner of 1994 Computer Press Award for "Best Introductory How-to" book. $29.95 *(1,032 pages)*

The PC is not a typewriter

Robin Williams

Ever wonder why some type looks more professional, more sophisticated than other type? The answer lies in the techniques and rules developed for professional typesetting. Not surprisingly, those methods are far different than the training given in Typing 1A. This book not only lays down the principles governing traditional type, but explains the logic behind them. The original bestselling version, entitled *The Mac is not a typewriter*, received scores of rave reviews and won the prestigious Benjamin Franklin Award from the Publishers Marketing Association. Tailored specifically for users of IBM-compatible computers, this new edition will introduce thousands more to the secrets of beautiful, sophisticated pages. $9.95 *(96 pages)*

Windows 95 is Driving Me Crazy

Kay Yarborough Nelson

Behind the hoopla and hype surrounding the release of Windows 95, there's one unavoidable reality: almost everybody's frustrated in one way or another with Microsoft's new operating system—its performance, its interface, its incompatibilities. This book is the ultimate problem-solving guide for making the most of this challenging situation. *Windows 95 is Driving Me Crazy* shows you ways to get around the worst problems, better ways of doing certain tasks, what you can and can't do in real-life situations, and where to turn for more help. You'll learn what Microsoft left out and what they don't tell you, how to keep the good parts of Windows 3.1, and hardware and software incompatibilities—and what to do about them. $24.95 *(400 pages)*

Windows 95: Visual QuickStart Guide

Steve Sagman

Windows 95, the long-awaited upgrade of Microsoft's operating system, offers an improved interface, faster performance, and numerous enhancements. This fast-paced, easy-to-read reference guide uses the same approach that's made other books in the Visual QuickStart series so popular: illustrations dominate, with text playing a supporting role. *Windows 95: Visual QuickStart Guide* provides a thorough tour of Windows 95, from introducing the basics, to managing your computer, to communicating online with Windows 95. $14.95 *(192 pages)*

Order Form

USA **800-283-9444** • **510-548-4393** • FAX **510-548-5991**
CANADA **800-387-8028** • **416-447-1779** • FAX **800-456-0536** OR **416-443-0948**

Qty	Title	Price	Total
	SUBTOTAL		
	ADD APPLICABLE SALES TAX*		
	SHIPPING		
	TOTAL		

Shipping is by UPS ground: $4 for first item, $1 each add'l.

*We are required to pay sales tax in all states with the exceptions of AK, DE, HI, MT, NH, NV, OK, OR, SC and WY. Please include appropriate sales tax if you live in any state not mentioned above.

Customer Information

NAME

COMPANY

STREET ADDRESS

CITY   STATE   ZIP

PHONE ( )   FAX ( )
[REQUIRED FOR CREDIT CARD ORDERS]

Payment Method

❏ CHECK ENCLOSED   ❏ VISA   ❏ MASTERCARD   ❏ AMEX

CREDIT CARD #   EXP. DATE

COMPANY PURCHASE ORDER #

Tell Us What You Think

PLEASE TELL US WHAT YOU THOUGHT OF THIS BOOK: TITLE:

WHAT OTHER BOOKS WOULD YOU LIKE US TO PUBLISH?

PC   **PEACHPIT PRESS** • **2344 Sixth Street** • **Berkeley, CA 94710**